Basic Computation and Programming with C

Undergraduate students of engineering and computer science will come across detailed coverage of the fundamentals of computation and programming in C language, in this textbook. Essential concepts including operators and expressions, input and output statements, loop statements, arrays, pointers, functions, strings and pre-processor are described in a lucid manner. For better comprehension of the concepts, the book is divided into three parts: Fundamentals of Computer, Programming with 'C' and Technical Questions.

A unique feature of the book is 'Learn by Quiz – Questions/Answers', which has questions designed through confidence-based-learning methodology. This helps readers to identify right answers with adequate explanation and reasoning as to why the other options are wrong. Plenty of computer programs and review questions are interspersed throughout the text.

The book can also be used as a self-learning book by beginners in Computer Programming.

Subrata Saha is Head of the Department of Computer Applications, Techno India Hooghly, West Bengal. His areas of interest include object oriented languages, image processing and cryptography.

Subhodip Mukherjee is Head of the Department of Computer Applications, Techno India College of Technology, Kolkata. His areas of interest include object oriented languages, software engineering, computer architecture and database management systems.

Basic Computation and Programming with C

Subrata Saha
Subhodip Mukherjee

CAMBRIDGE
UNIVERSITY PRESS

CAMBRIDGE
UNIVERSITY PRESS

4843/24, 2nd Floor, Ansari Road, Daryaganj, Delhi - 110002, India

Cambridge University Press is part of the University of Cambridge.

It furthers the University's mission by disseminating knowledge in the pursuit of education, learning and research at the highest international levels of excellence.

www.cambridge.org
Information on this title: www.cambridge.org/9781316601853

© Cambridge University Press 2016

First published 2016

Printed in India by Thomson Press India Ltd., New Delhi 110001

A catalogue record for this publication is available from the British Library

Library of Congress Cataloging-in-Publication Data
Names: Saha, Subrata, 1973- author. | Mukherjee, Subhodip, author.
Title: Basic computation and programming with C / Subrata Saha, Subhodip Mukherjee.
Description: New York : Cambridge University Press, 2016. | Includes bibliographical references and index.
Identifiers: LCCN 2016018907 | ISBN 9781316601853 (pbk.)
Subjects: LCSH: C (Computer program language) | Mathematics--Data processing.
Classification: LCC QA76.73.C15 S237 2016 | DDC 004.01/51--dc23 LC record available at
https://lccn.loc.gov/2016018907

ISBN 978-1-316-60185-3 Paperback

Additional resources for this publication at www.cambridge.org/9781316601853

To my father Late Kamal Krishna Saha and to my mother Geetasree Saha for what I am today.

— Subrata Saha

To my mother who sacrificed all sorts of entertainment for my education during my school life and to my father Professor S. G. Mukherjee whose addiction to books and simple living inspired me to be a teacher.

— Subhodip Mukherjee

Contents

PART A: Fundamentals of Computer

Figures

Tables

Preface

The C programming language is one of the most, academically as well as industrially, important programming languages in the world. It was unveiled in 1972 and since then, with gradual enhancements and enrichments, it has successfully established itself as a powerful language for programming microcontrollers, operating systems and various commercially significant software packages. Having unique features like block structure, stand alone functions and a rich set of keywords with very few restrictions, it is aptly regarded as the 'Mother Language' among programming languages. Hence it is necessary for every programmer to learn and, often, use C.

About the Book

Today, in any corner of the world, there is a necessity to learn computer programming for people to survive in any industry. All students do not possess technical background and therefore find learning C programming difficult. Keeping a strong focus on industrial requirements and the limitations of students from non-technical backgrounds, we have written this new book on C programming to enable students of non-technical as well as technical backgrounds learn this marvelous programming language in a completely new way.

This book is completely different from other popular C programming books available in the market. It teaches programming to someone who wants to learn how to program in C for the first time in his/her life with no programming knowledge at all. In other words, this book on C programming is for *absolute beginners* of programming but at the same time it outclasses several other C programming books in the market with its coverage. Although targeted at complete beginners, this book covers many advanced concepts in C programming and enables a non-programmer to develop into a competitive C programmer ready to face job interviews on C.

Structure of the Book

➢ This book is written presuming that the reader is not strong in English. All the explanations in each chapter are offered in simplest English to enable any reader to correctly understand a concept.

➤ Each chapter contains appropriate examples. It ends with a *'Learn by Quiz – Questions/Answers'*, having multiple choice questions with their respective answers (with clarifications) to ensure understandability.

➤ In order to make the presentation visually interactive for students, neat labeled diagrams are provided wherever necessary. For each topic, the explanations are clear and concise, avoiding verbosity as much as possible.

➤ Each programming topic is presented with an exercise set consisting of a large number of solved C programs. Each such solved program is presented with WHYs and HOWs for each new or next statement of a program.

➤ This book also includes a rich collection of commonly asked as well as most probable, new C programming *interview solved questions* and programs with step-by-step explanations to enable a student to be successful in an interview.

Students, we have prepared this book for you using a unique teaching approach based on our academic learnings so that it looks least intimidating and most interesting. We are sure that after studying this new book on C programming, those of you for whom C programming has been a source of sorrow will now find in it joy and fun. Though every attempt has been made to avoid errors, we will be grateful to our readers if they bring to our notice any oversight they find. If the content design and organization of this book meets all the expectations and requirements of our students, then only can this book be considered a worthwhile accomplishment.

Acknowledgments

I thank my, beloved, students for their constant motivation which made me write this book despite the availability of many best-selling C programming books in the market. My students are extremely fond of and fascinated by my 'teaching from the ground up' style and their demand inspired me to author this amazingly simple C book which is aimed at non-programmers or absolute beginners. My heartiest thanks to them.

I would like to thank T. K. Ghosh, Chief Executive Director of Techno India Group for providing me the platform to teach so many young minds.

I want to thank M. K. Chakraborty for his constant support and inspiration.

I would also like to thank Subir Hazra, my friend and ex-colleague, who helped us in preparing the 'Learn by Quiz - Questions/Answers' section.

Most important, heartiest thanks to my family specially my wife Sriparna Saha and my beloved daughter Shreya for their support, encouragement, quite patient and unconditional love which helped, conclude the book.

Finally, I would like to thank all the reviewers of this book for their critical comments and suggestions. I convey my gratitude to Rachna Sehgal and the entire editing team at Cambridge University Press, India for their great work.

Subrata Saha

Thanks to T. K. Ghosh (Chief Executive Director) who found in me suitability to be the head of three departments of a Techno India Group college. He gave me the opportunity to prove myself, to be a good teacher to thousand of students.

Thanks to my teacher Professor Ranjan Dasgupta (Head, Computer Science, NITTTR-Kolkata) who gave me the confidence to write a book.

Thanks to my ex-colleague Professor Sumana Chakraborty who participated actively in discussions to freeze the table of contents of this book.

Subhodip Mukherjee

PART A

Fundamentals of Computer

1

Computer-History, Classification and Basic Anatomy

The first electronic digital computer, called the Atanasoff–Berry Computer (ABC), was built by Dr John V. Atanasoff and Clifford Berry in 1937. An electronic computer called the Colossus was built in 1943 for the US army. Around the same time, many others were also trying to develop computers. The first general-purpose digital computer, the Electronic Numerical Integrator and Computer (ENIAC), was built in 1946.

Computers since 1946 are categorized in five generations:
- First Generation: Vacuum Tubes
- Second Generation: Transistors
- Third Generation: Integrated Circuits
- Fourth Generation: Microprocessors
- Fifth Generation: Artificial Intelligence

Follows a brief description of each generation:

1.1.1 First Generation (1946–1956) Vacuum Tubes

Vacuum tubes were used to make circuits of first generation computers. For building memory, magnetic drums were used that were huge in size and weight. First generation computers were so large in size that they often took an entire room. They were also very prone to error. They were too expensive to operate and in addition consumed huge electricity. It is worth mentioning the amount of heat they generated. Despite using liquid based cooling system, they often got damaged due to heat.

Programs for first generation computers were written in machine language, the lowest-level programming language understood by computers, to perform operations. They were designed to solve only one problem at a time. Punched cards and paper tapes were used to feed input, and output was displayed on printouts.

The ENIAC (**Electronic Numerical Integrator and Computer**) and UNIVAC (**Electronic Discrete Variable Automatic Computer**) computers are examples of first-generation computing devices.

Fig. 1.1   ENIAC

ENIAC was the first electronic general-purpose computer. It was capable of being reprogrammed to solve various numerical problems. ENIAC was primarily designed to calculate artillery firing tables. It was mainly used in the United States Army's Ballistic Research Laboratory. ENIAC was introduced to the public at the University of Pennsylvania in 1946 as "Giant Brain." ENIAC' was funded by the United States Army.

ENIAC had a modular design. It had individual panels to perform separate functions. Twenty modules among them were accumulators that could add, subtract and hold a ten-digit decimal number in memory. Numbers were passed between these modules through several general-purpose buses. The modules were able to send and receive numbers, compute, save the answer and trigger the next operation without any moving component. That is why it could achieve high speed. Key to its versatility was the ability for branching. It could switch to different operations, depending on the sign of a computed result.

ENIAC contained 17,468 vacuum tubes, 1500 relays, 70,000 resistors, 7200 crystal diodes, 10,000 capacitors. It had a whopping 5,000,000 hand-soldered joints. It weighed more than 27 tons, was roughly $8 \times 3 \times 100$ feet in size, occupied 1800 ft^2 and consumed 150 kW of electricity.

After ENIAC, a much improved computer named EDVAC (Electronic Discrete Variable Automatic Computer) was designed. EDVAC was a stored program computer. EDVAC was the first computer to work in binary number system. This is a major difference with ENIAC that used decimal number system.

1.1.2 Second Generation (1956–1963) Transistors

Transistors replaced vacuum tubes in the second generation of computers. The transistor was far superior to the vacuum tube in terms of size, generated heat and energy consumption. So computers made using transistors became smaller, faster, cheaper, more energy-efficient and more reliable.

Fig. 1.2   Transistor

The transistors also generated a lot of heat that subjected the computer to damage. But it was much better than the vacuum tubes in terms of size and heat.

Second-generation computers used symbolic or assembly languages instead of binary machine language that allowed programmers to specify instructions in words instead of machine code or binary.

Second-generation computers were still using punched cards for input and print-outs for output. At this time, high-level programming languages, like early versions of COBOL and FORTRAN were being developed. The first computers that were developed around this time were used in the atomic energy industry.

1.1.3   Third Generation (1964–1971) Integrated Circuits

Third generation computers were based on integrated circuits (IC circuits). Transistors were much smaller. They were placed on silicon chips, called semiconductors. This invention dramatically increased the speed and efficiency of computers.

In these computers, users interacted through keyboards and monitors and interfaced with an operating system. Many different applications were possible to run at one time. A central program usually resided in memory to monitor others. Computers for the first time became accessible to a mass audience because they became cheaper and smaller.

1.1.4   Fourth Generation (1971–Present) Microprocessors

Brain of the fourth generation of computers is **microprocessors.** Thousands of integrated circuits were built on a single silicon chip. Computers of the size of an entire room in first generation could now fit in palm. The Intel 4004 chip, developed in 1971, contained all the components of the computer like the central processing unit, memory and input/output controls on a single chip.

In 1981 IBM introduced its first computer for the home user, and in 1984 Apple introduced the Macintosh. Microprocessors also moved out of the realm of desktop computers and into many areas of life as more and more everyday products began to use microprocessors.

As these small computers became more powerful, they could now be linked together to form networks, which eventually led to the development of the Internet. Fourth generation computers were also equipped with the mouse and other handheld devices. Graphical user interface (GUI) was also designed for these computers.

1.1.5 Fifth generation (Present and Beyond) Artificial Intelligence

Fifth generation computing devices are based on artificial intelligence and are still being developed, while some applications, like voice and handwriting recognisers, are in use today. Fifth-generation computing aims to develop devices that will be responsive to natural language input and will also be able to learn and self-organize.

1.1.6 Evolution of Intel Processors

As Intel processors or compatible processors are most popular for desktop systems, it is worth mentioning the various microprocessors introduced by Intel. The first processor available to public was 8085 having 40 pin, 2 MHz clock frequency, 6500 transistors, 8 bit data bus and 16 bit address bus. But first personal computer made by IBM with Intel microprocessor was based on 8086 having 1 MB addressable memory and 30000 transistors. Then came 80286 followed by 386SX, 386DX, 486 SX and 486 DX.

The 486 processors contained up to 1.4 million transistors, reached 100 MHz frequency and can address up to 4 Gigabyte of memory (32 bit address bus so 2^{32} = 4 GB). After 486, came the decade of Pentium, Pentium with MMX (multimedia extended) and Pentium II processors. Then the Pentium III processor touched the 1 GHz clock frequency mark. From mid of year 2000 the market leader was various versions of Pentium IV for steady six years, achieved clock frequency up to 3.8 GHz and packed up to whopping 180 million transistors in it. Presently core-i3, core-i5 and core-i7 are ruling the market though Intel dual core processors are also available. (In this span, Intel marketed few other processors but they did not get good response.)

1.2 CLASSIFICATION OF COMPUTERS

Computers can be classified in many ways depending on various features and criteria. Many of them will be mentioned in this section. Though readers of this are being introduced to computer and do not have an in-depth knowledge of computer architecture, some classifications based on various architectural difference are also being listed. This will build interest of the readers in the subjects such as 'MICROPROCESSOR', 'ARCHITECTURE', 'COMPUTER ORGANIZATION', 'PARALLEL PROCESSING', 'ASSEMBLY LANGUAGE PROGRAMMING', and 'PIPELINING'.

> **Note** A computer's **architecture** is its abstract model and is the programmer's view in terms of instructions, addressing modes and registers. A computer's **organization** expresses the realization of the architecture. Architecture describes **what** the computer does and organization describes **how** it does it.

Here in this topic, following types of classifications will be discussed:
  i. Based on computation power.
 ii. Based on number of operands.
iii. Scalar VS Vector processor.

iv. Flynn's taxonomy

v. von Neumann vs. Harvard Architecture

vi. Big-endian vs. Little-endian

(i) Based on Size, Computing Power and Price

Based on their size, computing power and price the computers are broadly classified into four categories:

1. Microcomputers
2. Minicomputers
3. Mainframe computers
4. Supercomputer.

As the list descends, things will become large, expensive, complex and fast. Now follows a small introduction to all of them:

(1) Microcomputers are the most common kind of computers used by people today, whether in a workplace, at school or on the desk at home. These are microprocessor based systems. Microcomputers are small, low-cost and single-user digital computer. They consist of CPU, input unit, output unit, storage unit and the software. Microcomputers are stand-alone machines but they can be connected together to create a network of computers that can serve more than one user. Microcomputers include desktop computers, notebook computers or laptop, tablet computer, handheld computer, smart phones, etc. The most popular microprocessors in world are made by Intel and Apple for their Pentium based PCs and Apple Macintosh.

Here the evolution of Intel microprocessors will be worth mentioning. Intel first introduced the 8085 microprocessor having 8 bit data bus and 16 bit address bus but no personal computer was made based on it. The journey started with 8086 when IBM made IBM-AT based on it. Gradually came 80286, 386, 486 SX and 486 DX. Next processor was named Pentium with clock frequency 60 MHz to 300 MHz and introduced in the period 1993–1997. It had a 32 bit data bus and 32 bit address bus. The speed and internal cache memory size increased with time. Pentium II, Pentium III and Pentium IV were the successors. Then came Pentium DUAL CORE, Core2-DUO, and Quad-core processors having frequency in GHz level. Now the latest processors from Intel's stable are core-I3, core-I5 and core-I7.

(2) Minicomputer is a class of multi-user computers that lies in the middle range of the computing spectrum, in between the top end single-user systems (microcomputers or personal computers) and low end mainframe computers. They have high processing speed and high storage capacity than the microcomputers. Minicomputers can support up to 200 users simultaneously. The users can access the minicomputer through their PCs or terminal. They are used for various processor hungry applications in industries and research centers.

(3) Mainframe computers are multi-user, multi-programming and high performance computers. They operate at a very high speed, have huge storage capacity and can handle the workload of many users. The user accesses the mainframe computer via a terminal that may be a dumb terminal, an intelligent terminal or a PC. The terminals and PCs utilize the processing power and the storage facility of the mainframe computer. Mainframe computers are used primarily by corporate and governmental organizations for critical applications, bulk data processing such as census, industry and consumer statistics, enterprise resource planning and transaction processing.

(4) Supercomputers are the fastest and the most expensive machines. They have high processing speed compared to other computers. The speed of a supercomputer is generally measured in FLOPS (Floating point Operations Per Second). Some of the faster supercomputers can perform trillions of calculations per second. Supercomputers are built by interconnecting thousands of processors that can work in parallel. Supercomputers are used for highly calculation-intensive tasks, such as, weather forecasting, climate research, molecular research, biological research, nuclear research and aircraft design. Some examples of supercomputers are IBM Roadrunner, IBM Blue gene. The supercomputer assembled in India by C-DAC (Center for Development of Advanced Computing) is PARAM. PARAM Padma is the latest machine in this series. The peak computing power of PARAM Padma is One Tera FLOP.

(ii) Based on Number of Operands

The instruction-set of a computer is designed first, and then accordingly the architecture is designed. Just like a KEY is designed first then corresponding LOCK is assembled. A computer instruction should contain one operation code and zero or more operands on which the operation will be performed or where the result will be stored. Depending on maximum number of operands allowed in an instruction, computers can be classified:
1. Zero address machines (stack machine)
2. One address machine (accumulator machine)
3. Two address machine (Intel processors are of this type)
4. Three address machine

(iii) Scalar Processor vs Vector Processor

Each instruction executed by a scalar processor generally manipulates one or two data items at a time. On the contrary, instructions of a vector processor operate simultaneously on many data items.

(iv) By Flynn's Taxonomy

Flynn's taxonomy is a classification of computer architectures, proposed by Michael J. Flynn in 1966. There are four categories defined by Flynn. His classification is based upon the number of concurrent instruction (or control) and data streams available in the architecture:

1. Single Instruction, Single Data stream (SISD) A sequential computer which exploits no parallelism in either the instruction or data streams. Single control unit (CU) fetches single Instruction Stream (IS) from memory. The CU then generates appropriate control signals to direct single processing element to operate on single Data Stream.

2. Single Instruction, Multiple Data streams (SIMD) A computer which exploits multiple data streams against a single instruction stream to perform operations which may be naturally parallelized. For example, an array processor or GPU.

3. Multiple Instruction, Single Data stream (MISD) Multiple instructions operate on a single data stream. Uncommon architecture which is generally used for fault tolerance.

4. Multiple Instruction, Multiple Data streams (MIMD) Multiple autonomous processors simultaneously executing different instructions on different data. Distributed systems are generally recognized to be MIMD architectures; either exploiting a single shared memory space or a distributed memory space.

(v) von Neumann vs. Harvard Architecture

While talking about computers, there should be a topic on John von Neumann. This Hungary-born American mathematician gave the concept of stored-program architecture first but unfortunately in his life span no fully functional computer was made. His ideas will be discussed later on this chapter.

von Neumann architecture	Harvard architecture
1. Same memory for data & program	1. Separate data and code memory
2. Instructions are executed one by one. Execution requires at least two clock cycles. One for fetch and others for execution and pipelining is not possible.	2. Pipelining is possible.

(vi) Big-endian vs Little-endian

This is based on "How a large binary number is stored in 8 bit (byte) wide memory" (remember – each memory address can store 1 byte of data). Suppose the following 32 bit number have to be stored:

11111111 00000000 10101010 11110000

In case of **big-endian**, the most significant byte is stored in the smallest address. Here's how it would look:

Address	Data value
400	11111111
401	00000000
402	10101010
403	11110000

In case of **little-endian**, the least significant byte is stored in the smallest address. Here's how it would look:

Address	Data value
400	11110000
401	10101010
402	00000000
403	11111111

It can be easily understood by a little thought that "performing arithmetic operations are easier in little-endian computers where as comparing strings chronologically is easier in big-endian computers".

1.3   BASIC ANATOMY OF A COMPUTER

A digital computer is an electronic device that receives data, performs arithmetic and logical operations and produces results according to a predetermined program. It receives data from input devices and gives results to output devices. The central processing unit, also known as processor processes the data. Memory (primary and secondary) is used to store data and instructions. Follows, block diagram of a digital computer identifying the key components and their interconnection.

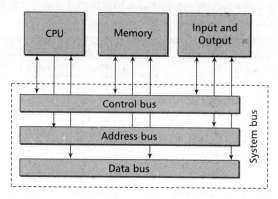

Fig. 1.3   Components of a computer

The Central Processing Unit (CPU) is like the brain of the computer. It is responsible for executing instructions. It controls the sequence of execution of instructions. It comprises a Control Unit (CU), an Arithmetic & Logic Unit (ALU) and huge number of registers. The CU controls the execution of instructions. First it decodes the instruction and then generates micro-operations in a particular order with the help of control memory. The ALU is responsible for performing arithmetic and logic operations.

The interconnections are referred as BUS. Buses are nothing but bunch of wires used to carry digital signals. There are three kinds of bus:
1. Address bus
2. Data bus
3. Control bus

Address bus carries address of memory from where to read/to where to write data. Size of address bus of a processor defines the amount of memory addressable by it. For example a processor with 16 bit address bus can access 2^{16} = 64 KB memory (2^6 = 64 and 2^{10} = 1024 = 1 K) and a processor with 32 bit address bus can access 2^{32}=4 GB memory (2^2 = 4 and 2^{30} = 1024 × 1024 × 1024 = 1024 × 1024 × 1 K = 1024 × 1 Mega = 1 Giga.). Address bus is unidirectional, i.e., it carries signal from CPU to other components (only CPU is intelligent enough to generate address).

Data bus is bidirectional. It carries data read from/to be written to a device. Its size and width of registers signify the size of data that can be crunched by the processor in one go.

Control bus carries control signals that activate/deactivate various circuits.

Block diagram of the common bus architecture follows:

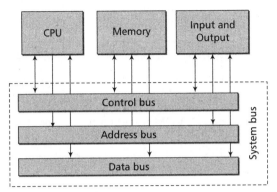

Fig. 1.4   Common bus architecture

1.4   VON NEUMANN ARCHITECTURE

While studying computer architecture, the name of Von Neumann comes first. Though he could not see any working model based on his proposal during his life span, design of all modern computers is based on the stored program model proposed by him. In 1945, the mathematician and physicist John von Neumann, along with others, had described computer architecture in the First Draft Report on the EDVAC. The Von Neumann architecture, which is also known as the Von Neumann model and Princeton architecture, is based on that. In this report a digital computer has been proposed that will contain the following parts:

- A processing unit containing an arithmetic logic unit and processor registers.
- A control unit containing an instruction register and program counter.
- Memory to store both data and instructions.
- External mass storage.
- Input and output mechanisms.

Stored-program computers were much advanced as compared to the program-controlled computers of the 1940s, like the Colossus and the ENIAC. These were programmed by switches and patches, which led to route data and could control the signals between the various functional units.

Some key points to remember about this architecture:

- A program should totally reside in the main memory prior to execution.[*]
- Data and code will reside in the same memory and will be indistinguishable.[†]

---

[*]As the programs became larger and larger, it was not possible to put the total program in the relatively smaller main memory. So **virtual memory** was introduced in operating systems. It is a technique that shows the free part of secondary storage as main memory. It keeps the total program in the secondary storage in blocks and fetches the required blocks to primary when necessary.

[†]Here **Von Neumann** design differs from **HAVARD ARCHITECTURE** that uses separate code and data memory on separate bus.

- Instructions will be fetched from memory and executed one at a time in a linear fashion.[‡] $$

1.5 MEMORY CLASSIFICATION AND HIERARCHY

Broadly classified, a computer system has two types of memory – Primary and Secondary.

RAM (Random Access Memory), ROM (Read Only Memory) and Cache memory (one kind of very fast random access memory) falls in the primary category where as Magnetic tape, CD-ROM, DVD, Hard disk, pen drive (flash memory) falls in the secondary mass storage category.

Computer system uses memory hierarchy to optimize hardware cost. For example, in a system where 4 megabyte of cache memory is being used, the size of RAM can be 2 GB or 4 GB. If a system is build with total 2 GB cache instead, the system cost will go beyond imagination but 'speed boost' will be only 10% of the system mentioned earlier.

If memory is classified in terms of access strategy then there are three categories:
1. Sequential access.
2. Random access.
3. Direct access.

In **sequential access memory**, access time is directly proportionate to address. Magnetic tapes falls in this category.

In **random access memory**, access time is constant, i.e., to access content at 1st location or at millionth location, same time will be required.

All sorts of circular and rotating memories like hard disk, CD, DVD fall in **direct access** category where access time can be expressed as a function $T = Ax + By$ where A, B are constants and x, y are variables. These sorts of memory are divided in tracks and sectors. Time required by the read/write head to reach a track is known as **seek time**. Time required by a sector to reach under read/write head is known as **latency time**.

1.6 INPUT AND OUTPUT DEVICES

In this section various input and output devices commonly used in computer systems will be discussed.

1.6.1 Input Devices

1.6.1.1 Keyboard

Text information is entered in the computer by typing on the computer keyboard. Most keyboards, for example – the 101-key US traditional keyboard or the 104-key Windows keyboard, have alphabetic and numeric characters, punctuation marks and function keys. Keyboards are generally connected to the computer by a PS/2 connector or USB port.

[‡] To speed up execution, multiple instructions are fetched in a queue in a pipelined computer.

Fig. 1.5   Keyboard

PS/2 port and cable   **USB port and cable**

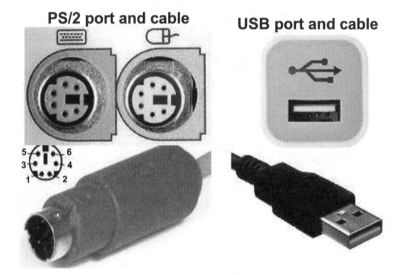

Fig. 1.6   USB and PS/2 ports

1.6.1.2 *Mouse*

Mouse is a pointing device. The **cursor** on the screen is moved by moving the mouse. A mouse have mainly two buttons – left and right. Newer mouses may contain other buttons and a roller for scrolling. In older models, a ball at the bottom of the mouse rolls on the surface as the mouse moves, and internal rollers sense the movement of the ball and transmit the information to the computer via the mouse cable. The newer optical mouse does not use a rolling ball, instead it uses a light and a small optical sensor to detect the motion of the mouse by tracking a tiny image of the desk surface. Even cordless mouse are very much affordable now a days, but they need regular battery change that reduces their popularity. Mouse sends two information to the computer – one is the X and Y coordinate of the pointer merged in a single number, another is the code of key pressed. Any activity on the mouse generates an interrupt that ultimately communicates an event such as mouse move, left click, double click, right click, and drag to the operating system. What incidents will happen with the mouse events, are completely programmable.

1.6.1.3 Scanners

A scanner is a device that converts a printed page or graphic to an image file that can be stored in a computer by digitizing it. It produces an image made of tiny pixels of different brightness and color values which are represented numerically and sent to the computer.

Fig. 1.7   Scanner

Pages containg text are also scanned and saved as images. To convert such images containing text to editable text files OCR (Optical Character Recognition) software is used.

Scanners are available in various sizes with various scan resolution capabilities. A4 size scanners (largest page size it can scan is A4-8.27" × 11.69") are most popular and affordable. Scanners with automatic document feeder are also available.

1.6.1.4 Microphone

A microphone can be attached to a computer through a sound card input or circuitry built into the motherboard to record sound. The sound is digitized and stored in the computer.

Fig. 1.8   Microphone

Our ear can hear analog sound of frequency range 20 to 20 MHz. But for storing sound in computer, the analog signal is converted to digital signal. Again when the sound is played back through speakers, the stored digital signal is converted to analog. (The process of digitization is beyond the scope of this book.)

1.6.2   Output Devices

1.6.2.1   Monitor

Monitor is the maximum used output device of a personal computers. At the begining, CRT- (Cathode Ray Tube) display in monochrome with low resolution was available. Gradually high resolution colour monitors were introduced. Presently bulky CRT monitors have been mostly replaced by LCD or LED monitors as LCD or LED displays consume less electricity, occupy less space and are capable of displaying more clear and flicker free images.

1.6.2.2   Printer

When some output on paper is needed, a printer is a must. The three most common types of printers are Dot matrix, Inkjet and Laser. Dot matrix printers provide poorest quality output at lowest cost. It is mainly used for text based outputs on pre-printed stationary such as cash-memo and ticket.

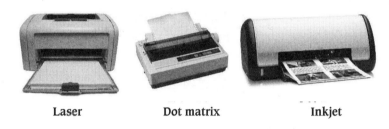

Laser   **Dot matrix**   **Inkjet**

Fig. 1.9   Printers

Laser printers produce best quality printouts using powder formed inks filled in toner cartiges. Cost of laser printers are high but printing cost is less than that of a deskjet printer that uses liquid inks with magnetic particles filled in ink cartiges.

EXERCISES

1. Write short notes on Von Neumann architecture.
2. Differentiate between Von Neumann and Havard architecture.
3. With a neat block diagram, describe various components on a computer.
4. Classify memories in terms of access strategy.
5. "All ROMs are RAM but all RAMs are not ROMs" – Justify.
6. For a medicine or grocery store what kind of printer you will suggest and why?
7. Write down various ports availble in a computer system.
8. What is a BUS? How many types of BUS is available?
9. Write full form of ENIAC.
10. What do you mean by Virtual Memory. What is the largest possible size of it? Why it is called virtual?

2

Introduction to Number System and Logic Gates

PLAYING WITH NUMBERS

2.1 INTRODUCTION

'Computer' as the name suggests is meant for computation. So knowledge of computer is not possible without the knowledge of various number systems, number formats and their advantages and drawbacks. That is why mathematicians always played a major role in the advancement of computer science.

From pre-historic age when human beings were formed by evolution, numbers are being used to count, label and measure. Initially tally marks were used for counting. Bones, cave pictures from pre-historic age have been discovered with marks cut into them that are similar to tally marks. It is assumed that these tally marks were used for counting elapsed time, such as numbers of days or to keep count of animals. Tally mark was not a positional number system. From tally mark evolved the Roman number system. All these systems have limitations of representing large numbers. Historically it is said that number system with place value was first used in Mesopotamia, from 3400 BC onwards. In India, Aryans used the word SHUNYA in Sanskrit to represent void. This is used as ZERO in mathematics. Greeks were confused about using zero. But eventually this place holder developed today's mostly used *positional number system* where the value of the number depends on the position of the digits. For example $349 = 3*10^2 + 4*10^1 + 9*10^0$ as 9 is at position 0, 4 is at position 1 and 3 is at position 2. And obviously the number 1000000 is larger than the number 999999. In fact the value of a number in a positional number system depends on two things, one position and the other is base of that number system.

2.2 BASE OF A NUMBER SYSTEM

Number of digits present in a number system is called **base** of that number system.

In general we use decimal number system, whose base is 10.

EXAMPLE

In **Decimal** base is *10* and the digits are: 0,1,2,3,4,5,6,7,8,9.

In **Binary** base is *2* and the digits are: 0,1.

In **Octal** base is *8* and the digits are: 0,1,2,3,4,5,6,7.

In **Hex**adecimal base is *16* and the digits are: 0,1,2,3,4,5,6,7,8,9,A,B,C,D,E,F.

A-10
B-11
C-12
D-13
E-14
F-15

So in a number system where base is 3, the digits will be 0, 1 and 2. Similarly in a number system where base is 13, the digits will be 0,1,2,3,4,5,6,7,8,9,A,B,C. Remember that the number 187 is not an octal number as the digit 8 cannot be presented in an octal number.

2.3 REASON BEHIND USING BINARY NUMBER SYSTEM

In computer we use binary number system and its variations (whatever may be the interpretation of a value of number, the digits present in a number used in computer are only 0 and 1). This is because today's computers are digital computers made with semiconductor switches that build the logic of the computer. The switches can be in either ON or OFF state (i.e., 0 or 1 state). In other simple word we have to deal with two voltages HIGH and LOW[*] to work in binary but if we have to design a computer that works in decimal internally we have to deal with 10 different, distinct voltages in the circuit and that is really complicated.

Now question may arise that 'if binary is used in computer then why learn Hex or octal?' the answer is simple: huge binary numbers can be represented in short Hex numbers that are easy to remember and understand by human being. For example the Hex number '3C4F' is equivalent to binary '0011110001001111'.

Again 'why Hex, why not decimal?' – "Converting a number from Binary to Hex or Binary to Octal and vice versa is easier and requires less computation than converting binary to Decimal".

> **Tip** Always remember that all positional number systems sing the same tune. You have to catch the perfect tune to play with them. If the pattern is perfectly recognized then one can handle huge numbers without using pen and paper. For example:
> There are 100 numbers from 00 to 99. If we divide them in two equal groups the numbers at the center are 49 and 50.
>
> Now if asked the same question for the set of numbers starting from 00000000 to 99999999 everybody will answer 49999999 and 50000000 without any calculation and just by pattern matching.

---

[*]though other voltages than HIGH and LOW exists in digital circuits, better not to bother about them until you start studying VLSI design.

2.4 CONVERSION AMONG DIFFERENT BASES

Rule

(i)   Divide the number to be converted by target base

(ii)   Store the remainder and divide the quotient by target base.

(iii)   Continue step II until quotient is 0.

(iv)   Write all stored remainders in reverse order to get equivalent result.

As example let us convert the decimal number 37 to different bases:

System	Octal	Hex	Binary
	8⌊37 8⌊4 ----5 0 ----4	16⌊37 16⌊2 ----5 0 ----2	2⌊37 2⌊18 ----1 2⌊9 ----0 2⌊4 ----1 2⌊2 ----0 2⌊1 ----0 0 ----1
Result	45	25	100101

```
Decimal  ◄────────  Other base
```

Rule   Sum up digit multiplied by base to the power position. i.e., Σdigit * base^{position}

As example let us return back to 37:

System	Octal	Hex	Binary
	$4*8^1+5*8^0$	$2*16^1+5*16^0$	$1*2^5+1*2^2+1*2^0$
Result	37	37	37

Tip   You do not have to follow the rule in order to convert from binary to decimal. Many easy shortcut methods are available. Before stating them, please mug up following tables thoroughly so that you can recite the values if asked randomly.

Table 2.1 Powers of 2

2^1	2
2^2	4
2^3	8
2^4	16
2^5	32
2^6	64
2^7	128
2^8	256
2^9	512
2^{10}	1024

Table 2.2 Binary values of decimal numbers

0	0000
1	0001
2	0010
3	0011
4	0100
5	0101
6	0110
7	0111
8	1000
9	1001
10	1010
11	1011
12	1100
13	1101
14	1110
15	1111

Remember that *"if we multiply a number by base a '0' is added at the end"* 35*10=350, 35*10^2=3500, 35*10^5=3500000 *and so on.*

Similarly in binary, notice that

Binary of 3= 11

Binary of 6= 110

Binary of 12= 1100

Binary of 24= 11000

Similarly in Octal

Octal of 2 = 2

Octal of 16 = 20

Octal of 128 = 200

Now you can use any of the following tricks for conversion

- *Notice that if you remember binary of 13 then you can say binary of 26, 52, 104 and so on.*
- *Let us take a larger example – Decimal equivalent of the binary number 11001110 is 206. As the number 11001110 = 11000000 + 1110 = 3*2^6 + 14= 192 + 14 = 206.*
- *Adding up power of 2 at the positions where there is 1 in the binary number gives equivalent decimal easily.*
- *128 = 2^7 so its binary will be 10000000 (7 zeros) hence binary of 127 will be 1111111 (7 ones) and binary of 129 will be 10000001*

Just write equivalent binary of the digits of the Hex number side by side using 4 bits for each Hex digit.

EXAMPLE

$3C4F_H = 0011110001001111$

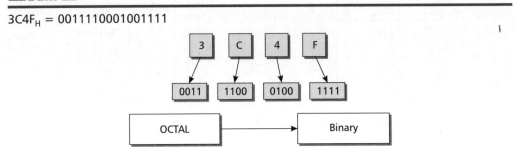

Just write equivalent binary of the digits of the octal number side by side using 3 bits for each octal digit.

EXAMPLE

$3746_8 = 011111100110$

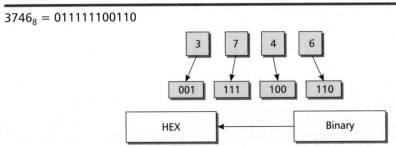

Group the digits of the binary number in four, taking from right. If required take extra 0 at left. Now write hex equivalent for each group.

EXAMPLE

$11110001001111 = 3C4F_H$

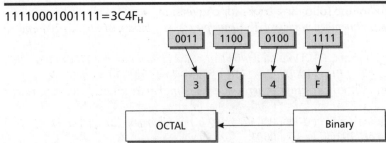

Group the digits of the binary number in three, taking from right. If required take extra 0 at left. Now write hex equivalent for each group.

EXAMPLE

$11111100110 = 3746_8$

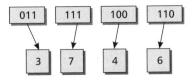

2.5 SIMILARITIES BETWEEN NUMBER SYSTEMS OF DIFFERENT BASES

I would like to repeat again the sentence – *"all positional number systems sing the same tune"*. From the following table the similarities will be clear.

Table 2.3   Similarity of different bases

	Decimal	Octal	Hex	Binary
Highest number using 3 digits	$10^3 - 1 = 999$	$8^3 - 1 = 777$	$16^3 - 1 = FFF$	$2^3 - 1 = 111$
Value of $1000 - 1 = ?$	999	777	FFF	111
Value of base	$10 = 10$	$8 = 10$	$16 = 10$	$2 = 10$
Subtracting 1	$30 - 1 = 29$	$30 - 1 = 27$	$30 - 1 = 2F$	$11110 - 1 = 11101$
Multiply by power of base	$37*10^3 = 37000$	$37*8^3 = 37000$	$37*16^3 = 37000$	$100101*2^3 = 100101000$

2.6 ADDITION OF TWO NUMBERS

Before stating the addition process, let us know two terms MSB and LSB. The leftmost digit of a number is called MSB (Most Significant Bit) and the rightmost digit of a number is called LSB (Least Significant Bit).

Now let us recap the addition process of two number, we are doing since our nursery classes:

- We start addition from adding LSB of two numbers.
- We divide the result by base to obtain quotient and remainder.
- We write remainder as sum and quotient goes to carry to next digit addition.

Pictorially it can be shown as:

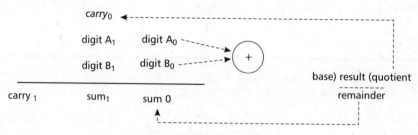

Fig. 2.1   Addition process

EXAMPLE

DECIMAL	STEP	RESULT (in decimal)	Quotient	Remainder
35	1(5+7)	12	1	2
67	2(3+6+1)	10	1	0
102				

In the above example the LSB of 35 is 5 and LSB of 67 is 7. So we first add them and get 12. We then divide 12 by base, i.e., 10 here to get 2 as remainder and 1 as quotient. So 2 is sum and 1 is carry. In the next step, we add 3, 6 and carry 1 from the previous addition to get 10. We repeat same process of division to get 0 as sum and 1 as carry. As there are no more digits left, the carry 1 will be written at the MSB.

Similarly addition of two numbers in different bases follows.

OCTAL(8)	STEP	RESULT (in decimal)	Quotient	Remainder
35	1(5+7)	12	1	4
67	2(3+6+1)	10	1	2
124				

HEX(16)	STEP	RESULT (in decimal)	Quotient	Remainder
3C	1(12+13)	25	1	9
6D	2(3+6+1)	10	0	A
A9				

BINARY(2)	STEP	RESULT (in decimal)	Quotient	Remainder
11	1	2	1	0
11	2	3	1	1
110				

Note that same procedure has been followed for all number systems. Only difference is that the division was done by corresponding base, e.g., 8 for Octal, 16 for Hexadecimal and so on.

We can add multiple binary numbers at a time in same process:

BINARY(2)	STEP	RESULT (in decimal)	Quotient	Remainder
110	1	4	2	0
101	2	5	2	1
111	3	7	3 (11 in binary)	1
011				
101				
100				
11110				

2.7 SIGNED BINARY NUMBERS

So far we were talking about unsigned numbers having only magnitude. In this section, we will see how to represent negative numbers in binary. The main hurdle is that we cannot store the symbol (–) minus in computers. We have only 0(zero) and 1(one) to use. There are many possible ways:

(A) **Signed magnitude form:** We can use the MSB as sign. For positive numbers we can use MSB = 0 and use MSB = 1 for negative numbers. Remaining bits used to store the magnitude. For example, in an 8 bit representation +5 = 00000101 and –5 = 10000101.

(B) **1's complement method:** To get the **1's** (one's) complement of a binary number we just have to invert all the bits in the binary representation of the number (replace 0 by 1 and 1 by 0). The 1's complement of the number then behaves like the negative of the original number. If 1's complement of a number is calculated we get the original number. This is like –(–5) = +5. Also if we add 1's complement of 2 with binary of 5 we get binary of 3 showing that 1's complement of 2 is behaving like –2.

(C) **2's complement method:** The two's complement of an N-digit binary number is defined as the complement with respect to 2^N, i.e., the result obtained by subtracting the number from 2^N. **Taking the 1's complement of the number and then adding 1 with the complement will give same result.** It can be easily verified that 2's complement of a number is the original number as in the case of 1's complement. *(Please note that any extra bit after MSB in 2's complement system is simple discarded.)*

Though both 1's complement and 2's complement system behaves almost same still 2's complement is mostly used for the two differences:

(i) In 1's complement value of 0 and –0 is different (0000 vs. 1111) but in 2's complement both zero and minus zero have same value, which is more realistic.

(ii) If we add P with –P in 1's complement we get –0 but in 2's complement we get 0. e.g. 5+(–5) → 0101 + 1010 = 1111 in 1's complement but 5+(–5) → 0101 + 1011 = 0000 in 2's complement.

While dealing with 2's complement numbers do not forget the range of numbers that can be represented using N bits. An N-bit 2's-complement number system can represent every integer in the range $-(2^{N-1})$ to $+(2^{N-1} - 1)$. Please refer to following table for the ranges.

Number of bits	Range in 2's complement	Range in unsigned representation
3	−4 to 3	0 to 7
4	−8 to 7	0 to 15
5	−16 to 15	0 to 31
8	−128 to 127	0 to 255
10	−512 to 511	0 to 1023
N	$-(2^{N-1})$ to $(2^{N-1} - 1)$	0 to $(2^N - 1)$
	Range of numbers using N bits	

Some examples of addition and subtraction using 2's complement system are given for ease of understanding.

i)

23−8=   23 =   00010111   23 =   00010111
23+(−8)   →   +8 =   00001000   →   −8 =   +11111000

                                      } =00001111   →   +15

ii)

8−23= 8+(-   8 =   00001000   8 =   00001000
23)   →   +23 =   00010111   →   −23 =   +11101001

                                         =11110001   →   −15

iii)

−8+23=   8 =   00001000   →   −8 =   11111000
          →   +23 =   00010111   +23 =   +00010111

                                         =00001111   →   +15

iv)

8+23=   8 =   00001000   →   8 =   00001000
          →   +23 =   00010111   +23 =   +00010111

                                         =00011111   →   +31

2.7.1 BCD (Binary Coded Decimal) Number

Binary-coded decimal (BCD) is a binary encoding of decimal numbers where each decimal digit is represented by a fixed number of binary bits (i.e., 0/1), usually four or eight.

For example BCD of the number 243 is <u>0010</u> <u>0100</u> <u>0011</u> where four bits are used for each digit.

Although BCD was used in many early decimal computers, now-a-days it is rarely used.

If 4 digits are used for every digit then it is called **packed BCD.**

If 8 digits are used for every digit then it is called **unpacked BCD.**

2.7.2 Advantage of BCD (Over Binary Number System)
- It gives more accurate representation and rounding of decimal quantities.
- Can be easily converted into human-readable representations.

2.7.3 Drawbacks of BCD
- Increase in the complexity of the circuits needed to implement basic arithmetic.
- More storage space required.

2.7.4 Addition of Two BCD Numbers
(i) First add two 4-bit BCD digits using normal binary addition.
(ii) If the 4-bit sum is less or equal to 9, the sum is in proper BCD and no correction is required but If the sum is greater than 9 or if a carry is generated from the sum then add 6 (0110) with the sum to get proper BCD result. If in this adjustment process a carry is generated then it will be added as carry to the next decimal place.

2.7.5 Excess-3 or XS-3 Code
The Excess-3 code of a decimal number is calculated by adding 3 (three) to each decimal digit of the given number and then replacing each digit of the newly generated decimal number by its four bit binary equivalent.

It is a biased BCD code. It was used on few older computers as well as in cash registers and old hand held portable electronic calculators of earlier days.

Number	0	1	2	3	4
BCD	0000	0001	0010	0011	0100
Excess-3	0011	0100	0101	0110	0111

Number	9	8	7	6	5
BCD	1001	1000	0111	0110	0101
Excess-3	1100	1011	1010	1001	1000

It is an example of **unweighted code** (as each position within the binary equivalent of the number is not assigned a fixed value).

Please note from the above table that excess-3 is self complimenting code or reflective code, as 1's compliment of any number (0–9) is available within these 10 numbers. For example 1's complement of 9 (1100) is 0011 which is excess-3 code of 0. Same phenomenon can be watched for 1–8, 2–7, 3–4 and 4–5.

The primary advantage of XS-3 coding over non-biased coding is that a decimal number can be nines' complemented (for subtraction) as easily as a binary number can be ones' complemented; just invert all bits.

2.8 ASCII (AMERICAN STANDARD CODE FOR INFORMATION INTERCHANGE)

The American Standard Code for Information Interchange (ASCII) is a character-encoding scheme originally based on the English alphabet that encodes 128 specified characters into the 7-bit binary integers. They can be classified as:

- The numbers 0–9.
- The letters a–z.
- The letters A–Z.
- Some basic punctuation symbols.
- Some control codes that originated with teletype machines.
- A blank space.

ASCII includes definitions for 128 characters. Among them there are 33 non-printing control characters that affect how text and space are processed and 95 printable characters, including the space.

Part of the ASCII table is given below:

Table 2.4   ASCII values

Character	Value			
	Dec	Hex	Binary	Oct
Null character	0	00	000 0000	000
Bell	7	07	000 0111	007
Backspace	8	08	000 1000	010
Horizontal tab	9	09	000 1001	011
Line feed	10	0A	000 1010	012
Carriage return	13	0D	000 1101	015
Escape	27	1B	001 1011	033
Space	32	20	0100000	040
*	42	2A	0101010	052
+	43	2B	0101011	053
−	45	2D	0101101	055
/	47	2F	0101111	057
0	48	30	0110000	060
9	57	39	0111001	071
A	65	41	1000001	101
Z	90	5A	1011010	132
a	97	61	1100001	141
z	122	7A	1111010	172

2.9 LOGIC GATES AND BOOLEAN ALGEBRA

All digital circuits can be classified into two broad categories:
1. Combinational Circuits
2. Sequential Circuits.

2.9.1 Combinational Circuits (Combinatorial Logic Circuits)

The digital circuits where the output(s) is/are totally dependent on the present input(s) are called combinational circuits.

When input(s) is/are changed, the information about the previous input(s) is lost. So we say that combinational logic circuits have no memory. This is in contrast to sequential logic, in which the output depends not only on the present input but also on the previous output.

In this chapter, we will concentrate on combinational circuits.

2.9.2 Sequential Circuits

The digital circuits in which the output depends both on the present input and the history of the input (previous output) are called sequential circuits. In other words, sequential logic has memory while combinational logic does not.

Sequential circuit can be described by following block diagram:

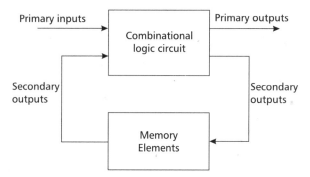

Fig. 2.2   Sequential circuit

2.10 GATES (LOGIC GATES)

Logic gates are combinational circuits having one or more input but only one output.

A logic gate performs a logical operation on one or more logic inputs and produces a single logic output. The logic performed is Boolean logic. Logic gates are implemented electronically using diodes or transistors.

2.11 BASIC GATES

AND gate OR gate NOT gate – These three are basic gates and we can create any Boolean logic circuit using combination of these three gates.

> ***Truth Table:*** A truth table is a table that describes the behavior of a logic gate. It lists the value of the output for every possible combination of the inputs.

> Boolean algebra is different from ordinary algebra in one major place. Boolean constants and variables can have only two possible values, 0 or 1.
>
> Boolean 0 and 1 are not actual numbers, on the contrary they represent the state of a voltage variable, or what is called its logic level.
>
> Common representation of 0 and 1 is:
> - Logic 0: False, Off, Low, No, Open Switch
> - Logic 1: True, On, High, Yes, Close Switch

2.11.1 AND Gate

AND gate is a logic gates having two or more inputs whose output is 1 if all of its inputs are 1 otherwise the output is 0.

AND gate is represented by the following block diagram:

If the inputs are a, b then the output is written as **a.b** or simply **ab (so '.' is the symbol of AND in Boolean expression).**

Truth table of a two-input and three-input AND gate follows

A	B	A.B
0	0	0
0	1	0
1	0	0
1	1	1

A	B	C	A.B.C
0	0	0	0
0	0	1	0
0	1	0	0
0	1	1	0
1	0	0	0
1	0	1	0
1	1	0	0
1	1	1	1

2.11.2 OR Gate

OR gate is a logic gates having two or more inputs whose output is 0 if all of its inputs are 0 otherwise the output is 1.

OR gate is represented by the following block diagram:

If the inputs are a, b then the output is written as **a+b (so '+' is the symbol of OR in Boolean expression).**

Truth table of a two input and three input OR gate follows:

A	B	A+B
0	0	0
0	1	1
1	0	1
1	1	1

A	B	C	A+B+C
0	0	0	0
0	0	1	1
0	1	0	1
0	1	1	1
1	0	0	1
1	0	1	1
1	1	0	1
1	1	1	1

2.11.3 NOT Gate

NOT gate can have only one input. The output is just reverse of the input. i.e., output is 1 if input is 0 & vice-versa.

NOT gate is represented by the following block diagram (also in composite circuit a bubble implies NOT).

The output is denoted by a bar over the input. If the input is A then output will be $\overline{A}$, if the input is $\overline{A}$ then the output will be A (double bar cancels).

If the input is A+B+C then the output will be $\overline{A+B+C}$ not $\overline{A} + \overline{B} + \overline{C}$, they are different. NOT gate is also known as **Astable Multivibrator**.

NAND gate Can be considered as NOT of AND. For inputs A, B the output will be $\overline{AB}$. Block diagram follows:

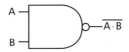

REMEMBER THE FOLLOWING IDENTITIES:

$A+A=A$

$A.A=A$

$A+1=1$

$A.1=A$

$A+0=A$

$A.0=0$

$A+\overline{A}=1$

$A.\overline{A}=0$

NOR gate Can be considered as NOT of OR. For inputs A, B the output will be $\overline{A+B}$. Block diagram follows:

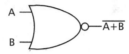

2.12 UNIVERSAL GATES

NAND and NOR are known as Universal Gates as by combining multiple NAND or NOR gates we can construct any Boolean logic without using any other gate.

Construction of three basic gates using NAND gate follows that sufficiently proves that NAND is a Universal Gate. (NOR is a Universal Gate-proof left to reader).

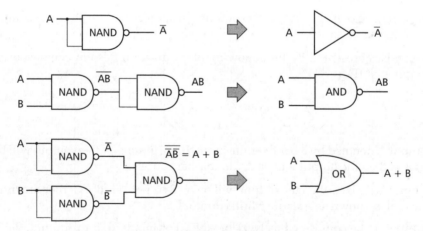

Fig. 2.3   NAND as universal gate

De Morgan's Laws:

1. $\overline{A+B} = \overline{A} \cdot \overline{B}$ (Proof by truth table is left for the reader)
2. $\overline{A} + \overline{B} = \overline{A \cdot B}$

Distributive Law

$$A + B \cdot C = (A+B) \cdot (A+C)$$

Proof

$$(A+B) \cdot (A+C) = A \cdot A + A \cdot B + A \cdot C + B \cdot C$$

$$= A + A \cdot B + A \cdot C + B \cdot C$$

$$= A \cdot (1+B+C) + B \cdot C$$

$$= A \cdot 1 + B \cdot C$$

$$= A + B \cdot C$$

XOR (Exclusive OR gate) It may have two or more inputs. The output is 1 if **odd number of input is 1** otherwise 0.

Denoted by $A \oplus B$ and the block diagram follows:

Truth table of a two input and three input XOR gate follows:

A	B	A⊕B
0	0	0
0	1	1
1	0	1
1	1	0

A	B	C	A⊕B⊕C
0	0	0	0
0	0	1	1
0	1	0	1
0	1	1	0
1	0	0	1
1	0	1	0
1	1	0	0
1	1	1	1

The XOR gate with inputs A and B implements the logical expression $\overline{A}B + A\overline{B}$.

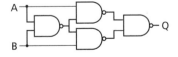

XOR gate constructed using only NAND gates

EXERCISES

1. Convert the Hexadecimal number 3F1D.3AB to Octal.
2. What is the advantage of 2's complement number over 1's complement.
3. Add the following numbers using 2's complement:
   (a) 5, 3
   (b) 5, 3
   (c) 5, 3
   (d) 16, 3
4. Which gates are called UNIVERSAL gates and why?
5. Draw circuit for $AB(\overline{A} + B)(A+\overline{B})$
6. Add the binary numbers: 100, 100, 110,011,111, 101.
7. Convert decimal 379 to Octal and Hex.
8. How to get output in POS form from Karnaugh map?
9. Write De Morgan's law.
10. Write distributive law.

3

Introduction to System Software and Operating Systems

3.1 INTRODUCTION TO ASSEMBLER

Initially when computer was invented, people used to communicate with them by on and off switches denoting primitive instructions. Then machine language was introduced, where programmer have to mention instructions as well as operands and addresses in binary format, i.e., using 0 and 1. Both writing and understanding a machine language program is difficult. The functionality of this program is difficult to understand, and a person going through it may not be sure of what can be achieved through the program. Assembly language program is one in which symbols such as letters, digits and special characters, are used for operation part, address part and other parts of instruction code. Both machine language and assembly language are referred as low level languages as the coding a problem is at the individual instruction level, i.e., for each line of a program written in these languages one and only one machine instruction is executed. Assembly language is considered as a second generation language. Computers based on different processors have got their own assembly languages which depend on the architecture of the processor. An assembler translates a program written in assembly language to machine language code.

Output of an assembler is an object file with extension '.obj'. It is the role of linker (another system-software) to make executable .exe file from it. Another system-software called loader, present in operating systems, loads the executable on memory when the program is required to run. The process is illustrated in Fig. 3.1. Process for producing executable file.

Typically, assemblers make two passes over the assembly file, i.e., reads the assembly program twice. (One pass assemblers with more complicated design are also available.)

In the first pass, it reads each line and records labels in a symbol table and in second pass, use info in symbol table to produce actual machine code for each line.

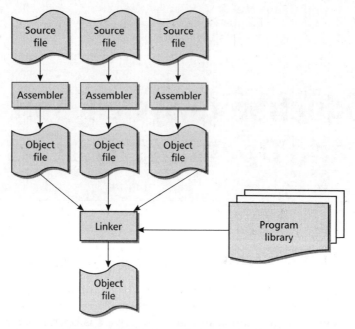

Fig. 3.1   Process for producing executable file

3.2   INTRODUCTION TO COMPILER

S1. A elephant is a huge animal.
S2. An elephant is small animal.

Carefully read the above two sentences. The sentence S1 has grammatical mistake as before 'elephant' we have to use 'An' not 'A'. This type of error is called syntax error. The second sentence S2 is grammatically correct but still sounds wrong as an elephant is not at all a small animal. This sort of error is known as semantic error or logical error.

A compiler checks a file containing a program or part of a program (written in high level language) only for syntax errors. However it is the programmers' responsibility to keep the program free from semantic errors. Semantic errors appearing in a program are removed by the programmers by means of debugging and various testing methodologies that are not our matter of interest here.

We have to remember that compiler always compiles file wise, i.e., if a program is spanned over 10 separate files, we have to compile 10 files separately and we will get 10 object files. Error in one file will not affect successful compilation of another file. After successful compilation of all the files, system software called **linker** creates a single executable file of the program from 10 object files. So it is the role of a **linker** to create executable file from object file.

Before questioning that 'how a compiler detects grammatical errors?' we in a nutshell will learn 'what is a grammar?'

3.2.1 Formal Definition of Grammar

A grammar G consists of the following components:
- A finite set N of non terminal symbols, none of which appear in strings formed from G.
- A finite set (Sigma) of terminal symbols that is disjoint from N.
- A finite set P of production rules.
- A distinguished symbol S as start symbol (S∈N).

The definition can be explained by an example of English grammar where
- Σ(Sigma) is the set of all English words.
- N is the set of non terminals that correspond to the structural components in an English sentence, such as <SENTENCE>, <SUBJECT>, <PREDICATE>, <NOUN>, <VERB>, <ARTICLE>, and so on.
- The start symbol would be <SENTENCE>.
- And we have the following production rules:
  - <SENTENCE> → <SUBJECT><PREDICATE>
  - <SUBJECT> → <NOUN>
  - <PREDICATE> → <VERB><NOUN>
  - <NOUN> → Ram
  - <NOUN> → Sam
  - <NOUN> → Jadu
  - <NOUN> → flower
  - <VERB> → loves

Now consider following three strings to check whether they are sentence or not
(i)   Ram loves flower.
(ii)   Sam loves flower.
(iii) Jadu flower loves.

Using the grammar defined above we can reach start symbol (goal symbol) <SENTENCE> from the first string in the following way:

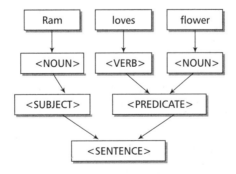

Fig. 3.2   **Parse tree of a sentence**

Similarly sentence can be formed from the second string but from the third string start symbol <SENTENCE> cannot be reached from the above defined grammar. (Readers having Bengali, Hindi or other Sanskrit based languages as mother tongue notice that in the grammar of their mother tongue a VERB usually comes after NOUN in the PREDICATE.)

Compiler does the same job as discussed above. It tries to reach the goal symbol of the high level language it is meant for, from the program written in the file it compiles using the grammar defined for the language. If it fails then it reports error. Though detail of a compiler is out of scope of this book, in the following section we will learn the different components of a compiler and their role.

3.2.2 Components of a Compiler

A compiler may have some or all of the following components:

(a) Lexical Analyzer or Lex It scans the source code as a stream of characters and breaks it into bunch of meaningful pieces called tokens. For identifying keywords or variables, it takes help of a symbol table.

(b) Parser Using the tokens supplied by the lex, parser tries to build a parse tree (Fig. 3.1) whose root will be the goal symbol of the language. If it succeeds then the program is free of syntax error and is passed to the next phase.

(c) Intermediate code generation The compiler generates an intermediate code of the source code for the target machine. The source program is converted to a program meant for an abstract machine. It is in between the high-level language and the machine language. The intermediate code is generated in such a way that it makes it easier to be translated into the target machine code.

(d) Code optimization In this phase, the intermediate code is optimized for faster execution. Some unnecessary lines are removed and code is sometimes rearranged for speedup and better memory management.

(e) Code generation The code generator takes the optimized representation of the intermediate code and maps it to the target machine language. The code generator translates the intermediate code into re-locatable machine code.

It should be noted that programs written in some high level languages are translated and executed by another kind of software called **INTERPRETERS.**

The basic difference between Interpreters and Compilers follows:
- Compiler takes entire program as input whereas interpreter takes single instruction as input, i.e., translates the source program line by line.
- Program needs to be compiled once but in case of interpreter, it converts higher level program into lower level program for every execution.
- In case of compiler, errors are displayed after the total program is checked. On the contrary, the interpreter displays error (if any) for every instruction interpreted.

3.3 INTRODUCTION TO OPERATING SYSTEM

Operating system is a system-software that acts as an interface between the user and the computer. It is a supervisory program that manages all sorts of hardware resources such as CPU, memory, disk and I/O devices. It also provides common services to computer programs. From the time of starting the computer till shutting it down, operating system resides in memory and can take commands from the user.

The digital computer was in its nascent stage in the 1940s and there were no operating systems. Machines of the time were in preliminary stage and programs could generally be entered one bit at a time on rows of machine switches. No programming languages, including assembly languages, were known at the time. The General Motors Research Laboratories implemented the first operating systems in early 1950s for their IBM 701. Various computer specific operating systems were developed till 1980 but never been used by mass audience. After that two operating systems have dominated the personal computer scene: MS-DOS, developed by Microsoft, for the IBM PC and other machines using the Intel 8088/8086 CPU and its successors, and UNIX, which is dominant on the large personal computers using the Motorola 6899 CPU family. Both of them were character based. User has to give input through keyboard and output was on the monitor displaying characters only. Then Graphical User Interface based OS such as Windows, GUI based UNIX and MAC OS came to make the computer acceptable to common people.

In the following section, brief description of DOS, UNIX and Windows are given:

3.3.1 MS-DOS

Microsoft Corporation wrote the version of DOS entirely in 8086 assembly language that IBM chose for its first line of personal computers. DOS is an acronym for the computer's 'Disk Operating System' program. It is named so as at that time it is the only small operating system that fits in a single floppy disk. Some information worth remembering about DOS follows:

- It requires three files – io.sys, msdos.sys and command.com to boot a system.
- It accepts commands from user at the command prompt (a command prompt looks like c:\> with a blinking _ called cursor).
- It allows only one program to run at a time.
- It supports two types of commands internal and external. Internal commands are inbuilt in 'command.com' and require no other file.
- It supports tree like hierarchical directory structure with '8.3' file name format.

Some useful DOS internal commands and their usage follows:

Table 3.1   Some DOS commands

Command	Purpose
MD	Make directory
CD	Change directory
RD	Remove directory
CLS	Clears screen
DATE	Show/set system date
TIME	Show/set system time
COPY	Copy one file to another or to console
TYPE	Displays content of file on screen
DEL	Deletes a file
DIR	Shows the content of a directory
PATH	Show/set current path
VOL	Shows volume label of a disk

3.3.2 Microsoft Windows^{TM}

Presently Microsoft Windows refers to the set of operating systems developed by Microsoft Corporation. In 1985, Microsoft ships Windows 1.0 a GUI operating system shell that runs under DOS. Then, rather than typing MS–DOS commands, moving a mouse to point and click way through screens, or 'windows' were possible. Drop-down menus, scroll bars, icons, dialog boxes and many other visual items were introduced in WINDOWS that make programs easier to learn and use. Switching among several programs without having to quit and restart each one was possible. Microsoft shipped Windows 1.0 with many utility programs like MS-DOS file manager, Paint – a drawing utility, Notepad to create and edit text files, Calculator, and a calendar, card file, and clock to help manage day-to-day activities. There was even a game – Reversi. Since its launch, Windows dominated the personal computer market. Windows 2.0, 2.1 3.0 and 3.11 were released and used till 1994. All of them were 16 bit and was a program that runs under MS-DOS as a shell. In 1995, Windows 95 was introduced, that was 32 bit version and was independent OS not a DOS shell. Seven million copies of Windows 95 were sold in the first month.

After Windows 95 there were several versions such as 98, XP, NT, Server 2000 and 2003, Windows CE, Vista, Windows 7 and 8 then presently Windows 10.

Beside support to old file allocation table of disk 'FAT' used in DOS, WINDOWS comes with two other file allocation tables named FAT32 and NTFS to support larger disks. NTFS also provides user access control to files and directory that increases security to disk contents.

Now a days, internet has become an integral part of daily life. To browse the content of a web page from internet, a software called browser is required. WINDOWS comes with a browser Internet Explorer built-in.

A program runs in a rectangular area called window in the WINDOWS operating system. Elements that may be present in a window are shown in the Fig 3.3 a sample window.

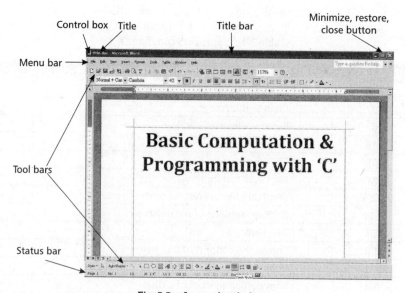

Fig. 3.3   A sample window

3.3.3   UNIX

In the year 1970, Ken Thompson, Dennis Ritchie and others developed UNIX which is a family of multitasking, multiuser operating system. It was designed to be used in the Bell labs where it was developed. Later American Telephone and Telegraph Company (AT&T) licensed it for outside parties. In a command-line operating system a text command is entered and the computer responds according to that command. With a graphical user interface (GUI) operating system, user interacts with the computer through a graphical interface with pictures and buttons by using the mouse and keyboard. Presently with UNIX both command-line (more control and flexibility) and GUI (easier) are available.

Follows some useful UNIX commands: (Please note that UNIX commands are case sensitive but DOS commands are not.)

Table 3.2   Some UNIX commands

Command	Purpose
cat	Display File Contents
cd	Changes Directory
chgrp	change file group
Chown	Change owner
compress	Compress files
Cp	Copy source file into destination
File	Determine file type
find	Find files
ftp	File transfer program
ftp	File transfer program
info	Displays command information pages online
kill	Send a signal to a process
logout	log off UNIX
ls	Display information about file type.
man	Displays manual pages online
mkdir	Create a new directory
mv	Move (Rename) an old name to new name
ps	Display the status of current processes
pwd	Print current working directory
rcp	Remote file copy
rm	Remove (Delete) filename
rmdir	Delete an existing directory provided it is empty
sort	Sort file data
uncompress	Uncompress files
uniq	Report repeated lines in a file

Command	Purpose
uniq	Report repeated lines in a file
vi	Opens vi text editor
wc	Count words, lines, and characters
who	List logged in users

Introduction to UNIX will be incomplete without knowledge of **UNIX shell**. To access the services of a kernel, users of an operating system have to use an interface. The software that provides that interface is called a shell. The UNIX shell, similarly, is a shell or command line interpreter that provides user interface for the UNIX or UNIX-like operating systems. Operation of the computer is directed by the user by entering commands as text, which is then executed by a command line interpreter. UNIX shells are of four types:

- Bourne shell (sh): Developed by Stephen Bourne at Bell Labs in 1974; Default prompt is $.
- C shell (csh): Developed by Bill Joy at the University of California at Berkeley in 1978; Default prompt is %.
- Korn shell(ksh): Developed by David Korn at Bell Labs in 1983;
- Bourne – again shell (bash): Default shell on Linux operating system; Runs on UNIX-like operating system and also available for Microsoft Windows systems.

In this section, a brief idea about the well known **vi editor** is given. Unix offers an editor named vi, which is a screen oriented text editor written by Bill Joy in the year 1976. vi editor is most suitable way to create a file because some operations like line change, caps lock, underline can be performed through this which could not be performed by the cat command. vi has three types of mode, Input mode (for entering text), Command mode (every key pressed is interpreted as a command to run on text) and the Last line mode or ex mode (commands can be entered in the last line of the screen to act on text).

Idea of the **UNIX file system** is provided in the following section. UNIX supports two basic objects, namely file and processes. A file is basically a store house of information that is represented as a sequence of bytes in the system. UNIX filenames can be up to 255 characters. A process is such a file that is being executed by the system, so it is a popular concept that UNIX treats everything as a file. File s in UNIX can be categorized into three sectors:

- Ordinary file or Regular file (Ex: text file)
- Directory file (Ex: any directory)
- Device file (Ex: Printer, Floppy drive, CD-ROMs)

Every file is associated with a table, which contain all information about the file except its name and content, this table is known as inode (index node) and is accessed by the inode number. A file has several attributes that are modifiable by some well-defined rules. "ls – l" command is used to display the file attributes.

UNIX files are integrated in a single directory structure. The file system is arranged in a structure like inverted tree (or hierarchical), i.e., Top of the tree is the root and is written as '/'(forward slash). root(/) is actually a directory file and it has all the sub-directories of the system under it.

Some features that are worth remembering about UNIX file system follows:
1. root directory(/) has no parent, every other has parent.
2. Directory contain the name of the file and the corresponding inode no.
3. root directory has an inode no. 2. inode no. 0 and 1 are not used.
4. The size of the directory is small because it contains only the name of the file and the inode no. It does not contain the data of the file.
5. Basically directory is the mount point consisting of files and file related information.
6. Mount means attached, so swap space has no mount point because it is a raw partition that is used by any file system for swapping.
7. User can make logical partition into a directory and mount it.
8. If user unmounts any directory means the pointer, i.e., the mount point is hidden.

In UNIX, a file is treated as a normal file if it resides in dormant state on the disk but when it is executed it is treated as a process. A process has several attributes among them two are important:
- PID: process id
- PPID: parent process id

UNIX operating system required three system calls for creation of process:
- fork(): Creates a new process
- exec(): For running the process
- Wait(): Executes by parent process to wait for the child process to complete.

In the process hierarchy, init is the first process whose PID is 1, sched is the parent of init whose PID is 0. UNIX is a popular operating system which is capable of handling activities from multiple users at the same time.

EXERCISES

1. After executing the command 'cd subhodip' at DOS prompt 'c:\book>' how the command prompt will look like?
2. What do you mean by 8.3 naming convention of files?
3. What you can do with the control box of a window?
4. What is the difference between one pass and two pass assembler?
5. What is full form of GUI?
6. What is a shell in UNIX?
7. Which commands are used to display contents of a directory in DOS and UNIX?
8. List different file types available in UNIX.
9. Where UNIX was developed?

4 Algorithms and Flow Chart

4.1 FLOW CHART

A flowchart is a type of diagram that represents an algorithm or process. The steps involved in the process are shown as boxes of various kinds. Arrows that connects the boxes depicts the correct order in which the steps should be performed. This diagrammatic representation illustrates a solution to a given problem. As a diagram is equivalent to 1000 words, flowcharts helps people working in a project to understand the problem very easily.

Flowcharts are broadly classified into two categories:
1. Program Flowchart
2. System Flowchart.

Program flowcharts are symbolic or graphical representation of computer programs in terms of flowcharting symbols. They contain the steps of solving a problem unit for a specific result; **System flowcharts**, on the other hand, contain solution of many problem units together that are closely related to each other and interact with each other to achieve a goal.

In this book, concentration will be on program flowcharts as this book is mainly on a programming language. A program flowchart is an extremely useful tool in program development activity in the following respects:
1. Any error, omission or commission can be easily detected from a program flowchart than it can be from a program.
2. A program flowchart can be followed easily and quickly.
3. It can be referred if program modifications are needed in future.

Follows a program flowchart to 'find maximum among three numbers' to give idea about the look of a program flowchart.

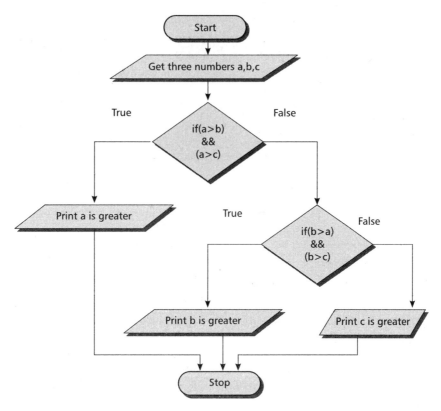

Fig 4.1   Flowchart of finding maximum of three numbers

Before drawing flowchart being familiar with the **standard symbols of flowchart** is required. Follows the list of symbols used in program flowchart along with their brief description:

The following rules should be followed while drawing program flowcharts:
- Only the standard symbols should be used in program flowcharts.
- Program logic should depict the flow from top to bottom and from left to right.
- Each symbol used in a program flowchart should contain only one entry point and one exit point, with the exception of the decision symbol.
- The operations shown within a symbol of a program flowchart should be expressed independent of any particular programming language.
- All decision branches should be well labeled.

Now follows some preliminary flowchart:

(Please note that the corresponding 'C' code is given along with each flowchart. First go through the flowcharts and ignore the codes. Revisit the 'C' codes when you complete PART-B Chapter-4 of this book.)

Table 4.1 Flowchart symbols

Symbol	Name	Usage
	Terminal	Used to show the beginning and end of a set of computer-related process.
	Input/output	Used to show any input/output operation.
	Computer processing	Used to show any processing performed by a computer system.
	Comment	Used to write any explanatory statement required to clarify something.
	Flow line	Used to connect the symbols.
	Document input/output	Used when input comes from a document and output goes to a document.
	Decision	Used to show any point in the process where a decision must be made to determine further action.
	On-page connector	Used to connect parts of a flowchart continued on the same page.
	Off-page connector	Used to connect parts of a flowchart continued to separate pages.

PROGRAM 1 Flowchart to show how sum of two numbers can be obtained.

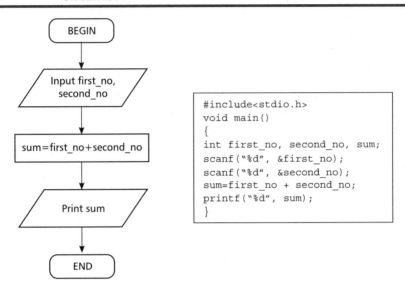

```
#include<stdio.h>
void main()
{
int first_no, second_no, sum;
scanf("%d", &first_no);
scanf("%d", &second_no);
sum=first_no + second_no;
printf("%d", sum);
}
```

PROGRAM 2 Flowchart to calculate area of triangle based on base and altitude.

Area of triangle = ½ × Base × Altitude

Accordingly the flow chart follows:

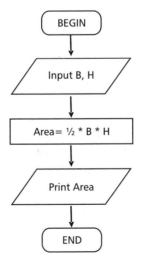

```
#include<stdio.h>
void main()
{
int B, H, Area;
scanf("%d", &B);
scanf("%d", &H);
Area=0.5 * B * H;
printf("%d", Area);
}
```

PROGRAM 3   Flowchart to show how to interchange values of two variables using a third variable.

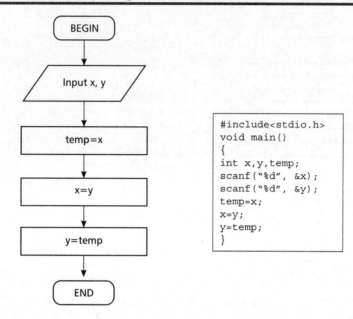

```
#include<stdio.h>
void main()
{
int x,y,temp;
scanf("%d", &x);
scanf("%d", &y);
temp=x;
x=y;
y=temp;
}
```

PROGRAM 4   Flowchart to show how to interchange values of two variables without using a third variable.

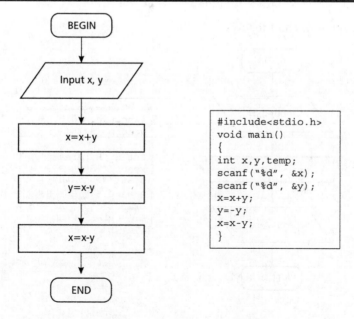

```
#include<stdio.h>
void main()
{
int x,y,temp;
scanf("%d", &x);
scanf("%d", &y);
x=x+y;
y=-y;
x=x-y;
}
```

4.1.1 Flow Charts with Conditional Branching

So far flowcharts of problems without any conditional branching have been drawn. Now problems involving decision-making will be discussed. It is implemented by a logic structure named SELECTION. Here a condition is checked to be TRUE or FALSE. If it is TRUE, a course of action is specified other wise another path of action is provided. In flowcharts, it is depicted as follows:

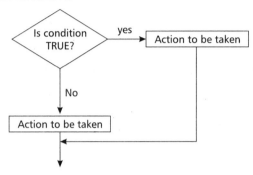

PROGRAM **5**   **Flowchart to display the greater number between two numbers provided by user.**

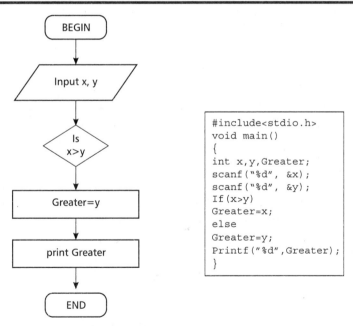

```
#include<stdio.h>
void main()
{
int x,y,Greater;
scanf("%d", &x);
scanf("%d", &y);
If(x>y)
Greater=x;
else
Greater=y;
Printf("%d",Greater);
}
```

PROGRAM **6**   **Flowchart to calculate roots of quadratic equation**
$ax^2+bx+c=0.$

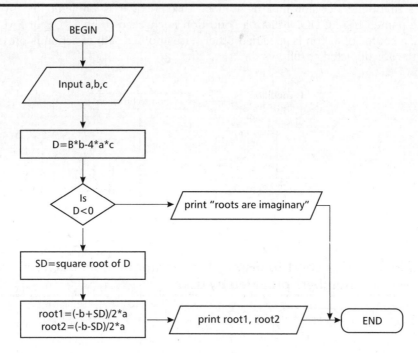

4.1.2   Flow Charts to Implement Loop

Now its time to explain **iteration** or **repetition** or most commonly said **loop.** Loop means repeating a set of operations again and again. Loop can be **pre-test loop** or **post-test loop.** In case of pre-test loop, a condition is tested to decide whether a set of operations is to be performed or not. If the condition is TRUE then operations are performed, if it is FALSE then the loop is terminated. In case of post-test loop, the condition is tested after performing the set of operations once to decide whether to repeat the set of operations or to terminate the loop. So in case of post-test the operations will be carried out at-least one time but in case of pretest it is possible that the operations are not performed at all. It can be understood from the following diagram.

Now some flow charts that involve loop follows:

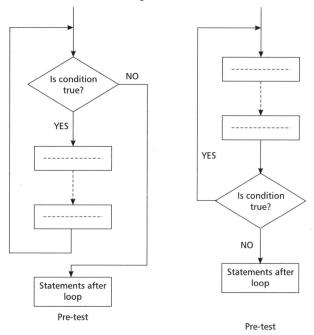

PROGRAM 7   Flowchart to find the sum of first 15 even natural numbers.

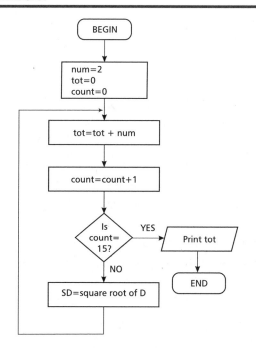

PROGRAM 8   Flowchart to print the numbers within 1–100 which are divisible by 5.

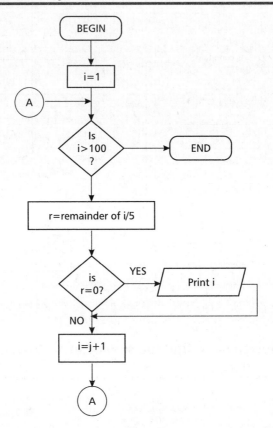

EXERCISES

1. Draw flowchart that determines area and perimeter of a circular plot.
2. Draw flowchart that determines cost of fencing a rectangular area at a given rate.
3. Draw flowchart that converts temperature value provided in centigrade to Fahrenheit.
4. Draw flowchart that determines highest of three numbers.
5. Draw a flowchart that determines whether a given number is even or odd.
6. Draw a flowchart that determines whether a given year is leap year or not.
7. Draw a flowchart that prints 1st 10 Fibonacci numbers.
8. Draw a flowchart that determines whether a number is Armstrong number or not.

PART B

Programming in 'C'

5

Introduction to C

We can define language as a mode of communication by which we can express ourselves to others. At different regions of the world, with respect to different geographical diversity, the residence, outfits, food habits and behaviour of the respective residents generally differ a lot. But one thing remains always common. Every individual has his own way of communication; which implies he has a language of his own. In this current digital era, even though human life has advanced immensely in every aspect but to express their heartiest feelings and emotions they have always taken the help of any suitable language (linguistic/non linguistic) since the earliest time. In that ancient age, the language did not sound very polished or flawless to hear and the early men used to apply some weird sounds or signals to communicate. Then, that was the ancient representation of the language. With the evolution of time, the language has also simultaneously evolved with ups and downs and has reached its present form. Naturally language differs from one region to another and exists in different forms and alphabets. Somewhere it is known as English, somewhere Bengali, somewhere Hindi, Spanish, French; and somewhere it is called German. It means in every particular region the language has a particular name. But no individual or group of people or organization have created this present form of language, instead this gradual development is spontaneous and has evolved from the 'Hoom', 'Haam' like sounds of the ancient era. Hence, this language is called *Natural Language*. Other than this, another form of language exists, the form of which has been developed by some people. Sitting together some people have settled the exact form of that language; like what symbols to be used, how to use those symbols, and what are the symbolic significances – everything has been decided there. For instance, in history we came to know about some letters where people used to apply different symbolic languages. Such a language may be considered under this category and it is called *Artificial Language*. Computer language is also a type of artificial language by which we can interact easily with the computers.

But as computer understands 0 and 1 only, so to interact with the computers we need to use these two binary numbers. During the evolution of computer language at the very beginning, only different combinations of 0s and 1s had been used; which means, to represent a single character, say 'A', we had to write 1000001. Here, you are hopefully able to predict how tough it was then to represent a full word or some instruction to a computer in this way. Really it was too complicated and so, to make it simpler the journey begins.

After passing several generations of languages we get today's form. In near future, we may get some other generation of language.

5.1 GENERATIONS OF PROGRAMMING LANGUAGES

Currently, programming language can be categorized into the following five categories:
- First Generation
- Second Generation
- Third Generation
- Fourth Generation
- Fifth Generation

5.1.1 First Generation Language

In first generation, programs are written as a string of 0s and 1s which is directly understandable to computer. It is also known as Machine Language. Here, all the instructions and data are executed directly by the CPU. As there is no translation needed, so the execution is quite fast. But it is very much difficult to understand and memorize such complicated combinations of 0s and 1s for human beings and as an effect, it was very hard to debug programs written in machine language. Moreover, as machine language depends on the type of processor, it is machine dependent. The instruction consists of two parts, an OP code (operation code) which specifies the operations such as add, subtract, move, etc. and an operand which gives the address of data item that is to be operated on. However, the programmer needs to keep track on the address parts of all data items along with the remembrance of various OP codes. Thus, programming in machine language is highly complicated and error prone.

5.1.2 Second Generation Language

As programming was very difficult and error prone with the machine language, a better understandable language for the programmer has been developed next. This is known as Assembly Language. It is similar to machine language but easier to programming. Here, instead of using binary codes, some meaningful, easily understandable English like abbreviations are used. For example, ADD for addition, SUB for subtraction, CMP for comparison, etc. These abbreviations are known as 'mnemonic'. Assembly Language is considered as second generation of language.

It was already mentioned that computer only understands 0 and 1; hence to interpret the English-like words, a translator is required. Assembler is such a translator using which assembly language program is converted into machine language code.

In comparison to machine language, assembly language is much easier to code and debug. Here, the complex binary sequence has been replaced by easily remembered English-like words. But keep in mind that it is also machine dependent. Programmer must have good knowledge of the architecture of the computer as well as its internal parts like registers, connections of ports to the peripherals, etc.

Machine language and assembly language both are referred to as low level languages because the coding for a problem is at the individual instruction level.

5.1.3 Third Generation Language

Though assembly language is much easier than machine language, still it is not that easy to program. So, third generation language has evolved next. Instead of mnemonics, here statements are used which has much resemblances with English and mathematics. The main advantage of this language is that it is not machine dependent and thus easily portable from one computer to another. Here, the programmers need not know the detail architecture of the machine and instead of concentrating on instruction set, they can focus on the procedures of solving the problem. Thus, it is also known as procedural language. These languages are problem oriented rather than instruction oriented. Third generation languages are known as high level languages. BASIC, COBOL, FORTRAN, C, etc. are examples of some high level languages.

Just like its ancestor 2G language, this 3G language also needs a translator to make the computer understand its own machine language. Basically, two types of translators are there; namely compiler and interpreter. Both of these translators convert a program written in some high level language into machine understandable 'object code'. But the conversion mechanism is different in each case. The main disadvantage of high level language is its slowness and as an effect of this the conversion needs an extra time.

5.1.4 Fourth Generation Language

The fourth generation language is often called 4GL. In comparison to third generation language this generation requires fewer instructions to accomplish a particular task. This language is non-procedural. Programmers need not specify the detailed procedure of accomplishing the task. Instead, they need to mention the required output. Fourth generation languages consist of report generators, query language, application generators, interactive database management programs, etc. The advantage of this language is that any non-technical persons can also use these languages to interact with the computer. SQL, FOCUS, NOMAD, Intellect, etc. are some examples of 4GL.

5.1.5 Fifth Generation Language

Fifth generation programming language is commonly known as 5GL. In 5GL problems are solved using the constraint given to the program, rather than specifying algorithmically how the problem is to be solved. These languages much resemble with the natural languages. It is similar to 4GL but eliminates the requirement to know the syntax of the language. These languages are designed to make the computer intelligent so that it is able to solve given problems without any help of the programmer. Programmers only need to specify the problems and the constraints need to be maintained. Most of the constraint based languages and logical programming languages are under 5GL. It is mainly used in research of Artificial Intelligence. Prolog, Mercury, etc. are some examples of 5GL.

5.2 HISTORY OF C LANGUAGE

C language is an imperative, high level, general-purpose computer programming language. It was developed by Dennis Ritchie in 1972 at AT & T's Bell Laboratories in U.S.A. for use with the UNIX operating system. Though first it was introduced for system programming, due to its unrivaled mix of power, portability, elegance and flexibility later it spread to many other operating systems and become one of the most widely used programming languages.

Initially there are several languages; each is used for a specific purpose. To develop a general purpose language by which one is able to write all possible applications, a new language named ALGOL 60 was developed. But it was too abstract. To reduce its abstractness 'Combined Programming Language (CPL)' was developed at Cambridge University. But the major drawback of CPL was that it was too large to use in many applications. In 1967 Martin Richards had created a scaled down simpler version of CPL retaining its basic features named 'Basic Combined Programming Language (BCPL)'. In 1970 Ken Thomson at AT & T's Bell lab developed another language named B which is another scaled down version of CPL written specifically for system programming. Finally in 1972, Dennis Ritchie inheriting the features of B and BCPL and adding some extra features developed a new language, C.

Later several versions of C had come into market. In the beginning of the summer of 1983 the American National Standards Institute (ANSI) established a committee to remove the discrepancy among various versions of C. Finally, in 1988 we got the standardized version of C, named ANSI C.

5.3 WHY IS C SO POPULAR?

There are several features in C that makes it so popular and the largest accepted language over the years. Here are some reasons behind its huge popularity:

- C is a highly portable language and is independent of machine architecture. It is often said that 'C is source code compatible'. It means that depending on the computer architecture, the compiler may be different. But the C source code remains the same. Same C program/source code can be compiled and executed in different machines without any modification.
- C is a common language. Today's many popular languages like C++, Visual C++, C#, Java, Perl, etc. are based on C. Their syntaxes are much common with C. If one learns C, then learning of other languages are becoming much easier for him.
- C has an important feature called extendibility. We can create our own library that would consist of several user-defined functions and macro and these can be used later in different programs.
- C is a structured programming language. All the basic structures, i.e., sequence, selection and iteration are used in C.
- C has low level programming features. It can directly access hardware components and also can operate at register level.
- C is rich in built in functions.
- C is simple, small and easy to learn.
- C has the facility for graphics programming.

5.4 POSITION OF C IN THE GENERATIONS OF LANGUAGES

C language stands in between high level language and machine language. C has all the features of high level language. C is a procedural language and machine independent. It supports structure programming as well as modular programming. On the other hand, C has low level programming features. It can directly access hardware components and also can operate at register level. It has features to create interface with high speed assembly language routine. That is why C is also known as middle level language. It merges the elements of high level languages with the low level bit manipulation facilities of assembly language. It can be used for system programming as well as application programming. Most of the UNIX commands are written in C. Several system tools are developed using C. A great number of games and business applications are also developed using C.

SUMMARY

➤ Machine language programs are written as string of 0s and 1s. Thus, it is directly understandable to computer.

➤ Programs written in machine language are executed very fast but it is machine dependent and difficult to understand.

➤ In assembly language programming, mnemonics are used.

➤ Assembly language programs are easier to machine language but not in comparison to high level language.

➤ Machine language and assembly language are referred to as low level languages.

➤ High level languages are machine independent and portable.

➤ C was developed in 1972 by Dennis Ritchie at AT & T's Bell lab.

➤ C is a high level, general purpose, portable, extensible, and structured programming language.

➤ C has both high level and low level programming features.

REVIEW EXERCISES

1. What do you mean by natural language?
2. What is the difference between natural language and artificial language?
3. What are the different generations of languages?
4. What are the advantages and disadvantages in machine language?
5. What are the advantages and disadvantages in assembly language?
6. Is assembly language program directly executable by computer? If not, how it is executed?
7. What do you mean by high level and low level language?
8. Why high level languages are known as procedural language?
9. Give some examples of high level languages?

10. What type of language is C?

11. What is the importance of C language?

12. When and by whom C is developed?

13. Which is the predecessor of C language?

14. Explain: 'C is a middle level language'.

15. Why it is stated that 'C is source code compatible'?

16. What is the purpose of compiler?

LEARN BY QUIZ – QUESTIONS

1. The programming language C was developed by

    (1) Dennis Ritchie

    (2) Niklaus Wirth

    (3) IBM & John Backus

2. What is true about C language?

    (1) It is source code level compatible.

    (2) It is machine independent.

    (3) It is platform independent.

3. What is true about C language?

    (1) It is a procedural language.

    (2) It is an unstructured language.

    (3) It is object-oriented language.

4. 'C' language was developed to implement which of the operating system?

    (1) Windows

    (2) Unix

    (3) Linux

5. What is needed to translate a C program to machine level language?

    (1) Interpreter

    (2) Compiler

    (3) Assembler

6. What type of error is identified by a compiler?

    (1) Syntactic error

    (2) Semantic error

    (3) Logical error

7. Which of the following is not a role of a compiler

    (1) Linking

    (2) Code optimization

    (3) Lexical analysis

8. What is the output of a compiler?

    (1) Executable code

    (2) Source code

    (3) Object code

9. Which statement is true about assembler?

    (1) Assembler translates programs written in high level language into machine language.

    (2) Assembler translates programs written in high level language into assembly language.

    (3) Assembler translates programs written in assembly language into machine language.

10. Which statement is true about compiler?

    (1) Compiler translates programs written in high level language into machine language.

    (2) Compiler translates programs written in high level language into assembly language.

    (3) Compiler translates programs written in machine language into high level language.

11. SQL is under which generation of language?

    (1) 3GL

    (2) 4GL

    (3) 5GL

12. What is not true about C language?

    (1) C is a portable language.

    (2) C is a structured programming language.

    (3) C is a natural language.

LEARN BY QUIZ – ANSWERS

Answer explanations

1. C language is an imperative, high level, general-purpose computer programming language. It was developed by Dennis Ritchie in 1972 at AT & T's Bell Laboratories in U.S.A. for use with the UNIX operating system. Though first it was introduced for system programming, due to its unrivaled mix of power, portability, elegance and flexibility later it spread to many other operating systems and become one of the most widely used programming languages.

    Pascal is also an imperative, procedural and influential computer programming language. It was designed in 1968/9 and published in 1970 by Niklaus Wirth.

    John Backus & IBM developed the programming language FORTRAN (Formula Translation System) in 1957.

2. A C program is source code level compatible. It implies that if we take the source code of a C program to a computer of different architecture or a computer running in different platform (Operating System) and compile it using the C compiler of that machine then the program will run fine.

C is not platform independent, i.e., the executable .exe file of one platform will not work in different platform. Note that JAVA is platform independent.

3. C is a procedural language. In procedural language, problems are considered as a sequence of tasks like reading, calculating, displaying, etc. For each task separate modules are written which is known as procedures or functions or subroutines. It follows top-down programming approach.

BASIC is an example of unstructured language.

C++, the successor of C is an example of Object-Oriented language.

4. C was developed to implement Unix. However, kernel of Microsoft Windows is developed in C and rest part in C++. Most of the parts of Linux are also developed in C and remaining portions using Python and C++.

5. Compiler is needed to translate a C program to Object Code. After compilation the linker links and converts one or multiple object code to executable code. A compiler is a system software (a special type of computer program) that translates the source code written in a high level language into machine level language known as object code.

Interpreter interprets a program line by line unlike a compiler that checks a program as a whole. If there is an error in 10th line of a program, then an interpreter will execute first 9 lines then stop giving error but the compiler will check first and show error at 10th line and will not start building object code until it is corrected. Primitive languages like BASIC uses interpreter.

Assembler is used to translate assembly language programs.

6. A compiler can trace out only syntax errors. The sentence 'A elephant is a huge animal' has syntax error as with elephant article An is used. More precisely, compiler finds out errors caused by violating the rules of grammar of a language.

Semantic error and logical error are synonymous. The sentence 'An elephant is a small animal' has semantic error as elephant is not a small animal. But this sort of error cannot be totally detected by compiler or any other software. The programmer, i.e., the human brain has to correct this sort of errors.

7. Generally, a compiler performs some or all of the following operations: lexical analysis, preprocessing, parsing, semantic analysis, code generation, and code optimization. But compiler does not link object files to executable file. It is the role of a linker.

8. The output of a compiler is object code. Source code is the input of a compiler. Executable code is created by a linker which is a software that takes the object codes generated by a compiler as input.

9. Assembler translates programs written in assembly language into machine language.

Compiler and interpreter translate programs written in high level language into machine language.

10. Compiler translates programs written in high level language into machine language.

Assembler translates programs written in assembly language into machine language.

11. Fourth generation languages consist of report generators, query language, application generators, interactive database management programs, etc. SQL is a query language and it is under 4GL.

12. C is a high level, general purpose, portable, extensible, and structured programming language.

    C is not a natural language. Computer languages are artificial languages. These are not created spontaneously. English, Bengali, Hindi, French, Spanish, etc. are examples of natural languages.

6

Constants, Variables
and Data Types

Before we write meaningful programs in C language, let us have a look at the various building block of C language. When we learn some natural language, first we learn about the alphabets, punctuation marks, etc., i.e., the symbols used in that language. Then using these symbols we learn how to construct word, sentence, etc. We follow the same strategy to learn C language. In this chapter, first we will learn about the symbols that can be used in C language. Then, step by step we will learn to construct constants, variables and will also learn about different data types. Constants and variables are the basic data objects that are manipulated in a program. Data type is the type of an object which determines the set of values it can have. These building blocks will be discussed in this chapter.

6.1 C CHARACTER SET

A character is a basic element used to construct commands and expressions. It may be any alphabet, digit or special symbol. The valid alphabets, numbers and special symbols allowed in C are followings:

Table 6.1   C character set

Alphabets	A, B, ..., Y, Z
	a, b, ..., y, z
Digits	0, 1, 2, 3, 4, 5, 6, 7, 8, 9
Special symbols	~ ' ! @ # % ^ & * ( ) _ - + = | \ { } [ ] :
; " ' < > , . ? /

6.2 CONSTANTS

A constant is an entity that does not change its value throughout the program. Constant may be of different types – integer constant, real constant, character constant, string constant, etc.

6.2.1 Integer Constants

An integer constant consists of one or more digits but within the range of −32768 to +32767. It is a whole number. So, it does not contain any decimal point. There should not be any spaces, commas or special characters within the digits. An integer constant may be positive or negative. But + sign is optional.

Some valid integer constants are:

    5
    +67
    −328
    2552
    etc.

Some invalid integer constants are:

    5.67   [As decimal point not allowed]
    23,725   [As comma not allowed]
    45 678   [As space not allowed]
    $235   [As special character not allowed]
    50000   [As the value not within the range]
    etc.

To represent larger values we have to use type qualifiers. The suffix **U** or **u** implies an unsigned integer, **L** or **l** implies long integer and **UL** or **ul** implies unsigned long integer.

Some valid unsigned integer constants are:

    54321u
    45986U
    etc.

Some valid long integer constants are:

    78564L
    689421
    etc.

Some valid unsigned long integer constants are:

    93455UL
    88888ul
    etc.

Again the constant preceded by a zero implies it is an octal number. In the octal number system, the base is 8, so there are 8 digits, 0–7. So, 033, 0752, etc. are valid octal constants. To represent a hexadecimal constant, the constant should be preceded by 0x or 0X. In the hexadecimal number system, the base is 16, so there are 16 digits, 0–9 and A–F or a–f. Some valid hexadecimal constants are 0X5A, 0x602, 0x2DA, etc.

6.2.2 Real Constants

Numeric values with fractional parts are known as real numbers or floating point numbers. The real constants consist of digits with a mandatory decimal point. Like integer constants, real constants also should not contain any spaces, commas or special characters within the digits. A real constant may be positive or negative and + sign is optional.

Some valid real constants are:

    3.141
    −0.07
    +1.11
    2.38161
    34.
    .56, etc.

Some invalid real constants are:

    52   [As decimal point missing]
    6,325.99   [As comma not allowed]
    #2.25   [As special character not allowed]

When the value is too small or too large, the real constant may also be represented in exponential form. In this form, there are two parts – mantissa and exponent. These are separated by the letter **e** or **E**. The mantissa may be an integer or real number but the exponent is an integer number. Both the part may have +ve or −ve sign.

So, 5e3, 1.44E5, 6.25e−3, etc. are valid real constant in exponential form. But 5e3.5 is an invalid real constant as exponent should be an integer number.

6.2.3 Character Constants

When a single character is enclosed within a pair of single inverted comma, it is known as character constant. It may be any alphabet, digit, space or any valid special symbols.

Some valid character constants are:

    'A'
    'b'
    '#'
    '7'
    etc.

6.2.4 String Constants

When set of characters are enclosed within a pair of double inverted comma, it is considered as a string constant. Each string constant is terminated by '\0' character. This '\0' character is automatically inserted by the compiler at the end of every string. That is why 'A' and "A" are not equivalent as 'A' is a character constant and "A" is a string constant. The string constant "A" consists of 2 characters. "A" is actually "A\0".

Some valid string constants are:

    "TIH"
    " C Language"
    etc.

6.3 KEYWORDS AND IDENTIFIERS

Every word in C language is either a keyword or an identifier. Keywords are reserve words and used for specific purpose. Thus, they cannot be used as a variable name. They serve as building blocks of a C program. The keywords in C are followings:

Table 6.2 Keywords in C

auto	double	int	struct
break	else	long	switch
case	enum	register	typedef
char	extern	return	union
const	float	short	unsigned
continue	for	signed	void
default	goto	sizeof	volatile
do	if	static	while

Identifiers refer to the names of variables, functions and arrays. These are user-defined names.

6.4 VARIABLES AND DATA TYPES

The first task in C program is to declare a variable. Variables are storage where we can store values of specific types. Each variable is identified by a variable name. The rules to declare a variable is:

1. A variable name consists of A–Z, a–z, 0–9 and special character underscore (_).
2. There will be no space embedded within a variable name.
3. Variable name starts only with a letter or underscore (_).
4. Uppercase is different from lowercase, so the names sum, Sum, and SUM specify three different variables.
5. Variable name should not be a keyword.

Though we can use uppercase letters in variable declaration, the convention is to use lower case letters only. And always we use meaningful variable name to increase the readability of the program. But try to avoid too lengthy name as it is tedious to type long names each time the variable is accessed. Though the variable names are case sensitive, i.e., var and Var are not same variables, but try to avoid such names as they make confusion and decrease readability. The followings are the examples of some variable names:

```
average              /* average of Marks */
basic_salary         /* Basic Salary of an employee */
number_of_employees  /* number of employees in office */
```

The following are not valid variable names:

```
1st_          /* Begins with a number */
roll no       /* Contains a space */
currency$     /* Contains a "$" */
int           /* Reserved word */
```

To declare a variable, the syntax is:

data type   variablename1, variablename2,... ;

Here, **data type** indicates the type of the data. C uses the following primary/basic data types:

Table 6.3   Basic data types in C

	Description	Keyword
1.	Integer	int
2.	Character	char
3.	Floating point	float
4.	Double precision floating point	double
5.	Void	void

Here, the first four data types will be discussed. The void data type will be discussed later (in 'Function' and 'Pointer' chapters). Along with the above data type, there also exist some type modifiers. These are **signed, unsigned, short** and **long. signed** and **short** are default type modifiers. While using type modifiers the following rules should be kept in mind:

- All the above mentioned type modifiers may be applied to the base type **int**.
- **signed** and **unsigned** modifiers may be applied to the base type **char**.
- The modifier **long** may be applied to **double**.
- If the base type is not mentioned, it will be considered as **int**.

Table 6.4   Size and range of data types on 16 bit machine

Type	Size (in bytes)	Range
char or signed char	1	−128 to 127
unsigned char	1	0 to 255
int or signed int or short int or signed short int	2	−32768 to 32767
unsigned int	2	0 to 65535
long int or signed long int	4	−2147483648 to 2147483647
unsigned long int	4	0 to 4294967295
Float	4	3.4 e−38 to 3.4 e+38 (accurate upto 7 digits)
double	8	1.7e−308 to 1.7e+308 (accurate upto 15 digits)

To store the integer value in a variable, the variable needs to be declared as integer and the corresponding keyword as '**int**'. An integer variable occupies 2 byte, i.e., 16 bits in memory. Among these 16 bits, the left most bit or MSB is used to maintain the sign of the number and others are used to store the data. As within n bits, the maximum value we can store is 2^n-1, an integer variable can store only any positive or negative value between −32768 and 32767 (-2^{15} to $+2^{15}-1$). We cannot store value beyond this range. Remember that, in C negative numbers are stored in 2's complement form. If we want to add 1 with 32767 (or want to store 32768), the resultant value will be overflowed and the variable will contain −32768. Similarly, if we want to store 32769, it will store −32767. To store only positive values (not the negative ones) or to store absolute values (where sign is not important), we can declare the variable as '**unsigned integer**'. By this declaration we can use the sign bit for storing data and then the range will be 0 to 65535($2^{16}-1$). To store any value larger than this, declare '**long int**'. As **long int** occupies 4 bytes, it can store data -2^{31} to $+2^{31}-1$. **long int** can also be **signed** or **unsigned**. An **unsigned long int** can store values 0 to $+2^{32}-1$. We cannot store values larger than this range as integer.

To store any character value in a variable, declare the variable as '**char**'. When we store some character into a variable, actually we store the ASCII value of that character. As a character variable occupies only 1 byte in memory, the possible range is −128 to +127(-2^7 to $+2^7-1$). To store the character whose ASCII value is larger than 127, we should declare the variable as '**unsigned char**'.

To store any real number (i.e., numeric value with fractional part), declare the variable as '**float**'. If we declare a variable as **float**, floating point values can be stored into it which is accurate up to 6 decimal places. For more accurate result and to store larger values, declare the variable as '**double**'. By this declaration, we can store floating point values which are accurate up to 14 decimal places.

EXAMPLE 6.1

```
char x;              /* To declare a character variable.   */
int marks;           /* To declare a integer variable.   */
int basic, da, hra;  /* To declare multiple integer variables.   */
float average;       /* To declare a floating point variable.   */
unsigned int roll_no; /* To declare a unsigned integer variable.   */
```

Every C statement terminated with the symbol '**;**' (semicolon). So, after declaring the variable we use **;** to mention the end of statement. Remember that we can write multiple statements in single line separated by **;**. Further, a single statement can span over multiple lines. The compiler will consider these multiple lines as a single statement till it finds a **;**.

At the time of declaration we can also assign value to the variables. If we do not assign, the variable will contain garbage value (i.e., some unpredictable value).

EXAMPLE 6.2

```
char x = 'A';
int marks = 0;
int basic = 5000, da, hra = 0;
```

In the above example, all variables will contain the specified value except the variable **da** which will contain a garbage value.

We can also use expression to initialize the variable.

EXAMPLE 6.3

```
int basic = 5000, da, hra = 0;
float net_salary = basic + basic*0.4 + hra;
```

If we use a variable to initialize another variable, the order in which the variable will be declared is important.

EXAMPLE 6.4

```
float net_salary = basic + basic*0.4 + hra;
int basic = 5000, da, hra = 0;
```

The above example will not work because here we are trying to use the variables **basic** and **hra** even before defining them.

Again we can initialize a set of variables with same value.

EXAMPLE 6.5

```
int basic, da, hra;
basic = da = hra = 0;
```

But the following statement will not work.

int basic = da = hra = 0;

Because in the above statement, only the variable **basic** is declared. Other variables are being tried to use before declaring them.

6.5 STORAGE TYPE QUALIFIER

There are two storage type qualifiers, const and volatile that control how the variables are modified and accessed.

6.5.1 Const

The keyword **const** is used to declare a variable as constant, i.e., not modifiable. In our program, if there is some requirement that value of one or more variables remain unchanged during the execution of program, we need to declare the variable as constant. For example,

const int max = 10;

The above statement tells that the value of the variable, **max**, is an integer variable which is initialized with 10 and through out the program its value remains unchanged and any assignment to the variable, **max**, causes an error.

6.5.2 Volatile

The keyword volatile is used to declare explicitly that the value of some variables may be changed by its own program as well as by some other program. For example,

> volatile int spl_var;

The above statement tells that the value, i.e., the content of the variable, spl_var, may be changed by some external program.

If we want that the value of the variable may be changed by some other program but not by own self, we have to declare the variable volatile as well as const.

> volatile const int x = 5;

The use of volatile is beyond the scope of this book. Typical use of volatile variable is in handling memory-mapped peripheral registers, updating global variables by some interrupt service routine, etc.

Summary

➤ A constant is an entity that does not change its value throughout the program.

➤ Variables are storage where we can store values of specific types.

➤ C has 32 keywords which serve as the building block of a program.

➤ data type indicates the type of the data.

➤ The five basic data types are: char, int, float, double and void.

➤ signed, unsigned, short and long are type modifiers. signed and short are default type modifiers.

➤ The keyword const is used to declare a variable as constant.

➤ Every C statement terminated with the symbol ';' (semicolon).

➤ Without declaring variables cannot be used.

➤ An integer variable can store only any positive or negative value between −32768 and 32767.

Review Exercises

1. What do you mean by constant?
2. Explain different type of constants with example.
3. What do you mean by identifier?
4. How many keywords are in C?
5. What is data type? What are the basic data types in C?
6. What is the size of an integer variable?
7. Is it possible to store 50000 in an integer type variable? Explain.
8. What is the utility of declaring a character type variable as unsigned?
9. What is the difference between float and double?

10. Which of the following declarations are correct?
    a. int x, int y, int z;
    b. char student name;
    c. char student's_name;
    d. float Rs., paisa;

11. Is the following statements are valid?
    a. int marks1 = marks2 = marks3 = 0;
    b. char roll = 5;
    c. float total = 100;
    d. int alpha = 'a';

12. How can we declare a variable as constant? What is its utility?

LEARN BY QUIZ – QUESTIONS

1. Which one of the following variable names is invalid?
   (1) 2A
   (2) A2
   (3) A2a

2. What is the size of an integer variable?

   (1) It depends on the word size of compiler in use

   (2) 2 bytes

   (3) 4 bytes

3. Which of the following is a valid identifier?
   (1) 123-45
   (2) Return
   (3) Kolkata_city

4. Which of the following is used to terminate every C statement?
   (1) .
   (2) ,
   (3) ;

5. A version of C recognizes only the first 8 characters of an identifier name, even if the identifier name is longer. In such a case, which of the following pairs will be considered identical?
   (1) name, names
   (2) answer, ANSWER
   (3) identifier1, identifier2

6. How many characters can a character variable store at a time?
   (1) 1 character
   (2) 8 characters
   (3) 16 characters

7. What is the size of a character variable?
   (1) 1 nibble (4 bits)
   (2) 1 byte (8 bits)
   (3) 2 bytes (16 bits)

8. Which of the following is not a valid variable name?
   (1) name of student
   (2) student_name
   (3) STNAME

9. Which of the following is an invalid name for a C constant?
   (1) 0XBCFC
   (2) 0XFCBC
   (3) 0XBGFC

10. Which one of the following is an invalid integer constant?
    (1) 743
    (2) 072
    (3) 36.0

11. Which one of the following is an invalid integer constant?
    (1) 490
    (2) 0490
    (3) 0X490

12. Which one of the following is a valid integer constant?
    (1) 12345
    (2) 12,345
    (3) 12,345.0

13. Which one of the following is an unsigned integer?
    (1) 4000U
    (2) U4000
    (3) 4U000

14. What is the size of an unsigned integer in a 16 bits system?
    (1) 8 bits
    (2) 16 bits
    (3) 32 bits

15. Which one of the following is a valid floating point constant?
    (1) 1.
    (2) 1
    (3) 1,00.0

16. Which one of the following is an invalid floating point constant?
    (1) 2E+10.2
    (2) 2E−10
    (3) 2.66E+10

17. How can the quantity 3×10^5 be represented in C?
    (1) 3e5
    (2) 30000.
    (3) 30E6

18. Which one of the following is an invalid character constant?
    (1) '5'
    (2) 'x'
    (3) 'xy'

19. Which one of the following is a valid character constant?
    (1) ' '
    (2) '30'
    (3) 'abc'

20. What is the ASCII value of A?
    (1) 41
    (2) 65
    (3) 97

21. How is a string terminated by a compiler?
    (1) \0
    (2) $
    (3) End

22. How will you compare the two constants 'A' and "A"?
    (1) These are equivalent
    (2) These are not equivalent
    (3) These are equal if used for same operator

23. How many characters does the string constant "w" consist of?
    (1) 1 character
    (2) 2 characters
    (3) Depends on declaration.

24. Which one of the following declarations is wrong regarding long integer variables?
    (1) int p,q long;
    (2) long int p,q;
    (3) long p,q;

25. A computer uses 2 bytes for integer quantity. What will be the value range of int a?
    (1) −32768 to + 32767
    (2) 0 to +32767
    (3) 0 to 65535

26. Which one of the following declarations of floating point variable sum is wrong?
    (1) float sum = 0.0;
    (2) float sum = 0.;
    (3) sum float = 0;

27. How much memory space is required to declare the string constant "California"?
    (1) 11 bytes
    (2) 10 bytes
    (3) 1 byte

28. What will be the declaration of a floating point variable *a* with an initial value of −8.2?
    (1) float a = −8.2;
    (2) float a = (minus)8.2;
    (3) A = −8.2f;

29. Which of the following is an incorrect declaration of *double precision variable n*?
    (1) double precision n;
    (2) double n;
    (3) long float n;

30. Which of the following is an incorrect declaration of floating point variable *b* with initial value 0.004?
    (1) float b = 0.004;
    (2) float b = 4E3;
    (3) float b = 4E−3;

31. What will be the declaration of the integer variable *c* with initial value −22?
    (1) int c = −22;
    (2) int −c = 22;
    (3) int c = (minus) 22;

32. What will be the declaration for character variable *c* with the initial value &?
    (1) char c = &;
    (2) char c = '&';
    (3) char c = "&";

33. What will be the declaration for the double precision variable x with initial value 3.2×10^{-16}?
    (1) double x = 3.2;
    (2) double x = 3.2E−16;
    (3) float x = 3.2E−16;

34. What will be the declaration for the double precision variable y with initial value -3.2×10^6?
    (1) double y = −3.2E6;
    (2) double y = 3.2E−6;
    (3) long double y = −3.2E6;

35. What will be the declaration of integer variable u in octal form with initial value equivalent to decimal 711?
    (1) int u = 711;
    (2) int u = 01307;
    (3) int u = 0X711;

36. What will be the declaration of integer variable v in hex with initial value fff?
    (1) int v = fff;
    (2) int v = 0Xfff;
    (3) int v = 0fff;

37. Which of the following declarations is wrong?
    (1) unsigned long char x;
    (2) long x;
    (3) unsigned char x;

38. Which of the following declarations is wrong?
    (1) unsigned long x;
    (2) unsigned long double x;
    (3) unsigned long int x;

LEARN BY QUIZ – ANSWERS

Answer explanations

1 2A is an invalid variable name.

   Variable name cannot start with a digit.

   Variable name can start with a letter or an underscore only.

   It can contain only digits and letters including the underscore character but no other characters.

   The letters can be upper case or lower case but they are treated as different characters. So, variable names in C are case sensitive.

   The variable name _A2 and A2a are valid in C.

2. The size of an integer variable in C depends on word size of compiler in use.

   Size of an integer is equal to the word size of the compiler being used. In a 16 bit compiler, an integer will be of 2 bytes but in a 32 bit compiler it will be 4 bytes.

3. Kolkata_city is the valid identifier since it satisfies all the rules of identifier naming as given below:

   Variable name can start with a letter or an underscore only.

It can contain only digits, letters and the underscore character (_).

The letters can be uppercase or lowercase but they are treated as different characters. So, variable names in C are case sensitive.

123-45 violates two rules. It starts with a number and it contains a hyphen.

return is a keyword and keywords or reserved words cannot be used as identifier names.

4. ; is used to terminate every C statement.

We can write multiple statements in single line separated by ;.

Further, a single statement can span over multiple lines. The compiler will consider these multiple lines as a single statement till it finds a ;.

5. identifier1, identifier2 will be considered identical in such a case.

The first 8 characters of both *identifier1*, *identifier2* are *identifi*. Characters after that will not be considered here. So *identifier1* and *identifier2* will be identical.

Had the compiler recognized the first 4 characters instead of the first 8, then *name* and *names* would have been identical. However, as that is not the case here, *name* and *names* are considered different words.

As C is case sensitive, *answer* and *ANSWER* will not be considered identical by the C compiler.

6. A character variable can store 1 character at a time.

A character variable is 1 byte in size and can store any one ASCII character.

For storing multiple characters, we have to use character array.

7. The size of a character variable is 1 byte (8 bits).

There are 128 ASCII (American Standard Code for Information Interchange) characters and 128 extended ASCII characters. Hence, there are a total of 256 characters. These may be represented using $\log_2 (256)$ bits, i.e., 8 bits. In other words, with 8 bits we can create $2^8 = 256$ combinations.

However, languages like Chinese have more than 256 characters. To support such languages a character set called UNICODE was introduced. A UNICODE character is 2 bytes in size, i.e., it supports 2^{16} combinations.

8. name of student is not a valid variable name since space is not allowed in a variable name.

The identifiers *student_name* and *STNAME* are valid as they satisfy the rules of identifier naming as given below.
   • Variable name can start with a letter or an underscore only.
   • It can contain only digits, letters and the underscore character.
   • The letters can be uppercase or lowercase but they are treated as different characters. So, variable names in C are case sensitive. ROSE, Rose and rose are not the same in C.

9. 0XBGFC is an invalid name for a C constant.

If the name of a constant starts with 0X, it indicates a HEXADECIMAL number. In the hexadecimal number system, there are 16 digits, 0–9 and A–F corresponding to 10–15 respectively. So G is invalid. Hence 0XBGFC is invalid and other two are valid.

10. 36.0 is an invalid integer constant.

Integer means whole number. A decimal point is not allowed in an integer. So 36.0 is invalid integer constant.

743 is a whole number so it is an integer constant.

072 is a valid octal integer.

11. 0490 is an invalid integer constant.

    The constant preceded by a zero implies it is an octal number. In the octal number system, the base is 8, so there are 8 digits, 0–7. The digit 9 is not valid. Hence, 0490 is an invalid integer.

    Decimal 490 is a valid integer.

    0X in 0X490 implies that it is a hexadecimal number. As 490 is a valid hexadecimal number, so 0X490 or 0x490 is a valid integer constant.

12. 12345 is a valid integer constant.

    , is not allowed in an integer constant. So 12,345 is invalid.

    , and . are not allowed in an integer constant. So 12,345.0 is invalid.

13. 4000U is an unsigned integer as the suffix *U* or *u* implies an unsigned number.

    U4000 have no meaning to the compiler, as *U* cannot be used in prefix form in an integer.

    U is not a valid digit in either decimal, octal or hexadecimal number system. *U* cannot be used in the middle of a number. Hence, 4U000 is invalid.

14. The size of an unsigned integer in a 16 bits system is 16 bits.

    Unsigned integer can take values from 0 to $2^{16}-1$, i.e., 0–65535. In case of signed integer, the size is same but the range is from -2^{15} to $+2^{15}-1$ as the left most bit (MSB – most significant bit) is used for sign. The signed numbers are kept in 2's complement form.

    The size of a short integer in some systems is 8 bits.

    Long integer takes 32 bits.

15. 1. is a valid floating point constant.

    1 is not valid as decimal point should be present in a floating point constant.

    , is not allowed in a floating point constant. Hence, 1,00.0 is invalid.

16. 2E+10.2 is an invalid floating point constant as the exponent part cannot be in fraction.

    2E−10 is valid as the exponent is negative and mantissa positive which implies that the original number is greater than 0 and less than 1.

    2.66E+10 is valid as the mantissa part of a floating point constant can be in fraction.

17. The quantity 3×10^5 can be represented in C by 3e5.

    Any floating point number converted into $p \times 10^q$, is written as *peq* or *pEq*. So 3×10^5 can be written as 3e5 or 3E5 or simply 300000 in C. Alternatively, if the mantissa is converted to 30 then the equivalent number will be 30E4.

18. 'xy' is an invalid character constant.

    'xy' is not a single character. Hence, it cannot be a character constant.

    '5' will be treated as a character and its value will be 53. The ASCII value of the characters 0–9 are 48–57, respectively.

19. ' ' is a valid character constant.

    There is only one space between the apostrophes.

    The ASCII value of a space character is 32 in decimal and 20 in Hex.

    '30' is invalid as multiple characters are not allowed.

    'abc' is invalid as multiple characters are not allowed.

20. The ASCII value of **A** is 65.

   41 is the hexadecimal ASCII value of **A**, which is equivalent to 65 decimal.

   97 is the ASCII value of **a**.

21. Every string is automatically terminated with a null character, i.e., \0 by the compiler.

22. '**A**' and "**A**" are not equivalent as '**A**' is a character constant and "**A**" is a string constant.

23. The string constant "w" consists of 2 characters.

   A null character \0 is automatically inserted by the compiler at the end of every string. So "w" is actually "w\0".

24. The declaration int p,q long; is wrong as *long* cannot be used after the variable names *p* and *q*.

   The declarations *long int p,q;* and *long p,q;* are the same and correct. In the declaration *long p,q;* no data type has been specified so by default *int* will be assumed.

25. The value range of int *a* will be −32768 to + 32767.

   2 bytes contain 16 bits. The leftmost bit is used as the sign bit. The remaining 15 bits contain the number. The range in these 15 bits will be -2^{15} to $+2^{15}-1$ in 2's complement form, i.e., −32768 to + 32767.

26. The declaration sum float = 0; is wrong as the float keyword should precede the variable name.

   The syntax is *<data type> <variable name> [= <expression>];*

27. The required memory space is 11 bytes.

   The compiler automatically inserts the null character \0 at the end.

28. The declaration of floating point variable *a* with an initial value -8.2 will be float a = −8.2;

29. double precision n; is an incorrect declaration of *double precision variable n* as it will give compilation error.

   Precision is not a keyword. If two double precision variables, say, *precision* and *n* have to be declared, a , (comma) has to be placed between them. Hence, the declaration will be *double precision, n;*.

   The declarations *double n;* and *long float n;* are correct.

30. 4E3 is equivalent to $4 \times 10^3 = 4000$. Hence, float b = 4E3; is an incorrect declaration of floating point variable *b* with initial value 0.004.

31. The declaration of integer variable *c* with an initial value of −22 will be int c = -22;.

32. The declaration for character variable *c* with initial value & will be char c = '&';

   Character constants have to be enclosed within single quotes.

33. The declaration for the double precision variable *x* with initial value 3.2×10^{-16} will be double x = 3.2E−16;.

   The declaration *double x = 3.2;* will not give any compilation error but in this case *x* will not have the value of 3.2×10^{-16}.

   float x = 3.2E−16; will not give any compilation error. But in this case, *x* will not be double precision.

34. The declaration for the double precision variable *y* with initial value -3.2×10^6 will be *double y = −3.2E6;*

The declaration **double y = 3.2E−6**; will initialize the value of **y** with 3.2 × 10^{-6}.

long double is a valid data type and it takes twice the memory space of the data type **double**.

35. The declaration of integer variable **u** in octal form with initial value equivalent to decimal 711 will be int **u** = 01307;. A number preceded by 0 implies that it will be treated as an octal number by the compiler. Octal 1307 is equivalent to decimal 711.

The declaration **int u = 711;** is valid and have same meaning but the declaration is in decimal not in octal as asked in the question.

The declaration **int u = 0X711;** will not give any compilation error but 0X711 implies it is a hex number and it is equivalent decimal is 1809.

36. The declaration of integer variable **v** in hex with initial value fff is int v = 0Xfff;. A number preceded by 0X or 0x implies it is a hex number and fff is a valid hex number.

int v = fff; will give compilation error as here fff is not preceded 0X. So the compiler will try to interpret it as a decimal number or another predefined variable fff. And the number fff is not a valid decimal number as **f** is not a decimal digit.

0fff will be treated as octal number but only fff cannot be an octal number.

37. unsigned long char x; is wrong.

While using type modifiers **signed**, **unsigned**, **short**, and **long** the following rules should be kept in mind:
- All the above mentioned type modifiers may be applied to the base type int.
- signed and unsigned modifier may be applied to the base type char.
- The modifier long may be applied to double.
- If the base type is not mentioned, it will be considered as int.

According to the above mentioned rules, **long** cannot be used with **char** data type so **unsigned long char x;** is wrong.

long x; is valid as it represents long **int**.

unsigned char x; is valid. **x** being an **unsigned** character will be able to take 256 different values unlike 128 possible in case of **signed char**.

38. unsigned long double x; is wrong.

While using type modifiers **signed**, **unsigned**, **short**, and **long** the following rules should be kept in mind:
- All the above mentioned type modifiers may be applied to the base type int.
- signed and unsigned modifier may be applied to the base type char.
- The modifier long may be applied to double.
- If the base type is not mentioned, it will be considered as int.

According to the above rules, **unsigned** cannot be used with **double** so **unsigned long double x;** is wrong. **unsigned long x;** and **unsigned long int x;** have same meaning.

7

Operators and Expressions

Operators are analogous with the verb of English language. It tells what operation has to be performed on operand(s). C language has a rich set of operators. It has 45 different operators. But it does not have any operator to calculate exponent. So, we cannot calculate a^b using some operators. For this, C provides a mathematical function named pow( ). In this chapter, we will discuss about most of the operators and their use. An Expression is a combination of variables, constants and operators to produce new values. Expressions are the backbone of C statement which is analogous with the sentence of English language. In this chapter, we will discuss about these building blocks.

7.1 OPERATORS IN C

Operators are the symbols that help the programmer to instruct the computer to perform certain arithmetic, relational or logical operation. Operators are used in C language program to operate on data and variables. One of the distinguished features of C language is its rich set of operators. The operators of C can be categorized as:

1. Arithmetic operators
2. Assignment operators
3. Increment and decrement operators
4. Relational operators
5. Logical operators
6. Conditional operators
7. Bitwise operators
8. Special operators

In addition to this classification operators can also be classified as unary, binary and ternary according to the number of operands associated with the particular operator.

7.1.1 Arithmetic Operators

All the basic arithmetic operations used in mathematics are available in C. These operators bear more or less same meaning in other languages also. C language supports both unary and binary arithmetic operators. The operators that have single operand are known as unary operators and the operators that have two operands are known as binary operators. For example, when unary – (minus) operator operates on some number, say 5, the result will be –5 and binary – (minus) operator subtract some value from other operand.

Table 7.1 Arithmetic operators and their role

Operators	Descriptions
+	Unary plus or addition
–	Unary minus or subtraction
*	Multiplication
/	Division
%	Modulo division

Examples of arithmetic operators are:

```
p + 5
var1 + var2
var1 - 10
-x + y
p * q - r
n/m
-a % b etc.,
```

Here p, var1, var2, x, y, q, r, n, m, a, b, 5, 10 all are operands as the operators are operating on them.

The operator '+' is used as binary plus operator for addition as well as unary plus operator. The unary '–' operator is used to change the sign, i.e., if a variable contain +ve value, after operation it will be –ve with same the magnitude. Similarly, –ve value will be converted to the +ve value.

```
int x = 5, y;
y = -x;
```

After execution of above statement, y will contain –5 and x will remain same, i.e., will contain 5.

When this operator used as binary operator, it subtracts 2nd operand from 1st operand.

```
int x = 7, y = 4, z;
z = x - y;
```

After execution of above statement, z will contain 3; x and y will remain same.

Though the use of '+' and '–' operator is same as mathematics but the notation of multiplication is different in C language. The operator '*' is used for multiplication.

To find the product of two variable, a and b, we cannot write:

      a b

or,   a . b

or,   a × b

we have to write a * b. Even 2(a + b) is a wrong statement; the valid statement will be 2 * (a + b).

The operator '%' is known as modulo division operator. It is used to compute the remainder value after division of two operands. For example,

    5 % 2 returns 1,

    2 % 5 returns 2.

It should be noted that, modulo division operator operates only on integer type value. Also remember that the sign of the first operand always is the sign of the result. So,

    −5 % 2 will return −1.

    5 % −2 will return 1.

    −5 % −2 will return −1.

7.1.1.1 Integer Arithmetic

If an arithmetic operation took place between two integers, it is known as integer arithmetic operation. The result of this operation is always an integer. Let var1 = 27 and var2 = 5 be two integer values. Now the integer operations on these two variables produce the following results.

```
var1 + var2 results 32
var1 - var2 results 22
var1 * var2 results 135
var1 % var2 results 2
var1 / var2 results 5
```

In case of integer division, only the integer part of the result is returned and if there is any fractional part, it is truncated.

7.1.1.2 Floating Point Arithmetic

If an arithmetic operation is performed between two real numbers or floating point numbers, it is known as floating point arithmetic. Let var1 = 27.56 and var2 = 5.2 be two floating point numbers. Now the floating point arithmetic operations on these two variables produce the following results.

```
var1 + var2 results 32.76
var1 - var2 results 22.36
var1 * var2 results 143.312
var1 / var2 results 5.3
```

7.1.1.3 Mixed Mode Arithmetic

If an arithmetic operation is performed between a real number and an integer, it is known as mixed mode arithmetic and the result of this operation is always real.

Let var1 = 10.6 and var2 = 2 then

```
var1 + var2 results 12.6
var1 - var2 results 8.6
var1 * var2 results 21.2
var1 / var2 results 5.3
```

Note The modulo division operator % is not applicable for floating point arithmetic or mixed mode arithmetic operations.

7.1.2 Assignment Operators

The assignment operator stores the value of its left side to the variable of its right side. The right side operand may be a variable, constant or any expression but the left side operand should be a variable. If there is any expression in right side, it will be evaluated first and then the result will be assigned to the left hand operand.

EXAMPLE 7.1

```
p = 5;
```

Here 5 will be stored within the variable p.

```
area = len * brd;
```

Here the expression len * brd will be evaluated first and this result will be stored within the variable area.

There is a set of shorthand assignment operators in C. The general form of these is:

variable operator = expression;

Here operator is any binary arithmetic operator. +=, -=, *=, /=, %= are the shorthand assignment operators. These operators are the combination of arithmetic operator and assignment operator. For example += operator is a combination of + and = operator. The statement m += n is same as m = m + n

Some commonly used shorthand assignment operators and their equivalent statement with simple assignment operator is given below:

Table 7.2 Shorthand assignment operators and their equivalent statement

Statement with shorthand operator	Statement with simple assignment operator
m += 10	m = m + 10
m -= 15	m = m - 15
m *= n	m = m * n
v /= (m + n)	v = v / (m + n)
v %= 5	v = v % 5

7.1.3 Increment and Decrement Operators

++ operator is known as increment operator and −− operator is known as decrement operator. These are unary operators. The general form of increment operator is:

        ++ variable;
Or   variable ++;

++ variable is known as pre-increment operator and **variable ++** is known as post-increment operator. Both the expressions are equivalent and increments the value of the variable by 1; i.e., it is equivalent to the statement,

    variable = variable + 1;

But if the increment operator is used along with some other operators, then both are not same. Pre-increment operator first increments the value of the variable and then that incremented value is used for other operators. But in case of post-increment operator first old value is used for other operators and at the end increments the value of the variable.

EXAMPLE 7.2

int a = 5, b = 5, c, d;

        c = ++a;   //Pre-increment operator

        d = b++;   //Post-increment operator

In the above example, first the value of the variable **a** will be incremented and then the incremented value, i.e., 6 will be stored within the variable **c**. But in the next statement as the post-increment operator is used, the old value of the variable **b** will be stored within the variable **d**. So, d will contain 5 and then **b** will be incremented to 6. In both cases, the operand of increment operator is incremented by 1 but the order is different. As a result, though the initial value is same, different value is returned.

Similarly, The general form of decrement operator is:

        −− variable;
Or   variable −−;

−− variable is known as pre-decrement operator and **variable −−** is known as post-decrement operator. Both the expressions are equivalent and decrements the value of the variable by 1, i.e., it is equivalent to the statement,

        variable = variable − 1;

Like increment operator, if the decrement operator is used along with some other operators, then both are not same. Pre-decrement operator first decrements the value of the variable by 1 and then that decremented value is used for other operators. In case of post-decrement operator first old value is used for other operators and at the end decrements the value of the variable.

EXAMPLE 7.3

```
int a = 5, b = 5, c, d;
        c = − −a;         //Pre-decrement operator
        d = b− −;         //Post-decrement operator
```

In the above example, first the value of the variable **a** will be decremented and then the decremented value, i.e., 4 will be stored within the variable **c**. But in the next statement as the post-decrement operator is used, the old value of the variable **b** will be stored within the variable **d**. So, **d** will contain 5 and then **b** will be decremented to 4. In both cases, the operand of decrement operator is decremented by 1 but the order is different. As a result, though the initial value is same, different value is returned.

7.1.4 Relational Operators

Relational operators are used to compare two numeric operands. When in a program we need to take some decision depending on some condition; relational operators are used to check that condition. Following are the relational operators in C language.

Table 7.3 Relational operators

Operators	Descriptions
>	is greater than
>=	is greater than or equal to
<	is less than
<=	is less than or equal to
==	is equal to
!=	is not equal to

These are binary operators and the operands may be variables, constants or any expressions. These operators are mainly used in conditional and iterative statements.

Some use of relational operators:

```
3.2 >= 14          results 0 (FALSE)
15 < (12 + 6)      results 1 (TRUE)
−22 > 0            results 0 (FALSE)
```

Always remember that in C, non-zero values are treated as TRUE and zero is treated as FALSE.

7.1.5 Logical Operators

C provides the following three logical operators. These operators are used to form logical expression which evaluate to 0 or 1.

Table 7.4 Logical operators

Operators	Description
&&	Logical AND
||	Logical OR
!	Logical NOT

7.1.5.1 Logical AND (&&)

It is a binary operator and used to combine two relational expressions..It returns TRUE, only if both the operands, i.e., expressions to the left and right of the logical operator is TRUE. When any one of the two operands is FALSE, it returns FALSE. Always remember that if first (i.e., left) operand is FALSE, then result of && operator must be FALSE. That is why C compiler does not check the second argument. This is called short-circuit in C.

EXAMPLE 7.4

```
salary < 25000 && sex == 'F'
```

The first operand `salary < 25000` is evaluated first. If it is TRUE then the second operand `sex == 'F'` is tested. If this is also true then only the whole expression will be TRUE.

7.1.5.2 Logical OR (||)

The logical OR is also a binary operator and used to combine two relational expressions. It returns TRUE if any one of the two expressions evaluates to TRUE. If both the expressions evaluate to FALSE then only the logical OR operator returns FALSE. Thus, if first (i.e., left) operand is TRUE, then result of || operator must be TRUE irrespective of the result of second expression. That is why C compiler does not check the second argument. This is also familiar as short-circuit in C.

EXAMPLE 7.5

```
salary >= 25000 || Service_year < 15
```

If any one of the operands of || operator is true or if both of them are true, the expression evaluates to true. The above expression evaluates to true if `salary` is greater than or equals to 25000 or `Service_year` is greater than 15.

7.1.5.3 Logical NOT (!)

It is a unary operator and negates the logical value of its operand. If its operand evaluates to FALSE, it returns TRUE and if the operand evaluates to TRUE, it returns FALSE.

EXAMPLE 7.6

```
!( salary < 25000 && sex == 'F' )
```

the above expression evaluates to true only if `salary` is neither less than 25000 nor sex is F.

7.1.6 Conditional Operator

The operator which is used to check condition is called conditional operator. This is denoted by ? and : symbol. The general form is:

(expression1) ? expresion2 : expression3;

First expression1 is evaluated. If the expression1 is true, then expression2 is evaluated otherwise expression3 is evaluated.

EXAMPLE 7.7

max = (a>b) ? a : b;

In the above example, larger number between a and b will be stored within the variable max.

As the operator has 3 operands it is also called **ternary** operator. We can use conditional operator within the expression of any conditional operator, i.e, conditional operator can be nested.

For example,

max = (a>b)? ((a>c)? a: c) : ((b>c) ? b: c);

The above statement finds the maximum between three inputted numbers. Here, after evaluation of expression1, it faces another conditional operator at the position of expression2 or expression3.

7.1.7 Bitwise Operators

C supports some operators that operate on bit level. These operators are used to test bits, to shift bit values, etc. These operators are:

Table 7.5   Bitwise operators

Operators	Description
&	Bitwise AND
|	Bitwise OR (Inclusive)
^	Bitwise Exclusive OR
~	One's Complement
<<	Left Shift
>>	Right Shift

Details of this operator will be discussed later in a separate chapter.

7.1.8 Special Operators

Apart from the above operators, C language supports some other operators. These are comma operator (,), sizeof operator, operators related to pointer (&, *, (.) and –>), array subscript operator ([ ]) and parenthesis or function call operator, i.e., '( )'. Here, we will discuss only the first two, others will be discussed later.

7.1.8.1 Comma Operator

The comma operator is used to combine related expressions. Already we have seen some use of comma operator at the time of variable declaration where more than one variable (of same data type) is declared in a single statement. This operator is also used with for statement which will be discussed at the next chapter. Here we will see its another use. Consider the following example,

$$r = (p = 5, q = 15, p+q);$$

Here, first the value 5 will be assigned to p, then 15 will be assigned to q and at the end, the expression p+q will be evaluated and will be assigned to r. So, after execution, 15+5, i.e., 20 will be stored within r.

7.1.8.2 sizeof Operator

The sizeof operator is used to find the number of bytes occupied in memory by a variable, a constant or a data type qualifier. For example,

sizeof(int) will return 2.
sizeof('a') will return 1.
      float f;
sizeof(f) will return 4.

This operator is effectively used to find the size of array and structure, if their sizes are not known to the programmer or there is a chance to change their size. It is also used at the time of dynamically memory allocation.

7.2 EXPRESSIONS

An **expression** is a combination of variables, constants, operators, and functions that evaluates to a certain value. It is executed according to the precedence rules and of associativity of operators.

For example, 5 + 6 is an arithmetic expression which evaluates to 11. Similarly, $x \geq 10$ is an example of a relational expression, which evaluates to true or false according to the value of the variable, x. Followings are more example of expressions:

p – q + r
2 * (a + b)
x * (y – z)/n etc.

We already have used some simple expressions. C can handle simple as well as complex expressions very efficiently. For complex expressions, precedence and of associativity of operators is very important because computation depends on these two factors.

7.2.1 Type Conversions in Expressions

An expression may contain variables or constants of same type or of different types. If all the variables and constants in an expression are of same data type, the resulting type is also of the same type. But if they are of different data type, conversions take place. These conversions are of two types.

1. Implicit type conversion
2. Explicit type conversion

7.2.1.1 *Implicit Type Conversion*

When a conversion occurs automatically by the compiler, it is called implicit type conversion. In a mixed-type expression, data of lower type is automatically converted to higher type during execution. It is also known as **coercion**. During evaluation C compiler follows the strict rules of type conversion. Conversion rules are shown in the following table:

Table 7.6 Conversion rules

Operand 1	Operand 2	Result
char	char	char
char	int	int
char	long int	long int
char	float	float
char	double	double
int	char	int
int	int	int
int	long int	long int
int	float	float
int	double	double
long int	char	long int
long int	int	long int
long int	long int	long int
long int	float	float
long int	double	double
float	char	float
float	int	float
float	long int	float
float	float	float
float	double	double
double	char	double
double	int	double
double	long int	double
double	float	double
double	double	double

EXAMPLE 7.8

Operation	Result
5/2	2
5.0/2	2.5
5/2.0	2.5
5.0/2.0	2.5

Operation	Result
2/5	0
2.0/5	0.4
2/5.0	0.4
2.0/5.0	0.4

7.2.1.2 Explicit Type Conversion

Sometimes automatic conversion cannot fulfil the programmer's requirement. Suppose in a program average marks of a class of n student need to calculate. To find the average marks, first we have to calculate total_marks by adding the individual marks of each student. Then average marks will be calculated by the following expression:

Average = total_marks/n;

Since total_marks and n both are of integer type, the resultant type will also be an integer. But the average marks may be a floating point value. Then the fraction part of the result will be truncated and a wrong answer will be produced.

To solve this problem, forcefully we have to convert one of the operand to float type as shown below.

Average = (float)total_marks/n;

Or

Average = total_marks/(float)n;

The operator float converts the variable total_marks or n to the data type **float**. Then the division is performed by floating point mode using the rule of automatic conversion. Now the expression produces the correct result which will contain value with the fractional part. The process of such forceful conversion is called **explicit conversion** or **type casting**. The general form of explicit type conversion is:

(data type) expression

7.2.2 Type Conversion in Assignments

Some times it may happen that the data type of the variable on the left-hand side of the assignment operator and the data type of the expression on the right-hand side of the assignment operator may not be same. In these situations the value of the expression is promoted or demoted depending on the data type of the variable on left-hand side of = operator.

Now consider the following assignment statements as example.

```
int  a;
float  f;
a = 3.141;
f = 45;
```

In the above example, consider the first assignment statement. As the float value cannot be stored in an int variable, the data type float is demoted to an int and then its value is stored. As a result, 3 will be stored within **a**. Again in the next assignment statement, 45 is promoted to 45.000000 and then stored in **b**. Though in the above example simple constant expressions are used, the same rules will be applied if any complex expressions are used.

So be cautious, unintended consequences may occur. When floating-point numbers are type-casted to integral values, the fraction part of the floating-point numbers are truncated (rounded towards zero). Thus data may be lost. Again, when integral values are type-casted to floating-point numbers, there is a chance of losing precision as the floating-point data types may not be able to represent the integer exactly.

7.3 PRECEDENCE AND ASSOCIATIVITY

If number of operators used in a expression is more than one, the order of execution depends on *precedence* and *associativity*. Precedence determines the priority or order in which the operations are performed. In C language some specific levels of precedence has been defined. All the operators belong to any one of that level. Expressions with higher-precedence operators are evaluated first. The highest precedence is given to the function expression operator, '( )' whereas the lowest precedence is given to the comma operator, ','. The grouping of operands can be forced by using parentheses.

For example, consider the expression,

x – y / z

Here the / operation is performed before – as the precedence of / is higher than that of –.

On the other hand, associativity is the right-to-left or left-to-right order of execution for a group of operands to operators that have the same precedence. The precedence of an operator is important only when the other operators in the expression are of higher or lower precedence but within same precedence associativity determines the order in which direction it will be executed.

Consider the following example:

x – y * z + p

Here as * operator has higher precedence than – and +, * is executed before + and –. But between + and –, who is executed first will be determined by their associativity as both have the same precedence. The associativity of + and – operators is left to right, hence in the above example the result of y * z is subtracted from x first, and then this result will be added with p .

Table 7.7   The precedence of operators and their associativity

Operator	Description	Associativity
() [] . -> ++ --	Parentheses (also called function call) Brackets (also called array subscript) Member selection via object name Member selection via pointer Postfix increment, decrement	left-to-right
++ -- + - ! ~ (datatype) * & sizeof	Prefix increment, decrement Unary plus, minus Logical negation, bitwise complement Cast (change to *datatype*) Dereference Address Determine size in bytes	right-to-left
* / %	Multiplication, division, modulus	left-to-right
+ -	Addition, subtraction	left-to-right
« »	Bitwise shift left, Bitwise shift right	left-to-right
< ≤ > ≥	Relational less than, less than or equal to Relational greater than, greater than or equal to	left-to-right
== !=	Relational is equal to, is not equal to	left-to-right
&	Bitwise AND	left-to-right
^	Bitwise exclusive OR	left-to-right
|	Bitwise inclusive OR	left-to-right
&&	Logical AND	left-to-right
||	Logical OR	left-to-right
?:	Ternary conditional	right-to-left
= += -= *= /= %= &= ^= |= «= »=	Assignment Addition, subtraction assignment Multiplication, division assignment Modulus, bitwise AND assignment Bitwise exclusive, inclusive OR assignment Bitwise shift left, right assignment	right-to-left
,	Comma	left-to-right

Note 1: The grouping of operands can be forced by using parentheses. When parenthetical expressions are nested, execution will start from innermost parenthetical expression and continued from inner to outer.

Note 2: Postfix increment and decrement operators have higher precedence, but the actual increment or decrement of the operand is delayed until the other related operations are not completed. So in the statement `a = b/c++;` the current value of `c` is used to evaluate the expression and after completion of all operations in the statement, `c` will be incremented.

SUMMARY

➤ Operators are the symbols that help the programmer to instruct the computer to perform certain arithmetic, relational or logical operations.

➤ Arithmetic operators are +, −, *, / and %.

➤ Assignment Operator is =. Shorthand assignment operators are +=, −=, *=, /= and %=.

➤ ++ and −− are increment and decrement operators, respectively.

➤ Relational operators are >, ≥, <, ≤, == and !=.

➤ Logical operators are &&, || and !.

➤ Conditional operator is ?:.

➤ Bitwise operators are &, |, ^, ~, » and «.

➤ An expression is a combination of variables, constants, operators, and functions that evaluates to a certain value.

➤ When a conversion occurs automatically by the compiler, it is called implicit type conversion.

➤ When a particular data type is converted to another data type forcefully, the process is known as explicit conversion or type casting.

➤ Precedence determines the priority or order in which the operations are performed.

➤ Associativity is the right-to-left or left-to-right order of execution for a group of operands to operators that have the same precedence.

REVIEW EXERCISES

1. What do you mean by operator?
2. What are the different types of operators available in C?
3. What are the unary operators available in C?
4. Is there any ternary operator available in C?
5. What do you mean by pre-increment and post-increment?
6. What is the use of sizeof( ) operator?
7. What type of value is returned on execution of relational operator?
8. By which value TRUE and FALSE are considered in C?
9. Why type conversion is required?
10. What is the difference between implicit type conversion and explicit type conversion?
11. What is coercion?
12. How precedence and associativity play their role in evaluating an expression.

LEARN BY QUIZ – QUESTIONS

1. Which of the following is not an arithmetic operator?
   (1) ^
   (2) *
   (3) %

2. What will be the result of the expression 10/4?
   (1) 2.5
   (2) 2
   (3) 3

3. What will be the result of the following expression 10/4.0?
   (1) 2.5
   (2) 2
   (3) 3

4. What will be the result of 5/(float)2?
   (1) 2
   (2) 3
   (3) 2.5

5. What will be the result of 5%2?
   (1) 1
   (2) 2
   (3) 2.5

6. Which one of the following expression is invalid?
   (1) 4.2/2
   (2) 2%3
   (3) 4.2%3

7. What will be the result of $-6/7$?
   (1) 0
   (2) -1
   (3) 0 or -1

8. What will be result of 15%-4?
   (1) 3
   (2) -3
   (3) -3.75

9. What will be the value of x after evaluating the expression x++, given the initial value of x is 5?
   (1) 5
   (2) 6
   (3) 7

10. Consider two integer variables x and y where x = 7; what will be the content of x and y after evaluating the expression y = ++x?
    (1) x = 7 and y = 7
    (2) x = 8 and y = 7
    (3) x = 8 and y = 8

11. What will be the result of the following arithmetic expression?
    20$-$2*7
    (1) 6
    (2) 126
    (3) 7

12. What will be the value of z after executing the following two statements?
    x = 5, y = 6;
    z = x + (y++);

    (1) 11
    (2) 12
    (3) Unpredictable

13. What will be the value of x? x = sizeof(123);
    (1) 3
    (2) 2
    (3) 2.5

14. What will be the value of c?

    c = (a = 5, b = 6, a + b);
    (1) 5
    (2) 6
    (3) 11

15. What will be the value of x and y after evaluating the following expression?

    x = 5;

    y = ++x + x++;
    (1) x = 7, y = 11
    (2) x = 6, y = 11
    (3) x = 7, y = 12

16. What will be the value of a?

    a = (5==5);
    (1) Invalid statement
    (2) 0
    (3) 1

17. What will be the value of a and b where a and b are integers?

    a = 100;

    b = sizeof(++a);
    (1) a = 100, b = 2
    (2) a = 101, b = 2
    (3) a = 102, b = 2

18. What will be the value of x? x = sizeof("HELLO");
    (1) 6
    (2) 5
    (3) 7

19. Which of the following is not a logical operator?
    (1) &
    (2) ||
    (3) &&

20. What will be the value of x? x = 10>5 && 6==5
    (1) 0
    (2) 1
    (3) 6

21. Which of the following expression is equivalent to the expression x ≥ y?
    (1) !(x==y)
    (2) !(x<y)
    (3) !(x>y)

22. What will be the value of x?

    a = 5;

    b = 6;

    x = (a > b)?a:b;
    (1) 6
    (2) 5
    (3) 1

23. What will be the value of m, n, p, and q?
    m = n = p = −1;
    q = ++m&&++n||++p;
    (1) m = 0, n = −1, p = 0, q = 0
    (2) m = −1, n = 0, p = 0, q = 0
    (3) m = 0, n = −1, p = 0, q = 1

24. Which of the following is not a bitwise operator?
    (1) &
    (2) ^
    (3) !!

25. Which of the following expression will produce unpredictable value? (the declaration is given as int x, a = 5;)
    (1) x = (++a) − (−−a);
    (2) x = ++a+a++;
    (3) x = a++;

26. What will be the value of b?

    int a = 5,b;

        b = !a;
    (1) 5
    (2) 1
    (3) 0

27. What will be the value of b?
    int a = 5,b;
        b = !!a;
    (1) 5
    (2) 1
    (3) 0

28. Consider that x is a variable of type int and x = 5. What will be the value of x after evaluating the expression x−−?
    (1) 4
    (2) 5
    (3) 6

29. Consider two integer variable x and y where x = 7; what will be the content of x and y after evaluating the expression y = −−x?
    (1) x = 6, y = 6
    (2) x = 6, y = 7
    (3) x = 7, y = 7

30. What will be the value of b?

    int a = 5, b;
        b = −a;

(1) 5

(2) −5

(3) 5 or −5

31. What will be the value of a and b?

    int a = 5, b = 6;

      a+=b;

  (1) a = 11, b = 6

  (2) a = 5, b = 6

  (3) Invalid expression

32. Which of the expression contains unnecessary parenthesis?

  (1) (a+b)*(c−d)

  (2) (a/b)*c

  (3) (a+b)*c/d

33. Which of the following expression is erroneous? (declaration of a and b is as int a = 5, b = 6;)

  (1) a+++b;

  (2) a+b++;

  (3) (a+b)++;

34. Which of the following expression is valid?

  (1) 'A'+1

  (2) 'A' = 1

  (3) 1 = 'A'

35. What will be result of the following expression?

    int x = 25, y = 8;

    x == 10+15 && y < 10;

  (1) 1

  (2) 0

  (3) 26

LEARN BY QUIZ – ANSWERS

Answer explanations

1. ^ is not an arithmetic operator in C. It is a bitwise operator.

In C the arithmetic operators available are as given below:

(i)   +   : this is used for addition

(ii) −   : this is used for subtraction

(iii) *   : this is used for multiplication

(iv) /   : this is used for division

(v)   %   : this is used for modulus

2. The result of the expression 10/4 will be 2.

Here both the operands are integers. In C, if all the operands are integers, the processing will be as integer arithmetic and it produces integer result. So, 10/4 will result in 2.

However if any of the operand is float then the other operand will be converted to float and the result will be float. 10.0/4 or 10/4.0 will be 2.5.

3. The result of the expression 10/4.0 will be 2.5.

   Since the value 4.0 is float, so 10 will also be converted into float. As a result, the whole expression will be float and the result will be 2.5.

4. The result of 5/(float)2 will be 2.5.

   Here although both the operands are actually integer, yet the result will be 2.5. Note that float data type is written within parenthesis with 2. This is known as type casting and it is done by cast operator i.e. the data type float here is playing the role of cast operator. Cast operator converts the data type of any operand during the evaluation of an expression. The original data type of that operand will not be changed.

   If float key word is omitted then both the operand will be integer. In any arithmetic operation if all the operands are integer then the result will also be an integer.

5. The result of 5%2 will be 1.

   % operator is called modulo operator and is used to directly find out the remainder. If 5 is divided by 2, then the remainder will be 1.

6. The expression 4.2%3 is Invalid.

   The % operator (modulo operator) can only be used with integers. Here, both the operands are not integers. So the expression is not valid.

7. The result of −6/7 will be 0 or −1. Here, both the operands are integer. Division of two integers always produce the result in integer. Fractional part (if any) is truncated. So our expected result is 0.

   But this expression needs a closer look before evaluation. If both the operands are integer and of same sign then the result will be zero. As one of them is negative so the result will be either 0 or −1. The actual result is completely machine dependent.

8. The result for 15%−4 will be 3.

   In modulo division, i.e., for finding out remainder using % (modulo) operator, the sign of the first operand always is the sign of the result. Hence, the result will be 3.

   The result will be −3 if the expression is −15%4

9. The value of *x* will be 6.

   The ++ is an incremental operator in C. This operator increments the content of a variable by 1.

   Note that the arithmetic expression *x*++ is equivalent to writing the assignment *x* = *x* + 1.

   Here, the expression x + 1 in the right hand side will be evaluated first and then the result will be stored in the left side variable *x*.

   So 1 will be added to the current value of *x*, i.e., 5, resulting the value 6 (5 + 1) and then it will be stored inside *x*.

   Note that the ++ operator can be written in the form of *x*++ or ++*x*.

   The first form is called prefix expression and the second one is called postfix expression.

   But both the expressions are equivalent to *x* = *x* + 1.

10. The content of *x* and *y* after evaluating the expression *y* = ++*x* will be *x* = 8 and *y* = 8.

    The ++ increment operator can be used either in prefix form (i.e., ++*x*) or in postfix form (i.e., *x*++). When they are used only with a variable alone then both the expression will produce the same value and will be equivalent to writing *x* = *x* + 1. But when they are used in an assignment statement, then their behaviour will be different. In the question, prefix expression has been used. So here first the value of **x** will be incremented by 1 and then it will be assigned to **y**. This is equivalent to evaluating the following two consecutive statements:

x = x + 1;

y = x;

Had it been written in the form of **y = x**++ (i.e., ++ in postfix form), then the result of **x** and **y** would have been 8 and 7. First the value of x will be assigned to y then the value of x will be incremented and this would be equivalent to evaluating the following two consecutive statements:

y = x;

x = x + 1;

11. The result of the arithmetic expression 20 − 2 * 7 will be 6.

Here two arithmetic operators are used i.e., − (subtraction) and * (multiplication). To evaluate any arithmetic expression, it is necessary to know the precedence of operators. C follows the following precedence rules.

*, /, % has high precedence

+, − has low precedence

So in the above arithmetic expression, first multiplication 2 * 7 will be done and then subtraction 20 − 14 will be done.

Writing the above expression in the form (20 − 2) * 7 will produce the result 126. Here, expression enclosed in parenthesis will be evaluated first.

12. The value of **z** will be 11.

Here ++ operator has been used in postfix form (i.e., ++ has been written after the variable y), which means that first the expression will be evaluated using older value of **y** and then value of **y** will be incremented. Although we know that () can be used to override the default precedence rules, but that is not applicable in ++ operator. So in the above expression, () has no role to play. As a result the older value of x and y (i.e., 5 and 6) will be added and the result 11 will be stored in z and at last value of y will be incremented. Hence, the final value of y will be 7.

13. The value of **x** will be 2.

C supports some special operators. *sizeof* is one of these. It is a compile time operator which determines how much memory space is required by a data type or variable in a particular environment when the actual size is not known to the programmer. Actual size of a data type varies from compiler to compiler.

But in most of C compiler, int occupies 2 bytes which is considered standard.

As for example in Turbo C compiler under DOS int data type occupies 2 bytes but in GCC compiler under Linux the size is 4 bytes.

123 is an integer value. So the value of **x** will be 2.

Size of a data type never becomes a fractional number.

14. The value of **c** will be 11.

Here comma (,) has been used in the expression. Comma (,) is considered as a special operator in C. It evaluates in a left to right manner but the result generated by the rightmost expression will be the final result of the whole expression. So the result of **a + b** (rightmost expression) will be finally stored in **c**. So first 5 will be assigned to a then 6 will be assigned to b and then a + b will be evaluated to 11 and will be assigned to c.

15. The correct answer is x = 7, y = 12.

    Here ++ operator is used twice with **x**. Prefix ++ will be evaluated first. As a result, the value of **x** will be incremented to 6. Since in the arithmetic expression both the operands are **x**, so 6 + 6 will be calculated and the result will be stored in **y**. After completion of the assignment, the value of **x** will again be incremented. So the final value will be **x** = 7, **y** = 12.

16. The value of **a** will be 1.

    Here in the right side of the assignment statement, one relational operator has been used, i.e., (==). C supports the following relational operators:

    >
    <
    >=
    <=
    ==
    !=

    These operators are used to compare two values. C has its own way to evaluate relational expression. The result of any relational expression is either 0 or 1. 0 is treated as the false value while 1 is treated as the truth value. In the above expression, == operator has been used which checks the equality. Since 5 is equal to 5, the truth value (i.e., 1) will be stored in **a**.

17. The value of **a** and **b** will be a = 100, b = 2.

    ++ operator increments the value of a variable by 1.

    Here, it is expected that the value of **a** should be 101, and **b** should be 2, i.e., the size of an int. But the value of **a** will be 100. The reason behind the queer output is that if sizeof operator is applied to an expression, the compiler does not compile it for an executable code. Hence in this case, the expression ++a will not have any effect when it is used with *sizeof* operator which was logically expected.

18. The value of **x** will be 6.

    In C, 'HELLO' is a string constant. A string constant is a set of character. C has its own way to store any character string in the memory. At the end of every string, one '\0' (null character) is stored. Thus, the string constant HELLO actually contains 6 characters. Each character is one byte. Hence the result is 6.

19. & is not a logical operator. It is a bitwise operator in C.

    C has got three logical operators: Logical AND (&&), logical OR (||), and NOT (!). Logical operators are used to combine two or more relational expression.

20. The value of **x** will be 0.

    Here two relational expressions 10 > 5 and 6 == 5 have been combined with &&. Every relational expression generates 1 when the expression is true and 0 when the expression is false. When these are combined in logical and (&&), they produce 0 or 1 according to the following rule:

    0 && 0 = 0
    0 && 1 = 1
    1 && 0 = 0
    1 && 1 = 1

    In the above question, the first expression 10 > 5 will generate 1 as it is true and the second expression 5 == 6 will generate 0 as it is false. So ultimately the result of 1 && 0 will be stored in **x**, which is 0 according to the rule mentioned above.

21. !(*x* < *y*) is equivalent to the expression *x* ≥ *y*.

   The expression *x* ≥ *y* will generate 1 whenever the value of *x* will be either greater than or equal to the value of *y*. ! is a logical operator which basically negates the result of any relational expression. ! TRUE means FALSE and ! FALSE means TRUE. So, !0 = 1 and !1 = 0. Naturally for all value of *x* which is greater then or equal to *y*, the expression (*x* < *y*) will generate 0 since it is false. So, !(*x* < *y*) will ultimately be !(0) which is 1, and will be equivalent to *x* ≥ *y*.

22. The value of *x* will be 6.

   Here a conditional expression has been evaluated with the help of ?: operator. This is known as ternary operator in C. It is used to write a conditional expression which has the following generalized form.

   expression1?expression2:expresson3.

   Expression1 is evaluated first if it is true, i.e., if the result is 1 or any non-zero value, then expression2 will be evaluated and if expression1 is false, i.e., if it generates 0 then expression3 will be evaluated. Here, the expression (*a* > *b*) is false resulting to 0. So expression3 will be evaluated and the value of *b* will be stored in *x*.

23. The values of *m*, *n*, *p* and *q* will be *m* = 0, *n* = −1, *p* = 0, *q* = 0.

   Here in the whole expression two logical operators have been used. Logical AND (&&) and logical OR (||). Precedence of && is higher than precedence of ||. ++*m* will be evaluated first for evaluation of logical &&. ++*m* will become 0.

   In logical AND, if both the operands evaluate to 1, then only the result will be 1. When ++*m* will become 0, there will be no need to evaluate ++*n*. So it will not be evaluated and value of *n* will remain −1 and the expression ++*m*&&++*n* will generate 0 (0 && any value = 0). It is combined with ++*p* using logical OR.

   In OR, result will be 1 if any one expression is 1(1 || any value = 1). Since the result of the first expression is 0, ++*p* has to be evaluated which will be evaluated to 0. Finally, the expression will become 0 || 0, which will generate 0 and will be stored in *q*. So ultimately *m* = 0, *n* = −1, *p* = 0, *q* = 0.

24. !! is not a bitwise operator.

   C supports a set of bitwise operators. The operators are as follows:
   (1) & (bitwise AND)
   (2) | (bitwise OR)
   (3) ^ (bitwise X-OR)
   (4) ~ (one's complement)
   (5) « (left shift)
   (6) » (right shift)

25. The result of x = (++a) − (−−a); will be Unpredictable.

   Here two operands of the addition operation are (++*a*) and (−−*a*). We know that pre increment or decrement operators work first. But in C there is no specific order of evaluation of the operands. It is left on the compiler. So whether (++*a*) will be evaluated first or (−−*a*) is not defined. Hence the result cannot be predicted.

26. The value of *b* will be 0.

   In C, evaluating any relational expression generates 1 if the expression is true, and 0 if the expression is false. But C itself treats any non zero value as truth value and 0 as false value.

Here, logical operator has not been used which basically negates the result. The interpretation is as follows:

!TRUE = FALSE

!FALSE = TRUE

So the expression !*a* means !5 which in turn means !TRUE which is a FASLE value and will generate 0. So the content of *b* will be 0.

27. The value of *b* will be 1.

The associativity of ! operator is right to left. So !*a* will be evaluated first. Then the result of !*a* will be evaluated by ! operator. The initial content of *a* is 5 which is a TRUTH value considered in C. Doing !*a* for the first time, i.e., !5 will produce 0 (FALSE). Then again doing !0 will produce 1 (i.e., TRUE). This value will ultimately be stored in *b*.

28. The value of *x* will be 4.

The $--$ is a decrement operator available in C. This operator is useful for decrementing the content of a variable by 1 only. Note that the arithmetic expression *x*$--$ is equivalent to writing the assignment $x = x - 1$. Here the expression in the right hand side will be evaluated first and then the result will be stored in the left side variable. So 1 will be subtracted from current value of *x* which will result in the value $5 - 1 = 4$ and then it will be stored inside *x*. Note that the $--$ operator can be written in the form of *x*$--$ or $--$*x*. The first form is called prefix expression and the second one is called postfix expression. But both the expressions are equivalent to $x = x - 1$.

29. The content of *x* and *y* after evaluating the expression $y = --x$, will be $x = 6, y = 6$.

The $--$ decrement operator can be used either in prefix form (i.e., $--x$) or in postfix form (i.e., *x*$--$). When it is used only with a variable alone then both will result in the same value and will be equivalent to writing $x = x - 1$. But when it is used in an assignment statement then their behaviour will be different. In the question, prefix expression has been used. So here first the value of *x* will be decremented by 1 then it will be assigned to *y*. This is equivalent to evaluating the following two consecutive statements:

$$x = x - 1$$
$$y = x$$

Had it been written in the form of $y = x--$ (i.e., $--$ in postfix form), then the result of *x* and *y* would have been 6 and 7 and this will be equivalent to evaluating the following two consecutive statements:

$$y = x$$
$$x = x - 1$$

30. The value of *b* will be is -5.

Here in the $-$ operator has been used with a single operand *b*. This is unary minus, means will work with only one operand. As a result the negative value of *a* will be evaluated first and then it will be stored inside *b*. So the value of *b* will be -5.

31. The value of *a* and *b* will be $a = 11, b = 6$.

This is an assignment operation. C supports short hand assignment statement which has the form variable op = expression, which is the equivalent to writing variable = variable + expression. So the above statement is equivalent to writing $a = a + b$. Value of *a* will be added with value of *b* and will be stored in *a*.

So final value of *a* and *b* will be 11 and 6, respectively.

32. The expression (*a/b*) * *c* contains unnecessary parenthesis.

    Arithmetic operators * and / have got the same precedence, and associativity is from left to right. Due to the associativity rule, *a/b* will be automatically evaluated first and then with the result **c* will be done. So putting parenthesis with *a/b* is totally redundant.

33. The expression (a+b)++; is erroneous.

    Here, increment operator ++ has been used. It is used in postfix form. But ++ operator can only be used with a variable, not with any constant value. In the above expression *a* is a variable, *b* is a variable. But the result of (*a* + *b*) is a constant, i.e., 11. So writing (*a* + *b*)++ is equivalent to writing (11)++ here, which is not legal.

    Hence, it is an erroneous statement.

34. The expression 'A' + 1 is valid and the result will be 66.

    Every character is represented with their ASCII value. The ASCII value is basically an integer value which is 65 for 'A'. So the arithmetic expression which involves one character and one integer will ultimately become 65 (i.e., ASCII value of 'A') and 1. So addition of 1 with 65 will produce 66.

    Constant is not allowed in the left hand side of an assignment operator. Thus other options are incorrect

35. The result of the expression will be 1.

    This is an expression involving arithmetic as well as logical and relational operators. The precedence rule says that arithmetic operators have got higher precedence than logical operators. So addition of 10 + 15 will be done first which will be 25. Since the value of *x* is 25. So ultimately the expression will be 25 == 25 && 8 < 10. Again the precedence rule says that relational operators enjoy higher precedence than logical operators. So 25 == 25 will result TRUE (1) and 8 < 10 will also result TRUE(1).

    Finally the logical expression will become TRUE&&TRUE, i.e., 1&1 and will be evaluated to 1.

8

Input and Output Statement

In the previous chapters we have learnt how variables can be declared and initialized, what are the different operators available in C and using these operators how a meaningful expression can be written. Now, we will discuss how the input and output operations are carried out in C.

C language does not have any input or output statement. All the input and output operations are accomplished using some library functions. These are included in stdio.h and conio.h header files. These input and output functions or in short, I/O functions are categorized into three groups. These are:
1. Console I/O functions which deal with keyboard and monitor,
2. Disk I/O functions which deal with hard disk or floppy disk and
3. Port I/O functions which deal with different port.

In this chapter, we will discuss only about some console I/O functions that are used frequently. These console I/O functions can be categorized into formatted I/O functions and unformatted I/O functions.

8.1 FORMATTED I/O FUNCTIONS

Formatted input refers to read or input data using keyboard in a particular format and formatted output refers to print or display (i.e., output) data or message in the VDU in a formatted way means when a set of values will be displayed, the sequence of the fields, their widths, spaces among the values, etc. can be specified. The standard library function *scanf( )* is used for formatted input operation and *printf( )* is used for formatted output operation.

8.1.1 The printf( ) Function

The printf( ) function is possibly the most versatile way to display data on the VDU for a program. It is defined in the stdio.h header file. The general form is:

    printf(format-string[,arguments,...]);

Here, format string, also known as control string, denotes how the output is formatted. There are three possible components of a format string. These are literal text, escape sequence and conversion specifier.

8.1.1.1 Literal Text

The literal text in a format string is basically anything that can be typed through keyboard except escape sequences and conversion specifier. It is printed as it is specified with in the double quotation mark (" "), including all spaces.

EXAMPLE 8.1

To display any message in the screen, the statement will be:

printf("Hello!");

Output: Hello!

8.1.1.2 Escape Sequence

An escape sequence is a sequence of characters that represent something else escaping from their original representation. It consists of a backslash (\) followed by a single or more characters. Though it is consist of sequence of characters but it is considered as a single character to the compiler. At the time of compilation the sequence of characters is converted into a single escaped character in the object code. For example, the escape sequence, '\n' is converted into a single character whose ASCII value is 10 and represented as a new line character. The following table lists the ANSI escape sequences and what they represent.

Table 8.1   Escape sequences

Escape sequence	Represents
\a	Bell (alert)
\b	Backspace
\f	Form feed
\n	New line
\r	Carriage return
\t	Horizontal tab
\v	Vertical tab
\'	Single quotation mark
\"	Double quotation mark
\\	Backslash
\?	Question mark
\0	Null character

EXAMPLE 8.2

printf("Hello \n Class!!");

Output: Hello

         Class!!

printf("Hello \t Class!!");

Output: Hello   Class!!

printf("Cat\rM");

Output: Mat

printf(" Cat\b\bu");

Output: Cut

printf("Welcome to the world of \'C\'");

Output: Welcome to the world of 'C'

printf(" \" India\" is great.");

Output: " India" is great.

8.1.1.3 *Conversion Specifier*

Conversion specifiers are used with printf( ) to display the content of variables in a specified data type format. It consists of a percent sign (%) followed by one or more single character. Commonly used specifier and their meaning are given in the following table:

Table 8.2   Conversion specifiers

Specifier	Meaning
%c	Prints a character
%d	Prints an integer (decimal value)
%i	Prints an integer
%e	Prints float value in exponential form
%f	Prints float value
%g	Prints using %e or %f whichever is smaller
%o	Prints octal value
%s	Prints a string
%x	Prints a hexadecimal integer (unsigned) using lower case a–f
%X	Prints a hexadecimal integer (unsigned) using upper case A–F
%p	Prints a pointer value
%u	Prints an unsigned decimal integer
%ud	Prints an unsigned decimal integer

EXAMPLE 8.3

To display the content of a variable, the statement will be:

int x = 5;

printf("%d",x);

Output: 5

To display any message along with the content of some variable, the statement will be:

int x = 5;

printf("The value of x is: %d",x);

Output: The value of x is: 5

We can display multiple variable with a single printf( ).

int x = 5, y = 7;

printf("%d, %d", x, y);

Output: 5, 7

int x = 5;

char ch = 'A';

printf("%d, %c", x, ch);

Output: 5, A

Along with variable, we can also use expression as argument.

int x = 5, y = 7;

printf("Sum = %d", x + y);

Output: Sum = 12

int x = 5, y = 2;

printf("%d / %d = %f", x, y,(float)x/y);

Output: 5/2 = 2.500000

If we want the output in more formatted way, we have to know more details of the printf( ) function's format string. The general form is:

%[Flag][Minimum Width][.Precision][Size Modifier][Conversion Specifier]

In the above form the percent sign(%) and conversion specifier are mandatory but others, i.e., Flag, Minimum Width, Precision and Size Modifier are optional. The list of conversion specifiers are already shown in **Table 8.2**. Minimum Width specifier specifies minimum number of characters used to display the value. Following table shows the possible set that can be used as width specifier.

Table 8.3 Minimum width specifiers

Width	Meaning
n	At least n characters will be printed. If the output value is less than n characters, the output will be padded with blank space. Output will be right justified. If the output value is wider than the specified width, the field will be expanded to accommodate the converted result.
0n	At least n characters will be printed. If the output value is less than n characters, the output will be padded with leading zeros.
*	The argument list will supply the value of the width specifier, which must be preceded the actual argument being formatted.

EXAMPLE 8.4

int x = 5, y = 125, z = 1234;

printf("%3d \n%3d\n%3d",x,y,z);

Output: 5
                125
                1234

int x = 5;

printf("%03d",x);

Output: 005

int x = 5,w = 3;

printf("%*d",3,x);

printf("\n%0*d",3,x);

printf("\n%0*d",w,x);

Output: 5
                005
                005

In the last example, as * is used as width specifier, actual value of width is supplied as argument. Here, it is 3. The advantage of it is programmer can specify the width dynamically using some variable as width specifier.

Precision specifier is used with real numbers and string. Its use related to strings is discussed in Chapter 12 where string handling is discussed. Here, we will discuss its use with real numbers, i.e., numbers with float and double data type. Precision specifier always preceded with a period(.) to separate it from width specifier. It is used to specify that the number of digits should be printed after decimal point. If the output value has more decimal places than the specified precision, the output will be rounded off up to the specified precision. Here also asterisk(*) can be used with or without the width specifier.

When asterisk is used, the actual value of the precision specifier is supplied through argument list and this argument must precede the data being formatted. If * is used for both width and precision specifier, the width argument must immediately follow the specifiers, then followed by the precision argument and next the actual argument (i.e., data) to be formatted. If precision specifier is omitted the default of 6 is assumed.

EXAMPLE 8.5

```
float x = 5;
printf("%f",x);
```
Output:

5	.	0	0	0	0	0	0

```
float x = 5;
printf("%.2f",x);
```
Output:

5	.	0	0

```
double x = 3.14159265;
printf("%.2lf",x);
```
Output:

3	.	1	4

```
float x = 234.5678;
printf("%.2f",x);
```
Output:

2	3	4	.	5	7

```
float x = 34.56;
printf("%.5f",x);
```
Output:

3	4	.	5	6	0	0	0

```
float x = 234.5678;
printf("%8.2f",x);
```
Output:

		2	3	4	.	5	7

```
float x = 234.5678;
int p = 3
printf("%.*f", p, x);
```

2	3	4	.	5	6	8

```
float x = 234.5678;
printf("%*.*f",8,2,x);
```

Output:

		2	3	4	.	5	7

The flag specifier specifies decimal points, numeric signs, output justification, trailing zeros, octal and hexa decimal prefixes. These are shown in the following table.

Table 8.4   Flag specifiers

Flag	Meaning
–	Produce left justified output
+	Always show positive or negative sign before value.
#	Specifies that specifier will use alternate form of specifier

If the # flag is used with printf, following conversion specifier can be attached with the # flag.

Table 8.5   Conversion specifiers that are used with flag specifiers

Flag values	Meaning
o	Adds a leading zero(0) before octal number
x or X	Adds a leading 0x or 0X before hexadecimal number
e E f	Always show a decimal point even if no digits follow the decimal point.
g G	Same as e and E. But trailing zeros are not removed.

EXAMPLE 8.6

```
int x = 12;
printf("%5d",x);
```

Output:

			1	2

```
int x = 12;
printf("%-5d",x);
```

Output:

1	2			

```
float x = 234.5678;
printf("%-8.2f",x);
```

Output:

2	3	4	.	5	7		

```
float x = 234.5678;
printf("%+8.2f",x);
```

Output:

	+	2	3	4	.	5	7

```
float x = 234.5678;
printf("%+−8.2f",x);
```

Output:

+	2	3	4	.	5	7	

```
int n = 11;
printf("%o",n);
```

Output: 13

```
int n = 11;
printf("%#o",n);
```

Output: 013

```
int n = 11;
printf("%X",n);
```

Output: B

```
int n = 11;
printf("%#X",n);
```

Output: 0XB

```
int n = 11;
printf("%.0f",n);
```

Output: 11

```
int n = 11;
printf("%#.0f",n);
```

Output: 11.

Following are the size modifiers that can be used with specific conversion specifier.

Table 8.6   Size modifiers with their conversion specifier

Size modifier	Used with conversion specifier	Meaning
h	d i o u x X	short
l	d i o u x X	long
l	e E f g G	double
L	e E f g G	long double

Only the corresponding type mentioned in the above table are used with the corresponding size modifiers. When 'h' will be added before a conversion specifier, it will indicate the short form of the corresponding type. Similarly inclusion of 'l' will specify long. Here are some examples of size modifiers:

Table 8.7   Examples of size modifiers

Specifier with size modifier	Meaning
%hd	Print a short integer
%ld	Print a long Integer
%lf	Print double value
%lo	Print an octal long
%hx	Print a hex short
%lu	Print an unsigned long decimal integer
%Lf	Print a long double value

Remember, on success, the printf( ) returns the total number of characters written but on failure, a negative number is returned.

EXAMPLE 8.7

```
printf("%d",printf("My Count="));
```
Output: My Count = 9

8.1.2   The scanf( ) Function

The scanf( ) function is used to take input from the keyboard for a program. It is also defined in the stdio.h header file. The general form is:

        scanf(format-string[,arguments,...]);

scanf() uses conversion specifiers in the format-string to take inputs through variable arguments. The arguments should be the addresses of the variables. For variables of primary data type, the address is passed by using the address-of operator (&) before the variable name. On success, the scanf( ) function returns the number of input fields successfully read, converted and stored but on failure, EOF is returned. The return value does not include read items that are not stored. If no items are stored, scanf( ) function returns 0 (zero).

EXAMPLE 8.8

```
int x;
scanf("%d",&x);

int x;
float y;
scanf("%d%f",&x,&y);
```

Like printf( ), inputs can also be taken in more formatted way. For that we need to follow the detail of format string of scanf( ) function. The general form is:

%[*][Maximum Width][Size Modifier][Conversion Specifier]

Here also the percent sign(%) and conversion specifier are mandatory but others, i.e., *, Minimum Width and Size Modifier are optional. The list of conversion specifiers and size modifiers are already shown in **Table 8.2** and **Table 8.6**, respectively. The asterisk (*) suppresses assignment of input field. When asterisk follow the % in the format string, the next input field will be scanned but would not be assigned to next address argument.

EXAMPLE 8.9

int x,y;

scanf("%d%*d%d",&x,&y);

Now if we provide the input value as 123 456 789, 123 will be assigned to **x**, 456 will be skipped due to * and 789 will be assigned to **y** variable.

Maximum width specifier specifies maximum number of characters to be read from the input field.

EXAMPLE 8.10

int x, y;

scanf("%2d%3d",&x,&y);

Now if we provide the input value as 12 345, 12 will be assigned to **x** and 345 will be assigned to **y** variable. But if the inputs are given as 123 45

12 will be assigned to **x** as %2d is specified and 3 will be assigned to **y** variable, i.e., the unread part of input field 123. The rest portion, i.e., 45 will remain in the buffer and will be assigned to first field of next scanf statement if any.

In scanf( ), if there is no separator between two conversion specifier or the separator is space, at the time of taking input we can use space or tab as separator. But if we want to use any other character as separator, we have to specify the corresponding character within the format string.

For example, if we want to take input of a date as DD/MM/YYYY format, the corresponding scanf( ) statement will be:

int d, m, y;

scanf("%d/%d/%d", &d, &m, &y);

For the above statement, we will give the input as 11/11/2011

Note On success, the printf( ) returns the total number of characters written and the scanf( ) function returns the number of items successfully read.

8.2 UNFORMATTED I/O FUNCTIONS

There are two types of unformatted I/O functions. These are character I/O functions and string I/O functions. The character I/O functions are:

- getch( )
- getche( )
- getchar( )
- putch( )
- putchar( )

getch( ):   It is a character input function defined in conio.h header file. It reads a single character directly from the keyboard not via input buffer. As soon as the character typed through keyboard, the value is assigned to the corresponding variable. Thus user needs not to press *Enter* key. Another important thing of this function that which character is inputted cannot be displayed/echoed in the VDU. The general form is:

> ch = getch( );

where ch is a character variable.

getche( ):   It is also a character input function defined in conio.h header file and like getch( ), it reads a single character directly from the keyboard not via input buffer. Here also user does not need to press *Enter* key. Only difference with the getch() is that it echoes the inputted character in the VDU. The general form is:

> ch = getche( );

where ch is a character variable.

getchar( ):   This is also a character input function defined in stdio.h. But it is a buffered function. When user provides the input from keyboard, instead of assigning to the corresponding variable the value is stored in the standard input buffer (**stdin**) temporarily. When the *Enter* key is pressed, the input moves to corresponding variable. The general form is:

> ch = getchar( );

where ch is a character variable.

putch( ):   This is a character output function defined in conio.h header file. It displays a single character directly to the VDU. The general form is:

> putch(ch);

where ch is a character variable.

putchar( ):   This is also a character output function defined in stdio.h header file. Instead of directly displays on VDU, it writes the character to the output buffer. Then it displays on the screen. The general form is:

> putchar(ch);

where ch is a character variable.

The operation of putch( ) and putchar( ) are almost same. The only difference is putch( ) cannot translate '\n' character into carriage-return/linefeed pairs. When putchar( ) executes '\n', control moves to the 1st column of next line but putch( ) moves to the same column of next line.

EXAMPLE 8.11

```
putch('A');
putch('B');
putch('\n');
putch('C');
```

Output: AB
        C

EXAMPLE 8.12

```
putchar('A');
putchar('B');
putchar('\n');
putchar('C');
```

Output: AB
        C

8.3 GENERAL STRUCTURE OF A C PROGRAM

Before writing a C program we have to know the basic structure of a C program. A C program may contain one or more following blocks.

Documentation Block
Preprocessor Directive Block
Global Declaration Block
main( ) Function Block
{
Local Declaration Block
Executable Code Block
}
Sub-Function Block

Documentation Block consists of comments regarding the problem definition. It may also include author name, date of program written and other related information regarding the program. Preprocessor Directive Block includes preprocessor directives if any is used in the program. If any global variables (i.e., the variables that are used in more than one function) are required in the program, that need to declare at this Global Declaration Block. Next comes the *main* function Block. Every C program must contain one and only one *main* function. *main* function consists of two Blocks: Local Declaration Block and Executable Code Block. Within the *main* function first task is to declare the local variables (i.e., the variables that are used only within the current function) of the *main* function. These are declared at Local Declaration Block. Within the *main* function block, next block is Executable Code Block where the required codes of the main function need to be written. The opening and closing brace ({....}) indicates block in C program. Here, it indicates *main* function Block. At the end of this block Sub-Function Block comes. If any user defined functions need to be written, that are written at this block.

Among the above mentioned blocks the *main* function block must exist in a C program. Other blocks may or may not exist according the requirement in the program.

8.4 FIRST C PROGRAM

Now we are able to write a complete C program. Here is a simple C program which will add two integer values.

PROGRAM 8.1   Write a C program to add two integer values.

```
/* Program to add two integer value */ } Documentation Block
#include<stdio.h>  ⎫
                   ⎬ Preprocessor Directive Block
#include<conio.h>  ⎭
                   } Global Declaration Block, here it is empty.
void main( )
{ int num1, num2, sum;           } Local Declaration Block
 clrscr( );
 printf("\nEnter 1st Number : ");
 scanf("%d",&num1);
 printf("\nEnter 2nd Number : ");  } Executable Code Block   main
 scanf("%d",&num2);                                          Function
 sum = num1 + num2;                                          Block
 printf("\nSum = %d", sum);
}
                   } Sub-Function Block, here it is empty.
Sample Test Run:
Enter 1st Number: 12
Enter 2nd Number: 53
Sum = 65
```

In the above program, first line is a comment line. Comment line is optional and can be used anywhere in our program. A 'comment' is any sequence of characters started with a forward slash followed by an asterisk combination (/*) and ended with an asterisk followed by a forward slash combination (*/). Compiler considers this total portion as a single white-space character or ignores it. Comments can be spread in multiple lines but nesting of comments is not allowed. The main purpose of the comments is to document our code. A comment may appear on the same line with code statements. For example:

    printf("Hello\n"); /* A comment may be written here */

The second line is a preprocessor directive (called file inclusion directive). It is used to include the stdio.h and conio.h header files. As printf() and scanf() are defined in stdio.h and clrscr() is defined in the conio.h, both files are included. There is no restriction, we can include file in any order. The detail of preprocessor directives will be discussed later.

The next line specifies a function named *main*. This is a special name that is recognized by the compiler. It points to the precise place in the program where execution begins. Every C program must have a *main* function. We cannot have more than one main function in a program.

Every C function has return type associated with it. When a function does not return any value, its return type is specified as *void*. As in most cases *main* function does not return any value, it is usually declared as *void*.

A pair of parenthesis follows the word *main* to indicate that it is a function. Next comes the character '{', called left brace. There is also matching '}' which appears at the end of the main function. These pair of matching braces encloses the body of the function. Within the body of the function, first task is to declare the variables. Next task is to write the statements according to algorithm. The clrscr() is used to clear the screen.

As we are able to write a program, our next task is to execute. So, now we will learn where we will write the program code and how this program will compiled and execute.

8.5 EXECUTING A C PROGRAM

To execute a C program first task is to write the program using any text editor. In windows environment, most of the C compiler has inbuilt editor to write C programs. Here we will discuss about Turbo C compiler. Though all the programs written in this book are compiled using Turbo C compiler, these programs can be executed on other compiler with very minor modifications or nothing at all.

The Turbo C compiler has its own Integrated Development Environment (IDE) that helps us in writing, compilation, debugging and executing C programs. We can load the Turbo C compiler by typing TC at the DOS prompt in the subdirectory where the compiler has been stored in hard disk or by clicking the icon of Turbo C on the desktop of the windows. In both cases, the TC IDE screen will be appeared. Here we can type our own program. The C program should be written in lower case. Only the symbolic constants are written in upper case. The program can be saved by selecting the save option from the File menu which will be activated by pressing ALT+F and then S. There is a shortcut key F2 to save a file. Now the save window will appear. Here we have to provide the filename. Filename may be any valid filename but extension should be .c. To compile the program, we will select Build All option from compile menu. If there is any compilation error, we need to recompile the program after rectifying the errors. Build All option is a combination of 3 tasks. These are compile, Link and Make exe. Instead of Build All option, we can execute these 3 tasks separately from compile menu. After successful compilation of a C program the corresponding object file(.obj) is created. That means if the name of source code is **sample.c**, the name of the object file will be **sample.obj**. Then linker links this object file with the system libraries and other object codes, if any. After linking, an executable file having .exe extension will be created. According to above example, the executable filename will be **sample.exe**. Finally to execute we can select Run option from Run menu or selecting the DOS shell from File menu and typing the filename at the shell prompt. If the executable filename is sample.exe, we have to type **sample** at shell prompt and then press enter key. The pressing of shortcut key CTRL+F9 is same as Build All + Run. All the 4 operations will be done in a single task.

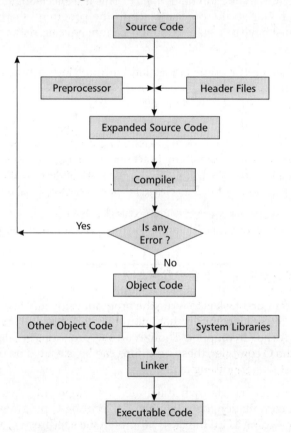

Fig. 8.1   Steps of compilation and execution

If we consider the **program 8.1**, when it will be executed, the first printf statement prints the message 'Enter 1st Number:' in the blank screen and wait for the first input. After taking the input, the message 'Enter 2nd Number:' will appear and wait for the second input. After taking the 2nd input, the result will be displayed as 'Sum = 65' if the inputs are given as 12 and 53. If we execute this program from DOS shell then we will not face any problem to see the output. But if we press CTRL+F9 from the IDE, we will not be able to see the output. To see the output we have to press ALT+F5. After observing the output when we want to return to the IDE, we need to press ENTER only. But to return from DOS shell, the command is EXIT.

8.6 EXECUTING FROM UNIX ENVIRONMENT

The basic procedure to execute a C program is same everywhere – develop, compile and execute. As there is no such IDE available in UNIX or LINUX environment, all the tasks need to be accomplished from command prompt. First we have to write the program using any text editor like vi, emacs, etc. and need to save with .c extension so that it can be identified as a C source code. Next task is to compile it. To compile a C source code in UNIX, the command is `cc`. If the name of the C file is sample.c, we have to write at the command prompt

```
cc sample.c
```

In LINUX operating system, the command is `gcc`. Thus it will take the form

```
gcc sample.c
```

In both cases, if there are any syntactical errors or warnings, it will be shown immediately. On successful compilation, it links with the library files and produces an executable file, named 'a.out'. We can include `-o` option with the `cc` or `gcc` command to provide our own name for the output file.

```
gcc -o sample sample.c
```

Now the executable output file will be `sample`.

To execute this file simply we need to type the name of the file.

```
sample
```

But if the directory in which the executable file resides is not in our PATH, the command will be,

```
./sample
```

'./' is put in front of the file name to explicitly inform the Unix shell that the program is run from the current directory.

8.7 DEVELOPING A PROGRAM

To develop a program the first task is to read and analyze the program thoroughly. Then we have to identify what are the inputs and what are outputs. Next step is to find the steps by which we can covert the inputs to the desire output. This is known as algorithm. Algorithm is the backbone of any program. Once the algorithm is generated, it is not any hard job to convert the algorithm to the corresponding C code. Thus to write a program first we have to develop the algorithm of the problem. Algorithm may be represented in step form or in flowchart. Here are some examples.

PROGRAM 8.1 Write a program in C to find the Area and Perimeter of a rectangle.

SOLUTION Here outputs are Area and Perimeter. We know, Area = Length * Breadth and Perimeter = 2(Length + Breadth). So our inputs will be Length and Breadth and using the above mentioned formula we will find the outputs. So, the algorithm of above problem will be:

Algorithm	Program
1. START	`void main( )`
2. PRINT "ENTER LENGTH:"	`{ int length, breadth, area,`
3. INPUT LENGTH	`peri;`
4. PRINT "ENTER BREADTH:"	`  printf("Enter Length");`
5. INPUT BREADTH	`  scanf("%d",&length);`
6. AREA = LENGTH * BREADTH	`  printf("Enter Breadth");`
7. PERI =	`  scanf("%d",&breadth);`
2*(LENGTH+BREADTH)	`  area = length * breadth;`
8. PRINT "AREA=", AREA	`  peri = 2*(length+breadth);`
9. PRINT "PERIMETER=", PERI	`  printf("Area=%d", area);`
STOP	`  printf("Perimeter= %d",peri);`
	`}`

Side by side the corresponding program is also shown.

PROGRAM 8.2   Write a C program to convert a given temperature in Centigrade scale to its equivalent Fahrenheit scale.

SOLUTION   Here input is temperature in centigrade and output is temperature in Fahrenheit. The convertion formula is, $f = 9*c/5+32$.

Algorithm	Program
1. START	`void main()`
2. PRINT "ENTER TEMP. IN	`{float c,f;`
CENTIGRADE"	`printf("Enter Temperature in`
3. INPUT C	`Centigrade:");`
4. F = 9*C/5+32	`scanf("%f",&c);`
5. PRINT "TEMP. IN	`f=9*c/5+32;`
FAHRENFEIT :", F	`printf("Equivalent Temperature`
6. STOP	`in Fahrenhite Scale: %f",f);`
	`}`

PROGRAM 8.3   Write a C program to find Simple Interest.

SOLUTION   Here output is Simple Interest. So, inputs will be principal amount, rate and interest. The conversion formula is, $si = p*r*t/100$.

Algorithm

1. START
2. PRINT "ENTER PRINCIPAL AMOUNT:"
3. INPUT P
4. PRINT "ENTER RATE OF INTEREST :"
5. INPUT R
6. PRINT "ENTER TIME :"
7. INPUT T
8. SI = P*R*T/100
9. PRINT "SIMPLE INTEREST : ", SI
10. STOP

Program

```c
void main()
{float p,r,t,si;
printf("Enter Principal Amount:");
scanf("%f",&p);
printf("Enter Rate of Interest:");
scanf("%f",&r);
printf("Enter Time:");
scanf("%f",&t);
si = p*r*t / 100;
printf("Simple Interest: %f",si);
}
```

8.8 PROGRAMMING EXAMPLES

Here are some programming examples to understand the features that we have learnt so far.

PROGRAM 8.4 Write a C program that accepts a decimal integer and prints it in the octal.

```c
/* Program that accepts a decimal integer and prints it in the octal. */
#include<conio.h>
#include<stdio.h>
void main( )
{ int number;
  clrscr( );
  printf("\nEnter any Number : ");
  scanf("%d",&number);
  printf("\nOctal equivalent of %d is %o", number, number);
}
```

PROGRAM 8.5 Write a C program that converts an upper case character to its lower case.

```c
/* Program that converts an upper case character to its lower case. */
#include<stdio.h>
void main( )
{    char ch_lwr,ch_upr;
     printf("\nEnter any Character in Upper Case: ");
     scanf("%c",&ch_upr);
```

```
ch_lwr = ch_upr + 32;   /*   ASCII value difference between up-
                             per case and lower case is 32. The
                             statement can also be written as:
                             ch_lwr = ch_upr + ('a' - 'A'); */
printf("\n\'%c\' in lower case is \'%c\'", ch_upr, ch_lwr);
}
```

PROGRAM 8.6 Write a C program to find the area of a circle.

```
/* Program to find the area of a circle */
#include<stdio.h>
void main( )
{ float radius, area;
  printf("\nEnter the Radius of the Circle : ");
  scanf("%f",&radius);
  area = 3.141 * radius * radius;
  printf("\nArea of the Circle is %.2f",area);
}
```

PROGRAM 8.7 Write a C program to calculate a^b.

```
/* Program to calculate a^b */
#include<stdio.h>
#include<math.h>
void main( )
{ double base, index, result;
  printf("\nEnter Base : ");
  scanf("%lf",&base);
  printf("\nEnter Index : ");
  scanf("%lf",&index);
  result = pow(base,index); /* pow() returns the value of base^index
                                and it is defined in math.h */
  printf("\n%lf^%lf = %lf",base,index,result);
}
```

PROGRAM 8.8 In any examination there are 5 subjects and maximum marks in each subject are 100. Write a C program to find the total marks and percentage of the marks obtain by any student.

```
/* Program to find the total marks and percentage of the marks */
#include<conio.h>
#include<stdio.h>
void main( )
{ int subject1,subject2,subject3,subject4,subject5,total_marks;
  float percentage;
  clrscr( );
  printf("\nEnter Marks of 1st Subject: ");
```

```
    scanf("%d",&subject1);
    printf("\nEnter Marks of 2nd Subject: ");
    scanf("%d",&subject2);
    printf("\nEnter Marks of 3rd Subject: ");
    scanf("%d",&subject3);
    printf("\nEnter Marks of 4th Subject: ");
    scanf("%d",&subject4);
    printf("\nEnter Marks of 5th Subject: ");
    scanf("%d",&subject5);

    total_marks = subject1+subject2+subject3+subject4+subject5;
    percentage = ((float)total_marks/500)*100;
    printf("\nTotal  =  %d  and  Percentage  =  %.2f",total_marks,
    percentage);
}
```

PROGRAM 8.9   In a shop, a discount of 10% on purchase amount is given. Write a C program to find net payable amount.

[Net Payable Amount = Purchase Amount – Discount]

```
/* Program to find net payable amount after giving Discount on Purchase
Amount */
#include<stdio.h>
void main( )
{ float pur_amt, discount,net_amt;
  printf("\nEnter Purchase Amount : ");
  scanf("%f",&pur_amt);
  discount = pur_amt * 0.1;
  net_amt = pur_amt - discount;
  printf("\nNet Payable Amount = %.2f", net_amt);
}
```

PROGRAM 8.10   In an organization, 55% of Basic Salary is given as Dearness allowance (DA) while House Rent allowance (HRA) is 15% of Basic Salary. Provident fund (PF) is deducted at the rate of 12.5% of Gross Salary. Write a C program to calculate Net Salary.

[Gross Salary = Basic + DA + HRA and Net Salary = Gross Salary – PF]

```
/* Program to find Net Salary */
#include<stdio.h>
void main( )
{ float basic, da, hra, gross, pf, net;
  printf("\nEnter Basic Salary : ");
  scanf("%f",&basic);
  da = basic * 0.55;
  hra = basic * 0.15;
```

```
   gross = basic + da + hra;
   pf = gross * 0.125;
   net = gross - pf;
   printf("\nNet Salary = %.2f", net);
}
```

PROGRAM 8.11   Write a C program that will demonstrate the difference between getch( ), getche( ) and getchar( ).

```
/* Program to demonstrate the difference between getch( ), getche()
and getchar() */
#include<stdio.h>
void main( )
{ char ch;
   printf("\nEnter any Character: ");
   ch=getch();
   printf("\nYou inputted %c",ch);
   printf("\nEnter any Character: ");
   ch=getche();
   printf("\nYou inputted %c",ch);
   printf("\nEnter any Character: ");
   ch=getchar();
   printf("\nYou inputted %c",ch);
}
```

PROGRAM 8.12   Write a program that will demonstrate the different format of integer number.

```
#include<stdio.h>
void main( )
{ int w;
   printf("\n|%d|",1234);
   printf("\n|%3d|",1234);
   printf("\n|%7d|",1234);
   printf("\n|%-7d|",1234);
   printf("\n|%+7d|",1234);
   printf("\n|%07d|",1234);
   printf("\nEnter Width:");
   scanf("%d",&w);
   printf("\n|%*d|",w,1234);
   printf("\n|%0*d|",w,1234);
}
```

Output:
```
|1234|
|1234|
|   1234|
|1234   |
|  +1234|
```

```
|0001234|
Enter Width: 10
|      1234|
|0000001234|
```

PROGRAM 8.12 Write a program that will demonstrate the different format of floating point number.

```
#include<stdio.h>
void main( )
{ int w,p;
   printf("\n|%f|",123.45);
   printf("\n|%e|",123.45);
   printf("\n|%.1f|",123.45);
   printf("\n|%.3f|",123.45);
   printf("\n|%8.2f|",123.45);
   printf("\n|%-8.2f|",123.45);
   printf("\nEnter Width");
   scanf("%d",&w);
   printf("\nEnter Precession");
   scanf("%d",&p);
   printf("\n|%*.*f|",w,p,123.45);
   printf("\n|%-*.*f|",w,p,123.45);
}
```

Output:
```
|123.450000|
|1.234500e+02|
|123.5|
|123.450|
|   123.45|
|123.45   |
Enter Width: 10
Enter Precession: 3
|   123.450|
|123.450   |
```

SUMMARY

➤ C provides several input and output statements.
➤ Console I/O functions can be categorized into formatted I/O functions and unformatted I/O functions.
➤ The standard library function scanf( ) is used for formatted input operation and printf( ) is used for formatted output operation.
➤ Escape sequences help us to format the output according to our requirement.
➤ Unformatted character I/O functions are getch( ), getche( ), getchar( ), putch( ) and putchar( ).
➤ Unformatted string I/O functions are gets( ) and puts( ).

➤ Minimum Width specifier specifies minimum number of characters used to display the value.

➤ Precision specifier is used to specify the number of digits should be printed after decimal point.

➤ The flag specifier specifies decimal points, numeric signs, output justification, trailing zeros, octal and hexadecimal prefixes.

REVIEW EXERCISES

1. Specify whether the following statements are true or false:
   a. getch( ) is used to take the input of integer numbers.
   b. printf() is an output statement.
   c. scanf() reads any possible variable type.
   d. Any C program may contain more than one main function.
   e. It is not possible to print multiple values using a single putch().

2. What are the formatted input and output functions available in C? Explain with example.

3. What are the unformatted input and output functions available in C? Explain with example.

4. Compare the three input functions: getch(), getche() and getchar().

5. Is there any difference between putch() and putchar()?

6. Is it possible to take input of a date in the format DD-MM-YYYY?

7. How can you set the field width at runtime?

8. How many decimal places are displayed by default when a number is printed with '%f' format specifier?

9. When '%u' format specifier is used?

10. As '−' sign is printed before negative number, is it possible to print a '+' sign before any positive number?

11. How can you print a left justified output when you print a numeric value?

12. Write a C program to find the area of a square.

13. Write a C program to find the average of three inputted numbers.

14. Write a C program that accepts a decimal integer and prints it as hexadecimal.

15. Write a C program to find the circumference of a circle.

16. Write a C program to convert a given temperature in Fahrenheit scale to its equivalent Centigrade scale.

17. Write a C program that converts a lower case character to its upper case.

LEARN BY QUIZ – QUESTIONS

1. Which function is used to show output?
   (1) printf()
   (2) print()
   (3) show()

2. What will be displayed by the following *printf()* statement?

> int *a* = 2;
>
> printf("%d", *a*);

(1) 2

(2) %d

(3) %2

3. What will be displayed by the following *printf( )* statement ?

> int *a* = 2;
>
> printf("The output is = %d", *a*);

(1) The output is = 2

(2) The output is = %d

(3) 2

4. Which function can display a single character on the screen?

(1) putchar( )

(2) put( )

(3) Print( )

5. What will be displayed after executing the following instructions?

> char x = 'A';
>
> printf("%d", x);

(1) 65

(2) A

(3) 0

6. What will be displayed by *printf* statement after executing the following instructions?

> int *i* = 65;
>
> printf("%c", *i*);

(1) A

(2) 65

(3) 0

7. What will be the output of the *printf( )* statement?

> printf("Hello\nWorld");

(1) Hello
    World

(2) Hello\nWorld

(3) HelloWorld

8. What will be the output of the following statement?

> printf("Hello\\nWorld");

(1) Hello\nWorld

(2) Hello
    World

(3) Hello\
    World

9. What will be the value of b?

> int *b*;
>
> *b* = printf("Hello");

(1) 5

(2) 6

(3) 7

10. What will be the output after executing the following statements?

     float *i* = 5.0

     printf("%f ", i);

(1) 5.000000

(2) 5

(3) 4.999999

11. Which one the following statement is valid?

(1) putchar('\n');

(2) printf("%n");

(3) putchar('\\n');

12. Which of the following functions is used to accept a single character from the keyboard?

(1) getchar( )

(2) get( )

(3) accept( )

13. What will be the output after executing the following statements?

     float *x* = 3.456789;

     printf("%.2f ", x);

(1) 2.45

(2) 3

(3) 3.46

14. What will be the output after executing the following statements?

     char *c* = '2';

     printf("%d", c);

(1) 50

(2) 2

(3) C

15. What will be the output after executing the following statement?

     printf("%%d");

(1) %d

(2) %

(3) d

16. Which of the following functions is used to accept input of various data types?

(1) scanf( )

(2) scanv( )

(3) scan( )

17. Which of the following statements will accept one integer value as input data?

Given declaration of variable *a* as:

     int *a*;

(1) scanf("%d", &a);

(2) scanf(a);

(3) scanf("%d" a);

18. Which one of the following format specifiers is used with **scanf** to accept a string as input data?
    (1) %s
    (2) %c
    (3) %d

19. Which statement is wrong about a C program?
    (1) A C program can be written without any function.
    (2) There should be at least one function
    (3) There may be multiple functions.

20. What will be the output after executing the following statements?

    int *a* = 15;

    printf("%x", *a*);
    (1) 0
    (2) 15
    (3) F

21. Which format specifier is used in **printf( )** for long int data type?
    (1) %ld
    (2) %d
    (3) %hd

22. What will be the output after executing the following statements?

    int *a* = 8;

    printf("%o", *a*);
    (1) 10
    (2) 8
    (3) 0

23. Consider the following declaration:

    unsigned int *a* = 65535;

    Which of the following statements is valid to print the content of *a*?
    (1) printf("%u", a);
    (2) printf("%d ", a);
    (3) printf("%f ", a);

24. Consider the following declaration:

    float *a* = 89.7564;

    Which statement will print the value 89.76 having two leading spaces?
    (1) printf("%7.2f ",a);
    (2) printf("%.2f ", a);
    (3) printf("%f ", a);

25. Consider the following declaration:

    float *a* = 89.7564;

    Which statement will print the value 89.76 having two trailing spaces?
    (1) printf("% -7.2f ",a);
    (2) printf("% +7.2f ",a);
    (3) printf("%f ",a)

26. Consider the following declaration:

    int *a* = 7658;

Which of the following statements will print the output 7658?
(1) printf("%2d",a);
(2) Printf("%%d");
(3) Printf("%.2d",a);

27. Consider the following declaration:

    int a=7658;

Which of the following statements will print the output 7658 having two leading spaces?
(1) printf("%d",a);
(2) printf("%6d",a);
(3) printf("%%d",a);

28. Consider the following declaration:

    int a = 7658;

Which of the following statements will print the output 7658 having two trailing spaces?
(1) printf("%-6d", a);
(2) printf("%d",a);
(3) printf("%6-d",a);

29. Which of the following is used to start the execution of a C program?
(1) main( )
(2) Begin
(3) start( )

30. What is the purpose of the header file?
(1) To refer to the library functions
(2) To store the source code
(3) To store the object code of the function

31. What is the escape sequence of apostrophe?
(1) \'
(2) \a
(3) \>

32. Which of the following set contains invalid escape sequence?
(1) \', \d, \t, \v
(2) \a, \b, \r, \n
(3) \\, \0, \t, \?

33. Programmers use comment in programs written in any language for documentation purpose. A well documented program is easy to understand by others and easy to modify or upgrade. In C, any thing written between /* and */ is a comment and compilers don't compile the comments.

Which of the following statements is true about comments used in a C program?
(1) Comments are never executed
(2) Comments are executed at run time
(3) Comments are executed at the time of debugging

34. How does an escape sequence always start?
(1) \
(2) /
(3) ~

35. What is the escape sequence of NULL?
(1) \0
(2) \n
(3) \t

36. How many lines does the string "text1 \n text2 \n text3" extend to?
   (1) 3 lines
   (2) 2 lines
   (3) 1 line

37. What will be the declaration of the character variable **c** with newline character as initial value?
   (1) char c = '\n';
   (2) char c = \newline character;
   (3) char c = 'newline character';

LEARN BY QUIZ – ANSWERS

Answer explanations

1. The function printf() is used to show output.

printf() can show output of any data type like *int*, *char*, *float*, etc., i.e., any datatype which is supported by C. The general syntax structure for this function is:

   printf("Control String", arg1, arg2, ...);

where, *control string* may contain format specifier which decides what type of data is going to be displayed. Several format specifiers are supported by C for various data types. For example %d is used for integer, %f is used for float and so on. So %d and %f are known as *format specifiers*.

arg1/arg2 are the data values which is displayed. There is no such function available in C named *print()* and *show()*.

2. The value of the variable *a*, i.e., 2 will be displayed.

printf() function displays everything written as control string, i.e., within " " marks. So if the statement is written as *printf*("Hello"), then Hello will be displayed. But if any control string contains a format specifier like %d, %c, %f, then *printf*() will recognize that this is not for direct display. Instead, it will recognize that some data values will be displayed against the format specifier. So it will go beyond the " " and pick up the data which will be replaced in place of %d.

In case of variables, *printf* ( ) will pick up the variable's content and in case of constant data, it will directly pick up the data. So here the variable *a* will be accessed and its value will be replaced in place of %d. Hence the output will be 2.

3. The output is = 2 will be displayed by the *printf*( ) function.

printf() displays the whole thing written within " " except the control string itself. So in the above statement the message **The output is =** will be displayed as usual but in place of %d, the content of variable *a*, i.e., 2 will be displayed.

4. The putchar( ) function can display a single character.

In C, *printf()* can be used to show any type of output. But C supports another function for showing output for a specific purpose. *putchar* function is written as:

   putchar(arg);

where the *arg* is character type data.

If the data is stored in a variable then the variable name is written in place of *arg* and if it is a constant character then that particular character is written within ' ' (single quotes).

For example, the statement *putchar('A');* will display *A* on the screen but if it is stored in a variable like *char c = 'A';* then *putchar(c);* will do the same job.

printf( ) can do the same task but then it has to be written in the following manner:

    printf("%c", c); or printf("%c", 'A');

5. 65 will be displayed after executing the instructions.

Here the control string of *printf( )* function contains the format specifier %d which says that the output should be an integer value. The variable *x* is of type character and it contains *A*. But every character is stored in the memory with their ASCII value. The ASCII value of *A* is 65. So it will be printed.

The format specifier %d in *printf( )* function can never display character. To display character, format specifier should be %c. So if the *printf( )* statement is written in the following form:

    printf("%c", x);

then the output will be *A*.

6. A will be displayed by *printf( )* statement.

In *printf* statement, the format specifier %c indicates that the output will be a character. Here the value stored in *i* will be displayed in the character form.

The value of *i* is the ASCII value of character *A* so it will be displayed.

The format specifier %c always displays the character. So *65* cannot be the output. Format specifier %d can display the value in integer format. So writing the *printf* in the form *printf("%d", i);* will show *65*.

7. The output will be

    Hello

    World

The two words will be displayed in two different lines.

Here the control string contains \n which is considered an escape sequence in C. \n causes printing a new line. As a result, after printing *Hello*, it will go to the next line and then *World* will be printed.

\n which is an escape sequence is not printed by *printf( )* function. Rather the effect is, it will go the next line. So \n inside *printf( )* will have the effect of going to next line but \n will not be displayed.

8. The output will be Hello\nWorld.

Here the control string contains \n (newline character) which causes generation of a new line. But before \n there is a \ character. \ is considered escape sequence in C. But preceding \ with another \ will suppress the meaning of escape sequence. As a result, the whole string becomes *Hello\nWorld*. Here \n loses its meaning of newline character. \ and *n* will be treated as two separate characters. So the output will be *Hello\nWorld*.

Preceding \n with a \ character suppresses the function of \n to be a newline character. So *Hello* and *World* will not be displayed in two different lines.

9. The value of *b* will be 5.

printf( ) function is used to display output of different data type.

printf( ) function always returns the number of characters it has been able to display on the screen.

Here **printf( )** has displayed the string **Hello** on the screen. Hence the **printf( )** will return 5.

Every string contains '**\0'** character at the end which is automatically supplied.

Since it is not displayed on the screen, so **printf( )**will not count it.

10. The output will be 5.000000.

    %f is the format specifier used in **printf** function to display any data of float type. Here the float variable **i** contains 5. So it has been displayed as 5.000000. Note 6 digits are taken after the decimal point which is the default behavior in C in case of floating point data. C has the provision to restrict the number of digits after decimal point.

    5 and 5.0 are different. One is integer and the other is float. Format specifier **%f** is used for float, and **%d** is used for int. So replacing **%d** in place of **%f** will generate the output 5.

11. The statement putchar('\n') is valid.

    \n is the newline character. Here **\n** is treated as a single character. **putchar( )** function can display a single character. So the statement

    > **putchar('\n');**

    will print a new line character.

    In putchar('\\n') statement, \\ will be interpreted as \ only and \\n will become \n. This is not the new line character any more but two consecutive characters \ and n. Since putchar can accept only one character, this statement is invalid.

12. The function getchar( ) is used to accept a single character from the keyboard.

    The function **getchar( )** accepts a single character and stores it in a variable.

    The syntax for writing **getchar( )** is:

    > **variable = getchar();**

13. The output will be 3.46.

    Here in the control string, the format specifier **"%.2f"** means some float value will be displayed and after the decimal point, only two digits will be taken even if the original data contains more digits. So the digit 2 indicates the width of the digits after decimal point. But during the truncation process it will check the third digit. If it is 5 or greater than 5, then 1 will be added with the second digit.

    Here the third digit after the decimal point is 6 which is greater than 5, so 1 will be added with the second digit and the final output will be 3.46.

14. The output will be 50.

    The content of the character variable **c** is character 2. All characters are represented with their ASCII value. The digits 0–9 when represented as characters will have their ASCII value. Here **%d** format specifier has been used as a control string which indicates that the result will be displayed as an integer. So the output will be 50.

15. The output will be %d.

    Format specifier used in control string starts with %. The format specifiers **%d, %f,** and **%c** are used for **int, float,** and **char data** respectively, depending on the data type going to be displayed. But when it is preceded by another % symbol, it loses its meaning of format specifier and is interpreted as string. So the output is **%d.**

16. The function **scanf( )** is used to accept input data of various types.

    scanf ( )has the following syntax structure:

    > **scanf("control string", arg1, arg2,.....);**

Control string contains format specifier which starts with a character % and may be like **%d**, **%f**, etc, which entirely depends on the input data type. **%d** is used for **int** data type and **%f** is used for **float** data type. **arg1**, **arg2** are the variables where the input data is going to be stored.

17. The statement scanf("%d", &a); will accept one integer value as input data.

    Here format specifier **%d** has been used which is used to accept data as integer.

    &a has been written as argument. It should be variable's address. & operator is used to find the address of any variable. So the above statement will work correctly and will accept one integer data which will be stored in the variable **a**.

    scanf(a); is an erroneous syntax and will not work.

    In option 3, & symbol has not been used with variable a, which is essential to store any input data in the variable a. So this is an error, but it will not be detected by C compiler.

18. The format specifier %s is used with **scanf** to accept character string.

    The statement should be written as follows:

        scanf("%s", a);

    Here **a** has been assumed as one character array. A string is always stored inside a character array. Note that & symbol is not required to store a string in a character array.

    %c is used to accept a single character.

    %d is used to accept integer.

19. Function is a self-contained block of statements that perform some specific job. Any C program is a collection of one or more functions. If it contains only one function, then it is the main function. In C program main function is a special function. Every C program starts its execution from main function and other functions are called from this function as well.

20. The output will be F.

    Here in the control string, the format specifier **%x** has been used which is used to get the output in hexadecimal number. The hexadecimal equivalent of 15 is **F**.

    Note that **%x** will work only for integer not for float. So if we try to print a hexadecimal equivalent of a number 15.15 using **%x** with **printf( )** function it will fail.

21. %ld is used for long int data type.

    %d format specifier can be prefixed with **l** or **h** for long and short integer, respectively. **l** can also be used with **%f** for double data type.

22. The output will be 10.

    The format specifier **%o** is used in **printf( )** for finding out the octal equivalent of a decimal integer. The octal equivalent of decimal integer 8 is 10. **%o** works for integer only. So if the data value is 8.8 in decimal, then by using **%o** we cannot get the octal equivalent.

23. printf("%u",a); is a valid statement to print the content of **a**.

    The format specifier **%u** is used to print the unsigned integer number. The range of unsigned integer is 0–65535.

    %d is used to print signed integer number. The range is −32768 to +32767. So **%d** will fail to print 65535.

    %f is used to print floating point numbers.

24. printf("%7.2f ",a); will print 89.76 having two leading spaces.

    Here the format specifier in the control string has the following generalized form:

    %w.pf

    where:

    w specifies Minimum Width i.e. minimum number of characters used to display the value. Here the value of **w** is 7.

    p specifies the number of digits should be printed after decimal point. If the output value has more decimal places than the specified precision, the output will be rounded off up to the specified precision. Here the value of **p** is 2.

    The data value which will be displayed will become 89.76. As there are a total of 7 positions reserved, so the **printf( )** statement will display the value 89.76 with leading two spaces.

25. printf("%-7.2f",a); will print the value 89.76 having two trailing spaces.

    Here the format specifier in the control string has the following generalized form:

    %w.pf

    where:

    w specifies Minimum Width, i.e., minimum number of characters used to display the value. Here the value of **w** is 7.

    p specifies the number of digits should be printed after decimal point. If the output value has more decimal places than the specified precision, the output will be rounded off upto the specified precision. Here the value of **p** is 2.

    The negative sign (−) indicates that if the output data is lesser than the number of digits reserved then the remaining positions are to be filled up with spaces and the spaces should be at trailing position.

    The data value which will be displayed will become 89.76. As there are a total of 7 positions reserved, so the **printf( )** statement will display the value 89.76 with two trailing spaces.

26. printf("%2d", a); will show the desired output.

    Here the format specifier in the control string has the following generalized form:

    % w d

    where,

    w specifies Minimum Width, i.e., minimum number of characters used to display the value. Here the value of **w** is 2.

    d indicates that the number to be printed is a decimal integer.

    However, if the number is greater than the specified field width, then no truncation of data will occur. It will be displayed in full. If the width is larger than the number to be displayed, then leading spaces will appear, i.e., the number will be right justified.

    Here the data value is 7658 which is larger than the width, which is 2. So no truncation of data will occur and the output will be 7658.

27. printf("%6d", a); will show the desired output.

    Here the format specifier in the control string has the following generalized form:

    % w d

    where,

    w specifies Minimum Width, i.e., minimum number of characters used to display the value. Here the value of **w** is 6.

    d indicates that the number to be printed is a decimal integer.

However, if the number is greater than the specified field width, then no truncation of data will occur. It will be displayed in full. If the width is larger than the number to be displayed then leading spaces will appear, i.e., the number will be right justified.

Here the data value is 7658 which is smaller than the width, i.e., 6. The output will be 7568 with two leading blank spaces.

28. The statement printf("%-6d", a); will show the desired output.

Here the format specifier in the control string has the following generalized form:

     % w d

where,

w specifies Minimum Width, i.e., minimum number of characters used to display the value. Here the value of **w** is 6.

d indicates that the number to be printed is a decimal integer.

However, if the number is greater than the specified field width, then no truncation of data will occur. It will be displayed in full. If the width is larger than the number to be displayed then leading spaces will appear, i.e., the number will be right justified. But having a negative (−) sign after **%** will cause the output to appear from the left. As a result, the spaces will be at the end.

Here the data value is 7658 which is smaller than the width, i.e., 6. Due to − (minus) sign the output will be 7658 with two trailing spaces.

29. The execution of a C program always starts from the main() function, irrespective of it's position in the program.

Even in a program divided in multiple files only one main function is allowed.

In C language, **begin** and **start()** have no special significance.

30. The purpose of the header file is to refer to the library functions.

Definitions of functions may also be written in header files but it is not done in practice.

Source program is generally stored in **.c** files.

Compiled code (object code) is stored in the library.

31. \' is the escape sequence of apostrophe.

Escape sequences available in C are given below.

     \a, \b, \n, \t, \r, \v, \', \", \\, \?, \0

These stand for bell(alert), backspace, newline (line feed), horizontal tab, carriage return, vertical tab, apostrophe ('), quotation mark ("), backslash (\), question mark (?) and null respectively.

     \a is escape sequence for Bell.

There is no escape sequence like \> in C.

32. In the set (\', \d, \t, \v), \d is an invalid escape sequence. Hence the set is invalid.

33. Comments are never executed.

Comments exist in the source file only. At the time of compilation, comments are discarded and they have no existence in the object file or the executable file.

34. An escape sequence always starts with \.

   Certain non-printable characters, the double quote ("), the apostrophe ('), the question mark (?) and the backslash (\), can be expressed in terms of escape sequences.

   An escape sequence always begins with a backward slash and is followed by one or more special characters.

   Escape sequences available in C are given below.

   \a, \b, \n, \t, \r, \v, \', \", \\, \?, \0

   These stand for bell (alert), backspace, newline (line feed), horizontal tab, carriage return, vertical tab, apostrophe ('), quotation mark ("), backslash (\), question mark (?) and null, respectively.

35. \0 is the escape sequence of NULL.

   \n is the escape sequence of new line.

   \t is the escape sequence of tab.

36. The string "text1 \n text2 \n text3" extends to 3 lines.

   For each **\n** there will be one line feed. The first one will be after **text1** and before **text2**. The second one will be after **text2** and before **text3**.

   So the given string extends to 3 lines.

37. The declaration of character variable **c** with new line character as initial value is char c = '\n';.

   Though it is consist of two characters but it is considered as single character. **\n** is the escape character for new line.

9

Branching Statement

In the previous chapter we have learnt to write simple C programs. The statements in the programs are executed sequentially, i.e., one after another as they appeared in the program. However, in practice, the problems are not so simple. We need to take decision whether a particular set of statements will execute or not; instead of one group of statements another group of statements may execute; even group of statements may execute repeatedly for known number of times or until certain condition are met. Thus the order of execution of statements has to be controlled. The statements which control the order of execution is known as *Control statement*. There are two type of control statement in C. These are:

- Branching and
- Looping

Branching statement decides what actions to take and loop statement decides how many times to take a certain action. In this chapter, we discuss on several branching statements.

Branching is so called because the program chooses to follow one branch or another. This type of statements is also known as conditional statement as depending on the condition a certain set of statement(s) executes. C has mainly two branching statements – **if** statement and **switch** statement.

9.1 IF STATEMENT

The most important branching statement is if statement. It handles one way as well as two way decision. The if statement consists of two parts – a test expression and one or more statements or block of statements. The decision is taken based on the expression given in parenthesis with the if statement. If the expression is true then a particular statement or block of statements gets executed. But if the expression is evaluated as false, then either these statements are skipped or another block of statements gets executed.

Note In C, non-zero values are treated as TRUE and zero is treated as FALSE. Thus any expression is considered as true if its evaluated value is non-zero.

if statements take the following forms:

```
  i)      if (expression)
          {
              statement(s);
          }
 ii)    if (expression)
          {
              statement(s);
          }
        else
          {
              statement(s);
          }
iii)    if (expression)
          {
              statement(s);
          }
        else
          { if (expression)
              {
                  statement(s);
              }
            else
              {
                  statement(s);
              }

          }
```

Here the expression can be any valid expression including a relational expression.

The first form represents, if the *expression* is true (i.e., non-zero), the *statement or block of statement* is executed. If the *expression* is false (i.e., zero), the *statement or block of statement* is ignored. If there is a single statement then the pair of braces ({ }) is optional. But for multiple statements, it is mandatory. This form of *if statement* can be represented by the following block diagram.

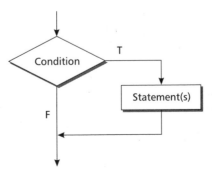

Fig. 9.1   Flowchart of if statement

Consider the following example.

PROGRAM 9.1   In a shop, a discount of 10% on purchase amount is given only if purchase amount exceeds Rs. 5000. Find net payable amount.

[Net Payable Amount = Purchase Amount − Discount]

```
#include<stdio.h>
void main( )
{   int pur_amt;
    float discount = 0, net_pay;
    printf("Enter Purchase Amount : ");
    scanf("%d", &pur_amt);
    if( pur_amt > 5000 )     /* Discount will be calculated only if */
        discount = pur_amt * 0.1;  /* purchase amount exceeds 5000 */
    net_pay = pur_amt - discount;
    printf("Net Payable Amount = %.2f ", net_pay);
}
```

Sample output

```
Enter Purchase Amount: 6000
Net Payable Amount = 5400.00

Enter Purchase Amount: 3500
Net Payable Amount = 3500.00
```

In the above example, discount will be calculated only if purchase amount exceeds Rs. 5000, otherwise this statement will be skipped. Thus in the first run 10% of purchase amount i.e. 600 is deducted from 6000 and net payable amount becomes 5400. But in second run, as purchase amount is less than Rs. 5000, the statement corresponding to calculation of discount is skipped. As a result, nothing is deducted from purchase amount.

In the second form of **if statement**, if the *expression* is true (i.e., non-zero), the *statement* or *block of statement* within *if block* is executed. If the *expression* is false (i.e., zero), the *statement* or *block of statement* within *else block* is executed. This can be represented by the following block diagram.

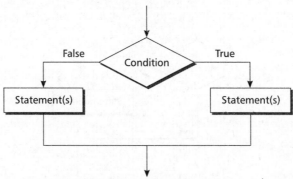

Fig. 9.2   Flowchart of if–else statement

Following example illustrate this.

PROGRAM 9.2   Find The Maximum Between Two Inputted Numbers.

```
#include<stdio.h>
#include<conio.h>

void main( )
{    int num1, num2;
     clrscr( );
     printf("\nEnter 1st Number : ");
     scanf("%d",&num1);
     printf("\nEnter 2nd Number : ");
     scanf("%d",&num2);
     if ( num1 > num2 )
          printf("Max = %d", num1);
     else
          printf("Max = %d", num2);
}
```

Sample output
```
Enter 1st Number: 15
Enter 2nd Number: 5
Max = 15

Enter 1st Number: 10
Enter 2nd Number: 20
Max = 20
```

In the above program, either *if block* or *else block* will execute depending on the condition given with the *if statement*. In the first run the expression corresponding to *if statement* becomes true, thus *if block* is executed but in 2nd run the expression becomes false, as a result *else block* executes.

Before proceeding further here we discuss some common mistakes related to if statement. Consider the following example.

```
 void main( )
 {
     int x;
     printf("Enter any Number : ");
     scanf("%d", &x);
     if( x > 10);
          printf("Inputted Number is grater than 10");
 }
```

Sample output
```
Enter any Number: 15
Inputted Number is grater than 10
```

```
Enter any Number: 5
Inputted Number is grater than 10
```

In the above program, first time the condition is true for the inputted value but in 2nd run the condition is false for the inputted value. But surprisingly the output is shown "Inputted Number is grater than 10" in both run. This is because a semicolon (;) is typed mistakenly after the if statement. But compiler would not produce an error because compiler consider the statement as:

```
if( x > 10)
{ ; }
    printf("Inputted Number is grater than 10");
```

Thus depending on the truth ness of the condition a do nothing statement, i.e., {;} will execute or skipped and the printf statement becomes the out of scope of *if statement*. So, whether the condition is true or false the printf statement always executes. Therefore, be careful about this mistake.

Now consider the following example.

```
void main( )
{
    int x;
    printf("Enter any Number : ");
    scanf("%d", &x);
    if( x > 10);
        printf("Inputted Number is grater than 10");
    else
        printf("Inputted Number is not grater than 10");
}
```

But the above code produces an error. Compiler treats the code snippet as:

```
if( x > 10)
{ ; }
    printf("Inputted Number is grater than 10");
else
    printf("Inputted Number is not grater than 10");
```

As the scope of *if statement* ends with the do nothing {;} statement, the *else statement* becomes out of scope of the above *if statement*. But without if, *else statement* cannot be written. Thus, compilation error will occur.

Consider another example.

```
void main( )
{
    int x;
    printf("Enter any Number : ");
    scanf("%d", &x);
    if( x = 10)
        printf("Inputted Number is equals to 10");
    else
```

```
                printf("Inputted Number is not equals to 10");
}
```

Sample output
```
Enter any Number: 10
Inputted Number is equals to 10

Enter any Number: 15
Inputted Number is equals to 10
```

This time no semicolon is given after condition of *if statement*. Still in either case the output shows the same result. Here another mistake took place. Instead of '==' we used '=' operator. In C, '==' is a relational operator used to check the equality of two numeric values where '=' is assignment operator. Thus, the *if statement* becomes **if (10)**. In case of C, any non-zero value is treated as true and zero is considered as false. As a result, the statement **if (10)** always evaluates to true. Hence we get this surprising output. Similarly if the condition written as **if(x = 0)**, the expression always evaluates to false.

The 3rd form of *if statement* shows the nesting of *if statement*. The statement under *if statement* can be any valid C statement including *if statement* in any form. We can write an entire *if-else* construct within either the body of the *if statement* or the body of an *else statement*. This is called '*nesting of if*'. There is no restriction on level of nesting. We can use as many as level of nesting is required.

To explain it, we consider another problem. Instead of two inputted numbers if we want to find the largest among three inputted numbers, a single if statement is not sufficient. After comparison of any two numbers we need to compare the larger one of these two with the third number. The algorithm is shown with the following flow chart.

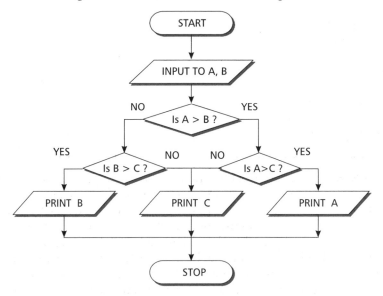

Fig. 9.3 **Flow chart to find the largest number among three inputted numbers**

The corresponding program of the above problem is given below.

PROGRAM 9.3   Find the maximum between three inputted numbers.

```c
#include<stdio.h>
#include<conio.h>
void main( )
{  int num1, num2, num3;
   clrscr( );
   printf("\nEnter 1st Number : ");
   scanf("%d",&num1);
   printf("\nEnter 2nd Number : ");
   scanf("%d",&num2);
   printf("\nEnter 3rd Number : ");
   scanf("%d",&num3);
   if ( num1 > num2 )
        if ( num1 > num3 )
             printf("Max = %d", num1);
        else
             printf("Max = %d", num3);
   else
        if ( num2 > num3 )
             printf("Max = %d", num2);
        else
             printf("Max = %d", num3);
}
```

Sample output

```
Enter 1st Number: 15
Enter 2nd Number: 5
Enter 3rd Number: 20
Max = 20


Enter 1st Number: 15
Enter 2nd Number: 25
Enter 3rd Number: 20
Max = 25
```

In the above example, first two inputted numbers, i.e., num1 and num2 will be compared first. If num1 is greater than num2, then num1 will be compared again to num3, i.e., with the 3rd inputted number. If num1 is greater than num3 also, num1 is largest. But if this condition fails, num3 is larger than num1 and as num1 is larger than num2, num3 is largest. But if the first condition, i.e., num1 > num2 fails, the larger among these two is num2 and the else part of the first if statement will be executed. Now, num2 will be compared with num3 and this if statement will be written in the else part of first if statement. If the condition num2 > num3 becomes true num2 is largest; otherwise num3 is largest.

Now if we want to find the maximum or minimum among five, six or seven inputted numbers, we can follow the above algorithm. But the program will be deeply nested and become slightly complicated. Instead, we can follow another algorithm where there will be no *nested if* but a sequence of *if statements*. Following example shows this.

Program 9.4   Find the maximum between five inputted numbers.

```c
#include<stdio.h>
#include<conio.h>
void main( )
{   int num1, num2, num3, num4, num5, max;
    clrscr( );
    printf("\nEnter 1st Number : ");
    scanf("%d",&num1);
    printf("\nEnter 2nd Number : ");
    scanf("%d",&num2);
    printf("\nEnter 3rd Number : ");
    scanf("%d",&num3);
    printf("\nEnter 4th Number : ");
    scanf("%d",&num4);
    printf("\nEnter 5th Number : ");
    scanf("%d",&num5);
    max = num1;
    if ( num2 > max)
        max = num2;
    if ( num3 > max)
        max = num3;
    if ( num4 > max)
        max = num4;
    if ( num5 > max)
        max = num5;
    printf("Max = %d", max);
}
```

Sample output
```
Enter 1st Number: 15
Enter 2nd Number: 5
Enter 3rd Number: 20
Enter 4th Number: 10
Enter 5th Number: 12
Max = 20
```

In the above example, num1 is first stored within max variable. Then each number is compared with max. If the number is greater than max, the number replaces the content of max variable. Finally, we will get the highest number within the max variable. By this algorithm, we can avoid deeply nested *if statement*. But always this is not possible. Whether set of simple *if statements* or nested *if statements*, which one is better, depends on the nature of the problem. In the following example, we will find another variation of nested *if statement* which will work effectively than the set of simple *if statements*.

PROGRAM 9.5 In a certain company, the commission of sales persons is calculated as per the following rules:

Sales value	Commission
Below Rs. 5000	5% of Sales value
Rs. 5000 to 7500	10% of Sales value + Rs. 100
Above Rs. 10000	15% of Sales

Find the commission of sales persons.

```
#include<stdio.h>
#include<conio.h>
void main( )
{   int sales_val;
    float com;
    printf("Enter Sales Value : ");
    scanf("%d", &sales_val);
    if( sales_val < 5000 )      /* when sales value below 5000 */
       com = sales_val * 0.05;
    else
        if(sales_val <= 7500)    /* sales value > 5000 but <=7500 */
            com = sales_val * 0.1 + 100;
        else                        /* sales value > 7500 */
            com = sales_val * 0.15;
    printf("\nCommission = %.2f", com);
}
```

Sample output
```
Enter Sales Value: 2000
Commission = 100.00

Enter Sales Value: 5100
Commission = 610.00

Enter Sales Value: 8000
Commission = 1200.00
```

In the above example, the first **if statement** checks whether the inputted sales value is below 5000 or not. If it is true the corresponding statement will be executed and the commission will be calculated. But if the condition becomes false, the **else part** of the **if statement** will be executed indicating sales value must be greater than or equal to 5000. Now the next **if statement** checks whether the sales value is less than or equal to 7500 which actually indicates that the sales value is in between 5000 and 7500 as it is in the **else part** of first **if statement**. Similarly, if this 2nd **if statement** becomes false, the **else part** indicates that the sales value must be greater than 7500.

In the above example, the true part of each **if statement** contains a single statement and thus parenthesis is not used. In the **else part** of each **if statement**, though it contains several lines but actually it contains a single **if statement**. So, no parenthesis is used in this case also. In the following example, we will add some extra constraints with the above problem where we will find the use of the pair of braces ({ }) within **if statement**.

PROGRAM 9.6 In a certain company, the commission of sales persons is calculated as per the following rules:

Sales value	Commission
Below Rs. 5000	5% of Sales value
Rs. 5000 to 7500	10% of Sales value + Rs. 100
	But subject to minimum of Rs. 650 and subject to maximum of Rs. 800
Above Rs. 10000	15% of Sales

Find the commission of sales persons.

```
#include<stdio.h>
#include<conio.h>
void main( )
{   int sales_val;
    float com;
    printf("Enter Sales Value : ");
    scanf("%d", &sales_val);
    if( sales_val < 5000 )
      com = sales_val * 0.05;
    else
      if(sales_val <= 7500)
      {   com = sales_val * 0.1 + 100;
        if (com < 650)
            com = 650;
        else
            if(com > 800)
               com = 800;
      }
      else
        com = sales_val * 0.15;

    printf("\nCommission = %.2f", com);
}
```

Sample output
```
Enter Sales Value: 2000
Commission = 100.00

Enter Sales Value: 5100
Commission = 650.00

Enter Sales Value: 6000
Commission = 700.00
```

In the above example, under the condition (sales_val <= 7500), we have two statements. First one calculates commission and second one is a nested if statement which takes necessary action when commission is less than 600 or greater than 800. So, here use of parenthesis is mandatory.

Instead of using nested if statement, we can use logical operators also. To understand the difference of nested if statement and logical operator, same problem is solved in two different ways: first using nested if and then using logical operators.

PROGRAM 9.7   Check whether an inputted year is leap year or not.

```c
#include<stdio.h>
void main( )
{  int year;
   printf("Enter The Year : ");
   scanf("%d", year);
   if( year % 100 == 0 )
   {
      if ( year % 400 == 0 )
          printf(" It is a Leap Year");
      else
          printf(" It is not a Leap Year");
   }
   else
   {
      if ( year % 4 == 0 )
          printf(" It is a Leap Year");
      else
          printf(" It is not a Leap Year");
   }
}
```

In the next example the same problem is solved with the logical operators.

```c
#include<stdio.h>
void main( )
{   int year;
    printf("Enter The Year : ");
    scanf("%d", year);
    if ( year % 400 == 0 || (year % 100 != 0 && year % 4 == 0))
         printf(" It is a Leap Year");
    else
         printf(" It is not a Leap Year");
}
```

Sample output

```
Enter The Year: 1996
It is a Leap Year

Enter The Year: 1900
It is not a Leap Year
```

Between nested if and use of logical operators, we cannot precisely mention which one is better. It depends on the problem. If there are several conditions and we have to take separate decisions for each condition, nested if is better. But for several conditions if we have to take limited decision then logical operators are more useful.

9.2 CONDITIONAL OPERATOR

To take decision instead of conditional statement (i.e., if statement) we can also use conditional operator which is more compact and effective for smaller situation.

PROGRAM 9.8 Check whether an inputted number is odd or even.

```
#include<stdio.h>
#include<conio.h>

void main( )
{    int num;
     clrscr( );
     printf("\nEnter Any Number : ");
     scanf("%d", &num);
     ( num % 2 == 0) ? printf("Even Number") : printf("Odd Number");
}
```

Sample output
```
Enter Any Number: 23
Odd Number

Enter Any Number: 32
Even Number
```

When the condition is true, i.e., **num%2** evaluates to 0, the message 'Even' will be printed otherwise 'Odd' will be printed in the screen.

We can also rewrite the last statement as :

```
( num % 2 ) ? printf("Odd") : printf("Even");
```

If the first expression, **num%2,** evaluates to 1 then it becomes true and the expression2, i.e., printf("Odd") will be executed. But if the expression **num%2** evaluates to 0 then it will be treated as false and the expression3, i.e., printf("Even") will be executed.

We can also rewrite this statement in more compact form as:

```
printf("%s",( num % 2 ) ? "Odd" : "Even");
```

Like if statement, conditional operator can also be nested.

PROGRAM 9.9　Find the maximum between three inputted numbers.

```
#include<stdio.h>
#include<conio.h>
void main( )
{   int num1, num2, num3, max;
    clrscr( );
    printf("\nEnter 1st Number : ");
    scanf("%d",&num1);
    printf("\nEnter 2nd Number : ");
    scanf("%d",&num2);
    printf("\nEnter 3rd Number : ");
    scanf("%d",&num3);
    max = (num1>num2) ? ((num1>num3)? num1: num3) : (
                                    (num2>num3) ? num2: num3);
    printf("Max = %d", max);
}
```

Sample output

```
Enter 1st Number: 15
Enter 2nd Number: 5
Enter 3rd Number: 20
Max = 20
```

Here, instead of using nested if statement we are able to find the maximum between 3 inputted numbers. But for complicated and lengthy nested if statement, use of conditional operator decreases the readability of the program. Conditional operator is effective for smaller situation where the condition has both true and false part and each part execute single statement.

9.3　SWITCH STATEMENT

Some times we faced situations where we are required to choose a particular option among a set of alternatives. We can handle this situation with nested if statement. But if the alternatives increase, the program lost its readability as it is deeply nested. A better alternative is **switch statement** which represents the case-structure.

Switch statement compares a variable or expression to several 'integral' values. Integral values are such values that can be expressed as an integer. The value of type int and char can be considered as integral. When a match is found, the control continues executing the program from that point until a break statement is encountered or end of switch statement is reached.

The general form of switch statement is:

```
switch (expression)
{
case constant-value1: statement-list
                    break;
```

```
case constant-value2: statement-list
                      break;
case constant-value3: statement-list
                      break;
          . . . . . . . . . . .
          . . . . . . . . . . .
default:                  statement-list


}
```

where the *expression* is any valid C statement which results some integral value and *constant-value* is a constant integral value, i.e., integer constant or character constant.

When a program executes a switch statement, the value of its expression is first evaluated. Then this value compared with the constant values that follow the case statement. If this matches any of the constant values in a case, the statements following that case are executed. If the value does not match any of the case value, the **default** is chosen. The **default** is optional and if no matching constant value is found and no **default** is given, the whole switch is skipped.

The following program shows the use of switch.

PROGRAM 9.10   Program to demonstrate the use of switch statement.

```
#include <stdio.h>
void main()
{
      int number;
      printf("Enter Any Number :");
      scanf("%d", &number);

      switch ( number )
      {
        case 1 :    printf ( "We are in case 1 \n" );
                    break;
        case 2 :    printf ( "We are in case 2 \n" );
                    break;
        case 3 :    printf ( "We are in case 3 \n" );
                    break;
        default :   printf ( "We are in default \n" );
      }
}
```

The above program displays in which case it is executing according to the input. If the input of the above program is 1, output will be:

```
We are in case 1
```

If the input of the above program is 3, output will be:

```
We are in case 3
```

But if the input of the above program is 5, output will be:

```
We are in default
```

Break statement is optional and in absence of break statement, when a condition is met in switch case then execution continues into the next case clause. The following example illustrates this.

```c
#include <stdio.h>
void main()
{
        int number;
        printf("Enter Any Number :");
        scanf("%d", &number);
        switch ( number )
        {
          case 1 :     printf ( "We are in case 1 \n" );

          case 2 :     printf ( "We are in case 2 \n" );

          case 3 :     printf ( "We are in case 3 \n" );

          default :    printf ( "We are in default \n" );
        }
}
```

If the input of the above program is 1, output will be:

```
We are in case 1
We are in case 2
We are in case 3
We are in default
```

If the input of the above program is 3, output will be:

```
We are in case 3
We are in default
```

The following example shows how we can use integral value.

PROGRAM 9.11   Write a program that will describe the grade in words.

```c
#include <stdio.h>
void main()
{
        char Grade;
        printf("Enter Grade :");
        scanf("%c", &Grade);
        switch( Grade )
        {
          case 'A' : printf( "Excellent\n" );
                     break;
```

```
        case 'B' : printf( "Good\n" );
                   break;
        case 'C' : printf( "OK\n" );
                   break;
        case 'D' : printf( "Not so good\n" );
                   break;
        case 'F' : printf( "Very Bad\n" );
                   break;
        default  : printf( "Invalid Grade\n" );

    }
}
```

Sample output

```
    Enter Grade: B
    Good

    Enter Grade: D
    Not so good
```

Some time we may not include any statement in some cases. We can use this feature to implement OR operation between different cases. When same set of statements is required to execute for different cases, we can simply use empty cases.

Consider the above example. It will work fine if our input is in upper case. But what happens when our input is in lower case? Obviously it will not work because 'A' and 'a' are not same and so on. We can rewrite the program in the following way so that it can work irrespective of upper or lower case.

```
#include <stdio.h>
void main()
{
    char  Grade;
    printf("Enter Grade :");
    scanf("%c", &Grade);
    switch( Grade )
    {
      case 'a' :
      case 'A' : printf( "Excellent\n" );
                 break;
      case 'b' :
      case 'B' : printf( "Good\n" );
                 break;
      case 'c' :
      case 'C' : printf( "OK\n" );
                 break;
      case 'd' :
      case 'D' : printf( "Not so good\n" );
                 break;
      case 'f' :
```

```
        case 'F' : printf("Very Bad\n" );
                   break;
        default  : printf("Invalid Grade\n" );

    }
}
```

Sample output
    Enter Grade: B
    Good

    Enter Grade: d
    Not so good

Remember that we can put the cases in any order. And like if statement, a switch may occur within another. This is called nested switch. But it is rarely used.

9.4 GOTO STATEMENT

There is another branching statement in C. The goto statement is used to jump unconditionally to any statement in the program using a label. Label is any valid identifier followed by a colon(:). The general form of the goto statement is as follows:

```
goto label;
```

The following example shows the use of goto statement.

```
int a=1;
if ( a < 5)
{
    a++;
    printf("%d ",a);
    goto abc;
}
printf("%d",++a);
---
---
abc:
printf("%d ",++a);
```

output: 2 3

Any structured programming is called goto avoid program, because it reduce the program readability. So, we have to careful to use goto statement. goto is useful only to come out from deeply nested loop (discussed later).

9.5 PROGRAMMING EXAMPLES

Here are some programming examples to understand the various uses of branching statement.

PROGRAM 9.13 Write a program to check whether an inputted number is positive, negative or zero.

```
#include<stdio.h>
void main( )
{ int num;
    printf("Enter any Number :");
    scanf("%d",&num);
    if(num == 0)
        printf("It is Zero");
    else
        if(num > 0)
            printf("It is a Positive Number");
        else
            printf("It is a Negative Number");
}
```

PROGRAM 9.14 Write a program to check whether an inputted character is a digit or not.

```
#include <stdio.h>
void main()
{
    char  ch;
    printf("Enter any character:");
    scanf("%c", &ch);
    if(ch >= '0' && ch<= '9')
        printf("Inputted Character is a digit");
    else
        printf("Inputted Character is not a digit");
}
```

PROGRAM 9.15 In a certain university grade is calculated as per following rules:

Marks	Grade
Above or equals to 90	O
>= 80 but < 90	E
>= 70 but < 80	A
>= 60 but < 70	B
>= 50 but < 60	C
>= 40 but < 50	D
Below 40	F

Write a program to calculate grade.

```
#include <stdio.h>
void main()
{
     int marks;
     char  grade;
     printf("Enter Marks :");
     scanf("%d", &marks);
     if(marks>=90)
        grade = 'O';
     else if(marks>=80)
        grade = 'E';
     else if(marks>=70)
        grade = 'A';
     else if(marks>=60)
        grade = 'B';
     else if(marks>=50)
        grade = 'C';
     else if(marks>=40)
        grade = 'D';
     else
        grade = 'F';
     printf("\nYour Grade is:%c",grade);
}
```

PROGRAM 9.16   In a certain city telephone bill is calculated as per the following rules:

for first 75 calls, charge is fixed and is equal to Rs. 250;

for next 75 calls, the rate is Rs. 0.80 per call;

for next 75 calls, the rate is Rs. 1.00 per call;

for calls beyond that, the rate is Rs. 1.20 per call.

Write a program to calculate the telephone bill for the subscriber of that city.

```
#include<stdio.h>
void main()
{   int calls;
    float chrg;
    printf("Enter Number of Calls:");
    scanf("%d",&calls);
    if(calls <= 75)
       chrg = 250;
    else
       if(calls <= 150)
           chrg = 250+(calls - 75)*0.80;
       else
```

```
        if(calls <= 225)
            chrg = 250+75*0.80+(calls - 150)*1.00;
        else
            chrg = 250+75*0.80+75*1.00+(calls - 225)*1.20;
    printf("Charge is : %.2f", chrg);
}
```

PROGRAM 9.17 In a courier company, charges for parcel is calculated as per the following rules:

For first 20 gms, charge is fixed and is equal to Rs. 25;

For next each 10 gms and their part of charge is Rs. 5.

Write a program to calculate the charges for the parcel.

```
#include<stdio.h>
void main()
{   int weight,net,times,rem;
    float chrg;
    printf("Enter weight:");
    scanf("%d", &weight);
    if(weight<=20)
        chrg = 25;
    else
    {
        net = weight - 20;
        times = net /10;
        rem = net % 10;
        if(rem != 0)    /* Some part of 1o exist */
            times++;    /* Thus one more Rs. 5 is required */
        chrg = 25+times*5;
    }
    printf("Charge = Rs. %.2f",chrg);
}
```

PROGRAM 9.18 Write a program which will accept the length of three sides of a triangle and check the validity of the lengths and decides what type of triangle it is.

```
#include<stdio.h>
void main()
{   int s1,s2,s3;
    printf("Enter The Three Sides of a Triangle: ");
    scanf("%d%d%d",&s1,&s2,&s3);
    if(s1<=0||s2<=0||s3<=0)
        printf("\nAll sides must be geater than Zero.");
    else
        if(s1>=s2+s3 || s2>=s1+s3 || s3>= s1+s2)
```

```
    { printf("Sum of Any Two Sides of A Triangle Must Be
                                    Greater than 3rd Side");
    }
    else
        if(s1==s2&&s2==s3&&s3==s1)
            printf("It is an Equilateral Triangle");
        else
            if((s1==s2&&s1!=s3)||(s2==s3&&s2!=s1)||(s1==s3&&s1!=s2))
                printf("It is an Isosceles Triangle ");
            else
                printf("It is an Scalene Triangle ");
}
```

PROGRAM 9.19   Write a program in C to find the roots of a quadratic equation. Your program should print the imaginary roots in the form of a+ib

```
#include<stdio.h>
#include<math.h>
void main()
{ int a,b,c,inter;
  float t;
  printf("Enter the coeficients of Quadratic Equation: ");
  scanf("%d%d%d",&a,&b,&c);
  inter= b*b - 4*a*c;
  if(inter<0)
  { puts("Imaginary Roots.");
    printf("Roots are %d+i%d and %d-i%d",a,b,a,b);
  }
  else
      if(inter==0)
  printf("Roots are Equal and it is %d", -b/(2*a));
      else
      { t=sqrt(inter);
        printf("Roots are %f and %f", (-b+t)/(2*a),(-b-t)/(2*a));
      }
  }
}
```

PROGRAM 9.20   Write a menu driven program to carry out the simple arithmetic operations like addition, subtraction, multiplication and division between two inputted numbers.

```
#include<stdio.h>
void main()
{
    float number1,number2,result;
```

```
    int opt;
    printf("\n==============================");
    printf("\n\t Menu");
    printf("\n==============================");
    printf("\nEnter 1 for Addition");
    printf("\nEnter 2 for Subraction");
    printf("\nEnter 3 for Multiplication");
    printf("\nEnter 4 for Division");
    printf("\n==============================");
    printf("\nEnter your option:");
    scanf("%d", &opt);
    printf("============================");
    if(opt<1||opt>4)
    {   printf("\nInvalid Option...");
        exit(0);
    }
    printf("\nEnter Two Numbers:");
    scanf("%f%f", &number1,&number2);
    switch(opt)
    {
        case 1:  result = number1+number2;
                    break;
        case 2:  result = number1-number2;
                    break;
        case 3:  result = number1*number2;
                    break;
        case 4:  result = number1/number2;
    }
    printf("\nResult = %f", result);
}
```

PROGRAM 9.21   Write a program in C to test whether an inputted character is vowel or not.

```
#include<stdio.h>
void main()
{
    char chr;
    printf("Enter any chracter:");
    scanf("%c",&chr);
    switch(chr)
    {
        case 'a':
        case 'e':
        case 'i':
        case 'o':
        case 'u':
        case 'A':
```

```
        case 'E':
        case 'I':
        case 'O':
        case 'U': printf("It is vowel.");
                        break;
        default : printf("It is not a vowel");
    }
}
```

SUMMARY

➤ Control statement controls the order of execution in a program.

➤ Branching and looping are two different type of control statement.

➤ Branching statement decides which group of statements will execute among different group of statements.

➤ **if** statement and **switch** statement are two branching statements.

➤ In C, non-zero values are treated as TRUE and zero is treated as FALSE.

➤ Generally relational operators are used to check the condition.

➤ Without if, else statement can't be used but without else, if statement can be used.

➤ If set of statements are need to execute depending on some condition, those statements should be enclosed within the pair of parenthesis ({...}).

➤ Instead of nested if statement, logical operators can also be used.

➤ **switch** statement is used to choose a particular option from a set of alternatives.

➤ **goto** statement is another branching rather jumping statement that can send the control anywhere in the program using a label.

REVIEW EXERCISES

1. What do you mean by control statement?
2. What is the utility of branching statement?
3. What are the different types of branching statement available in C?
4. Explain the different form of **if** statement.
5. What is the purpose of **switch** statement?
6. Compare and contrast between **if** statement and **switch** statement.
7. Compare conditional statement and conditional operator.
8. Why structured programming is called **goto** avoid program?
9. Write a program to check whether an inputted number is odd or even.
10. Write a program to check whether an inputted character is an alphabet or not.
11. Write a program to find the smallest number between 3 inputted numbers.
12. Professional Tax is calculated as per the following rules:

Basic Salary	Tax
Below 5000	Nil
5000 – 10000	Rs. 75
10000 – 20000	Rs. 125
Above 20000	Rs. 180

Write a program to calculate Professional Tax of the employees.

13. A contractor pays the workers at the end of each week on the basis of hours worked in the week. The rate of payment varies as the hours worked as per the following rules:

   For the first 35 hours the rate is Rs. 14 per hour; for the next 25 hours the rate is Rs. 18 per hour; for hours beyond that the rate is Rs. 25 per hour. No worker is allowed to work for more than 80 hours in a week. Write a program to calculate wages for the workers.

14. Write a menu driven program to convert the temperature from one scale to another. Your program should able to convert Centigrade to Fahrenheit, Fahrenheit to Centigrade, Centigrade to Reaumur, Reaumur to Centigrade, Fahrenheit to Reaumur and Reaumur to Fahrenheit.

   [Hint: $C/5 = (F - 32)/9 = R/4$]

15. Write a program to check whether an inputted number is positive, negative or zero using conditional operator.

16. Write a program to find the smallest number between 3 inputted numbers using conditional operator.

LEARN BY QUIZ – QUESTIONS

1. What will be the output of any expression containing only relational operators?
   (1) 0 or 1
   (2) always 1
   (3) any nonzero number

2. For condition evaluation any nonzero number is treated as
   (1) True
   (2) False
   (3) depends on the condition

3. If the value of a variable COUNT is 50 what will be the output of relational expression COUNT <=100
   (1) 1
   (2) 0
   (3) 50

4. If the value of the variables 'a' and 'b' be 100 and 150 respectively what will be the value of the relational expression a >= b
   (1) 50
   (2) 1
   (3) 0

5. To evaluate the value of the expression a > b the actual operation that takes place is
   (1) Subtraction
   (2) Addition
   (3) value comparison

6. Which of the following is not true regarding if-else control statement
   (1) it is an assignment statement
   (2) it is a conditional statement
   (3) it is a decision making statement

7. Which of the following *if* construct is meaningless
   (1) if (abp > 10);
       printf(" abp is greater than 10");
   (2) if (abp > 10)
       printf(" abp is greater than 10");
   (3) if (abp>10)
       {printf(" abp is greater than 10");}

8. For the if control statement what statements to be executed if the condition is true is written within
   (1) braces after the if
   (2) brackets after the if
   (3) in a separate block linked with this if

9. What will be the output of the following program segment if the input is 9?
   ```
   int i;
   scanf("%d",&i);
   if(i%4==0)
   printf("Number entered is divisible by 4");
   ```
   (1) compilation error
   (2) number entered is divisible by 4
   (3) no output shown

10. What will be the output of the following program segment if the input is 16?
    ```
    int i;
    scanf("%d",&i);
    if(i%4==0)
    printf("Number entered is divisible by 4");
    ```
    (1) number entered is divisible by 4
    (2) no output shown
    (3) compilation error

11. What will be the output of the following program segment if the input is 10?
    ```
    int s;
    float f;
    printf("enter the value of f");
    s=scanf("%f",&f);
    if (s==0)
    printf(" the input is not a floating point number");
    ```
    (1) blank output
    (2) compilation error
    (3) the input is not a floating point number

12. What will be the output of the following program segment if the input is 10.03?
    ```
    int s;
    float f;
    ```

```
printf("enter the value of f");
s=scanf("%f",&f);
if (s!=0)
printf(" the input is a floating point number");
if (s==0)
printf(" the input is not a floating point number");
```
(1) the input is a floating point number
(2) this is not a floating point number
(3) blank output

13. What will be the output of the following program segment?

```
int a,b,c,x;
printf("Input a,b,c\n");
scanf("%d%d%d", &a, &b, &c);

x=a;
if(b>x) x=b;
if(c>x) x=c;
printf("%d",x);
```
(1) Print the value of the variable c.
(2) print the smallest among the three inputs
(3) print the largest among the three inputs

14. What will be the output of the following program if the input is 10?

```
int s;
float f;
printf("enter the value of f");
s=scanf("%f",&f);
if (s==0)
printf(" the input is not a floating point number");
else
printf(" the input is a floating point number");
```
(1) the input is a floating point number
(2) the input is not a floating point number
(3) blank output

15. What will be the output of the following program segment if the input is zero?

```
int i;
printf("input an integer");
scanf("%d",&i);
if (i)
printf("it is nonzero\n");
else
printf("it is zero\n");
```

(1) it is zero
(2) it is nonzero
(3) compilation error showing message relational operator required

16. Which of the following is invalid C segment?
(1)
```
if(x>y)
{
if(y>z)
printf("x is greater than z");
else
{
printf("y is less thn z");
else
printf("x is less than y");
}
}
```
(2)
```
if(x>y)
{
if(y>z)
printf("x is greater than z");
else
printf("y is less than z");
}
else
printf("x is less than y");
```
(3)
```
if(x>y)
if(y>z)
printf("x is greater than z");
else
printf("y is less than z");
else
printf("x is less than y");
```

17. What will be the output of the following C segment if a=30, b=20, c=25?
```
if(a>b)
if(b>c)
printf("a is greater than c");
else
printf("b is less than c");
```
(1) b is less than c
(2) a is greater than c
(3) compilation error

18. What will be the output of the following program segment? Given i=2, j=4, k=3, l=5.
```
int i,j,k,l;
if (i==j)
printf("i and j are equal\n");
else if (i==k)
printf("i and k are equal\n");
else if (i==l)
printf("i and l are equal\n");
else
printf("i is not equal to j,k,l\n");
```

(1) i is not equal to j, k, l
(2) i and j are equal
(3) i and l are equal

19. What will be the output of the following segment?

```
int x,y,i=3;
if(i>3)
x=4;
y=5;
else
x=6;
printf("value of x is %d",x);
```

(1) compilation error
(2) blank output
(3) 6

20. What will be the output for basic salary 2000?

```
float bs,gs,da,ha;
printf("enter basic salary");
scanf("%f",&bs);
if(bs<1500)
{
ha=bs*10/100;
da=bs*80/100;
}
else
{
ha=500;
da=bs*90/100;
}
gs=bs+ha+da;
printf("gross salary=Rs%d",gs);
```

(1) gross salary=Rs 3800
(2) gross salary=Rs 4300
(3) gross salary=Rs 4000

21. What will be the output of the segment?

```
int a=10,b=5;
if(a>3 && b!=3)
printf("condition satisfies");
else
printf("condition does not satisfy");
```

(1) condition satisfies
(2) condition does not satisfy
(3) error in condition expression

22. What will be the output of the segment?

```
int a=10,b=5;
if((a!=3) && (b=3))
printf("condition satisfies");
else
printf("condition does not satisfy");
```

(1) condition satisfies
(2) condition does not satisfy
(3) error in condition expression

23. What will be the output of the segment?
```
int a=10, b=5;
if((a==3)||(b!=3))
printf("condition satisfies");
else
printf("condition does not satisfy");
```
    (1) condition satisfies
    (2) condition does not satisfy
    (3) error in condition expression

24. What will be the output of the segment?
```
int x=55, y=11, z=44;
if(!x>=45)
y=33;
z=22;
printf("y=%d,z=%d",y,z);
```
    (1) y=11,z=22
    (2) y=11,z=44
    (3) y=33,z=22

25. What will be the output of the segment?
```
float a=10.76,b=12.68;
if(a=b)
printf("a and b are equal");
else
printf("a and b are not equal");
```
    (1) a and b are equal
    (2) a and b are not equal
    (3) compilation error

26. What will be the output of the segment?
```
if('A'<'a')
printf("condition satisfies");
else
printf("condition does not satisfy");
```
    (1) condition satisfies
    (2) condition does not satisfy
    (3) compilation error

27. What will be the output of the segment?
```
int x=5;
if x>=2
printf("%d",x);
```
    (1) compilation error
    (2) 5
    (3) 1

28. What will be the output of the segment?
```
float p=0.7;
if(p<0.7)
printf("p is less than 0.7");
else
printf("p is not less than 0.7");
```
    (1) p is less than 0.7
    (2) p is not less than 0.7
    (3) error in condition expression

29. What will be the output of the segment?
```
int a=10, b=20;
if(!(!a)&&a)
printf("%d",x);
else
printf("%d",y);
```
 (1) 0
 (2) 10
 (3) 20

30. Which of the following statement is false for goto statement?
 (1) goto can transfer control to a statement of other program
 (2) goto transfers control to a labeled statement in the same program
 (3) use of goto should be avoided

31. A switch statement is used for which of the following purpose?
 (1) to choose from multiple possibilities which may arise due to different values of a single variable
 (2) switch from one variable to another
 (3) switch between functions of a program

32. What will be the output of the following program segment?
```
int know=3;
switch(know)
{
case 1:
    printf("one");
    break;
case 3:
    printf("three");
    break;
case 5:
    printf("five");
    break;
default:
    printf("odd");
    break;
}
```
 (1) The output will be three
 (2) The output will be threefiveodd
 (3) The output will be onethreefiveodd

33. What will be the output of the following program segment?
```
int know=3;
switch(know)
{
case 3:
    printf("three");
    break;
case 1:
    printf("one");
    break;
case 5:
    printf("five");
    break;
```

```
      default:
         printf ("odd");
         break;
      }
```
(1) three
(2) odd
(3) five

34. What will be the output of the following program segment?
```
      int know=3;
      switch (know)
      {
        case 1:
           printf ("one");
        case 3:
           printf ("three");
        case 5:
           printf ("five");
        default:
           printf ("odd");
      }
```
(1) three five odd
(2) one three five odd
(3) three

35. What will be the output of the following program segment?
```
      int know=3;
      switch (know)
      {
        case 1:
           printf ("one");
           break;
        case 1+1+1:
           printf ("three");
           break;
        case 3+2:
           printf ("five");
           break;
        default:
           printf ("odd");
           break;
      }
```
(1) three
(2) compilation error
(3) odd

36. What will be the output of the following program segment?
```
      int knowledge=1, factor=2;
      switch (knowledge+factor)
      {
      case 1:
           printf ("one");
           break;
      case 3:
```

```
        printf("three");
        break;
    case 5:
        printf("five");
        break;
    default:
        printf("odd");
        break;
    }
```
(1) three
(2) compilation error
(3) odd

37. What will be the output of the following program segment?
```
    float know=3.3;
    switch(know)
    {
      case 1.1:
        printf("one point one");
        break;
    case 3.3:
        printf("three point three");
        break;
    case 5.5:
        printf("five point five");
        break;
    default:
        printf("odd");
        break;
    }
```
(1) compilation error
(2) three point three
(3) odd

38. What will be the output of the following program segment?
```
    int know=67;
    switch(know)
    {
    case 'A':
        printf("one");
        break;
    case 'B':
        printf("three");
        break;
    case 'C':
        printf("five");
        break;
    default:
        printf("odd");
        break;
    }
```
(1) five
(2) odd
(3) compilation error

39. What will be the output of the following program segment?

```c
char know='C';
switch(know)
{
 case A:
    printf("one");
    break;
 case B:
    printf("three");
    break;
 case C:
    printf("five");
    break;
 default:
    printf("odd");
    break;
}
```

(1) will produce compilation error
(2) five
(3) odd

40. What will be the output of the following program segment?

```c
int know=3;
switch(know)
{
printf("Knowledge");
case 1:
    printf("one");
    break;
case 3:
    printf("three");
    break;
case 5:
    printf("five");
    break;
default:
    printf("Factor");
    break;
}
```

(1) three
(2) knowledge Factor
(3) knowledge three

41. What will be the output of the following program segment?

```c
int know=2;
switch(++know)
{
case 1:
    printf("one");
    break;
case 3:
    printf("three");
    break;
```

```
case 5:
    printf("five");
    break;
default:
    printf("Factor");
    break;
}
```
(1) three
(2) five
(3) Factor

42. What will be the output of the following program segment if the input is b or B?
```
char choise;
scanf("%c", &choise);
switch(choise)
{
case 'A':
case 'a':
    printf("one");
    break;
case 'B':
case 'b':
    printf("three");
    break;
case 'C':
case 'c':
    printf("five");
    break;
default:
    printf("odd");
    break;
}
```
(1) three
(2) odd
(3) blank output

43. What will be the output of the following program segment if input is 3?
```
int a=10, b=5, choice;
printf("enter 1 to add\n");
printf("enter 2 to subtract\n");
printf("enter 3 to multiply\n");
printf("enter 4 to divide\n");
printf("enter your choice");
scanf("%d", &choice);
switch(choice)
{
case 1:
        printf("%d", a+b); break;
case 2:
        printf("%d", a-b); break;
case 3:
        printf("%d", a*b); break;
case 4:
        printf("%d", a/b); break;
```

```
        default:
                printf ("wrong choice");
        }
```

(1) 50
(2) wrong choice
(3) 502wrongchoice

44. What will be the output of the following program segment if the input is a?

```
int know=1,p=10,q=5; char factor='a';
switch (know)
{   case 1:
            switch (factor)
            {
                case 'a': p = p + q; break;
                case 'b': p = p - q; break;
                default:  p = p * q; break;
            }
            break;
    default:
        p=p/q;
}
printf ("%d", p);
```

(1) 15
(2) 5
(3) 2

LEARN BY QUIZ – ANSWERS

Answer explanations

1. C permits the following relational operators

    < (less than)

    > (greater than)

    == (equal to)

    <= (less than or equal to)

    >= (greater than or equal to)

    != (not equal to)

    All the relational operators are comparisons between two variables. So the result of this comparison should be either true or false. A true value is represented by 1 and a false value is represented by 0 in C. So the output of any relational expression will be either 1 or 0.

2. Zero is treated as false and any nonzero number is treated as true value. These are fixed values and they do not depend on what condition has been given for evaluation.

3. <= is a relational operator. It checks here whether the value of the variable COUNT is less than or equal to the numeric 100. As the value of the variable COUNT is given 50, so the comparison returns a true value. A true value is represented by 1, so 1 will be the required answer.

4. >= is a relational operator which compares whether 'a' is greater than or equal to 'b', but according to the given value 'a'=100 and 'b'=150. So 'a' is smaller than 'b'. So the comparison returns a false result. Zero represents false. So 0 is the output here.

5. To evaluate a>b the actual operation performed is (a−b). If the subtraction result is zero that means a is equal to b, so the comparison a>b returns a false result. If the subtraction result is a positive integer it shows that that the value of a is greater than b, so the comparison a>b returns a true result. If the subtraction result is negative integer then a is smaller than b, so the comparison a>b returns a false result.

6. When we want to do some action depending upon the truth value or upon the false value of a condition the if-else control statement is used. So it can be treated as conditional statement or a decision making statement where the decision depends on the condition given. No assignment is done here.

7. if (abp>10);

   printf("a is greater than 10"); is meaningless as for the (;) after the if condition the if statement is terminated there and the printf will execute irrespective of **abp** is greater than 10 or not.

   in the statement if (abp>10)

   {printf("abp is greater than 10");} the curly braces {} is not necessary as there is only one statement for the *if* condition but this is neither a syntax nor logical error.

8. The syntax of the if construct clearly shows that multiple or compound statements are to write in braces after the if.

9. % is a modulo operator. If the value of i is 9 then 9% 4=1 which is not equal to zero. As the condition checks whether the result of the modulo operator is equal to zero so the condition is false here. The message will be shown only if the condition becomes true. So no output will be shown here.

   There is no syntactical error in this program statement. So no compilation error will occur.

10. % is a modulo operator. If the value of i is 16 then 16% 4=0 which is equal to zero. As the condition checks whether the result of the modulo operator is equal to zero so the condition is true here. The message will be shown only if the condition becomes true. So the message 'number entered is divisible by 4' will be shown here.

    There is no syntactical error in this program statement. So no compilation error will occur.

11. The scanf() function returns zero only if there is any problem regarding input. So here the value returned by scanf() will not be zero and so the value of s will also not be zero. So no output will be shown.

12. The scanf() function returns zero only if there is any problem regarding input. So here the value returned by scanf() will not be zero and so the value of s will also not be zero. Hence, the first if condition satisfies and first printf() statement will be executed to show the output "the input is a floating point number".

13. The variable x first holds the value of the variable a. Then a comparison with b and x is executed. If b is greater then x then x will take the value of b. That is now x takes the greater value among a and b. Then similar comparison is done between x and c, and x takes the value of c if it is less than c. That is at the end x takes the greatest value among the three inputs.

14. The scanf() function returns zero only if there is any problem regarding input. So here the value returned by scanf() will not be zero and so the value of s will also not be zero. So the else part of the if-else construct will be executed and as a result 'the input is a floating point number' will be shown.

15. The value of the condition variable i will decide whether the else part of if-else construct will run or not. Here the value of i is given zero. So the else part of the if-else construct will be executed as the zero value of i indicates the false of the condition.

Explicit use of relational operator is not a mandatory regarding condition expression. Actually here the condition variable i is compared with zero or nonzero value which uses the relational operator ==. So no compilation error will be detected.

16. The second else in the else block is used without any associated if. An if construct can be used without using any else block but no else part can be used without any if part. else is only a part of if-else.

17. The segment shown in the question is a very popular typical problem encountered in programs. It is called the dangling else problem. There are two ifs and one else. So the problem is with which if the else should be attached with. C solves this problem by considering that the last unmatched else should be associated with last unmatched if. So here the else will be attached with the last if.

18. According to the value given the value of i, j, k, l all are unequal; so the last option attached with the else will be executed.

19. Here there are multiple statements within the true part of the if-else construct but no brace is used. So the compiler will treat the construct as only a if construct and x=4 be its only statement. So it can not associate the else with anything and tries to find another if for this else and fails. So a compilation error rather warning will be generated.

20. It is a simple if-else construct. According to the input, the else part of the if-else construct will be executed. So the gross salary will be Rs 4300.

21. For a>3 && b!=3 the first condition evaluates to be true, so it is replaced by 1. Similarly second part is also true and hence 1. So the result of the and (&&) is also 1. As 1 represents the true so the condition for the if is true here and as a result it will display the condition it satisfies.

22. a!=3 evaluates to be true, so it results 1. b=3 is an assignment statement. So the condition becomes 1 && 3. Any nonzero value is treated as true in C. So the output of the and operator is true here. So the condition for the if is true here and as a result it will display the condition it satisfies.

23. a==3 evaluates to be false, so it results 0. b!=3 evaluates to be true. So the condition becomes 0||1. So the output of the or operator is 1 here. As 1 represents the true so the condition for the if is true here and as a result it will display the condition it satisfies.

24. According to the precedence of operators in C, out of ! and >= , ! enjoys a higher priority. Therefore, !55 will be performed first which returns 0, it is then compared with 45 and returns false. So the condition fails and the controls automatically jumps to z=22. So the value of y will not be changed. So the output will be y=11, z=22

25. The assignment operator used in if statement simply assigns the value of b to a which is a nonzero positive constant. So it returns a true value and hence the condition satisfies and executes the first printf() statement. If the programmer's intension is to compare a with b then comparison operator == has to be used instead of assignment operator =.

26. Any character enclosed within a pair of quotes is replaced by the ASCII value of the character. The ASCII value of A is 65 whereas that of a is 97. So the condition in if satisfies and the first printf() will be executed.

27. if statement is missing a pair of parentheses surrounding the condition which is a must. So compilation error will occur.

28. When 0.7 is stored in p, due to precision consideration, it is stored as something less than 0.7. So when it is compared with 0.7, the condition evaluates to be true.

29. 'a' has a true value so !a results 0. !(!a) is !(0) that is 1. So the output of the and operation is 1 which again satisfies the condition of the if because of its 1 value. So the first printf() will be executed.

30. The correct option is goto can transfer control to a statement of other program.

The functionality of goto is that it can transfer control of execution within a program but cannot transfer control to another program. A goto less program is always desirable.

31. The correct option is to choose from multiple possibilities which may arise due to different values of a single variable.

32. The output will be three.

Here the switch variable is know whose value is 3. So the control jumps to label case 3, print three, encounters break and moves the control out of switch.

33. The output will be three. As the value of know is three the execution will start from case 3: irrespective of its order (position) in the switch statement and will continue until a break is encountered.

34. The output will be three five odd.

Here the switch variable is know whose value is 3. So the control jumps to label case 3, print three, as no break statement is associated with this case so control goes to next statement, prints five and for the same reason goes to the next statement and also prints odd and then only moves the control out of switch by encountering }.

35. The output will be three.

As the value of the switch variable is 3, control goes to the case 1+1+1 as its value is 3, prints three, encounters break and moves control out of switch. Any arithmetic operator can be used in the case statement that will give the desired value.

36. The output will be three.

Here switch variable is an expression. An expression can also be used in a switch statement (provided it should be a constant expression). According to the value given, this expression results in 3 so control goes to the case 3, prints three, encounters break and moves control out of switch.

37. The program segment will result in compilation error.

No float variable or constant can be used in the case construct of a switch statement.

38. The output will be five.

Here the case values are character constants. The ASCII equivalent of 'C' is 67. Here the switch variable value is also 67. So case 'C' will be chosen, control will jump there, prints five, encounters break, control jumps out of switch.

39. The execution of the program will produce compilation error.

The case construct can take only integer or character constants. But here missing of single quotes prevent A, B, C to be character constant, so it will produce compilation error.

40. The output will be three.

Any statement can be written within the switch statement other than the case constructs. C will not produce any compilation error but switch will bypass all those statements and only considers case constructs. As the value given for the switch variable know=3 so control goes to the case 3, prints three, encounters break and moves control out of switch.

41. The output will be three.

Here switch variable is an expression. An expression can also be used in a switch statement. According to the value given, this expression results in 3, so control goes to the case 3, prints three, encounters break and moves control out of switch.

42. The output will be three.

No statement is written for case 'B'. So if B is given as choice, execution automatically goes to the case 'b'. So for both the inputs 'B' or 'b', three will be printed and control will jump after switch because break has been encountered.

43. The output will be 50.

As the value of the switch variable is 3, control goes to the case 3, prints the value of the expression a*b which is 50, encounters break and moves control out of switch.

44. The output will be 15.

It is an example of nested switch. The outer switch variable is know whose value is 1, so control jumps to case 1 where the inner switch starts. Its switch variable is factor whose value is 'a', so control jumps to case 'a', adds values of p and q, encounters break, jumps from inner switch, again encounters break, jumps from outer switch, then prints the value of p which is 15.

10

Loop Statements

In the last two chapters, we have learnt to develop programs that used simple sequential statements or conditional statements. In the first case, each statement in the program is executed in a fixed order; whereas in the second case, depending on some condition a particular set of statements gets executed, skipped or another set of statements gets executed. But most of the time we have to execute same series of actions. The mechanism, which helps us to perform an action over and over, is the 'loop' or 'iteration'.

Loops are of two types, **entry controlled loop** and **exit controlled loop**. When condition is checked before the execution of the body of the loop, it is called entry controlled loop or pre-test iteration. It is described by the following block diagram.

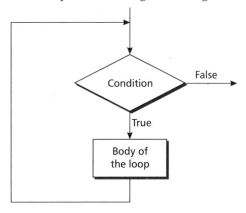

Fig. 10.1   Entry controlled loop

As the block diagram described, first condition will be checked. If the condition is true, the control will enter in the loop and body of the loop will execute. Then control will loop back and the condition will be tested again. This process will be continued until the condition becomes false. When the condition becomes false, control will terminate the loop and execute the next statement followed by the loop statement.

But when condition is checked after the execution of the body of the loop, it is called exit controlled loop or post test iteration. Here, first body of the loop will execute. Then condition will be checked to determine whether the loop will execute next time or not. If the condition is true, the control will loop back. When the condition becomes false, control will terminate the loop and execute the next statement followed by the loop statement. It is described by the following block diagram.

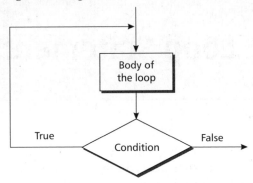

Fig. 10.2   Exit controlled loop

The difference between entry control and exit control loop is that entry control loop may not execute single time but exit control loop must execute at least once. C supports both type of loop structure. In C, **while** and **for** are of entry controlled type loop statement and **do-while** is of exit-controlled type loop statement.

10.1   WHILE STATEMENT

In 'C', while statement is a pre-test iteration or entry controlled loop statement. Here condition is tested first. If the condition is true, then body of the loop is executed. This continues until the condition becomes false. **As the condition is tested first, body of the loop may not execute at all**. Body of the loop may be a single statement or a block of statements. For single statement parentheses are optional. The general form of while loop:

```
while (condition)
{
    ...    /* body of the loop */
    ...
}
```

Generally any loop statement contains a loop control variable. Depending on its value, how long a loop will execute is decided. This loop control variable or loop index is initialized before entering the loop. Before entering the while loop, this loop index is tested by the condition attached with the while statement. If it satisfies the condition, body of the while loop executes. Within the body of the loop the value of loop index is changed. After execution of all statements of body of the loop, control return to the top of the while statement and the condition will be checked again with the new value of the loop index. This procedure continues until the condition becomes false.

EXAMPLE 10.1

```
int i = 5;
while(i<= 10)
{  printf("%d ", i);
    i++;
}
printf("%d ", i);
```

The above example will print: 5 6 7 8 9 10 11.

In the above example, first the variable **i** is initialized with 5. Then the condition is checked. As the condition is true body of the loop (i.e. the statements within the parenthesis) executes. Thus printf prints 5 and **i** becomes 6. As the control reaches at the end of loop, the control returns to the top of loop and the condition is checked again. This process continues and printf statement prints up to 10. When **i** become 11, the condition becomes false and control comes out from the loop and the statement followed by the while loop is now executes. So, 11 will be printed at end. Following flow chart illustrates the above program clearly.

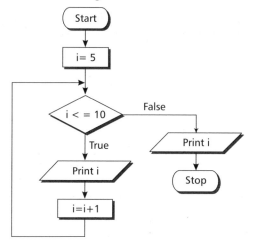

Fig. 10.3 Flow chart to illustrate while statement

Now, consider the following example:
```
int i = 5;
while(i>= 10)
{  printf("%d ", i);
    i++;
}
```

The above example will print nothing as the condition is false at very beginning.

Be cautious, there will be no semicolon immediately after the condition. Consider the following example:
```
int   i = 5 ;
while ( i <= 10 ) ;
```

```
{      printf ("%d ", i ) ;
          i++;
}
```

This is an infinite loop, and it does not give any output. Because, we have carelessly given a ';' after the while. This would make the loop work like this...

```
int    i = 5 ;
while ( i <= 10 )
{  ;  }
{      printf ("%d ", i ) ;
          i++;
}
```

Instead of original body of the loop, the semicolon act as a dummy do nothing block. So, the loop counter would not get chance to increment. As a result, condition is always true and becomes an infinite loop.

Let us develop some C programs to understand the use of *while* statement.

PROGRAM 10.1   Write a program to display first 10 natural numbers.

```
#include<stdio.h>
void main( )
{   int i=1;
    while(i <= 10)
    {
        printf ("%d ", i ) ;
        i++;
    }
}
```

Output: 1 2 3 4 5 6 7 8 9 10

The above program prints the first 10 natural numbers. But if we want to generalize the program, i.e., instead of 10 if we want to print n natural number, we have to take the input of n and at the condition of while statement 10 will be replaced by n. Following program shows this. Notice that, whatever changes are incorporated is shown in bold face.

PROGRAM 10.2   Write a program to display first n natural numbers.

```
#include<stdio.h>
void main( )
{   int i=1, n;
    printf("Enter the value of n : ");
    scanf("%d", &n);
    while(i <= n)
    {
        printf ("%d ", i ) ;
        i++;
    }
}
```

Sample output

Enter the value of n : 5

1 2 3 4 5

Enter the value of n : 10

1 2 3 4 5 6 7 8 9 10

Now instead of displaying if we want to add first n natural number, we need to modify a small portion. Instead of displaying each value of **i** we have to add these values. So, printf statement would be replaced by the addition statement. Here is the program.

PROGRAM 10.3   Write a program to add first n natural numbers.

```
#include<stdio.h>
void main( )
{   int i=1, n, sum = 0;
    printf("Enter the value of n : ");
    scanf("%d", &n);
    while(i <= n)
    {
        sum = sum + i ;
        i++;
    }
    printf ("Sum = %d ", sum ) ;
}
```

Sample output

Enter the value of n : 5

Sum = 15

Enter the value of n : 10

Sum = 55

In the above program the variable **sum** is taken to store the summation value and it is initialized with zero at the very beginning of the program. Within the loop as **i** generates the each value of the series, that value is summed up and stored within the variable **sum**. When the control comes out from the loop, the value of **sum** will be printed.

In the next program we will try to write a program which will add first n odd numbers. For that we have to consider two extra points. First, how we generate odd numbers and this is very simple. As the gap between each odd number is 2, within the loop **i** will be incremented by 2. Second is how the count is maintained in the program. For that we have to take an extra variable which will be incremented by 1 in each iteration. Here is the program.

PROGRAM 10.4:   Write a program to add first n odd numbers.

```
#include<stdio.h>
void main( )
{   int i=1, n, sum=0, count=1;
    printf("Enter the value of n : ");
    scanf("%d", &n);
    while(count <= n)
    {
        sum = sum + i ;
        i=i+2;
        count++;
    }
    printf ("Sum = %d ", sum ) ;
}
```

Sample output

Enter the value of n : 3

Sum = 9

It is not necessary that how many times a loop will execute that depends solely on the loop index. A user choice may control the loop execution. Consider the following example. Here user input will decide how long the loop will execute.

PROGRAM 10.5   Write a program to find the summation of n inputted numbers.

```
#include<stdio.h>
void main()
{    int num,sum=0;
     char ch = 'y';
     while(ch == 'y' || ch == 'Y')
     {
         printf("Enter any Number:");
         scanf("%d",&num);
         sum+=num;
         fflush(stdin);
         printf("Enter More Number? (y/n)");
         scanf("%c",&ch);
     }
     printf("Sum = %d",sum);
}
```

Sample output

Enter any Number: 5

Enter More Number?(y/n) y

Enter any Number: 8

Enter More Number?(y/n) y

Enter any Number: −2

Enter More Number?(y/n) n

Sum = 11

By the above program user can add as many number as he/she wants. The Input procedure will be over when user negates in response of the question 'Enter More Number?(y/n)'.

Body of the loop not only contains sequential statement, but also may contain conditional statement or another iterative statement. Following example shows conditional statement within a loop.

PROGRAM 10.6 Program to display all two digited numbers which are divisible by 3 but not divisible by 9.

```c
#include<stdio.h>
void main( )
{   int num = 10;
    while(num <= 99)
    {
        if( num % 3 = = 0   && num % 9 != 0)
            printf("%d ", num);
        num++;
    }
}
```

In the above program, the while loop is used to generate all two digited numbers and then each number is tested with the specified condition. If the condition is satisfied, the number is displayed.

10.2 NESTED LOOP

Like conditional statement, a loop can also be nested. When a loop is defined under another loop it is called nested loop. There is no restriction on number of levels of nesting. In nested loop, for each iteration of outer loop the inner loop executes its total iteration. The following code snippet illustrates nested loop:

```c
i=1;
while(i<= 3)
{   j=1;
    while(j <= 4)
    {
        printf("%d   ", j);
        j++;
    }
    printf("\n");
    i++;
}
```

The output of the above code snippet is:

```
1 2 3 4
1 2 3 4
1 2 3 4
```

In the above code snippet, for each value of **i**, the inner loop executes 4 times as each time j is incremented from 1 to 4 and prints the value of j (i.e., 1 2 3 4). After completion of the execution of inner loop, new line is printed. Thus we get 3 lines in the output as the outer loop executes 3 times.

Following program shows the use of nested while loop.

PROGRAM 10.7   Program to find the sum of the following series:

1! + 3! + 5! + ... upto n number of terms

```
#include<stdio.h>
#include<conio.h>
void main()
{ int i=1,c=1, a=1,n;
  long int fact, sum=0;
  clrscr();
  printf("Enter No. of Terms: ");
  scanf("%d", &n);
  while(c<=n)
  {
      fact = 1;
      i = 1;
      while(i <= a)        Calculates Factorial of a number
      {   fact *= i;
          i++;
      }
      sum += fact;  /* fact variable contains the factorial value of
                                           variable a */
      c++;
      a = a + 2;
  }
  printf("Sum = %ld", sum);
}
```

In the above program the variable **a** generates the series 1, 3, 5.... . The inner loop calculates the factorial value of **a**, i.e., 1!, 3!, 5! and so on. Then these factorial values are summed up within the variable **sum**. The number of terms is controlled by the variable **c**.

10.3 TEST YOUR PROGRESS

What will be the output for the following programs?

```
(a)  #include<stdio.h>
     void main()
     {    int i=1;
              while(i--)
          {
                  printf("%d ",i);
          }
          printf("%d ",i);
     }
```

Output: 0 −1

```
(b)  #include<stdio.h>
     void main( )
     {    int i= 0;
          while(++i)
          {
              printf("%d ",i);
          }
          printf("%d ",i);
     }
```

Output: 1 2 3 4 5 .... −4 −3 −2 −1 0

```
(c)  #include<stdio.h>
     void main()
     {    char ch=255;
          while(ch)
          {
              printf("%c ",ch--);
          }
     }
```

Output: prints all the ASCII characters in reverse order.

10.4 FOR STATEMENT

In 'C', *for* statement is a pre-test iteration or entry controlled loop statement and it is more compact loop structure. The *for* allows us to specify three main things about a loop in a single line. These are – setting a loop index to an initial value, testing the loop condition to determine whether the loop will execute or not and increment/decrement of loop index.

The general form of for loop:

```
for (initialization ; condition ; increment )
{
    ...  /* body of the loop */
    ...
}
```

Here initialization is done first. Then condition is tested. If the condition is true, then body of the loop is executed and at the end of executing the body of the loop, increment statement is executed. Then condition is checked again. This continues until the condition become false. Remember, initialization part executes always once and iteration continues in the order – condition -> body of the loop -> increment -> condition and so on until the condition become false.

EXAMPLE 10.2

```
for ( i = 5; i<= 10 ; i++)
{   printf("%d ", i);
    i++;
}
```

The above example will print: 5 6 7 8 9 10

All the three parts in the for statement may contain zero or multiple values.

Consider the following example:

PROGRAM 10.8 Program to find the sum of the following series:

1 + 3 + 5 + ... Upto n number of terms

```
#include<stdio.h>
#include<conio.h>
void main()
{
    int i, c, n, sum;
    clrscr();
    printf("Enter No. of Terms: ");
    scanf("%d", &n);

    for( c = 1, i = 1, sum =0; i<= n ; c++, i += 2)
    {
        sum += i;
    }
    printf("Sum = %d", sum);
}
```

Sample output

Enter the value of n : 3

Sum = 9

In the above program, there are three statements in the initialization section. These statements are separated by comma (,). Similarly, the increment section also contains two statements. In any *for* statement, all the three sections may contain any number of statements. These statements should be separated by the comma operator (,) and these sections should be separated by semicolon (;).

We can also omit any one or all the three sections in the *for* statement. But the separator two semicolons in the *for* statement should be there.

PROGRAM 10.9   Program to find the sum of the digits of a number.

```
#include<stdio.h>
#include<conio.h>
void main()
{ int num, sum = 0, rem;
  clrscr();
  printf("Enter Any Positive Integer: ");
  scanf("%d", &num);
  for( ; num > 0 ;)
  {
        rem = num % 10;
        sum = sum + rem;
        num = num / 10;
  }
  printf("Sum of the digits = %d", sum);
}
```

In the above program, no initialization is required as well as there is no such increment or decrement statement. That is why the initialization section and increment section is empty in the *for* statement. But the separator semicolons are given as they are required.

If the condition part is omitted, it is assumed to result in a 'true' value and the loop never terminates. A common way of writing never-ending loops or infinite loop is:

for(; ;)

We can also write the infinite loop using following while statement:

while(1)

We will see its use later.

10.4.1 Nested for Statement

Like *while* statement, *for* statement can also be nested. The following code snippet illustrates nested for loop:

```
      for( i=1; i<= 3 ; i++)
      {    for( j=1 ; j <= 4 ; j++)
              printf("%d    ", j);
           printf("\n");
      }
```

The output of the above code snippet is:

    1 2 3 4

    1 2 3 4

    1 2 3 4

In the above code snippet, for each value of **i**, the inner loop executes 4 times as each time j is incremented from 1 to 4 and prints the value of j (i.e., 1 2 3 4). After completion of the execution of inner loop, new line is printed. Thus, we get 3 lines in the output as the outer loop executes 3 times. From the above code, snippet it is cleared that the number of lines is controlled by outer loop and number of column, i.e., how many value will print in each line is controlled by inner loop. So, we can modify the code snippet in the following way:

```
for( i=1; i<= 4 ; i++)
    {   for( j=1 ; j <= i ; j++)
            printf("%d    "; j);
        printf("\n");
    }
```

As the outer loop executes 4 times, the above code snippet prints 4 lines. In each iteration the inner loop executes i number of times, i.e., when the value of i is 1, inner loop executes once; when i is 2, inner loop executes twice and so on. Thus we get the following output.

1

1 2

1 2 3

1 2 3 4

But if we want the following figure, what change we have to make?

    1

   1 2

  1 2 3

1 2 3 4

It is very simple. As we cannot print from right to left, first we have to print some spaces in each line first and then the numbers. So, now in each line we have two tasks. First one is to print space and then print numbers. If we look carefully, we will see that in first line number of space is 3, in second line number of space is 2, in third line number of space is 1 and in fourth line number of space is 0. The number of space is decreasing with the increase of line number. So, we can say we have to print (4–i) number of spaces. It can be easily implemented with a *for* loop which will execute (4–i) times and print a single space (' ') in each iteration. Next task is number printing and it is same as previous example. The following program illustrates this.

PROGRAM 10.10   Write a program to display the following figure for n number of lines.

    1

   1 2

  1 2 3

1 2 3 4

....

....

```
#include<stdio.h>
void main()
{   int n,i,j;
    printf("Enter no.of lines:");
    scanf("%d", &n);
    for( i=1; i<= n ; i++)              /* Controls number of lines to print */
    {   for(j = 1; j <= n-i; j++)       /*Controls number of spaces to print
                                                             in each line */
            printf(" ");
        for( j=1 ; j <= i ; j++)    /* Prints number from 1 to line number i.e. i */
            printf("%d", j);
        printf("\n");               /* Prints new line character to move to next line */

    }

}
```

Now consider the next example.

PROGRAM 10.11   Write a program to display the following figure for n number of lines.

```
      1
     1 2 3
    1 2 3 4 5
   1 2 3 4 5 6 7
   ................
   ................
```

```
#include<stdio.h>
void main( )
{   int n,i,j;
    printf("Enter no.of lines:");
    scanf("%d",&n);
    for(i=1;i<=n;i++)              /* Controls number of lines to print */
    {   for(j=1;j<=n-i;j++)        /*Controls number of spaces to print in each line */
            printf(" ");
        for(j=1;j<=2*i-1;j++)      /* Prints numbers */
```

```
        printf("%d",j);
      printf("\n");
  }
}
```

This program is similar to **program 10.10**. Only difference is in number printing. In each line printing starts from 1 but ended not with the line number. In 1st line it is 1, in 2nd line it is 3, in 3rd line it is 5 and so on. If **i** is the line number, the final value is (2*i–1). Thus in last *for* loop instead of j<=i the condition is written as **j<=2*i–1**.

But what happens in case of following figure.

PROGRAM 10.12   Write a program to display the following figure for n number of lines.

```
    1
   1 2 1
  1 2 3 2 1
 1 2 3 4 3 2 1
................
................
```

```c
#include<stdio.h>
void main()
{   int n,i,j;
    printf("Enter no.of lines:");
    scanf("%d", &n);
    for(i=1;i<=n;i++)          /* Controls number of lines to print */
    {   for(j=1;j<=n-i;j++)    /* Controls number of spaces to print in each line */
            printf(" ");
        for(j=1;j<=i;j++)      /* Prints increment part */
            printf("%d",j);
        for(j=i-1;j>=1;j--)    /* Prints decrement part */
            printf("%d",j);
        printf("\n");
    }
}
```

Here, in each line the numbers are incremented first and after mid point they are decremented. Thus the above program is same as previous one with an extra job in each line. That is why an extra *for* loop is required. In this loop, the number is decremented up to 1.

As *while* and *for* loop both are entry controlled loop, we can use the loops interchangeably (i.e., we can use *while* in place of *for* loop and vice-versa). Notice the program 10.4 and program 10.7, same problem is solved twice. First time using while loop and next time using for loop. But the question is when to use which one? The general concept is that when initialization, final value of loop index, proper increment or decrement are known, *for* statement is a better option. But when final value of loop index is not known or there is no proper increment or decrement of loop counter, *while* statement is better. As *for* statement generally contain all the 3 basic part of a loop, one can easily calculate exactly how many times the loop will execute. Thus *for* statement is also known as **definite** loop. But these 3 parts are not directly included in the *while* loop syntax. So, it is not always possible to calculate exactly how many times the loop will execute. At run time depending on the values of the variables it is decided. Thus *while* statement is known as **indefinite** loop.

10.5 TEST YOUR PROGRESS

What will be the output for the following programs?

(a)
```
#include<stdio.h>
void main()
{    int i=5;
     for(i--;i--;i--)
     {
          printf("%d ",i);
     }
     printf("%d ",i);
}
```

Output: 3 1 –1

(b)
```
#include<stdio.h>
void main()
{    int i=1;
     for(--i; --i; --i)
     {
          printf("%d ",i);
     }
     printf("%d ",i);
}
```

Output: –1 –3 –5 –7 –9 ....

(c)
```
#include<stdio.h>
void main()
{    int i=1;
     for(i++;i++;i++)
```

```
        {
              printf("%d ",i);
        }
        printf("%d ",i);
    }
```

Output: 3 5 7 .... –7 –3 –1 1

10.6 DO-WHILE STATEMENT

In 'C', do-while statement is a post-test iteration or exit controlled loop statement. Here body of the loop is executed first. Then the condition is tested whether the loop will execute next time or not. If the condition is true, the control continues to evaluate the body of the loop once again. When the condition becomes false, the loop will be terminated. As the body of the loop is executed first before the condition checked, the body of the loop is always executed at least once. The general form of do-while loop :

```
    do
        {
        ...  // body of the loop
        ...
        } while (condition);
```

We should pay close attention to that semicolon – it is not optional.

EXAMPLE 10.3

```
        int i = 5;
        do
        {  printf("%d ", i);
            i++;
        }  while(i<= 10);
```

The above example, will print: 5 6 7 8 9 10

But, consider the following example.

```
    int i = 5;
        do
        {  printf("%d ", i);
            i++;
        }  while(i>= 10);
```

The above example, will print: 5 . Because before condition checking, body of the loop will execute and will print 5. So, be careful in using do-while statement. This loop statement is useful in such situation where the loop executes at least once.

Now we will discuss two important statements which are related to loop statement. These are *break* statement and *continue* statement.

10.7 BREAK STATEMENT

We often face some situations when it is required to jump out from a loop instantly, without waiting to get back to the conditional test. For example, if we want to search a particular element from a list of 100 elements, we need to write a loop statement which will iterate 100 times and in each iteration it will read and check the element. But as soon as the desired element will be found, we need not to proceed further to check the rest elements. The keyword *break* allows us to do this. When *break* is encountered inside any loop, control automatically passes to the first statement after the loop. Following example illustrate this.

EXAMPLE 10.4

```
int i = 5;
while(i<= 10)
{   printf("%d ", i);
      if( i == 7)
            break;
      i++;
}
printf("%d ", i);
```

The above example will print : 5 6 7 7

In the above program as **i** is initialized with 5, condition is true and the control enters into the while loop. So, printf statement prints 5 as the current value of **i** is 5. In the next statement, condition related to *if* statement becomes false. Thus *break* statement will not execute. Next **i** will be incremented to 6 and looped back. The condition related to while loop is till true and control enters into while loop again. Thus 6 will be printed and incremented to 7. Similarly, in next iteration 7 will be printed. But this time, the *if* statement becomes true and the *break* statement will execute. So, control comes out from the loop and the printf statement immediate after the loop will execute and again prints 7.

If a *break* statement is encountered with in nested loop, the *break* statement sends the control out from the loop containing it, i.e., from the innermost loop and the first statement after the innermost loop will execute. Following example illustrate this.

EXAMPLE 10.5

```
int i = 1, j;
while(i<= 5)
{   printf("\n%d\t", i);
      j = 1;
      while( j<=5)
      {   printf("%d ", j);
            if(i == j)
                break;
```

```
        j++;
    }
    i++;
}
```

The above example will print : 1   1
                                2   1 2
                                3   1 2 3
                                4   1 2 3 4
                                5   1 2 3 4 5

In the above example, after printing the value of **i**, i.e., 1, control enters into inner loop and prints **j**, i.e., 1. As both **i** and **j** contains 1, if condition becomes true and the *break* statement is encountered. So, control jumps to the first statement after this loop and **i** incremented to 2. Similarly in next iteration of outer loop after printing the value of **i** as 2, **j** prints 1 and 2 before executing *break* statement. This process continues and we get the above output.

PROGRAM 10.13   Write a program to determine whether a number is prime or not.

```c
#include<stdio.h>

#include<conio.h>

void main( )
{
    int num, i, r = 1;
    printf ( "Enter a number " ) ;
    scanf ( "%d", &num ) ;

    for(i = 2; i<= num/2; i++)
    {
        r = num % i;
        if(r == 0)            /* once a number is divisible, need not to check further */
            break;
    }
    if ( r == 0)
        printf("%d is not a Prime Number", num);
    else

        printf("%d is a Prime Number", num);
}
```

Here, in the above program the moment the value of **r** becomes zero (i.e., num is exactly divisible by i), we need not check further. So, *break* statement is used and the control forcefully terminates the *for* loop.

But now we have to check in which way the control comes out from the loop. Because there are two possibilities by which the control could have reached outside the *for* loop:

i)   Due to the execution of *break* statement.

ii) The loop came to an end because the value of **i** became greater than num/2.

This problem can be solved in many ways. Here the value of **r** is tested. If control comes out due to *break* statement, the value of **r** must be zero. Otherwise **r** will contain some non zero value. Accordingly, when **r** becomes zero, the number will be treated as non prime number and when **r** becomes non-zero, the number will be treated as prime number.

10.8   USE OF GOTO

There are some situations where we need to come out forcefully from deeply nested loops. But *break* statement sends the control out from the innermost loop only and the first statement after the innermost loop will execute. That is control executes within the second innermost loop. There is no way to come out from deeply nested loop directly. *goto* statement helps us in this situation. Using *goto* statement we can easily come out from deeply nested loop. This is the only situation where *goto* statement is useful. Following example illustrates the use of *goto* statement in deeply nested loop.

EXAMPLE 10.6

```
void main( )
 {  int i, j, k, l;
    for(i=1; i<10; i++)
    {
        for( j=1; j<10; j++)
        {
            for(k=1; k<10; k++)
            {
                for( l=1; l<10; l++)
                {
                    printf("\n%d %d %d %d", i, j, k, l);
                    if ( l == 3)
                        goto out;
                }
            }
        }
    }
    out:
    printf("\nWe are out from deeply nested loop.");
 }
```

Output:

1 1 1 1

1 1 1 2

1 1 1 3

We are out from deeply nested loop.

10.9 CONTINUE STATEMENT

Some times in a program when we are continuing in a loop, it may happen that we need not to continue the rest portion of the body of the loop; instead next iteration needs to be started. In such situation, we need to bypass the rest statements inside the loop and sends control to the beginning of the loop. C provides a statement named *continue* which helps us to do this. The *continue* statement is used to transfer the control to the beginning of the loop, bypassing the statements between the *continue* statement and end of loop. Following example illustrates this.

Suppose we have to write a program which will take n number of inputs and among them find the average of only positive integers.

PROGRAM 10.14   Write a program to find the average of positive integers among n inputted numbers.

```
#include<stdio.h>
void main()
{
    int num, sum = 0, i, n, c = 0;
    float avg;
    printf("Enter Number of Elements:");
    scanf("%d",&n);
    for(i=1;i<=n;i++)
    {
        printf("Enter any Number:");
        scanf("%d",&num);
        if( num<=0)     /* to ignore the negative inputted numbers, if any */
            continue;
        sum+=num;
        c++;
    }
```

```
   avg=(float)sum/c;
   printf("Average = %f",avg);
}
```

In the above program when user inputs any negative number or zero the control will jump to the beginning of the loop bypassing the rest two statements in the loop. Thus, these values will not be considered in calculation of average.

10.10 TEST YOUR PROGRESS

What will be the output for the following programs?

(a)
```
#include<stdio.h>
void main()
{ int a = 1;
  while(a<10)
  {    printf("%d ",a);
       if(a==3)
            continue;
       a++;
  }
}
```

Output: 1 2 3 3 3 3 ......

(b)
```
#include<stdio.h>
void main()
{ int a = 1;
  while(a<10)
  { printf("%d ", a++);
    if(a==4)
       continue;
    a++;
  }
  printf("%d ",a);
}
```

Output: 1 3 4 6 8 10

10.11 PROGRAMMING EXAMPLES

Here are some programming examples to understand the various uses of loop statement.

PROGRAM 10.15   Write a program to find the factorial of a number.

```c
#include<stdio.h>
#include<conio.h>
void main( )
{    int num, i=1;
     long int fact =1;
     clrscr( );
     printf("Enter any Number : ");
     scanf("%d",&num);
     while(i <= num)
     {
         fact = fact * i;
         i++;
     }
     printf("Factorial of %d is %ld", num, fact);
}
```

PROGRAM 10.16   Write a C program to find the average of n numbers.

```c
#include<stdio.h>
void main()
{    int num,sum=0,i,n;
     float avg;
     printf("Enter Number of Elements:");
     scanf("%d",&n);
     for(i=1;i<=n;i++)
     {   printf("Enter any Number:");
         scanf("%d",&num);
         sum+=num;
     }
     avg=(float)sum/n;
     printf("Average = %f",avg);
}
```

PROGRAM 10.17   Write a C program to find the GCD and LCM *of* two positive integer numbers.

```c
#include<stdio.h>
void main()
{    int a,b,i,lcm;
     printf("Enter Any Two Non Negative Integers:");
     scanf("%d%d",&a,&b);
     i=b;
     while(i>1)
     {    if( a%i==0 && b%i==0)
             break;
```

```
        i--;
    }
    /*Now i becomes the GCD of a and b. */
    printf("GCD of %d,%d is %d",a,b,i);
    lcm=a*b/i;
    printf("\nand LCM of %d,%d is %d",a,b,lcm);
}
```

PROGRAM 10.18 Write a program in C which prints the smallest divisor of an integer, for example smallest divisor of 77 is 7.

```
#include<stdio.h>
void main()
{   int i,n,r;
    printf("Enter any Number : ");
    scanf("%d",&n);
    for(i=2;i<=n;i++)
    {   r = n%i;
        if(r==0)
        {   printf("Smallest Divisor of %d is %d",n,i);
                break;
        }
    }
}
```

PROGRAM 10.19 Write down the following program in C:

Input an M-digit number. Print its digit one by one (least significant but first).

```
#include<stdio.h>
void main( )
{   int n;
    printf("Enter any Number: ");
    scanf("%d",&n);
    printf("Digits of the number are : ");
    while( n>0)
    {   printf("%d, ", n%10);
        n=n/10;
    }
}
```

PROGRAM 10.20 Write a C function to reverse the digits of an integer.

```
#include<stdio.h>
void main()
{   int num,rev=0, result;
    printf("Enter any Number:");
```

```
    scanf("%d",&num);
    while(num>0)
    {    rev=rev*10+num%10;
         num=num/10;
    }
    printf("The Reverse Number is : %d", rev);
}
```

PROGRAM 10.21   Write a program to check a number is palindrome or not.

```
#include<stdio.h>
void main()
{
    while(num>0)
    {   rev=rev*10+num%10;
        num=num/10;
    }
    if(old==rev)
        printf("The number is Palindrome");
    else
        printf("The number is not a Palindrome");
}
```

PROGRAM 10.22   Write a C program, which accepts an integer numbers and prints the multiplication of the digits.

```
#include<stdio.h>
void main()
{
    int num,product=1,old;
    printf("Enter any Number:");
    scanf("%d",&num);
    old=num;
    while(num>0)
    {
        product = product * num%10;
        num=num/10;
    }
    printf("Multiplication of the digits of %d is %d", old, product);
}
```

PROGRAM 10.23   Write a program to accept a number and find sum of its individual digits repeatedly till the result is a single digit.

```
#include<stdio.h>
void main()
```

```
{   int num,sum;
    printf("Enter any Number:");
    scanf("%d",&num);
    while(num>9)
    {       sum=0;
            while(num>0)
            {       sum=sum+num%10;
                    num=num/10;
            }
            num=sum;
    }
    printf("Sum = %d",sum);
}
```

PROGRAM 10.24: The equation $x^2 + y^2 = r^2$ represents a circle with centers at origin and radius is r. Write a program that read r from the keyboard and print the number of points with integer co-ordinate that lie on the circumference of the circle.

```
#include<stdio.h>
#include<math.h>
#include<conio.h>
void main()
{ int x,y,r;
  clrscr();
  printf("Enter Radious : ");
  scanf("%d",&r);
  for(x=0;x<=r;x++)
  {     y=sqrt(r*r-x*x);
        printf("\n(%d, %d)",x,y);
        printf("\n(%d, %d)",x,-y);
  }
  for(x=-1;x>=-r;x--)
  {     y=sqrt(r*r-x*x);
        printf("\n(%d, %d)",x,y);
        printf("\n(%d, %d)",x,-y);
  }
}
```

PROGRAM 10.25 Write a program to print the series as given along with the sum

1−2+3−4+5 .... n.

```
#include<stdio.h>
void main()
{     int num,sum=0,i,n;
```

```
        printf("Enter Number of Terms:");
        scanf("%d",&n);
        for(i=1;i<=n;i++)
        {       printf("%d",i);
                if(i%2==1)
                {       sum+=i;
                        printf("-");
                }
                else
                {       sum-=i;
                        printf("+");
                }
        }
        printf("\b=%d",sum);
}
```

PROGRAM 10.26   Write a program to print the summation of the following series:

$$1 + \frac{1}{2^2} + \frac{1}{3^2} + \frac{1}{4^2} + \dots\dots\dots + \frac{1}{N^2}$$

```
#include<stdio.h>
void main()
{       int i,c,n;
        float sum=0;
        printf("Enter No. of Terms: ");
        scanf("%d",&n);
        for(c=1;c<=n;c++)
        {
                sum += (float)1/(c*c);
        }
        printf("Sum = %f",sum);
}
```

PROGRAM 10.27   Write a program to print the sum of the following series of n terms:

$$s = 1 + (1 + 2) + (1 + 2 + 3)+\dots\dots\dots$$

```
#include<stdio.h>
void main()
{       int i,c,n,s,sum=0;
        printf("Enter No. of Terms: ");
        scanf("%d",&n);
        for(c=1;c<=n;c++)
        {   s=0;
```

```
        for(i=1;i<=c;i++)
                s += i;
        sum += s;
    }
    printf("Sum = %d",sum);
}
```

PROGRAM 10.28   Write a program to add the following series:

1 + 2/2! + 3/3! + ... + n/n!, value of n given by user.

```
#include<stdio.h>
void main()
{    int i,c,n;
     float fact,sum=0;
     printf("Enter No. of Terms: ");
     scanf("%d",&n);
     for(c=1;c<=n;c++)
     {      fact=1;
            for(i=1;i<=c;i++)        /* Calculates factorial of c */
                fact *= i;
            sum += c/fact;
     }
     printf("Sum = %f",sum);
}
```

PROGRAM 10.29   Write a program to evaluate the series.

$1 + x/1! + x^2/2! + x^3/3! + \ldots\ldots\ldots + x^n/n!$

```
#include<stdio.h>
#include<math.h>
void main()
{       int i,c,n, x;
        float fact,sum=0;
        printf("Enter value of n: ");
        scanf("%d",&n);
        printf("Enter value of x: ");
        scanf("%d",&x);

        for(c=0;c<=n;c++)
        {       fact=1;
                for(i=1;i<=c;i++)     /* Calculates factorial of c */
                        fact *= i;
                sum += pow(x,c)/fact;
        }
        printf("Sum = %f",sum);
}
```

PROGRAM 10.30   Write a program to find the result of the following series:
$\sin(x) = x - x^3/3! + x^5/5! + x^7/7! + \ldots\ldots + x^n/n!$ (where the value of x and n are supplied by the user as an input).

```c
#include<stdio.h>
#include<math.h>
void main()
{   int i,c,n,x;
    float fact,sum=0;
    printf("Enter the value of n: ");
    scanf("%d",&n);
    printf("Enter the value of x: ");
    scanf("%d",&x);

    for(c=1;c<=n;c=c+2)
    {   fact=1;
        for(i=1;i<=c;i++)          /* Calculates factorial of c */
          fact *= i;
        if(c==3)                   /* When value of c is 3, then only value will */
            sum -= pow(x,c)/fact;  /*be subtracted, otherwise it will be added */
        else
            sum += pow(x,c)/fact;
    }
    printf("Sum = %f", sum);
}
```

PROGRAM 10.31   Write C code to print

```
1
2    3
4    5    6
7    8    9    10
11   12   13   14   15
```

```c
#include<stdio.h>
void main()
{   int n,i,j,k=1;
    printf("Enter no.of lines:");
    scanf("%d",&n);
    for(i=1;i<=n;i++)
    {
       for(j=1;j<=i;j++)
          printf("\t%2d",k++);
       printf("\n");
    }
}
```

PROGRAM **10.32** Write a program to print

A
A B
A B C
A B C D
A B C D E

```c
#include<stdio.h>
void main()
{   int n,i,j;
    char ch;
    printf("Enter no. of lines:");
    scanf("%d", &n);

    for(i=1; i<=n; i++)
    {
        for(j=1, ch='A'; j<=i; j++, ch++)
            printf("%c",ch);
        printf("\n");
    }
}
```

PROGRAM **10.33** Write a program to print

1
0 1
1 0 1
0 1 0 1
1 0 1 0 1

```c
#include<stdio.h>
void main()
{   int n,i,j,k;
    printf("Enter no. of lines:");
    scanf("%d",&n);

    for(i=1;i<=n;i++)
    {
        for(j=1,k=i;j<=i;j++,k++)
            printf("%d",k%2);
        printf("\n");
    }
}
```

PROGRAM 10.34   Write a C program to print

```
      1
    1 0 1
  1 0 1 0 1
1 0 1 0 1 0 1
```

```c
#include<stdio.h>
void main( )
{    int n,i,j;
     printf("Enter no. of lines:");
     scanf("%d",&n);
     for(i=1;i<=n;i++)
     {    for(j=1;j<=n-i;j++)
              printf(" ");
          for(j=1;j<=2*i-1;j++)
              printf("%d", j%2);
          printf("\n");
     }
}
```

PROGRAM 10.35   Write C code to print

```
A   B   C   D   E   F   E   D   C   B   A
A   B   C   D   E       E   D   C   B   A
A   B   C   D               D   C   B   A
A   B   C                       C   B   A
A   B                               B   A
A                                       A
```

```c
#include<stdio.h>
void main()
{    int i,j,n;
     char ch;
     printf("Enter number of lines: ");
     scanf("%d",&n);
     for(i=0;i<=n;i++)
     {    for(j=0,ch='A';j<=n-i;j++)
              printf("%c",ch++);
          for(j=0;j<=2*i-2;j++)
              printf(" ");
          if(i == 0)
              ch--;
          for(;ch>'A';)
              printf("%c",--ch);
          printf("\n");
     }
}
```

SUMMARY

➤ The mechanism, which helps us to perform an action over and over, is the 'loop' or 'iteration'.

➤ Loops are of two types, **entry controlled loop** and **exit controlled loop**.

➤ When condition is checked before the execution of the body of the loop, it is called entry controlled loop or pre test iteration.

➤ But when condition is checked after the execution of the body of the loop, it is called exit controlled loop or post test iteration.

➤ In C, **while** and **for** are of entry controlled type loop statements and **do-while** is of exit-controlled type loop statement.

➤ In comparison to *for* and *while* statements, when initialization, final value of loop index, proper increment or decrement are known, *for* statement is a better option. But when final value of loop index is not known or there is no proper increment or decrement of loop counter, *while* statement is better.

➤ In comparison to *for* and *while* statement with the *do-while* statement, the *for* and *while* loop may not execute single time whereas the *do-while* will execute at least once.

➤ When a loop is defined under another loop, it is called nested loop.

➤ When *break* statement is encountered inside any loop, control automatically passes to the first statement after the loop.

➤ If a *break* statement is encountered with in nested loop, the *break* statement sends the control out from the innermost loop only.

➤ The continue statement is used to transfer the control to the beginning of the loop, bypassing the statements between the continue statement and end of loop.

REVIEW EXERCISES

1. What do you mean by iteration?
2. What is the utility of loop or iterative statement?
3. What is entry control loop? What is exit control loop?
4. What are the different types of loop statement available in C?
5. Differentiate between while loop and do-while loop.
6. Differentiate between break and continue statements.
7. Differentiate between break and goto statements.
8. Write a C program to find the maximum between n inputted numbers.
9. Write a program in C to print all numbers between 100 and 200 which are divisible by 5 but not divisible by 15.
10. What will be the output for the following programs?

    (a)
    ```c
    #include<stdio.h>
    void main()
    { int i=1;
      for(i--;i--;i--)
    ```

```
    {
        printf("%d ",i);
    }
    printf("%d ",i);
}
```

(b)   ```
      #include<stdio.h>
      void main()
      { int i=2;
        for(--i;--i;--i)
        {
            printf("%d ",i);
        }
        printf("%d ",i);
      }
      ```

(c)   ```
      #include<stdio.h>
      void main()
      { int i=6;
        for(--i;--i;--i)
        {
            printf("%d ",i);
        }
        printf("%d ",i);
      }
      ```

(d)   ```
      #include<stdio.h>
      void main()
      { int a = 1;
        while(a<10)
        { printf("%d ",a++);
          if(a==3)
             continue;
          a++;
        }
        printf("%d ",a);
      }
      ```

11. Write C programs to display the following series:

(a) 1, 4, 7, 10, 13 ................. upto n terms

(b) 1, 1, 2, 4, 7, 11, 16 ........... upto n terms

(c) 2, 5, 10, 17, ................. upto n terms

(d) 1, 10, 101, 1010 ................. upto n terms

12. Write C programs to calculate the sum of the following series:

(a) 2 + 4 + 6 + 8 + ................. upto n terms

(b) 1 + 2 + 4 + 7 + 11 + 16 + ................. upto n terms
      ```

(c) $1 + 11 + 111 + 1111 + \ldots\ldots\ldots\ldots$ upto n terms

(d) $1^2 + 3^2 + 5^2 + 7^2 + \ldots\ldots\ldots\ldots$ upto n terms

(e) $1 + 2^2 + 3^3 + 4^4 + \ldots\ldots\ldots\ldots$ upto n terms

(f) $1 - 2^2/3! + 3^2/5! - 4^2/7! + \ldots\ldots\ldots$ upto n terms

13. Write a C program to reverse an integer number, subtract 9 from the reversed number and print the result. [For example, *if* the given number is 678; then its reverse is 876. Subtracting 9 will give 867.]

14. If the sum of the factors of a number (excluding the number itself) is equal to the number itself, the number is known as Perfect Number. Write a C program to check whether an inputted number is a perfect number or not [For example, $6 = 1+2+3$, $28 = 1+2+4+7+14$].

15. Write a C program to display all three digited Armstrong number. Three digited Armstrong numbers are the numbers whose sum of cube of the digits of the number is equals to the number [For example, $153 = 1^3+5^3+3^3$].

16. Write a C program to check whether an inputted number is Peterson number or not. A Peterson number is a number whose sum of factorial of digits equals to the number [For example, $145 = 1! +4! +5!$].

17. Write a C program to display the following triangle:

(a) *
```
   *  *
   *  *  *
   *  *  *  *   ..... upto n lines
```

(b)
```
        4
      4 3
    4 3 2
  4 3 2 1   ..... upto n lines
```

(c)
```
4 3 2 1
  4 3 2
    4 3
      4   ..... upto n lines
```

(d)
```
        1
      2   2
    3   3   3
  4 4   4 4   ..... upto n lines
```

(e)
```
        4
      4 3 4
    4 3 2 3 4
  4 3 2 1 2 3 4   ..... upto n lines
```

(f)
```
  4 3 2 1 2 3 4
    4 3 2 3 4
      4 3 4
        4         ..... upto n lines
```

(g)   4
            4 3 4
          4 3 2 3 4
        4 3 2 1 2 3 4
          4 3 2 3 4
            4 3 4
              4   ..... upto n lines

(h)   1
            1 2 1
          1 2 3 2 1
        1 2 3 4 3 2 1
          1 2 3 2 1
            1 2 1
              1   ..... upto n lines

(i) * * * * *
      * * * * *
        * * * * *
      * * * * *
    * * * * *   ..... upto n lines

(j)   * * * * *
        * * * * *
      * * * * *
        * * * * *
          * * * * * ..... upto n lines

(k) * * * * *
    *   *
    *   *
    *   *
    * * * * *   ..... upto n lines

LEARN BY QUIZ – QUESTIONS

1. What will be the output?

```
printf("1");
printf("2");
goto calcutta:
printf("3");
printf("4");
printf("5");
printf("6");
calcutta:
printf("7");
printf("8");
```

(1) 1278
(2) 12345678
(3) 12783456

2. What will be the output?

```
int know;
know=5;
comehere:
printf("%d", know);
know=know+1;
if (know<10) goto comehere:
```

(1) 56789
(2) 5678910
(3) 5

3. Which statement is true regarding loop?
   (1) a loop terminates when a particular condition is satisfied.
   (2) a loop executes always a specific number of times.
   (3) a loop terminates when the first printf() is encountered.

4. What will be the output of the following program segment?

```
int know;
for(know=0;know<=5;know=know+1)
printf("%d", know);
```

(1) 012345
(2) 01234
(3) 0123456

5. What will be the output of the following program segment?

```
int know;
for(know=5;know>=0; know=know-1)
printf("%d",know);
```

(1) 543210
(2) 54321
(3) 543210-1

6. What will be the output of the following program segment?

```
int i, sum;
sum=0;
for(i=1;i<=5;i++)
{
sum=sum+i;
printf("sum=%d\n",sum);
}
```

(1) sum=1 sum=3 sum=6 sum=10 sum=15
(2) sum=1 sum=2 sum=3 sum=4 sum=5
(3) sum=15

7. What will be the output of the following program segment?

```
int ab;
for(ab=0; ab<256;ab++)
printf("%c\n", ab);
```

(1) All ASCII characters
(2) all integers in the range 0 to 255
(3) compilation error

8. What will be the output of the following program segment if a 16 bit compiler is used?

```
int abc;
for(abc=0; abc<=32767;abc++)
printf("%d\n", abc);
```

(1) infinite loop
(2) all numbers from 0 to 32767
(3) all numbers from 0 to 32766

9. What will be the output of the following program segment?

```
int know, factor;
for(know=1,factor=1; factor<10; ++factor)
{
know=know*factor;
printf("%d", know);
}
```

(1) 46
(2) 37
(3) 29

10. for the program segment

```
int know;
for(know=1;know<=10;know=know+1)
printf("%d\n",know);
```

which of the following is correct alternative?

(1)
```
int know=1;
for(;know<=10;)
{
printf("%d\n",know);
know=know+1;
}
```

(2)
```
int know;
for(;know<=10;know=know+1)
{
printf("%d\n",know);
}
```

(3)
```
int know;
for(know=1;know<=10;)
printf("%d\n",know);
```

11. What will be the output of the following program segment?

```
int know1,know2,know3;
for(know1=1, know2=20; know1<=know2; know1++, know2-)
know3=know1+know2;
printf("%d##%d##%d", know1,know2,know3);
```

(1) 11##10##21
(2) 10##10##21
(3) 10##10##20

12. What will be the output of the following program segment?

```
int i, sum=0;
for(i=1;i< 20 &&  sum<100; i++)
sum+=i;
printf("%d %d", i, sum);
```

(1) 15 105
(2) 15 100
(3) 20 210

13. What will be the output of the following program segment?

```
int know, m=60, n=4;
for(know=(m+n)/2;know>1;know=know/2)
printf("%d\t", know);
```

(1) 32   16   8   4   2
(2) 16   8   4   2   1
(3) 2   4   8   16   32

14. What will be the output of the following program segment?

```
int know;
for(know=0;know++<5;)
printf("%d", know);
```

(1) 12345
(2) 01234
(3) 05101520

15. What will be the output of the following program segment?

```
int know;
for(know=5;know;know--)
printf("%d", know);
```

(1) 54321
(2) 543210
(3) condition part is incomplete

16. What will be the output of the following program segment?

```
int know;
for(know=1;know++<=5;printf("%d",know));
```

(1) 23456
(2) 12345
(3) compilation error

17. What will be the output of the following program segment?

```
int magic=5;
for(;magic!=20;)
{
printf("%d", magic);
magic=magic+5;}
```

(1) 51015
(2) 5101520
(3) 123451015

18. What will be the output of the following program segment?

```
for(know=10;know>0;know--);
printf("%d",know);
```

(1) 0
(2) 10987654321
(3) 1

19. What will be the output of the following program segment?

```
int k1,k2,sum=0;
for(k1=1;k1<3;k1++)
{
    for(k2=1;k2<=2;k2++)
        sum=sum+k1+k2;
}
printf("%d", sum);
```

(1) 12
(2) 11
(3) 13

20. In a for loop with a multi-statement loop body ; should appear following
     (1) each statement of the loop body
     (2) the for statement itself
     (3) the closing brace of the multiple statement loop body.

21. What will be the output of the following program segment?

```
#include<stdio.h>
void main(void)
{
int x,y;
for(x=1;x<=4;x++)
{
  for(y=0;y<x;y++)
  printf("*");
  printf("\n");
}
}
```

(1) *
     * *
     * * *
     * * * *

(2)   *
           * *
         * * *
       * * * *

(3) * * * *
     * * *
     * *
     *

22. What will be the output of the following program segment?

```
#include<stdio.h>
void main(void)
{
int x,y,z;
for(x=0;x<5;x++)
{
```

```
for(y=0; y<(4-x); y++)
printf(" ");
 for(z=0; z<x; z++)
 printf("*");
 printf("\n");
}
}
```

(1)
```
*
* *
* * *
* * * *
```

(2)
```
      *
    * *
  * * *
* * * *
```

(3)
```
* * * *
* * *
* *
*
```

23. What will be the output of the following program segment?
```
#include<stdio.h>
void main(void)
{
int x,y;
for(x=4; x>0; x--)
{
for(y=0; y<x; y++)
printf("*");
printf("\n");
}
}
```

(1)
```
*
* *
* * *
* * * *
```

(2)
```
      *
    * *
  * * *
* * * *
```

(3)
```
* * * *
* * *
* *
*
```

24. What will be the output of the following program segment?
```
int know=1;
while(know<=5)
{
printf("%d",know);
know=know+1;
}
```

    (1) 12345
    (2) 123456
    (3) 13579

25. What will be the output of the following program segment?

```
int know=5;
while(know>=1)
know--;
printf("%d",know);
```

    (1) 0
    (2) 1
    (3) −1

26. What will be the output of the following program segment?

```
int know=1;
while(know<=10)
printf("%d",know);
```

    (1) it will go for infinite loop
    (2) it will generate compilation error
    (3) it will print 1 to 10

27. What will be the output of the following program segment?

```
float xx=5.0;
while(xx<=5.5)
{
printf("%f\t",xx);
xx=xx+0.1;
}
```

    (1) 5.0000 5.1000 5.2000 5.4000 5.5000
    (2) loop variable cannot be a floating point number
    (3) 5.5000

28. What will be the output of the following program segment?

```
int know=1;
while(know<=32767)
{
printf("%d\n", know);
know++;
}
```

    (1) it will go for infinite loop
    (2) it will print all positive integer values
    (3) only 32767 will be displayed

29. What will be the output of the following program segment?

```
int know=1;
while(know<=10);
{
printf("%d\n", know);
know++;
}
```

    (1) it will go infinitely
    (2) 12345678910
    (3) 123456789

30. What will be the output of the following program segment?

```
int know=1;
while (++know<5)
printf ("%d\n", know);
```

(1) 234
(2) 1234
(3) 12345

31. What will be the output of the following program segment?

```
int know=1,factor=1;
while (know<4)
{        while (factor<3)
         {     printf ("%d\t", know+factor);
               factor++;
         }
         know++;
}
```

(1) 2 3
(2) 2 3 3 4 4 5
(3) 2 3 4 5 6 7

32. What will be the output of the following program segment if the input is 'y'

```
char c;
do{
printf ("enter y to terminate");
scanf ("%c", &c);
printf ("loop executed");
}while (c!= 'y');
```

(1) loop executed
(2) blank output
(3) y

33. What will be the output of the following program segment?

```
int digit, num, sum=0;
scanf ("%d", &num);
do{
digit=num%10;
sum+=digit;
num/=10;
}while (num!=0);
```

(1) it will display the sum of the digits of a number.
(2) it will display the sum of the numbers taken as input.
(3) it will display the sum of the numbers those are divisible by 10.

34. What will be the output of the following program segment?

```
int know=1;
do{
know++;
printf ("Hello#");
}while (know<4);
```

(1) Hello# Hello# Hello#
(2) Hello#
(3) Hello# Hello# Hello# Hello#

35. Fill the blank

A do-while loop is useful when we want that the statements within the loop must be executed_____

  (1) at least once

  (2) only once

  (3) more than once

36. Choose the appropriate sequence of the actions **INITIALIZATION, TESTING and EXECUTION OF BODY** done in a do-while loop?

  (1) **INITIALIZATION ,EXECUTION OF BODY ,TESTING**

  (2) **EXECUTION OF BODY , INITIALIZATION , TESTING**

  (3) **INITIALIZATION , TESTING , EXECUTION OF BODY**

37. What will be the output of the following program segment?

```
int know;
for(know=1; know<=10; know++)
{
if (know==5) break;
else
printf("%d\n",know);
}
```

  (1) 1 2 3 4

  (2) 1 2 3 4 5

  (3) 1 2 3 4 5 6 7 8 9 10

38. What will be the output of the following program segment if the input is 13?

```
int i,num;
i=2;
scanf("%d", &num);
while(i<=num-1)
{    if(num%i==0)
     {
          printf("not a prime number");
          break;
     }
i++;
}
if(i==num)
printf("prime number");
```

  (1) prime number

  (2) not a prime number

  (3) blank output

39. **break** statement is used to exit from which of the following?

  (1) a **for** loop

  (2) a program

  (3) an **if** statement

40. What will be the output of the following program segment?

```
int know, factor;
for(know=1; know<=2; know++)
{     for(factor=1; factor<=2; factor++)
      {    if(know==factor) continue;
```

```
                    printf("%d %d \n", know, factor);
          }
  }
```

(1) 12   21
(2) 11   12   21   22
(3) blank output

41. Which of the following statements is used to take the control to the beginning of the loop for next pass?
    (1) continue
    (2) break
    (3) exit

42. Which of the following loop will not iterate infinitely?
    (1)
```
int y,x=0;
do{
y=x;
}while(x==0);
```

    (2)
```
int i=1;
while(1)
i++;
```

    (3) `for(;;);`

43. What will be the output of the following program segment?
```
int factor,know=1;
do
{     for(factor=1;;factor++)
        {
            if(factor>2) break;
            if(know==factor) continue;
            printf("%d%d\n", know,factor);
        }
know++;
}while(know<3);
```

    (1) 12   21
    (2) 11   12   21   22
    (3) 11   22

44. How many times the string **KnowledgeFactor** will be printed by the following program segment?
```
while(1)
{
    if(printf("%d", printf("KnowledgeFactor")))
        break;
    else
        continue;
}
```

    (1) 1
    (2) 2
    (3) infinite times

45. What will be the output of the following program segment?

```
int know=3;
while(know<6)
know>0?know++:know--;
printf("%d",know);
```

(1) 6
(2) 3
(3) 0

46. which of the following keyword is used to jump out of a loop without waiting to get back to the conditional test
(1) break
(2) continue
(3) exit

47. What will be the output of the following program segment?

```
int i,j,tag;
for(i=1;i<=30;i++)
{    tag=1;
     for(j=2;j<=i-1;j++)
     {    if(i%j==0)
          {    tag=0;
               break;
          }
     }
     if(tag==1)
         printf("%d",i);
}
```

(1) it will print all the prime numbers from 1 to 30
(2) it will print all the numbers from 1 to 30
(3) it will print all the odd numbers from 1 to 30

48. What will be the output of the following program segment?

```
int i,j,fact=1;
float val=0;
for(i=1;i<=5;i++)
{for(j=1;j<=i;j++)
fact*=j;
val+=i/fact;
}
printf("%f",val);
```

(1) It will print the series (1/1!)+(2/2!)+(3/3!)+(4/4!)+(5/5!)
(2) It will print the series 1!+2!+3!+4!+5!
(3) It will print the series (1/1!)+(1/2!)+(1/3!)+(1/4!)+(1/5!)

49. What will be the output of the following program segment?

```
int num1,num2=0,digit;
scanf("%d",&num1);
while(num1>0)
{  digit=num1%10;
   num2=num2*10+digit;
   num1=num1/10;
}
printf("%d",num2);
```

(1) it will print the reverse of the input number
(2) it will print the input number
(3) it will print the sum of the digits of the input number

50. Which statement is wrong regarding the following program segment?

```
int i,num1,num2=0,digit;
printf("enter a number");
scanf("%d",&num1);
i=num1;
while(num1>0)
{   digit=num1%10;
    num2=num2*10+digit;
    num1=num1/10;
}
if(i==num2)
printf("succeed");
```

(1) it will print succeed if the input number is divisible by 10
(2) it will print succeed if the input number is a palindrome
(3) it will print nothing if the input number is not a palindrome

51. What will be the output of the following program segment?

```
int i,num1,num2=0,digit;
printf("enter a 3 digit number");
scanf("%d",&num1);
i=num1;
while(num1>0)
{   digit=num1%10;
    num2=num2+pow(digit,3);
    num1=num1/10;
}
if(i==num2)
printf("succeed");
```

(1) it will print succeed if the input is an Armstrong number
(2) it will print succeed if the input is not an Armstrong number
(3) it will print succeed if the input can be represented as the cube of a number.

52. If the annual rate of interest is r% and interest is given q times per year, the principle amount p will be compounded to the amount a in n years using the formula:

$$a=p(1+r/q)^{nq}$$

Which of the following program segment can not do the above computation for 5 years?

(1)
```
double p,a=0;
float r,q;
int n;
scanf("%lf,%f%f%d",&p,&r,&q,&n);
for(n=0;n<5;n++)
{
a=p*pow((1+(r/q)),(n*q));
printf("%lf",a);
}
```

(2)
```
double p,a=0;
float r,q;
```

```
int n;
scanf("%lf,%f%f%d",&p,&r,&q,&n);
n=1;
while(n<=5)
{
a=p*pow((1+(r/q)),(n*q));
printf("%lf",a);
n++;
}
```

(3)
```
double p,a=0;
float r,q;
int n;
scanf("%lf,%f%f%d",&p,&r,&q,&n);
n=1;
do
{
a=p*pow((1+(r/q)),(n*q));
printf("%lf",a);
n++;
} while(n<=5);
```

53. What will be the output of the following program segment?
```
int i,j,num1=1,num2=10;
for(i=1;num1<=num2;i++)
{   for(j=1;j<(num2/2)-i;j++)
        printf(" ");
    for(j=1;j<=i;j++)
    {
        printf("%d",num1++);
        printf(" ");
    }
    printf("\n");
}
```

(1)
```
        1
       2 3
      4  5  6
   7   8  9 10
```

(2)
```
        1
        23
        456
        78910
```

(3)
```
        1
        234
        5678910
```

54. What will be the output of the following program segment?
```
int i=3,fib1=1,fib2=1,temp;
printf("%d\n%d\n",fib1,fib2);
while(i<=10)
{   temp=fib1+fib2;
    fib1=fib2;
    fib2=temp;
```

```
    printf("%d\n",fib2);
    i++ ;
}
```

(1) it will print the first 10 Fibonacci numbers
(2) it will print the sum of first 10 numbers
(3) it will reversely print the first 10 Fibonacci numbers

LEARN BY QUIZ – ANSWERS

Answer explanations

1. The output will be 1278. **goto** is an unconditional jump statement. After printing 12 the control will jump to label **Calcutta**. So the statements after **Calcutta**: will be executed, i.e., 78 will be printed.

2. The output will be 56789. goto is an unconditional jump statement. The role of goto is to transfer program control to the label name specified along with. But here it has been used clubbed with conditional statement **if**. So the jump to **comehere:** will continue until value of know reaches 10. When know will be 10 the goto statement will not execute anymore.

3   a loop terminates when a particular condition is satisfied. If no terminating condition is specified a **loop** will run forever.

    There are two general categories of loop. 1. Deterministic loop 2. Non-deterministic loop. For a deterministic loop observing code it can be said that how many times the loop will iterate. i.e., the loop executes a specific number of times but in case of non deterministic loop the number of iteration changes and cannot be predicted earlier.

4. The output will be 012345.

    the for loop → for(know=0;know<=5;know=know+1) will run starting with value of know = 0 and exit when value of know will be 6 and value of know will be incremented by one in each iteration due to know=know+1. So the body of the for loop, i.e., the printf() statement will be executed for know=0,1,2,3,4,5.

5. The output will be 543210.

    The for loop → for(know=5;know>=0;know=know−1) will run starting with value of know 5 and each time decrementing the value by 1 and exit when value of know will be −1. So the body of the for loop, i.e., the printf() statement will be executed for know=543210.

6. The output will be **sum=1 sum=3 sum=6 sum=10 sum=15**.

    The for loop for(i=1;i<=5;i++) will run starting the value of i as 1, incrementing it by 1 in each iteration and exit when it becomes 6. During each iteration of the for loop, the variable sum will be changed by adding its current value with the loop variable i. As the printf() statement is within the for loop, it will print the value of the variable sum in each iteration.

7. The output will be **All ASCII characters**.

    The for loop runs by initializing the loop variable to 0 and run up to the loop variable becomes 255. It is a single statement for loop body, so the printf() will be executed for each iteration of the for loop. As the character equivalent of the integer variable ab has been printed each time, it will print the ASCII characters as their value ranges from 0 to 255.

8. The output will be **infinite loop**.

    The for loop starts with the value of the loop counter as 0, increments in each iteration by 1 and reaches to 32767. as the loop now wants to increment abc whose value is 32767 by 1, it does not changes to 32768 rather changes to −32768 as we have already know that in the integer value range the number after 32767 is −32768. Here in the program segment, the loop terminating condition is abc's value will be 32768 which never comes. So the loop will never end and will go for infinite times.

9. The output will be 46.

Here the initialization part of the for loop initializes two variables know and factor. The loop goes until the value of factor becomes 10. As the printf() statement is within the for loop, it will print the changed value of know in each iteration.

10. The correct alternative is

```
int know=1;
for(;know<=10;)
{
printf("%d\n",know);
know=know+1;
}
```

the for loop syntax has three parts – initialization, condition checking and step value each separated by a ;. Each of these 3 parts is optional if they are properly placed elsewhere. In this case, the initialization should be prior to the loop and step value should be mentioned prior to the end of loop brace. Mentioning of these parts in proper places is mandatory otherwise loop will not execute as desired. So a for loop syntax with initialization, condition checking and step value is equivalent to a for loop syntax without mentioning them and mentioning them elsewhere.

11. The output will be **11##10##21**.

The for loop in the program segment has two loop variables – know1 and know2. The first one increases and the second one decreases in each iteration. The loop terminates when the value of know1 exceeds know2. So when the value of know1=11 and know2=10 the loop ends. know3 will hold the sum of know1 and know2 that is 11+10=21.

12. The output will be **15 105**.

Here the condition part of the for loop contains the relational operator &&. So the loop will run until both the conditions are satisfied. If any one of them becomes false the loop will not further be executed. Here the value of i when becomes 14, the sum takes the value 105 thus violating the second condition. So the loop will end but before it happened it will increment the value of i to 15.

13. The output will be **32   16   8   4 2**.

the for loop → for(know=(m+n)/2;know>1;know=know/2) will run starting with value of know (60+4)/2, i.e., 32 and each time decrementing the value by ½ the value of know and exit when value of know will be 1. So the body of the for loop, i.e., the printf() statement will be executed for know= 32 16 8 4 2.

14. The output will be **12345**.

The for loop syntax has three parts – initialization, condition checking and step value each separated by a ;. Each of these 3 parts is optional.

The for loop will start running with the value of know as 0. The condition checking part itself increments the value of know by 1 after completing the value of checking. So the printf() statement will print the incremented value. As step value is already given in the condition part, it is no longer needed to be mentioned elsewhere.

15. The output will be **54321**.

    The for loop → for(know=5;know;know− −) will run starting with value of know 5 and each time decrementing the value by 1 and runs till the value of know is a nonzero one, i.e., until it reaches 0. So the body of the for loop, i.e., the printf() statement will be executed for know = 54321.

16. The output will be **23456**.

    The for loop will start running with the value of know as 1. The condition checking part itself increments the value of know by 1 after completing the value of checking. So the printf() statement will print the incremented value. As step value is already given in the condition part, it is no longer needed to be mentioned elsewhere.

17. The output will be **51015**.

    The for loop syntax has three parts – initialization, condition checking and step value each separated by a ;. Each of these 3 parts is optional if they are properly placed elsewhere. In this case, the initialization should be prior to the loop and step value should be mentioned prior to the end of loop brace. Mentioning of these parts in proper places is mandatory. So a for loop syntax with initialization, condition checking and step value is equivalent to a for loop syntax without mentioning them and mentioning them elsewhere.

18. The output will be **0**.

    The for loop → for(know=10;know>0;know− −) will run starting with value of know 10 and each time decrementing the value by 1 and runs till the value of know is a nonzero one, i.e., until it reaches 0. But a semicolon(;) is given just after the for loop syntax which means that the for loop will execute without executing any body of the loop. So the printf() statement will be executed once after the for loop completes and will print the value of final know = 0.

19. The output will be **12**.

    It is an example of a nested for loop. The outer for loop that is for(k1=1;k1<3;k1++) will start from k1=1 and will go up to k1=2 and for each value of k1 the inner for loop, i.e., for(k2=1;k2<=2;k2++) will start from k2=1 and will go up to k2=2. The printf() statement will print the final value of sum which is 12.

20. In a **for** loop with a multi-statement loop body ; should appear following each statement of the loop body as usual as in the case of normal compound statements of C and there should not be any ; after the closing brace of the compound statement.

    If a ; is applied after the for statement itself then it will not give any error but the for statement will have no relationship with the following compound statement. Whatever times the for loop repeats, the compound statement will execute only once.

21. The internal for loop →
    ```
    for(j=0;j<i;j++)
    printf("*");
    ```
    will print * for i number of times.
    The external for loop can be viewed as follows:–
    ```
    for(i=1;i<5;i++)
    {
    Internal For Loop.
    Print New Line Character To Send The Cursor To Next Line.
    }
    ```
    This external for loop will iterate 4 times with value of i = 1,2,3 and 4, respectively.

(1) In the first iteration, one star will be printed for the internal loop. Then cursor will go to next line.

(2) In the second iteration, two stars will be printed for the internal loop. Then cursor will go to next line.

(3) In the third iteration, three stars will be printed for the internal loop. Then cursor will go to next line.

(4) In the fourth iteration, four stars will be printed for the internal loop. Then cursor will go to next line. Then the program will terminate.

So the output will be

```
*
* *
* *   *
* *   *   *
```

22.
```
              *
        *   *
     *   *   *
   *   *   *   *
```

23. ** * *
```
  * *   *
  * *
  *
```

24. Here the loop counter is initialized at 1 and according to the test expression the loop will go until the value of the loop counter becomes 5. Each time the loop counter will be incremented by 1. So the printf() statement within the loop will print the value of know for each execution of the loop body and as a result it will print 12345.

When the loop terminates the value of the loop counter becomes 6 but as this is the loop terminating condition this time the body of the loop will not be executed, so 6 will not be printed.

25. Here the loop counter is initialized to 5 and it each time the loop executes it is decremented by 1 until it reaches to 1. When the value of the counter is 1, then also the test condition satisfies and the body of the loop executes, thus decrements the value of the variable know to 0. Here the loop test expression fails and the loop terminates. As the printf() statement is written outside the loop, it will print the final value of know that is 0.

26. Here the loop variable is initialized to 1. The test condition checks whether the value of know is less than or equal to 10 or not, but here the counter is not incremented or decremented. So know remains equal to 1 forever. So the test condition remains true always and the loop will never terminate.

27. It is not necessary that a loop counter must only be an int. It can even be a float.

28. **It will go for infinite loop.**

The for loop starts with the value of the loop counter as 0, increments in each iteration by 1 and reaches to 32767. As the loop now wants to increment abc whose value is 32767 by 1, it does not change to 32768 rather changes to -32768 as we have already known that in the integer value range the number after 32767 is –32768. Here in the program segment, the loop terminating condition is abc's value will be 32768 which never comes. So the loop will never end and will go for infinite times.

29. The output will be **it will go infinitely.**

Here a semicolon has been given just after the while loop; so the statements within the brace just after the while loop will not be treated as the body of the while loop. As the loop variable know is not changed in the while loop, it will always satisfy the condition know<=10 and will run infinitely.

30. The output will be **234**.

The while loop will start running with the value of know as 1. The condition part of the loop first increments the loop variable by 1 and then checks the condition. So the printf() statement which is the part of the while loop will print 234.

31. The output will be **2 3**.

It is an example of the nested while. The outer while loop will start with the value know=1 and will go till know=3. For each value of know the inner while loop should run until its loop variable factor becomes 3. When know=1 the inner while loop goes from factor=1 to factor=2 and prints the corresponding sum and this inner loop terminates when factor becomes 3. For the next consecutive run of the outer while loop, the inner while loop will not be executed as the inner loop variable factor has not been initialized and as a result it is still 3 which violates the inner while loop condition and so the inner while loop will not be executed further and no more value will be printed.

32. The output will be **loop executed.**

The difference between while and do-while loop is that the do while loop will be executed once if the condition part of the while fails at the very first time as here the condition checking is done after the execution of the body, but there will be no execution of the loop body in the case of while loop if the condition fails initially as there the condition checking is done before the execution of the body. Here the case is the same. The condition fails at the fist time but as it is a do-while loop the printf() statement will be executed showing the string loop executed.

33. The output will be **it will display the sum of the digits of a number.**

The first statement of the do-while loop separates the rightmost digit of the given number by taking the modulo operator. The next statement performs the sum of the digits of the number. Now the number is divided by 10 so that the next iteration of the loop can separate the next left digit. As for example if the number is 123, then digit=123%10=3, sum=0+3=3, num=123/10=12. Each time the number will be decremented and finally when it becomes zero the sum of all the digits have been added.

34. The output will be **Hello# Hello# Hello#.**

It is an example of a simple do-while construct. Here the do-while loop starts with loop variable know=1 and each time incremented by 1 it will run up to know=3. As the printf() statement is within the loop, Hello# will be printed thrice.

35. The output will be **at least once.**

The difference between while and do-while loop is that the do while loop will be executed once if the condition part of the while fails at the very first time that is it will execute at once, but there will be no execution of the loop body in the case of while loop if the condition fails initially.

36. The appropriate sequence is **INITIALIZATION, EXECUTION OF BODY, TESTING**

The difference between while and do-while loop is that the do while loop will be executed once if the condition part of the while fails at the very first time as here the condition checking is done after the execution of the body, but there will be no execution of the loop body in the case of while loop if the condition fails initially as there the condition checking is done before the execution of the body.

37. The output will be

   1

   2

   3

   4

   The break statement is used to move the control out of the corresponding loop. In the question, when the for loop variable know becomes 5 it satisfies the if condition associated with the break, and the break executes by moving the control out of the for loop. But before that the loop will execute 4 times during know=1 to know=4. So it will show the above output.

38. The output will be **prime number.**

   A prime number is one which is divisible by 1 and the number itself. So to check whether a number is prime or not we have to divide it by 2 to the previous number. This is done by the outer while loop. If the given number is divisible by any number it will no longer prime then and we do not have to check it for further division. This is done through the conditional break statement within the while loop. If the number is prime which is the case for 13 the while loop variable i will be incremented until it reaches 13 which is equal to the number itself and will print it as a prime number.

39. The correct statement is **a for loop.**

   A break statement can only be used to move the control out of a loop.

40. The output will be **12.**

   21

   The continue statement is used to skip the current iteration of the loop where it is being used and start from the next iteration of the same loop. Here continue is used conditionally when the outer loop variable know's value equals to the inner loop variable factor's value. So the printf() statement will only be encountered when the value of know and factor are different. So it will print 12 and 21.

41. Continue is used to take the control to the beginning of the loop for next pass. The **continue** statement passes control to the next iteration of the **do, for,** or **while** statement in which it appears, bypassing any remaining statements in the **do, for,** or **while** statement body.

42. The correct option is
   ```
   int y, x=0;
   do{
   y=x;
   }while(x==0);
   ```

   In the do-while the termination condition is x==0 which is also the initial value of x. So the condition fails at the very beginning. But as it is a do-while the loop body will execute once. The other options i.e., while(1) anf for(; ;) are two infinite loop.

43. The output will be **12**

   21

   more than one loop construct can also be used in C's nested within one another.

The continue statement is used to skip the current iteration of the loop where it is being used and start from the next iteration of the same loop. Here continue is used conditionally when the outer loop variable know's value equals to the inner loop variable factor's value. So the printf() statement will only be encountered when the value of know and factor are different. So it will print 12 and 21. The inner loop termination condition is given through the break statement. It is another way to give the termination condition.

44. The answer is **1**.

    The loop termination condition is given through the conditional break statement. The break will work if the printf() statement returns nonzero value. When the printf() statement prints "KnowledgeFactor" first time the printf() returns 15, as a result the if condition is satisfied and the control jumps out from the while loop. So the string will be printed once.

45. The output will be **6**.

    Here the step value of the while loop variable know depends on a condition, so it can be expressed through the ternary operator. As the printf() statement is out of the while loop, it will be the final value of know which is 6.

46. The output is **break**.

    Break is the keyword to skip the remaining total iteration of the loop and jump control to the out of the loop.

47. The output will be **it will print all the prime numbers from 1 to 30.**

    The outer for loop increments the loop variable i from 1 to 30 and for each value of i the inner for loop and the if statement check whether it is prime or not. A prime number is one which is divisible by 1 and the number itself. So to check whether a number is prime or not we have to divide it by 2 to the previous number. This is done by the inner for loop. If the given number is divisible by any number, it will be no longer prime then and we do not have to check it for further division. This is done through the conditional break statement. If the number is prime its value will be printed.

48. The output is **it will print the series (1/1!)+(2/2!)+(3/3!)+(4/4!)+(5/5!).**

    The outer for loop will increment the loop variable from 1 to 5, the inner for loop will produce the factorial of each value of i as well as the value of the summation of i/i!.

49. It will print the reverse of the input number. In every iteration, it will extract a digit of num1 starting from right side taking the remainder using the modulo operator and put it in num2 starting from left. As per example, if the input is 376 then it will extract 6, 7 and 3 and make num2 6, 67 and 673 at last.

50. It will print succeed if the input number is a palindrome. As the loop will put reverse of num1 in num2.

51. It will print succeed if the input is an Armstrong number. As per definition of Armstrong number, sum of cube of digits is equal to the number itself.

52. Option1 cannot do the specific job as in the first iteration value of n is 0 but in other options initial value of n is 1.

53. The output will be option1.

54. It will print the first 10 Fibonacci numbers. Fibonacci series goes like 1,2,3,5,8,13, etc. A number is obtained by adding previous two numbers.

11

Array

The number of variables used so far in a program is very limited. But in real life, plenty of elements are required to be dealt with. Like, we have already written programs to find out maximum between two, three or four variables, but if our task is to find the highest marks in a class of 60 students or more, then it will become a tedious job for us. Which means 60 variables are to be declared to store marks of 60 students, so 60 *scanf* statements have to be used to take input the marks of each student and finally 60 *if* statements to find the maximum of these marks and so on. Not only that, if another class contain less or more than 60 students, we could not use this program for that class. We have to rewrite the program according to that new class. Thus this approach of processing a large set of data is too cumbersome and surely not flexible enough. The **C** language (rather all modern high level languages) provides a more convenient way of processing such collections. The solution is **Array** or Subscripted variables.

11.1   WHAT IS AN ARRAY?

An array is a collection of homogeneous (i.e., same data type) data elements described by a single name and placed in contiguous memory locations. Each individual element of an array is referenced by a subscripted variable, formed by affixing to the array name a subscript or index enclosed in brackets.

Thus by declaring an array we can store a set of values, say 60 of type *int* in a single variable without declaring 60 different variables of different names. All these values will be stored under a unique identifier (array name).

11.2   DECLARATION OF AN ARRAY

Like other variables, it is also needed to declare arrays before they can be used in the program. The general form to declare an array is:

   data_type variable_name[size_of_array];

Here

data_type	:	specifies the data type of the elements which are going to be stored in the array.
variable_name	:	specifies the name of array.
size_of_array	:	specifies the size of an array, i.e., maximum number of elements that can be stored within that array. It should be an integer **constant** greater than zero.

As array is a block of non-dynamic memory, its size must be determined before execution, i.e., during compilation time.

EXAMPLE 11.1

```
int marks[60];

char name[30];

double height[100];

float width[20];
```

The elements of the array occupy adjacent locations in memory. Each element in the array is identified by its position known as array index or array subscript. In C language, array index starts from position 0 and upper limit should be size of the array – 1.

For example, to store 5 integer values with in an array named **arr** could be declared as:

    int arr[5];

and represented like this:

	0	1	2	3	4
arr					

Here each blank cell represents an element of the array. As the data type of the array is declared as **int**, all the elements of this array will be of type **int**. They are numbered from 0 to 4 since the first index of array is always 0.

11.3 INITIALIZING ARRAYS

When an array is declared, the elements of the array will not be initialized automatically. They will contain garbage values. But we have the scope to assign initial values at the time of declaring an array to each one of its elements by enclosing the values within braces { }. Consider the following example:

    int arr [5] = {26, 3, 89, 41, 12073};

This declaration will create an array like this:

	0	1	2	3	4
arr	26	3	89	41	12073

The number of initial values mentioned within the braces { } must not be larger than the size of the array declared between square brackets [ ]. For example, the array **arr** is declared with its size as **5**, so the list of initial values within braces { } contains 5 values, one for each element.

However, we can specify lesser number of elements than its size. For example:

int arr [5] = {26, 3, 89};

First three elements get values 26, 3 and 89, respectively; the rest initializes with zero automatically.

	0	1	2	3	4
arr	26	3	89	0	0

If the initialization list is provided, it is possible to omit the size of the array leaving the square brackets empty [ ]. In this situation, the compiler checks the number of values included within the braces { } and according to this initialization list provides the size for the array.

int arr [ ] = {26, 3, 89, 41, 12073};

After this declaration, the size of the array **arr** would be 5, since we have provided 5 initialization values.

11.3.1 Space Allocated for Array Elements and their Addresses

As array is a collection of elements, total memory required for the array is **product of size of the array and memory required for each element**. But the total memory requirement of each element differs according to its data type. Like, in case of character arrays, each element takes 1 byte (8 bit) of memory space, similarly elements of an int type array occupies 2 bytes (16 bit) of consecutive memory location and so on. Elements of an array are always stored in contiguous memory locations. So address of an element of a character array will be greater by 1 than its previous element whereas the increment will be 2 in case of integer array, 4 for float and 8 for double, likewise.

Hence, the declaration

char arr1[5] allocates 5*1 = 5 bytes (Fig. 11.1) and int arr2[5]; allocates 5*2 = 10 bytes (Fig. 11.2), etc.

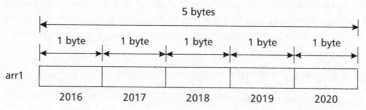

Fig. 11.1 Allocation of memory for character array

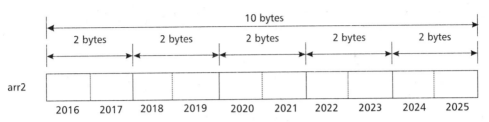

Fig. 11.2   Allocation of memory for integer array

The allocation of memory for different data types will be clear from the following example program and their output:-

PROGRAM 11.1   Write a program to print how much memory is required in terms of bytes for array of different data types.

```
# include <stdio.h>
void main( )
{
    char arr1[5];
    int arr2[5];
    long arr3[5];
    float arr4[5];
    printf ("\'char\'reserves %d Byte in memory", sizeof(char));
    printf ("\n\'int\'reserves %d Bytes in memory", sizeof(int));
    printf ("\n\'long\'reserves %d Bytes in memory", sizeof(long));
    printf ("\n\'float\'reserves %d Bytes in memory", sizeof(float));

    printf ("\nMemory required for a character array of size 5 is %d
            Bytes ",sizeof(arr1));
    printf ("\nMemory required for an integer array of size 5 is %d
            Bytes ",sizeof(arr2));
    printf ("\nMemory required for an array of type 'long' of size 5
            is %d Bytes ",sizeof(arr3));
    printf ("\nMemory required for an array of type 'float' of size 5
            is %d Bytes ",sizeof(arr4));
}
```

Output:

'char' reserves 1 Byte in memory

'int' reserves 2 Bytes in memory

'long' reserves 4 Bytes in memory

'float' reserves 4 Bytes in memory

Memory required for a character array of size 5 is 5 Bytes

Memory required for an integer array of size 5 is 10 Bytes

Memory required for an array of type 'long' of size 5 is 20 Bytes

Memory required for an array of type 'float' of size 5 is 20 Bytes

11.4 ACCESSING ELEMENTS OF AN ARRAY

Once an array is declared, we can access individual elements in the array. These elements are accessed with the help of array index which is nothing but the position of the element in that array. It is already mentioned earlier that the first position of an array is 0, second is 1, and so on. To access an array element we need to mention the array name followed by the array index enclosed within [ ]. The general format to access an array element is:

Array_name[index]

If we declare an array as: int arr[5];

Then to access the first element of the above array we have to write arr[0] as in C array index always starts from 0. Similarly to access the next elements we have to write arr[1], arr[2] and so on.

	arr[0]	arr[1]	arr[2]	arr[3]	arr[4]
arr	26	3	89	0	0

These elements can be accessed individually just like a normal variable. We can read as well as modify its value. For example, to assign the value 72 in the second cell of **arr**, we can write the statement as:

arr[1] = 72;

Similarly, to assign the value of the second element of **arr** to a variable called **num**, we can write:

num = arr[1];

Thus, the expression arr[1] act just like a variable of type int. Not only assignment it can be used in input statement, output statement, in any arithmetic expression – everywhere its use is similar to an integer variable.

Notice that the second element of **arr** is specified as **arr**[1], since the first one is **arr**[0]. Therefore, the third element will be **arr**[2], fourth element will be **arr**[3] and last element will be **arr**[4]. Thus, if we write **arr**[5], it would be the sixth element of the array **arr** and therefore exceeding the size of the array.

C compiler does not check or impose any restriction on the subscript value used to access an array element. If the subscript value exceeds the size of the array, compiler will not produce any error; even if any −ve number is used as subscript value, then also the program will be compiled successfully. When subscript value exceeds the array size, it refers to a memory address which is outside the allocation of the array. In case of −ve subscript value, it refers to a memory address which is some prior location to the base address of the array. However in both cases, we are not accessing the required memory locations and if we assign some values on those locations, which may overwrite other variables in the program or the program itself and that leads to some unpredictable result. Thus, it is entirely the programmer's botheration and not the compiler's that we do not reach beyond the array size.

We can use variable as a subscript or array index to access the array elements. At runtime this variable may contains several values and thus different array elements are accessed accordingly. This facility of using variables as subscripts makes array so useful.

Note Remember if we write −ve number or number larger than the array size as subscript or array index compiler will not show any error. But we may not get the proper output as these memory locations may be used by another variables. So, it is totally programmer's responsibility to restrict the array index with in 0 to size of the array − 1 to execute the program efficiently.

The following code snippet shows how easily we can take 60 inputs in an array using a variable as subscript:

```
int arr[60], i;
for(i = 0; i < 60; i++)
{
        printf("Enter any number: ");
        scanf("%d",&arr[i]);
}
```

Similarly, we can display the content of an array of size 60 as:

```
for(i = 0; i < 60; i++)
{
        printf ("%d ", arr[i]);
}
```

Some other valid operations with arrays:

```
arr[0] = a;
arr[a] = 75;
b = arr [a+2];
arr[2] = arr[0] + arr[1];
arr[arr[a]] = arr[2] + 5;   etc..
```

Now we will write a complete program that will demonstrate the operations of the array.

PROGRAM 11.2   Program to find the highest marks in a class of 60 students.

```
#include<conio.h>

#include<stdio.h>

void main( )
{   int marks[60], i, maxm;
    for(i = 0; i < 60; i++)        /* Input to array */
    {
            printf("Enter Marks of Student%d: ",i+1);
```

```
        scanf("%d",&marks[i]);
    }
    maxm = marks[0];            /* Assigning 1st element to maxm variable */
    for(i = 1;i < 60; i++)      /* Other elements will be compared with maxm */
    {
        if(marks[i]>maxm)
            maxm = marks[i];
    }
    printf("The Highest Marks is : %d", maxm);
}
```

In the above program, first we declare an array named marks of size 60 with the statement – int marks[60]; next we take the input to the array. To find the highest marks we store the first element into the **maxm** variable and compare it with the rest elements of the array. If the array element is larger than **maxm**, it will be stored within the **maxm** variable. So, **maxm** variable contains the highest marks.

From the above program, we can see now with a single statement we are able to store marks of 60 students. A **for** loop and a **scanf** statement are able to take input the marks of 60 students and similarly a **for** loop and an **if** statement are able to find the maximum of these marks. This is the advantage of using an array.

Next program shows the addressing and allocation of memory for the array elements.

PROGRAM 11.3   Write a program to print the addresses of array elements.

```
# include <stdio.h>
void main (void)
{
    int num[5]={1,2,3,2,5};
    printf ("\n num[0] = %d Address : %u",num[0], &num[0]);
    printf ("\n num[1] = %d Address : %u",num[1], &num[1]);
    printf ("\n num[2] = %d Address : %u",num[2], &num[2]);
    printf ("\n num[3] = %d Address : %u",num[3], &num[3]);
    printf ("\n num[4] = %d Address : %u",num[4], &num[4]);
}
```

Sample Output

num[0] = 1 Address : 5516

num[1] = 2 Address : 5518

num[2] = 3 Address : 5520

num[3] = 2 Address : 5522

num[4] = 5 Address : 5524

Not only a single array, we can use as many as array is required in a program. Here is another example where we use two arrays in a program.

PROGRAM **11.4** **Write a program that will store the positive numbers first, then zeros if any, and the negative numbers at the end in a different array from a group of numbers.**

```c
#include<conio.h>
#include<stdio.h>
#define SIZE 15
void main( )
{
    int element[SIZE],arranged[SIZE],i,j=0;
    for(i=0;i<SIZE;i++)                      /* Input to array */
    {
        printf("Enter Element %d: ",i+1);
        scanf("%d",&element[i]);
    }
    for(i=0;i<SIZE;i++)                      /* copy of positive elements */
    {
        if(element[i]>0)
        {   arranged[j++]=element[i];
        }
    }
    for(i=0;i<SIZE;i++)                      /* copy of zeros */
    {
        if(element[i]==0)
        {       arranged[j++]=element[i];
        }
    }

    for(i=0;i<SIZE;i++)                      /* copy of negative elements */
    {
        if(element[i]<0)
        {       arranged[j++]=element[i];
        }
    }
    printf("The Newly Arranged Elements are : ");
    for(i=0;i<SIZE;i++)                      /* Printing of array elements */
    {
        printf("%d ", arranged[i]);
    }
}
```

In the above program, we have used a new preprocessor directive, i.e., #define. The processor directive #define is used to define symbolic constant. It increases the speed and readability of the program and also helps the programmer to modify the program. When the above program will execute all the occurrence of the symbolic constant, 'SIZE' will be replaced by 15. This is very effective in the program where we use array. If it is required to change the size of the array, we need not to change every position which is related to the size of the array. We only have to change at the definition of the symbolic constant.

In the above program we just grouped together the positive numbers, zeros and negative numbers. But the array is not sorted properly. To sort an array properly, we have to follow some specific technique. Now we discuss about sorting.

11.5   SORTING

Sorting is a process by which we can arrange the elements in a specific order. The order may be increasing or decreasing. By default it is increasing. There are several algorithms to sort an array. Here we discuss few of them.

11.5.1   Bubble Sort

It is very simple and most common sorting technique to the beginners. In this sorting technique, the adjacent elements are compared. If the previous element is larger than the successor, elements are being interchanged. This continues from first two elements to last two elements. At the end of comparison of last two elements, first pass is completed. At the end of first pass, we will find that the largest element has moved to last position. This process continues. As in each pass, a single element will move to its required position, there are n–1 pass will be required to sort the array. The following example illustrates the working principle of Bubble sort.

arr	85	33	57	12	40	2

arr	85	33	57	12	40	2

First arr[0] will be compared with arr[1], i.e., 85 with 33. As the first element is larger than the next one, elements will be interchanged and we will get the next state.

arr	33	85	57	12	40	2

Next arr[1] will be compared with arr[2], i.e., 85 with 57. Again 85 is larger than 57. So, elements will be interchanged. This process continues.

arr	33	57	85	12	40	2

arr	33	57	12	85	40	2

arr	33	57	12	40	85	2

arr	33	57	12	40	2	85

This is end of first pass and we get the largest element at the last position. Now second pass will be started.

arr	33	57	12	40	2	85	(no interchange)

arr	33	57	12	40	2	85	(interchange)

arr	33	12	57	40	2	85	(interchange)

arr	33	12	40	57	2	85	(interchange)

arr	33	12	40	2	57	85	(no interchange)

This is end of second pass and the second largest element, i.e., 57 is now in its proper position. In this way in each pass a single element will got its proper position. Resemble with the formation of bubbles, in this sorting technique the array sorted gradually from bottom. That is why it is known as Bubble sort. As the sorting process involves exchange of two elements, it is also known as **exchange sort**. Other passes are described below:

Third pass:

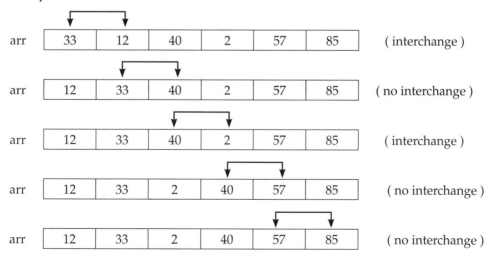

arr	33	12	40	2	57	85	(interchange)

arr	12	33	40	2	57	85	(no interchange)

arr	12	33	40	2	57	85	(interchange)

arr	12	33	2	40	57	85	(no interchange)

arr	12	33	2	40	57	85	(no interchange)

Fourth pass:

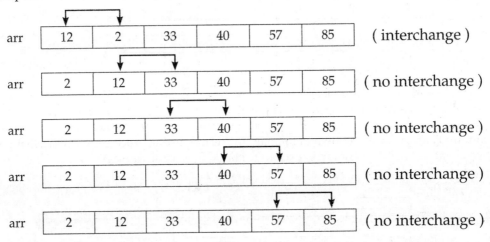

Fifth pass:

Now the array becomes sorted.

On the basis of this algorithm now we can write the corresponding program.

PROGRAM 11.5   Program to sort an array using bubble sort algorithm.

```
#include<stdio.h>
#define SIZE 15

void main( )
{
    int element[SIZE], i, j, temp;
    for(i=0;i<SIZE;i++)
```

```
    {
        printf("Enter Element %d: ",i+1);
        scanf("%d",&element[i]);
    }

    for( i = 0; i < SIZE -1; i++ )
    {
        for( j = 0; j < SIZE -1; j++ )
        {
            if( element[j] ) > element[j+1] )
            {
                temp = element[j];
                element[j] = element[j+1];
                element[j+1] = temp;
            }
        }
    }
    printf("\n\nThe Sorted Elements are : ");
    for(i=0;i<SIZE;i++)
    {
        printf("%d ", elements[i]);
    }
}
```

In the above code, we can make some modification to increase the efficiency of the program. In the second pass as the largest element is in last position, unnecessarily we compare the last two elements. Similarly, in third pass last two comparisons are unnecessary. We can modify our code in such a way so that in the first pass n–1 comparisons are made, in the second pass n–2 comparisons are made, in the third pass n–3 comparisons are made and so on. In this way, in last pass, i.e., n–1th pass only one comparison will be required. Thus, the process speeds up as it proceeds through successive passes.

Another drawback of this algorithm is that if the elements are already sorted or the array becomes sorted in any intermediate stage, till we have to proceed for n–1 passes. But if we carefully notice that if the elements become sorted, then no further interchange is made. In other words, if no interchange took place in a pass, we can say that the elements are sorted and it can be easily implemented by using an extra variable say flag. Considering these two modifications, the modified version of the basic technique of bubble sort is given below.

PROGRAM 11.6 Modified version of Bubble sort algorithm.

```
#include<stdio.h>
#define SIZE 10

void main( )
{
    int element[SIZE], i, j, temp, flag;
    for(i=0;i<SIZE;i++)
```

```
{
    printf("Enter Element %d: ",i+1);
    scanf("%d",&element[i]);
}

for( i = 0; i < SIZE -1; i++ )
{   flag = 0;
    for( j = 0; j < SIZE - i -1; j++ )
    {
        if( element[j] ) > element[j+1] )
        {
            temp =  element[j];
            element[j] =  element[j+1];
            element[j+1] =  temp;
            flag = 1;
        }
    }
    if(flag == 0)
        break;
}

printf("\n\nThe Sorted Elements are : ");
for(i=0;i<SIZE;i++)
{
    printf("%d ", elements[i]);
}
}
```

11.5.2 Selection Sort

In this sorting technique, first the smallest element is selected and then this element will be interchanged with the element of first position. Now first element is in its proper position and rest elements are unsorted. So, consider the rest elements. The second element is now logically first element for the rest sets. Again we select the smallest element from this rest set and interchange with the currently logical first position. This process continues by selecting the smallest element from the rest and placed it into its proper position by interchanging with the logical first element. As in each iteration corresponding smallest elements are selected and placed into their proper position, this algorithm is known as Selection sort. As in each pass a single element will move to its required position, there are n−1 pass will be required to sort the array. The following example illustrates the working principle of Selection sort.

arr	33	85	57	12	40	2

arr	33	85	57	12	40	2

Here, the smallest element is 2. So, it will be interchanged with first element, i.e., 33 and we get the next state.

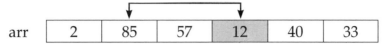

arr

| 2 | 85 | 57 | 12 | 40 | 33 |

Now 2 is placed in its proper position. So, we consider only the rest elements. Among the rest elements 12 is the smallest. It will be interchanged with the second position which is currently the logical first position.

arr

| 2 | 12 | 57 | 85 | 40 | 33 |

This process continues.

arr

| 2 | 12 | 33 | 85 | 40 | 57 |

arr

| 2 | 12 | 33 | 40 | 85 | 57 |

arr

| 2 | 12 | 33 | 40 | 57 | 85 |

On the basis of this algorithm now we write a program to sort an array using selection sort.

PROGRAM 11.7 Program to sort an array using Selection sort algorithm.

```c
#include<conio.h>
#include<stdio.h>
#define SIZE 10

void main( )
{
   int element[SIZE], i, j, temp, min, posn;
   clrscr();
   for(i=0;i<SIZE;i++)
   {
        printf("Enter Element %d: ",i+1);
        scanf("%d",&element[i]);
   }

   for( i = 0; i < SIZE -1; i++ )
   {
        min = element[i];
        posn = i ;
        for( j = i+1; j < SIZE; j++ )   /* Finding smallest element and its position */
```

```
        {
                if ( element [j] ) < min )
                {
                        min = element [j];
                        posn = j ;
                }
        }
        if ( posn != i)      /* Interchange with ith element and smallest element */
        {
                temp = element [i];
                element [i] = element [posn];
                element [posn] = temp;
        }
    }

    printf ("\n\nThe Sorted Elements are : ");
    for (i=0; i<SIZE; i++)
    {
            printf ("%d ", elements [i]);
    }
}
```

11.5.3   Insertion Sort

The basic theory of this sorting technique is that each element is inserted into its proper position in a previously sorted array. The process starts from the 2nd element of the array. Before this element there is a single element only and it can be considered as a sorted array which has only one element. Now insert the 2nd element in this array so that we get a sorted array of two elements. Next consider the 3rd element. Before this element, we have a sorted array of two elements. Insert the 3rd element into its proper position in this sorted array and we will get first three elements sorted. This process continues up to last element to become the array fully sorted. As the sorting technique grows by inserting each element into its proper position, this sorting technique is known as Insertion sort. The following example illustrates the working principle of Insertion sort.

Consider the initial array is:

arr	85	33	57	12	40	2

According to this technique, the sorting procedure starts from the 2nd position of the array. So, we have to consider the 2nd element, i.e., arr[1] which is 33 and the situation is:

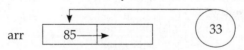

To become sorted 85 will shifted to its next position, i.e., into arr[1] and 33 will be inserted to arr[0] position. So, the new state will be:

arr	33	85	57	12	40	2

In next iteration we have to consider the 3rd element, i.e., arr[2]. Now the situation is:

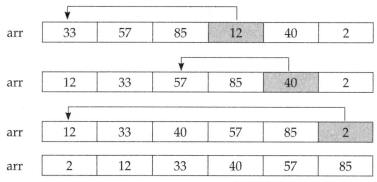

As 57 is smaller than 85 but larger than 33, 57 should be inserted in between these two. So, 85 will be shifted to arr[2] position and 57 will be inserted in arr[1] and we will get:

| arr | 33 | 57 | 85 | 12 | 40 | 2 |

This process continues and we get the following states:

| arr | 33 | 57 | 85 | 12 | 40 | 2 |

| arr | 12 | 33 | 57 | 85 | 40 | 2 |

| arr | 12 | 33 | 40 | 57 | 85 | 2 |

| arr | 2 | 12 | 33 | 40 | 57 | 85 |

The following code shows the implementation of above algorithm.

PROGRAM 11.8 Program to sort an array using Insertion sort algorithm.

```
#include<stdio.h>
#define SIZE 10

void main( )
{
    int element[SIZE], i, j, temp, min, posn;
    for(i=0;i<SIZE;i++)
    {
        printf("Enter Element %d: ",i+1);
        scanf("%d",&element[i]);
    }
    for( i = 1; i < SIZE ; i++ )
    {
        temp = element[i];
        j = i - 1;
        while ( temp < element[j]  &&  j>=0 )
        {
            element[j+1] = element[j];
            j = j - 1;
        }
        element[j+1] = temp;
    }
```

```
printf("\n\nThe Sorted Elements are : ");
for(i=0;i<SIZE;i++)
{
    printf("%d ", elements[i]);
}
}
```

11.6 SEARCHING

Searching is a process by which we can check whether an element is present within a set of elements or not. If it is present we can also find the position of the element in the list. Like sorting, we can also implement searching algorithms using array. There are two algorithms to search an element from an array.
- Linear search
- Binary search

11.6.1 Linear Search

The algorithm which checks each element of a list starting from first position is known as Linear search. As this algorithm checks each element in a list sequentially it is also known as sequential search. When the elements in a list are unsorted, i.e., not in proper order, this searching technique is used.

Here is the implementation of linear search technique:

PROGRAM 11.9   Program to implement Linear Searching.

```
#include<stdio.h>
#define SIZE 15

void main( )
{    int element[SIZE],num,i;
     for(i=0;i<SIZE;i++)
     {   printf("Enter Element %d: ",i+1);
         scanf("%d",&element[i]);
     }
     printf("\nEnter The Element to be searched: ");
     scanf("%d",&num);
     for(i=0;i<SIZE;i++)
     {   if(element[i]==num)
         {   printf("The element is in %dth position",i+1);
             break;
         }
     }
     if(i==SIZE)
         printf("The Element not found");
}
```

11.6.2 Binary Search

To implement binary search the array needs to be sorted. According to binary search algorithm, the search key value is compared with the middle element of the sorted array. If it matches the array index is returned. Otherwise, if the search key is less than the middle element, then the algorithm repeats its action on the sub-array to the left of the middle element or if the search key is greater, then the algorithm repeats its action on the sub-array to the right of the middle element. This process continues until the match is found or the remaining array to be searched becomes empty. If it is empty, it indicates that the search element is not found. This algorithm runs much faster than linear search.

Here is the implementation of binary search technique:

PROGRAM 11.10   Program to implement binary searching.

```c
#include<stdio.h>
void main()
{
    int ar[20],i,number,key,low,high,mid,flag=0;
    printf("Enter number of elements:");
    scanf("%d",&number);
    printf("Enter the values in ascending order:");
    for(i=0;i<number;i++)
        scanf("%d", &ar[i]);
    printf("Enter the number you want to search:");
    scanf("%d",&key);
    low=0;
    high=number - 1;
    while(low<=high)
    {   mid= (low+high)/2;
        if( key==ar[mid])
        {   flag=1;
            break;
        }
        else
            if(key<ar[mid])
                high = mid-1;
            else
                low= mid+1;
    }
    if(flag)
        printf("The number is in %dth position", mid);
    else
        printf("Number not found");
}
```

11.7 TWO DIMENSIONAL ARRAY

So far, we have discussed arrays with only one dimension. It is also possible to declare two or more dimensions for arrays. In one dimensional array, we can store a list of values but in two dimensional array we can store values in tabular format.

A two dimensional array consist of some rows and columns. The conceptual view of a two dimensional array named arr2d, whose number of rows is 3 and number of column in each row is 5, is shown in the following figure:

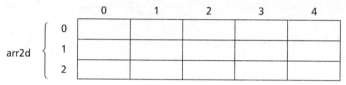

Fig. 11.3   Conceptual view of a two dimensional array

The General form to declare a two dimensional array is:

data_type variable_name[rows][columns];

Here data_type specifies the data type of the element which is going to be stored in the array, variable_name specifies the name of array, rows specifies total number of rows and columns specifies total number of columns. Like one dimensional array, we cannot use variables in place of rows and columns. It must be constant.

EXAMPLE 11.2

```
int sales[10][12];

char name[50][30];

double myarray[100][80];
```

11.7.1 Initializing 2D Arrays

Like one dimensional array, we can also initialize two dimensional arrays at the time of declaration in the following way:

```
int  sales[4][3] = {
                      { 534,   96, 221},
                      { 112, 435, 27 },
                      { 777, 800, 660},
                      {  62, 780, 500}
                    };
```

or

```
int sales[4][3] = { 534, 96, 221, 112, 435, 27, 777, 800, 660, 62, 780, 500 } ;
```

Both are same but the first one is more readable.

Remember that it is essential to specify the second dimension (columns), while the first dimension (rows) is optional when initializing a two dimensional array. Thus the declarations,

> int myarr[2][3] = { 10, 20, 30, 40, 50, 60 } ;

is same as:

> int myarr[ ][3] = { 10, 20, 30, 40, 50, 60 } ;

But the following declarations produce errors.

> int myarr[2][ ] = { 10, 20, 30, 40, 50, 60 } ;

or   int myarr[ ][ ] = { 10, 20, 30, 40, 50, 60 } ;

11.7.2   Accessing Elements of an 2d Array

To access an element of an 2D array we have to specify the row number and column number of the element. The general format is:

> Array_name[row][column]

EXAMPLE 11.3

As described in the picture, row number and column number both start from zero. So, to access the second element vertically and fourth horizontally from the array named arr2d the expression would be:

> arr2d[1][3]

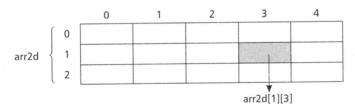

Fig. 11.4   **Accessing elements in a two dimensional array.**

Other operations are same as one dimensional array. Some valid operations with two dimensional arrays:

```
arr2d[0][0] = a;        /* a is an integer variable    */
arr2d[i][j] = 75;       /* i and j are integer variables    */
a = arr2d [i+2][j];
```

The following program illustrates the use and operation of two dimensional array.

PROGRAM **11.11**   **Program to add two matrix.**

```
#include<conio.h>
#include<stdio.h>
void main()
{
int ar1[4][4], ar2[4][4],ar3[4][4],i=0,j=0,t;
printf("\nEnter the elements of 1st Matrix:-\n");
for(i=0;i<4;i++)                              /* Input to 1st Matrix   */
{    for(j=0;j<4;j++)
        {  printf("Enter element[%d][%d] : ",i,j);
           scanf("%d",&ar1[i][j]);
        }
}
printf("\nEnter the elements of 2nd Matrix:-\n");
for(i=0;i<4;i++)                              /* Input to 2nd Matrix   */
{    for(j=0;j<4;j++)
        {  printf("Enter element[%d][%d] : ",i,j);
           scanf("%d",&ar2[i][j]);
        }
}


clrscr();
printf("1st Matrix:-\n");
for(i=0;i<4;i++)                              /* Print 1st Matrix   */
{    for(j=0;j<4;j++)
           printf("%d\t",ar1[i][j]);
     printf("\n");
}
printf("\n2nd Matrix:-\n");
for(i=0;i<4;i++)                              /* Print 2nd Matrix   */
{    for(j=0;j<4;j++)
           printf("%d\t",ar2[i][j]);
     printf("\n");
}


for(i=0;i<4;i++)                              /* Addition of two matrix   */
{    for(j=0;j<4;j++)
     {
           ar3[i][j] = ar1[i][j] + ar2[i][j];
     }
}
printf("\nSum of two Matrix:-\n");
for(i=0;i<4;i++)                              /*  Printing of Resultant matrix */
{    for(j=0;j<4;j++)
           printf("%d\t",ar3[i][j]);
     printf("\n");
}
}
```

Using 2D array we can easily solve the problems related to matrix. But not only the matrix, 2D array may be used in other situation also. Here is an example.

PROBLEM 11.11   The following figure is known as Pascal's triangle.

```
1
1  1
1  2  1
1  3  3  1
1  4  6  4  1
1  5 10 10  5  1
. . . . .
. . . . .
```

Write a program to display the Pascal's Triangle up to specified number of rows.

PROGRAM 11.12   Program to generate Pascal's Triangle.

```c
#include<stdio.h>
void main( )
{
    int ar[20][20],i,j,line;
    printf("Enter number of lines:");
    scanf("%d",&line);
    for(i=0;i<line;i++)
    {
        for(j=0;j<=i;j++)
        {   if(j==0 || i==j)          /* To set 1 in 1st column and diagonal */
                ar[i][j] = 1;
            else
                ar[i][j]= ar[i-1][j] + ar[i-1][j-1];
            printf("%2d  ",ar[i][j]);
        }
        printf("\n");
    }
}
```

11.8   MULTIDIMENSIONAL ARRAY

Not only two dimensional, we can declare array of any dimension according to our requirement. Actually number of dimension depends on number of constraint to represent data. For example, to store sales amount of some employee of an organization one dimensional array is sufficient. But if we want to store the sales amount of each employee of each month of that organization in a year, two dimensional array is required. Because each data value, i.e., sales amount is represented by two constraints. These are employee and month. For example, in January sales amount of 3rd employee is Rs. 65000. So, if there is 30 employee and we want to store the data of a year, we have to declare an array of size 30 × 12. Suppose now we want to store more specific data. For example the organization has 5 types of product and we want to store the sales amounts of each employee of each month of each product. Now, our constraint is three (i.e., employee, month and product type). So, we have to declare a three dimensional array and according to the above example its size will be 30 × 12 × 5. In this way as the number of constraint increases the number of dimension also increases.

The syntax of declaring a multidimensional array is:

>   data type   array name[dim1][dim2] ......[dim n];

EXAMPLE 11.4:

int arr1[5][6][7];	/* 3-D integer array of size 5 × 6 × 7. */
float arr2[3][5][7][4];	/*4-D float array of size 3 × 5 × 7 × 4. */

All operations on multidimensional array are same as two dimensional array. Only number of index or subscript will increase with increase of dimension. The following program illustrates the use and operation of three dimensional array.

PROGRAM 11.13   Program to find the total sales of each employee and total sales of each product. Available data are the sale figure of 10 employees of 6 months and of 5 types of products.

```
#include<stdio.h>
void main( )
{   int sales[10][6][5], i, j, k, tot;

    for(i=0;i<10;i++)             /* Input to 3D Array   */
        for(j=0;j<6;j++)
          for(k=0;k<5;k++)
          {
              printf("\nEnter the Sales amount of Employee%d of Month%d
                                  of Product%d:",i+1,j+1,k+1);
              scanf("%d",&sales[i][j][k]);
          }

    for(i=0;i<10;i++)
    {
        tot = 0;
        for(j=0;j<6;j++)        /* Calculation of Total sales of each employee */
          for(k=0;k<5;k++)
          {
              tot = tot + sales[i][j][k];
          }
          printf("\nTotal Sales amount of Employee%d = %d", i+1, tot);
    }
```

```
    for(k=0;k<5;k++)
    {
        tot = 0;
        for(j=0;j<6;j++)      /* Calculation of Total sales of each Product */
            for(i=0;i<10;i++)
            {
                tot = tot + sales[i][j][k];
            }
        printf("\nTotal Sales amount of Product%d = %d", k+1, tot);
    }
}
```

From the above program we can see that the 3D array is declared here as:

sales[10][6][5]

and input is given to the array by the statement :

scanf("%d",&sales[i][j][k]);

The array is accessed by the statement sales[i][j][k] which denotes the sales amount of **i**th Employee on the **j**th Month of the **k**th product.

11.9 PROGRAMMING EXAMPLES

Here are some programming examples to understand the various uses of array.

PROGRAM 11.14   Write a program to print the addresses of character array.

```
# include<stdio.h>
void main( )
{
    int i=0;
    char c_arr[7]={'P','A','S','C','A','L'};
    for(i=0;i<7;i++)
    {
        printf("\n[%c] is at %u memory location ",c_arr[i],&c_arr[i]);
        i++;
    }
}
```

Sample Output

    [P] is at 1054 memory location
    [A] is at 1055 memory location
    [S] is at 1056 memory location
    [C] is at 1057 memory location
    [A] is at 1058 memory location
    [L] is at 1059 memory location

Program 11.15   Write a program to store n numbers in an array and find their average.

```c
#include<stdio.h>
#define SIZE   20
void main()
{
    int arr[SIZE],sum=0,i,num;
    float avg;
    printf("Enter Number of Elements(<=20) :");
    scanf("%d",&num);
    for(i=0;i<num;i++)                    /*Storing of numbers into the array */
    {   printf("Enter any Number :");
        scanf("%d",&arr[i]);
        sum+=arr[i];                      /* Summation of array numbers */
    }
    avg=(float)sum/num;                   /* Calculation of Average */
    printf("\nAverage = %.2f",avg);
}
```

Sample Output

Enter Number of Elements(<=20) : 5

Enter any Number : 12

Enter any Number : 25

Enter any Number : 49

Enter any Number : 78

Enter any Number : 33

Average = 39.40

Program 11.16   Write a Program to input five numbers through the keyboard. Compute & display addition of even numbers and product of odd numbers.

```c
# include <stdio.h>
void main()
{
    int a=0,m=1,i,num[5];
    for (i=0;i<5;i++)
    {
        printf ("\nEnter Number %d:",i+1);
        scanf ("%d",&num[i]);
    }
    printf ("\n");
    for (i=0;i<5;i++)
    {
        if (num[i]%2==0)   /* Checking of Even Numbers */
```

```
        {
            printf ("\n Even Number  : %d",num[i]);
            a=a+num[i];                    /* Addition of Even Numbers */
        }
        else
        {
            printf ("\n Odd Number   : %d",num[i]);
            m=m*num[i];                    /* Multiplication of Odd Numbers */
        }
    }
    printf ("\n\n Addition of Even Numbers : %d",a);
    printf ("\n Product  of Odd  Numbers :%d",m);
}
```

Sample Output

Enter Number 1: 1
Enter Number 2: 2
Enter Number 3: 3
Enter Number 4: 4
Enter Number 5: 5

Odd Number : 1
Even Number : 2
Odd Number : 3
Even Number : 4
Odd Number : 5

Addition of Even Numbers : 6
Product of Odd Numbers : 15

PROGRAM 11.17 Write a program to find the intersection of two sets of numbers.

```
#include<conio.h>
#include<stdio.h>
#define SIZE    20
void main()
{
    int arr1[SIZE],arr2[SIZE],arr3[2*SIZE],i,j,k=0;
    printf("Enter Numbers for the First Set:- \n");
    for(i=0;i<SIZE;i++)                /* Inputs to first array */
    {   printf("Enter Number %d:",i+1);
        scanf("%d",&arr1[i]);
    }
    printf("\nEnter Numbers for the Second Set:- \n");
    for(i=0;i<SIZE;i++)                /* Inputs to Second array */
    {   printf("Enter Number %d:",i+1);
```

```
        scanf("%d",&arr2[i]);
    }
    for(i=0;i<SIZE;i++)                    /* Checking for Intersection */
    for(j=0;j<SIZE;j++)
    {
        if(arr1[i]==arr2[j])
        {   arr3[k++]=arr1[i];
            break;
        }
    }
    printf("\n The Intersection of above Two sets of numbers :\n");
    for(i=0;i<k;i++)
        printf("%d  ",arr3[i]);
}
```

Sample Output

Enter Numbers for the First Set:-

Enter Number 1: 1

Enter Number 2: 3

Enter Number 3: 5

Enter Number 4: 7

Enter Number 5: 9

Enter Numbers for the Second Set:-

Enter Number 1: 2

Enter Number 2: 3

Enter Number 3: 4

Enter Number 4: 5

Enter Number 5: 6

The Intersection of above Two sets of numbers:

   3 5

PROGRAM 11.18   Write a program to rearrange an array in reverse order without using a second array.

```
#include<stdio.h>
#define SIZE   15
void main()
{   int arr[SIZE],i,num,j,t;

    printf("Enter Number of Elements(<=15):");
    scanf("%d",&num);
    for(i=0;i<num;i++)
    {   printf("Enter any Number:");
        scanf("%d",&arr[i]);
    }
```

```
    for(i=0,j=num-1;i<j;i++,j--)    /* swapping of elements to reverse the array */
    {    t = arr[i];
         arr[i] = arr[j];
         arr[j] = t;
    }
    printf("\n Array elements in reverse order :\n");
    for(i=0;i<num;i++)
         printf("%d  ",arr[i]);
}
```

Sample Output

Enter Number of Elements(<=20) : 5

Enter any Number : 1

Enter any Number : 3

Enter any Number : 5

Enter any Number : 7

Enter any Number : 9

Array elements in reverse order:

9 7 5 3 1

PROGRAM 11.19   Write a program to insert an element into an array in a particular position..

```
#include<conio.h>
#include<stdio.h>
#define ASIZE    15
void main()
{
    int arr[ASIZE],n,posn,i,j;

    for(i=0;i<ASIZE-1;i++)              /* Inputs of 9 numbers */
    {    printf("Enter any number: ");
         scanf("%d",&arr[i]);
    }
    printf("\nEnter the number to be inserted : ");
    scanf("%d",&n);
    printf("Enter the position where the number will be inserted : ");
    scanf("%d",&posn);
    for(i=ASIZE-1;i>=posn;i--)          /* Shifting of elements towards end up to */
         arr[i]= arr[i-1];              /* the insertion position */
    arr[posn]=n;                        /* Insertion of elements */
    clrscr();
    printf("\nList of elements after insertion :\n");
    for(i=0;i<ASIZE;i++)
         printf("%d ",arr[i]);
}
```

Sample Output

Enter any number : 5
Enter any Number : 32
Enter any Number : 12
Enter any Number : 73
Enter any Number : 22
Enter any Number : 55
Enter any Number : 42
Enter any Number : 63
Enter any Number : 10

Enter the number to be inserted : 33
Enter the position where the number will be inserted : 4

List of elements after insertion :
5 32 12 33 73 22 55 42 63 10

PROGRAM 11.20   Write a program to multiply two matrices.

```
#include<conio.h>
#include<stdio.h>
void main()
{    int ar1[3][3], ar2[3][3],ar3[3][3],i,j,k,t;

printf("\nEnter the elements of 1st Matrix:-\n");
for(i=0;i<3;i++)                              /* Input to 1st Matrix   */
{   for(j=0;j<3;j++)
       {  printf("Enter element[%d][%d]  : ",i,j);
          scanf("%d",&ar1[i][j]);
       }
}
printf("\nEnter the elements of 2nd Matrix:-\n");
for(i=0;i<3;i++)                              /* Input to 2nd Matrix   */
{   for(j=0;j<3;j++)
       {  printf("Enter element[%d][%d]  : ",i,j);
          scanf("%d",&ar2[i][j]);
       }
}

clrscr();
printf("\n\n1st Matrix:-\n");
for(i=0;i<3;i++)                              /* Print 1st Matrix   */
{   for(j=0;j<3;j++)
          printf("%d\t",ar1[i][j]);
    printf("\n");
}
printf("\n\n2nd Matrix:-\n");
```

```
for(i=0;i<3;i++)                              /* Print 2nd Matrix   */
{    for(j=0;j<3;j++)
         printf("%d\t",ar2[i][j]);
     printf("\n");
}

for(i=0;i<3;i++)                              /* Multiplication of two matrix */
{    for(j=0;j<3;j++)
     {    ar3[i][j] = 0;
          for(k=0;k<3;k++)
              ar3[i][j] += ar1[i][k] * ar2[k][j];
     }
}
printf("\n\nAfter Multiplication the resultant Matrix is :-\n");
for(i=0;i<3;i++)                              /*  Printing of Resultant matrix */
{    for(j=0;j<3;j++)
         printf("%d\t", ar3[i][j]);
     printf("\n");
}
}
```

Sample Output

Enter the elements of 1st Matrix:-

    Enter element[0][0] : 1

    Enter element[0][1] : 2

    Enter element[0][2] : 3

    Enter element[1][0] : 4

    Enter element[1][1] : 5

    Enter element[1][2] : 6

    Enter element[2][0] : 7

    Enter element[2][1] : 8

    Enter element[2][2] : 9

Enter the elements of 2nd Matrix:-

    Enter element[0][0] : 2

    Enter element[0][1] : 3

    Enter element[0][2] : 4

    Enter element[1][0] : 5

    Enter element[1][1] : 6

    Enter element[1][2] : 7

    Enter element[2][0] : 8

    Enter element[2][1] : 9

    Enter element[2][2] : 10

1st Matrix:-

1	2	3
4	5	6
7	8	9

2nd Matrix:-

2	3	4
5	6	7
8	9	10

After multiplication the resultant Matrixis :-

36	42	48
81	96	111
126	150	174

PROGRAM 11.21   Write a program to find transpose of a matrix.

```c
#include<conio.h>
#include<stdio.h>
void main()
{    int matrix[3][3],i=0,j=0,t;

     printf("\nEnter the elements of a Matrix:-\n");

     for(i=0;i<3;i++)
     {    for(j=0;j<3;j++)
          {    printf("Enter element[%d][%d] : ");
               scanf("%d",&matrix[i][j]);
          }
     }

     clrscr();
     printf("\n\nOriginal Matrix:-\n");
     for(i=0;i<3;i++)
     {    for(j=0;j<3;j++)
               printf("%d\t",matrix[i][j]);
          printf("\n");
     }
     for(i=0;i<3;i++)
          for(j=0;j<i;j++)
          {    t= matrix[i][j];
               matrix[i][j]=matrix[j][i];
               matrix[j][i]=t;
          }
```

```
printf("\n\nTranspose of the Matrix:-\n");

for(i=0;i<3;i++)
{    for(j=0;j<3;j++)
          printf("%d\t",matrix[i][j]);
     printf("\n");
}
}
```

Sample Output

Enter the elements of a Matrix:-
Enter element[0][0] : 10
Enter element[0][1] : 20
Enter element[0][2] : 30
Enter element[1][0] : 40
Enter element[1][1] : 50
Enter element[1][2] : 60
Enter element[2][0] : 70
Enter element[2][1] : 80
Enter element[2][2] : 90

Original Matrix:-
    10   20   30
    40   50   60
    70   80   90

Transpose of the Matrix:-
    10   40   70
    20   50   80
    30   60   90

SUMMARY

- An array is a collection of homogeneous data elements.
- Array elements are always stored in contiguous memory locations.
- Array index always starts with 0.
- only valid type of declaration for array is:
    datatype arrayname[Size1][Size2-*optional*][[Size3-*optional*]..;
    where Size should be any **integer** constant or symbolic constant with **integral value**.
- The subscript or array index may be any valid integer constant, integer variable or integer expression.
- C does not perform any bound checking. So accessing array elements beyond size will not produce any error.
- Negative array index will not produce any error.
- Array name is a constant pointer (Will be discussed in Chapter 14 (Pointer)).

➤ When an array is passed as an argument to a function, base address of the array is actually passed.

➤ For sending array containing string to function, there is no need to send the size along with but for other types of array, sending the size is required as they are not null terminated (Will be discussed in Chapter 13 (Function)).

REVIEW EXERCISES

1. What is an array? What is its need?
2. What are subscripts?
3. Suppose in the initialization list less number of values is provided than the array size – What happens?
4. What happens if the array subscript exceeds the size of the array?
5. Write a C program to find the smallest element among N inputted numbers.
6. Write a C program to find the largest difference in a set of numbers.
7. Write a C program to calculate variance of N numbers.
8. Write a C program to count odd numbers in a set of integers.
9. Write a C program to find binary equivalent of a decimal number.
10. Write a C program to delete an element from the *k*-th position of an array.
11. Write a C program to sort an array in descending order.
12. Write a C program to insert an element at its proper position in a previously sorted array.
13. Write a C program to find the union of two sets of numbers.
14. Write a C program to merge two sorted array.
15. Write a C program to find the frequency of each element in an array.
16. Write a C program to find the determinant of a matrix.
17. Write a C program to find the sum of diagonal elements of a square matrix.
18. In an organization, there are 15 employees. The monthly sale figures of a whole year of each employee are available. Write a C program to find the total sales of each employee and total sales of each month. Also find the grand total sales of the company.

LEARN BY QUIZ – QUESTIONS

1. What is an array?
   (1) Collection of homogeneous data elements.
   (2) Collection of heterogeneous data elements.
   (3) Collection of homogeneous or heterogeneous data elements that depends on compiler.
2. Which of the following is true in respect to array?
   (1) Array elements are always stored in contiguous memory locations.
   (2) Array elements are always stored in scattered way in the memory.
   (3) There is no fixed rule about allocation of an array. Depending on the availability of memory, Operating system allocates memory for an array.

3. Which of the following is true in respect to array?
   (1) An array consists of homogeneous element and its allocation is scattered in memory.
   (2) An array consists of homogeneous element and its allocation is contiguous.
   (3) An array consists of heterogeneous element and its allocation is contiguous.

4. What is the syntax of array declaration?
   (1) datatype arrayname[Size];
   (2) Declare array arrayname[size];
   (3) Dim arrayname(size) as datatype;

5. Which of the following array declaration is correct?
   (1) int apple[5];
   (2) float apple[3.5];
   (3) int apple[n]; *where n is an integer variable.*

6. Which of the following declaration is correct?
   (1) int arr[5] = [2,4,6,8,10];
   (2) int arr[5] = {2,4,6,8,10};
   (3) int arr[5] = (2,4,6,8,10);

7. Which of the following is not correct?
   (1) int arr[4] = {2 4 6 8};
   (2) int arr[4] = { 2,4};
   (3) int arr[4] = {2,4,6,8};

8. Which of the following array declaration is not correct?
   (1) int a[];
   (2) int a[4] = {1,3};
   (3) int a[] = {1,3,6,9};

9. Which of the following array initialization statement is correct?
   (1) int sample[3] = {,5, };
   (2) int sample[3] = {5, };
   (3) int sample[3] = { , ,5};

10. In 'C' language the array index always starts with
    (1) 0
    (2) 1
    (3) −1

11. Which of the following is not true?
    (1) The array index may be a floating value.
    (2) The array index may be an integer.
    (3) The array index may be any expression which yields an integer.

12. void main()
    { int arr[3]={1,2,3};
      printf("%d",arr[3]); }
    Which of the following option is the correct output in respect to the above program segment?
    (1) 3
    (2) Garbage value
    (3) As in the printf statement, array crosses its boundary limit it produce compilation error.

13. Which of the following produce compilation error to access an array element?
    (1) a(1)
    (2) a[−1]
    (3) a[2*(i+3)]

14 Which one is incorrect to access the (i+1)th element of an array named arr
   (1) arr[i+1]
   (2) arr[i]
   (3) i[arr]

15. How much memory will be allocated by the declaration (in a 16bit compiler): int a[5];
   (1) 6 bytes
   (2) 5 bytes
   (3) 10 bytes

16. If the declaration is: double data[5][7];
   Which one will be the last element?
   (1) data[4][6]
   (2) data[5][7]
   (3) Data[4][7]

17. If the declaration is: float data[7][5];
   Which one will be the first element?
   (1) data[0][0]
   (2) data[1][1]
   (3) data[0][1]

18. void main()
   {   int arr[3]={576};
       printf("%d",arr[1]); }
   Which of the following option is the correct output of the above program segment?
   (1) 7
   (2) 576
   (3) 0

19. Array can be used to store
   (1) Price of Cars.
   (2) Roll no, Name, Address, Age of a student
   (3) Total weekly expenditure of an organization.

20. Array can be used to store
   (1) Name of a student
   (2) Age of a student
   (3) Fees paid by a student

21. If the declaration is: double data[100];
   What will be the subscript of the last element?
   (1) 200
   (2) 100
   (3) 99

22. If less number of values are provided in the initialization list than the array size, what happens?
   (1) The elements will be initialized from first by the values in the initialization list and rest array elements will contain zero.
   (2) Compilation error will occur.
   (3) The elements will be initialized from first by the values in the initialization list and rest array elements will contain garbage value.

23. If more values are provided in the initialization list than the array size, what happens?
   (1) Compilation error will occur.
   (2) Array will be initialized properly and the extra elements in the list will be lost.
   (3) Array will be initialized properly and the extra elements overwrite the adjacent memory locations.

24. What is the syntax of 2 dimensional array declaration?
    (1) datatype arrayname[row_size X col_size];
    (2) datatype arrayname[row_size,col_size];
    (3) datatype arrayname[row_size][col_size];

25. For storing which of the following data 2-D array is required?
    (1) Sales amount of each sales man for each month in an organization
    (2) Sales amount of each sales man for each month for each product in an organization
    (3) Sales amount of each sales man in an organization

26. What is the syntax of multi dimensional array declaration?
    (1) datatype arrayname[s1][s2][s3]...[sn];
        where s1,s2, ... are the size of 1st dimension, 2nd dimension, ...
    (2) datatype arrayname[s1,s2,s3,.....sn];
        where s1,s2, ... are the size of 1st dimension, 2nd dimension, ...
    (3) datatype arrayname[s1 X s2 X s3 X ....X sn];
        where s1,s2, ... are the size of 1st dimension, 2nd dimension, ...

27. Which of the following array declaration is correct?
    (1) `int arr[2] [3] = { {2,4},`
                          `{3,5},`
                          `{6,7},`
                      `};`
    (2) `int arr[2] [3] = { [2,4,6],`
                          `[3,5,7]`
                      `};`
    (3) `int arr[2] [3] = { (2,4,6),`
                          `(3,5,7)`
                      `};`

28. `int arr[2] [3] = { (2,4,6),`
                      `(3,5,7)`
                  `};`
    what will be the value of arr[1][2]?
    (1) 0
    (2) 7
    (3) The code will face syntactical error.

29. `int arr[2][3]={ {2,4,6}, };`
    what will be the value of arr[1][2]?
    (1) 0
    (2) 6
    (3) Garbage value

30. `int arr[2] [3] = { {11,12},`
                      `{22}`
                  `};`
    what will be the value of arr[0][2]?
    (1) Garbage value
    (2) 22
    (3) 0

31. To represent a matrix, it is better to use
    (1) 2 dimensional array
    (2) 1 dimensional array
    (3) 3 dimensional array

32. To represent a graph, which one of the following is used?
   (1) 2-D array
   (2) 1-D array
   (3) Multidimensional array

33.
```
int arr[] [3] = { {2,4,6},
                  {3,5,7}
                };
```
   what the above statement will do?
   (1) Will produce an error as row size is not mentioned.
   (2) Will declare a 1-D array because row size is not mentioned and it will be considered as a single dimensional array.
   (3) Will declare a 2-D array which will consist of 2 rows and 3 cols and will be initialized by the initialization list.

34. Which one of the following is correct?
   (1) int arr[2][3] ={11,12,13,21,22,23};
   (2) int arr[2][]= { {11,12,13}, {21,22,23} };
   (3) int arr[][] = { {11,12,13}, {21,22,23} };

35.
```
void main()
{ int arr[3] [3], i;
   for(i=0;i<3;i++)
      printf("%d ",arr[0] [i]); }
```
   The above code will print
   (1) The first row elements only
   (2) The first column elements only
   (3) The diagonal elements only

36.
```
void main()
{ int arr[] [3] = { {2,4,6},
                    {3,5,7}
                  };
   printf("%d", sizeof(arr));
}
```
   What will be the output of the program? Assume that we are using 16 bit compiler.
   (1) 3
   (2) 6
   (3) 12

37.
```
void main()
{ int arr[3] [3], i;
   for(i=0;i<3;i++)
      arr[i] [i]=0; }
```
   The above code will initialize
   (1) The diagonal elements
   (2) The first row only
   (3) The first column only

38. Which of the following function prototype is appropriate for a function that will find the largest number among the integers stored in an array?

(1) int largest(int arr[], int n);

(2) int largest(int arr, int n);

(3) int largest(int arr);

39. What will be the function call statement to call the function:

int largest(int a[], int n); where n is the size of the array.

Suppose the name of the array in calling function is arr and its size is 10.

(1) p=largest(arr, 10);

(2) p=largest(arr[],10);

(3) p=largest(arr[10],10);

40.
```
void main()
{ int arr[3][3], i;
   for(i=0;i<3;i++)
      arr[i][0]=1; }
```
The above code will initialize

(1) The first column elements only

(2) The first row elements only

(3) The diagonal elements only

41.
```
void main()
{ int arr[3]={1,2,3};
  printf("%d",arr[0]); }
```
Which of the following option is correct output in respect to the above program segment?

(1) 1

(2) Error because array index cannot be 0.

(3) Garbage value

42 Assume that we are using 16 bit compiler.

What will be the size of the following array in bytes?

int sales[3][4][5];

(1) 120

(2) 24

(3) 60

43
```
void main()
{ int arr[2][3]={{1,2,3}, {4,5,6}};
   int i, j;
   for(i=0;i<2;i++)
     for(j=0;j<3;j++)
        printf("%d ",arr[i][j]); }
```
What will be the output of the above program?

(1) 1 2 3 4 5 6

(2) Garbage value

(3) 0 1 2 0 4 5

44.
```
void main()
{ float arr[2][3];  int i, j;
   for(i=0;i<2;i++)
     for(j=0;j<3;j++)
        printf("%u ",&arr[i][j]); }
```
What will be the output of the above program if the starting address of the array is 2000?

(1) 2000 2002 2004 2006 2008 2010

(2) 2000 2004 2008 2012 2016 2020

(3) Cannot determined

45.
```
void main()
{ float arr[3]={1.15,2.6,3.79};  int i;
  for(i=0;i<3;i++)
      printf("%u ",&arr[i]); }
```
What will be the output of the above program if the starting address of the array is 2000?

(1) 2000 2004 2008

(2) 2000 2001 2002

(3) 2000 2002 2004

LEARN BY QUIZ – ANSWERS

Answer explanations

1. An array is a collection of homogeneous data elements described by a single name, and each individual element of an array is referred by a subscripted variable.

   example:

   int a[10]; /* the declaration of an integer array having 10 elements a[0] to a[9] */

   a[2]=5; /*assigning the value 5 to the third element*/

   i=a[2] /* reading value of third element of the array and assigning to a variable*/

2. An array is a collection of homogeneous data elements described by a single name. **Array elements are always stored in contiguous memory locations.** In any circumstances, allocation of an array cannot be scattered.

3. An array consists of homogeneous element and its allocation is contiguous.

   homogeneous:- all the elements are of same datatype.

   contiguous allocation:- all the elements will reside in successive locations of memory. For example the following case is not possible:

   first 5 elements of a ten element character array are in memory location 1000–1004 and other five element at 1500–1504 is not possible.

4. In C language the only valid type of declaration for array is:

   datatype arrayname[Size];

   where Size should be any constant or symbolic constant.

   example:

   int a[10]; /* the declaration of an integer array having 10 elements a[0] to a[9] */

5. The syntax to declare an array is : *datatype arrayname[Size];*

   int apple[5]; is correct. Here, **int** is the data type, **apple** is array name and **5** is size of the array, i.e., atmost 5 integers can be stored in the array.

   float apple[3.5]; is wrong. Size of an array cannot be float or double. It should be any integer constant or symbolic constant with integral value.

   int apple[n]; Size of an array cannot be any variable.

6. int arr[5] = {2,4,6,8,10}; is correct.

   int arr[5] = [2,4,6,8,10]; or int arr[5] = (2,4,6,8,10); are wrong as [] or () are not applicable here. Instead we should use {}.

7. At the time of initialization, the values in the list must be separated by commas not by space. So int arr[4] = {2 4 6 8}; is not correct statement.

The initialization list may contain lesser number of values than its size. Then remaining cells will contain zero instead of garbage values. So int arr[4] = { 2,4}; is equivalent to int arr[4]={2,4,0,0};

int arr[4] = {2,4,6,8}; is correct. It is declaring an integer array of 4 elements where a[0]=2, a[1]=4, a[2]=6 and a[3]=8.

8. To declare an array, the size of the array must have to be mentioned, unless it is initialized at the same time. So the declaration **int a[];** is incorrect.

   The initialization list may contain lesser number of values than its size. Then remaining cells will contain zero instead of garbage values. So int a[4] = {1,3}; will work fine and is equivalent to int a[4]={1,3,0,0} or int a[]={1,3,0,0}.

   If the array is initialized when it is declared, it is optional to mention the size of the array. Hence int a[] = {1,3,6,9}; have nothing wrong.

9. The initialization list may contain lesser number of values than its size. In the statement **int sample[3] = {5, };** the comma after 5 in the initialization list is optional.

   int sample[3] = {,5, }; or int sample[3] = { , ,5}; will give compilation error.

10. In 'C' language the array index always starts with 0. As per example, in the declaration int a[4]; 4 elements will be created with index 0,1,2 and 3. They can be accessed by a[0], a[1], a[2] and a[3].

11. The subscript or array index may be any valid integer constant, integer variable or integer expression but cannot be a floating point value.

12. In the printf statement, arr[3] refers the 4th element. But here the array size is 3. So **it will print some garbage value.**

    As array index starts with 0, arr[3] refers the 4th cell or element. And 3 is the 3rd element. So, **3 will not be the ouput.**

    C does not perform any bound checking. That is why **arr[3] will not produce any error.**

13. To access an array element, ( ) is not allowed. Only [ ] have to be used. So,

    a(1) will produce compilation error to access an array element.

    Negative array index will not produce any error. But it refers the cell in backward direction starting from first cell. And it **should be avoided** as it does not refer any position within the array bound.

    a[2*(i+3)] is correct. Because any expression which results some integer can be used as array index or subscript.

14. As array index starts with 0, (i+1)th element will be arr[i]. Instead of arr[i], it can be written as i[arr]. arr[i] and i[arr] refers to the same element.

    So, to access the (i+1)th element of an array named arr, any one of arr[i] or i[arr] can be used. arr[i+1] is the incorrect statement.

15. **10 bytes will be allocated by the declaration: int a[5];**

    An integer takes 2 bytes in memory. So, for an integer array of size 5, number of bytes required is 5 * 2 = 10 bytes.

16. If the declaration is: double data[5][7];

    The last element will be data[4][6]. Array index for row as well as column start with 0. So, the first element is data[0][0], next data[0][1], and so on.

17. If the declaration is: float data[7][5];

    the first element will be data[0][0].

Array index for row as well as column start with 0. So, the first element in 2-D array named data is data[0][0], next data[0][1], and so on.

18. The output of the above program is 0.

   int arr[3]={576}; – in this statement, array size is 3 and no. of initializing element is one. So, 576 will be stored at arr[0]. arr[1] and arr[2] will contain zero(0).

19. These are some integer or float values, i.e., homogeneous elements. So, **Array can be used to store Price of Cars.**

   Roll no may be integer, **name** and **address** are of character type **age** may be integer or float. These are heterogeneous elements. So, **these cannot be stored in an array.**

   Total weekly expenditure of an organization – is not a set of elements. It is a single figure. So, **Array cannot be used.** To store it a single integer or float variable is required.

20. **Name of a student** – it is set of characters. So, **to store it array will be required.**

   Age and **fees paid by a student** are single element. That is why normal integer or float variable will be required – not an array. Always remember array is **Collection of homogeneous data elements.**

21. The subscript of the last element will be 99 in the declaration: double data[100];

   As the subscript starts with 0 always, the last element will be 99 as there are total 100 elements.

22. The elements will be initialized from first by the values in the initialization list and rest array elements will contain zero.

23. **The compiler will produce an error message** as the initialization list contains more elements than the declared size.

24. In C language the only valid type of declaration for 2 dimensional array is:

   datatype arrayname[row_size][col_size];

   where row_size indicates the total no. of rows and col_size indicates the total no. of cols. row_size and col_size should be any integer constant or symbolic constant.

   Example:

   int A[2][3]; /* A is a two dimensional integer array having two rows and three columns*/

   the elements can be visualized as following:-

   A[0][0], A[0][1], A[0][2] /*FIRST ROW */

   A[1][0], A[1][1], A[1][2] /*SECOND ROW */

   Similarly declaration of a three dimension array will be int A[2][3][2];

25. Instead of list of values, when we have to store a table of values, 2-D array is better option. If the no. of constraint (i.e., depending factor) of the data is two, it will be better we use 2-D array for writing a program. Though we can store the data in 1-D array, but it will lost the readability and retrieval of data to face different query will be complicated.

   So, to store Sales amount of each sales man for each month in an organization, a 2-D array will be required. Here no. of constraints is 2 and these are salesman and month.

   Sales amount of each sales man for each month for each product in an organization cannot be stored within the 2-D array. Here no. of constraints is 3 and these are **salesman**, **month** and **product**. So, we cannot use 2-D array. For this 3-D array will be required.

   Sales amount of each sales man in an organization cannot be stored within the 2-D array. Here no. of constraints is 1 and this is only **salesman**. So, we cannot use 2-D array. For this 1-D array will be required.

26. In C language the only valid type of declaration for multi dimensional array is:

    datatype arrayname[s1][s2][s3]...[sn];

    where s1,s2, ... are the size of 1st dimension, 2nd dimension, ...

    and these s1,s2,.... should be any constant or symbolic constant.

27. ```
    int arr[2][3]={  {2,4,6},
                     {3,5,7}
                  };
    ```

    The above declaration is correct. It declares 2-D array which consists of 2 rows and 3 cols and it will also be initialized by the initialization list.

    We can also write it as :

    `int arr[2][3]={ 2,4,6,3,5,7};` But it will lose the readability as the size increased.

    ```
    int arr[2][3]={  [2,4,6],
                     [3,5,7]
                  };
    ```

    The above declaration is incorrect. Because at the time of initialization we have to use { } and not [ ].

    ```
    int arr[2][3]={  {2,4},
                     {3,5},
                     {6,7},
                  };
    ```

    The above declaration is incorrect. Here initialization list is not written properly. The above code will produce error. Here, no. rows are 2 and initialization list containing values for 3 rows.

28. Instead of '{ }' here '( )' is used. So, the statement (2,4,6) will return 6 according to the associativity property of comma(,) operator within '( )'. That's why, only 6 will be stored at arr[0][0] and 7 will be stored at arr[0][1]. Rest will contain zero. **The correct answer, i.e., the value of arr[1][2] will be 0 (zero).**

29. If less number of values are provided in the initialization list than the array size, the elements will be initialized from first by the values in the initialization list and rest array elements will contain zero. So, the correct answer is **0 (Zero)**. As only the first row is initialized here, rest element will contain zero(0).

30. The correct answer is **0 (Zero)**. The first two elements of the first row will be initialized by 11 and 12, respectively. The first element of the second row will contain 22 and other elements will be initialized by zero.

31. As a matrix consists of some rows and cols, **2-dimensional array is used to represent a matrix.**

32. In computer, graph is represented by adjacency matrix and incidence matrix. As matrix consist of some rows and cols, **to represent a graph 2-D array is used.**

33. ```
    int arr[][3]={  {2,4,6},
                    {3,5,7}
                 };
    ```

The above statement will declare a 2-D array which will consist of 2 rows and 3 cols and will be initialized by the initialization list.

While initializing an array it is essential to specify col_size, while row_size is optional. It will be determined by the initialization list.

34. Memory does not contain rows and columns. In memory whether it is one-dimensional or a two-dimensional array, the array elements are stored in one continuous chain. So, **int arr[2] [3] ={11,12,13,21,22,23};** is correct.

   While initializing an array, **it is necessary to mention the col_size, whereas the row_size is optional**. It will be determined by the initialization list. So,

   int arr[2][ ]= { {11,12,13}, {21,22,23} }; and

   int arr[ ][ ] = { {11,12,13}, {21,22,23} }; are wrong.

35. By the above code, arr[0][0], arr[0][1] and arr[0][2] will only be printed.

   So, the above code will print first row elements only.

36. Correct answer is **12**. sizeof operator returns the total size (i.e., allocation in memory) of any variable or datatype in terms of byte. The array arr contains 2 rows each with 3 cols. So, total no. of elements is 2 * 3 = 6. As each int occupies 2 bytes in memory, the total allocation = 6 * 2 = **12**.

37. By the above code, arr[0][0], arr[1][1] and arr[2][2] will only be initialized by 0.

   So, the above code will initialize the diagonal elements.

38. **int largest(int arr[], int n);** is the correct answer. Here 1st argument is array itself and 2nd argument is the size of the array. As there is no way to find the array boundary in numeric array, we have to mention the size of the array.

   The function body may be as following:-

```
int largest(int arr[], int n)
{
int i,maximum;
maximum=arr[0];
for(i=1;i<n;i++)
if (arr[i]>maximum) maximum=arr[i];
return maximum;
}
```

39. When we want to pass an entire array, we have to pass the base address of the array by specifying its name or by the statement &arr[0].

   So, p=largest(arr, 10); is the correct answer.

   p=largest(arr[],10); is wrong because arr[] is used to declare an initialized array. This cannot be used at function call.

   p=largest(arr[10],10); is wrong because arr[10] represents only a particular element (though this position is out of array boundary. Here limit will be 0–9.) not the entire array.

40. By the above code, arr[0][0], arr[1][0] and arr[2][0] will only be initialized by 1.

   So, the above code will initialize the first column elements only.

41. **The output of the program will be 1.** Array index always starts with 0. arr[0] indicates the first element in the array.

42. We can get the no. of elements by multiplying the sizes. So, no. of elements in the array sales = 3*4*5=60.

    To get size of the array, this value will be multiplied with the size of each element(here it is 2 as int requires 2 bytes for allocation in memory).

    So total size = 60 * 2 = 120.

43. By the statement **int arr[2][3]={{1,2,3}, {4,5,6}};** a 2-D array will be declared and by its initialization list the array elements will be initialized. So, arr[0][0] will contain 1, arr[0][1] will contain 2, a[0][2] will contain 3, a[1][0] will contain 4, arr[1][1] will contain 5 and arr[1][2] will contain 6. So, **the output will be**

    1 2 3 4 5 6

44. **The correct output will be 2000 2004 2008 2012 2016 2020.**

    Memory does not contain rows and columns. It is always linear. Whatever may be the dimension of an array, in memory it is always allocated in contiguous locations.

    And any float value takes 4 bytes in memory. If the starting address is 2000, then address of arr[0][0] will be 2000,address of arr[0][1] will be 2004, address of arr[0][2] will be 2008, address of arr[1][0] will be 2012 and so on.

45. **The correct output will be 2000 2004 2008**. Any float value takes 4 bytes in memory. If the starting address is 2000, then address of arr[1] will be 2004 and address of arr[2] will be 2008.

12

String Handling

In the last chapter, we discussed about single and multi dimensional array. We already learnt how to define arrays of different sizes and dimensions, how to initialize them, how to operate on arrays of different dimensions, etc. With this knowledge, we are ready to handle **strings**, which are, simply a special kind of array. String handling basically consists of:

- Input and output strings from/to keyboard/monitor or files.
- Copying and comparing strings with library functions.
- Finding substrings, determining length, extracting substring, concatenating strings with library functions.
- Manipulating case of characters in a string with library functions.
- Writing equivalent functions of string manipulating library functions.

We will discuss all important string manipulating library functions in this chapter; however a complete list of string manipulating library functions along with explanation is given in **Appendix**.

We will learn to write equivalent functions of string manipulating library functions in functions chapter.

12.1 STRING

A string is a sequence of characters terminated with a null character ('\0'). It is usually stored as one-dimensional character array. A set of characters arranged in any sequence defined within double quotation is known as string constant. To manipulate text such as words and sentences, strings, i.e., character arrays are used. The way a group of integers can be stored in an integer array, is similar with a group of characters stored in a character array.

12.1.1 Declaration of String

The general form to declare a string is:

```
char string_name[string_size];
```

Here **string_size** denotes the number of characters stored within the character array. As every string is terminated by '\0' character, the size of the array would be equal to the *maximum number of characters in the string plus one.*

For example, to store the string "Subrata", the array size needs to be declared as at least of size 8. i.e., 7 letters + 1 null character ('\0') as:

> char name[8];

Whenever we declare a string constant, C automatically creates an unnamed array of characters that will contain the string terminated by the '\0' character.

For example, for a string constant, "Hello, world!" an unnamed character array of size 14 will be declared and the string will be stored within that array with a '\0' character at the end. It can be represented as follows:

0	1	2	3	4	5	6	7	8	9	10	11	12	13
H	e	l	l	o	,		w	o	r	l	d	!	\0

12.1.2 Initializing Strings

Like numeric array, we can initialize a string also at the time of declaration.

> char name[8] = {'S', 'u', 'b', 'r', 'a', 't', 'a', '\0'};

or simply,

> char name[8] = "Subrata";

When we use the string constant to initialize a string, '\0' character is not required to mention. It is inserted automatically at end.

Like numeric array, it is possible to omit the size of the array also if we initialize at the time of declaration.

> char name[] = "Subrata";

These declarations would have created an array like this:

	0	1	2	3	4	5	6	7
name	S	u	b	r	a	t	a	\0

12.1.3 Writing Strings to Screen

To print strings on to the VDU the *printf()* is used. The array name is passed as argument. The *printf()* along with format specifier %s starts display each character starting from the first position of the array until the null character is encountered. For example,

```
printf("%s",strn);
```

The above statement will display the contents of the array `strn`.

With the %s format specifier, we may include the width and precision specifier. It takes the form:

> **%w.ps**

here **w** specifies the width specifier which defines the minimum width for the output field. If the string is shorter, then unused positions of the field are filled with white space and the string will be printed as right justified. If we include minus sign with the format specifier, the output will be left justified. However, smaller width does not make any sense; and the entire string will be printed.

p specifies the precision specifier which defines the maximum number of characters to display and these characters taken from the beginning of the string. For example,

```
printf("%25.8s",strn);
```

The above statement will display the first eight characters of the string strn in the total field width of 25 characters.

The following example illustrates various usage of %s specifier.

PROGRAM 12.1   Program to demonstrate the use of width and precession specifier in case of string.

```
#include<stdio.h>
void main()
{    char strn[25]="Computer Programming";
     printf("\n!%s!",strn);
     printf("\n!%25s!",strn);
     printf("\n!%-25s!",strn);
     printf("\n!%10s!",strn);
     printf("\n!%25.8s!",strn);
     printf("\n!%-25.8s!",strn);
     printf("\n!%.8s!",strn);
}
```

Sample Output

```
!Computer Programming!
!      Computer Programming!
!Computer Programming      !
!Computer Programming!
!                Computer!
!Computer                 !
!Computer!
```

We can also use wildcard at the place of width and precision. Then the printf( ) statement takes the form

```
printf("%*.*s", w, p, strn);
```

where w indicates the width for the output field and p indicates the first p number of characters of string strn.

PROGRAM 12.2   Program to demonstrate the use of wildcard at the place of width and precision specifier.

```
#include<stdio.h>
#include<string.h>
void main()
{
    char strn[]="Computer Programming";
    int i,l;
    l=strlen(strn);    /* strlen() is used to find the length of a string */
    for(i=0;i<=l;i++)
    printf("\n%*.*s",l,i,strn);
}
```

Sample Output

```
                   C
                  Co
                 Com
                Comp
               Compu
              Comput
             Compute
            Computer
            Computer
           Computer P
          Computer Pr
         Computer Pro
        Computer Prog
       Computer Progr
      Computer Progra
     Computer Program
    Computer Programm
   Computer Programmi
  Computer Programmin
 Computer Programming
```

We can also use the puts( ) function to display strings on the screen. This function is also defined at stdio.h file.

The General form of puts( ) is:

```
puts(array_name);
```

EXAMPLE 12.1

```
puts(name);
```

Both the functions print the content of the array from the beginning to the null character. But the difference between printf( ) and puts( ) is that puts( ) adds an extra new line character at the end of the print statement.

For example,

```
          printf(" First ");
          printf(" Second");
output:   First Second

          puts(" First ");
          puts(" Second");
output:   First
          Second
```

12.1.4   Reading Strings from the Terminal

To read a string from the terminal we can use the library function scanf( ) with %s format specifier. Following program illustrate this:

PROGRAM 12.3

```
void main()
{
     char name[40];
     printf("Enter a name: ");
     scanf("%s",name);
     printf("The name is: %s",name);
}
```

Sample Output

Enter a name: Subrata
The name is: Subrata

Note that, here in the scanf statement the ampersand symbol is not used before the variable name as the array name returns the base address of its own self required by the scanf statement. Hence, no explicit use of '&' is needed in this case.

But, scanf statement is limited in certain extent. It stops reading as soon as a white space is found.

For instance, if we run *Program 8.3* with a different string like "Subrata Saha" then only the first word of the string, i.e., "Subrata" will be read because after the word "Subrata" there is a white space.

Sample Output

Enter a name: Subrata Saha
The name is: Subrata

The rest portion of the string will be stored in the buffer and will be read by the next scanf statement with the %s format specification, if any.

Let us consider another example.

PROGRAM 12.4

```
#include<stdio.h>
void main()
{
    char firstnm[30],lastnm[30];
    printf("Enter your first name:");
    scanf("%s",firstnm);
    printf("Enter your last name:");
    scanf("%s",lastnm);
    printf("\nFirst Name: %s",firstnm);
    printf("\nLast Name: %s",lastnm);
}
```

Sample Output

Enter your first name: Subrata Kumar Saha
Enter your last name:
First Name: Subrata
Last Name: Kumar

In this example, only "Subrata" has been stored in firstnm, as a space was encountered after it and then "Kumar" has been stored in lastnm and the remaining string was ignored as there was another space found after Kumar. If we provide the third scanf statement here with a %s specifier then "Saha" will also be read by it.

12.2 OVERCOMING THE LIMITATION WITH THE HELP OF SCANSET

We can get rid of this problem by using scanset specifiers. This facility helps us to specify the acceptable characters or to mention the terminating character(s). scanset specifiers are represented by %[ ]. To define the scanset, characters are needed to put inside the square brackets. If '^' is put as first character of scanset, then reading will be stopped as soon as it encounters the character(s) specified after '^'. Remember that the scansets are case-sensitive.

Here is some example to illustrate the use of scanset. The following scanset in *Program 8.5* will read all characters but stops after first occurrence of 'h'.

PROGRAM 12.5

```
void main()
{
    char strn[80];
    printf("Enter a string: ");
    scanf("%[^h]s", strn);
```

```
    printf("Inputted String is: %s", strn);
}
```

Sample Output

Enter a string: Subrata Saha

Inputted String is: Subrata Sa

Similarly, in *Program 8.6* scanf will read the complete string given by the user unless it will encounter a carriage-return/enter.

Program 12.6

```
void main()
{
    char strn[100];
    printf("Enter a string with spaces and terminate by pressing enter:");
    scanf("%[^\n]s", strn);
    printf("Inputted String is: %s", strn);
}
```

Sample Output

Enter a string with spaces and terminate by pressing enter: Subrata Saha

Inputted String is: Subrata Saha

If the user wants to give a multiline input, then any symbol (For instance "#") other than "\n" can be put inside the scanset formatting.

Program 12.7

```
void main()
{
    char strn[150];
    printf("Enter multi line string and end with a # sign:");
    scanf("%[^#]s", strn);
    printf("Inputted String is: %s", strn);
}
```

Sample Output

Enter multi line string and end with a # sign: This is first line.
And this is second line.#

Inputted String is: This is first line.
And this is second line.

From the above examples, it is clear that using scanset we can take multiword string input.

We can also include multiple terminating characters. In the following example, reading will be terminated while encountering a ';' or a ':'.

PROGRAM 12.8

```
void main()
{
    char strn[150];
    printf("Enter any string and end with : or ; sign:");
    scanf("%[^;:]s", strn);
    printf("Inputted String is: %s", strn);


}
```

Sample Output

Enter any string and end with : or ; sign: This is first line; o.k.
Inputted String is: This is first line

Enter any string and end with : or ; sign: This is first line: o.k.
Inputted String is: This is first line

Another added feature of scanset is that, we can specify single character as well as range of characters inside scanset. The following example will read only the digits. It will stop reading as soon as the other character is encountered and the remaining portion will be in the buffer and will be read by the next scanf statement with the %s format specification, if any.

PROGRAM 12.9

```
void main()
{
    char strn[80];
    printf("Enter a string: ");
    scanf("%[0-9]s", strn);
    printf("Inputted String is: %s", strn);
}
```

Sample Output

Enter a string: 5836SF2
Inputted String is: 5836

Another approach can be followed to take the input of strings with the *scanf()*. Instead of %s, we can use %c with a count associated with it. The count specifies the number of characters to be read in. The disadvantage of this approach is that it demands exact number of character input. If we give wrong numbers of characters as input, the first n number of characters (where n is the count) will be read and the rest portion will be stored in the buffer and will be read by the next *scanf()* statement, if any. The following program illustrates this.

PROGRAM 12.10

```
void main()
{
    char arr[10];
    int i;
    for(i=0;i<4;i++)
    {
        printf("\nEnter a string: ");
        scanf("%9c",arr);
        printf("Inputted String is: %s",arr);
    }
}
```

Sample Output
```
Enter a string: Subrata Saha
Inputted String is: Subrata S
Enter a string: 1234567890
Inputted String is: aha
12345
Enter a string: 12
Inputted String is: 67890
12
Enter a string: 12
45
78
Inputted String is: 12
45
78
```

In *Program 12.10*, the for loop runs 4 times.

In the *first iteration*, the inputted string is *Subrata Saha* which consists of 12 characters including the space. We can see that in the output first 9 characters are displayed i,e **Subrata S**. Please note that, here the space is also included with the help of format specifier %9c. However, this would not be possible with a %s format specifier.

In the *second iteration*, an input of size 10 (i.e., *1234567890*) was given. Here, the 3 unconsumed characters (*aha*) of first inputted string, which were previously stored in the input buffers are shown initially. Then one new line character was read. Even though we use an enter key for the termination purpose of the input, but here it was treated as a character and also be read by *scanf()* statement as an inputted character. Finally the first 5 characters of the 2nd inputted string (*12345*), means in total 3+1+5=9 characters were read and shown. The remaining 5 characters (*67890*) stored in the input buffer for the next reference.

In the *third iteration* only two input characters 12 were given and as an output we obtained the 5 leftover characters of last iteration (i.e., *67890*) + a new line character + 2 characters of the newly inputted string(i.e., 12) + a newline character. Hence in total (5+1+2+1) = 9 characters displayed after run.

In the final iteration, first *12* was given and then an enter key was pressed, then *45* was given and again an enter key was pressed and lastly *78* was given and an enter key was pressed. Here, every time the enter key was treated as an individual character and hence a total 9 characters including 3 new-line characters were read by the *scanf()* statement and also displayed at the same time as there was neither any unconsumed characters left from the earlier entry, nor any left-over characters would be stored from the current entry, from/to the input buffer, respectively.

One point is noticeable, that no matter how many characters are given as input, and only 9 characters are to be read by the scanf statement due to % 9c format specifier. The remaining unconsumed characters are stored in the buffer for the next reference.

12.2.1 Using gets( )

We have already learnt the various use of scanf( ) statement for string input. But the most convenient way to string input is to use **gets( )** function. This function is defined at stdio.h file. Using this function we can take multiword string input also as it terminates reading on encounter of new line character('\n'). The general form of gets( ) :

```
gets( array_name);
```

Following program shows the use of gets( ) function.

PROGRAM: 12.11

```
void main()
{
  char nm[40];
  printf("Enter a name: ");
  gets(nm);
  printf("The name is: %s", nm);
}
```

Sample Output

```
Enter a name: Subrata Saha
The name is: Subrata Saha
```

Here is a sample program that will demonstrate how we can declare, store and access a string.

PROGRAM 12.12   Program to count the number of characters in a string.

```
#include<conio.h>
#include<stdio.h>
void main()
{    char string[100];
     int i=0;
     puts("Enter Any String : ");
     gets(string);

     while( string[i] != '\0')
     {
          i++;
     }
     printf("\nTotal number of characters in the string \"%s\" is
     %d", string, i);
}
```

Sample Output

Enter Any String:
This is a sample string.
Total number of characters in the string "This is a sample string." is 24.

In the above program, first we take the input using gets( ). Then each character of the string is checked and counted. When the '\0' is encountered, the while loop is terminated.

12.3   sscanf( ) AND sprintf( ) FUNCTION

The sscanf() and sprintf() are two special versions of printf() and scanf() statement used to handle string in a different approach. These two functions are mainly used in file handling. The utility and usage of sscanf() and sprintf() are explained below:

12.3.1   sscanf() Function

sscanf() function is used for formatted string read purpose. It helps to extract strings from a given string. It implies that the data is to be taken out from the character array according to the conversion specifier and stored them into respective variables. A terminating null character is automatically appended after the content.

12.3.1.1   Syntax

sscanf(characterArray, "Conversion specifier", address of variables);

Here, sscanf() will read subsequent characters from 'characterArray', until a whitespace is found (whitespace characters are blank, newline and tab) and return the number of characters that was read and stored.

For instance: if a string contains Roll, Name and Percentage of Marks of a student like:

char str[ ] = "12 Subrata 34.43";

If we want to extract Roll, Name and Percentage of Marks, i.e., "12", "Subrata" and "34.43" from the character array 'str' and store them individually into separate variables, then it can be implemented using sscanf() function.

Consider the following example for further illustration:

PROGRAM 12.13 Program to demonstrate the use of sscanf( ) function.

```
#include <stdio.h>
void main()
{
char name[20],str[60];
int roll;
float marks;
printf("Enter Roll, Name and Percentage of Marks: ");
gets(str);
sscanf(str, "%d %s %f",&roll,name,&marks);
printf("Roll: %d, Name: %s, Percentage: %f\n", roll, name, marks);
}
```

Output

Enter Roll, Name and Percentage of Marks: 12 Subrata 34.43

Roll: 12, Name: Subrata, Percentage: 34.430000

In the above example, first Roll, Name and Percentage of Marks was taken as input in the string str. Next using sscanf() statement, individual Roll, Name and Percentage of Marks were extracted from the string str and stored in the variables roll, name and marks, respectively.

12.3.2 sprintf() Function

sprintf() function is exactly opposite to sscanf() function. It composes a string with the same text, but instead of being printed, the content is stored as a *C string* in the buffer.

If successful, this function returns the total number of characters written excluding the null character which is appended at the end of the string, otherwise a negative number is returned.

12.3.2.1 *Syntax*

sprintf (CharacterArray,"Conversion Specifier", variables);

This function works like `printf()` with the only difference is that the composed string is not output to the standard output, but is placed in array of characters passed as the first parameter.

Consider the following example for further illustration:

PROGRAM 12.14   Program to demonstrate the use of sprintf( ) function.

```
#include <stdio.h>
void main()
{
    char name[20],str[60];
    int roll;
    float marks;
    printf("Enter Roll:");
    scanf("%d",&roll);
    printf("Enter Name: ");
    fflush(stdin);
    gets(name);
    printf("Enter Percentage of Marks: ");
    scanf("%d",&marks);
    printf("Constructed string using sprintf: ");
    sprintf(str, "%d %s %f",roll,name,marks);
    puts(str);
}
```

Output:

```
Enter Roll: 12
Enter Name: Subrata
Enter Percentage of Marks: 34.43
Constructed string using sprintf: 12 Subrata 34.43
```

In the above example, 12, "Subrata" and 34.43 was taken individually as input in the variables roll, name and marks, respectively. Then using sprint() statement, the string "12 Subrata 34.43" has been constructed with the inputted values and stored within "str".

12.4 CHARACTER HANDLING FUNCTIONS

Before we proceed writing more programs, let us discuss about some library functions that operate on characters. These functions are defined in **ctype.h** header file and take a character as argument.

12.4.1 toupper( ) Function

This function converts and returns the upper case letter. The general form of toupper( ) is:

x = **toupper(ch);**

where x and ch both are character variables.

PROGRAM 12.15   Program to convert a lower case character to its upper case.

```c
#include<ctype.h>
#include<stdio.h>
void main()
{
    char ch1, ch2;
    printf("Enter any character: ");
    scanf("%c", &ch1);
    ch2 = toupper(ch1);
    printf("\nInputted character in upper case: %c", ch2);
}
```

Sample Output

```
Enter any character: a
Inputted character in upper case: A
```

12.4.2   tolower( ) Function

This function converts and returns the lower case letter. The general form of tolower( ) is:

> x = **tolower(ch);**

where x and ch both are character variables.

PROGRAM 12.16   Program to convert a upper case character to its lower case.

```c
#include<ctype.h>
#include<stdio.h>
void main()
{
    char ch1, ch2;
    printf("Enter any character: ");
    scanf("%c", &ch1);
    ch2 = tolower(ch1);
    printf("\nInputted character in lower case: %c", ch2);
}
```

Sample Output

```
Enter any character: A
Inputted character in lower case: a
```

12.4.3   islower( ) Function

This function checks whether a character is in lower case. On success it returns 1, otherwise 0. The general form of islower( ) is:

> x = **islower(ch);**

where **ch** is a character variable and **x** is an integer variable.

PROGRAM 12.17   Program to check whether an inputted character is in lower case or not.

```c
#include<stdio.h>
#include<ctype.h>
void main()
{
    char chr, x;
    printf("Enter any character: ");
    scanf("%c", &chr);
    if(islower(chr))
        printf("\nYou entered a lower case character.");
    else
        printf("\nYou have not entered a lower case character.");
}
```

Sample Output

Enter any character: d
You entered a lower case character.

Enter any character: D
You have not entered a lower case character.

12.4.4   isupper( ) Function

This function checks whether a character is in upper case. On success it returns 1, otherwise 0. The general form of isupper( ) is:

   x = isupper(ch);

where **ch** is a character variable and **x** is an integer variable.

PROGRAM 12.18   Program to check whether an inputted character is in upper case or not.

```c
#include<ctype.h>
#include<stdio.h>
void main()
{
    char chr;
    printf("Enter any character: ");
    scanf("%c", &chr);
    if (isupper(chr))
        printf("\nYou entered a upper case character.");
    else
        printf("\nYou have not entered a upper case character.");
}
```

Sample Output

Enter any character: d

You have not entered a upper case character.

Enter any character: D
You entered a upper case character.

12.4.5   isdigit( ) Function

This function checks whether a character is digit (i.e., 0–9) or not. On success it returns 1, otherwise 0. The general form of isdigit( ) is:

  x = isdigit(ch);

where **ch** is a character variable and **x** is an integer variable.

PROGRAM 12.19   **Program to check whether an inputted character is a digit or not.**

```
#include<stdio.h>
#include<ctype.h>
void main()
{
    char chr;
    printf("Enter any character: ");
    scanf("%c", &chr);
    if(isdigit(chr))
        printf("\nYou entered a digit");
    else
        printf("\nYou have not entered a digit.");
}
```

Sample Output

Enter any character: d
You have not entered a digit.

Enter any character: 3
You entered a digit.

12.4.6   isalpha( ) Function

This function checks whether a character is an alphabet. Alphabetic characters are Lowercase letters and Uppercase letters. On success it returns 1, otherwise 0. The general form of isalpha( ) is:

  x = isalpha(ch);

where **ch** is a character variable and **x** is an integer variable.

PROGRAM 12.20 **Program to check whether an inputted character is an alphabet or not.**

```
#include<ctype.h>
#include<stdio.h>
void main()
{
    char chr;
    printf("Enter any character: ");
    scanf("%c", &chr);
    if(isalpha(chr))
        printf("\nYou entered an alphabet.");
    else
        printf("\nYou have not entered any alphabet.");
}
```

Sample Output

Enter any character: d
You entered an alphabet.

Enter any character: 3
You have not entered any alphabet.

12.4.7 isalnum( ) Function

This function checks whether a character is an alpha numeric character. Alpha numeric characters are Digits, Lowercase letters and Uppercase letters. On success it returns 1, otherwise 0. The general form of isalnum( ) is:

   x = isalnum(ch);

where **ch** is a character variable and **x** is an integer variable.

PROGRAM 12.21 **Program to check whether an inputted character is an alpha numeric character or not.**

```
#include<ctype.h>
#include<stdio.h>
void main()
{
    char chr;
    printf("Enter any character: ");
    scanf("%c", &chr);
    if(isalnum(chr))
        printf("\nYou entered an alpha numeric character.");
    else
        printf("\nYou have not entered any alpha numeric character.");
}
```

Sample Output

Enter any character: d
You entered an alpha numeric character.

Enter any character: 3
You entered an alpha numeric character.

Enter any character: #
You have not entered any alpha numeric character.

12.4.8 ispunct( ) Function

This function checks whether a character is a punctuation. Punctuation characters are ! " #
$ % & ' ( ) * + , – . / : ; < = > ? @ [\ ] ^ _ ` { | } ~. On success it returns 1, otherwise 0. The
general form of ispunct( ) is:

> x = ispunct(ch);

where **ch** is a character variable and **x** is an integer variable.

PROGRAM **12.22**   **Program to check whether an inputted character is a
punctuation mark or not.**

```
#include<ctype.h>
#include<stdio.h>
void main()
{
  char chr;
  printf("Enter any character: ");
  scanf("%c", &chr);
  if(ispunct(chr))
      printf("\nYou entered a punctuation character.");
  else
      printf("\nYou have not entered any punctuation character.");
}
```

Sample Output

Enter any character: !
You entered a punctuation character.

Enter any character: P
You have not entered any punctuation character.

12.4.9 isspace( ) Function

This function checks whether a character is a white-space. White-space characters are
tab, newline, vertical tab, form feed, carriage return, and space. On success it returns 1,
otherwise 0. The general form of isspace( ):

> x = isspace(ch);

where **ch** is a character variable and **x** is an integer variable.

PROGRAM 12.23   Program to check whether an inputted character is a space or not.

```
#include<ctype.h>
#include<stdio.h>
void main()
{
    char chr;
    printf("Enter any character: ");
    scanf("%c", &chr);
    if(isspace(chr))
        printf("\nYou entered a white-space character.");
    else
        printf("\nYou have not entered any white-space character.");
}
```

Sample Output

Enter any character:
You entered a white-space character.

Enter any character: 0
You have not entered any white-space character.

12.4.10   isxdigit( ) Function

This function checks whether a character is a hexadecimal digit. Hexadecimal digits are 0, 1, 2, 3, 4, 5, 6, 7, 8, 9, a, b, c, d, e, f, A, B, C, D, E, F. On success it returns 1, otherwise 0. The general form of isxdigit( ):

   x = isxdigit(ch);

where **ch** is a character variable and **x** is an integer variable.

PROGRAM 12.24   Program to check whether an inputted character is a hexadecimal digit or not.

```
#include<ctype.h>
#include<stdio.h>
void main()
{
    char chr;
    printf("Enter any character: ");
    scanf("%c", &chr);
    if(isxdigit(chr))
        printf("\nYou entered a hexadecimal digit");
    else
        printf("\nYou have not entered any hexadecimal digit.");
}
```

Sample Output

Enter any character: X
You have not entered any hexadecimal digit.

Enter any character: D
You entered a hexadecimal digit.

The following programs illustrate some more operations on string.

PROGRAM 12.25   Write a program to display all Punctuation characters.

```
#include<stdio.h>
#include<ctype.h>
void main()
{    int i;
     printf("Punctuation characters are \n");
     for(i=0;i<128;i++)
     {    if(ispunct(i))
               printf("%c ",i);
     }
}
```

Sample Output

Punctuation characters are

! " # $ % & ' ( ) * + , - . / : ; < = > ? @ [\ ] ^ _ ` { | } ~

PROGRAM 12.26   Write a program to count the number of vowels, consonants, digits, spaces and punctuation marks in a string.

```
#include<conio.h>
#include<stdio.h>
#include<ctype.h>
void main()
{    char string[80], chr;
     int i=0,v=0,c=0,d=0,s=0,p=0;
     puts("Enter Any String : ");
     gets(string);

     while( string[i] != '\0')
     {
          chr = toupper(string[i]);
          if(chr == 'A'||chr == 'E'||chr == 'I'|| chr == 'O' || chr == 'U')
               v++;
          else
               if(chr>'A' && chr <='Z')
                    c++;
```

```
                else
                    if ( chr>='0' && chr <='9')
                        d++;
                    else
                        if ( chr == ' ')
                            s++;
                        else
                            if (ispunct (chr))
                                p++;
            i++;
        }


    printf ("\nTotal number of Vowels is %d", v);
    printf ("\nTotal number of Consonants is %d", c);
    printf ("\nTotal number of Digits is %d", d);
    printf ("\nTotal number of Spaces is %d", s);
    printf ("\nTotal number of Punctuation marks is %d", p);
}
```

Sample Output

Enter Any String : My roll no. is: 53

Total number of Vowels is 3
Total number of Consonants is 7
Total number of Digits is 2
Total number of Spaces is 4
Total number of Punctuation marks is 2

We can also rewrite this program using library functions as follows.

```
/* Program to count the number of vowels, consonants, spaces, digits
and punctuation marks in a string using library functions. */
#include<stdio.h>
#include<conio.h>
#include<ctype.h>
void main()
{   char string[80], chr;
    int i=0,v=0,c=0,d=0,s=0,p=0;
    puts("Enter Any String : ");
    gets(string);

    while( string[i] != '\0')
    {
        chr = toupper(string[i]);
        if ( chr == 'A' || chr == 'E' || chr == 'I' || chr == 'O' || chr == 'U')
            v++;
        else
            if (isaplha(chr))
                c++;
```

```
            else
                 if ( isdigit(chr))
                       d++;
                 else
                     if ( isspace(chr))
                           s++;
                     else
                         if (ispunct(chr))
                               p++;
        i++;
    }
    printf("\nTotal number of Vowels is %d", v);
    printf("\nTotal number of Consonants is %d", c);
    printf("\nTotal number of Digits is %d", d);
    printf("\nTotal number of Spaces is %d", s);
    printf("\nTotal number of Punctuation marks is %d", p);
}
```

Sample Output

Enter Any String : My roll no. is: 53

Total number of Vowels is 3
Total number of Consonants is 7
Total number of Digits is 2
Total number of Spaces is 4
Total number of Punctuation marks is 2

12.5 STRING HANDLING FUNCTIONS

C library supports a large number of string handling functions. These functions help us to carry out various string manipulations. Here we will discuss some common functions defined in 'string.h' header file.

12.5.1 strlen( ) Function

This function finds the length of the given string. It counts the number of characters in a string excluding the null character and then returns it. The general form of strlen():

>   **ln = strlen(string);**

where **ln** is an integer variable which stores the length of the string.

EXAMPLE 12.2

```
    len=strlen("Subrata");
```

The function will assign 7 to the integer variable len.

12.5.2 strcat( ) Function

To concatenate two strings, strcat( ) function is used. The general form of this function is:

```
strcat(strn1,strn2)
```

strn1 & strn2 are two character arrays. On execution of the function strcat( ), at the end of first string strn1 the second string strn2 is appended. The second string, i.e., strn2 remains unchanged.

EXAMPLE 12.3

```
char string1[30] = "Ram";
char string2[30] = "Krishna";
strcat(string1,string2);
puts(string1);
puts(string2);

output:   RamKrishna
          Krishna
```

From the output, we can see that value of string1 becomes "RamKrishna". The string at string2 remains unchanged as "Krishna". The size of string1 should be large enough to store the concatenated string.

12.5.3 strncat( ) Function

This function *concatenates* two strings by copying the first n characters of second string at the end of the first string. The general form of this function is:

```
strncat(strn1,strn2,n)
```

strncat( ) function appends the first n character of strn2 to strn1 and then appends a null character. strn2 may be a string constant or a character array variable.

EXAMPLE 12.4

```
char string1[30] = "Ram";
char string2[30] = "ananda";
strncat(string1,string2,2);
puts(string1);
puts(string2);

output:   Raman
          ananda
```

12.5.4 strcpy( ) Function

It is not possible to assign a string to a character array directly using '=' operator. Instead we need to use the strcpy( )function to copy the content of one character array to another. The general form of this function is:

```
strcpy(t_strn, s_strn);
```

strcpy function assigns the contents of source string s_strn to the target string t_strn. t_strn may be a string constant or a character array variable.

EXAMPLE 12.5

```
char string1[30];
char string2[30];
strcpy(string1, "Techno");
strcpy(string2,string1);
puts(string1);
puts(string2);
```

output: Techno
             Techno

In the above example, first the string constant "Techno" is assigned to the string **string1**. Then string1 is copied to string2.

12.5.5   strncpy( ) Function

This function is similar to strcpy( ) function. But instead of copies the total string it copies only the first **n** characters of the source string **s_strn** to the target string **t_strn**. The general form of this function is:

   strncpy(t_strn, s_strn, n);

strncpy function assigns the first n character of s_strn to t_strn. T_strn may be a string constant or a character array variable. The target string, **t_strn**, might not be null-terminated if the length of the source (i.e., s_strn) is greater than or equals to n.

EXAMPLE 12.6

```
char string1[30];
strncpy(string1, "Techno",4);
string1[4] = '\0';
puts(string1);
```

output: Tech

In the above example, strncpy( ) will copy first 4 character of the string constant. Thus the content of string1 will be "Tech". As '\0' will not be inserted automatically, we have stored it in the next statement.

12.5.6   strcmp( ) Function

In C, we cannot directly compare two strings using relational operators. For this we have to use the strcmp( ) function. If two strings are identical this function returns zero, otherwise it returns a non zero number. The general form of strcmp() is:

   strcmp(strn1, strn2)

where strn1 & strn2 are two string constants or character array variables. strcmp( ) returns negative value if the first string **strn1** is alphabetically less than the second string **strn2** and a positive value if **strn1** is alphabetically greater than the **strn2**. The comparison starts from the first character of each string. If the character matches then it checks the next character. When a mismatch occurs the function returns the difference of ASCII values of the compared characters. If both the strings are identical it returns a zero.

EXAMPLE 12.7

```
strcmp("Techno","Techno");
```

will return zero because two strings are identical.

```
strcmp("Technical","Technology");
```

will return −6 which is the numeric difference between ASCII value of 'i' and that of 'o'.

```
strcmp("Techno","techno")
```

will return −32 which is the numeric difference between ASCII value of 'T' and that of 't'.

```
strcmp("techno","Techno")
```

will return 32 which is the numeric difference between ASCII value of 't' and that of 'T'.

12.5.7   strcmpi( ) Function

This function is similar to `strcmp()`. It also compares two strings but the only difference is that, it checks the strings ignoring the case sensitivity.

EXAMPLE 12.8

```
strcmpi("TECHNO","techno");
```

will return 0.

12.5.8   strncmp() Function

This function compares the first n characters of two strings.

EXAMPLE 12.9

```
strncmp("their","there",3);
```

It will return 0 as the first three characters in both the strings are same.

12.5.9   strncmpi() Function

This function compares the first n characters of two strings ignoring the case sensitivity.

EXAMPLE 12.10

```
strncmpi("Their",  "there",3);
```

will return 0.

12.5.10   strupr( ) Function

This function converts all lower case letters into a string of upper case. The general form of strupr() is given below:

strupr(string);

EXAMPLE 12.11

```
strupr("Techno India");
```

converts to TECHNO INDIA.

12.5.11 strlwr( ) Function

This function converts all upper case letters into a string of lowercase. The general form of strlwr() is given below:

strlwr(string);

EXAMPLE 12.12

```
strlwr("TECHNO INDIA");
```

converts to techno india.

12.5.12 strrev( ) Function

This function reverses the characters in a string. The general form of strrev() is given below:

strrev(string);

EXAMPLE 12.13

```
strrev("program") ;
```

It reverses the characters into a string containing "margorp".

Here is a sample program to demonstrate the use of library functions.

PROGRAM 12.27   Write a program to check whether a string is a palindrome or not.

```
#include<conio.h>
#include<stdio.h>
#include<string.h>
void main()
{
    char st[30], dup[30];
    int l, i= 0;
    printf("Enter any String: ");
    gets(st);
    l = strlen(st) - 1;
    while ( l > 0)
    {
```

```
        dup[ i++] = st [ l--];
    }
    dup [ i ] = '\0';
    if( strcmp( st, dup) == 0)
        printf("The String is Palindrome");
    else
        printf("The String is not a Palindrome");
}
```

Sample Output

Enter any String: madam
The String is Palindrome

Enter any String: Teacher
The String is not a Palindrome

12.6 TWO-DIMENSIONAL ARRAY OF CHARACTERS

To store a string, one dimensional character array is required. To handle multiple strings, we need array of strings. This can be implemented using a 2-dimensional character array where each row of a 2-dimensional character array stores an individual string. We can declare a 2-dimensional character array as,

```
    char arr[10][20];
```

The above array arr can store 10 strings and the length of each strings should be less than 20. We can also initialize a 2-dimensional character array as following:

```
    char days[] [10] = {   "Sunday",
                           "Monday",
                           "Tuesday",
                           "Wednesday",
                           "Thursday",
                           "Friday",
                           "Saturday"
                       };
```

We can access an element by specifying the row number and column number of the element similar to accessing elements in 2D numeric array. But as it is used mostly as array of strings, first row is considered as the first element of the array and so on. If we consider the above example by mentioning days[0] we can access the first row i.e. the string "Sunday", by mentioning days[1] we can access the second row, i.e., the string "Monday" and so on. So, to take input in a 2D character array we can write the following code snippet.

```
    char mystrings[10][30];
    int i;
    for(i=0;i<10;i++)
```

```
{        printf("Enter any String: ");
         fflush(stdin);
         gets(mystrings[i]);
}
```

The statement fflush(stdin) is used to flush the stdin buffer which makes the input procedure smooth. fflush( ) is a library function defined in stdio.h header file.

Here is a sample program that will demonstrate how we can declare, store and access a 2-dimensional character array or array of strings.

PROGRAM 12.28   Write a program that would sort a list of names in alphabetic order.

```
#include<conio.h>
#include<stdio.h>
#define SIZE 8
void main()
{   char names[SIZE][30], temp[30];
    int i,j;
    for(i=0;i<SIZE;i++)                  /* Taking Inputs */
    {    printf("Enter Name%d: ",i+1);
         fflush(stdin);
         gets(names[i]);
    }
     for(i=1;i<SIZE;i++)                 /* Sorting on Names */
         for(j=0;j<SIZE-i;j++)
             if(strcmp(names[j], names[j+1])>0)
                 {    strcpy(temp, names[j]);
                      strcpy(names[j], names[j+1]);
                      strcpy(names[j+1], temp);
                 }
         printf("\nList of Names in Ascending order :\n");
         for(i=0;i<SIZE;i++)            /* Displaying Names */
             puts(names[i]);
}
```

Sample Output

```
Enter Name1: Rabin Mandol
Enter Name2: Bipul Sarkar
Enter Name3: Sriparna Saha
Enter Name4: Mrinal Chakraborty
Enter Name5: Animesh Das
Enter Name6: Tito Dasgupta
Enter Name7: Srabasti Mukherjee
Enter Name8: Dibyendu Modok
```

List of Names in Ascending Order
Animesh Das
Bipul Sarkar
Dibyendu Modok
Mrinal Chakraborty
Rabin Mandol
Srabasti Mukherjee
Sriparna Saha
Tito Dasgupta

12.7 PROGRAMMING EXAMPLES

Here are some programming examples to understand the various use of array.

PROGRAM 12.29 Write a program to count the number of words in a string. (Words may separated by one or more spaces.)

```
#include<conio.h>
#include<stdio.h>
void main()
{    int i= 0,count=1;
     char st[80];
     printf("Enter any String:");
     gets(st);
     while (st[i])
     {
         if(st[i]==' '&& st[i+1] != ' ')
              count++;
         i++;
     }
     printf("\nTotal number of words = %d", count);
}
```

Sample Output

Enter any String: Ram is a good boy

Total number of words = 5

PROGRAM 12.30 Write a program to convert a binary number to equivalent decimal number.

```
#include<stdio.h>
#include<math.h>
#include<string.h>
void main()
{    int l,num=0,i=0;
     char bin[17];
```

```
printf("Enter any Binary Number: ");
scanf("%s",bin);
l = strlen(bin) - 1;
while(l>=0)
{    num = num + (bin[l]-48)*pow(2,i);
     i++;
     l--;
}
printf("Decimal Equivalent of %s is %d", bin, num);
}
```

Sample Output

Enter any Binary Number: 1101
Decimal Equivalent of 1101 is 13

Enter any Binary Number: 101010
Decimal Equivalent of 101010 is 42

PROGRAM 12.31 Write a program that will convert each character (only alphabet) of a string into the next alphabet.

```
#include<stdio.h>
#include<conio.h>
#include<ctype.h>
void main()
{    int i= 0;
     char st[80],ch;
     clrscr();
     printf("Enter any String:");
     gets(st);
     while (st[i])
     {    ch = st[i];
          if(isalpha(ch))
          {    if(ch=='z')        /* To convert 'z' to 'a' */
                    st[i] = 'a';
               else
                    if(ch=='Z')
                         st[i] = 'A';
                    else
                         st[i] = ch +1;
                         /* To convert other alphabet to next alphabet */
          }
          i++;
     }
     printf("The converted string is: %s",st);
}
```

Sample Output

Enter any String: 33 A. P. C Road
The converted string is: 33 B. Q. D Spbe

PROGRAM **12.32**   Write a program to capitalize first character of each
                     word of a string.

```
#include<stdio.h>
#include<ctype.h>
void main( )
{    int i= 0;
     char st[80];
     printf("Enter any String:");
     gets(st);
     st[i]=toupper(st[i]);
     while (st[i])
     {
         if(st[i]==' '&& st[i+1] != ' ')
                       /* st[i+1] is the first character of a word */
            st[i+1]=toupper(st[i+1]);
         i++;
     }
     printf("Converted string is: %s", st);
}
```

Sample Output

Enter any String: ram is a good boy.
Converted string is: Ram Is A Good Boy.

PROGRAM **12.33**   Write a program to find the Abbreviation of your
                     name.

```
#include<stdio.h>
#include<string.h>
void main()
{    int i=0,j=0,position=-1,l;
     char st[80],abr[20];
     printf("Enter Your Name: ");
     gets(st);
     l=strlen(st);
     while(st[--l]==' ');   /* To remove the trailing blanks */
     st[l+1]='\0';
     while(st[i]==' ')       /* To ignore the leading blanks */
         i++;
     abr[j++]=st[i++];       /* storing 1st letter of the name into abr array */
     position=i;
      while (st[i])
```

```
    {
    if (st[i]=='  '&& st[i+1] != ' ')
    {     abr[j++]  = '.';
          abr[j++]  = st[i+1];      /* storing 1st letter of each word */
          position = i+2;           /* for storing position of 2nd letter
                                        of surname */
    }
    i++;
    }
    while (st[position])
          abr[j++]  = st[position++];
    abr[j]  = '\0';
    printf("Your Abbreviated Name is : %s", abr);
}
```

Sample Output

Enter Your Name: Vangipurapu Venkata Sai Laxman
Your Abbreviated Name is: V.V.S. Laxman

SUMMARY

➤ A String is an array of characters terminated by '\0'.

➤ The general form to declare a string is:

   char string_name[size];

   Here size denotes the number of characters stored within the character array.

➤ The size of the array would be equal to the maximum number of characters in the string plus one.

➤ Strings allow shorthand initialization.

➤ Best way to sting input is to use gets( ) function.

➤ For multi line string input we can use scanset specifier with scanf( ).

➤ printf( ) with %s or puts( ) can be used to print a string.

➤ Character handling functions are defined in ctype.h header file.

➤ In C Strings can be neither copied nor compared using operators. We have to use library functions or write own functions to do so.

➤ String handling functions are defined in string.h header file.

➤ To create an array of strings a 2D character array needs to be declared.

REVIEW EXERCISES

1. What do you mean by String? How can a String be initialized?
2. What is the difference between scanf( ) with %s and gets( )?
3. What is the difference between "A" and 'A'?
4. Discuss any three string handling functions?

5. What is the difference between strcat( ) and strcpy( )?

6. Write a C program to read and display a line character by character.

7. Write a C program that accepts a word from the user and prints it in the following way. If the word is PROGRAM, the program will print it as

```
      P
      R
      O
PROGRAM
      R
      A
      M
```

8. Write a C program that accepts a word from the user and prints it in the following way. If the word is PROGRAM, the program will print it as

```
P
PR
PRO
PROG
PROGR
PROGRA
PROGRAM
```

9. Write a C program to find the frequency of a particular letter in an inputted string.

10. Write a C program that will remove extra spaces from an inputted string.

11. Write a C program that will print a sub-string within a string. Program will take the input of the length of the sub-string and the starting position in the string.

12. Write a C program to find the frequency of a particular word in an inputted string.

13. Write a C program that will delete a particular word from a line of text.

14. Write a C program that will replace a particular word with another word in a line of text.

15. Write a C program to convert an amount into words. For example, 12345 should be printed as, 'Twelve Thousand three hundred forty five'.

16. Write a C program to search a city among a set of cities.

LEARN BY QUIZ – QUESTIONS

1. Which of the following is a string constant?
   (1) "HELLO"
   (2) 'H'
   (3) 2

2. Which of the following is suitable for storing a character string?
   (1) One character array
   (2) One character variable
   (3) Integer array

3. Which of the following statements is true regarding string?
   (1) Every string is terminated with a null ('\0') character.
   (2) Every string is terminated with a full stop ('.').
   (3) Every string is terminated with a space.

4. Which of the following declarations will store the string, HELLO, in a character array named s?
   (1) char s[7] = "HELLO" ;
   (2) char s[5] = "HELLO" ;
   (3) char s = "HELLO" ;

5. Which of the following statements will print the string "HELLO"?
   (1) printf("\"HELLO\"") ;
   (2) printf(""HELLO"") ;
   (3) puts(""HELLO"") ;

6. Which of the following answers contains correct statement(s)?
   (1) 2 is a numeric constant.
       '2' is character constant.
       "2" is string constant.
   (2) 2 ,'2' and "2" are same
   (3) 2 and '2' are same but "2" is different

7. Which of the following declarations of string with initial value SAMPLE is correct?
   (1) char text[ ] = "SAMPLE";
   (2) char text[ ] = "SAMPLE\0";
   (3) char text = "SAMPLE";

8. To store the string "Hello World!" in an array, what will be the declaration statement?
   (1) char arr[]="Hello World!";
   (2) char arr[]={Hello World!};
   (3) char arr[]={H,e,l,l,o, ,W,o,r,l,d,!,\0};

9. To store the string "Hello World!" in an array, what will be the minimum size of the array?
   (1) 13
   (2) 12
   (3) 11

10. Which of the following is suitable for storing multiple strings in the memory?
    (1) A 1-D character array
    (2) A 2-D character array
    (3) A 3-D character array

11. Which of the following initialization statements is appropriate for storing multiple strings?
    (1) char city[3][30] = { "Kolkata", "Delhi", "Mumbai" } ;
    (2) char city[3][30] = { "Kolkata, Delhi, Mumbai" } ;
    (3) char city[3][ ] = { "Kolkata", "Delhi", "Mumbai" } ;

12. Given, array declaration:
    char st[10] ;

    Which of the following consecutive statements will not work correctly?
    (1) st[0] = 'C' ;
        st[1] = 'A' ;
        st[2] = 'T' ;
        puts(st) ;
    (2) st[0] = 'C' ;
        st[1] = 'A' ;
        st[2] = 'T' ;
        st[3] = '\0' ;
        puts(s) ;
    (3) st[0] = 'C' ;
        st[1] = 'A' ;

```
st[2] = 'T' ;
st[3] = '\0'
printf("%s", st) ;
```

13. Which of the following statements is true regarding the initialization statement given below?

    char st[10] = "BABI" ;

    (1) st[0] = 'B', st[1] = 'A', st[2] = 'B', st[3] = 'I', st[4] = '\0' and the remaining locations, from s[5] to s[9] will contain '\0' characters.

    (2) st[0] = 'B', st[1] = 'A', st[2] = 'B', st[3] = 'I', st[4] = '\0' and the remaining locations, from s[5] to s[9] will contain garbage values.

    (3) st[0] = 'B', st[1] = 'A', st[2] = 'B', st[3] = 'I', st[4] = '\0' and the remaining locations, from s[5] to s[9] will contain blank spaces.

14. What should be the minimum size of the character array for storing a character string of length n?

    (1) n

    (2) n − 1

    (3) n+1

15. Consider the following program segment:

```
main ( )
{
    char c, s [30] ;
    int i = 0 ;
    While(c = getchar())! = '\n')
        s [i++] = c;
    s [i] = '\0' ;
}
```

    What will the above program be equivalent to?

    (1) gets function

    (2) getline function

    (3) scanf function with %s format specifier

16.
```
void main ( )
{
    int s [10] = "GOOD", i = 0 ;
    while(s [i] != '\0') {
    putchar(s [i]) ;
    i++ ;
    }
}
```

    What will the above program segment be equivalent to?

    (1) puts(s)

    (2) putline(s)

    (3) printf(s) ;

17. How are two strings compared?

    (1) Using the library function strcmp

    (2) Using comparison operators like <, >, == etc

    (3) Using special operators

18. What will be returned by the following strcmp function?

    strcmp ("RAM", "RAN") ;

    (1) 1

(2) −1

(3) 1 or −1 depends on the compiler

19. Consider the following declaration:

    Char s[2] = "Hello", t[20] = "World" ;

    Which of the following invocations of strcmp( )is correct?
    (1) strcmp(s , t)
    (2) strcmp("s", "t")
    (3) strcmp(s[20] , t[20])

20. How are two strings concatenated?
    (1) Using the library function, strcat( )
    (2) Using the + operator
    (3) Using the ++ operator

21. Consider the following declaration:

    char s[20] = "RAM", t[20] = "ANANDA" ;

    Which of the following statements will store RAMANANDA in the character array, s?
    (1) strcat(s , t)
    (2) starcat(t , s)
    (3) strcat(s + t)

22. Consider the following program segment:

```
void main( )
{
    chars[20] = {'H','E','L','L','O','\0','W','O','R','L','D','\0'};
    puts(s) ;
}
```

    What will be the output of the program segment given above?
    (1) HELLO
    (2) HELLO WORLD
    (3) HELLOWORLD

23. Which of the following header files contains the declaration of all string handling functions?
    (1) string.h
    (2) stdio.h
    (3) ctype.h

24. Which of the following string handling library functions calculates the length of a string?
    (1) strlen function
    (2) length function
    (3) stringlength function

25. Consider the following program segment:

```
main( )
{
    char s[10] = "HELLO" ;
    int x, y ;
    x = strlen(s) ;
    printf("%d", x) ;
}
```

    What will be the output of the program segment given above?
    (1) 5

(2) 6
(3) 7

26. Consider the following program declaration:

    char s[10] ;

Which of the following statements will copy the string, HELLO, into the character array, s?
(1) strcpy(s, "HELLO") ;
(2) s = "HELLO" ;
(3) stringcopy(s, "HELLO") ;

27. Consider the following declaration:

    Char s[10] = "HELLO", t[10] = "Hi" ;

Which of the following string copy operations is illegal?
(1) strcpy("HI", s) ;
(2) strcpy(s, t) ;
(3) strcpy(t, s) ;

28. Consider the following declaration:

    char x[20] = "RUBY", y[20] = "ROY", z[20] ;

Which of the following sequence of statements will store RUBY ROY in the array, z?
(1) strcpy(z, x) ;
    strcat(z, " ") ;
    strcat(z, y) ;
(2) strcat(z, x) ;
    strcat(z, " ") ;
    strcat(z, y) ;
(3) strcat(z, x, y) ;

29. Which of the following string comparisons will return 0?
(1) strcmp("HELLO", "HELLO") ;
(2) strcmp("HELLO" , "hello") ;
(3) strcmp("HELLO" , "HELL") ;

30. Which of the following string handling functions treat uppercase and lowercase alphabets equally?
(1) strcmpi function
(2) istrcmp function
(3) Icasestrcmp function

31. Consider the following declaration:

    Char city[ ][10] = { "Kolkata", "Delhi", "Mumbai" } ;

Which of the following program segments will display all the strings in different lines?
(1) for(i = 0 ; i < 3 ; i++)
       puts(city[i]) ;
(2) for(i = 0 ; i < 3 ; i++)
       puts(city) ;
(3) puts(city) ;

32. Which of the following functions will copy at most n characters from one string to another?
(1) nstrcpy function
(2) strcpy function
(3) strncpy function

33. Consider the following code segment:

```
main( )
{
    Char s[30] = "good" ;
    int i ;
    for(i = 0 ; s[i]! = '\0' ; i++)
    s[i] = toupper(s[i]) ;
}
```

What will happen when the above program segment is executed?
(1) It will convert the content of array, s, "good" to upper case "GOOD".
(2) The content of array, s, will remain the same.
(3) The content of array, s, will be replaced by garbage values.

34. Consider the following declaration:

```
char s[10] = "KOLKATA", t[10] ;
```

Which of the following statements will copy KOL in the array, t?
(1) strncpy(t, s, 3) ;
    t[3] = '\0' ;
(2) strncpy(t, s, 3) ;
(3) strcpy(t, s) ;

35. Which of following functions compares two strings of at most n characters each?
(1) strncmp function
(2) strcmpn function
(3) nstrcmp function

36. Consider the following declaration:

```
char s[20] = "SUBIR" ;
```

Which of the following statement(s) will make SUBIR ROY the content of the array, s?
(1) strcat(s, " ") ;
    strncat(s, "ROYCHOWDHURY", 3) ;
(2) strcat(s, "ROYCHOWDHURY") ;
(3) strncat(s, "ROYCHOWDHURY",3) ;

37. Which of the following functions is used to search for the occurrence of a given character in a string?
(1) strchr function
(2) search function
(3) sccurrence function

38. What will be the output of the following program segment?

```
main( )
{.
    if( strchr('B', "KOLKATA') != NULL)
      printf(" B is absent ") ;
    else
      printf("B is present ") ;
}
```

(1) B is present
(2) B is absent
(3) There will be no output.

39. Which of the following functions is used to search for the last occurrence of a given character in a string?
   (1) strrchr function
   (2) strchr function
   (3) search function

40. Which of the following functions is used to search for the occurrence of a string within a string?
   (1) strstr function
   (2) substr function
   (3) str function

41. What will be the output of the following program?

```
main ( )
{
        if(strstr("This", "is") == NULL)
            printf("Good morning")
        else
            pritntf("Good  evening") ;
}
```
   (1) Good evening
   (2) Good morning
   (3) Blank space

42. Which of the following functions is used to set all the characters in the string with a particular character?
   (1) strset function
   (2) set function
   (3) setstring function

43. What will be the output of the following program after calling strset function?

```
main ( )
{
        char s[10] = "1234" ;
        puts(s) ;
        strset(s, 'c') ;
        puts(s) ;
}
```
   (1) 1234
      cccc
   (2) 1234c
   (3) 1234cccc

44. Consider the following program:

```
main ( )
{
        char s[30] = "KOLKATA", t[30] ;
        int i ;
        for(i = 0 ; s[i] != '\0' ; i++)
            t[i] = s[i] ;
        t[i] = '\0' ;
}
```

What will the above program be equivalent to?

(1) strcat function
(2) strncpy function
(3) strcpy function

45. Consider the following program code:

```
main( )
{
    char s[10] = "KOLKATA", t[30] = "DELHI" ;
    int i, j ;
    for(i = 0 ; s[i] == t[i] ; i++)
    {    if ( s[i] == '\0')
         j = 0 ;
         j = s[i] - t[i] ;
    }
}
```

What will the above program be equivalent to?
(1) strcmp function
(2) strncmp function
(3) strlen function

46. Consider the following declaration:

        char city[3][20] ;

Which of the following program codes will accept input strings in all the three rows?
(1) for(i = 0 ; i < 3 ; i++)
    scanf("%s", city[i]) ;
(2) gets(city)
(3) scanf("%s", city)

47. Consider the following program:

```
main(                                                    )
{
    char s[20] = "KOLKATA" ;
    int i ;
    for( i = 0 ; s[i]! = '\0' ; i++) ;
}
```

What will the above program code be equivalent to?
(1) strlen( )
(2) strlen( ) + 1
(3) strlen( ) − 1

48. Consider the following program segment:

```
main( )
{
    char s[20] = "SHREYA", t[20] = "SAHA" ;
    int i, j ;
    for(i = 0 ; s[i] != '\0'; i++) ;
    for(j = 0 ; t[j] != '\0'; j++)
    s[i++] = t[j] ;
    s[i] = '\0' ;
}
```

What will the above program be equivalent to?
(1) strncat function
(2) strcat function
(3) concat function

49. To store name of 10 students in an array named 'name' (expected length of names are less than 30), what will be the declaration?
(1) char name[10][30];
(2) char name[10];
(3) char name[30][10];

50. What will be the declaration statement of the array, if we want to store the name of basic three colors (i.e., Red, Green & Blue) in an array?
(1) char color[][10]={"Red", "Green", "Blue"};
(2) string color[3][10] ={"Red", "Green", "Blue"};
(3) char color[3][10]={ {Red}, {Green}, {Blue}};

LEARN BY QUIZ – ANSWERS

Answer explanations

1. "HELLO" is a string constant.

A string can be defined as a sequence of characters that are treated as a single data item. In C, string constants are written within double quotes (" ").

"HELLO" contains a sequence of characters and hence is a string. It is a constant since it has a fixed set of characters, and is written within double quotes (" ").

Character constants are written within single quotes (' '). So 'H' is a character constant and not a string constant. However, had H been written within double quotes (" "), i.e., "H", then it would have been a string constant.

2. One character array is suitable for storing a character string.

A string can be defined as a sequence of characters that are treated as a single data item. This type of memory space requirement is fulfilled by character array.

For example:

We can store a string, "Techno India", in a user defined character array, company_name, as:

   char company_name[ ] = "Techno India" ;

One character variable is suitable for storing a single character.

For example:

We can store a character, 'K', in a user defined character variable, one, as:

   char one = 'K' ;

Integer array is suitable for storing a set of integers.

For example:

   int number[ ] = {1, 2, 3, 4, 5}

Here, number is declared as an integer array, in which 5 integer numbers – 1, 2, 3, 4, and 5 will be stored.

3. Every string is terminated with a null ('\0') character, is the true statement.

   A string is a data structure, which is stored in an array, and is not a data type in C. Since the length of the array need not be equal to the length of the string, it often becomes larger than the string. So a string needs to be terminated and '\0' represents the terminating position of a string.

4. The declaration, char s[7] = "HELLO" ;, will store the string, HELLO.

   The array size should be at least one more than the actual string to be stored in the array.

   The string, HELLO, consists of 5 characters. So an array of at least length 6 is required. One extra space is required to store the end of string marker, '\0' (null character). The string will be internally stored as s[7] = "HELLO\0" by the compiler.

   So char s[7] = "HELLO" is the correct declaration.

   The declaration, char s[5] = "HELLO" is syntactically valid. The array size is one less than the required size. This is logically incorrect and generates problem at the time of execution. But there will be no compilation error. The compiler does not check the boundary of an array; it has to be done by the programmer.

   The declaration, char s = "HELLO" ; is wrong since a character variable cannot store a string. It can store only a character.

5. The statement, printf("\"HELLO\"") ; will print "HELLO".

   Double quotes have to be included with a backslash in a string, as is shown in the printf function.

6. 2 is numeric constant.

   '2' is character constant.

   "2" is string constant.

   These are correct.

   2 is a number. Hence it is treated as numeric integer constant. One integer variable is sufficient to store this data in memory.

   '2' is a character constant. So it is represented with its ASCII value, 50. It requires one byte memory space in the memory. One character variable is sufficient to store this data.

   "2" is a string constant. It consists of two consecutive characters, '2' followed by a '\0' character. So in the memory, two characters are stored. One character array, of size 2, is the minimum space required to store this in the memory. No arithmetic operation is possible on "2".

7. The correct declaration for a string variable with the initial value SAMPLE is char text[ ] = "SAMPLE".

   A null character \0 will automatically be inserted at the end by the compiler.

   The declaration char text = "SAMPLE"; will raise the error message "can't convert 'char*' to 'char'".

   "SAMPLE" is a string that can be put in a character array or be pointed by a character pointer, i.e., char* but text is declared here as char.

8. char arr[]="Hello World!"; is the correct declaration to store the string "Hello World!" in an array.

   char arr[]={Hello World!}; is wrong because string constants need to enclose with double quotation(" ") not with braces ({ }).

char arr[]={H,e,l,l,o, ,W,o,r,l,d,!,\0}; is wrong because to mention individual character constant, each character needs to enclose with single quotation. 'H' is character constant but H indicates an identifier or variable.

9. Minimum size of the array will be 13.

   In the string constant, there are 10 alphabet, 1 space and 1 punctuation character. These 12 characters and one extra character for terminating '\0' character; total 13 byte for these 13 characters are required.

10. A 2-D character array is suitable for storing multiple strings in the memory.

    A 1-D character array is suitable for storing only one string and is considered a single unit. For example:

    char names [3] [10] = {"Subir", "Anurag", "Darshana"};

    There are 3 rows and 10 columns here. The number of strings is 3 and length of each string is less than 10.

    A 3-D array can be logically thought of as a collection of 2-D arrays. So a 3-D array can also be used to store multiple strings. But handling of these strings becomes unnecessarily complicated and hence is not feasible for use.

11. The declaration, char city[3][30] = { "Kolkata, Delhi, Mumbai" } ; is appropriate for storing multiple strings.

    The 2-D character array, city, has 3 rows and 30 columns. A total of 3 cities have been provided and the length of each is less than 30. So the above initialization will store all the three strings.

    The declaration, char city[3][30] = {"Kolkata, Delhi, Mumbai"} ; will not store multiple strings in the 2-D array, city. A string constant has to be enclosed within double quotes (" "). But here the data, i.e., Kolkata, Delhi and Mumbai, has been enclosed together in double quotes. As a result, "Kolkata, Delhi, Mumbai" will be treated as a single string.

    When initializing a 2-D array, omitting of the column size is not allowed. Hence it will be an error.

12. The following consecutive statements will not work correctly:

    st[0] = 'C' ;

    st[1] = 'A' ;

    st[2] = 'T' ;

    puts(st) ;

    After the execution of the statements, st[0] will contain 'C', st[1] will contain 'A' and st[2] will contain 'T'. So these three characters will be stored sequentially in the array. A null character has to be stored at the end, in the location st[3] of the array, st, to terminate the string. But the location st[3] is vacant which means that garbage value has been stored. As a result, the puts function will fail to print CAT. After printing CAT, it will print garbage values and then abnormally terminate.

13. After the initialization, st[0] = 'B', st[1] = 'A', st[2] = 'B', st[3] = 'I', st[4] = '\0' and the remaining locations, from s[5] to s[9] will contain '\0' characters.

    So when a character array is initialized with a string constant and if the string length is lesser then the array size, then the remaining locations will be filled with '\0' characters.

14. The minimum size of the character array should be n + 1.

Any character string ends with a null character ('\0'). A null character is an extra character that is stored in the character array. It acts as the end of string marker. So a minimum of one extra location is required. Hence the length of the character array should be n + 1.

15. The above program will be equivalent to gets function.

gets function accepts a string containing any sequence of characters. It reads characters sequentially, stores them in a character array, stops when it encounters a newline character and stores a '\0' character at the end. The given program will also work in a similar fashion and will be equivalent to gets function.

There is no function called getline.

scanf function with format specifier, %s, can accept string but it stops when it encounters a whitespace character.

16. The above program will be equivalent to puts(s).

puts function displays a string. If the string is stored in a character array, then the array name should be written in the argument of puts( ). The above program will display all the characters of the string, i.e., the whole string will be displayed.

There is no function called putline in C.

printf(s) can display the whole string stored within the character array, s. So apparently it seems to us that it is also equivalent to the program. But printf(s) fails to print the string, if the string itself contains % character. So the correct statement to print the string is printf("%s", s).

17. Two strings are compared using the library function strcmp.

strcmp function accepts two strings as its arguments and returns one integer value. The return value can either be a positive number, a negative number or zero.

General form of strcmp function is:

    strcmp(strn1,strn2);

where,

strn1 and strn2 are the two strings to be compared. They may either be string constants or strings stored within character array.

Comparison operators will not work for string.

There are no special operators available for string comparison.

18. The return value of strcmp("RAM", "RAN") will be −1.

strcmp works as follows:

It performs character by character comparison of both the strings. But stops where it encounters the first mismatched characters and returns the difference of the ASCII values of the character in the first string and that in the second string.

Here, the strcmp function will start comparing the first characters of both the strings. The first character is R in both the strings, so they match. The second character is A in both, which also matches. The mismatch occurs in the third character. So it will compute the difference of M and N. The ASCII value of M is 78 and that of N is 79. So M − N will be −1.

If the strcmp function is invoked as strcmp("RAN","RAM"); then the value of N − M will be returned, which is, 1.

If both the strings are equal, then strcmp function will return 0. Hence, strcmp("RAM","RAM"); will return 0.

Let us take another example to compare the two strings viz. RAN and RUN.

strcmp("RAN","RUN"); the first character is R in both the strings, so they match. The difference is in the second character of both the strings, so it will return the difference of the ASCII value A and U, i.e., 65 − 87, i.e., −22.

It never depends on the compiler

19. The invocation, strcmp(s, t) is correct.

    strcmp function accepts two strings as its arguments. If the two strings are string constants, then they have to be written within double quotes (" "). If the two strings are stored within a character array, then the name of the array has to be written. In any function, the name of the array, which is passed, is written. No subscripts are written.

    Enclosing s and t within double quotes (" ") will make them string constants. So they will not be considered as arrays and comparison will be performed between two strings, i.e., "s" and "t".

20. Two strings are concatenated using the library function, **strcat( )**.

    strcat function accepts two strings in the following form:

    strcat(strn1, strn2) ;

    where,

    strn1 has to be a character array containing a string.

    strn2 is a character array variable containing a string or a string constant.

21. **strcat(s, t)** will store **RAMANANDA** in the character array, **s**.

    strcat function concatenates the content of the first array with that of the second array and stores the resultant string in the first.

    The strcat function accepts two strings in the following form:

    strcat(strn1, strn2) ;

    where,

    strn1 has to be a character array containing a string.

    strn2 is a character array variable containing a string or a string constant.

    starcat(t, s) will store **ANANDARAM** in the character array, **t**.

22. The output of the program segment will be **HELLO**.

    Every string should have one null character at the end. But in the array, s, there are two null characters. So the first null character will be treated as the end of string. If any character is stored after this, it will be ignored by the string handling functions. Hence, WORLD will be ignored here by the first null character (of HELLO) and will not be displayed.

23. The header file, **string.h**, contains the declaration of all the string handling functions.

    Any C program using a string handling function includes string.h in the following manner:

    #include<string.h>

24. **strlen function** calculates the length of a string.

    strlen function accepts one string as its argument and returns the length of the string – including the spaces and excluding the null character. The argument may either be a string constant or an array containing string.

For example:

int l ;

l = strlen("Subhodip Mukherjee") ;

Here, the strlen function will return the length of the string, "Subhodip Mukherjee", i.e., 18, including the spaces and excluding the null character. The length that is returned will be stored in the integer variable, l.

There are no string handling library functions called **length( )** or **stringlength( )** in C.

25. The output will be **5**.

The character array, s, has been passed as the argument of strlen function. When the array is passed as function argument, only the name of the array is written. strlen function will calculate the length of the string, HELLO and store the result in x.

Every string terminates with a null character. But **strlen** function calculates the length of the string, excluding the null character.

26. **strcpy(s, "HELLO")** ; will copy the string, **HELLO**, in the character array, **s**.

strcpy is a library function which performs string copy operation. The function accepts two arguments, which are strings. It is invoked as follows:

strcpy(string1, string2);

where,

string1 is the destination.

string2 is the source.

string1 should be a character array since the source string will be copied into the destination string. But string2 may either be a constant string or a character array containing a string.

s = "HELLO"; is invalid because assignment statement is not permitted for a string.

There is no function named, **stringcopy()** in C.

27. **strcpy("HI", s)** ; is an illegal string copy operation.

strcpy is a library function which performs string copy operation. The function accepts two arguments, which are strings. It is invoked as follows:

strcpy(string1, string2) ;

where,

string1 is the destination.

string2 is the source.

string1 should be a character array since the source string will be copied into the destination string. But string2 may either be a constant string or a character array containing a string.

28. The following sequence of statements will store **RUBY ROY** in the array, **z**:

strcpy(z, x) ;

strcat(z, " ") ;

strcat(z, y) ;

strcpy(z, x) will copy the content of array x, i.e., RUBY in the array z.

strcat(z," ") will concatenate " ", i.e., a space at the end of RUBY.

strcat(z, y) will append ROY at the end and make the content of array z as RUBY ROY.

strcat(z, x) ;

strcat(z, " ") ;

strcat(z, y) ;

is not valid. Here strcat(z, x) will fail because initially the array z was empty.

strcat(z, x, y) ;

is not valid since strcat function cannot accept 3 arguments.

29. The string comparison, **strcmp("HELLO" , "HELLO") ;** will return 0.

strcmp function performs string comparison taking two strings as its arguments and returns 0 when two strings are equal.

Uppercase and lowercase alphabets are treated differently by **strcmp** function. **"HELLO"** and **"hello"** are different. Hence this comparison will not return 0.

30. **strcmpi function** treats uppercase and lower case alphabets equally.

strcmpi function accepts two strings as its arguments. The result which it returns after comparison may either be a positive number, negative number or zero. While performing the comparison, it ignores the case (i.e., uppercase or lowercase) of the string.

For example:

    strcmpi("Hello", "hello") ;

Here although the case of the two strings are different (i.e., "Hello" is in uppercase and "hello" is in lowercase), strcmpi( ) will return 0. This is because strcmpi function performs the comparison irrespective of the case of the string.

There are no functions called **istrcmp( )** or **icasestrcmp( )** in C.

31. The following program segment will display all the strings in different lines:

    for(i = 0 ; i < 3 ; i++)

    puts(city[i]) ;

puts function displays a string, but it automatically prints a newline after printing the string. If a 1-D array contains a string, only array name should be written in the argument of the puts function. But in case of 2-D array containing multiple strings, array name with first subscript should be written as the argument of the puts function, where first subscript indicates the row number.

Writing only array name as argument of the puts function is valid in case of 1-D array.

32. **strncpy** function will copy the first **n** characters from a source string to the destination array.

strncpy function takes arguments in the following way:

    strncpy(string1, string2, n) ;

where,

string1 is a character array and is the destination where n number of characters will be copied.

string2 is a character array variable containing a string or a constant string.

n is the number of characters that are to be copied from string2 to string1.

Note that strncpy copies at most n characters and the destination array is not null terminated. So we have to manually include '\0' after the end of the string else the compiler will include some garbage value after the string.

For example:

```
char full[20 ] = "Good Morning" ;
char initial [10 ] ;
strncpy(initial, full, 4) ;
initial [4] = '\0' ;
```

This will copy the first 4 characters of the string stored in the array, full, to the array, initial. So initial will now contain "Good". To terminate the string we have to add a null character at the end of "Good" else the compiler will include some garbage value after Good.

33. The above program **will convert the content of array, s, "good" to upper case "GOOD".**

   toupper function converts one lowercase alphabet to its corresponding uppercase alphabet. In the above program, each character will be accessed from the array with the for loop. Then each character will be stored in that same array after conversion to uppercase, and ultimately the entire content will be converted to uppercase.

34. The following two consecutive statements will copy **KOL** in the array, t.

   strncpy(t,s,3);

   t[3] = '\0' ;

   strncpy function copies at most n characters from a source string to the destination array.

   strncpy function takes arguments in the following way:

   strncpy(string1, string2, n) ;

   where,

   string1 is a character array and the destination where n number of characters will be copied.

   string2 is a character array variable containing a string or a constant string.

   n is the number of characters that are to be copied from string2 to string1.

   Note that strncpy copies at most n characters and the destination array is not null terminated.

35. **strncmp function** performs string comparison of at most **n** characters from both the strings.

   strncmp function has the following syntax:

   strncmp(string1, string2, n) ;

   where,

   string1 and string2 are the two strings that are to be compared.

   n is the number of characters to be compared at most. It returns a value (the difference of the two mismatched ASCII characters), which may either be greater than 0, less than 0 or 0(Zero).

   Note that string1 and string2 may either be string constants or character array containing strings.

   For example:

```
int l ;
char str1 [ ] = "Good Morning" ;
```

```
char str2 [ ] = "Good Evening" ;
l = strncmp(str, str2, 4);
```

In the above example, the strncmp function will compare the first 4 characters of the two strings. Since they match, it will return 0.

There are no functions called **strcmpn( )** or **nstrcmp( )** in C.

36. The following two consecutive statements will make **SUBIR ROY** the content of the array, s.

strcat(s, " ") ;

strncat(s, "ROYCHOWDHURY", 3) ;

strcat function is used to concatenate/join the two strings.

So here, strcat(s, " ") ; will append one space at the end of the array, s, making its content, SUBIR, followed by a blank space.

The strncat function concatenates n number of characters from the second string to those in the first string and the result is stored in the first array.

So the statement, strncat(s, "ROYCHOWDHURY", 3) will concatenate the first 3 characters from the second string, "ROYCHOWDHURY", i.e., ROY, with the content of the array, s. Thus the final content of the array, s, will be SUBIR ROY.

37. **strchr function** is used to search for the first occurrence of a given character in a string.

It takes two arguments and its syntax is as follows:

strchr(character, string) ;

where,

character is the required character to be searched for in the string.

string is the word from where the character is to be searched.

The strchr function searches for the first occurrence of the character in the string and returns the address where the character occurs. It returns NULL if the character is absent.

38. The output will be **B is absent**.

strchr function searches for the first occurrence of a given character in a string. It takes two arguments.

Its syntax is as follows:

strchr(character, string) ;

where,

character is the required character to be searched for in the string.

string is the word from where the character is to be searched.

The strchr function searches for the first occurrence of the character in the string and returns the address where the character occurs. It returns NULL if the character is absent.

Here, B is not present in the string, "KOLKATA". So the strchr function will return NULL and the output will be B is absent.

39. **strrchr function** is used to search for the last occurrence of a given character in a string.

It takes two arguments and its syntax is as follows :

strrchr(character, string) ;

where,

character is the required character to be searched for in the string.

string is the word from where the character is to be searched.

The strrchr function searches for the last occurrence of the character in the string and returns the address where the character occurs. It returns NULL if the character is absent.

strchr function is used to search for the first occurrence of a character in a string.

40. **strstr function** is used to search for the occurrence of a string within a string.

It takes two arguments and has the following syntax:

strsr(string1, string2) ;

Here string2 is searched for within string1. If string2 is present in string1, then the address of string2 is returned, otherwise NULL is returned.

For example:

int I ;

char str1 [ ] = "Welcome to Confidence Based Learning" ;

char str2 [ ] = " Learning" ;

I = strstr(str1, str2) ;

Since "Learning" is found in the content of str1, the strstr function will return the address of "Learning" from str1.

Let us take another example:

char str1 [ ] = "Welcome to Confidence Based Learning" ;

char str2 [ ] = " Mastery" ;

I = strstr(str1, str2) ;

Since "Mastery" is not found in the content of str1, it will return NULL.

There are no functions called **substr( )** or **str( )** in C.

41. The output of the program will be **Good evening**.

Here, the strstr function will search for the occurrence of the string, "is", within the string "This". Since "is" is present in "This", the strstr function will return the address where it occurs, which is a not a NULL address. So the output will be Good evening.

42. **strset function** is used to set all the characters in the string with a particular character.

strset function accepts two arguments and has the following syntax:

strset(string, character) ;

where,

string is a set of characters which are to be set to a particular character specified by the second argument, character.

character is the character to which the argument, string, is to be set.

The strset function sets all the characters of the string with a character.

There are no such functions called **set( )** or **setstring( )** in C.

43. The output of the program after calling **strset** function will be:

1234

cccc

The character array, s, contains the string "1234". So the puts function will print 1234 first. The strset function will set all the characters of the string with character, 'c'. Four characters will be replaced by 'c' since the string contains only four characters.

44. The above program will be equivalent to **strcpy** function.

In the program, the array, s, contains the string, "KOLKATA". In each iteration of the for loop, starting from the 0th position, one character of the string, "KOLKATA" will be taken from array, s, and stored in array, t. One '\0' character will be stored at end in array, t. Finally array, t, will hold all the characters of array, s. This is the function of strcpy( ).

45. The above program will be equivalent to **strcmp** function.

strcmp function starts character by character comparison from the 0th position and returns 0 if all characters in both the strings are equal till the '\0' character. Otherwise, it stops where the first mismatch occurs and returns the difference of the ASCII values of the character in the first string and that in the second string.

In this program, the first character of array, s, is 'K' and that of array, t, is 'D'. The ASCII value of 'K' is 75 and that of 'D' is 68. So 'K' − 'D', i.e., 7 will be stored in j.

46. The following program code will accept input strings in all the 3 rows:

for(i = 0 ; i < 3 ; i++) ;

scanf("%s", city[i]);

In a 2-D character array, while taking input string, array name with first subscript should be written. First subscript indicates the row number where the input string is to be stored.

In the above program, the for loop will continue with i, varying from 0 to 2 with an increment of 1. This i has been used as the first subscript of the array, city. So with the loop structure, three strings will be accepted in three rows of the array, city.

If **city** is declared as a **1-D array**, then **gets(city)** or **scanf("%s", city)** can accept one string. **gets(city)** is not a correct command for accepting multiple strings.

47. The above program will be equivalent to **strlen( )**.

In the given program, the for loop will start from the 0th position and continue till a NULL character (\0) is found. Each iteration will increment i by 1. The final value of i will be 7 which is the length of the string, "KOLKATA".

48. The above program will be equivalent to **strcat** function.

strcat function concatenates/joins the first string with the second string and stores the whole concatenated string in the first array. Care should be taken that the first array should be large enough to hold the concatenated string.

In the above program, the first for loop will proceed up to the '\0' character of the array, s. So i will hold the position of the '\0' character of the array, s. Now the second loop will start with the variable, j, and will continue up to the '\0' character of the array, t. In each step, one character will be appended in the array, s, from the array, t. Finally in the array, s, one '\0' character will be stored. So the final content of the array, s, will be SHREYASAHA\0.

strcat(s, t) will also perform the same job.

There is no function called concat( ) in C.

49. Correct answer is **char name[10][30];**. To store a single name, we need a single dimensional array of size 30. To store 10 such name, 10 arrays will be required. Instead of 10 several array, a 2-D array is the better option because it becomes a single unit and operations on the elements will be much easier.

char name[10]; is wrong because this can able to store only 9 characters.

char name[30][10]; is wrong because this declaration can store 30 names. And maximum length of names will be less than 10 – which is not our requirement.

50. **char color[ ][10]={"Red", "Green", "Blue"};** is the correct answer. The first string "Red" will be stored at 1st row, The second "Green" will be stored at 2nd row and the third string "Blue" will be store at 3rd row.

string color[3][10] ={"Red", "Green", "Blue"}; is wrong because string is not a valid datatype in C.

char color[3][10]={ {Red}, {Green}, {Blue}}; is wrong because the name of the colors are string. So, these have to write within double courts. Ex: "Red", "Green", etc.

13

Function

The basic principle to define a function is to divide a large program into some smaller modules so that a complicated task can be broken into simpler and more manageable form that can be handled easily. These smaller modules are used to accomplish a definite task.

Function is a self-contained block of statements that perform some specific job. In C language, we achieve the modular programming using function. Functions in C are categorized into two groups. They are *Library function* and *User defined function*. *Library functions* are defined within several header files as per individual category of the functions. We already discussed some library functions and some other will be discussed later. Though C supports a large number of library functions, but this is not sufficient. According to our requirement we need to define our own functions. These are called *user defined function*. In this chapter we will discuss how a user defined function can be defined and how it can be accessed, etc.

Basically, any C program is a collection of one or more functions. If it contains only one function, then it is the main function. In C program **main** function is a special function. **Every C program starts its execution from main function and other functions are called from this function as well. Every C program must have a main function and more than one main function is not possible in a single program.** However, a C program may contain more than one user defined function and there is no restriction on this. If more than one function is present in a C program, they may appear in any sequence. Though there are many other functions, we can understand the basic logic of the program by reading only the main function. It is the heart of the program as the control flow of the program is totally under the control of this main function.

13.1 WHY FUNCTION

Till now whatever programs we wrote are very small and simple. But in real life, it is not that easier. Rather they are large enough and quite complicated. As programs become more complex and large, several problems may arise. It is always better to handle some smaller programs than a large one. That is why the modular programming concept arises – where a large program is divided into some smaller modules. In C programming, these modules are known as functions. There are several advantages of use of functions. These are:

Increases readability: Functions are used to split up long lines of code into smaller ones called modules. Every module in a program is designed to perform a specific task. A module may be split into further modules called sub modules. Those smaller modules or functions can be invoked from the main functions. Hence instead of reading the whole code including all the modules or sub modules of program, if someone just read the main function and know only the purpose of different functions defined in the program, easily he/she will be able to understand the basic algorithm of the program even without knowing the detail code of each function. But in absence of functions to understand the algorithm we need to read the total program. For example, a program of 3000 lines may be split into 10 functions whose main function may consist of 250 lines. Then by reading these 250 lines any one can understand the algorithm of the program. He/she need not to read 3000 lines. In this way the readability certainly gets increased.

Decreases LOC (Line of Code): A function may be called several times from main function or from other functions according to the requirement. If any user needs to do same kind of work several times he can easily do it just by invoking the corresponding function instead of writing the codes several times. He has to write the code only once, i.e., at the time of defining the particular function and whenever that particular code will be required he just need to call the particular function. This means if that function contains 100 lines of code and if we need to do the particular job defined within the function 5 times, then we do not have to write $100 \times 5 = 500$ lines of code for this as we will invoke the defined function 5 times only, the required LOC will be 100 plus 5 = 105 which is very small compared to non-function version of code (i.e., just 1/5th). Thus functions decrease the **Line of Code** effectively.

Minimize the effort in testing, debugging and maintenance: Testing is one of the expensive phases in software development. Much more effort is required during this process and so a programmer's objective would always be to minimize the testing effort. It is always easier to test a smaller module than a larger one. So, testing a function with 100 lines of code is always desirable than a big program with 1000 lines of code. It reduces the effort and the testing cost both at the same time. Not only this, as a function may be required to call several times, in a non-function version code that particular code will be in several places in the code. So, each portion has to test. But if we write function, then testing only a particular module would be sufficient. The same is applicable for debugging purpose as well. If we use function, then we need to remove/correct errors at only one place instead of everywhere. Thus, it decreases the effort and cost of a debugger like testing.

Maintenance is the costliest phase amongst all. So an utmost care is needed to reduce both the corrective and adaptive maintenance cost of the software. If any modification is needed in the code, the cost for the modification and corresponding testing and debugging in a larger module is always costlier than a smaller one. In modular programming, we will make change only at the particular module. The other module will remain untouched. So, the corresponding testing-debugging will also be required for that particular module – not for all modules. Thus, using function would always provide a much more cost effective maintenance than a larger LOC.

Increases reusability: As mentioned earlier usage of function increases the reusability of code as the programmers do not need to write down the same lines of code over and over again to perform the same task. For instance, if we want to sort an array of elements 5 times, then instead of writing the code of sorting 5 times repeatedly, we will write the code only once within the function definition body and will call the function 5 times. Again, a function may be reused in multiple programs. Like C standard library, we can also create our own library where several functions may be stored. Then instead of starting from scratch, a programmer can just use those functions from that library any time and for any program. In this way, function increases the reusability.

Helps in top down modular programming: We already know that modular programming is a top down approach and functions help the programmer to implement it. From the main program sub function may be invoked and similarly from the sub function another sub-sub function can be called and likewise. For instance, to solve the problem of permutations and combinations, we have to determine the value of ^nP_r or ^nC_r, which are considered to be two separate modules or functions. The programmer needs the help of another sub function which will find the value of the factorial to get the value of both ^nP_r and ^nC_r. In this way functions helps to achieve the top down approach.

Helps to distribute tasks among team members: It is always better to work on team than single handedly to achieve a better product. In the software industry, it is a great challenge to deliver the product within the stipulated time. Only distribution of works can solve this problem. Using modular programming concept, we can split a large program into some smaller functions and those functions can be distributed among team members. Hence, the total development time will be reduced.

13.1.1   General Form of a User-Defined Function

A user defined function consists of function header and function body. Function header consists of return type of the function, function name and arguments to pass through the function. Function body is basically a set of valid C statements enclosed within parentheses.

The general form of a user-defined function is:

```
return_type function_name (list of Arguments )} Function Header
{
    ....

    ....                                          } Function Body
    [return [(expression)];]

}
```

Here, **return_type** determines the type of the value which will be returned by the function. If a function does not return any value, then its return type is specified as **void**. And if it returns some value, then corresponding data type is mentioned in function definition. Similarly, if no argument is passed through a function, we can define the parameter/ argument list as void. Note that if we do not mention the return type in function definition, by default it will be treated as integer. **function_name** is the name of the function. The rules to declare a function name is same as declaring a variable name with an extra care that it should not be match with any library function name. Body of the function consists of any valid C statement(s). The **return** statement returns some value (if any) as well as the control to the calling point. The **return** statement is optional if the return type is void. It just returns the control to the calling point. If **return** statement is not mentioned and control reaches at the end of function, then also control returns at the calling point. But in case of non-void return type we must have to use **return** statement with some constant, variable or expression. This value will be returned to the calling point. Always remember that a function can accept any number of arguments but it can return only one value per call. A **return** statement may occur anywhere within the body of a function and as many times as it is required.

13.2 CALLING A FUNCTION

Like library functions, the user defined functions are invoked or called simply by the function name including arguments, if any, enclosed within parentheses. These parentheses must follow the function name even if there is no argument to be passed. The general form of the function calling statement is

   function_name(list of arguments);

If there is no argument to be passed, then the function calling statement would be

   function_name( );

When the function call statement executes, the program control is transferred to the called function. When the specified task of the function is over, the program control is returned to the calling point in the calling function.

The following program illustrates how we can define a user defined function and how the function can be invoked from main( ) function.

PROGRAM 13.1   Function to find the factorial of a number and its use from main.

```
/* Function to find the factorial of a number */
    int factorial(int n)
    {    int i, f=1;
         for(i=1;i<=n;i++)
             f=f*i;                        Function Definition
         return(f);
    }

void main( )
    {    int x,fact;
         printf("Enter any Number : ");
         scanf("%d",&x);
         fact = factorial(x);       /*  Function call  */
         printf("Factorial of %d is %d", x, fact);
    }
```

Here, factorial( ) is a user-defined function whose return type is integer and it has a single argument of integer type. This function is called from the main( ) function. When we execute the above program, execution starts from main( ). After taking input when the statement:

fact = factorial(x);

executes, control jumps to the function **factorial( )** defined above. The value of **x** will be copied to the variable **n**. Within the function the factorial of n will be calculated and the calculated value will be returned to the calling point by the **return** statement and will be assigned to the variable, **fact**. Remember, the variable **x** and **fact** are local to the main( ) and are not accessible within the function, **factorial( )**. Similarly, the variable, **i, f** and **n** are local to the function, **factorial( )**. So, they are not accessible from **main( )**.

Depending on the arguments passed to any function, invoking of functions can be classified into two groups. These are:
1. Call by value
2. Call by reference

When we pass the arguments as a call by value, we pass the value of variables to the function. In this mechanism a copy of the actual arguments are passed. In this chapter, we only follow call by value mechanism. Call by reference mechanism will be discussed in next chapter, i.e., Chapter 14 where we discuss about the pointer.

13.3 TYPES OF FUNCTION ARGUMENTS

We can classify the arguments into two types - actual argument and formal argument. The arguments we send at the time of function call is known as actual arguments. They are called actual arguments because these arguments hold the actual value. The actual arguments can be constants, variables or any valid C expressions. Whereas the arguments defined at the argument list in a function definition is known as formal arguments. They are called formal arguments because they are formal place holder. The formal arguments should be variables. It cannot be constants or expressions.

Following example shows the formal arguments and actual arguments.

PROGRAM 13.2 Define a function to find the average of two numbers and show its use from main function.

Formal Arguments

```
float average(int n1, int n2)
    {    float avg;
         avg = (n1 + n2) / 2.0;
         return(avg);
    }
```

```
void main( )
{    int m,n;
     float avrg;
     printf("Enter any Number : ");
     scanf("%d",&m);
     printf("Enter another Number : ");
     scanf("%d",&n);
```

Actual Arguments

```
     avrg = average(m, n);      /* Function call */
     printf("Average of %d and %d is %d", m, n, avrg);
}
```

In the above example, **m** and **n** are actual arguments in the statement

avrg = average(m,n);

and **n1** and **n2** are formal arguments in the function definition. Remember that, the data type of actual argument and formal argument should be same.

We can pass zero or any number of arguments into a function. If the number of arguments is zero, i.e., if we do not pass any argument we can mention it as void or simply omit the argument list. For example,

```
void display(void)
{
     printf("Welcome to the world of C function");
}
```

The above function can also be written as:

```
void display( )
{
     printf("Welcome to the world of C function");
}
```

When we pass argument(s) into a function we have to mention the data type of the formal arguments in function definitions. For example:

```
int square(int n)
{
     int sq;
     sq = n * n;
     return(sq);
}
```

This is a single argument function. It takes only one argument, **n** of integer type. Using this variable square of the number is calculated and returned.

```
int max(int m, int n)
{
     int max;
```

```
    if ( m > n)
        max = m;
    else
        max = n;
    return(max);
}
```

This is a two argument function. It takes two integer arguments, **m** and **n**. Depending on these variables max is calculated and stored within the **max** variable. Finally the value of the **max** variable is returned through the statement **return(max)**.

```
float simple_interest( int amount, float rate, float time)
    {
        float si;
        si = amount * rate * time /100;
        return(si);
    }
```

The above function takes three arguments: one integer type and two float type. Using these arguments this function calculates simple interest and stores it into the variable **si**. As this value is a real number we declare the return type of the function as float. At end, the statement **return(si)** return back the control as well as the value of the variable **si** to the calling point.

It is not necessary that always we have to calculate and store within a variable and then only we can return the value. We may return the value directly without storing in a variable. The above function can be written as:

```
float simple_interest( int amount, float rate, float time)
    {
        return(amount * rate * time /100);
    }
```

Here, the calculation will be done first and then will be stored in some unnamed memory location. The return statement will return the value from that unnamed memory location.

13.4 ARRAY AS FUNCTION ARGUMENT

As we pass individual variables we can pass an entire array to a function as a function argument. To pass a numeric array, we need to mention the array name and its size along with functions arguments.

For example, to find the smallest element within a set of element we need to pass the array as a function argument. If the function name is smallest, the corresponding function call statement may look like:

     smallest(my_arr, n);

where **my_arr** is the array name and **n** indicates the size of the array. As the array name only indicates the starting address of the array and there is no scope to find end of the array in case of numeric array, we need to mention size of the array. Thus, the above statement passes all the elements of the array **my_arr**. The called function also has to define appropriately. The function header may be defined as:

int smallest(int num_arr[], int size);

The function has two arguments. First one is the name of the array and second argument is the size of the array. Here size specifies the number of elements in the array. You may note that the formal argument array is declared as follows:

int num_arr[];

Here, to declare the array, size is not mentioned. It is optional here. This is possible because the array will be initialized with the values of the array passed as actual argument. In this example, the array num_arr will be initialized with the values of my_arr, i.e., the elements of my_arr will be copied to num_arr.

When an array is passed to a function as an argument one major point should always remember. Unlike normal variable any changes occur on the array elements persists in the original array that passed to the function. Here instead of copying the contents of the array into the formal parameter array, the starting address of the array is passed on to the function. Thus, all the changes occur in the called function are truly reflected in the original array in the calling function.

Here is a complete program to show how an array can be passed to a function.

PROGRAM 13.3 Write a function to find the smallest element in an array.

```c
/*  Function to find the smallest element in an array  */
#include<stdio.h>
#include<conio.h>
int smallest(int num_arr[ ], int size)
{
    int i, minimum;
    minimum = num_arr[0];
    for( i = 1; i < size; i++ )
    {
        if( num_arr[i] < minimum )
            minimum = num_arr[i];
    }
    return( minimum);
}

void main( )
{   int my_arr[20], i, min;
    for(i = 0; i < 20; i++)
    {
        printf(„Enter Element%d: „,i+1);
        scanf(„%d",& my_arr[i]);
    }
    min = smallest(my_arr, 20);
```

```
        printf("The smallest element is %d", min);
    }
```

Like numeric array, we can pass a string as function argument. As the end of the string is determined by the '\0' character, we need not send the size of the array as argument like numeric array. The following program illustrates how we can pass a string as function argument.

PROGRAM 13.4 Write a function to count the number of words in a string.

```
/*  Function to count the number of words in a string    */
#include<stdio.h>
#include<conio.h>
int count_word( char str[ ])
{   int c = 0, i = 0;
    while( str[i] != '\0')
    {
        if( str[i] =   ' ' && str[i+1] != ' ' )   /* Checking for more
                                                      than one consecutive
                                                      space   */
                c++;
        i++;
    }
    return(c+1);
}

void main( )
{   char strng[80];
    int count, i=0;
    puts("Enter Any String : ");
    gets(strng);
    count = count_word(strng);
    printf("Total number of words in the string \"%s\" is %d, strng, count);
}
```

Sample output

Enter Any String : He is a good boy
Total number of words in the string "He is a good boy" is 5

13.5 FUNCTION PROTOTYPE

So far in the chapter, we have defined the function before its use, i.e., before the main function. But it is not mandatory. But for this, we need to declare the *function prototype* before calling the functions. *Function prototype* provides the information to the compiler about a function which will be defined at a later point in the program. To declare the prototype, we have to write the function header with a semicolon at end. Mentioning the name of the formal arguments is optional. But the data types of the formal arguments are mandatory. The prototype of the above function will be declared as:

int count_word(char str[ ]);

or simply,   int count_word(char [ ]);

Here is a complete program showing the function prototype declaration.

PROGRAM 13.5   Write a program to display all two digit Prime numbers.

```
/*  Program to display all two digit Prime numbers  */
#include<conio.h>
#include<stdio.h>
int isprime(int);       /* Function prototype declaration */

void main( )
{
    int i;
    printf("Two digited Prime Numbers are : ");
    for(i = 10; i<=99; i++)
    {
      if(isprime(i))             /* Function call */
         printf("%d", i);
    }
}

int isprime(int n)     /* Function Definition to check whether a number
                         is Prime or not */
{     int r=1,i;
    for(i=2;i<=n/2;i++)
    {    r=n%i;
         if(r= =0)
         break;
    }
    return(r);
}
```

Sample output

Two digited Prime Numbers are:

11 13 17 19 23 29 31 37 41 43 47 53 59 61 67 71 73 79 83 89 97

In the above example, isprime( ) function accepts an integer as argument and checks whether it is prime or not. In the main( ) function, all two digited numbers, i.e., 10–99 is generated and checked through the isprime( ) function. If the function returns any non-zero value, i.e., true, then the number is printed. As the function isprime( ) is written after main(), it is necessary to declare the function prototype. But it is good habit to declare function prototype always whether it is required or not.

Here is another example where we will see the prototype declaration of a function whose argument is an array.

PROGRAM 13.6   Write a program to sort an array using bubble sort algorithm.

```
/* Program to sort an array using bubble sort algorithm */
#include<conio.h>
#include<stdio.h>
#define SIZE 10
void bubble_sort( int [ ], int );   /* Prototype declaration of the
                                       function */
void main()
{
    int element[SIZE],i;
    for(i=0;i<SIZE;i++)
    {
        printf("Enter Element %d: ",i+1);
        scanf("%d",&element[i]);
    }

    bubble_sort(element, SIZE);            /* Function call */


    printf("\n\nThe Sorted Elements are : ");
    for(i=0;i<SIZE;i++)
    {
        printf("%d ", elements[i]);
    }
}

void bubble_sort( int my_arr[], int n)
{
    int i, j, temp;
    for( i = 0; i < n -1; i++ )
    {
        for( j = 0; j < n -1 - i; j++ )
        {
            if(my_arr[j] >  my_arr[ j + 1] )
            {
                temp =  my_arr[j];
                my_arr[j] = my_arr[j+1];
                my_arr[j+1] =  temp;
            }
        }
    }
}
```

Sample output

```
Enter Element 1: 42
Enter Element 2: 63
Enter Element 3: 5
Enter Element 4: 27
Enter Element 5: 39
Enter Element 6: 12
Enter Element 7:  2
Enter Element 8: 44
Enter Element 9: 31
Enter Element 10: 19
```

The Sorted Elements are : 2 5 12 19 27 31 39 42 44 63

13.6 PASSING MULTIDIMENSIONAL ARRAY AS FUNCTION ARGUMENT

Like single dimensional array, we can pass multidimensional array as function arguments. When we declare the multidimensional array as formal argument in the function definition, we need to specify the dimensions second onwards. The first dimension value can be omitted. Following example illustrates how multidimensional array can be passed as function argument.

PROGRAM 13.7 Write separate functions to take input in a matrix, print a matrix and add two matrix. Write a program to add two matrix using these functions.

```
/*   Program to add two matrix  using function*/
#include<stdio.h>
#include<conio.h>
void input( int a[][3]);
void print( int a[][3]);
void add_matrix( int a[][3], int b[][3], int c[][3]);
void main()
{
    int a[3][3], b[3][3],c[3][3];
    clrscr();
    printf("\nEnter the elements of 1st Matrix:-\n");
    input( a );                /* Input to 1st Matrix    */
    printf("\nEnter the elements of 2nd Matrix:-\n");
    input( b );                /* Input to 2nd Matrix    */
    clrscr( );
    printf("\n\n1st Matrix:-\n");
    print( a );                /* Print 1st Matrix    */
    printf("\n\n2nd Matrix:-\n");
    print( b );                /* Print 2nd Matrix    */
```

```
        add_matrix( a, b, c);          /* Addition of two matrix   */

        printf("\n\nSum of two Matrix:-\n");
        print( c );                    /* Printing of Resultant matrix  */
}

void input( int a[][3])         /* Function to take Input into a Matrix */
{   int i, j;
    for(i=0;i<3;i++)
    {    for(j=0;j<3;j++)
        {    printf("Enter element[%d][%d] : ",i,j);
             scanf("%d",&a[i][j]);
        }
    }
}

void print( int a[][3])         /* Function to Print Matrix      */
{   int i, j;
    for(i=0;i<3;i++)
    {    for(j=0;j<3;j++)
             printf("%d\t",a[i][j]);
         printf("\n");
    }
}

void add_matrix( int a[][3], int b[][3], int c[][3])
                                /* Function to Add two matrix */
{   int i, j;
    for(i=0;i<3;i++)
    {    for(j=0;j<3;j++)
        {
             c[i][j] = a[i][j] + b[i][j];
        }
    }
}
```

13.7 STORAGE CLASS

Before we proceed to more on functions, we need to understand storage class. Storage class specifies the scope and life time of variables and/or functions within a C Program.

A scope specifies the part of the program where a variable name is visible, that is the accessibility of the variable by its name. In other word, scope of a variable means in which portion that variable is accessible. Scopes are of two types – local and global. The scope of a variable depends on the type of storage class. "Scope is local" means the variable is accessible only from the block in which it is declared but the variable is not accessible from outside this block. "The scope is global" means variable is accessible from not only within the block it is declared, but also from outside this block and from all other functions in a program file.

A global variable and a local variable can have same name in a program. Two local variables of same name can be declared inside two different functions of a program.

In these cases, the compiler will choose the variable local to a function, when accessed inside that function.

But two local variables of same name inside same function are not allowed. Two global variables of same name in same program is not allowed.

Life time (persistence) of a variable specifies how long the variable is accessible within its scope. When the life time of a variable is over, the variable is de-allocated from memory.

In C language, storage class is categorized into four groups. These are:
- Automatic
- Register
- Static
- External

13.7.1 Automatic

The keyword to declare an automatic storage class is **auto**. The use of this keyword is very rare as it is the default storage class. So far in this book, the variables declared are of automatic storage class as they are declared without specifying any storage class. These variables are declared inside any function. More specifically the activities of this type of variable is limited within the block in which they are defined. When the function is invoked and the corresponding block comes into action; they are created and as soon as the control exits from this block, these variables are destroyed. Automatic variables are accessed only from the block in which they are defined; from outside this block they cannot be accessible. Thus they are local to the block. Automatic variables are allocated in the memory and unless initialized they contain garbage value. Following program illustrates the scope and life time of automatic variables.

PROGRAM 13.8 **Program to demonstrate the life time of automatic variable.**

```
#include<stdio.h>
void main( )
{
    auto int   auto_var = 30 ;
    {   auto int   auto_var = 20 ;
        {
            auto int   auto_var = 10 ;
            printf ("%d ", auto_var ) ;
        }
        printf ("%d ", auto_var ) ;
    }
    printf ("%d ", auto_var ) ;
}
```

Output: 10 20 30

In the above program, the variable **auto_var** is declared thrice. As they are defined in three different blocks compiler treats them as different variables. Within the innermost block, the value of the variable **auto_var** is printed as 10, since within this block this third version of **auto_var** is only accessible. When the control comes out from this block the variable **auto_var** with value 10 is destroyed and hence the **auto_var** in the second block becomes visible. So, the printf( ) in this block prints 20. Similarly, when the control comes out from this second block, the variable **auto_var** with value 20 is destroyed and the third printf( ) refers to the variable **auto_var** with value 30.

13.7.2 Register

When a variable is declared generally it is allocated in the memory. If the storage class of a variable is declared as register, it will be allocated within the CPU register. The variables stored in registers are accessed much faster than the variable stored in memory. So, if the variables that are accessed frequently are kept in the register, the execution of the program becomes faster. Its property is same as automatic variable with only difference in its allocation place. The keyword to declare a register storage class is register. This is done as follows:

```
register int i;
```

If we declare the storage class of any variable as register, we cannot say surely that it will be a register variable. Because the number of registers in the CPU is limited and no one knows currently how many of them are idle. If there is no free register, compiler treats the storage class of the variable as auto.

13.7.3 Static

The static storage class is declared with the keyword static. The scope of static variable is local but the value given to a static variable persists until the end of the program. Because they are not destroyed until the program comes to an end. By default static variables are initialized with zero. Following program illustrates features of static storage class.

PROGRAM 13.9   **Program to demonstrate the scope and life time of static variable.**

```
#include<stdio.h>
void stat_func( )
{
    static int s;
    s++;
    printf("s=%d\n",s);
}

void main( )
{
    stat_func();
    stat_func();
    stat_func();
/* The statement printf("s=%d\n",s); will not execute from here. It is local
to stat_func() and can be accessed only within stat_func() function. */
}
```

> SCOPE and LIFE TIME are different in case of static variables.

Output: s = 1

           s = 2

           s = 3

In the above program during the first call to the function, stat_func, s is incremented to 1 (default initial value of static variable is 0) and prints s = 1. As s is static, this value persists and therefore in the next call s is incremented by 1 and the value of s becomes 2. Similarly in the next call, s becomes 3. But if we declare the storage class of s as auto then we get the output as:

s=1

s=1

s=1

13.7.4 External

When a variable is declared outside of all functions, it is known as external variable. By default, external variables are initialized with zero. The scope of external variables is global and its life exists till the execution of the program does not come to an end.

PROGRAM 13.10   Program to demonstrate the scope and life time of external variable.

```
#include<stdio.h>
int i = 10;
void function1( )
{
    printf("%d", i);
    i++;
}
void function2( )
{
    printf("%d", i);
    i--;
}
void main()
{
    printf("%d", i);
    function1();
    function2();
    printf("%d", i);
}
```

Output: 10 10 11 10

From the above program, it is cleared that the variable is accessible from function1( ), function2( ) and main(). It becomes possible because the variable i is declared as global variable.

We can define local variable and global variable of same name. But within the block where local variable is declared, only local variable will be accessed as local variables have higher precedence than the global variables.

PROGRAM 13.11   Program to demonstrate the local and global variables.

```
#include<stdio.h>
int x = 100;

void function1( )
{    int x = 50;
     printf ("%d", x);
}

void main()
{
     function1();
     printf ("%d", x);
}
```

Output: 50 100

In the above program, x is defined twice. First time outside main( ) function and second time inside function1( ). When function1 is called there arises a confliction as both x is available here. In such situation, local variable gets preference over the global variable. Thus the printf() statement prints 50. When control comes back to main( ) there is no such confliction. Only the global variable x is visible here. So, this time printf() statement prints 100.

Usually at the beginning of the program, i.e., before all functions, global variables are declared without specifying any storage class. But it is not necessary. We can declare the global variable anywhere but obviously outside of any function. Suppose we have five functions in a program. We can declare the variable after defining three or four functions, even if at the end also. But the problem is that the functions which are defined before its declaration unable to access this variable. The keyword **extern** helps us to solve this problem. In each such function, the variable needs to re-declare with the keyword **extern.** If a variable declared with the keyword **extern** it tells the compiler that the variable is defined somewhere else in the program. As the allocation is done with the definition not with the declaration, the declaration of a variable as external does not allocate memory for it. It just provides the information about the external variable to the said function. Following program illustrate this.

PROGRAM 13.12   Program to demonstrate the properties of global variable.

```
#include<stdio.h>
void function1( )
{    extern int i;
     i = 20;
```

```
    printf("%d", i);
}

int i = 10;

void main( )
{
    function1( );
    printf("%d", i);
}
```

Output: 20 20

In the above program, i is first declared within the function1( ) and defined later. They are not different variables. First it is initialized to 10 at the time of defining the variable. Next when function1 is invoked, it is initialized to 20. So, it prints 20. Next when the control come back to main( ) then it again prints 20 as the variable retains its value.

13.8 MULTI-FILE PROGRAMS

When a project or software is developed with C it is not necessary that it consists of a single file. Multiple C files can be developed separately which can be linked later to create executable object code. The advantage of this approach is that if any changes required in one file, only that file have to be compiled again. The entire program needs not to recompile. If any variable is need to share among multiple program files it should be declared as **extern**. In one file it will be declared as global and in other files as external. Consider the following example.

PROGRAM1.C

```
int x;
main()
{
    int y;
    ...
    ...
}

function1()
{
    int z;
    ...
    ....
}
```

Program2.c

```
function2()
{
    extern int x;
    int p;
    ...
}
function3()
{
    int q;
    ...
    ....
}
```

In the above example, the variable x is declared as global in Program1. This variable is not accessible from Program2 unless we declare it as extern in Program2.

The features of different storage class & their comparative studies are given in the following table:

Storage class	Storage	Default value	Scope	Life time
Auto	Memory	Garbage value	Local to the block in which the variable is declared.	Till the control remains within the block in which it is defined.
Register	CPU registers	Garbage value	Local to the block in which the variable is declared.	Till the control remains within the block in which it is defined.
Static	Memory	Zero	Local to the block in which the variable is declared.	Value of the variable persists between different function calls.
Extern	Memory	Zero	Global, i.e., visible to all functions	Till the program execution terminates.

13.8.1 Nesting of Function Calls

Any C function can call any other C functions including main( ). In turn that function may call other function and so on. Nesting of function calls is allowed in C and there is no limitation on how deeply the function calls is nested. Following program illustrates this:

Program 13.13 Program to demonstrate nesting of function calls.

```
#include<stdio.h>
void function3 ( )
{
    printf("\nI am in function 3");
}
void function2 ( )
{   printf("\nI am in function 2");
    function3();
```

```
        printf("\nBack to function 2");
}
void function1( )
{    printf("\nI am in function 1");
     function2();
     printf("\nBack to function 1");
}

void main()
{    printf("\nI am in main");
     function1();
     printf("\nBack to main");
}
```

Output: I am in main
　　　　　I am in function 1
　　　　　I am in function 2
　　　　　I am in function 3
　　　　　Back to function 2
　　　　　Back to function 1
　　　　　Back to main

In the above program, main function first calls the function1 after executing the first printf statement. So, control goes to function1. Then it executes the printf statement in function1 and jump to function2. Then again it executes the printf statement in function2 and jump to function3. Now after executing the printf statement in function3, control comes back to its calling point, i.e., in function2. So, now it executes the last printf statement in function2. In this way control comes back to main and we get the above output.

13.9 RECURSION

Not only from other functions, a function in 'C' may be called from itself also. When a function is called by itself, the function is called Recursive function. And the process is called Recursion. So, we can define, **Recursion** is the process where a function is called by itself. Though it is more memory consuming process, it is very effective in implementation where algorithm demands same repetitive process.

For example, n! is calculated as n * (n–1)! i.e., to calculate n!, first we have to find out (n-1)!. Similarly to calculate (n-1)!, first we have to find out (n-2)!. Thus if a function is defined to find the factorial of n, it will call ownself for (n-1) and to find (n-1)! it will call again ownself for the value (n-2) and so on. This call will continue upto 1 or 0 as 1! 0r 0! is a constant and it is 1. So, we can easily implement it using recursion.

```
int    factorial(int num)
{    if (num <= 1)
          return(1);
     else
          return(num * factorial(num - 1));
}
```

Here, if we want to calculate factorial(4), the second return statement of the function will be executed as return(4 * factorial(3)); but this statement cannot be executed until factorial(3) is executed. Again, for this function call return(4 * factorial(3)); – this statement will execute. This will continue until **num** become 1. Then return(1) statement will execute and returns the control to its calling point. Then its previous return statement will return 2*1, i.e., 2. In this way, factorial(4) will be calculated as 4*3*2*1.

```
factorial(4)
    ↓↑ 24
  return(4 * factorial(3))
          ↓↑ 6
        return(3 * factorial(2))
                ↓↑ 2
              return(2 * factorial(1))
                      ↓↑ 1
                    return(1)
```

Always remember that though recursion is the process where a function is called itself, but this is not for infinite times. Stack will be overflowed in that case. Thus a terminating condition is must. In the above example, the terminating condition is: (num <= 1). Here is the complete program.

PROGRAM 13.14   Program to find the factorial of a positive integer using recursive function.

```
/* Recursive function to find the factorial of a positive integer */
int    factorial(int num)
{
    if (num <= 1)
        return(1);
    else
        return(num * factorial(num-1));
}

void main( )
{    int fact, n;
    clrscr();
    printf("Enter any positive Integer:");
    scanf("%d",&n);
    fact = factorial(n);
    printf("Factorial of %d is : %d",n,fact);
}
```

Depending on the function call recursion can be categorized into following types:
1. Linear recursion
2. Tail recursion
3. Binary recursion
4. Mutual recursion
5. Nested recursion

13.9.1 Linear Recursion

It is the simplest one. Here only a single recursive function call exists in the function to call own self and a terminating condition to terminate.

13.9.2 Tail Recursion

It is a special form of linear recursion. When recursive call is the last statement of the function, the recursion is known as tail recursion. In most cases, tail recursion can be easily converted to iteration. Instead of recursive call, a loop can be used. Here is an example of tail recursion.

EXAMPLE 13.1

```
int    factorial(int a)
{
    if (a <= 1)
        return(1);
    else
        return(a * factorial(a-1));
}
```

13.9.3 Binary Recursion

In this recursion, in place of once the function is called twice at a time. That is why its name is binary recursion. This type of recursion is found in the implementation of binary tree data structure, finding Fibonacci numbers, etc. Consider the following example.

PROGRAM 13.15   Function to find the n-th Fibonacci number.

```
/* Function to find the nth Fibonacci number */
int FibNum(int n)
{
    if (n < 1)
        return (-1);
    if (n <= 2)          /* For n =1 and 2 */
        return (1);
    else
        return (FibNum(n - 1) + FibNum(n - 2));
}
```

In the above function, at a time two recursive functions are called, that is why it is treated as Binary Recursion. As we know, the first two term of Fibonacci series is 1, the terminating condition is written as

$$if (n <= 2)$$

$$return (1);$$

Thus when value of n will be 1 or 2, function will return 1. Zero or −ve value of n indicates invalid value, thus returns −1. The other terms of this series are generated by adding the two predecessor value of this series. So, to find the nth term of this series, we need to add (n–1)th and (n–2)th term and the statement becomes,

return (FibNum(n – 1) + FibNum(n – 2));

13.9.4 Mutual Recursion

A recursive function does not always call itself directly. Some times it may happen that the first function calls the second function, second function calls the third function and the third function again calls the first function. In this way, each function is called by own self but not directly rather via one or more functions. This is known as **Mutual Recursion**. So, it can be defined as an indirect form of recursion when one method calls another, which in turn calls the first.

Following example illustrate this.

PROGRAM 13.16   Program to check whether an inputted number is odd or even.

```
int iseven(int n)
{
    if (n==0) return 1;
    else return(isodd(n-1));
}

int isodd(int n)
{
    return (!iseven(n));
}

void main( )
{
    int num;
    printf("Enter any number: ");
    scanf("%d", &num);
    if(iseven(num))
        printf("The number is Even");
    else
        printf("The number is Odd");
}
```

In the above program both the function mutually calls each other to check whether a number is even or odd. In the main function instead of iseven( ), isodd( ) can also be used.

13.9.5 Nested Recursion

If one of the arguments of any recursive call statement contains another recursive function call, then it is known as **Nested recursion**. Implementation of classical mathematical function, Ackermann's function, is a good example of nested function.

PROGRAM 13.17

```
int ackerman(int m, int n)
{
    if (m == 0)
        return(n+1);
    else
        if (n == 0)
            return(ackerman(m-1,1));
        else
            return(ackerman(m-1,ackerman(m,n-1)));
}
```

13.10 ADVANTAGE AND DISADVANTAGE OF RECURSION

13.10.1 Advantages

The advantages of recursion are:
1. Reduce the code.
2. Helps in implementation of Divide and conquer algorithm.
3. Helps in implementation where algorithms use STACK.
4. Helps to reverse the order of some sequence.

13.10.2 Disadvantages

The major drawbacks of using recursion are it is not as good as iteration regarding time and space complexity. Recursion achieves repetition through repeated function calls.

In iteration same set of variables is used. But in recursion, every time the function is called, the complete set of variables is allocated again and again. So, a significant space cost is associated with recursion.

Again there is also a significant time cost associated with recursion, due to the overhead required to manage the stack and the relative slowness of function calls.

13.11 IMPLEMENTATION OF SOME STANDARD LIBRARY FUNCTIONS

As now we are able to write our own function, we can implement some standard library functions. Here are few of them.

PROGRAM 13.18   Implementation of toupper( ):

```
char my2upr( char ch)
{
    if (ch >= 'a' && ch <= 'z')
```

```
        ch = ch - 32;      /* we can also write:  ch = ch - ('a' - 'A'); */
    return(ch);
}
```

PROGRAM 13.19   Implementation of isdigit( ):

```
int myisdigit( char ch )
{
    if( ch >= '0' && ch <= '9')
        return(1);
    else
        return(0);
}
```

In the above function, when the condition is true, we are returning 1 and when the condition is false, we are returning 0. So, the function can be written in more compact form as follows.

```
int myisdigit( char ch )
{
    return ( ch >= '0' && ch <= '9');
}
```

PROGRAM 13.20   Implementation of strlen( ):

```
int stringlength( char st[ ] )
{
    int i=0;
    while( st[i] )
        i++;
    return(i);
}
```

PROGRAM 13.21   Implementation of strcmp( ):

```
int stringcomparison( char st1[ ], char st2[ ] )
{
    int i=0;
    while( st1[i] )
    {
        if( st1[i] != st2[i])
            break;
        i++;
    }
    return(st1[i] - st2[i]);
}
```

13.12 PROGRAMMING EXAMPLES

Here are some programming examples to understand the various use of function.

PROGRAM 13.22 Write a C function to copy a string without using any library function and show its use in a program.

```
#include<conio.h>
#include<stdio.h>
void mystrcpy( char [ ], char [ ]);
void main()
{
    char string1[30], string2[30];
    puts("Enter any String:");
    gets(string1);
    mystrcpy(string2,string1);
    printf("\nSource String : %s", string1);
    printf("\nDestination String : %s", string1);
}

void mystrcpy( char dest[ ], char sorc[ ])
{
    int i=0;
    while(src[i])
    {
        dest[i] = sorc[i];
        i++;
    }
    dest[i] = '\0';
}
```

Sample output
```
Enter any String:
This is a string.
Source String : This is a string.
Destination String : This is a string.
```

PROGRAM 13.23 Write a function that will print the binary equivalent of a given decimal number.

```
#include<conio.h>
#include<stdio.h>

void d2b(int m)
{    int rem;
     if(m>0)
     {    rem = m%2;
          d2b(m/2);
```

```
              printf("%d",rem);
          }
      }

  void main()
  {     int no, sum=0,old;
        printf("Enter any decimal Number:");
        scanf("%d",&no);
        printf("Binary Equivalent of %d is :   ",no);
        d2b(no);
  }
```

Sample output
  Enter any decimal Number: 13
  Binary Equivalent of 13 is : 1101

PROGRAM 13.24   Write a program to convert binary number to equivalent decimal number.

```
  #include<stdio.h>
  #include<conio.h>
  #include<math.h>
  #include<string.h>
  int b2d( char [ ] );

  void main()
  {
        int dec;
        char bin[17];
        clrscr();
        printf("Enter any Binary Number:");
        scanf("%s",bin);

        dec = b2d(bin);

        printf("Decimal Equivalent of %s is %d", bin, dec);
  }

  int b2d( char bin[ ])
  {
        int l, num=0, i=0;
        l = strlen(bin) - 1;
        while(l>=0)
        {   num = num + (bin[l] - 48) * pow(2, i);
            i++;
            l--;
        }
```

```
        return( num );
}
```

Sample output
Enter any Binary Number: 1101
Decimal Equivalent of 1101 is 13

PROGRAM 13.25   Write a program to add the following series:

1 + 2/2! + 3/3! + ... + n/n!, value of n given by user.

```
#include<conio.h>
#include<stdio.h>
int factorial( int );

void main()
{    int c, no;
     float sum=0;
     printf("Enter No. of Terms: ");
     scanf("%d",&no);
     for(c = 1; c <= no; c++)
     {
          sum += (float)c/factorial(c);
     }
     printf("Sum = %f",sum);
}

int factorial(int n)
{
     int i, f=1;
     for(i=1; i<=n; i++)
          f=f*i;
     return(f);
}
```

Sample output
Enter No. of Terms: 3
Sum = 2.500000

PROGRAM 13.26   Write a program in C using function to reverse a number and calculate the difference of these two numbers.

```
#include<conio.h>
#include<stdio.h>
#include<math.h>
int reverse( int );
```

```
int reverse( int n)
{    int rev=0;
     while( n > 0 )
     {    rev = rev * 10 + n % 10;
          n = n / 10;
     }
     return( rev );
}


void main()
{
     int no, rev, result;
     printf("Enter any Number:");
     scanf("%d", &no);
     rev = reverse(no);
     result = rev - no;
     printf("The Difference between original and reverse
            number is : %d", abs(result));
}
```

Sample output

Enter any Number: 876
The Difference between original and reverse number is: 198

PROGRAM 13.27   Write a program to print Fibonacci series using recursion.

```
#include<conio.h>
#include<stdio.h>
int fibo(int n)
{
     if(n<=2)
          return(1);
     else
          return(fibo(n-1)+fibo(n-2));
}


void main()
{
     int term,i;
     clrscr();
     printf("How many term Required:");
     scanf("%d",&term);
     printf("The Fibonacci Series : ");
     for(i=1; i<=term; i++)
          printf("%d ",fibo(i));
}
```

Sample output
```
How many term Required: 6
The Fibonacci Series : 1 1 2 3 5 8
```

PROGRAM 13.28   Write a recursive function for GCD calculation.

```c
#include<conio.h>
#include<stdio.h>
int gcd(int n1, int n2)
{   if(n1%n2==0)
        return(n2);
    else
        return(gcd(n2, n1%n2));
}

void main()
{   int num1,num2,result;
    printf("Enter Any Two Positive Integers:");
    scanf("%d%d",&num1,&num2);
    result = gcd(num1, num2);
    printf("GCD of %d,%d is %d",num1, num2, result);
}
```

Sample output
```
Enter Any Two Positive Integers: 25  15
GCD of 25, 15  is 5
```

PROGRAM 13.29   Write a recursive function to calculate a^b, where a and b are positive integers.

```c
int  pwr(int a, int b)
{   if(b==0)
        return(1);
    else
        return(a*pwr(a,b-1));
}
```

PROGRAM 13.30   Write a C program to implement the Tower of Hanoi problem using recursion.

```c
#include<stdio.h>
void move_disk(char p1,char p2,char p3,int n)
{
    if(n<=0)
        printf("\n Invalid Entry");
    if(n==1)
        printf ("\n Move disk from %c to %c", p1, p3);
    else
```

```
        {
            move_disk(p1,p3,p2,n-1);
            move_disk(p1,p2,p3,1);
            move_disk(p2,p1,p3,n-1);
        }
    }

    void main ()
    {
        int no;
        printf("\n Enter number of disk:");
        scanf("%d", &no);
        printf("\n Tower of Hanoi for %d disks", no);
        move_disk('X','Y','Z',no);
    }
```

Sample output

Enter number of disk: 3

Tower of Hanoi for 3 disks
Move disk from X to Z
Move disk from X to Y
Move disk from Z to Y
Move disk from X to Z
Move disk from Y to X
Move disk from Y to Z
Move disk from X to Z

SUMMARY

➤ A function is a self-contained block of statements that perform some specific job.

➤ The general form to declare a user-defined function is:

```
            return_type    function_name( list of Arguments )
            {      . . . .
                   . . . .   // Body of the function
                   [ return [(expression)];]
            }
```

Here return_type determines the type of the value returned by the function. function_name is the name of the function. The return statement returns some value (if any) as well as the control to the calling point.

➤ A function may or may not return any value. If returns, it can return only one value.

➤ By default a function returns int type data.

➤ Function arguments are of two types – actual argument and formal argument.

➤ The data type of actual argument and formal argument should be same.

➤ Single dimensional array as well as multidimensional array can be passed as function argument.

➤ Every C program starts its execution from main function.

➤ More than one main function is not possible in a single program.

➤ Recursion is the process where a function is called by itself.

➤ Storage class specifies the scope and life time of variables and/or functions within a C Program.

➤ Scope defines the visibility of any variable.

➤ Life time of a variable specifies how long the variable is accessible within its scope.

➤ Automatic, register, static and external are the four storage class available in C.

REVIEW EXERCISES

1. What is a function? What are the advantages of using functions in 'C' programming?

2. Distinguish between actual argument and formal argument with the help of simple program.

3. When is it necessary to declare prototype of a function?

4. Explain the storage classes available in C.

5. What do you mean by scope of the variable?

6. What are automatic variables? List the limitations of register variables.

7. What is the purpose of a static variable? What is its scope?

8. What do you mean by local variable and global variable?

9. What do you mean by recursion? What advantages are there in its use?

10. Write a C function to convert an upper case letter to lower case without using library function.

11. Write a C function to check whether a character is an alphabet or not without using library function.

12. Write a C function to concatenate two strings without using any library function and show its use in a program.

13. Write a program that uses a function to reverse a string.

14. Write a program that uses a function to check whether a number is palindrome or not.

15. Write a C function that will convert a decimal number to a number of any base.

16. Write a program that uses a function to transpose of a matrix.

17. Write a recursive function in C to produce nth Fibonacci number.

18. Write a recursive function in C to find the sum of the digits of a number.

LEARN BY QUIZ – QUESTIONS

1. Which of the following is not true about C function?
   (1) Defining a function inside a function is allowed.
   (2) Calling multiple functions from inside a function is allowed.
   (3) Calling same function from inside it is allowed.

2. Which of the following is not an advantage of a function?
   (1) It makes program execution faster.
   (2) It makes a program more readable.
   (3) It facilitates top-down modular programming,

3. Which of the following is not an advantage of a function?
   (1) It reduces size of source code.
   (2) It makes program debugging easier.
   (3) It makes program execution faster.

4. Identify which of the following is not a function call?
   (1) i=my_func(x,y);
   (2) my_func(int x, int y);
   (3) my_func(x,y);

5. If no return type is specified at the beginning, by default what is the return type of a C function?
   (1) integer
   (2) void
   (3) character.

6. What type of function is main()?
   (1) User defined function
   (2) library function
   (3) Header function

7. The body of a function is executed by
   (1) function declaration.
   (2) function definition.
   (3) function call.

8. Suppose a function has been declared but no where defined. The function has been called in a program. What type of error this will give?
   (1) Linking error.
   (2) compilation error
   (3) runtime error.

9. Which of the following case is a procedure?
   (1) Dropping a postcard in post box.
   (2) Paying electricity bill.
   (3) Sending a letter by registered post.

10. Which of the following is not a valid function declaration in C? (given that no datatype named function has been defined)
    (1) add(int x, int y);
    (2) function add(int x, int y);
    (3) int add(int x, int y);

11. Which of the following is not a valid function declaration in C
    (1) add int x, int y;
    (2) add(int x, int y);
    (3) int add(int x, int y);

12. Which of the following is allowed?
    (1) local variable and function have same name.
    (2) global variable and function have same name.
    (3) function have same name as a keyword.

13. Functions in C pass arguments by
    (1) reference
    (2) value
    (3) name

14. Which of the following function prototype is appropriate for a function that will add two integers and return their sum?
    (1) int add(int first, int second);
    (2) float add(int first, int second);
    (3) void add(int first, int second, int* sum);

15. Which of the following functions (factorial1, factorial2, factorial3) for calculating factorial is not recursive?
    (1) unsigned int factorial1(int a)
```
    {
        int accu = 1;
        int i;
        for(i = 1; i <= a; i++)
        {
            accu *= i;
        }
        return accu;
    }
```
    (2) unsigned int factorial2(int a) {
```
        return a>=1 ? a * factorial2(a-1) : 1;
    }
```
    (3) unsigned int factorial3(unsigned int a){if (a == 1)return 1;else{a = a*factorial3(a-1);return a;}}

16. Which of the following is not a valid recursive function?
    (1) unsigned int factorial1(unsigned int a){a=a*factorial1(a-1);returna;}
    (2) unsigned int factorial2(int a) {
```
        return a>=1 ? a * factorial2(a-1) : 1;
    }
```
    (3) int Fibonacci(int n){if(n==0||n==1)return 1;elsereturn Fibonacci(n-1)+Fibonacci(n-2);}

17. A collection of recursive functions is executed in a
    (1) first in first out order
    (2) last in first out order
    (3) parallel fashion

18. To execute recursive function compiler uses a
    (1) tree
    (2) queue
    (3) stack

19. Which of the following statement is false?
    (1) return statement is compulsory in a function
    (2) return statement may not be present in a function
    (3) In a function there may be multiple return statements.

20. A function can return
    (1) exactly one value
    (2) multiple value
    (3) only 0 or 1.

21. If the statement *int sp;* occurs outside any function then a function f()
  (1) can't access sp.
  (2) considers sp as local variable.
  (3) considers sp as global variable.

22. What is the output of the following program?

```
void sum1(int sa)
{
static k;
printf("%d", k+sa);
k++;
}
void main()
{
int a=0;
while (a<5)
{
sum1(a);
a++;
}
}
```

  (1) 02468
  (2) 01234
  (3) 13579

23. What is the output of the following program?

```
void main()
{
int a=11, b=12;
printf("%d", f(a,b));
}

int f(int a, int b)
{
static i;
i++;
if(a<b) return(f(b,a));
if (b==0) return(a);
return(i);
}
```

  (1) 2
  (2) compilation error
  (3) runtime error

24. Consider the following two functions

```
int f1(int a)
{
int x=0;
do
x+=a--;
while(a>0);
return(x);
}
```

```
int f2(int a)
{
int x=0;
while(a>0)
x+=a--;
return(x);
}
```

Which of the following statement is true?
(1) value of f1(10) and f2(10) is 55.
(2) f1() and f2() are identical function
(3) value of f1(−1) and f2(−1) is the same.

25. consider the following function
```
void main()
{
int a=1, b=5;
printf("%d %d", sqrr(a+b), sqrr(++a));
}
int sqrr(int x)
{
return x*x;
}
```
(1) 49 4
(2) 36 4
(3) 36 1

26.
```
void abc(int a)        void def(int a)        void ghi(int a)
    {                      {                      {
    int b;                 int b;                 int b;
    ....                   ....                   ....
    return b;              return;
    }                      }                      }
```
In the three above functions named abc(), def() and ghi() which one will not run if used in a program?
(1) abc()
(2) def()
(3) ghi()

27. What will be the output of the following program
```
void main()
{
int i=45; float c;
c=f(i);
printf("%f", c);
}
f(int ch)
{
ch>=45 ? return(3.14) : return (6.28);
}
```
(1) 3.000
(2) 3.14
(3) Generate error.

28. Which of the following is general format of function definition?

   (1)
```
function_type function_name1(parameter list)
{
local variable declaration;
executable statement 1;
executable statement 2;
........
.......
return statement;
}
```

   (2)
```
function_type function_name2(parameter list)
{
executable statement 1;
local variable declaration;
executable statement 2;
........
.......
return statement;
}
```

   (3) function_type function_name3(parameter list);

29. In function call we provide
   (1) formal parameter
   (2) actual parameter
   (3) dummy parameter

30.
```
int sum(int a, int b)
{
return (a+b);
}

void main(void)
{
int x,y,z,w;
x=5; y=10;
z=sum(x,y);
w=sum(5,10);
}
```

   In the above program which are formal parameter?
   (1) a, b
   (2) x, y
   (3) 5,10

31. What is used to convert a string to integer?
   (1) stringtoint
   (2) atol
   (3) atoi

32. Which function is used to calculate power of a number?
   (1) pow
   (2) power
   (3) sqrt

33. Which function is used to calculate square root of a number?
   (1) sqrt

(2) squareroot

(3) rootof

34. Which of the following does not return a random number?

    (1) randomize

    (2) rand

    (3) random

35. Which of the following is not a trigonometric function?

    (1) abs

    (2) sin

    (3) cos

36. What will be the output of the following program segment?

```
#include<stdio.h>
#include<math.h>
void main(void)
{
    float f;
    f = floor( 2.7 );
    printf( "%f###", f );
    y = floor(-2.7 );
    printf( "%f", f );
}
```

    (1) 2.000000###−3.000000

    (2) 2.000000###3.000000

    (3) 2.000000###−2.000000

37. What will be the output of the following program segment?

```
#include<stdio.h>
#include<math.h>
void main(void)
{
    float f;
    f = ceil( 2.7 );
    printf( "%f###", f );
    f = ceil(-2.7 );
    printf( "%f", f );
}
```

    (1) 3.000000##−2.000000

    (2) 3.000000##2.000000

    (3) 3.000000##−3.000000

38. Which of the following program segment will not print "yes it is a digit"?

    (1) `if(isdigit(3))`
         `    printf( "yes it is a digit" );`

    (2) `if(isdigit(51))`
         `    printf( "yes it is a digit" );`

    (3) `if(isdigit('3'))`
         `    printf( "yes it is a digit" );`

39. Which of the following statement is true about kbhit() function

    (1) If the function returns a nonzero value, a keystroke is waiting in the buffer.

    (2) If the function returns a zero value, a keystroke is waiting in the buffer.

    (3) It echoes the keystroke if it is a printable character.

40. What does exit() function do?
    (1) terminates a program
    (2) terminates a loop
    (3) terminates a function

41. What does the system() function do?
    (1) executes a DOS command
    (2) terminates a program and exit to system prompt
    (3) opens the command prompt

42. Which library function is used to convert a character to lower case?
    (1) uptolow
    (2) islower
    (3) tolower

43. Which library function is used to convert a character to upper case?
    (1) toupper
    (2) isupper
    (3) lowtoup

44. Which function is used to find common logarithm of a number
    (1) log10
    (2) log
    (3) logarithm

45. Which function is used to retrieve the system time
    (1) gettime
    (2) clock
    (3) time

46. Which function is used to retrieve the system date?
    (1) getdate
    (2) date
    (3) sysdate

47. Which of the following will define the scope of a variable that will be known only to the function in which it is declared?
    (1) auto
    (2) register
    (3) extern

48. Which of the following local variables will always retain its value?
    (1) static
    (2) auto
    (3) extern

49. Which one of the following statements is true about static variable?
    (1) The scope is local but the lifetime is global
    (2) The lifetime is local but the scope is global
    (3) Both scope and lifetime are global

50. Which storage class is preferred for faster processing?
    (1) register
    (2) auto
    (3) Static

51. Which of the following function prototype is appropriate for a function that will sort the list of 20 names? Assume maximum length of name is less than 30.
    (1) void name_list(char names[][30]);

(2) void name_list(char names[20][]);
(3) void name_list(char names[][]);

52. Which of the following function prototype is appropriate for a function that will transpose a 4×4 matrix of integer type?
    (1) void trans(int a[][], int m, int n); where m is used to store the no. of rows and n is used to store the no. of cols.
    (2) void trans(int a[4][], int n); where n is used to store the no. of cols.
    (3) void trans(int a[][4], int n); where n is used to store the no. of rows.

53. Which of the following function prototype is appropriate for a function to pass a 3-D integer array of size 3×4×5?
    (1) void pass3d(int a[][4][5]);
    (2) void pass3d(int a[][][5]);
    (3) void pass3d(int a[][][]);

54. What will be the function prototype for a function that will copy the all elements of one array to another array?
    (1) void copy_arr(int arr1[], int m, int arr2[], int n);
    (2) void copy_arr(int arr1[], int m);
    (3) copy_arr(arr1, m,arr2,n); where m & n are integer and is used to pass the the size of the array.

55. Which of the following function prototype is appropriate for a function that will find the total number of words in a string of length 80?
    (1) int count_word(char st);
    (2) char count_word(char st[], int n);
    (3) int count_word(char st[]);

56. What will be the function call statement to call the function:
    `int cout_word( char st[]);`
    Suppose the name of the array in calling function is str and its size is 80.
    (1) n=count_word(str);
    (2) n=count_word(char str[]);
    (3) n=count_word(st[80]);

LEARN BY QUIZ – ANSWERS

Answer explanations

1. Defining a function inside a function which is also known as nested function definition is not allowed in C. The only commonly used language that supports nested function definition is JAVA™.

   Multiple functions can be called from inside a function.

   Calling same function from inside a function is also allowed in C and it is known as recursion.

2. Program execution gets slower by function call. At the time of a function call the current location of execution (known from a register of a CPU called program counter) and current contents of CPU registers are kept in stack and the control jumps to the start of a function and after the function is finished the control returns to the next line from where the call was made. This time the address and CPU register values are popped from stack. All these extra burdens make function call slower than linear execution of a function less program.

   The main philosophy of structured programming is function. The program becomes more readable and easy to debug by use of function.

Function facilitates top-down modular programming. In this programming style, the high level logic of the overall problem is solved first while the details of each lower level function are addressed later.

3. Program execution gets slower by function call. A function call involves many extra processing other than the program code that makes a program written using functions run slower than the same program logic written without using functions.

Function makes program debugging easier. When a compilation error is shown inside a function or a function returns any illogical value then the programmer have to concentrate on the function only which is a small part of the total program.

Function reduces size of source code. Suppose a function consists of 100 lines of code and is called 10 times inside a program. Then only one copy of the function, i.e., 100 lines will be in the source code as well as in main memory at the time of execution instead of $10 \times 100 = 1000$ lines of code if the program was written without using function. So using function also reduces main memory requirement of a program.

4. my_func(int x, int y); is not a function call. It is the declaration of the function my_func. As no return type is specified at the beginning, by default it will be integer type.

In the line i=my_func(x,y); my_func is called and its reurn value has been assigned to the variable i.

For the line my_func(x,y); either or both of the following two guesses are correct:
1. the rerurn value of my_func is not used.
2. my_func is a void type function, i.e., it returns nothing.

5. If no return type is specified by default a C function returns int (integer).

6. main() is an user defined function. The programmer has to define the return type and the body of main. However, the parameters that main can accept is predefined. Either the programmer will not use any parameter in main or he/she have to use two predefined parameters **int argc** and **char* argv[]** which is beyond the scope of this topic.

7. The body of a function is executed when a **function call** is encountered.

8. This will not give a compilation error. Compiler just matches the prototype of function call with the declaration. Compilation is done file wise. If the prototype matches the compiler will give green signal to proceed assuming that the definition is in another file. But **this will give a linking error** as when linker will encounter a function call it will search for the function body. It is the job of the linker to link all the files together to make the executable file.

There is no question of runtime error as the linker will not generate executable file so the program cannot be run.

9. Dropping a post card is a procedure. After completion of the job there is no result to return. But in other two cases transaction number along with some receipt will be returned.

10. function add(int x, int y); is not valid. Function is not a keyword and it should not precede the declaration.

11. add int x, int y; is invalid as the parameters are not within a ().

12. Local variable and function can have same name as local variable has no visibility outside its scope. Even we can declare a variable of same name inside the function.

function cannot have same name as keyword as for function same rules are applicable as for identifier naming.

13. Functions in C pass all arguments by value. A copy of the value of the variable is created and passed to the called routine. The called routine can modify the copy of the argument but it cannot modify the original argument. The variable's value might be changed by the procedure or function, but the variable's original value in the calling program is not changed.

   Passing arguments by reference is required in programs but as it is not supported by C, it is in practice forcefully done by sending the address of the actual parameters and using pointers as formal parameter. But pass by reference is beyond the scope of this topic.

   Pass by name and pass by value reference is supported by some programming languages but not by C.

14. int add(int first, int second); is perfect prototype as per requirement. The function add will take two integer parameter first and second and return the sum which will be integer. The body of the fuction may be something as following:

```
int add(int first, int second)
{
 return first+second;
}
```
   or in a novice way as following:-
```
int add(int first, int second)
{
int sum;
sum=first+second;
 return sum;
}
```

15. factorial1 function is calculating factorial in iterative method. Note that inside factorial1 no where factorial1 has been called. factorial2 and factorial3 are recursive function of factorial and if carefully observed they have same logic but written in a different way.

16. factorial1() is not valid recursive function as it is calling itself but there is no terminating condition.

   Note: A recursive function:
   - Calls itself
   - contains a terminating condition where this self calling will stop.

   Observe that
   - in factorial2() the terminating condition is a<1

   in Fibonacci() the terminating condition is (n==0||n==1)

17. A collection of recursive functions is executed in a first in first out order as other statements execute in C. Next function is not called until control returns from one recursive function.

18. To execute recursive function compiler uses a stack.

19. In a **void** type function **return** statement is not required. So return statement is not necessary in a function.

   Through some conditional block multiple return statements are provided in a function. For example
```
int pass(int marks)
{     if(marks>=50)
            return(1);
      else
            return(0);
}
```

20. One function can have only one return type. It cannot have multiple return values as well as return_type of a function cannot change. For example, our common printf function can print different data types but its return type will be always int.

21. The function f() will consider sp as global variable. If sp was declared inside the function f() then it would have been considered as local variable. If it was declared inside some other function than f() then f() will not be able to access sp.

22. The output will be 02468.
    Initially a is 0 and k is 0.
    The while loop will run 5 times for five values of a(0,1,2,3,4).
    The sum1 function will be called for those five values of a.
    As k is a static variable then its changed values will be retained until next increment by K++.
    Value of actual parameter a will be copied to formal parameter sa.
    The printf function in sum1 will be called 5 times with the following pair value of k and sa.
    k=0 and sa=0
    k=1 and sa=1
    k=2 and sa=2
    k=3 and sa=3
    k=4 and sa=4

23. The output will be 2. f() will be called 2 times:
    1. from main as f(11,12)
    2. from f as f(12,11)

    So value of static variable will increment two times and will become 2.

24. Value of f1(10) and f2(10) is 55. In fact f1() and f2() will return same value for all positive value passed to them. They will differ in output if 0 or negative values are passed to them as in those case the do-while loop of f1() will run once but the while loop of f2() will not run.

25. The output will be 49 4.
    The parameters of printf function are evaluated from right to left.
    So sqrr(++a) will be evaluated first. That will make value of a=2 and sqrr(++a) will return 4.
    Secondly sqrr(a+b) will be evaluated where a=2 and b=5. So it will return 49.
    Hence the output will be 49 4.

26. abc() will not run as an integer is returned in a void function.
    ghi() is perfect as in void function no return statement has been used. The blank return statement of function def() is not harmful.

27. The output will be 3.000.
    • The function will be called with the value of i = 45.
    • So the ternary operator in f() will run return(3.14).
    • But the return type of the function is not declared so by default it will be int.
    • So f() will return 3 after truncating 3.14.
    • The printf function will print 3 as 3.000 as %f is provided.

28. function_name1() is general format of function definition.
    function_name2() is not valid as in C function all local variable declaration should precede all executable statement.
    function_name3() is not a definition of function it is the declaration.

29. In function call, we provide actual parameter. Formal parameter and dummy parameter are equivalent word and they are used in function declaration or definition.

30. a,b are formal parameters used in the definition of sum(). x,y and 5,10 are actual parameters used in function call.

31. atoi is used to convert a string to integer.
    atoi – – – Macro that converts string to integer

32. pow is used to calculate power of a number.
    Declaration:
    double pow(double x, double y);
    returns x^y.
    output of the following code will be 8:
    double i;
    i=pow(2,3);
    printf("%lf",i);

33. sqrt is used to calculate square root of a number.
    prototype: double sqrt(double x);
    output of the following code will be 25:
    double i;
    i=625;
    printf("%lf", sqrt(i));

34. *randomize* does not return a random number rather it initialize the random number generator.
    If Randomize is not used, the Rnd function (with no arguments) uses the same number as a seed the first time it is called, and thereafter uses the last generated number as a seed value.
    rand and *random* both returns a random number.
    rand function do not take any argument and returns a number of arbitrary range.
    random function takes an integer as argument [int random(int n)] and returns a random number in the range of 0 to (n−1).

35. abs is a macro used to get the absolute value of a number. It is not a trigonometric function. The following program explains the use of abs.
    ```
    #include <stdio.h>
    #include <math.h>
    void main()
    {
       int num = -345;
       printf("Absolute value of %d is: %d\n", num, abs(num));
    }
    ```
    Output:
    Absolute value of −345 is: 345
    sin and cos are trigonometric function. Other commonly used trigonometric functions are tan, asin, acos, atan.
    sin, cos and tan have similar prototype as:
    double sin(double x);
    where x is the angle to be provided in radian.
    asin, acos and atan are used to calculate arc sine, arc cosine and arc tangent respectively.

36. The output will be 2.000000###−3.000000.
    The floor(x) function returns a floating-point value representing the largest integer that is less than or equal to x. So the largest integer less than 2.7 is 2 and that of −2.7 is −3. Do not forget to include math.h when using floor function.

37. The output will be 3.000000##−2.000000. The **ceil** function returns a **double** value representing the smallest integer that is greater than or equal to x. So the smallest integer greater than 2.7 is 3 and that of −2.7 is −2. **Do not forget to include math.h when using ceil function.**

38.
```
if(isdigit(3))
      printf( "yes it is a digit" );
```
will not print "yes it is a digit". To the function isdigit() if the parameter is ASCII value of a digit, i.e., 0–9 then it returns non-zero. 51 is the ASCII value of 3 so remaining two statements are equivalent and the y will print "yes it is a digit".

39. If the function returns a nonzero value, a keystroke is waiting in the buffer. The program can then call **getch** or **getche** to get the keystroke. But kbhit itself do not read the buffer or show anything. The following loop can be used to pause a program until user intervention.
```
while(!kbhit());
```
So the following code will print series of 0 and 1 until the user press any key:
```
int i=0;
while(!kbhit())
{
i=!i;
printf("%d", i);
}
```

40. Exit terminates the program. So at any point of a program if we want to terminate it we may call the exit function.
Declaration:
void exit(int status);
Before termination, exit function closes all files and writes buffered output if any. Typically a 0 value of status indicates normal termination where non zero value indicates some error.

41. system() Issues a DOS command
Declaration:
int system(const char *command);
system( ) invokes the DOS command interpreter file from inside an executing C program to execute a DOS command, batch file, or other program named by the string "command". Include process.h to use system() function.

42. The **int tolower(int ch)** function returns the character **ch** converted to lower case if it is in the range of **A to Z** otherwise it returns ch unchanged.

43. The **int toupper(int ch)** function returns the character **ch** converted to upper case if it is in the range of **a to z** otherwise it returns **ch** unchanged.
int isupper(int ch) function returns non-zero value if ch is a uppercase character. So it is used to check whether a character is in uppercase or not.

44. **double log10(double x)** is used to calculate common logarithm(base 10) of x.
So the output of the following code segment will be 2:
double x=100;
int i;
i=log10(x);
printf("%d", i);
double log(double x) is used to calculate natural logarithm(base e) of x.

45. The **void gettime(struct time* timep)** functions fills a time structure with system time. Its use can be understood from the following example:
```
#include    <stdio.h>
#include    <dos.h>
void main( )
{
    struct  time cur_time;
```

```
    gettime(&cur_time);
    printf("It is : %2d:%02d:%02d now.",
    cur_time.ti_hour, cur_time.ti_min, cur_time.ti_sec);
}
```

clock function returns number of processor ticks since the starting of the program.

time function returns current time in seconds elapsed since 00:00:00 GMT, January 1, 1970. It stores that value in the location *timer; timer is not a null pointer.

46. **void getdate(struct date *datep)**
getdate fills in the date structure *datep with the system's current date. Without going in details, from the following example that will display system date, month and year the use getdate function will be clear:

```
#include <dos.h>
#include <stdio.h>
int main(void)
{
    struct date today;
    getdate(&today);
    printf("Today is: %d/%d/%d", today.da_day, today.da_mon,
                                                     today.da_year);

}
```

47. The keyword **auto** may be used for declaring local variables. However, it is not mandatory in C as **auto** is the default.

48. **static** will always retain its value.
Local variables which always retain their values are **static**.
For **auto** variables, values are destroyed as the program flow goes outside the scope.
extern variables are not local variables.

49. The statement, **The scope is local but the lifetime is global**, is true about a **static** variable.
A **static** variable declared inside a function is not accessible from outside the function but it retains its value throughout the program. When a function is executed for the first time, space is allocated in the memory for the **static** variables declared in the function. These variables are kept in the memory till the program terminates.
However, local variables of **auto** type are deleted from memory as soon as control comes out of the code block where it is declared.

50. The storage class **register** is preferred for faster processing.
The storage class *register* requests the compiler to store the variable being declared in a CPU register. This optimizes access. This is done only if some register is unused at runtime.

51. Whatever may be the datatype integer or character, while an array will be declared as an argument in the function declaration, it is necessary to mention the col_size , whereas the row_size is optional. So,
void name_list(char names[ ][30]); is the correct answer.
void name_list(char names[20][ ]); and void name_list(char names[ ][ ]); are wrong because in both case col_size is missing.

52. While an array will be declared as an argument in the function declaration, it is necessary to mention the col_size , whereas the row_size is optional. So,
void trans(int a[ ][4], int n); is the correct answer.
void trans(int a[4][ ], int n); and void trans(int a[ ][ ], int m, int n); are wrong because in both case col_size is missing.

53. While an array will be declared as an argument in the function declaration, we can omit the value of first dimension of the array, not others. So,

    void pass3d(int a[ ][4][5]); is the correct answer.

    void pass3d(int a[ ][ ][5]); is wrong because here 1st and 2nd both dimensions are missing.

    void pass3d(int a[ ][ ][ ]); is wrong because here all the three dimensions are missing.

54. The function prototype for a function that will copy the all elements of one array to another array is:

    void copy_arr(int arr1[], int m, int arr2[], int n);

    Among these one array is source array from which the elements will be copied and another array is target array to which the elements will be copied.

    void copy_arr(int arr1[], int m); is wrong. Instead of two array single array is taken as argument.

    copy_arr(arr1, m,arr2,n); is wrong. This is basically function call statement, not the function prototype.

55. As every string (i.e., array of character) is terminated by '\0' character, the size of the array is not needed to pass. So, **int count_word(char st[]);** is the correct answer.

    char count_word(char st[ ], int n); is wrong because total no. of words is integer, so return type should be int. And array size also needs not to pass.

    int count_word(char st); is wrong because char st means st is a character variable. But we have to pass the entire array.

56. To pass the entire array, the base address (i.e., starting address) of the array have to pass along with its size. By specifying the **name of the array**, we sending the **base address of the array**. But in case of string (i.e., array of characters) '\0' character indicates the end of string. So, in case of string array size need not to pass. And correct answer is **n=count_word(str);**

    n=count_word(char str[ ]); is wrong. Because we have to pass the base address of the array to call the function. But char str[] declares an array.

    n=count_word(st[80]); is wrong because, st[80] represents a particular element (though this position is out of array boundary. Here limit will be 0–79.) not the entire array.

14

Pointer

Any physical entity can be accessed by its name as well as its address. For example, if address of the building, 'Chatterjee International Centre' is '33A, Chowringhee Road, Kol-71', then to mention the building we can say 'Chatterjee International Centre' or the building at '33A, Chowringhee Road, Kol-71'. The same concept is applicable for accessing variables also. This means even though we accessed the variables by its name so far but we can access them by their address also. In this chapter, we will discuss about the accessibility of the variables by means of their addresses.

(Note that 'a building having address but not having any name' is possible but 'a building having a name but not having any address' cannot exist. Similarly all variables should have a unique memory address, but a memory address not having a unique variable name can still be accessed by its address using the pointer pointing to it.)

14.1 POINTER

Pointer provides a flexible, powerful and efficient method to manipulate data in our programs. In C language, a pointer is a variable that can store the address of some memory location. Each memory location in the computer, i.e., in the RAM has an address. By storing that address a pointer variable actually points to or references the particular memory location where the data are stored. As now a pointer variable can be used to access memory locations, the content of the memory locations can be accessed and modified easily.

Before starting the discussion on pointer variable, we need to be familiar with two operators which are related to pointer operation. These are: '&' called 'address of' operator and '*' called 'content at address' operator.

The & operator returns the base address (i.e., starting address) of the variable or data. For example, if we declare a variable as int x=5; and if it is allocated, say, at 4062 and 4063 memory location (as integer variable take two bytes in memory to being allocated), &x returns 4062.

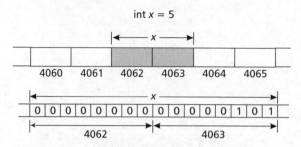

Fig. 14.1   Memory map of variable allocation

& Address of Operator
contents of Address Operator *

The * operator returns the content that is stored at a particular address. This operator is also known as 'indirection' operator as it accesses the value indirectly using a pointer variable. In the above example, as 4062 is the base address of the variable x, *(4062) returns the content of the address 4062, i.e., 5.

Now, to access the variable by its address we need to store the address in some other variable. But we cannot store the address in any ordinary integer variable. As we discussed above that only pointer variable can store address, here we need to declare a pointer variable for storage purpose.

A pointer variable is declared as:

datatype *pointer_variable;

Here, the data type indicates that the pointer variable will hold the address of variable of which type. In other word, it indicates the data type of the variable whose address will be stored by the pointer variable. Here, the asterisk sends the message to the compiler that we are declaring a pointer variable.

EXAMPLE 14.1

int *pntr;

Here, pntr is a pointer variable which is able to store the address where an integer value can be stored. Similarly,

char *q_pntr;

denotes q_pntr is a pointer variable which is able to store the address where a character value can be stored.

Note that space taken by all types of pointer variable is that taken by an integer, as pointers hold address of memory and that is an integer. In the above examples, both pntr and qpntr will take 2 bytes of memory (considering a 16 bit compiler) but pntr will point to two bytes of memory and q_pntr will point to one byte of memory.

Here is a program that demonstrates what we have been discussing.

PROGRAM 14.1   Program to demonstrates the use of & and * operator.

```
#include<stdio.h>
void  main( )
{
    int  var = 14 ;
    int  *pntr ;
    pntr  = &var ;

    printf ( "\nContent of var = %d", var ) ;
    printf ( "\nAddress of var = %u", &var ) ;
    printf ( "\nContent of var = %d", * ( &var ) ) ;
    printf ( "\nContent of pntr = %u", pntr ) ;
    printf ( "\nAddress of pntr = %u", &pntr ) ;
    printf ( "\nContent of var = %d", *pntr ) ;
}
```

Output: Content of var = 14
            Address of var = 4062
            Content of var = 14
            Content of ptr = 4062
            Address of ptr = 6069
            Content of var = 14

(Assuming the integer variable **var** is allocated at 4062 and the pointer variable **pntr** is allocated at 6069)

The following memory map would illustrate the above output clearly.

         var   pntr
      ┌────────┐   ┌────────┐
      │   14   │   │ 4062 │
      └────────┘   └────────┘
         4062   6069

Again as pntr is a variable we can store the address of pntr in some other pointer variable. Like –

$$pptr = \&pntr;$$

So, in memory it will look like

           pptr
        ┌────────┐
        │ 6069 │
        └────────┘
           5032

But before use we have to declare the variable pptr.

How can we declare it? See, we cannot declare as *int * pptr;* as this declaration indicates that pptr is a variable which can store the address of an integer. Here pptr holds the address of another pointer variable. That is one level deep. That is why it will be declared as:

int **pptr;

This implies that pptr is a variable which can store the address of a variable that will store the address of an integer, or in short pptr is a variable which is able to store the address of an integer pointer.

The following program illustrates this.

PROGRAM 14.2   Program to demonstrate the concept of pointer to pointer.

```
#include<stdio.h>
void  main( )
{
     int  var = 14 ;
     int  *pntr ;
     int **pptr;
     pntr  = &var ;
     pptr= &pntr;

     printf ( "\nContent of var = %d", var ) ;
     printf ( "\nAddress of var = %u", &var ) ;
     printf ( "\nContent of var = %d", *( &var ) ) ;
     printf ( "\nContent of pntr = %u", pntr ) ;
     printf ( "\nAddress of pntr = %u", &pntr ) ;
     printf ( "\nContent of var = %d", *pntr ) ;
     printf ( "\nContent of pptr = %u", pptr ) ;
     printf ( "\nAddress of pptr = %u", &pptr ) ;
     printf ( "\nAddress of var = %u", *pptr ) ;
     printf ( "\nContent of var = %d", **pptr ) ;
}
```

Output: Content of var = 14
Address of var = 4062
Content of var = 14
Content of pntr = 4062
Address of pntr = 6069
Content of var = 14
Content of pptr = 6069
Address of pptr = 5032
Address of var = 4062
Content of var = 14

We can extend the above program still further by creating a pointer to a pointer to an integer pointer. In principle, it may be possible to declare a pointer to a pointer to a pointer to a pointer to a pointer and so on and actually there is no limit. We can extend this definition as deep as we want. But in practice, a pointer to a pointer is sufficient in most cases.

Here is an example that will show the use of & and * operator.

Program 14.3 Program using pointer to find the maximum between two inputted numbers.

```
#include<conio.h>
#include<stdio.h>
#define SIZE 20
void main( )
{
    int num1, num2, maxm, *ptr_num1, *ptr_num2, *ptr_max;
    ptr_num1 = &num1;
    ptr_num2 = &num2;
    ptr_max = &maxm;
    clrscr( );
    printf("Enter 1st number : " );
    scanf("%d", ptr_num1);
    printf("Enter 2nd number : " );
    scanf("%d", ptr_num2);
    if( * ptr_num1 > * ptr_num2 )
        * ptr_max = * ptr_num1;
    else
        * ptr_max = * ptr_num2;
    printf("Max = %d", *ptr_max);
}
```

Sample output
```
Enter 1st number : 10
Enter 2nd number : 15
Max = 15
```

14.2 ARRAY AND POINTER

Like simple variable we can access an array with pointer also.

Let us take an array as follows:

int my_arr[5] = {12,22,33,42,56};

To access this array with pointer we need to declare a pointer which will store the base address of this array. As the array name itself returns the base address of the array, our statements will be:

int *ptr;
ptr = my_arr;

> Remember that array name is a constant pointer and cannot be used at the left hand side of an assignment operator.

We can also write the statement as:

ptr = &my_arr[0];

Now ptr is an integer pointer pointing to an integer array. If the array is allocated at, say, 7030 memory location, the content of ptr will be 7030 and *ptr will be 12.

	0	1	2	3	4	ptr
my_arr	12	22	33	42	56	7030
	7030	7032	7034	7036	7038	

To access other elements of the array, we need to apply the pointer arithmetic.

14.3 POINTER ARITHMETIC

Pointer variable does not support all arithmetic operations like simple variable because here operations are related to address arithmetic. The valid operations that can be performed on pointers are:

(1) **Addition of an integer number and a pointer:** We can add integer value with a pointer. The resultant value will be a pointer. By the addition of **n** with a pointer, the result will indicate the address which is **n** cell apart from the pointer. For example,

```
int my_arr[5] = {12,22,33,42,56};
int *ptr1, *ptr2 ;
ptr1 = my_arr ;
ptr1++ ;
ptr2 = ptr1 + 3 ;
```

The above mentioned addition is different from a simple arithmetic addition.

To explain this, let us suppose the above declared array is allocated at, say, 7030 memory location. So, the content of ptr1 is now 7030. When the expression ptr1++ will execute, the value of ptr1 will not be 7031. Instead it will be 7032. Because addition of 1 to a pointer means pointer will point to the next element. It is actually calculated as:

```
ptr + n => ptr + n * sizeof(data type)
```

Here ptr is a pointer variable and n is an integer variable. So, from the above example the value of ptr1 will be calculated as $7030 + 1 * 2 = 7032$ [as size of integer is 2 considering a 16 bit compiler] and then ptr2 will be $7032 + 3 * 2 = 7038$.

(2) **Subtraction of a number from a pointer:** Like addition we can subtract integer value from a pointer. Here also the resultant is of type pointer. By the subtraction of **n** with a pointer, the result will indicate the address, which is **n** cells away from the pointer.

For example,

```
int my_arr[5] = {12,22,33,42,56};
int  *ptr1, *ptr2 ;
ptr1 = &my_arr[4] ;
ptr1-- ;
ptr2 = ptr1 - 3 ;
```

The subtraction operation follows the same methodology of addition. It is calculated as:

```
ptr - n => ptr - n * sizeof(data type)
```

Here ptr is a pointer variable and n is an integer variable. So, according to the above example, here also the content of ptr1 is the address of fifth element of the array, i.e., 7038 (considering base address as 7030). When the expression ptr1-- will execute, the value of ptr1 will be calculated as 7038 – 1 * 2 = 7036 and then ptr2 will be 7036 – 3 * 2 = 7030.

Note that the += and –= operator can be used with the pointer if the left hand side operand is a pointer and right hand side operand is an integer variable or integer constant.

(3) **Subtraction of one pointer from another:** One pointer variable can be subtracted from another pointer variable. This is possible only if both the pointer variables point to elements of the same array. The resultant value indicates the number of elements between two pointers. This is illustrated below:

```
int my_arr[5] = {12,22,33,42,56};
int  n, *ptr1, *ptr2 ;
ptr1 = &my_arr[4] ;
ptr2 =  &my_arr[0] ;
n = ptr2 - ptr1;
```

Similarly, the subtraction operation between two pointer variable is not simple arithmetic subtraction. As it indicates the number of cells in between two addresses, it is calculated as:

> **Simple arithmetic subtraction between two pointer / sizeof(data type)**

So, according to the above example, the content of ptr1 is the address of fifth element of the array, i.e., 7038 (considering base address as 7030) and the content of ptr2 is the address of first element of the array, i.e., 7030. When the expression ptr2 – ptr1 will execute, the value of n will be calculated as (7038 – 7030)/2 = 8/2 = 4 which indicates the occurrence of 4 cells in between these two addresses.

(4) **Comparison of two pointer variables:** Pointer variables can be compared if both are of same type. Using relational operators, pointers can be compared. If two pointers compare equal to each other, it indicates that they point to the same memory address. If one pointer compares less than another, it indicates that the first pointer points to a lesser memory address which means it is on the left side if compared to the second pointer. It is useful when both pointers point to elements of same array. Consider the following program:

```
int my_arr[5] = {12,22,33,42,56};
int  n, *ptr1, *ptr2 ;
ptr1 = &my_arr[4] ;
ptr2 =  &my_arr[0] ;
if( ptr1 > ptr2)
    n = ptr1 - ptr2;
else
    n = ptr2 - ptr1;
printf("There are %d elements between two pointer");
```

Following are the Invalid Operations on Pointer

i)   Addition of two pointers
ii)   Multiplication of a pointer with a constant
iii)   Multiplication of two pointers
iv)   Division of a pointer with a constant
v)   Division of two pointers

Now consider the following example.

```
int my_arr[5] = {12,22,33,42,56};

int  *pntr ;

pntr = my_arr ;
```

The memory map of the above example looks like:

	0	1	2	3	4		pntr
my_arr	12	22	33	42	56		7030
	7030	7032	7034	7036	7038		6087

From the above example we can find,

```
pntr + 0  ≡  7030  ≡  & my_arr[0]
pntr + 1  ≡  7032  ≡  & my_arr[1]
pntr + 2  ≡  7034  ≡  & my_arr[2]
pntr + 3  ≡  7036  ≡  & my_arr[3]
pntr + 4  ≡  7038  ≡  & my_arr[4]
```

From these we can conclude,

$$\boxed{\text{pntr + i} \quad \equiv \quad \text{\& my\_arr[i]}}$$ .... (1)

Again,

```
* (pntr + 0)  ≡   12  ≡  my_arr[0]
* (pntr + 1)  ≡   22  ≡  my_arr[1]
* (pntr + 2)  ≡   33  ≡  my_arr[2]
* (pntr + 3)  ≡   42  ≡  my_arr[3]
* (pntr + 4)  ≡   56  ≡  my_arr[4]
```

From these we can conclude,

$$\boxed{\text{* (pntr + i)} \quad \equiv \quad \text{my\_arr[i]}}$$ .... (2)

Again, as an array name represents the base address of an array variable, we can also write:

```
my_arr + i        ≡    & my_arr[i]
```
and   `* (my_arr + i)   ≡    my_arr[i]`

Another interesting thing we can conclude that,

```
my_arr[i]    ≡      * (my_arr + i )
             ≡      * ( i + my_arr )
             ≡      i [my_arr]
```

From the conclusion 1 and 2, we can rewrite the programs now with the pointer notation which were earlier written using array. The following program illustrates the operation of pointer.

PROGRAM 14.4 Program to find the maximum from a set of elements.

```
#include<conio.h>
#include<stdio.h>
#define SIZE   20
void main( )
{    int my_arr[SIZE], *ptr, i, maxm;
     ptr = my_arr;
     for(i = 0; i < SIZE; i++ )
     {   printf("Enter Number : ");
         scanf("%d",(ptr + i));
     }
     maxm = *ptr;
     for( i = 1; i < SIZE; i++)
     {
         if(*(ptr+i) > maxm)
             maxm = *(ptr+i);
     }
     printf("\nMaximum Number : %d", maxm);
}
```

In the above example, first the base address of the array is assigned to the pointer, ptr so that we can access the array through the pointer. Now to take the input in the array **(ptr+i)** is written instead of **&my_arr[i]** to use the pointer notation. Similarly, **my_arr[0]** is substituted by ***ptr** and **my_arr[i]** by ***(ptr+i)**.

14.4 ARRAY VS POINTER

An array name represents the base address of an array variable. Now, if a pointer variable points to the base address of an array, the array name and the pointer variable looks alike in most operations. For example,

```
char arr[20];
char *ptr;
ptr = arr;
```

Now to take input in the array, we can write, **gets(arr)** as well as **gets(ptr)**. Similarly to print the content of the array we can write, **puts(arr)** as well as **puts(ptr)**. If we want to copy a string to the array we can write, **strcpy(arr,"Hello")** as well as **strcpy(ptr,"Hello")** and so on.

Again, the aforesaid two conclusions (1 & 2) derived in the previous section can be written as:

$$\& \; my\_arr[i] \quad \equiv \quad my\_arr + i \quad \equiv \quad ptr + i$$
$$and \; my\_arr[i] \quad \equiv \quad *(my\_arr + i) \quad \equiv \quad *(ptr + i)$$

In this way, most operations what are done on pointer are also applicable to array name but both are not same. When we declare an array, compiler allocates some memory place to store a set of values. But in case of pointer declaration, compiler allocates just 2 bytes (considering 16 bit compiler) to store the memory address of a variable which may be an array. Using the **sizeof** operator we can show this difference. Consider the following example.

PROGRAM 14.5   Program to show the difference between array name and a pointer.

```
void main( )
{
    int my_arr[12];
    int * pntr;
    pntr = my_arr;
    printf("Size of the array : %d", sizeof(my_arr));
    printf("\nSize of the pointer : %d", sizeof(pntr));
}
```

Output:
   Size of the array : 24
   Size of the pointer : 2

In the above example an integer array of size 12 is declared. So, memory allocated for the array is 12 × 2 = 24 bytes. The sizeof operator returns this value. In the next statement, size of a pointer variable is always 2 in a 16 bit compiler.

Another difference is that the content of array name cannot be changed. An array name is a constant pointer.

For example,   int a[10],*p;

              p=a;

Now, p++ is a valid statement and it will points to the second element in the array. But, we cannot write a++. Because by writing this, we are actually changing the base address of an array and compiler would not allow it.

14.5   POINTER AND FUNCTION

Like other variables, we can pass pointers as function argument. Depending on the arguments passed to any function, **invoking of functions can be classified into two groups**. These are:

       1. Call by value   **2.** Call by reference

14.5.1   Call by Value

When we pass the arguments as a call by value, we pass the value of variables to the function. In the previous chapter whatever functions are written, all those functions were followed the call by value mechanism. In this mechanism, a copy of the actual arguments are passed. For example, consider the following code snippet.

PROGRAM 14.6   Program to demonstrate call by value mechanism.

```
#include<stdio.h>
int sum(int n1, int n2)
{
    int s;
    s = n1 + n2;
    return(s);
}

void main( )
{
    int num1,num2,total;
    printf("Enter any two Numbers:");
    scanf("%d%d",&num1,&num2);
    total = sum(x,y);
    printf("Sum =%d ",total);
}
```

Sample output

Enter any two Numbers: 10 15
Sum = 25

Here, value of num1 and num2 will be passed to sum( ) and those value will be accepted by the formal arguments of sum( ), n1 and n2.

But there is a problem in this mechanism. If we make any change in the formal arguments, that change will not affect the actual arguments. Consider the following example.

PROGRAM 14.7   Program to demonstrate the limitation of call by value mechanism.

```
#include<stdio.h>
void swapping(int v1, int v2)
{
    int temp;                         v1              v2
    temp = v1;                     ┌────────┐      ┌────────┐
    v1 = v2;                       │ 12̶ 15  │      │ 1̶5̶ 12  │
    v2 = temp;                     └────────┘      └────────┘
}                                     3044            4323

void main( )
{                                                n1              n2
    int n1,n2;                                ┌──────┐        ┌──────┐
    printf("Enter any two Numbers: ");        │  12  │        │  15  │
    scanf("%d%d",&n1,&n2);                    └──────┘        └──────┘
    printf("\nBefore swapping, 1st Number= %d  2nd Number= %d",n1,n2);
    swapping(n1,n2);
    printf("\nAfter swapping, 1st Number= %d  2nd Number= %d",n1,n2);
}
```
5225 under n1, 5300 under n2

Sample output

Enter any two Numbers: 12 15

Before swapping, 1st Number = 12 2nd Number = 15
After swapping, 1st Number = 12 2nd Number = 15

In the above program, when the **swap** function is called two new variables **v1** and **v2** is created and the value of **n1**, i.e., **12** is copied to **v1** and the value of **n2**, i.e., **15** is copied to **v2**. The operation done in the **swapping** function, swaps the value of **v1** and **v2**. So, **v1** becomes **15** and **v2** becomes **12**. But the value of **n1** and **n2** will remain unchanged as they are different variables. Thus, we do not get our required output.

Another point is any function can return at most one value. So, it is really a problem if any function needs to return more than one value.

Both the problems can be solved using call by reference mechanism.

14.5.2   Call by Reference

When we pass the address of variables to the function as arguments, it is known as call by address or call by reference. Actually there is no concept of reference in C language. Here call by reference means call by address. In this mechanism, like call by value the address of the variable is copied to the formal argument from actual argument. The main advantage of call by reference is that we can change/modify the content of more than one variable through some function. Consider the following code snippet.

PROGRAM 14.8   Program to demonstrate call by reference mechanism.

```
#include<stdio.h>
void swapping(int *p1, int *p2)
{
    int temp;                    p1                    p2
    temp = *p1;               ┌──────┐             ┌──────┐
    *p1 = *p2;                │ 5225 │             │ 5300 │
    *p2 = temp;               └──────┘             └──────┘
}                               3044                 4323

void main( )
{                                           n1                   n2
    int n1,n2;                          ┌───────┐           ┌───────┐
    printf("Enter any two Numbers:");   │ 12 15 │           │ 15 12 │
    scanf("%d%d",&n1,&n2);              └───────┘           └───────┘
    printf("\nBefore swapping, 1st        5225                5300
       Number= %d  2nd Number= %d",n1,n2);
    swapping(&n1,&n2);
    printf("\nAfter swapping, 1st Number= %d  2nd Number= %d",n1,n2);
}
```

Sample output

Enter any two Numbers: 12 15

Before swapping, 1st Number = 12 2nd Number = 15
After swapping, 1st Number = 15 2nd Number = 12

Here, instead of value of n1 and n2, address of n1 and n2 is sent to swapping( ). So, from swapping() function, we directly access the address of n1 and n2 variable and change the content of those locations. As these changes occur at the original memory location of the actual argument, not at the local variable of the function, the effect of this change persists in the calling function.

In the above example, we passed the address of two integer variables. We can pass an entire array also. Consider the following example.

PROGRAM 14.9 Program to sort an array using bubble sort algorithm.

```c
#include<conio.h>
#include<stdio.h>
#define ARR_SIZE 10
voidbubble_sort(int*,int);    /*Prototype declaration of the function*/

void main()
{
    int element[ARR_SIZE],i;
    clrscr();
    for(i=0;i< ARR_SIZE;i++)
    {
        printf("Enter Element %d: ",i+1);
        scanf("%d",&element[i]);
    }
    bubble_sort(element, ARR_SIZE);
    printf("\n\nThe Sorted Elements are : ");
    for(i=0;i< ARR_SIZE;i++)
    {
        printf("%d ", elements[i]);
    }
}

void bubble_sort( int *p, int size)
{
    int i, j, t;
    for( i = 0; i < size -1; i++ )
    {
        for( j = 0; j < size -1 - i; j++ )
        {
            if( * ( p + j ) > * ( p + j + 1) )
            {
                t = * (p + j);
                * (p + j) = * (p + j + 1);
                * (p + j + 1) = t;
            }
        }
    }
}
```

Sample output
```
Enter element 1: 25
Enter element 2: 49
Enter element 3: 5
Enter element 4: 37
Enter element 5: 16
Enter element 6: 22
Enter element 7: 8
Enter element 8: 31
Enter element 9: 13
Enter element 10: 28
```

The Sorted Elements are : 5 8 13 16 22 25 28 31 37 49

In the above example, consider the function call statement. We are sending the base address of the array named **element** and its size. In the function definition that address is accepted by a pointer and the size by an integer variable. As soon as the base address of the array is available, we can easily access the array. This is another example of call by reference or call by address. Always remember that an array can pass to a function only through call by reference.

14.6   POINTER AND STRING

As strings are basically a character array, we can access the strings with the pointer as like numeric single dimensional array. Here is some examples to access strings through pointers.

PROGRAM 14.10   Program to find the frequency of a word in an inputted string.

```
#include<conio.h>
#include<stdio.h>
#include<string.h>
int wordfrequency(char *, char *);
void main()
{
    char str[80],word[25];
    int n;
    printf("Enter any String: ");
    gets(str);
    printf("Enter any word: ");
    fflush(stdin);
    gets(word);
    n = wordfrequency(str,word);
    printf("\nThe frequency of the word \'%s\' is : %d",word, n);
}
int wordfrequency(char *str, char *wrd)
{   int i=0,j=0,c=0;
    char temp[25];
```

```
     while(*(str+i))
     {    j=0;
          while(*(str+i)!=' '&&ispunct(*(str+i))!=1&&*(str+i)!='\0')
          {
               temp[j++]=*(str+i);
               i++;
          }
          temp[j]='\0';
          if(strcmp(wrd,temp)==0)
               c++;
          if(*(str+i)!='\0')
               i++;
     }
     return(c);
}
```

Sample output
> Enter any String: the earth moves round the sun
> Enter any word: the
>
> The frequency of the word 'the' is: 2

14.7 FUNCTION RETURNING POINTER

A function can return pointer also. As returning pointer means returning the base address of some variable, we can return an entire array or the portion of an array from any function. This is true for string also. It is one of the advantages of using pointer. Here is an example.

PROGRAM 14.11 Program to merge two sorted arrays such that after merging the merged array maintains the sorted order.

```
/* Program to Merge two sorted array */
#include<conio.h>
#include<stdio.h>
#define SIZE1 5
#define SIZE2 5
int* merge(int [], int []);
void main()
{    int arr1[SIZE1],arr2[SIZE2],i;
     int *ptr;
     clrscr();
     printf("Enter Elements for first array:-\n");
     for(i=0;i<SIZE1;i++)
     {    printf("Enter Element %d: ",i+1);
          scanf("%d",&arr1[i]);
     }
```

```
        printf("\nEnter Elements for Second array:-\n");
        for(i=0;i<SIZE2;i++)
        {    printf("Enter Element %d: ",i+1);
             scanf("%d",&arr2[i]);
        }
        ptr=merge(arr1,arr2);
        printf("\nMerged Array: ");
        for(i=0;i<SIZE1+SIZE2;i++)
             printf("%d ",*(ptr+i));
}

int* merge(int a1[], int a2[])
{
        static int arr3[SIZE1+SIZE2];
        int i=0,j=0,l=0;
        while(i<SIZE1 && j<SIZE2)
        {
             if(a1[i] < a2[j])
                  arr3[l++]=a1[i++];
             else
                  arr3[l++]=a2[j++];
        }
        while(i<SIZE1)
        {
             arr3[l++]=a1[i++];
        }
        while(j<SIZE2)
        {
             arr3[l++]=a2[j++];
        }
        return(arr3);
}
```

Sample output

```
Enter elements for first array:
Enter element 1: 1
Enter element 2: 3
Enter element 3: 5
Enter element 4: 7
Enter element 5: 9

Enter elements for second array:
Enter element 1: 2
Enter element 2: 4
Enter element 3: 6
Enter element 4: 8
Enter element 5: 10

Merged Array: 1  2  3  4  5  6  7  8  9  10
```

14.8 POINTERS AND MULTIDIMENSIONAL ARRAYS

Using pointer we can access 2D array also. A 2D array can be treated as array of arrays. Means each row of a two-dimensional array can be considered as a one-dimensional array. If we have an array – int arr2d[3][4]; then arr2d[0] gives the address of the zeroth one-dimensional array, arr2d[1] gives the address of the first one-dimensional array and so on. So, arr2d[i] gives the address of the i-th one-dimensional array. Thus, the address of j-th element in the i-th row will be arr2d[i] + j and to get the content at this address we need to write the statement * (arr2d[i] + j). So, we can say,

$$\begin{aligned}\text{arr2d[i][j]} &\equiv \text{*(arr2d[i] + j)} \\ &\equiv \text{*(* (arr2d + i) + j)} \\ \text{and, \&arr2d[i][j]} &\equiv \text{(* (arr2d + i) + j)}\end{aligned}$$

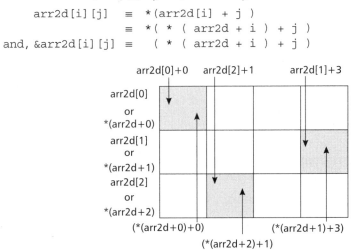

Fig. 14.2   Address calculation for the elements of 2D array

Thus for 3-D array, instead of arr3d[i][j][k], we can write : *(* (* (arr3d + i) + j) + k) and instead of &arr3d[i][j][k], we can write : (* (* (arr3d + i) + j) + k).

In this way we can handle any multidimensional array.

Here is an example which shows how we can handle a two dimensional array with the pointer notation.

PROGRAM 14.12   Program to find transpose of a matrix.

```
/* Program to transpose of a matrix. */
#include<conio.h>
#include<stdio.h>
void main()
{   int matrix[3][3], i=0, j=0, t;
    clrscr();
    printf("\nEnter the elements of a Matrix:-\n");
    for(i=0;i<3;i++)
    {   for(j=0;j<3;j++)
        {   printf("Enter element[%d][%d] : ", i, j);
```

```
            scanf("%d", ( * (matrix + i) + j));
        }
    }
    clrscr();
    printf("\n\nOriginal Matrix:-\n");
    for(i=0;i<3;i++)
    {   for(j=0;j<3;j++)
            printf("%d\t", *( * (matrix + i) + j));
        printf("\n");
    }
    for(i=0;i<3;i++)
        for(j=0;j<i;j++)
        {   t   = *( * (matrix + i) + j);
            *( * (matrix + i) + j) = *( * (matrix + j) + i);
            *( * (matrix + j) + i) = t;
        }
    printf("\n\nTranspose of the Matrix:-\n");
    for(i=0;i<3;i++)
    {   for(j=0;j<3;j++)
            printf("%d\t",*( * (matrix + i) + j));
        printf("\n");
    }
}
```

Sample output

Enter the elements of a Matrix:
　　Enter element[0][0] : 11
　　Enter element[0][1] : 12
　　Enter element[0][2] : 13
　　Enter element[1][0] : 14
　　Enter element[1][1] : 15
　　Enter element[1][2] : 16
　　Enter element[2][0] : 17
　　Enter element[2][1] : 18
　　Enter element[2][2] : 19
Original Matrix:
　　11　　12　　13
　　14　　15　　16
　　17　　18　　19
Transpose of the Matrix:
　　11　　14　　17
　　12　　15　　18
　　13　　16　　19

14.9　ARRAY OF POINTERS

Like numeric or character array, we can declare the array of pointers also. Array of pointers means an array consists of pointers. As pointer variable contains an address, an array of pointer is basically a collection of addresses. The addresses stored in the array of pointers are mainly addresses of isolated variables or addresses of some array or any other addresses. The rules applicable for array of pointers are similar to that of array.

EXAMPLE 14.2

```
int *arr[3];
int x, y[5],z[10];
arr[0]= &x;
arr[1]= y;
arr[2]= z;
```

Here, arr is an array of pointers which contains the address of variable x and the base address of two array y and z.

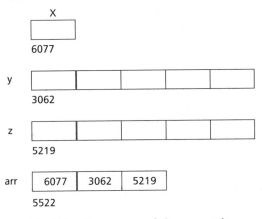

Fig. 14.3 Memory map of above example

Array of pointer is very much used in handling multiple strings. We can declare and initialize it in the following way:

```
char *days[] = {  "Sunday",
                  "Monday",
                  "Tuesday",
                  "Wednesday",
                  "Thursday",
                  "Friday",
                  "Saturday"
               };
```

Here, all the strings will be allocated in some unnamed places in memory and the base address of each string will be stored in the array of pointers in sequence. Base address of the string, 'Sunday' will be stored at days[0], base address of the string, 'Monday' will be stored at days[1] and so on.

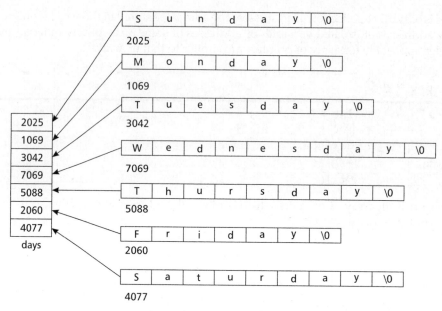

Fig. 14.4   **Memory map of array of pointer to string**

As we access strings with its base address, simply accessing the array of pointer we can access the strings. Here is an example:

PROGRAM 14.13   Program to change the date format DD/MM/YYYY to Month DD, YYYY. [For example: 12/05/1987 will be May 12, 1987]

```c
#include<stdio.h>
#include<conio.h>
void main( )
{
    char month[] [10] = { "January",
                          "February",
                          "March",
                          "April",
                          "May",
                          "June",
                          "July",
                          "August",
                          "September",
                          "October",
                          "November",
                          "December"
                    };
```

```
      int dd, mm, yy;
      clrscr();
      printf("Enter a Date(DD/MM/YYYY) : ");
      scanf("%d/%d/%d", &dd, &mm, &yy);
      printf("The inputted Date in new format is:
                           %s %d, %d",month[mm-1],dd,yy);
  }
```

Sample output
Enter a Date (DD/MM/YYYY) : 12/05/1987
The inputted Date in new format is : May 12, 1987

The purpose of array of pointers to string and 2D character array are almost same. You also note that accessing strings in both cases are also same. But allocations in memory are not same. In case of 2D array we need to declare a table whose number of columns is same as the length of the string which has the highest number of characters. But in case of array of pointers to string for each string requires memory according to its size. Thus if the length of the string varies a lot, a significant amount of memory will be wastage.

In contrast to the above example if we want to store the same set of strings into a 2D array, we have to declare it as:

```
      char days[][10] =  { "Sunday",
                           "Monday",
                           "Tuesday",
                           "Wednesday",
                           "Thursday",
                           "Friday",
                           "Saturday"
                        };
```

The memory map of the above declaration will be:

S	u	n	d	a	y	\0			
M	o	n	d	a	y	\0			
T	u	e	s	d	a	y	\0		
W	e	d	n	e	s	d	a	y	\0
T	h	u	r	s	d	a	y	\0	
F	r	i	d	a	y	\0			
S	a	t	u	r	d	a	y	\0	

It is clear from the above figures that the allocation for 2D array is 70 bytes whereas in case of array of pointer it is 57.

Another advantage we may find. Suppose we want to sort a set of strings. To do that, we need to exchange strings. In case of 2D array, we have to swap each character of those strings but in case of array of pointers only two addresses are need to exchange.

Thus we can see that array of pointers to string is much better than 2D character array to store multiple string of varying length.

Now we will discuss some special types of pointer.

14.9.1 Void Pointer

Pointer to void, or a void pointer, is a special type of pointer that has a great facility of pointing to any data type. This is also known as generic pointer. Except void pointer, all pointer variables can store the address of only corresponding data type. The address placed in a pointer must have the same type as the pointer. Consider the following example:

```
int i;
float f;
int* p;
p = &f;
```

The above statement will produce an error. The address of the float variable is stored in an integer pointer that is incorrect. The void pointer is a special type of pointer that the programmer can use to point to any data type. We can declare void pointer in this manner:

```
void* sample;
```

Using the above example's definition and assigning the void pointer to the address of an integer or float variable is perfectly correct.

```
sample = &i;  or,
sample = &f;
```

So, the **advantage** of void pointer is that it can be used to store address of any data type.

PROGRAM 14.14　　Program to increase the value of an integer variable as well as a character type variable by a single function.

```
#include<conio.h>
#include<stdio.h>
void increment (void* data, int size)
{
    if ( size == sizeof(char) )
    {
        char* c_ptr = (char*)data;
        (*c_ptr)++;
    }
    else
        if (size == sizeof(int) )
        {
            int* i_ptr = (int*)data;
            (*i_ptr)++;
        }
}
```

```
void main ( )
{
    int n = 1203;
    char ch = 'A';
    increment (&n, sizeof(n));
    increment (&ch, sizeof(ch));
    printf("%d, %c ", n , ch);
}
```

The output of the above program is: 1204, B

The above example shows that irrespective of data type, a single function can operate on integer as well as character variable. This is possible due to void pointer only.

There is some disadvantage of void pointer. The disadvantage of void pointer is that as the void pointer does not know what type of variable it is pointing to, it cannot be dereferenced. Rather, the void pointer must first be explicitly cast to another pointer type before it is dereferenced. Similarly, **it is not possible to do pointer arithmetic on a void pointer**.

14.9.2 Wild Pointer

When we declare a pointer variable, like other variable it is also contain some garbage value. We cannot use this pointer until a meaningful address is assigned to it. This uninitialized pointer is known as **wild pointer**. The use of wild pointer may cause segmentation fault (which means the pointer variable points to some invalid area of memory) or may behave abnormally.

```
int *ptr;
*ptr = 5;
```

Here, ptr is a wild pointer and may point to anywhere in memory. So performing the assignment *ptr = 5 may cause some runtime error or may makes some undefined behavior.

14.9.3 Null Pointer

As use of wild pointer causes abnormal behavior or produce error, it is our duty to initialize the pointer variables. But for the time being if the actual address is not available to us to initialize we can initialize the pointer variable with NULL values. Initializing Pointer Variable to NULL Value means the pointer is not pointing to anywhere; which means that it does not point to any variable or array cell or anything else. A pointer initialized with NULL value (i.e., zero) is known as **Null pointer**. Null pointer may also be used with the return statement in a function. A function that returns pointer values can return a null pointer when it is unable to perform its task.

The most easiest way to declare a null pointer in our program is by using the predefined symbolic constant NULL defined in several header files like <stdio.h>, <stdlib.h>, etc. Following code shows how we can initialize a pointer with null value.

```
#include <stdio.h>

int *pntr = NULL;
```

To check that whether a pointer is a null pointer or we may use code like

```
if(pntr == NULL)
      printf("It is a Null Pointer");
```

It is also possible to refer to the null pointer by simply assigning 0 (zero).

```
int *pntr = 0;
```

14.10 DYNAMIC MEMORY ALLOCATION

So far the variables we declared that are allocated statically. We are not able to declare array whose size will be determined at run time. The most amazing advantage of pointer is that if we use pointer we will be able to allocate memory dynamically, i.e., at the time of execution we can decide the size of the array.

The process of allocating memory at the time of program execution, i.e., at run time is called dynamic memory allocation. The advantage of dynamic memory allocation is that we can allocate memory according to our requirement. So, like static allocation we do not have any wastage of memory neither we face lack of memory. 'C' supports some memory management functions by which during the program execution memories can be allocated and de-allocated. C language provides the following functions to efficiently manage the memory.

Function name	Purpose
malloc	Allocates a block of memory of specified size and returns the base address of the allocated block.
calloc	Allocates multiple blocks in memory and initializes them to zero and returns the base address of the allocated space
free	De-allocate memories previously allocated by malloc or calloc function.
realloc	Redefines the size of previously allocated memory block.

14.10.1 malloc( )

The **malloc( )** function allocates a block of memory whose size is specified in the function argument and returns the base address of the allocated block. The return type of malloc( ) function is **void ***. So, it can be assigned to any type of pointer using type casting. This function is defined in alloc.h and stdlib.h header files. The general form of this function is:

```
pntr=(type-to-cast*)malloc(block_size);
```

pntr is a pointer of type `type-to-cast`. The above statement returns a pointer of type void* with an area of memory of size `block-size`. Then it is type casted to `type-to-cast` type and is assigned to the pointer **pntr**. If it fails to allocate the required memory, it returns NULL.

Example 14.3

```
int *pntr;
pntr = (int*)malloc(30 * sizeof(int));
```

On successful execution of this statement a memory equivalent to 30 times the size of int is allocated and the base address of allocated memory is assigned to the pointer pntr of type int. And on failure, it will return NULL.

14.10.2 calloc( )

The **calloc( )** is also a memory allocation function and works similar to malloc( ) function. It is generally used to allocate multiple blocks of storage whose each block are of same size. After allocation calloc( ) function sets all bytes to zero. This function is also defined in alloc.h and stdlib.h header files. It takes the following form:

```
pntr=(type-to-cast*)calloc(n, element-size);
```

Here also **pntr** is a pointer of type `type-to-cast`. **n** is the number of blocks to allocate and `element-size` indicates the size of each block. The calloc( ) function allocates contiguous space for **n** blocks each size of **element-size** bytes and after allocation it initializes all bytes to zero. Like malloc( ) function it also returns a pointer to the first byte of the allocated area. As it is also return a pointer of type void* it is needed to type cast it according to requirement. If the function fails to allocate required memory, a null pointer is returned.

EXAMPLE 14.4

```
int *pntr;
pntr = (int*)malloc(30, sizeof(int));
```

On successful execution of this statement a contiguous space for 30 blocks each size of 2 bytes (i.e., size of int) is allocated and initialized with zero. But on failure, it will return NULL.

14.10.3 free( )

Already we have seen that compile time storage of a variable is allocated and de-allocated automatically according to its storage class. But in case of dynamic runtime allocation, the allocation is permanent in nature (unless the power become off). So, it is responsibility of a programmer to de-allocate the memory space when it is no longer required. We can implement it using free( ) and general form of free( ) is:

```
free(pntr);
```

pntr is a pointer which is pointing to a memory block allocated by using malloc( ) function or calloc( ) function.

14.10.4 realloc( )

Sometimes it may happen that the memory allocated previously using calloc( ) function or malloc( ) function is not sufficient. It may be insufficient or excess. In both cases, we need to change the size of previously allocated memory block. C language provides a memory management function named **realloc( )** function for this purpose, i.e., for reallocation of memory. The general form of realloc() function is:

```
pntr = realloc(pntr, newsize);
```

The above statement allocates new memory space of size `newsize` and returns the base address of the newly allocated memory block to the pointer variable **pntr**. This reallocation may or may not be took place at the same memory location.

The following program illustrates dynamic memory allocation. We already write the same program using static allocation. Now, follow the differences.

PROGRAM 14.15 **Program to find the maximum from a set of elements. The number of elements will be decided during the execution of the program.**

```
#include<conio.h>
#include<stdio.h>
void main( )
{    int  *ptr, i, maxm, n;
     printf("Number of elements :");
     scanf("%d", &n);

     /* Dynamic Allocation according to Input  */

     ptr = (int*)malloc( n * 2);          /* As size of integer is 2.*/
     if(ptr == NULL)
     {
          puts(" Insufficient Memory");
          exit(0);
     }

     for(i = 0; i < n; i++ )
     {    printf("Enter Number %d: ",i+1);
          scanf("%d",(ptr + i));
     }
     maxm = *ptr;
     for( i = 1; i < SIZE; i++)
     {
          if(*(ptr+i) > maxm)
               maxm = *(ptr+i);
     }
     printf("\nMaximum Number is : %d", maxm);
     free(ptr);     /* Releasing the used space */
}
```

Sample output
```
Number of elements: 10
Enter Number 1: 15
Enter Number 2: 8
Enter Number 3: 23
Enter Number 4: 17
Enter Number 5:  6
Enter Number 6: 42
```

Enter Number 7: 35
Enter Number 8: 20
Enter Number 9: 28
Enter Number 10: 30

Maximum Number is: 42

14.11 FUNCTION POINTER

A pointer variable is able to store the address of a function also. When a pointer points to a function, i.e., holds the address of a function is called **pointer to a function** or simply **function pointer**. Before execution a program is first loaded into the memory, i.e., it is allocated in the memory. Thus all the functions defined in the program have their own address. Pointer variables can point these functions just like other variables. So, we can invoke functions through pointer also. We can declare a function pointer as:

```
return_type (* function_pointer_name)( list of Arguments );
```

for example if **fptr** is a function pointer pointing to a function whose return type is float and take two integers as argument, the declaration statement will be:

```
float (*fptr)(int, int);
```

To assign the address of the function to the pointer, we just need to mention the function name. If average is a function with the prototype:

```
float average(int, int);
```

Then to assign the address of this function to the above function pointer, we have to write the statement,

```
fptr = average;
```

Using the function pointer, we can invoke a function in two ways. To invoke the above average( ) function through fptr we may write,

```
fptr(5, 6);
```

or

```
(*fptr)(5, 6);
```

Following example illustrates the operations of pointer to a function.

PROGRAM 14.16   Program to illustrate the use of function pointer.

```
#include<conio.h>
#include<stdio.h>
int sum(int n1, int n2)
{    int s;
     s=n1+n2;
     return(s);
}
```

```
float average(int n1, int n2)
{    float avg;
     avg=(float)(n1+n2)/2;
     return(avg);
}

void main()
{
     int (*fptr1)(int, int);  /* Declaration of pointer to a function
                                    returning int. */
     float (*fptr2)(int, int);  /* Declaration of pointer to a function
                                    returning float. */
     int num1,num2,s;
     float avg;
     fptr1 = sum; /* Assign address of function sum to the function
                    pointer.*/
     fptr2 = average;  /* Assign address of function average to the
                         function pointer. */
     printf("Enter 1st number:");
     scanf("%d",&num1);
     printf("Enter 2nd number:");
     scanf("%d",&num2);

     s=fptr1(num1,num2);              /* Invoking the function sum(). */
     avg=(*fptr2)(num1, num2);  /* Invoking the function average(). */
     printf("Sum = %d",s);
     printf("\nAverage = %.2f",avg);
}
```

Sample output
```
Enter 1st number:  5
Enter 2nd number:  6
Sum = 11
Average = 5.50
```

14.12 RETURNING A TWO DIMENSIONAL ARRAY FROM FUNCTION

Like single dimensional array, we can return a two dimensional array from any function. But it is not so simple due to the construction mechanism of 2D array. So, we need to follow some tricky solution. The simplest way to return a 2D array is returning the base address and access all the elements (i.e., row * column elements) sequentially.

```
#include<stdio.h>
#include<conio.h>

int* input(int arr[][3])
{    int i,j;
```

```
        printf("\nEnter the elements of Matrix :-\n");
        for(i=0;i<3;i++)
        {    for(j=0;j<3;j++)
             {    printf("Enter element[%d][%d] : ",i,j);
                  scanf("%d",&arr[i][j]);
             }
        }
        return(&arr[0][0]);
}

void main()
{    int a[3][3],i,j,*p;
     clrscr();

     p=input(a);
     printf("\n\nElements of the Matrix:-\n");
     for(i=0;i<3;i++)
     {    for(j=0;j<3;j++)
                printf("%d\t",*(p++));
          printf("\n");
     }
}
```

But in this representation, the logical tabular representation of array is lost. So, a better way to return a 2D array is returning pointer to an array. Size of this array will be size of the column of 2Darray. Consider the following example.

```
#include<stdio.h>
#include<conio.h>

int (*(input)(int arr[][3]))[ ]
{    int i,j;
     printf("\nEnter the elements of Matrix:-\n");
     for(i=0;i<3;i++)
     {    for(j=0;j<3;j++)
          {    printf("Enter element[%d][%d] : ",i,j);
               scanf("%d",&arr[i][j]);
          }
     }
     return(arr);
}

void main()
{    int a[3][3],i,j;
     int (*p)[3];  /* declaration of pointer to an array of integers */
     clrscr();

     p=input(a);        /* assigning */
     printf("\n\n Elements of the Matrix:-\n");
     for(i=0;i<3;i++)
```

```
{    for(j=0;j<3;j++)
         printf("%d\t",p[i][j]);
     printf("\n");
}
}
```

14.13 DANGLING POINTER

Dangling pointer is not a special pointer. It is a special case in operation with the pointer. If any pointer is pointing the memory address of any variable but after some time the variable has deallocated from that memory location while pointer is still pointing that memory location. Such pointer is known as **dangling pointer**. A pointer may become a dangling pointer in several situations. Consider the following example.

```
void main( )
{
    int *ptr = (int *) malloc(10 *2);
    .....
    .....
    free(ptr);
    .....    /* ptr is now a dangling pointer */
}
```

In the above example, an integer pointer **ptr** is declared and initialized with the base address of a memory block allocated dynamically by the malloc( ) function. After some times if we deallocate this memory with the statement **free(ptr)**, the pointer **ptr** becomes dangling pointer as the pointer **ptr** is still pointing to a memory location where actually there is no allocation.

Now consider another situation.

```
void main()
{
    int *ptr = NULL;
    .....
    .....
    {
        int var;
        ptr = &var;
    }
    ...../* ptr is now a dangling pointer */
}
```

Here, first an integer pointer **ptr** is declared. Next, within the inner block an integer variable **var** is declared and address of this variable is assigned to the pointer variable **ptr**. Though the integer variable **var** is not visible in Outer Block, the pointer **ptr** is still pointing to same invalid memory location in Outer block. Thus the pointer **ptr** becomes dangling pointer.

A pointer may become a dangling pointer due to a common mistake in returning the address of a local variable. Once a called function returns, the space allocated for the local variables declared within the function get deallocated. So, practically the returning address points to a memory location where there is no allocation.

```
int* f1( )
{
     int var = 5;
     . . . . .
     . . . . .
     return &var;
}

void main( )
{
     int *pntr;
     . . . . .
     . . . . .
     pntr = f1( );
     . . . . .          /* pntr is now a dangling pointer */
}
```

14.14 IMPLEMENTATION OF SOME STANDARD LIBRARY FUNCTIONS

As now we are able to use pointers in our own function, we can implement some another set of library functions. Here are few of them.

PROGRAM 14.17   Function to Implement gets( ):

```
char* my_gets(char *strn)
{    int i=0;
     char ch;
     while((ch=getchar())!='\n')
     {    *(strn+i)=ch;
          i++;
     }
     *(strn+i)='\0';
     return(strn);
}
```

PROGRAM 14.18   Function to Implement puts( ):

```
void my_puts(char *strn)
{
     while(*strn)
```

```
{
    printf("%c",*strn);
    strn++;
}
printf("\n");
}
```

PROGRAM **14.19**   Function to Implement strlen( ):

```
int slen(char *s)
{   int l=0;
    while(*(s+l))
        l++;
    return(l);
}
```

PROGRAM **14.20**   Function to Implement strcpy( ):

```
char* scopy(char *tr, char *sr)
{
    int i=0;
    while(*(sr+i))
    {   *(tr+i) = *(sr+i);
        i++;
    }
    *(tr+i)='\0';
    return(tr);
}
```

PROGRAM **14.21**   Function to Implement strcat( ):

```
char* sconcat(char *str1, char *str2)
{
    int i=0,j=0;
    while(*(str1+i))
        i++;
    while(*(str2+j))
    {   *(str1+i) = *(str2+j);
        i++;
        j++;
    }
    *(str1+i)='\0';
    return(str1);
}
```

PROGRAM **14.22**   Function to Implement strrev( ):

```
char* srev(char *str)
{    char temp;
     int i=0,j=0;
     while(*(str+i))
          i++;
     i--;
     while(j<i)
     {    temp = *(str+i);
          *(str+i) = *(str+j);
          *(str+j) = temp;
          i--;
          j++;
     }
     return(str);
}
```

PROGRAM **14.23**   Function to Implement atoi( ):

```
int my_a2i(char *strn)
{
     int num = 0;
     while(*strn)
     {
          if(*strn>= '0' && *strn<= '9')
               num = num * 10 + (*strn - 48);
          else
               return(0);
          strn++;
     }
     return(num);
}
```

14.15 ADVANTAGES OF POINTER

Through out the chapter, we discussed how we can declare, initialize and access the pointer variable. We also discussed the advantages of using pointer variables. Here the advantages of pointers are summarized. Using pointers we can

- Return more than one value from a function using call by reference method.
- Pass arrays and strings more efficiently to a function as arguments.
- Allocate memory dynamically.
- Implement Complex data structures such as linked list, trees, and graph.
- Increase execution speed.
- Implement better memory utilization.

14.16 INTERPRETING COMPLICATED POINTER DECLARATIONS

Sometimes pointer declarations are very confusing, especially when function pointer is included in the pointer declarations. To understand these complicated declarations, we have to follow some simple rules. Here is an algorithm.

From the declaration, first find the identifier and consider it as declarant. From this point, we have to start interpreting. start the interpretation as 'Identifier is a/an'.

Next look immediate right of the declarant. If it is an array subscript operator([]), add the string 'array of' with the interpreted string. If function call operator, i.e., '( )' is found, add the string 'function returning'. If some argument type is mentioned within function call operator, then add the string 'expecting', argument list and the string 'and returning' with the interpreted string. Now declarant would be considered along with this operator. Continuing the process, we have to move right until a ')' or ';'is encountered.

If ')' or ';'is encountered move left to the declarant. Now some data type or '*' may be found. If any data type is found add it with the interpreted string. If '*' is found, add the string 'pointer to' with the interpreted string. Now this data type or '*' will be incorporated with the declarant. Move left until '(' is encountered or reached beginning of the string.

If '(' is encountered, again move to right to the declarant. Repeat steps 2 and 3 until the total declaration string read.

Here is an example. Consider the following declaration.

```
int ( * ptr [] ) ( );
```

In the above declaration, ptr is the identifier. So, interpretation starts with 'ptr is a/an'. Now '[]' is its immediate right. Thus the interpreted string becomes 'ptr is an array of' and the declarant becomes 'ptr []'. Next ')' is encountered. So, We have to move left to the declarant and '*' is found. Thus the interpreted string becomes 'ptr is an array of pointer to' and the declarant becomes '* ptr [])'. Next '(' is encountered. Move right to the declarant. Now '( )' is right to the declarant. So, the interpreted string becomes 'ptr is an array of pointer to function returning' and the declarant becomes '(* ptr []) ( )'. Next character is ';'. So, again we move to the left and the datatype int is found. So, the interpreted string becomes 'ptr is an array of pointer to function returning int'.

Here is some simple and complicated declaration of pointer and their interpretations.

int *ptr;	ptr is a pointer to int (i.e., an integer pointer)
int **ptr;	ptr is a pointer to pointer to int
int *ptr[];	ptr is an array of pointer to int
int *ptr( );	ptr is a function returning pointer to int
	(or function returning pointer to integer pointer)
void *ptr( );	ptr is a function returning pointer to void
int (*ptr)( );	ptr is a pointer to function returning int

int (*ptr)(int*, int);	ptr is a pointer to function expecting (int*, int) and returning int
int (*ptr) [];	ptr is a pointer to array of int
int **ptr( );	ptr is a function returning pointer to pointer to int
char ***ptr;	ptr is a pointer to pointer to pointer to char
int (**ptr) [];	ptr is a pointer to pointer to array of int
int (**ptr) ( );	ptr is a pointer to pointer to function returning int
int * (*ptr) [];	ptr is a pointer to array of pointer to int (i.e., a pointer to an array of integer pointers)
int * (*ptr) ( );	ptr is a pointer to function returning pointer to int (i.e., a pointer to a function returning an integer pointer)
int (*ptr) [] [];	ptr is a pointer to array of array of int
int (*ptr[]) [];	ptr is an array of pointer to array of int
int (*ptr[]) ( );	ptr is an array of pointer to function returning int
int (* ptr( )) [];	ptr is a function returning pointer to array of int
int (* ptr( )) ( );	ptr is a function returning pointer to function returning int
char (* (*ptr[]) ( )) [];	ptr is an array of pointer to function returning pointer to array of char
char (* (*ptr( )) []) ( );	ptr is a function returning pointer to array of pointer to function returning char

14.17 PROGRAMMING EXAMPLES

Here are some programming examples to understand the various uses of pointers.

PROGRAM 14.24 **Write a program to declare a two-dimensional array dynamically.**

```
#include<stdio.h>
#include<stdlib.h>
#include<conio.h>
void main()
{    int row,col,i,j;
     int **pntr;
     clrscr();
     printf("Enter No. of Rows :");
     scanf("%d",&row);
     printf("Enter No. of Cols :");
     scanf("%d",&col);

     pntr=(int**)malloc(row*sizeof(int*));
```

```
    for(i=0;i<row;i++)
        *(pntr+i)=(int*)malloc(col*sizeof(int));

    for(i=0;i<row;i++)
    for(j=0;j<col;j++)
    {   printf("Enter data for row %d & col %d:",i+1,j+1);
        scanf("%d",(*(pntr+i)+j));
    }

    for(i=0;i<row;i++)
    {   for(j=0;j<col;j++)
            printf("%d\t",*(*(pntr+i)+j));
        printf("\n");
    }
}
```

Sample output

Enter No. of Rows: 2
Enter No. of Cols: 3
Enter data for row 1 & col 1: 10
Enter data for row 1 & col 2: 11
Enter data for row 1 & col 3: 12
Enter data for row 2 & col 1: 13
Enter data for row 2 & col 2: 14
Enter data for row 2 & col 3: 15

10   11   12
13   14   15

PROGRAM 14.25 Write a function to sort the characters of the string passed to it as argument. Also write a suitable main function to show the use of this function.

```
#include<conio.h>
#include<stdio.h>

void bubble_sort_str( char *c_pntr)
{
    int i, j, n;
    char temp;
    n = strlen(c_pntr);
    for( i = 0; i < n - 1; i++ )
    {
        for( j = 0; j < n - 1 - i; j++ )
        {
            if( * ( c_pntr + j ) >  * ( c_pntr + j + 1) )
            {
                temp =  * (c_pntr + j);
```

```
                    * (c_pntr + j) = * (c_pntr + j + 1);
                    * (c_pntr + j + 1) =  temp;
                }
            }
        }
    }

    void main()
    {
        char string[80];
        puts("Enter Any String :");
        scanf("%s",string);

        bubble_sort_str(string);

        printf("\n\nafter Sorting the string becomes : ");
        puts(string);
    }
```

Sample output

```
Enter Any String: TECHNO
after Sorting the string becomes: CEHNOT
```

PROGRAM 14.26 Write a program to sort a list of strings using pointer.

```
#include<stdio.h>
#include<conio.h>
#define SIZE 20
void sort_list( char* [], int);
void main( )
{
    char *ptr[SIZE];
    int i,num;
    clrscr();
    printf("Enter Number of Strings: ");
    scanf("%d",&num);
    for(i=0;i<num;i++)
    {
        printf("Enter String%d: ",i+1);
        fflush(stdin);
        ptr[i]=(char*)malloc(30);
        gets(ptr[i]);
    }

    sort_list(ptr,num);

    printf("\nSorted List :- ");
    for(i=0;i<num;i++)
        puts(ptr[i]);
}
```

```
void sort_list( char *pntr[], int n)
{
    char *tptr;
    int i,j;
    for( i = 0; i < n - 1; i++ )
    {
        for( j = 0; j < n - 1 - i; j++ )
        {
            if( strcmp(*(pntr+j), *(pntr+j+1)) > 0)
            {
                tptr =  * (pntr + j);
                * (pntr + j) = * (pntr + j + 1);
                * (pntr + j + 1) = tptr;
            }
        }
    }
}
```

Sample output

Enter Number of Strings: 5
Enter String1: Kolkata
Enter String2: Chennai
Enter String3: Pune
Enter String4: Bengaluru
Enter String5: Delhi

Sorted List:
Bengaluru
Chennai
Delhi
Kolkata
Pune

SUMMARY

➤ Pointer is a variable that holds the address of another variable.

➤ The & operator, known as 'address of' operator, returns the base address of a variable.

➤ The * operator, known as 'content at address' or 'indirection' operator, returns the value stored at a particular address.

➤ The data type of a pointer variable indicates the data type of the variable whose address will be stored by the pointer variable.

➤ An integer can be added with a pointer variable, an integer can be subtracted from a pointer variable and one pointer variable can be subtracted from another pointer variable. Multiplication and division are not allowed with the pointer variable.

➤ A function can be invoked either by value or by reference.

➤ When an array is passed to a function, it always follows the call by reference mechanism.

➤ Array of pointers to string is much better than 2D character array to store multiple string of varying length. In 2D character array, there is a lot of wastage of memory.

➤ Void pointer is a special type of pointer that can point to a variable of any data type.

➤ Always initialize the pointer variables before access it.

➤ Initializing Pointer Variable to NULL Value means the pointer is not pointing to anywhere.

➤ Using pointer variable we can allocate memory dynamically.

➤ Function pointer holds the address of a function.

REVIEW EXERCISES

1. What is a pointer variable? How is the pointer initialized?
2. What do you mean by NULL pointer?
3. What are the different characteristics of a pointer?
4. What are the advantages of pointer?
5. "Pass by address refers to the address of a variable passed as an argument to the called function." Justify the statement.
6. What is meant by dynamic memory allocation?
7. Are the expressions *ptr++ and ++*ptr same? Explain.
8. What do you understand by pointer to pointer?
9. Differentiate between malloc ( ) and calloc ( ).
10. What are call by value and call by reference? Explain with examples.
11. Write a function to swap the value of 2 variables without using any additional variable. The change should be permanent.
12. What is the relationship between an array name and pointer?
13. What is the difference between array of pointers and pointer to an array?
14. What is special about void pointer and what are the advantage and disadvantage of using void pointer?
15. How can the indirection operation (*) be used to access multidimensional array element?
16. What are the operations permissible on pointers?
17. Using pointer write a program to find out length of the given string without using strlen ( ) function.
18. Write a program segment that dynamically allocates a two dimensional array of size m × n, where m and n are to be supplied during execution.
19. Write a function that will receive a character string and remove all leading and trailing blanks. Function should return the trimmed string.
20. Write a function to concatenate two strings without affecting the original string. Function should return the concatenated string.

Learn by Quiz – Questions

1. Consider the following code
```
main()
{
    int a[]={ 1,2,3,4,5}, i, *p ;
    for(p=arr+4,i=0; i<5; i++)
    printf("%d", p[-i];);
}
```
Which of the following is true?
   (1) The above code will print 5,4,3,2,1;
   (2) The above code will generate error message as subscript cannot be negative
   (3) The above code will print 1,2,3,4,5

2. Consider the code segment
```
main()
{
    int a[3]={2,4,6},*p[3],i;
    for(i=0; i<3; i++)
    p[i]=a+i;
    for(i=0; i<3; i++)
    printf("%d", *p[i]);
}
```
What will be the output?
   (1) 2,4,6
   (2) Address of a[0], a[1], a[2]
   (3) 6,4,2

3. Consider two form of pointer declaration
   int *a[10] and int (*a)[10];
   Which of the following is true?
   (1) Both the declarations are correct and equivalent.
   (2) The second declaration is incorrect
   (3) Both the declarations are correct but have got different meaning

4. ```
main()
{
    void *p;
    int a=5;
    p=&a;
    printf("%d", *(int *)p);
}
```
What will be the output?
   (1) 5
   (2) Garbage value
   (3) 0

5. Which of the following code segment is incorrect to print the string Kolkata?
   ```
   char s[]="Kolkata", *p;
   ```
   (1) ```
   while (*s!='\0')
   { putchar(*s);
     s++;
   }
   ```

```
(2) for(p=s,i=0; p[i]!='\0';i++)
       putchar(p[i]);
(3) puts(s)
```

6. When an array is passed as an argument to a function, what is actually passed?
   (1) Any element of the array.
   (2) First element of the array.
   (3) Base address of the array.

7. ```
   main()
   {
   int arr[3][3]={11,22,33,44,55,66,77,88,99};
   int index;
   for(index=0; index<3; index++)
   printf("%d", *arr[index]);
   }
   ```

   What will be the output?
   (1) 11,22,33
   (2) Address of arr[0][0], arr[1][0], and arr[2][0] element
   (3) 11,44,77

8. ```
   main()
   {
       int a[3][3]={ 1,2,3,4,5,6,7,,8,9},i;
       int *p[3]={ a[0], a[1],a[2] };
       int **ptr=p;
       for( i=0; i<=2; i++)
       {
           printf("%d", **ptr);
           ptr++;
       }
   }
   ```

   What will be the output?
   (1) 1,4,7
   (2) Address of a[0][0], a[1][0], a[2][0]
   (3) 1,2,3

9. Consider the following declaration
   ```
   int a[3][4];
   ```

   If the starting address of the 2-D array is 100 and int occupies 2 bytes then what will be value of a+1?
   (1) 108
   (2) 102
   (3) 101

10. Consider the following code segment
    ```
    register int i=5;
    int *p;
    p=&i;
    ```

    Which of the following statement is true?
    (1) Compiler will produce error message
    (2) Address of i will be stored in p
    (3) NULL will be stored in p

11. Returning the address of a local variable of auto storage class from a function is
    (1) Syntactically correct but logically incorrect.
    (2) Both syntactically and logically incorrect
    (3) Both syntactically and logically correct.

12. Consider the following code segment.
```
main()
{
    int a[5],i
    for(i=0; i<10; i++)
     a[i]=i ;
    for(i=0; i<10; i++)
    printf("%d", a[i]);
}
```

What will happen if the above program is executed
(1) The program will print 1 2 3 4 5
(2) The program will run and give the output 1 2 3 4 5 6 7 8 9
(3) The program will run but during execution the behavior will be undefined.

13. Consider the following program
```
void f1();
main()
{
    void (*ptr)();
    ptr=f1;
    (*ptr)();
}

void f1()
{
    printf("Hello\n");
}
```

Which of the following statement is true?
(1) The above program will run successfully and gives the output Hello
(2) The above program will run but nothing will be displayed
(3) The above program will generate compilation error

14.
```
main()
{
    char s[]="Kolkata";
    printf("%c", *(&s[2]));
}
```
What will be the output?
(1) Address of s[2]
(2) l
(3) lkata

15.
```
main()
{
    char s[30]="Kolkata", t[30];
    strcpy(t,s+2);
    puts(t);
}
```

What will be the output?
(1) lkata
(2) Kolkata
(3) Kol

16. Consider the following declaration

```
char *s=NULL;
```

If a character string is to be taken input in s then which of the following statement is true?
(1) Memory should be allocated first either by library function malloc or calloc. Starting address of the allocated memory space should be stored inside s then gets(s) can take the input string
(2) By just writing gets(s) can take the input string
(3) Memory should be allocated by calling malloc function only. And then gets(s) can accept the input string

17. Consider the following program

```
main()
{
    int a[]={ 5,15,25,35,45,55};
    int *p;
    for(p=a+5; p>=a; p--)
    printf("%d", a[p-a]);
}
```

What will be the output?
(1) 55,45,35,25,15,5
(2) 5,15,25,35,45,55
(3) 0,0,0,0,0,0

18. Consider the following program

```
main()
{
    int x[]={ 5,15,25,35,45,55};
    static int *pntr[]={ x, x+1, x+2, x+3, x+4};
    int **p_pntr=pntr;
    p_pntr++;
    printf( "%d", *p_pntr-x);
}
```

What will be the output?
(1) 1
(2) 5
(3) 15

19.
```
main()
{
    int **p;
    int m=3, n=5, i,;
    p=( int **)malloc(m*sizeof(int *));
    for(i=0; i<n; i++)
    p[i]=(int *)malloc(n*sizeof(int));
}
```

Which of the following code will work correctly to free all the allocated spaces?
(1) for(i=0; i<m; i++)
    free(p[i]);
    free(p);
(2) free(p)
(3) free(*p);

20. Consider the program code
```
main()
{
    char s[]="Kolkata";
    printf("%s\n%s", s, s+2);
}
```
What will be the output?
(1) Kolkata
    lkata
(2) Kolkata
    Kolkata
(3) Kolkata
    olkata

21. Which of the following assignment will not work?
(1) char name[20];
    name="Hello"
(2) char *name;
    name="Hello";
(3) char name[20]="Hello";

22. Consider the following program code
```
main()
{
    char *s;
    s=(char *)malloc(10);
    strcpy(s,"Hello");
    s=(char *)realloc(s,20);
    puts(s);
}
```
What will be the output?
(1) 00000000000000000000
(2) Garbage string
(3) Hello

23. Consider the program code
```
main()
{
    int *p, i;
    p=(int *)calloc(5,sizeof(int));
    for(i=0; i<5; i++)
    printf("%d", p[i]);
}
```
What will be the output?
(1) Five different addresses
(2) All garbage values
(3) 0 0 0 0 0

24.
```
main()
{
    char s[30], *p;
    p=s;
    strcpy(p,"Hello");
}
```

What will be stored in the array s?
(1) Hello
(2) Nothing will be stored in array s so there will be garbage.
(3) '\0' will be stored in the array s

25. Which one will be called array of pointers to function returning int?
(1) int *p[3]()
(2) int (*p)[3];
(3) int *p[3];

26.
```
main()
{
    int **p;
    int m=3, n=5, i, j;
    p=( int **)malloc(m*sizeof(int *));
    for(i=0; i<n; i++)
    p[i]=(int *)malloc(n*sizeof(int));
}
```

The above program code will
(1) Dynamically allocate an array of 3 integers
(2) Dynamically allocate an array of 5 pointers to integer
(3) Dynamically allocate 2-D array of integer of size 3×5

27. Consider the following declaration
```
    int a[3][3];
```
if p is a pointer variable then which type of declaration of p is correct to write the statement like p=a ?
(1) int (*p)[3];
(2) int *p;
(3) int *p[3];

LEARN BY QUIZ – ANSWERS

Answer Explanations

1. The code will print 5,4,3,2,1. On the code segment the printf function is taking an argument p[−i]. The expression p[−i] will be converted as *(p−i). The pointer variable p is initialized to the address of the 5th element of that array. So p−i is representing an address and *(p−i) is the content.

   If one is sure that p−i is a valid address then writing p[−i] is also valid. If p is an array name then p[−i] will be definitely invalid because array name is the base address of that of array and there is no valid address before the first element of that array.

2. The output is 2,4,6. P has been declared as array of pointers. In the for loop that statement p[i]=a+i will store the address of a[0], a[1] and a[2] to p[0], p[1] and p[2]. So in the second for loop the statement printf("%d", *p[i]) will display he content of a[0], a[1], and a[2] element.

3. Both the declarations are true and have got the different meaning. The first declaration says that a is an array of pointer to integer of 10. And the second declaration says that a is a pointer array of 10 integer. In the first case there are 10 pointers but in the second case there is only one pointer.

4. The output is 5. P has been declared as void pointer which called generic pointer. It means any type of address can be stored inside this pointer variable. Here the a is an integer and address of a has been stored in p. So p pointes to a. But the expression *p cannot access the content of a because p is a void type pointer and does not know how many bytes should be accessed to get the content. The statement (int *)p is typecasting operation means the address stored in p will be converted to integer type address. As a result *(int *)p will give he content of a, i.e., 5.

5. The code segment
```
while (*s!='\0')
{
    putchar(*s);
    s++;
}
```

Is incorrect to print the string Kolkata. Here s has been declared as a character array. The array name s is the base address of that array but it is a constant not a variable. So s+i is a valid expression to get the address of the i-th element but writing s++ is an invalid expression. That is why it is incorrect.

6. When an array is passed as an argument to a function, base address of the array is actually passed. If the array is numeric, the size/no. of elements also has to be passed. Otherwise it is not possible to understand the end of array or how many elements are there.

7. The output is 11,44,77. In case of 2-D array, the array name along with first subscript denotes an address of staring element of a particular row. The subscript gives the row number. So in the program segment arr[index] gives the address of the first element of that array and *arr[index] gives the content of the first element of index-th row.

8. The output will be 1,4,7

In this program a has been declared as 2-D array. In case of 2-D array the expression a[i] denote the starting address of the i-th row. So a[0], a[1], a[2] is the address of the a[0][0], a[1][0], and a[2][0] element which has been stored in array of pointers p, i.e., in p[0], p[1], p[2], respectively. Now p is array name of the array of pointers which is base address of the p array. Naturally, it is a pointer to pointer and has been stored in ptr variable. Now in the for loop ptr is de-referenced twice in the printf function and incremented so it will generate the output 1,4,7.

9. The value of a+1 will be 108. In case of a 2-D array, array name is the starting address of that array but type of the pointer is pointer to array. In the declaration a is a 2-D array of 3 rows and 4 columns. So the array name 'a' is a pointer to array of 4 integers. It means adding 1 to a will cause the instrumentation of a row size that is 8 byte (size of 1 row) in this case. Staring address is 100. So a+1 means 100+1 and the value will be 108.

10. The statement 'Compiler will produce error message' is true. The declaration register int i=5 tells the compiler that the variable i belongs to register storage class means the variable will be placed inside CPU register instead of memory. So the variable will not have any address. As a result &i which gives the address of a variable will generate error message.

11. Returning the address of a local variable of auto storage class from a function is

syntactically correct but logically incorrect. As soon as the program control will return from a function all the local variables belong to storage class auto will be destroyed from the memory. As a result retuning the address a variable which does not exist in the memory when program control returns to the caller will ultimately become meaningless and logically incorrect. But there is no syntactical error.

12. If the program is executed then it will run but during execution the behavior will be undefined.

In C it is the responsibility of the C programmer to check the boundary of the array. This is not done by C compiler. In the program array size is 5 but the program is accessing array location beyond that. When array elements are accessed by writing the expression a[i] it is expanded in the form of *(a+i) by the C compiler. Here array name a is the base address of that array and adding i with it, i.e., a+i will give the i-th element's address. Now in this case a+4 is logically the last valid address for this program as array size is 5. But beyond that address other addresses are not valid for this program. There may be other important information is stored. So accessing those location by writing a+i(for all the values of i greater that 4) for storing data values will not generate any error message but will cause the behavior of the program undefined.

13. The program will run successfully and gives the output **Hello**

In the program f1 is a function which returns nothing that is void return type. ptr is pointer to a function having void return type. Just like array name function name is a pointer to that function. So the statement ptr=f1 will store the address of the function f1 in ptr. So dereferencing the pointer variable by the expression (*ptr)() will invoke the function f1 and will generate output Hello.

14. The output is l. &s[2] is the address of the s[2] location of character array s where the character string 'Kolkata'. So the expression *(&s[2]) is the content of the s[2] location, i.e., l. It can be said that * and & nullifies each other.

15. The output will be lkata. The argument of strcpy is two character pointer. In the program the first argument is the array name t which is the starting address of the destination array. But the second argument is s+2 is the address of the 3rd element of the array s and it is the source array. So, lkata will be copied to array t. Hence the output is lkata.

16. To accept a character string 'Memory should be allocated first either by library function malloc or calloc. Starting address of the allocated memory space should be stored inside s then gets(s) can take the input string'.

Here s is pointer variable. So s can hold address. To accept a string memory locations should be allocated contiguously. Since there is no such memory allocated so memory should be allocated first with malloc or calloc function and starting address of the reserved location will have to be stored in s. Then gets(s) function can store input string.

17. The output will be 55 45 35 25 15 5.

In the program inside the for loop the statement p=a+5 will store the address of a[5] in p. As a is the array name, it is the starting address of the array. Subtraction of two pointers gives an integer value, i.e., no of elements beyond the starting address. So in for loop the expression a[p−a] will become a[5] for the first time and as p is decremented each time so next time a[p−a] will be a[4] and so on. So the output will be 55 45 35 25 15 5.

18. The output will be 1. Here p_pntr is a pointer to pointer points to an integer and pntr is an array of pointers. The base address of the array pntr is assigned to p_pntr. The array of pointers pntr contains the addresses of the integer array x[].

The statement p_pntr++ causes incrimination of p_pntr which points to the nest element of array pntr[], i.e., address of pntr[1]. Now *p_pntr means content at that address, i.e., content of pntr[1] which is address of x[1]. So *p_pntr−1 can be thought as x+1−x. So the value is 1.

19. The code

    ```
    for(i=0; i<m; i++)
    free(p[i]);
    free(p);
    ```

    will work correctly to free all the allocated spaces. In the program first an array of pointers of size 3 will be allocated. Now each pointer of the array of pointer will store the starting address of dynamically allocated array of 5 integers. So to free the total space first 3 array of 5 integers have to be released. This is done with help of for loop. Next array of 3 pointers has to be released. This is done by free(p).

20. The output is

    Kolkata

    lkata

    Using %s format string in printf function it is needed to pass the address of the string to be printed. The addresses being passed to printf function are s and s+2, i.e., base address and the address of 3rd element of the string. Hence the output is Kolkata and lkata. So it can be concluded that with proper use of pointer part of the string can be displayed using printf function.

21. The assignment statement

    char name[20];

    name="Hello";

    will not work.

    Here name has been declared as a character array. So the array name is a pointer to the starting address of that array. But array name is constant not a variable. So the assignment will not work. For an assignment statement left hand side should be variable.

22. The output is Hello

    In this program, s has been declared as character pointer. First malloc function reserved 10 bytes of memory location whose starting address is stored in s. Then the string Hello has been stored in the reserved memory locations by strcpy function. Next realloc function will resize the location to 20. Obviously these are new memory locations but the stating address has been stored in s but the content of the older memory locations will remain intact. So the output will be the string Hello.

23. The output will be 0 0 0 0 0.

    Calloc function can reserve memory locations at the time of execution. The invocation of calloc function will allocate memory locations for five integers and returns the starting address in pointer p. Calloc function initializes all the reserved memory locations with 0 so the output is 0 0 0 0 0.

    If the memory space for five integers is allocated by malloc function then the output will be all garbage values because malloc function, after reserving the memory location does not initialize it with 0 or any other values.

24. The string Hello will be stored in array s. The library function strcpy takes two parameters. First is the destination address where the character string will be stored (copied) and second is the source address from where the character string will be copied. The starting address of array s has been stored in a pointer variable p. Now strcpy(p,"Hello") will copy the source string Hello from the starting location of the destination address. As p contains the string address of array s so in the array he string Hello will be stored.

25. The declaration int *p[3]() tells that p is an array of pointers to function returning integer.

26. The program code will dynamically allocate 2-D array of integer of size 3×5. P has been declared as a pointer to a pointer pointing to an integer. The statement p=(int **)malloc(m*sizeof(int *)); will allocate an array of pointers to integer of size 3 whose staring address will be stored in the pointer variable p. And the next for loop each iteration will create an array of integer of size 5 whose starting address will be stored in p[i]. So finally a 2-D array of integers of size will be allocated in the memory.

27. The declaration int (*p)[3] is correct to write the statement p=a. Here 'a' has been declared as a 2-D array of integer. In case of 2-D array, the array name is considered as the base address of that array but it is treated as a pointer to integer. In the case the size of the two dimension array is 3 by 3. As the column size is 3 so the array name a is considered as a pointer to array of 3 integers. So, if any pointer variable is declared to store it naturally, it has to be a pointer to array of the 3 integers. So the declaration int (*p)[3] is correct and means p is a pointer to array of three integers.

15

Structure

So far the data types that are used in our programs are primitive or basic data types. However, C language provides the facilities to construct our own data types. These are known as user-defined data types. User-defined data type, also known as derived data type is constructed using primitive data types and/or other user-defined data type.

Already we have seen that array is a collection of homogeneous elements. But in real life, we need to store heterogeneous elements that are highly related to each other and thus demands to store as a single logical unit. For example, to store the information about a student, we need to store roll number which is integer, name which is a string, fees may be of type float and so on. Structure helps us to handle this situation.

15.1 STRUCTURE

A structure is a collection of heterogeneous elements. Basically it provides a template to define a set of similar or dissimilar elements under a single name. It helps programmers to group heterogeneous but highly related data elements into a single logical unit. It is a user-defined data type that constructed using primitive data types. To declare a structure, the keyword **struct** is used. The general form to declare a structure the statement is given below:

```
struct structure name
{
    data type     member1;
    data type     member2;
    data type     member3;
    ......
    ......
} ;
```

where **struct** is a keyword to define a structure. The *structure name* is called tag and it specifies the name of the structure being defined. Members of the structure may be of same or different data types. They may be of primitive data type or any derived data type.

A structure to store information about students may be defined as:

```
struct student { int roll;
                 char name[30];
                 float grade_point;
               };
```

The above declaration has not declared any variable. This statement defines a new data type called **struct student**. Once a new structure data type has been defined, we can declare one or more variables of that type. Each variable of this data type will consist of an integer variable named roll, a character array named name and a float variable named grade_point. We can declare the structure variable as,

struct student s1, s2, s3 ;

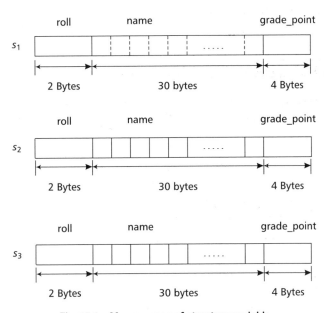

Fig. 15.1   Memory map of structure variable

The variables s1, s2, s3 are declared of the type **struct student** and in memory each variable occupies 2 + 30 + 4 = 36 bytes.

Defining a specific structure and declaring variables of that structure type can be combined in one statement. The declaration looks like:

```
struct student {  int roll;
                  char name[30];
                  float grade_point;
               }  s1, s2, s3;
```

The tag or structure name is optional in definition of a structure. So, the following statement is also perfectly valid statement.

```
struct {  int roll;
          char name[30];
          float grade_point;
       }  s1, s2, s3;
```

The only problem in the above declaration is that we cannot further declare variables of this type in other functions or elsewhere.

Declaration of structure and its variable can be local or global just like other variables. That means we can declare it within main or within any other functions or we can declare it outside of any function definition. Even if we can declare a structure in separate header file and can be included to the different source files according to requirement. If we declare a structure within a function it is accessible within that function only. It cannot be accessed in other functions. If we need to access from other functions also, we have to declare it globally.

15.2 STRUCTURE INITIALIZATION

Like primitive data types or an array we can also initialize structure variables at the time of declaration. The syntax is almost similar to that used to initialize an array. For example,

```
struct student {  int roll;
                  char name[30];
                  float grade_point;
               };
struct student s1 = {5, "Anubhab", 9.2};
struct student s2 = {43, "Sania", 8.9};
```

And obviously we can initialize the structure variable at the time of defining a structure.

```
struct student {  int roll;
                  char name[30];
                  float grade_point;
               }  s1 = {5, "Anubhab", 9.2}, s2 = {43, "Sania", 8.9};
```

15.2.1 Accessing Structure Members

After declaration, we need to access the individual member elements of a structure variable. The dot (.) operator is used to access elements or members of a structure variable. The general form for accessing members of a structure using dot operator is:

```
Structre_variable_name . member_name
```

Considering the previous example, if we want to access the roll of student s1, we have to write

```
s1.roll
```

Similarly, to access name and grade point of s1, we will write

```
s1.name

s1.grade_point
```

So in the previous example, to access the members of the structure variable s2 we have to write,

```
s2.roll

s2.name

s2.grade_point
```

Now these member variables can be accessed as ordinary variable. Values can be assigned, inputs can be taken within these variables, these variables can be used to assign values to other variables, etc. Here is some example.

```
s1.roll = 5;

s1.grade_point = 8.2;
```

The above two statements assigned 5 and 8.2 to the s1.roll and s1.grade_point, respectively. But we cannot use '=' to store some name to the s1.name as name is a character array. So, we have to use strcpy( ) as following:

```
strcpy(s1.name, "Shreya");
```

Similarly to take input we will write:

```
scanf("%d", & s1.roll);

gets(s1.name);

scanf("%f", & s1.grade_point);
```

To print the content of these variables the statements can be written as,

```
printf("%d",s1.roll);

printf("%s",s1.name);

printf("%f",s1.grade_point);
```

To store these values into other variables statements can be written as,

```
int roll_no;

char student_name[30];

float grade;


roll_no = s1.roll;

strcpy(student_name, s1.name);

grade = s1.grade_point;
```

To store these values into other corresponding structure variables statements will be,

```
s2.roll = s1.roll;

strcpy(s2.name, s1.name);

s2.grade_point = s1.grade_point;
```

Here is a complete program to understand the above discussions about structures.

PROGRAM 15.1   Define a structure named student which contains roll no, name and total marks. Using this structure write a program to show the input and output operation on structure variable.

```c
#include<stdio.h>
struct student
    {   int roll;
        char name[30];
        int total;
    };
void main()
    {
        struct student s;

        printf("\nEnter Roll No: ");
        scanf("%d",&s.roll);
        printf("Enter Name : ");
        gets(s.name);
        printf("Enter Total Marks : ");
        scanf("%d",&s.total);

        printf("\nYou entered: ");
        printf("\nRoll : %d", s.roll);
        printf("\nName : %s",s.name);
        printf("\nTotal :%f",s.total);
    }
```

Sample output

```
Enter Roll No: 1
Enter Name: Subhodeep Mukherjee
Enter Total Marks: 98

You entered:
Roll: 1
Name: Subhodeep Mukherjee
Total: 98
```

15.2.2 Operations on Structure Variables

There are only two operators that can be operated on structure variable. These are '='(assignment operator) and '&'(address-of operator). Using the '=' operator the content of one structure variable can be assigned to another variable of same structure type. This is a very useful feature as we need not assign each member of a structure variable to corresponding members of another structure variable.

If s1 and s2 are two structure variables of type struct student, then to assign the content of s1 variable to s2 variable, the statement

```
s2 = s1;
```

is sufficient instead of writing the following sets of statement.

```
s2.roll = s1.roll;

strcpy(s2.name, s1.name);

s2.grade_point = s1.grade_point;
```

Following program illustrate this.

PROGRAM 15.2 Write a program that will interchange the content of two structure variable.

```c
#include<stdio.h>
struct student
    {    int roll;
         char name[30];
         int total;
    };

void main()
    {
         struct student s1, s2, temp;

         printf("\nEnter Information for the First student:- ");
         printf("\nEnter Roll No: ");
         scanf("%d",&s1.roll);
         printf("Enter Name : ");
         gets(s1.name);
         printf("Enter Total Marks : ");
         scanf("%d",&s1.total);

         printf("\nEnter Information for the Second student:- ");
         printf("\nEnter Roll No: ");
         scanf("%d",&s2.roll);
         printf("Enter Name : ");
         gets(s2.name);
         printf("Enter Total Marks : ");
         scanf("%d",&s2.total);
```

```
temp = s1;     /* all the members of s1 are assigned to temp */
s1 = s2;
s2 = temp;

printf("\nAfter interchangeing :");
printf("\nFirst Student: ");
printf("\nRoll : %d", s1.roll);
printf("\nName : %s",s1.name);
printf("\nTotal :%f",s1.total);

printf("\n\nSecond Student: ");
printf("\nRoll : %d", s2.roll);
printf("\nName : %s",s2.name);
printf("\nTotal :%f",s2.total);
}
```

Sample output

Enter Information for the First student:
Enter Roll No: 15
Enter Name: Animesh Roy
Enter Total Marks: 68

Enter Information for the Second student:
Enter Roll No: 23
Enter Name: Bikash Pathak
Enter Total Marks: 73

After interchanging:
First Student:
Roll: 23
Name: Bikash Pathak
Total: 73

Second Student:
Roll: 15
Name: Animesh Roy
Total: 68

15.3 ARRAYS OF STRUCTURES

C does not limit a programmer to storing simple data types inside an array. User-defined structures too can be elements of an array. For example, to store the information of all 60 students in a class, we have to declare an array of type struct student.

```
struct student s[60];
```

The above statement declares an array named **s** which has 60 elements. Each element inside the array is of type struct student. As each structure variable of type struct student occupies 36 (2 + 30 + 4) bytes in memory, size of each element of array s will be 36 and the total size of the array s will be 36 * 60 = 2160 bytes.

Referencing an element in the array is quite simple.

```
s[0].roll
s[0].name
s[0].grade_point...
```

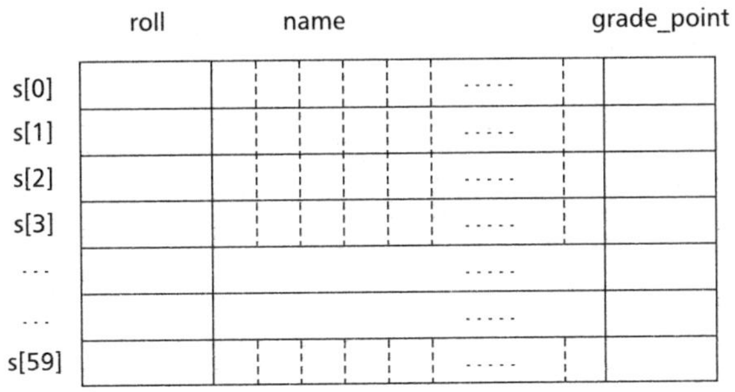

Fig. 15.2 Array of structure

Initialization of structure arrays is similar to initialization of multidimensional arrays:

```
struct student s[10] = {{5, "Anubhab", 9.2}, {43, "Sania", 8.9} };
```

will initialize the first two elements of the array **s** as shown in the following figure.

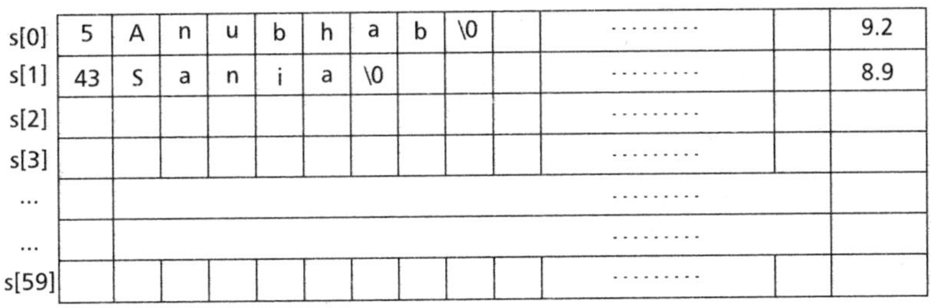

Fig. 15.3 Initialized array of structure s

The following program illustrates how input can be given; elements can be accessed in an array of structure.

PROGRAM 15.3 Write a program to find the highest marks among a set of students and also display his/her name.

```c
#include<stdio.h>
#define SIZE 10

struct student0
    {   int roll;
        char name[30];
        int total;
    };
```

```
void main()
    {   struct student s[SIZE];
        int i,j=0,max=0;
        for(i = 0;i < SIZE; i++)
        {   printf("\nEnter Roll No: ");
            scanf("%d",&s[i].roll);
            printf("Enter Name : ");
            fflush(stdin);
            gets(s[i].name);
            printf("Enter Total Marks : ");
            scanf("%d",&s[i].total);
            if(s[i].total>max)
            {
                max= s[i].total;  /* max stores the highest marks */
                j=i;     /* j stores the corresponding array index */
            }
        }
        printf("\n\nThe details of the Student having the
                                Highest Total Marks:-\n ");
        printf("\nRoll No    : %d",s[j].roll);
        printf("\nName       : %s",s[j].name);
        printf("\nTotal Marks: %d",s[j].total);
    }
```

Sample output

Enter Roll No: 1
Enter Name: Subhodeep Mukherjee
Enter Total Marks: 89

Enter Roll No: 2
Enter Name: Animesh Tarafder
Enter Total Marks: 76

Enter Roll No: 3
Enter Name: Jyoti Sinha
Enter Total Marks: 43

Enter Roll No: 4
Enter Name: Arunangshu Das
Enter Total Marks: 57

Enter Roll No: 5
Enter Name: Oli Debnath
Enter Total Marks: 84

Enter Roll No: 6
Enter Name: Ushashi Chakraborty
Enter Total Marks: 93

Enter Roll No: 7
Enter Name: Priya Roy
Enter Total Marks: 49

Enter Roll No: 8
Enter Name: Aritra Pal
Enter Total Marks: 62

Enter Roll No: 9
Enter Name: Nandita Dey
Enter Total Marks: 77

Enter Roll No: 10
Enter Name: Gautam Dey
Enter Total Marks: 58

The details of the Student having the Highest Total Marks:
Roll No   : 6
Name   : Ushashi Chakraborty
Total Marks : 93

15.4 NESTED STRUCTURES

We can declare one structure within another structure, i.e., C permits nesting of structures. Using this facility complex data types can be created. Only restriction on nesting of structures is that a structure cannot contain a member of own type.

For example, suppose we want to include additional information regarding date of birth of the student in the student structure. As a date consists of three parts – day, month and year – to represent a date, structure is the best option. So, the total requirement can be easily implemented using the nested structure as follows:

```
struct date
    {   int dd;
        int mm;
        int yy;
    };
```

Now using this structure **date** we can add an additional member date of birth which basically stores a date in the structure **struct student**.

```
struct student
    {   int roll;
        char name[40];
        struct date dob;
        float grade_point;
    };
```

The above structure is a nested structure. We can define a structure within another structure directly.

```
struct student
    {   int roll;
        char name[40];
        struct
            {   int dd;
                int mm;
```

```
                      int yy;
             }    dob;
         float grade_point;
    };
```

Both the style of declaring nested structure works same. But the advantage of declaring first one is that the date structure can be used in other purpose also.

If we declare a variable of struct student as,   struct student s1, then we can access the elements of nested structure as,

```
        s1.dob.dd

        s1.dob.mm

        s1.dob.yy
```

The nesting of structures need not be single level depth. A structure can be nested within a structure, which can be nested within another structure and so on – up to any level.

PROGRAM 15.4   Define a structure named employee which contains name, date of birth, date of joining and basic salary of an employee. Write a program using this structure to show the input and output operation on nested structure variable.

```c
#include<stdio.h>

struct date
{    int dd;
     int mm;
     int yy;
};
struct employee
{    char name[30];
     struct date dob;
     struct date doj;
     int basic;
};

void main()
{
     struct employee emp;

     printf("Enter Name : ");
     gets(emp.name);
     printf("Enter Date of Birth (dd/mm/yyyy): ");
     scanf("%d/%d/%d", &emp.dob.dd, &emp.dob.mm, &emp.dob.yy);
     printf("Enter Date of Joining (dd/mm/yyyy): ");
     scanf("%d/%d/%d", &emp.doj.dd, &emp.doj.mm, &emp.doj.yy);
```

```
    printf("Enter Basic Salary : ");
    scanf("%d", &emp.basic);

    printf("\nYou entered: ");
    printf("\nName                    : %s", emp.name);
    printf("\nDateofBirth:%d/%d/%d",emp.dob.dd,emp.dob.mm,emp.dob.yy);
    printf("\nDate of Joining: %d/%d/%d", emp.doj.dd,
                                  emp.doj.mm, emp.doj.yy);

    printf("\nBasic Salary : %d", emp.basic);
}
```

Sample output

    Enter Name: Anirban Debnath
    Enter Date of Birth (dd/mm/yyyy): 27/12/1974
    Enter Date of Joining (dd/mm/yyyy): 15/10/1996
    Enter Basic Salary: 25000

    You entered:
    Name   : Anirban Debnath
    Date of Birth   : 27/12/1974
    Date of Joining : 15/10/1996
    Basic Salary   : 25000

15.5 STRUCTURES AND FUNCTIONS

Like primitive data type and array, any structure variable can be passed as function arguments. When a structure variable is passed as an argument the members of the structure are passed as a whole to the called function. We can pass structure variable to a function using call by value mechanism as well as call by reference. In case of call by value mechanism, all the members of the structure are copied but in case of call by reference only the base address of the structure variable is passed and using that address the members of the structure variable are accessed from the calling function. Passing of structure variable using call by reference mechanism will be discussed in the next section along with the pointer. The following program shows how a structure variable can be passed using call by value mechanism.

PROGRAM 15.5   Define a structure date. Write a function to display a date in the DD/MM/YYYY format.

```
#include<stdio.h>

struct date
{   int dt;
    int mn;
    int yr;
};
```

```
void display(struct date);

void main( )
{    struct date d1;
     printf("Enter Date in the DD/MM/YYYY format : ");
     scanf("%d / %d / %d", &d1.dt, &d1.mn, &d1.yr);
     display(d1);
}

void display(struct date ddt)
{
     printf(" Date : "%d / %d / %d", ddt.dt, ddt.mn, ddt.yr);
}
```

Sample output
Enter Date in the DD/MM/YYYY format: 20/11/1972
Date: 20/11/1972

In the above program, d1 is a structure variable of type **struct date**. It is passed to the function display( ). So, the members of the structure variable, i.e., dt, mn and yr is copied to the structure variable ddt. Thus it prints the same date as the inputted date.

15.6 FUNCTION RETURNING STRUCTURE

As structure is a user defined data type, any function can return any structure variable also. Following program illustrates how a structure variable can be returned.

PROGRAM 15.6 Define a structure date. Write a function to calculate the age of a person.

```
#include<stdio.h>
#include<conio.h>

struct date
{    int dd;
     int mm;
     int yy;
};

struct date  calc_age(struct date, struct date);

void main( )
{    struct date dob, cur_dt, age;
     clrscr( );
     printf("Enter Date of Birth in the DD/MM/YYYY format : ");
     scanf("%d / %d / %d", &dob.dd, &dob.mm, &dob.yy);
```

```
      printf("Enter Current Date in the DD/MM/YYYY format : ");
      scanf("%d / %d / %d", &cur_dt.dd, &cur_dt.mm, &cur_dt.yy);

      age = calc_age(dob, cur_dt);

      printf("\nYour Age is : %d years %d months and %d days",
                                         age.yy, age.mm, age.dd);
}

struct date  calc_age(struct date b_dt, struct date c_dt)
{
      struct date age;
      if(c_dt.dd >= b_dt.dd)
          age.dd = c_dt.dd - b_dt.dd;
      else
      {   age.dd = c_dt.dd +30 - b_dt.dd;
          c_dt.mm--;
      }
      if(c_dt.mm >= b_dt.mm)
           age.mm = c_dt.mm - b_dt.mm;
      else
      {   age.mm = c_dt.mm +12 - b_dt.mm;
          c_dt.yy--;
      }
      age.yy = c_dt.yy - b_dt.yy;

      return(age);
}
```

Sample output
Enter Date of Birth in the DD/MM/YYYY format: 20/11/1978
Enter Current Date in the DD/MM/YYYY format: 12/09/2014

Your Age is: 35 years 9 months and 22 days

Age is not a single value it consists of 3 integers, i.e., day, month and year. But a function cannot return more than one value. Thus in the above program to encapsulate these three values we use the same structure that is used to represent a date. In the function **calc_age**, we individually calculate the days, months and years of the age and stores them in the structure variable, **age** and then return it.

15.6.1 Using typedef keyword

Another important feature of C language is that it provides a scope to the programmers to create an alias name of existing data types. This is possible due to the keyword *typedef*. For example:

```
      typedef unsigned long int ULI;

      ULI roll_no;
```

Here we have typedefined an unsigned long integer as ULI. Now we can use ULI in our program as like any other data type and it will work as unsigned long integer. Variables can be declared using this alias name as shown in above example. Similarly we can typedef a structure too.

```
typedef struct student Student;
```

Then we can use the newly defined data type, as in the following example:

```
Student s1;
```

We can also use the keyword typedef at the time of defining a structure.

```
typedef struct student
{       int roll;
        char name[30];
        int total;
}       Student;
```

Here Student is not a variable of the above structure. The alias name of above structure is defined as Student. So, we can use 'Student' in place of 'stuct student' in the program.

typedef statement is very much useful in the programs where structure is used. When structure variables are declared, formal arguments contain structure variable, we need not write the keyword struct followed by the tag name. We simply use some alias name. Here is an example. The program 15.5 is rewritten here using typedef statement.

PROGRAM 15.7   Define a structure date and rename it using typedef statement. Write a function to display the inputted date.

```
#include<stdio.h>

typedef  struct date
{    int dd;
     int mm;
     int yy;
}    Date;

void display( Date );

void main()
{    Date d1;
     clrscr();
     printf("Enter Date in the DD/MM/YYYY format : ");
     scanf("%d / %d / %d", &d1.dd, &d1.mm, &d1.yy);
     display(d1);
}
```

```
void display( Date dt)
{
    printf(" Date : %d / %d / %d", dt.dd, dt.mm, dt.yy);
}
```

Sample output
Enter Date in the DD/MM/YYYY format: 20/11/1972
Date: 20/11/1972

In the above program at the time of defining the structure its alias name 'Date' is assigned using typedef statement and thus the every occurance of 'struct date' is replaced by the new name 'Date'.

15.7   STRUCTURES AND POINTERS

As we can declare a pointer of any primitive data type, it is possible to declare a pointer of any structure type also. And to pointing to a structure variable we need to assign the base address of a structure variable to the corresponding pointer variable. As a pointer can store the address of corresponding type only, we need to declare the pointer of specific structure type. For example,

```
struct student s, *ptr ;

ptr = &s;
```

So, to access the content of the member elements we have to write,

```
(*ptr).roll

(*ptr).name

(*ptr).total
```

Instead of using these two operators, C provides a single operator called arrow operator(->) to access the content of the member elements of a structure. So, we can write the above statement as,

```
ptr -> roll

ptr -> name

ptr -> total
```

Here is an example that shows how a structure variable can be accessed using pointer.

PROGRAM 15.8   Program to demonstrate the use of structure pointer.

```
#include<stdio.h>
typedef   struct date
{     int dd;
      int mm;
      int yy;
}     Date;
```

```
void display( Date* );

void main()
{    Date d1;
     printf("Enter Date in the DD/MM/YYYY format : ");
     scanf("%d / %d / %d", &d1.dd, &d1.mm, &d1.yy);
     display(&d1);
}

void display( Date *ptr)
{
     printf(" Date : %d / %d / %d", ptr ->dd, ptr ->mm, ptr ->yy);
}
```

Sample output

Enter Date in the DD/MM/YYYY format: 20/11/1972
Date: 20/11/1972

The program 15.7 is rewritten here to show the call by reference mechanism to pass a structure variable.

We can allocate memory dynamically for the structure variables as well as array of structure also. We know, to allocate memory dynamically we have to use malloc( ) function or calloc( ) function. In both cases first we need to declare a pointer variable of the corresponding type. So, to declare an array of structure dynamically first we declare a structure pointer. Next by using malloc( ) or calloc( ) function we will allocate the required memory and then the base address of the allocating place will be assigned to the structure pointer. Following example shows how to declare an array of structure and access the members.

PROGRAM 15.9   **Define a structure Batsman containing Batsman's name, match played and total runs scored. Write a program to store the information of some batsman and list them in descending order of total runs scored. Number of batsman is given as input at run time.**

```
#include<stdio.h>
#include<conio.h>
#include<alloc.h>
typedef struct player
{    char name[30];
     int match;
     int runs;
}    Batsman;
```

```c
void main()
{
    Batsman  *bptr, temp;
    int n,i,j;
    printf("Enter number of batsman: ");
    scanf("%d",&n);
    bptr = (Batsman*)malloc(n*sizeof(Batsman));
    if (bptr==NULL)
        puts("Allocation not possible");
    else
    {
        for(i=0;i<n;i++)              /* Input of information */
        {
            printf("\nEnter information for batsman%d:-", i+1);
            printf("\nEnter Name: ");
            fflush(stdin);
            gets((bptr+i)->name);
            printf("Total number of match played: ");
            scanf("%d",&(bptr+i)->match);
            printf("Total runs scored: ");
            scanf("%d",&(bptr+i)->runs);
        }
        for(i=0;i<n-1;i++)            /* Sorting based on runs  */
        {
            for(j=0;j<n-1-i;j++)
            {
                if((bptr+j)->runs < (bptr+j+1)->runs)
                {
                    temp = *(bptr+j);
                    *(bptr+j) = *(bptr+j+1);
                    *(bptr+j+1) = temp;
                }
            }
        }
        clrscr( );
        printf("List of Batsman");
        printf("\n---------------------------------------------");
        printf("\n Name            Match Played    Runs Scored");
        printf("\n---------------------------------------------");
        for(i=0;i<n;i++)
        {   printf("\n%-30s  %5d  %5d",(bptr+i)->name,
                                (bptr+i)->match,(bptr+i)->runs);
        }
        printf("\n---------------------------------------------");
    }
}
```

Sample output

    Enter number of batsman: 5

    Enter information for batsman1:
    Enter Name: Sourav Ganguly
    Total number of match played: 311
    Total runs scored: 11363

    Enter information for batsman2:
    Enter Name: Rahul Dravid
    Total number of match played: 344
    Total runs scored: 10889

    Enter information for batsman3:
    Enter Name: Sachin Tendulkar
    Total number of match played: 463
    Total runs scored: 18426

    Enter information for batsman4:
    Enter Name: Brian Lara
    Total number of match played: 299
    Total runs scored: 10405

    Enter information for batsman5:
    Enter Name: Ricky Ponting
    Total number of match played: 375
    Total runs scored: 13704

List of Batsman

Name	Match Played	Runs Scored
Sachin Tendulkar	463	18426
Ricky Ponting	375	13704
Sourav Ganguly	311	11363
Rahul Dravid	344	10889
Brian Lara	299	10405

15.8 BIT FIELDS

Structures can contain special members called bit fields. This is used when we store smaller values which require much smaller space compare to 16 bit to store an integer. The data type of these members is either int, unsigned int or signed int. The length of bit fields is specified in terms of bits. A signed bit field should have at least 2 bits (one bit for sign). The general form to declare a member as:

```
data type  member: bit-length
```

Consider the following example.

```
struct student
     {    int roll;
          char sname[40];
          unsigned  sex : 1;
          unsigned  age : 7;
     };
```

the address of bit fields cannot be obtained. So, we cannot take the input to the bit fields using scanf( ). We can store values in the following way:

```
     struct student s;
     scanf("%d %d", &msex, &mage);
     s.sex = msex;
     s.age = mage;
```

But we have to be careful that assigned values should be within the range of their size. The largest value that can be stored is 2^n-1, where n is the bit-length.

Remember that a pointer cannot be used to access bit fields and array of bit fields is not permitted.

Here is a complete program to demonstrate the use of bit fields.

PROGRAM 15.10   Program to demonstrate the use of bit field.

```
#include<stdio.h>
struct student
     {    int roll;
          char name[30];
          unsigned   sex : 1;
          unsigned   age : 7;
     };

void main( )
     {
          struct student s;
          int msex, mage;
          printf("\nEnter Roll No: ");
          scanf("%d",&s.roll);
          printf("Enter Name : ");
          fflush(stdin);
          gets(s.name);
          printf("Enter Sex(0 for Male, 1 for Female): ");
          scanf("%d", &msex);
          s.sex = msex;     /* Assigning value to the bit field sex */
          printf("Enter Age : ");
          scanf("%d", &mage);
          s.age = mage;     /* Assigning value to the bit field age */

          printf("\nYou entered:- ");
```

```
        printf("\nRoll : %d", s.roll);
        printf("\nName : %s",s.name);
        printf("\nSex  : ");
        if(s.sex == 0)
            printf("Male");
        else
            printf("Female");
        printf("\nAge : %d", s.age);
    }
```

S3ample output:
Enter Roll No: 12
Enter Name: Reenu Srivastav
Enter Sex (0 for Male, 1 for Female): 1
Enter Age: 35

You entered:
Roll   : 12
Name : Reenu Srivastav
Sex   : Female
Age   : 35

In the above program, we save 3 bytes of memory as the value of sex and age field is stored in a single byte memory location. Instead of using bit-field if two integer variable is used for sex and age, the structure variable would occupy 36 bytes. But now it occupies just 33 bytes. Thus bit-field helps us to save memory efficiently.

15.8.1 Union

Another user-defined data type is Union. Like structures, Union is also used to group a number of elements of different type and size in single logical unit. But its allocation in memory is different in comparison to structure. While all the members of a structure have their own separate memory, the members of a union share the common space in memory. Thus, in case of union same memory location sometimes may be treated as a variable of one type, and sometimes may be considered as different type. So, in the group of elements if all elements may require at a time, the choice is structure. But every time if any one among different data type is required, not all elements at a time, the choice is union. The syntax to declare a union is almost similar to that of a structure:

```
union sample_union
{   char v1;
    int v2;
    float v3;
}   u1;
```

Each member element in union shares the common memory space. Compiler allocates a chunk of memory which is large enough to hold the largest member of the union. Here, v3 requires 4 bytes which is the largest among members. So, the size of the union variable, u1 will be 4.

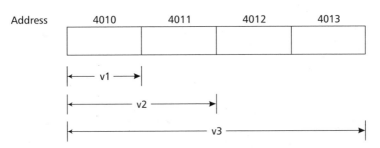

Fig. 15.4 Sharing of memory location by the members of a union

The members of the union variable are also accessed in the same way as structure variable. For example,

u1.v1

u1.v2

u1.v3

Following program illustrates the use of a union.

PROGRAM 15.11 Sometimes grade of marks are given as a grade point which basically is a real number (for example 8.4, 5.6, 9.2, etc) and sometimes it is given as AA, AB+, A++, etc. Write a C program which is able to handle both type of grade.

```c
#include<stdio.h>
union grade
{    char grade_name[4];
     float grade_point;
};

void main( )
{
     union grade grd;
     printf("Enter Grade : ");
     scanf("%s",  grd.grade_name);
     printf("Your Grade is : %s",grd.grade_name);

     printf("\nEnter Grade Point: ");
     scanf("%f",  &grd.grade_point);
     printf("Your Grade Point is : %.2f",grd.grade_point);

     printf("\nThe size of the union variable is : %d", sizeof(grd));
}
```

Sample output
    Enter Grade: A+
    Your Grade is: A+

    Enter Grade Point: 9.21
    Your Grade Point is: 9.21

    The size of the union variable is: 4

The above program shows that a single union variable **grd** is capable to handle a string as well as a float variable but it occupies only 4 bytes in memory which is required to store any one member of the union variable. Thus use of union is very efficient in respect to memory allocation where among a set of data types any one will be get allocated.

As there can be arrays within structures, structures within structures, there can be arrays within unions, unions within structures, unions within union, structures within unions. Consider the following example:

```
struct   st1 {  int a[10];
                char b[15];
             };

struct   st2 {  int c[10];
                float d[5];
             };

union   un1  {  struct st1 s1;
                struct st2 s2;
             };
```

here un1 is a union of structures. Again,

```
union   uni1 {  int p[10];
                char q[15];
             };

union uni2  {  int r[10];
               float s[5];
            };

struct   st_un1 { union uni1 u1;
                  union uni1 u1;
                };
```

here st_un1 is a structure of unions. Again, we can combine both of them.

```
struct   st_un2 { struct st1 su1;
                  union uni1 u2;
                };

union   st_un3  { struct st1 su2;
                  union uni1 u3;
                };
```

In the above example st_un2 is a structure containing structure and union both as member element and st_un3 is a union containing structure and union both as member element.

PROGRAM 15.12 **Define a structure named student which contains registration number, name and grade. Grade may be alphabetical grade or grade point. Write a C program that will store the information of students having different type of grade.**

```c
#include<conio.h>
#include<stdio.h>
#include<ctype.h>

typedef union grade
{    char grade_name[4];
     float grade_point;
}    Grade;

typedef struct student
{    int reg_no;
     char name[30];
     char grade_indicator;
     Grade grd;
}    Student;

void main( )
{    Student s[3];
     int i; float gr;
     printf("Enter Information for students:-\n");
     for(i=0;i<3;i++)
     {    printf("Enter Registration No: ");
          scanf("%d",&s[i].reg_no);
          printf("Enter Name: ");
          fflush(stdin);
          gets(s[i].name);
          printf("What is your Grade? Alphabetical Grade or Grade Point?");
          printf("\nFor Alphabetical Grade Press A");
          printf("\nFor Grade Point Press G : ");
          scanf("%c",&s[i].grade_indicator);
          if(toupper(s[i].grade_indicator)=='A')
                    /* grade_indicator decides which type of value */
          {         /* will be stored within the union */
               printf("Enter Alphabetical Grade : ");
               scanf("%s", s[i].grd.grade_name);
          }    else
               {    printf("Enter Grade Point: ");
                    scanf("%f", &gr);
                    s[i].grd.grade_point=gr;
               }
     }
}
```

```
            clrscr();
            printf("List of students:-");
            for(i=0;i<3;i++)
            {   printf("\n Registration No: %d", s[i].reg_no);
                printf("\nName : %s", s[i].name);
                if(toupper(s[i].grade_indicator)=='A')
                    printf("\nGrade : %s", s[i].grd.grade_name);
                else
                    printf("\nGrade : %.2f", s[i].grd.grade_point);
            }
    }
```

Sample output

Enter Information for students:
Enter Registration No: 2561
Enter Name: Sreyashkar Mukherjee
What is your Grade? Alphabetical Grade or Grade Point?
For Alphabetical Grade Press A
For Grade Point Press G: A
Enter Alphabetical Grade: AA

Enter Registration No: 2562
Enter Name: Moumita Das
What is your Grade? Alphabetical Grade or Grade Point?
For Alphabetical Grade Press A
For Grade Point Press G: G
Enter Alphabetical Grade: 8.62

Enter Registration No: 2563
Enter Name: Amitava Dhar
What is your Grade? Alphabetical Grade or Grade Point?
For Alphabetical Grade Press A
For Grade Point Press G: A
Enter Alphabetical Grade: A+

List of students:

Registration No : 2561
Name   : Sreyashkar Mukherjee
Grade   : AA
Registration No : 2562
Name   : Moumita Das
Grade   : 8.62
Registration No : 2563
Name   : Amitava Dhar
Grade   : A+

15.8.2 Enumerated Data Type

Enumerated data type is another user defined data type by which we can define a group of named integer constants. An enumeration type declaration provide us an enumeration tag and under this tag defines set of named integer constants which are known as "enumeration set," "enumerator constants," "enumerators," or "members". Enumeration type variables store any one of the defined values of the corresponding enumeration set. As the enumerator constants are always of type integer, they can be used in those situations where any integer expression is used. Its definition is similar to structure or union. It is defined with the keyword enum. The syntax is:

```
enum identifier { enumerator-list }
```

EXAMPLE 15.1

```
enum COLOUR   {    Violet,
                   Indigo,
                   Blue,
                   Green,
                   Yellow,
                   Orange,
                   Red
              }    vibgyor;
```

The above example defines an enumeration type named COLOUR and declares a variable named vibgyor of that type.

The value 0 is associated with Violet by default. The remaining constants are initialized with the values 1 through 6 by default. Thus Indigo will be associated with 1, Green will be associated with 3 and so on.

A value from the set COLOUR is assigned to the variable favorite_colour by the statement:

```
enum COLOUR favorite_colour;
favorite_colour = Indigo;
```

We can directly assign integer values to enumerated variable. Thus the assignment,

```
favorite_colour = 1;
```

is same as

```
favorite_colour = Indigo;
```

It is possible to assign values explicitly to the enumeration constants. This also affects following constants in the list in initialization. Assigning same values to more than one constant is also allowed. For example:

```
enum sample { m, n, o=30, p=20, q, r, s=20, t };
```

Here, 0 will be assigned to m, 1 to n, 30 to o, 20 to p, 21 to q, 22 to r, 20 to s and 21 will be assigned to t.

PROGRAM 15.13   Define a enumeration data type named Boolean to handle two Boolean value False and True. Use it to write a function that check whether a number is odd or even.

```
typedef enum bool{False, True} Boolean;
                        /* 0 will be assigned to False, 1 to True */
Boolean isOdd(int n)
{
    if(n%2 == 0)
        return False;
    else
        return True;
}

void main()
{
    int num;
    printf("Enter any number:");
    scanf("%d",&num);
    if(isOdd(num))
        printf("The Inputted number is an Odd number");
    else
        printf("The Inputted number is an Even number");
}
```

Sample output

Enter any number: 26
The Inputted number is an Even number

15.9   PROGRAMMING EXAMPLES

Here are some programming examples to understand the various uses of structures.

PROGRAM 15.14   Write a 'C' program that implements a structure person that would contain person name, date_of_ joining & salary.

```
#include<conio.h>
#include<stdio.h>
struct person

{    char name[30];
     char doj[11];
      int salary;
};

void main()
{    struct parson p;
```

```
    int i,j=0,max=0;
    clrscr();
    printf("Enter Name : ");
    fflush(stdin);
    gets(p.name);
    printf("Enter Date of joining : ");
    fflush(stdin);
    gets(p.doj);
    printf("Enter Salary : ");
    scanf("%d",&p.salary);

    printf("\n\nThe details of the Person :-\n ");
    printf("\nName : %s",p.name);
    printf("\nDate of Joining : %s",p.doj);
    printf("\nSalary : %d",p.salary);
}
```

PROGRAM 15.15 Define a structure called 'employee', to store information about an employee (e-no,e-name,basic-pay, DA, HRA and gross pay). Write a program to input the e-no,e-name and basic-pay of several employees. The program will calculate the DA (65% of basic), HRA (15% of basic) and gross pay (basic + DA + HRA) of all employees. Also display the details of the employee having the highest salary.

```
#include<conio.h>
#include<stdio.h>
#define SIZE 15

struct employee
{   int e_no;
    char e_name[30];
    int basic_pay;
    float da,hra,gross;
};

void main( )
{   struct employee emp[SIZE];
    int i,j=0,max=0;
    clrscr();
    for(i=0;i<SIZE;i++)
    {   printf("\nEnter Employee No: ");
        scanf("%d",&emp[i].e_no);
        printf("Enter Name : ");
        fflush(stdin);
        gets(emp[i].e_name);
        printf("Enter Basic Pay : ");
```

```
        scanf("%d",&emp[i].basic_pay);
        emp[i].da    = emp[i].basic_pay * 0.65;
        emp[i].hra = emp[i].basic_pay * 0.15;
        emp[i].gross = emp[i].basic_pay + emp[i].hra + emp[i].da;
        if(emp[i].gross>max)
        {    max=emp[i].gross;   /*max stores the highest gross salary*/
             j=i;         /* j stores the corresponding array index */
        }
    }
    printf("\n\nThe details of the Employee having the
                                    Highest Salary :-\n ");
        printf("\nEmployee No      :    %d",emp[j].e_no);
        printf("\nEmployee Name    :    %s",emp[j].e_name);
        printf("\nBasic Pay        :    %d",emp[j].basic_pay);
        printf("\nDA               :    %f",emp[j].da);
        printf("\nHRA              :    %f",emp[j].hra);
        printf("\nGross Pay        :    %f",emp[j].gross);
}
```

PROGRAM 15.16 Write a C program to take two distances, in the form of feet and inch and store them in two structure variables. Now calculate the sum of two distances and display it.

```
#include <stdio.h>
struct Distance
{
    int ft;
    float inch;
}    dist1,dist2,sum;

int main()
{    printf("Enter information for 1st distance\n");
    printf("Enter feet: ");
    scanf("%d",&dist1.ft);
    printf("Enter inch: ");
    scanf("%f",&dist1.inch);
    printf("\nEnter information for 2nd distance\n");
    printf("Enter feet: ");
    scanf("%d",&dist2.ft);
    printf("Enter inch: ");
    scanf("%f",&dist2.inch);
    sum.ft=dist1.ft+dist2.ft;
    sum.inch=dist1.inch+dist2.inch;
```

```
        if (sum.inch>=12.0)   /* If inch is greater than or equals to 12,
                            changing it to feet. */
        {   sum.inch=sum.inch-12.0;
                ++sum.ft;
        }
        printf("\nSum of distances=%d\' %.1f\"",sum.ft,sum.inch);
        return 0;
}
```

Sample output
Enter information for 1st distance
Enter feet: 5
Enter inch: 7.32
Enter information for 2nd distance
Enter feet: 6
Enter inch: 5.2
Sum of distances=12' 0.52"

PROGRAM 15.17 Write a C program to calculate the difference between two time periods. The two time periods will be stored within two variables. Perform this task using a function.

```
#include <stdio.h>
typedef struct time
{   int sec;
    int min;
    int hrs;
}   TIME;

void time_gap(TIME, TIME, TIME *);

void main()
{   TIME tm1, tm2, differ;
    printf("Enter start time: \n");
    printf("Hours, minutes and seconds respectively: ");
    scanf("%d%d%d",&tm2.hrs,&tm2.min,&tm2.sec);

    printf("Enter stop time: \n");
    printf("Hours, minutes and seconds respectively: ");
    scanf("%d%d%d",&tm1.hrs,&tm1.min,&tm1.sec);

    time_gap(tm1,tm2,&differ);

    printf("\nTimeDifferenceis:%d:%d:%d- ",tm1.hrs,tm1.min,tm1.sec);
    printf("%d:%d:%d ",tm2.hrs,tm2.min,tm2.sec);
    printf("= %d:%d:%d\n",differ.hrs,differ.min,differ.sec);
}
```

```
void time_gap(TIME tm1, TIME tm2, TIME *diff)
{
    if(tm2.sec>tm1.sec)
    {    --tm1.min;
         tm1.sec+=60;
    }
    diff->sec=tm1.sec-tm2.sec;

    if(tm2.min>tm1.min)
    {    --tm1.hrs;
         tm1.min+=60;
    }
    diff->min=tm1.min-tm2.min;
    diff->hrs=tm1.hrs-tm2.hrs;
}
```

Sample output

Enter start time:
Enter hours, minutes and seconds respectively: 8 25 20

Enter stop time:
Enter hours, minutes and seconds respectively: 11 35 52

Time difference is: 11:35:52 − 8:25:20 = 3:10:32

PROGRAM 15.18   Write a function to increment a date by one day. Using this function write a program to print tomorrow's date. Today's date will be taken as Input.

```
#include<conio.h>
#include<stdio.h>

struct date
{    int dd;
     int mm;
     int yy;
}    Date;

void increment(Date *d);

void main()
{
    Date d;
    clrscr();
    printf("Enter Today's Date :- ");
    printf("\nEnter the day: ");
    scanf("%d", &d.dd);
    printf("Enter the month: ");
    scanf("%d", &d.mm);
    printf("Enter the year: ");
```

```
        scanf("%d", &d.yy);
        increment(&d);
        printf("Tomorrow is: %d/%d/%d", d.dd, d.mm, d.yy);
}

void increment(Date *d)
{
        int day, month, year;
        int arr[13]={0,31,28,31,30,31,30,31,31,30,31,30,31};
                                    /* Storing last date of each month */
        day=d->dd;
        month=d->mm;
        year=d->yy;
        if(year%400==0 || (year % 100 !=0 && year%4==0)
        {                                   /* Checking for leap year */
            arr[2]=29;
        }
        if(day==arr[month])
        {   day=1;
            month=month+1;
        }
        else
        {
            day=day+1;
        }
}
```

Sample output

Enter Today's Date:
Enter the day: 31
Enter the month: 12
Enter the year: 2014

Tomorrow is: 1/1/2015

SUMMARY

➤ A structure is a collection of heterogeneous elements.

➤ The elements of a structure variable are accessed using a dot (.) operator.

➤ An array can be a member of a structure as well as a structure can be a member of an array, i.e., an array of structure can be formed.

➤ One structure can be declared within another structure. It is known as nesting of structures.

➤ Structure variables can be passed as function arguments as well as a function can return a structure variable.

➤ When a structure variable is passed as function arguments, it can be passed as call by value and/or call by reference mechanism.

➤ typedef statement does not create new data type; it renames any existing datatype.

➤ Arrow operator(->) is used to access the member elements of a structure when it will be accessed by pointer.

➤ A structure can define bit-field which is a set of adjacent bits. Bit fields are used for efficient memory management.

➤ Members of Union share the same storage.

➤ Enumerated data type is used to create named integer constants.

➤ Structure, Union, Enumerated data type all are user-defined data types.

REVIEW EXERCISES

1. What are the user defined data types? Explain briefly.

2. Which of the user defined data types store(s) different types of data in a single location?

3. What is structure? How a structure member accessed?

4. What is an array of structures described with an example?

5. What is the difference between arrays within a structure and the array of structure?

6. What is the difference between array and structure?

7. How the structure members are accessed with the corresponding pointer variable?

8. What is union? How a union member accessed?

9. Compare and contrast between structure and union in C.

10. What is the importance of typedef statement?

11. What is enumeration variable? What is the advantage of using enumeration variable?

12. Define a structure Account containing account number, Customer's name, Branch name and balance amount. Write a program to store the information of bank account holders and prints the list of customers for the given branch.

13. Define a structure Product containing Product Code, Description, Unit of measurement, Balance quantity and reorder level. Using this structure write a function that will display the list of items whose balance quantity is less than its reorder level.

14. Define a structure complex that would contain two parts – real and imaginary. Write a menu driven program to perform the following tasks:

a. Add two complex numbers.

b. Subtract one complex number from another.

c. Multiply two complex numbers.

15. Define a structure **Address** containing house number, street, city, state and pin code. Define a nested structure **Student** containing student's name, father's name, address. Use the above Address structure to store student's address.

LEARN BY QUIZ – QUESTIONS

1. Consider the following program segment:
```
struct accounts
{
    int acc_no;
```

```
      char holder_name[40];
      float balance;
};
struct accounts a;
scanf("%d", &a.acc_no); /* line number 1 */
scanf("%s", &a.holder_name); /* line number 2 */
scanf("%f", &a.balance); /* line number 3 */
```

Which & is not required?
(1) /* line number 1 */
(2) /* line number 2 */
(3) /* line number 3 */

2. Structure elements of a structure variable are accessed using
   (1) . (dot) operator
   (2) -> (arrow) operator
   (3) ^ (carat) operator

3. structure is used to ____
   (1) combine dissimilar data types into a single entity
   (2) combine similar data types in single entity
   (3) Create different entities in single declaration.

4. Which of the following variable declaration is correct?
   (1) `struct account_info`
   ```
   {   int accno;
       char holder_name[40];
       int balance;
       char holder_address[200];
   }; struct account_info a1, a2;
   ```
   (2) `struct account_info`
   ```
   {   int accno;
       char holder_name[40];
       int balance;
       char holder_address[200];
   }  struct account_info p1, p2;
   ```
   (3) `struct account_info`
   ```
   {   int accno;
       char holder_name[40];
       int balance;
       char holder_address[200];
   }; account_info x1, x2;
   ```

5. Which of the following variable declaration is correct?
   (1) `struct account_info`
   ```
   {   int accno;
       char holder_nm[40];
       int bln;
       char holder_address[200];
   }  a1, a2;
   ```
   (2) `struct account_info`
   ```
   {   int accno;
       char holder_nm[40];
       int bln;
       char holder_address[200];
   }; x1, x2;
   ```

```
(3) struct account_info p1, p2
    {  int accno;
       char holder_nm[40];
       int bln;
       char holder_address[200];
    };
```

6. Which of the following variable declaration is correct?
   ```
   (1) struct
       {  int acc_no;
          char holder_name[80];
          float balance;
          char holder_address[200];
       } a1, a2;
   (2) typedef struct p1
       {  int acc_no;
          char holder_name[80];
          float balance;
          char holder_address[200];
       } p2;
   (3) struct x1
       {  int acc_no;
          char holder_name[80];
          float balance;
          char holder_address[200];
       };
   ```

7. Elements of structure variable are kept in memory_____
   (1) in contiguous locations
   (2) contiguously or in scattered way decided by compiler.
   (3) contiguously or in scattered way decided by programmer.

8. Which of the following is correct declaration of array of structure?
   (1) struct employee knowledge[10];
   (2) struct employee knowledge;
   (3) struct employee[10] knowledge;

9. struct acnt_info
   ```
   {  int accno;
      char holder_nm[40];
      int balance;
      char holder_address[200];
   } knowledge[10];
   ```
   which of the following is correct for accessing account balance of third account?
   (1) struct knowledge.balance[2]
   (2) account_info[2].balance
   (3) knowledge[2].balance

10. Which of the following statement is correct?
    (1) A structure variable can be assigned to another structure variable of same type.
    (2) A structure variable cannot be assigned to another structure variable of same type; we have to copy element by element.
    (3) A structure variable can be assigned to another structure variable of same type if all of its elements are integer.

11. To access structure elements through a pointer the operator used is
    (1) -> (arrow) operator
    (2) . (dot) operator
    (3) ^ (carat) operator

12. Which of the following is incorrect declaration of nested structure variable?
    (1)
```
struct engine
{  int displacement;
   char fueltype;
};
struct car1
{  char make[30];
   char model_name[30];
   struct engine eng;
}; struct car1 mycar1;
```
    (2)
```
struct car2
{  char make[30];
   char model_name[30];
   struct engine
   {  int displacement;
      char fueltype;
   } eng;
};
struct car2 mycar2;
```
    (3)
```
struct engine
{  int displacement;
   char fueltype;
};
struct car3
{  char make[30];
   char model_name[30];
   engine eng;
}; struct car3 mycar3;
```

13. Given a nested structure variable declaration
```
struct point
{  int xco;
   int yco;
};
struct rectangle
{  struct point startp;
   struct point endp;
   int color;
} rec1;
```
    which of the following assignment is correct?
    (1) rec1.startp.xco=10;
    (2) rec1.(startp.xco)=10;
    (3) rec1.startp(xco)=10

14. Memory consumed by a structure variable is _____
    (1) sum of memory consumed by all elements
    (2) largest of memory consumed by all elements
    (3) smallest of memory consumed by all elements

15. Memory consumed by a union variable is _____
    (1) smallest of memory consumed by all elements
    (2) sum of memory consumed by all elements
    (3) largest of memory consumed by all elements

16. Which of the following is true about passing structure variable to a function?
    (1) can be passed as ordinary variable
    (2) have to be passed by reference
    (3) The elements have to be sent individually.

17. What will be output of the following program segment if a 16 bit compiler is used?

```
    union test
    {  int knowledge;
       char factor[2];
    }  x;
x.knowledge= 519;
printf("%d", x.factor[0]);
printf("%d", x.factor[1]);
```

    (1) 72
    (2) 27
    (3) 519

18. Which of the following declaration is wrong?

    (1)
```
typedef struct stud_struct
{  int roll;
   char name[80];
}  student;
struct student a,b;
```

    (2)
```
typedef struct stud_struct
{  int roll;
   char name[80];
}  student;
student c,d;
```

    (3)
```
typedef struct
{  int roll;
   char name[80];
}  student;
student e,f;
```

19. Consider the following declaration:

```
typedef struct pers
{  char name[80];
   float salary;
}  person[10];
person vivek;
```

    What is true about vivek?
    (1) vivek is a 10 element array of structures of type pers
    (2) the declaration will give compilation error.
    (3) vivek is a structure type variable of type pers.

20. Consider the following declaration:

```
typedef struct
{int day, mnth, yr;}date;
typedef struct
{  char name[80];
```

```
      date dob;
   } person;
   person x;
   person *y=&x;
```
which of the following assignment is correct?
(1) y->dob.day=5;
(2) y.dob->day=5;
(3) y->dob->day=5;

21. Which of the following operation is legal?
    (1) assigning structure variable to another structure variable of same type.
    (2) adding two structure variables of same type.
    (3) comparing two structure variable by == operator.

22. Which of the following operation is illegal?
    (1) comparing two union variable by == operator.
    (2) assigning union variable to another union variable of same type.
    (3) Extracting address of a union variable by address_of(&) operator.

23. Which of the following process of copying string is not legal?
    (1) `char a[30]="knowledge";`
        `char b[30];`
        `b=a;`
    (2) `char a[30]=" knowledge ";`
        `char b[30];`
        `strcpy(b,a);`
    (3) `struct str`
        `{ char s[30];`
        `} x={"knowledge"};`
        `struct str y;`
        `y=x;`

24. Consider the following declaration:
    ```
    union flag_id{
    int size;
    char colour;
    }
    struct {
    char country;
    union flag_id fid;
    int date;
    } flags;
    ```
    to assign a colour to flags, the correct statement would be
    (1) flags.fid.colour='B';
    (2) flags.colour='B';
    (3) Flags.i.colour='Blue';

25. Which of the following option is true in respect to the following statement?
    NurserySchool.Nursery.Student=5;
    (1) Nursery is nested within the structure NurserySchool
    (2) The structure NurserySchool is nested within the structure Nursery
    (3) The structure Student is nested within the structure Nursery

26. Which of the following is true about the following statement?
    ```
    struct s
    {int i; float f; };
    ```

(1) it defines a structure type s but no memory is allocated to it as no variable of type s is declared here.

(2) It tells the compiler to reserve the space for its data member i and f.

(3) s is a structure type variable having two elements i and f.

27. What will be the output?

```c
#include<string.h>
#include<stdio.h>
struct test{char s[10];};
void my_func(struct test temp)
{
strcpy(temp.s,"factor");
}
void main()
{
struct test temp;
strcpy(temp.s,"knowledge");
printf("%s", temp.s);
my_func(temp);
printf("%s", temp.s);
}
```

(1) knowledgeknowledge

(2) knowledgefactor

(3) knowledgeknowledgefactor

28. Consider the following declaration

```c
union un{
int x;
char ch;
float f;
} u;
```

if the size of integer, floating point and character variable s are 2bytes, 4 bytes and 1 byte respectively then the size of the variable u is

(1) 4 bytes

(2) 7 bytes

(3) 14 bytes

29. Consider the following declaration:

```c
struct s
{
int p;
char q[30];
};
union un{
int x;
char ch;
float f;
struct s us;
} u;
```

if the size of integer, floating point and character variable s are 2bytes, 4 bytes and 1 byte respectively then the size of the variable u is

(1) 30bytes

(2) 32 bytes

(3) 39bytes

30. Identify the most appropriate sentence to describe union
    (1) union contains members of different data types which share the same storage area in memory.
    (2) unions are like structures
    (3) unions are less frequently used in programs

31. Which of the following is true
    (1) structure can be a member of union and vice-versa.
    (2) union cannot be member of a structure
    (3) structure cannot be member of a union

32. Which of the following is true?
    (1) A global anonymous union must be static.
    (2) A local anonymous union must be static.
    (3) A local anonymous union may be external.

33. Consider the following declaration:
    enum Player{Sachin, Sourav, Laxman, Rahul, Kumble};

    what will be the value of Sourav?
    (1) 1
    (2) 2
    (3) the string "Sourav"

34. Consider the following declaration:
    enum myenum{m, n, o, p=20, q, r, s=20, t};
    What will be the value of t?
    (1) 21
    (2) 7
    (3) garbage

35. What is the purpose of enum?
    (1) Good alternative of multiple #define
    (2) creating new data type
    (3) Alternative to integer variable declaration with initialization.

36. Which of the following enum declaration is correct?
    (1) enum Player{Sachin, Sourav, Laxman, Rahul, Kumble};
    (2) enum Player[Sachin; Sourav; Laxman; Rahul; Kumble];
    (3) enum Player(Sachin, Sourav, Laxman, Rahul, Kumble);

37. Which of the following enum declaration is wrong?
    (1) enum Days[Sunday,Monday,Tuesday] ;
    (2) enum Days{Sunday,Monday,Tuesday };
    (3) enum {Sunday,Monday,Tuesday };

38. Which one of the following is used to give a new name to a built-in or pre-defined data type?
    (1) typedef
    (2) int
    (3) Float

39. What does the declaration typedef int BYTE; mean?
    (1) BYTE is given a new name for the built-in data type int.
    (2) int is a new name against built in data type BYTE
    (3) A complete new data type BYTE is created.

LEARN BY QUIZ – ANSWERS

Answer Explanations

1. & sign in the statement scanf("%s", &a.holder_name); /* line number 2 */ is not required. scanf() function takes address of the variable where input value has to be stored. a.holder_ name itself is the starting address of the character array holder_name inside structure variable a. So we should write a.holder_name instead of &a.holder_name.

2. Structure elements of a structure variable are accessed using the (.) dot operator.

   The -> operator is used to access elements of a structure using a structure pointer.

   Example:
   ```
   struct demo
   {  int knowledge;
      char factor;
   }  x, *y;
   y=&x;
   x.knowledge=5;
   x.factor='a';
   y->knowledge=10;
   y->factor='b';
   ```

3. Structure is used to combine dissimilar data types into a single entity.

   Example:
   ```
   struct account_info
   {  int acc_no;
      char holder_name[40];
      float balance;
      char holder_address[200];
   };
   ```

   Here account number, holder name, account balance and holder address have different data types but they are merged in a single data type named account_info.

4. The declaration of structure variable a1 and a2 is correct.

   in the declaration of structure variable p1 and p2 the structure declaration should be terminated with a semicolon.

   in the declaration of structure variable x1 and x2 the variable declaration should be preceded by the struct keyword, i.e., it should be struct account_info x1, x2;

5. The declaration of structure variable a1 and a2 is correct. Here a1 and a2 is declared along with the structure declaration. If some other variable say x of type account_info is required to be declared somewhere else in the program then we have to write struct account_info x;

6. The declaration of structure variable a1 and a2 is correct. As we are declaring a1 and a2 along with the structure, giving a name to the structure like
   ```
   struct
   {  int acc_no;
      char holder_name[80];
      float balance;
      char holder_address[200];
   }  a1, a2;
   ```

   is not required but later in other places of the program other variable of same type cannot be declared as the structure has no name.

In 2nd declaration p2 is not a variable; it is the alias name of the structure.

7. Elements of structure variable are kept in memory in contiguous locations

8. struct employee knowledge[10]; is the correct declaration of array of structure. Here knowledge is a 10 element array of structure type employee.

9. knowledge[2].balance refers to account balance of third account.

10. A structure variable can be assigned to another structure variable of same type as it can be done to other variables of built in data types.

   Example:
```
struct stud
{  int roll;
   char name[80];
};
struct stud a, b={2, "ram sharma"};
   a=b;
```

11. To access structure elements through a pointer the -> (arrow) operator is used.

   Example:
```
struct demo
{  int knowledge;
   char factor;
}  x, *y;
y=&x;
y->knowledge=10;
y->factor='b';
```

12. The declaration of car1 is correct. Here first a structure type engine is declared.
```
struct engine
{  int displacement;
   char fueltype;
};
```
Then in the structure type declaration of car1 a structure type variable eng of type engine is included by:
```
struct engine eng;
```
Declaration of car2 is also correct. It is another form of declaring nested structure.

The incorrect declaration is car3 as struct keyword is missing in declaring the variable of struct engine in nested structure.

13. rec1.startp.xco=10; is correct.

rec1.startp will access the structure(point) type variable startp as rec1 is a structure type variable of type rectangle which has a member named startp.

To access the integer element xco of the structure (point) type variable startp we write startp.xco.

So combining the two we get rec1.startp.xco.

14. Memory consumed by a structure variable is sum of memory consumed by all elements.
   Example:
```
struct demo
{  int knowledge;
   char factor;
}  x;
```
here size of x will be 2+1=3 bytes in a 16 bit compiler.

15. Memory consumed by a union variable is largest of memory consumed by all elements.

    Example:

```
unionemo
{  int knowledge;
   char factor;
}  x;
```

Here size of x will be 2 byte as largest element is knowledge being an integer.

16. Structure variable can be passed as ordinary variable to a function and it will be pass-by-value. No special syntax is required to send structure variable to a function.

17. The output will be 72.

    Binary equivalent of 519 in 16 bit is 0000001000000111. This will be stored in two bytes. 00000010 in one byte and 00000111 in another byte. The C compiler will put 00000111 in first location of memory allocated for variable x and 00000010 in the second location. So x.factor[0] will be equal to 00000111(decimal 7) and x.factor[1] will be equal to 00000010(decimal 2). So the output will be 72.

    Note that a if 32 bit number is stored at memory location say 0X2000 then it will be stored as follows:

```
                                          1010101  0X2003
                                          1111111  0X2002
                                          0000000  0X2001
   1010101 1111111 0000000 1111000    →    1111000  0X2000
```

18.
```
typedef struct stud_struct
       {  int roll;
          char name[80];
       }  student;
struct student a,b;
```

    is wrong.
    Here we have renamed structure type stud_struct to student. So declaration should be student a,b;
    The struct keyword is not required.
    Remaining two declarations are perfect.
    In the declaration of e,f stud_struct is not provided as it is not mandatory.

19. vivek is a 10 element array of structures of type pers

20. y->dob.day=5; is correct.

    y is a structure pointer in which there are two elements name and dob. So to access element by y we have to use arrow. e.g., y->name or y->dob.

    dob is a structure type variable. So to access element of it we should use (.) dot operator e.g. dob.day or dob.mnth or dob.yr.

21. Using assignment operator a structure variable can be assigned to another structure variable of same type. Unlike strcpy() is used in copying string no function is required to copy elements of a structure variable to another structure variable even if one or more elements of the structure variable is string.

    Adding or comparing of two structure variables like variables of inbuilt data types are not allowed in C.

22. Comparing two union variable by == operator is not allowed.

    Assigning union variable to another union variable of same type is legal.

    Extracting address of a union variable by address_of(&) operator is legal.

23. Writing b=a is illegal. We cannot assign string to another string by assignment operator. To be more precise it will give an error message: '=': left operand must be l-value. As array name is a constant pointer it cannot be used at left hand size of the assignment operator.

    But x and y are structure type variable containing string. So they can be copied by assignment operator.

24. To assign a colour to flags, the correct statement will be flags.fid.colour='B';
    fid is an element of structure variable flags so to access it we have to write
    flags.fid
    fid is a union variable of type flag_id whose element is the character variable colour. So to assign it we should write
    fid.colour='B';
    so the complete assignment statement will be flags.fid.colour='B';
    flags.colour='B'; is wrong as there are no element named colour of the structure variable flags.
    flags.fid.colour='Blue'; is wrong as colour is a character type variable and we cannot assign multiple characters in that fashion.

25. The structure Nursery is nested within the structure NurserySchool. Student is a variable (element) of the structure Nursery.
    NurserySchool.Nursery implies that Nursery is an element of the structure variable NurserySchool.
    Nursery.Student implies that Nursery is not a variable of basic data type. It is either structure type or union type as it contains element student inside it.

26. It defines a structure type s but no memory is allocated to it as no variable of type s is declared here.

27. The output will be knowledgeknowledge.
    t is a local variable in main() which has been passed to function my_func() by value so it will be copied on local variable temp of my_func().
    Modifying temp of my_func() will not affect temp of main(). temp is assigned value "knowledge" in main(). It will be printed twice.

28. The size of the variable u is 4 bytes. Union variable takes space equal to its largest member which is here of float having size of 4 bytes.

29. The size of the variable u is 32bytes.
    Union variable takes space equal to its largest member.
    Structure variable takes space equal to sum of space taken by its all members.
    Size of the structure variable us of type s will be 32 (2+30).
    Size of union variable u will be max(2, 1, 4, 32) = 32bytes.

30. Union contains members of different data types which share the same storage area in memory.
    The size of a union variable is equal to the size of the largest element in it.
    In a union variable at a time only one of its element is stored. If another element is assigned then the previous element is overwritten.

31. Structure can be a member of union and vice-versa.

32. A global anonymous union must be static.   A local anonymous union may be static or automatic. A local anonymous union cannot be external.

33. The value of Sourav will be 1
    The value of Sachin will be 0
    The value of Laxman will be 2
    The value of Rahul will be 3

The value of Kumble will be 4

The enumerator constants are always of integer type. Unless specified the values starts from 0 and assigned serially.

34. m = 0
    n = 1
    o = 2
    p = 20
    q = 21
    r = 22
    s = 20
    t = 21

    Unless specified the values of the enumeration constants starts from 0 and assigned serially. If any specific value is assigned, the successor constants are increased by one successively. It is possible to assign same values to more than one constant.

35. enum is good alternative of multiple #define for example
    #define a 0
    #define b 1
    #define c 2
    can be replaced by enum item{a,b,c};
    We can declare variables of item type by writing
    item x,y; and assign them like x=b; y=c;
    but in that case x, y are nothing but integer variables and any integer variable can be assigned in the same way. e.g.
    int p;
    p=c;

36. enum Player{Sachin, Sourav, Laxman, Rahul, Kumble};
    is correct enum declaration.
    enumerated elements should be in curly braces{} and should be separated by a comma(,) and the declaration should be terminated by a semicolon(;).

37. enum Days[Sunday,Monday,Tuesday]; is wrong.
    Enumerated elements should be in curly braces{} and should be separated by a comma(,) and the declaration should be terminated by a semicolon(;).
    Other two are correct. We may omit the optional tag as in
    enum {Sunday,Monday,Tuesday}; the tag Days is omitted.

38. typedef is used to give a new name to a built-in or pre-defined data type.
    int and float are built-in data types of C.

    The declaration typedef int BYTE; means that BYTE is given a new name for the built in data type int. The typedef specifier defines a name that can be used as a synonym for a type or derived type.

    The syntax for typedef statement is

    typedef <type definition> <new_name> ;

    An example of typedef statement is

    typedef unsigned char byte;
    So in the declaration BYTE is a synonym for int.

16

File

So far the programs are written following the console I/O operations. The inputs are taken through keyboard, these inputs and calculated data are stored in the memory, i.e., in the RAM and output is shown through VDU. But there are some problems related to this system when we need to handle large volume of data. As the data are stored in the main memory, the entire data set is lost as soon as the program is terminated. So for next execution of the program we need to enter the entire inputs. It is very tedious and time consuming to take input a large volume of data through keyboard every time the program executes. Thus it would be much better if we able to store these data permanently so that we can read back whenever required. The solution is file as file is the only place where the data can be stored permanently. C supports a large set of library functions for file handling. These are known as disk I/O or file I/O functions. In this chapter, we will discuss about files I/O functions which help us to know how to write data in files and how to read data from files. These are almost similar to console I/O functions except that these are operated on files.

16.1 WHAT IS A FILE?

A file can be defined as a repository of data or more preciously collection of bytes stored on a secondary storage device as it is permanent storage of data. Depending on the interpretation of these bytes several types of file may form. It may form textual document, a database file, an image file or file of any other form. The type of a particular file is decided entirely by the data structures and operations used by a program to process the file.

Depending on the way a file is opened for processing, a file can be classified as a text file or a binary file. The mode of opening a particular file differs in three main areas. These are:

i) Storage of numbers: In text files, numbers are stored as strings of characters. Thus, to store 1234 in a text file we require 4 bytes whereas in binary file numbers are stored in binary format. So, only 2 bytes is required to store any integer value. Similarly, the floating-point number 1234.56 would occupy 7 bytes in text file but 4 bytes in binary file.

ii) Handling of newlines: In text mode, the newline character is considered as the combination of carriage return and a linefeed. Thus while writing to a file, the newline character is converted into these characters and stored in the file. Similarly at the time of reading, when the carriage return-linefeed combination is read it is converted back to a newline. But, if a file is opened in binary mode these conversions will not take place. Hence the size of a file differs if it read separately in two different modes.

iii) Representation of end of file: In text mode, to mark the end of file a special character is inserted at the end of file, i.e., after the last character in the file. This character is generated by pressing ^Z and its ASCII value is 26. It indicates the end of file in a text file. But in binary files, no such character is there to indicate end of file. Instead, the file size which is present in the directory entry is used to realize the end of file.

16.2 PROCESSING A FILE

A program related to file involves the following operations:
1. Opening a file.
2. Reading from a file and/or writing into a file.
3. Closing the file.

16.2.1 Opening a File

The first task in file processing is to declare a FILE pointer; where FILE is a structure defined in the stdio.h header file. This structure contains information about the file being used, such as its location in memory and block size. We can declare File pointer as,

```
FILE *fp;
```

Next task is to open a file. The general format for opening a file is:

```
fopen( "Filename", "mode" );
```

There are several file opening mode. These are given below:

Table 16.1   File opening mode

Mode For Text File	Mode For Binary File	Purpose
r	rb	Reading from the file. File must exist.
w	wb	Writing into the file. If file already exists, its content is overwritten.
a	ab	Data will be added at the end of the existing file, if exist. Otherwise new file will be created.
r+	rb+	Reading and modifying existing content. File must exist.
w+	wb+	Writing new contents, reading them back and modifying existing content. If file already exists, its content is overwritten.
a+	ab+	Reading existing content, appending new content at the end of the file but cannot modify existing content.

EXAMPLE 16.1

```
FILE *fp;

fp = fopen("Test.txt", "r");
```

will request the operating system to open the file for reading purpose only. **On success**, the file pointer, fp will point the starting address of the file and **on failure** it will return NULL.

A filename may contain the path information. This is basically the location of the file which contains the drive name and/or directory/folder and their sub-directories/sub-folder names. For example, if the file **Test.txt** is resides in the **Cproject** subdirectories under the **MyProject** directories in **C** drive, it will be written as:

```
C:\MyProject\Cproject\Test.txt
```

When a file name is specified without mentioning its path, by default it is considered that the file is in the current path. If the file is in different path, we need to mention the path along with the filename. It is better programming approach to specify the path as part of the filename always. Though '\' is used to separate the drive, directories, filename when specifying the path, but '\' is s special character in C which is used to indicate the escape sequence when it is in a string. So, we have to use '\\' to represent '\'. Thus in a C program the above path has to be written as:

```
"C:\\MyProject\\Cproject\\Test.txt"
```

So, the file open statement would be:

```
FILE *fp;

fp = fopen("C:\\MyProject\\Cproject\\Test.txt", "r");
```

It is not necessary that always we have to specify the filename directly in the code. User can provide the filename as input.

EXAMPLE 16.2

```
FILE *fp;

char filenm[40];

printf("Enter the filename : ");

scanf("%s",filenm);

fp = fopen( filenm, "r");
```

Remember, when the filename is entered through keyboard do not use double backslash as a separator in mentioning the path, instead use single backslash.

16.2.2 Trouble Opening a File

When fopen() is used to open a file, there is no guarantee that the fopen() is succeed to open the file. There may be several possibilities for failure. When a file is trying to open in 'r' mode, fopen() may fails due to misspelling of file name or mentioning wrong path or the specified file may not present in the disk etc. If a file is trying to open in 'w' mode, fopen() may fails due to lack of sufficient disk space or the disk may be write protected etc. Whatever may be the reason it is necessary to check whether a file is opened properly before further proceeding. As we know if fopen() fails to open a file it returns NULL, we can handle the situation by the following way.

```
fp=fopen("Test.txt", "r");
if ( fp == NULL )
{       puts("Cannot open file");
        exit(0);
}
```

16.2.3 Closing a File

When all operation on file is over we must have to close the file. When a file is closed, the corresponding buffer is flushed, i.e., if the file is opened for writing the content of the buffer is written to the disk but if the file opened for reading the buffer's content is cleared. The general format for closing a file is:

```
fclose( file pointer);
```

For example, fclose(fp);

On success fclose( ) returns 0 but if any error occurs returns EOF.

16.3 INPUT-OUTPUT OPERATIONS ON FILES

C supports following type of I/O functions for reading and writing:
- Character I/O
- Integer I/O
- String I/O
- Formatted I/O
- Record I/O

16.3.1 Character I/O

First we will discuss character I/O, i.e., single character wise read-write operation on file. For this purpose we have a set of functions and a set of macros. The functions are:

fgetc( ) : to read a character from a file and

fputc( ) : to write a character into a file

Both the functions are in stdio.h header file. Following example illustrate the use of these functions.

If **ch** is a character type variable and **fp** is a file pointer pointing to a specific file then to read a character from that file, the statement would be,

```
ch = fgetc(fp);
```

On successful opening, the file pointer points to the first byte, i.e., the first character of the file. fgetc( ) reads the pointed character and returns it. After reading, the file pointer automatically advanced to the next byte. Unlike normal pointer, file pointer need not be incremented manually.

Similarly to write a character in a file pointed by the file pointer **fp**, the statement would be,

```
fputc( ch, fp);
```

In case of fputc( ) also, after writing the character at the pointed memory position file pointer moves to next byte position automatically.

The same operation can be done through a set of macros – **getc( )** and **putc( )**. Its syntax is similar to fgets() and fputs(), respectively.

Here is a program to create a text file.

PROGRAM 16.1 Write a Program to create a text file.

```
#include<stdio.h>
#include<conio.h>

void main( )
{    char ch;
     FILE *fptr;
     clrscr();
     fptr=fopen("Test.txt", "w");   /* File opened in writing mode */
     if ( fptr == NULL )
     {    puts("Cannot open file");
          getch( );
          exit(0);
     }
     while((ch=getchar())!=EOF)    /* Taking inputs until ^z is pressed */
     {
          putc(ch,fptr);   /* Writing inputted characters into the file */
     }
     fclose(fptr);      /*closes the file*/
}
```

As our task is to create a file, i.e., we are going to write some thing in the file. So we need to open the file in writing mode. Thus file opening mode used is 'w'. Next the file pointer, fptr is checked whether the file opened properly in writing mode. In case of failure its value would be NULL. So, program will terminate displaying suitable message. If the file is opened successfully, each character will be taken through keyboard and will be written into the file until the user pressed ^z. EOF is a macro defined at stdio.h header file. It is used to indicate the end of file. Its value is same as the value returned when ^z is pressed. In this program to write the characters putc() is used. Instead of it fputc( ) may be used. The result will be same. Only difference is that the first one is macro and other one is function.

Thus with fputc() there will be some extra overhead in operation. Details will be discussed in the chapter 18 where preprocessors are discussed.

Now we will write a program to read the file created by the previous program and then it will be displayed on the screen.

PROGRAM 16.2　Write a program to read a text file.

```
#include<conio.h>
#include<stdio.h>

void main( )
{    char ch;
     FILE *fptr;
     clrscr();

     fptr=fopen("Test.txt", "r");       /* File opened in read mode */
     if ( fptr == NULL )
     {   puts("Can not open file");
         exit(0);
     }
     while((ch=getc(fptr ))!=EOF) /* Reading characters from file */
     {                            /* until end of file is reached*/
         putchar(ch);             /* Displaying each character in VDU */
     }
     fclose(fptr);
}
```

The above program will print the content of the file, Test.txt on the screen. In this program, we can also use fgetc( ) instead of getc( ).

Not only a single file, we can access more than one file in a single program. Here is the program to handle multiple files at a time.

PROGRAM 16.3　Write a program to copy a text file.

```
#include<conio.h>
#include<stdio.h>

void main( )
{    char ch;
     FILE *fp1, *fp2;
     clrscr();
     fp1 = fopen("Test.txt", "r");   /* 1st File opened in read mode */
     if ( fp1 == NULL )
     {   puts("Cannot open file");
         exit(0);
     }
     fp2 = fopen("Sample.txt", "w");    /* 2nd File opened in write mode */
     if ( fp2 == NULL )
     {   puts("Cannot open file");
```

```
        fclose(fp1);
        exit(0);
    }
    while((ch=getc(fp1 ))!=EOF)
                        /* Reading characters from first file */
    {
        putc(ch, fp2);    /* Writing characters into second file */
    }
    fclose(fp1);          /*closes 1st file*/
    fclose(fp2);          /*closes 2nd file*/
}
```

16.3.2 Integer I/O

There are another set of functions which are used to operate on integer data. These are:

> **getw( )** : Reads an integer from a file and
>
> **putw( )** : Writes an integer to the file

These functions are useful when the problem deals with only integer data. Both the functions are in stdio.h header file and are used when the file is opened in binary mode. Following example illustrates the use of these functions.

If **n** is an integer variable and **fp** is a file pointer pointing to a specific file then to read an integer from that file, the statement would be,

```
        n = getw(fp);
```

Similarly to write an integer, **n** in a file pointed by the file pointer **fp**, the statement would be,

```
        putw( n, fp);
```

Next program shows how integers can be stored in a binary file.

PROGRAM 16.4   Write a program that will store 10 integers in a binary file. Numbers are generated randomly. Again read back the file to display the numbers from the file.

```
#include<stdlib.h>
#include<conio.h>
#include<stdio.h>

void main()
{   FILE *fp;
    int n,i;
    clrscr();
    fp = fopen("Number.dat","wb");   /* Binary File opened in write mode */
    if ( fp = = NULL )
    {   puts("Cannot open file");
        exit(0);
    }
    for(i=0;i<10;i++)
```

```
{    putw(rand(),fp);   /* Here rand( ) is used to generate random
                            numbers */
}
fclose(fp);

fp=fopen("Number.dat","rb");   /* Created Binary File opened now
                                  in read mode */
for(i=0;i<10;i++)
{
    n = getw(fp);              /* Reading from files */
    printf("%d ",n);
}
fclose(fp);
}
```

16.3.4   String I/O

Though character I/O operation is very powerful and useful, there are some situations where instead of individual character operation reading or writing entire string from and to files is more efficient. C provides the facility to read and write the entire string instead of a single character. The functions are:

fgets( ) : to read a string from a file and

fputs( ) : to write a string into a file

Both the functions are in stdio.h header file. If **str** is a character array of size **n** and **fp** is a file pointer then following statement shows the use of fgets( ).

```
fgets ( str, n, fp ) ;
```

fgets( ) reads from the file pointed by **fp** and stores them in the array **str**. It stops reading when it reads either **n–1** characters or a new line character or end of file marker, which one comes first. On success fgets() returns the string pointed to by str but when the end of file is encountered or any error occurs it returns NULL.

If **str** is a character array and **fp** is a file pointer then following statement shows the use of fputs( ).

```
fputs ( str, fp ) ;
```

fputs( ) copies the string **str** to the position pointed by **fp** in the file. It does not append a new line character nor copy the terminating null character.

The following program shows the use of fputs( ).

PROGRAM 16.5   Write a program to create a file reading strings from keyboard.

```
#include<conio.h>
#include <stdio.h>

void main( )
{    FILE  *fp ;
```

```
    char  str[80] ;
    fp = fopen ( "Test_str.txt", "w" ) ;   /* File opened in writing mode */
    if ( fp == NULL )
    {
        puts ( "Cannot open file" ) ;
        exit(0) ;
    }
    printf ( "\nEnter  strings, Press Just enter at the
                              beginning of a line to finish\n" ) ;
    while ( strlen ( gets ( str ) ) > 0 )
    {
        fputs(str,fp); /*Writing the content of array, str into the file*/
        fputs("\n",fp); /*Adding new line character at end of each line*/
    }
    fclose ( fp ) ;
}
```

The above program accepts strings when we press enter key. To terminate the execution of the loop, we have to press the enter key at the very beginning of a line. This produces a zero length string. Then the loop terminates. As fputs() does not append new line character like puts(), to place the each inputted string in separate line in the file the statement **fputs("\n", fp);** is used.

The following program reads the file created by the previous program and then it will be displayed on the screen.

PROGRAM 16.6   Write a program to read strings from the file.

```
#include<conio.h>
#include <stdio.h>

void main( )
{   FILE   *fp ;
    char   str[80] ;
    fp = fopen ( " Test_str.txt ", "r" ) ;
    if ( fp == NULL )
    {
        puts ( "Cannot open file" ) ;
        exit(0) ;
    }
    while ( fgets ( str, 80, fp ) != NULL )   /* Reading each line from file */
    {
        puts( str ) ;
    }

    fclose ( fp ) ;
}
```

16.3.4. Formatted I/O

Instead of handling simple unformatted text, C is able to handle formatted data which are mainly used to store records in a text file. Like formatted I/O functions printf and scanf, here is also two functions named **fprintf** and **fscanf**, which are almost similar to those functions for accessing files except that the fprintf and fscanf take the file pointer as an additional first argument. The general form of fprintf( ) is:

```
fprintf(file pointer,  format-string[, arguments,...]);
```

The following program demonstrates the use of fprintf( ).

PROGRAM 16.7   **Write a program to create a data file which will store the records of students.**

```c
#include<conio.h>
#include<ctype.h>
#include <stdio.h>

struct student
{    int roll;
     char name[30];
     int total;
};

void main( )
{
     FILE   *fp;
     char   ch = 'Y';
     struct student  s;

     fp = fopen ( "Student.dat", "w" );
     if ( fp == NULL )
     {
          puts ( "Cannot open file" );
          exit(0) ;
     }

     while ( toupper( ch) == 'Y' )
     {
          printf ( "\nEnter Roll, Name and Total Marks:" );
          scanf ( "%d %s %d", &s.roll, s.name, &s.total );
                                  /* Taking inputs from user */
          fprintf ( fp, "%d %s %d\n", s.roll, s.name, s.total );
                                  /* Writing into file */

          printf ( "Add another record? (Y/N) " );
          fflush ( stdin );
          scanf("%c", &ch);
     }
     fclose ( fp ) ;
}
```

To read the formatted data written by the fprintf( ) we have to use fscanf( ). The general form of fscanf( ) is:

```
fscanf(file pointer,  format-string[, arguments,...]);
```

where, arguments should be the addresses of the variables. If successfully read, the fscanf( ) returns the number of items that are successfully read. Returns EOF when end of file is reached.

The following program demonstrate the use of fscanf( ). Using fscanf( ) the program reads all records from student.dat file which is created by the previous program and displays on the screen.

PROGRAM 16.8   Write a program to read formatted data from a file and displays in the screen.

```c
#include<conio.h>
#include <stdio.h>

struct student
{    int roll;
     char name[30];
     int total;
};

void main( )
{    FILE  *fp ;
     struct student s ;
     fp = fopen ( "Student.dat", "r" );
     if ( fp == NULL )
     {
         puts ( "Cannot open file" );
         exit(0) ;
     }
     clrscr( );
     printf("\n List of Students: ");
     while ( fscanf ( fp, "%d %s %d", &s.roll, s.name, &s.total) != EOF )
     {                               /* Reading data of each student */
         printf ("\n%2d   %30s  %3d", s.roll, s.name, s.total );
     }
     fclose ( fp ) ;
}
```

fscanf( ) suffers in some problem. Format string of fscanf( ) should be same as fprintf(). Another problem is reading strings. If a string, say name, consists of multiple word, fscanf( ) reads only first part. For each part of the name we need to use different distinguish arrays. But the number of parts in any name varies person to person. Handling this type of situation with fscanf( ) is really difficult. Thus to handle this situation we can opt an alternative way. Following section describes this.

16.3.5   Record I/O

A more efficient way of reading and/or writing records from/to the file is to use another set of functions. These are fread( ) and fwrite( ). Here instead of reading or writing individual fields of a record we can able to handle the record as a whole if we put them in a structure variable. The general form of fwrite( ) is:

```
fwrite(&var, sizeof(var), n, file pointer);
```

where **var** is any variable and **n** is the number of such variables to be written at one time.

Following program shows how records can be written to a file.

PROGRAM 16.9   Write a program to create a binary file which will store the records of students.

```
#include<conio.h>
#include<ctype.h>
#include <stdio.h>

struct student
{    int roll;
     char name[30];
     int total;
};

void main( )
{    FILE   *fp ;
     char   ch = 'Y' ;
     struct student   s ;

     fp = fopen ( "Student.dat", "wb" ) ;
     if ( fp == NULL )
     {
         puts ( "Cannot open file" ) ;
         exit(0) ;
     }
     while ( toupper( ch) == 'Y' )
     {
         printf ( "\nEnter Roll, Name and Total Marks: " ) ;
         scanf ( "%d %s %d", &s.roll, s.name, &s.total ) ;
         fwrite ( &s, sizeof ( s ), 1, fp ) ;
                         /* Writing each record into the file */

         printf ( "Add another record? (Y/N) " ) ;
         fflush ( stdin ) ;
         scanf("%c", &ch);
     }
     fclose ( fp ) ;
}
```

The above program is similar to the **Program 16.7** written earlier. Instead of fprintf( ), here fwrite( ) is used and thus instead of writing separate fields total structure is written. Another difference is the file 'Student.dat' has now been created in binary mode.

The argument list of fread( ) is same as fwrite( ). The general form of fread( ) is:

```
fread(&var, sizeof(var), n, file pointer);
```

where **var** is any variable and **n** is the number of such variables to be written at one time. The fread( ) returns the number of records read. If end-of-file is encountered, it returns 0.

Now we will write a program that would read records from the file and display them on the screen.

PROGRAM 16.10   Write a program to read records from a binary file and display them on the screen.

```c
#include<conio.h>
#include <stdio.h>
struct student
{    int roll;
     char name[30];
      int total;
};

void main( )
{    FILE  *fp ;
     struct student  s ;
     fp = fopen ( "Student.dat", "rb" ) ;
     if ( fp == NULL )
     {
          puts ( "Cannot open file" ) ;
          exit(0) ;
     }
     clrscr( );
     printf("\n List of Students: ");
     while ( fread ( &s, sizeof ( s ), 1, fp ))
                          /* Reading each record into the file */
     {
          printf ("\n%2d    %30s  %3d", s.roll, s.name, s.total ) ;
     }
     fclose ( fp ) ;
}
```

You can note one thing that while writing the records, the entire structure is written. Similarly, while reading the file entire structure is read back. Thus it does not matter how many parts are there in the name field or in which format the records are written.

16.4   MORE FILE FUNCTIONS

So far we have discussed the file functions that are useful for read and write operations in various ways. But by these functions we can access files sequentially only. But C supports sequential access as well as random access in a file. The following three functions *ftell()*, *fseek()* and *rewind()* helps us in random access to a file. These functions play an important role in file manipulations.

ftell( ): This function is used to know the current position of the file pointer in a file. It returns a long integer which indicates how far the file pointer is in bytes from the beginning of a file. If any error occurs, `ftell()` returns −1. The prototype of this function is:

```
long int ftell(FILE *fp);
```

fseek( ): The function `fseek()` sets the file pointer to the required position in a file. Prototype of this function is as shown below:

```
int fseek(FILE *fp, long int offset, int location);
```

Here *fp* is the file pointer, *offset* is the number of bytes to move. The *offset* value may be positive or negative, denoting forward or backward movement of the file pointer in the file. *location* is the reference position from which the offset is applied, this can be one of the following:

Table 16.2   Reference positions

Symbolic constants	Value	Reference position
SEEK_SET	0	Beginning of the file
SEEK_CUR	1	Current position in the file
SEEK_END	2	End of the file

EXAMPLE 16.3

To set a file pointer at the beginning of file, the statement would be
```
        fseek( fp, 0, 0 );
```
or,   `fseek( fp, 0, SEEK_SET );`

To set a file pointer at the end of the file, the statement would be
```
        fseek( fp, 0, 2 );
```
or,   `fseek( fp, 0, SEEK_ END );`

To move the file pointer 10 bytes from current position,
```
        fseek( fp, 10, 1 );
```
or,   `fseek( fp, 10, SEEK_ CUR );`

To move the file pointer 10 bytes in backward direction from current position,
```
        fseek( fp, -10, 1 );
```
or,   `fseek( fp, -10, SEEK_CUR );`

rewind( ): The rewind( ) set the file pointer at the beginning of file, irrespective of where it is right now. It is used as,

```
        rewind( file pointer);
```

So, we can say rewind(fp) is equivalent to fseek(fp, 0, 0);

PROGRAM 16.11   Write a program to find the size of the file and count the number of records in a file.

```c
#include <stdio.h>
#include<conio.h>

struct student
{     int roll;
      char name[30];
      int total;
};

void main( )
{     FILE  *fp ;
      struct student  s ;
      int size,count;
      fp = fopen ( "Student.dat", "rb" ) ;
      if ( fp == NULL )
      {
          puts ( "Cannot open file" ) ;
          exit(0) ;
      }
      fseek(fp,0,2);     /* File pointer set at end of file */
      size = ftell(fp);  /* Returns bytes apart from BOF, i.e., filesize */
      count = size / sizeof(s);
      printf("\n The size of the file is %d Bytes", size ) ;
      printf("\n and Number of Records in the file is %d", count ) ;

      fclose(fp);
}
```

In the above program we set the file pointer at the end of the file using fseek( ) function. Now ftell( ) is used to know how far the position is from the beginning of the file which is basically the size of the file. As the records are of same size, we divide the size of the file with size of the records and obtain the number of records in the file.

feof( ): feof( ) is a macro which is also used to check whether a file pointer is reached at end of file. It returns a non-zero value when the end of file is reached, otherwise returns 0.

So, to read a file we can use it in the following way:

```c
while ( !feof( fp ))
{
    ch = fgetc( fp );
    .....
    .....
}
```

ferror( ): ferror( ) is a macro which is used to detect any error that might have occurred during a read or write operation on a file. It returns non zero value if any error is detected on read or write operation, otherwise returns 0(zero).

The following program illustrates the use of feof() and ferror():

PROGRAM 16.12   Write a program to show the use of feof( ) and ferror( ).

```
#include<stdio.h>

void main( )
{
    FILE *fptr;
    char ch;
    fptr = fopen("A.TXT", "r");
    while( !feof(fptr))
    {
        ch = getc(fptr);
        if( ferror( ))
        {
            printf("Error in reading file");
            break;
        }
        else
            printf("%c",ch);
    }
    fclose(fptr);
}
```

remove( ): remove( ) is a macro which is used to delete a file. It is defined in the stdio.h header file. If the file successfully removed from the disk it returns 0, otherwise it returns −1. Remember, the file to be removed should be closed properly before use this function. The prototype of this function is:

```
int remove ( const char *filename);
```

the string *filename may include the full path name. If path not included, it checks only at current directory.

rename( ): rename( ) is a library function defined in the stdio.h header file. It is used to rename, i.e., to change the name of an existing file. On success it returns 0, otherwise it returns −1. The prototype of this function is:

```
int rename(const char *oldfilename, const char *newfilename);
```

Using rename( ) we can rename a file as well as move a file from one directory to another. When mentioning the old file name and new filename, if the paths of the filenames differ the file will be moved.

Following program illustrates the use of remove( ) and rename( ).

PROGRAM 16.13   write a program to remove all blank lines from a file.

```
#include<conio.h>
#include<stdio.h>

void main()
```

```
{    FILE *fp1,*fp2;
     char s[120];
     fp1=fopen("A.TXT","r");
     if(fp1==NULL)
     {    printf("Unable to open the 1st file for reading.");
          getch();
          exit(0);
     }

     fp2=fopen("B.TXT", "w");
     if(fp2==NULL)
     {    printf("Unable to open the file for writing.");
          getch( );
          fclose(fp1);
          exit(0);
     }

     while(fgets(s,120,fp1)!=NULL)
     {
          if(strlen(s)>1)
          fputs(s,fp2);
     }
     fclose(fp1);
     fclose(fp2);
     remove("A.TXT");         /* Removes old file */
     rename("B.TXT", "A.TXT");
                         /* Newly created file is renamed to old file */
     printf("Removed blank lines successfully");
}
```

Using C language we cannot delete lines from a file. Not only lines, we cannot delete a single byte also. So, to delete any thing – that may be text, that may be records – first we have to copy the total content of the file into a new file except the portion to be deleted. Then the old file has to delete and rename the new file to old one. It seems to the user that the portion is deleted from the file. This logic is followed in the above program.

16.5 COMMAND LINE ARGUMENTS

Command line arguments are the parameters supplied to a 'C' program when the program will execute. Using command line argument, we can supply inputs to a program. This input may contain filename as well as any other value. In any 'C' function number of argument is fixed. But the advantage of command line argument is that we can supply variable number of arguments to a program. To accept command line argument in a 'C' program, we have to define the main function as:

```
main( int argc, char*argv[])
{
     .....
}
```

The argument **argc** tells the number of arguments (i.e., argument count) on the command line and **argv** represents argument value, i.e., arguments.

For example, if we want to execute a 'C' program (named mycopy) that copy the content of one file to another, we may write the command line as:

```
C:\TC> mycopy      A.TXT      B.TXT
```

Then, argc will contain 3 and argv[0], argv[1] and argv[2] will store the address of three string 'mycopy', 'A.TXT', 'B.TXT', respectively. These values will act as the inputs of the program.

Here is the program.

PROGRAM 16.14   Write a program to copy a text file. File names are supplied through command line arguments.

```c
#include<conio.h>
#include<stdio.h>

void main(int argc, char* argv[])
{   FILE *fptr1,*fptr2;
    char ch;
    if(argc<3)
    {   printf("Too few Arguments.");
        getch();
        exit(0);
    }
    else
        if(argc>3)
        {   printf("Too many Arguments.");
            getch();
            exit(0);
        }

    fptr1= fopen(argv[1], "r");
    if(fptr1==NULL)
    {   printf("Unable to open the file for reading.");
        getch();
        exit(0);
    }

    fptr2=fopen(argv[2], "w");
    if(fptr2==NULL)
    {   printf("Unable to open the file for writing.");
        getch();
        fclose(fptr1);
        exit(0);
    }

    while((ch=getc(fptr1))!=EOF)
        putc(ch,fptr2);
    printf("File copied successfully");
```

```
        fclose(fptr1);
        fclose(fptr2);
}
```

Remember that the command line argument is a feature of C language not for file handling alone though it is discussed in the file handling chapter. In any C program that related or not related to files, the inputs can be supplied through command line argument. Following program shows how any number of integers can be summed up using this feature.

PROGRAM 16.15 Write a program to find the sum of any number of integers.

```
#include<stdio.h>
#include<stdlib.h>
void main(int argc, char* argv[])
{
    int sum =0, i;
    for(i=1;i<=argc;i++)
        sum = sum + atoi(argv[i]);  /* atoi() is used to convert alpha-
                                       numeric string to integer */
    printf("\nSum = %d",sum);
}
```

If the name of the above program is sum.c, its execution may look like:

C:\cprograms> sum 5 10 15
Sum = 30

C:\cprograms> sum 2 4 6 8 10 12
Sum = 42

C:\cprograms> sum
Sum = 0

16.6 PROGRAMMING EXAMPLES

Here are some programming examples to understand the various uses of files.

PROGRAM 16.16 Write a C program which passes a string 'This is a test' in command line and print those arguments one by one and also print the number of arguments.

```
#include<conio.h>
#include<stdio.h>

void main(int argc, char* argv[])
{    int i;
     clrscr();
     printf("Arguments are:-\n");
```

```
    for(i=1;i<argc;i++)
        puts(argv[i]);
    printf("Number of arguments = %d",argc-1);
    getch();
}
```

PROGRAM 16.17   Write a program to count the number of characters, spaces, tabs and new lines in a file using command line arguments.

```
#include<conio.h>
#include<stdio.h>

void main(int argc, char* argv[])
{   char ch;
    FILE *fp;
    int tot_ch=0,tot_sp=0,tot_tab=0,tot_ln=0;
    clrscr();
    if(argc != 2)
    {   puts("Invalid number of arguments.");
        getch();
        exit(0);
    }
    fp=fopen(argv[1],"r");
    while((ch=getc(fp))!=EOF)
    {   tot_ch++;
        if(ch==' ')
            tot_sp++;
        if(ch=='\t')
            tot_tab++;
        if(ch=='\n')
            tot_ln++;
    }
    printf("\nTotal number of characters = %d",tot_ch);
    printf("\nTotal number of spaces = %d",tot_sp);
    printf("\nTotal number of tabs = %d",tot_tab);
    printf("\nTotal number of lines = %d",tot_ln);
    fclose(fp);
}
```

PROGRAM 16.18   Write a program which will merge the content of two files and copy into another blank file.

```
#include<conio.h>
#include<stdio.h>

void main()
{   FILE *fp1,*fp2, *fp3;
    char ch;
```

```
    clrscr();
    fp1=fopen("A.TXT","r");
    if(fp1==NULL)
    {   printf("Unable to open the 1st file for reading.");
        getch();
        exit(0);
    }
    fp2=fopen("B.TXT","r");
    if(fp2==NULL)
    {   printf("Unable to open the 2nd file for reading.");
        getch();
        fclose(fp1);
        exit(0);
    }

    fp3=fopen("C.TXT","w");
    if(fp3==NULL)
    {   printf("Unable to open the file for writing.");
        getch();
        fclose(fp1);
        fclose(fp2);
        exit(0);
    }
    while((ch=getc(fp1))!=EOF)
        putc(ch,fp3);
    while((ch=getc(fp2))!=EOF)
        putc(ch,fp3);

    printf("File Merged successfully");

    fclose(fp1);
    fclose(fp2);
    fclose(fp3);
}
```

PROGRAM 16.19 Write a C program to create a file contains a series of integer numbers and then reads all numbers of this file and writes all even numbers to a file named even and writes all odd numbers to another file named odd.

```
#include<conio.h>
#include<stdio.h>

void main()
{   int i,num;
    FILE *fp1, *fp2, *fp3;
    clrscr();
    fp1=fopen("number.dat","w");
```

```
        while(1)
        {    printf("Enter any number (-1 to stop):");
             scanf("%d",&num);
             if(num== -1)
                   break;
             putw(num,fp1);
        }
        fclose(fp1);


        fp1=fopen("number.dat","r");
        if(fp1==NULL)
        {    printf("Unable to open the file for reading.");
             getch();
             exit(0);
        }
        fp2=fopen("odd","w");
        if(fp2==NULL)
        {    printf("Unable to open the file for writing.");
             getch();
             fclose(fp1);
             exit(0);
        }
        fp3=fopen("even","w");
        if(fp3==NULL)
        {    printf("Unable to open the file for writing.");
             getch();
             fclose(fp1);
             fclose(fp2);
             exit(0);
        }
        while(( num=getw(fp1)) != EOF)
        {    if(num%2==0)
             putw(num,fp3);         /* Even numbers are written into even file */
             else
             putw(num,fp2);         /* Odd numbers are written into odd file */
        }
        fclose(fp1);
        fclose(fp2);
        fclose(fp3);
}
```

PROGRAM 16.20   Write a C program to display the lines along with the line number which contains the inputted string. File name and inputted string should be supplied as command line argument.

```
#include<conio.h>
#include<stdio.h>
```

```
void main(int arc, char *arv[])
{    FILE *fp;
     char ch, line[100], filename[15];
     int line_no=1;
     fp = fopen(arv[1],"r+");
     if(fp == NULL)
     {    printf("Unable to open the file %s for reading.", arv[1]);
          getch();
          exit(0);
     }

     while((fgets(line,100,fp))!=NULL)
     {    if(strstr(line,arv[2]))  /* Checks inputted string is present
                                       in the line */
              printf("[%d]: %s",line_no,line);
          line_no++;
     }
     fclose(fp);
}
```

Program 16.21 Write a C program to replace all occurrence of *'can'* with *'may'* in a text file.

```
#include<conio.h>
#include<stdio.h>

void main()
{  FILE *fp;
   char ch, word[30],flname[15];
   int i=0,posn;
   printf("Enter file name: ");
   scanf("%s",&flname);
   fp = fopen(flname, "r+");
   while((ch=getc(fp))!=EOF)
   {  if(isspace(ch) || ispunct(ch))  /* As words are separated by
                                          space or punctuation mark*/
      {   word[i]= '\0';
          i=0;

          if(strcmp(word,"can")==0)
          {  posn=ftell(fp); /* stores the position of read pointer */
             fseek(fp,-4,1); /* Moving back 4 character, 3 for can and
                                 1 for space */
             fputs("may",fp);
             fseek(fp,posn,0);            /* Resetting file pointer */
          }
      }
      else
          word[i++]=ch;
   }
   fclose(fp);
}
```

PROGRAM 16.22   Write a program to read an employee file which contains employee number, employee name, salary and address. Create a file which will contain the informations of the employees whose salary is >30000.

```c
#include<conio.h>
#include <stdio.h>

struct employee
{    int emp_no;
     char name[40];
     int salary;
     char address[60];
};

void main( )
{    FILE  *fp1, *fp2 ;
     struct employee  emp ;
     fp1 = fopen ( "employee.dat", "rb" ) ;
     if ( fp1 == NULL )
     {    puts ( "Cannot open file" ) ;
          exit(0) ;
     }
     fp2 = fopen ( "emp_out.dat", "wb" ) ;
     if ( fp2 == NULL )
     {    puts ( "Cannot open file" ) ;
          fclose(fp1);
          exit(0);
     }
     clrscr( );
     while ( fread ( &emp, sizeof ( emp ), 1, fp1))  //reading old file
     {    if( emp.salary>30000)
          fwrite ( &emp, sizeof ( emp ), 1, fp2);  // writing into new file
     }
     fclose ( fp1);
     fclose ( fp2);
}
```

PROGRAM 16.23   Write a complete C program to implement a simple Database Management System. Program should maintain the information of students and able to-

i) store new records,
ii) edit/modify existing records,
iii) delete records,
iv) display the list of students
v) search whether a student information is in the database or not and
vi) count total number of records.

```c
#include <stdio.h>
#include<conio.h>
#include<ctype.h>

struct student
{    int roll;
     char name[30];
     int total;
};
void add_rec(FILE *);
void display_rec(FILE *);
void find_rec(FILE *, int);
void edit_rec(FILE *, int);
void delete_rec(int);
int count_rec(FILE *);

void main()
{    FILE  *fp ;
     struct student s ;
     int mroll,n;
     char choice, ans;
     do
     {    clrscr();
          printf("DATABASE MANAGEMENT SYSTEM ");
          printf("\n=============================");
          printf("\n\n1.Add ");
          printf("\n2.Edit ");
          printf("\n3.Display");
          printf("\n4.Delete");
          printf("\n5.Find");
          printf("\n6.Count");
          printf("\n7.Exit");
          printf("\n\nEnter your Choice : ");
          fflush(stdin);
          scanf("%c", &choice);
          switch(choice)
          {  case '1':                 /* Add Records */
               fp = fopen ( "Student.dat", "ab" ) ;
               if ( fp == NULL )
               { puts( "Cannot open file" ) ;
                  exit(0);
               }
               add_rec(fp);
               fclose(fp);
               break;
             case '2':                 /* Edit a Record */
               fp = fopen ( "Student.dat", "rb+" );
               printf("\nEnter Roll Number:");
               scanf("%d",&mroll);
```

```
                    edit_rec(fp,mroll);
                    fclose( fp );
                    break;
                case '3':                  /* Display Records */
                    fp = fopen ( "Student.dat", "rb" );
                    display_rec(fp);
                    fclose ( fp );
                    getch();
                    break;
                case '4':                  /* Delete a Record */
                    printf("\nEnter The roll number whose Record You Want
                                                To Delete : ");
                    scanf("%d",&mroll);
                    delete_rec(mroll);
                    getch();
                    break;
                case '5':                  /* Find a Record */
                    fp = fopen ( "Student.dat", "rb" );
                    printf("\nEnter Roll Number:");
                    scanf("%d",&mroll);
                    find_rec(fp,mroll);
                    fclose( fp );
                    getch();
                    break;
                case '6':                  /* Count Records */
                    fp = fopen ( "Student.dat", "rb" );
                    n=count_rec(fp);
                    printf("\nTotal number of students = %d", n );
                    fclose( fp );
                    getch();
                    break;
                case '7':
                    printf("\n\nQuiting.......");
                    getch();
                    exit(0);
                default:
                    printf("Invalid choice. Please Enter Correct Choice");
                    getch();
            }
    } while(choice !='7');
}

void add_rec(FILE *fp)                     /* Add Records */
{   char ch='Y';
    struct student s;
    while ( toupper( ch) == 'Y' )
    {   printf ( "\nEnter Roll No.:");
        scanf("%d",&s.roll);
        printf("\nEnter Name :");
```

```
          fflush(stdin);
          gets(s.name);
          printf("Total Marks: " );
          scanf ( "%d",&s.total );
          fwrite( &s, sizeof ( s ), 1, fp );

          printf( "Add another record? (Y/N) " );
          fflush( stdin );
          scanf("%c", &ch);
     }
     fclose( fp );
}


void edit_rec(FILE *fp, int mroll)    /* Edit a Record */
{    struct student s;
     int flag = 1,m;
     while ( fread ( &s, sizeof ( s ), 1, fp ))
     {    if(mroll == s.roll)
          {    printf ("\n Roll: %d", s.roll);
               printf ("\n Name: %s", s.name);
               printf ("\n Total: %d", s.total );

               printf("\nEnter Name :");
               fflush(stdin);
               gets(s.name);
               printf("Total Marks: " );
               scanf ( "%d",&s.total );
               m=sizeof(s)*(-1);
               fseek(fp,m,1);
               fwrite( &s, sizeof(s),1,fp);

               flag = 0;
               break;
          }
     }
     if(flag)
     {    puts("Record not found...");
          getch();
     }
}

void delete_rec(int mroll)                /* Delete a Record */
{    FILE *fp, *temp;
     char ch;
     struct student s;
     int flag = 1;
     fp = fopen ( "Student.dat", "rb" ) ;
     while ( fread ( &s, sizeof ( s ), 1, fp ))
     {    if(mroll == s.roll)
```

```
        {    printf ("\n Roll: %d", s.roll);
             printf ("\n Name: %s", s.name);
             printf ("\n Total: %d", s.total ) ;
             flag = 0;
             break;
        }
    }

    if(flag)
    {    puts("Record not found...");
         fclose(fp);
    }
    else
    {
         printf ("\n\nDelete record?(Y/N)");
         fflush ( stdin ) ;
         scanf("%c", &ch);
         if (toupper(ch)=='Y')
         {    rewind(fp);
              temp=fopen("Temp.dat","wb");
              while ( fread ( &s, sizeof ( s ), 1, fp ))
              {
                   if(mroll != s.roll)
                   fwrite ( &s, sizeof ( s ), 1, temp );
              }
              fclose(fp);
              fclose(temp);
              remove("Student.dat");
              rename("Temp.dat","Student.dat");
              printf("\nRecord Deleted Successfully...");
         }
    }
}

void find_rec(FILE *fp, int mroll)    /* Find a Record */
{    struct student s;
     int flag = 1;
     while ( fread ( &s, sizeof ( s ), 1, fp ))
     {    if(mroll == s.roll)
          {    printf ("\n Roll: %d", s.roll);
               printf ("\n Name: %s", s.name);
               printf ("\n Total: %d", s.total);
               flag = 0;
               break;
          }
     }
     if(flag)
          puts("Record not found...");
}
```

```
void display_rec(FILE *fp)                /* Display Records */
{      struct student s;
       clrscr( );
       printf("\n              List of Students ");
       printf("\n-------------------------------------------");
       printf("\nRoll  Name                          Total");
       printf("\n-------------------------------------------");
       while ( fread ( &s, sizeof ( s ), 1, fp ))
       {
            printf ("\n%2d   %-30s %-3d", s.roll, s.name, s.total );
       }
}

int count_rec(FILE *fp)                   /* Count Records */
{      struct student s;
       int count = 0;
       while ( fread ( &s, sizeof ( s ), 1, fp ))
       {
            count++;
       }
       return(count);
}
```

SUMMARY

➤ A file is a collection of bytes stored on a secondary storage device.

➤ If large volume of data needs to be inputted or data needs to store permanently, use of file is the best option.

➤ fopen( ) is used to open a file and fclose( ) is used to close a file.

➤ There are several sets of functions and macros for file I/O.

➤ File I/O are almost similar to character I/O except an additional parameter for file pointer.

➤ Random file access is achieved through *ftell()*, *fseek()* and *rewind()*.

➤ Any number of arguments can be passed to main function through command line arguments.

REVIEW EXERCISES

1. What are the advantages of using a file?
2. How a binary file differs from a text file?
3. What do you mean by 'FILE'?
4. Discuss about several file opening mode.
5. What is the importance of closing a file?
6. How the *end of file* is detected in a file?
7. Compare the file opening mode a+ and w+.
8. What is the use of fseek( )?

9. Write a program that will count number of lines in a file.

10. Write a program that will convert all upper case letters to lower case.

11. Write a program to concatenate two files one after another into a new file.

12. Write a program to compare two files line by line and display those lines where they differ.

13. Write a program to display last n lines from a file. File name and number of lines should pass through command line.

14. Write a program to find the frequency (i.e., number of occurrence) of a given word in a text file.

15. Write a program to replace the all occurrence of a particular word with another word.

16. Write a program to display the lines along with the line number that does not contain the given word.

17. Write a program to read a text file and display the total number of four letter words in the text file.

18. Write a program to read a text file and print each word in reverse order.

   For example,   Input: THIS IS A SAMPLE TEXT

                        Output: SIHT SI A ELPMAS TXET

19. Write a program that will create a data file containing Item Code, Item Group, Description, Stock in Hand and Reorder Level of Items in an Inventory. Also include functions:
   (a) to display list of items whose stock is below reorder level.
   (b) to find whether a item is present in the inventory.
   (c) to list the items of a particular group.

20. Write a menu driven program to maintain database of employees. The information needs to store about employee code, name, designation, department and basic salary. The program should be able to add new records, modify an existing record, delete an existing record, prepare department wise employee list and pay slip of each employee.

LEARN BY QUIZ – QUESTIONS

1. What is a file?
   (1) Collection of bytes stored on a secondary storage device.
   (2) Collection of bytes stored on primary memory.
   (3) Collection of records stored on primary memory.

2. Which one is the correct statement?
   (1) File stores data permanently.
   (2) Array stores data permanently.
   (3) Structure stores data permanently.

3. Which one is the correct statement?
   (1) In text file, data are stored as a character.
   (2) In binary file, data are stored as a character.
   (3) In text file, data are stored according to their datatype.

4. In binary file how data is stored?
   (1) always as a character.
   (2) as the binary equivalent of the data
   (3) as a number but the digit of each number is stored as its binary equivalent.

5. How many bytes are required to store an integer number, 24968 in a text file?
   (1) 2
   (2) 5
   (3) 6

6. How many bytes are required to store a floating point number, 24.968 in a text file?
   (1) 6
   (2) 4
   (3) 5

7. How many bytes are required to store an integer number, 24968 in a binary file?
   (1) 2
   (2) 5
   (3) 6

8. How many bytes are required to store an floating point number, 24.968 in a binary file?
   (1) 4
   (2) 5
   (3) 6

9. How end-of-file is detected in text file?
   (1) By the character ^Z (whose ASCII value is 26)
   (2) By the character . (whose ASCII value is 46)
   (3) By the key End (whose scan code is 79)

10. Which function is used to open a file?
    (1) fopen()
    (2) fileopen()
    (3) openfile()

11. What is the prototype of fopen()?
    (1) FILE fopen(const char*filename, const char *mode);
    (2) void fopen(char * filename);
    (3) int fopen(const char* filename);

12. To create a text file named myfile.txt, the file open statement will be:
    (1) FILE *fp;
        fp=fopen("myfile.txt","w");
    (2) char *fp;
        fp=fopen("myfile.txt","w");
    (3) FILE *fp;
        fp=fopen("myfile.txt");

13. What will be the correct statement to open a text file named myfile.txt for reading only?
    (1) FILE *fp;
        fp=fopen("myfile.txt","r");
    (2) FILE *fp;
        fp=fopen("myfile.txt","a");
    (3) FILE *fp;
        fp=fopen("myfile.txt");

14. At most how many files can be opened with a single fopen()?
    (1) 1
    (2) 2
    (3) Any number of files.

15. At most how many files can be opened at a time?
    (1) 1
    (2) 2
    (3) Any number of files.

16. Which function is used to close a file?
    (1) fclose()
    (2) fileclose()
    (3) flclose()

17. Which one of the following is correct to close the file a.txt and b.txt?
    (1) fclose("a.txt");
        fclose("b.txt");
    (2) fclose("a.txt","b.txt");
    (3) fclose("a.txt && b.txt");

18. To read a character from a file, the function is:
    (1) fgetc()
    (2) freadc()
    (3) fputc()

19. To write a character into the file, the function is:
    (1) fputc()
    (2) putchar()
    (3) fgetc()

20. What will be the correct statement to open a binary file named myfile.dat for reading only?
    (1) FILE *fp;
        fp=fopen("myfile.dat","rb");
    (2) FILE *fp;
        fp=fopen("myfile.dat","ab");
    (3) FILE *fp;
        fp=fopen("myfile.dat","r");

21. Consider the following declaration:
    FILE *fp;
    fp=fopen("myfile.dat","r");
    if the file opening fails due to some reason (like, incorrect filename, incorrect path, etc.), what will be the value of fp?
    (1) NULL
    (2) −1
    (3) Nothing will be stored within fp, but program will be terminated.

22. Which one of the following reads a character from file?
    (1) getc()
    (2) getch()
    (3) getchar()

23. Which one of the following writes a character into a file?
    (1) putc()
    (2) putch()
    (3) putchar()

24. If we want to modify the existing content of a file, what will be the file opening mode for a text file?
    (1) r+
    (2) w
    (3) a+

25.
```
void main()
{ FILE *fptr;
  char chr;
  fptr=fopen("newfile.txt","r");
  while((chr=fgetc(fptr))!=EOF)
  putchar(chr);
  fclose(fptr);
}
```
What does the above program segment do?
(1) Display the content of the file, "newfile.txt".
(2) Display only the first character from file "newfile.txt".
(3) Display only the last character from file "newfile.txt".

26. If we want to create a file containing only a series of integer numbers, which function is appropriate for storing (writing) the number into the file?
(1) putw()
(2) putint()
(3) putc()

27. If we want to read numbers from a file containing only a series of integer numbers, which function will be appropriate?
(1) getint()
(2) getw()
(3) getc()

28. Which of the following header files contain the declaration of all file handling functions?
(1) stdio.h
(2) string.h
(3) ctype.h

29. Which function is appropriate for reading a total line instead of a single character from a text file?
(1) *fgets* function
(2) *fline* function
(3) *fgetline* function

30. Which function is appropriate for storing (writing) a string instead of a single character into a text file?
(1) *fputs* function
(2) *fline* function
(3) *fputline* function

31. Instead of a single character or integer, if we want to write a group of mixed data into a text file, which library function is used?
(1) *fprintf* function
(2) *printf* function
(3) *sprintf* function

32. Which function is used to write a record (structure) into a binary file?
(1) fwrite()
(2) fputs()
(3) fputc()

33. Which function is used to read a record (structure) from a binary file?
(1) fread()
(2) fgets()
(3) fgetc()

34. Which function is used to move the file pointer to a desired location within the file?
    (1) fset()
    (2) fmove()
    (3) fseek()

35. Which of the following invocations of fseek() sets the file pointer, fp at the beginning of file?
    (1) fseek(fp,0,0);
    (2) fseek(fp,0,1);
    (3) fseek(fp,1,1);

36. Which of the following invocations of fseek() sets the file pointer, fp at the end of file?
    (1) fseek(fp,0,2);
    (2) fseek(fp,2,0);
    (3) fseek(fp,0,0);

37. Which of the following invocations of fseek() is equivalent to *rewind()*?
    (1) fseek(fp,0,0);
    (2) fseek(fp,0,2);
    (3) fseek(fp,0,1);

38. How can we know the current position of file pointer in a file?
    (1) Using ftell()
    (2) Using fseek()
    (3) Using fposition()

39. Consider the following program segment:
```
void main( )
{  FILE *fp;
   int n;
   fp=fopen("newfile.txt","r");
   fseek(fp,0,2);
   n=ftell(fp);
   printf("%d",n);
   fclose(fp);
}
```
    What will be the output of the program segment given above?
    (1) Size of the file,"newfile.txt".
    (2) 0
    (3) Garbage value.

40. Which function is used to delete a file?
    (1) remove()
    (2) delete()
    (3) fdelete()

41. Which function is used to rename a file?
    (1) rename()
    (2) rem()
    (3) frename()

42. How can we detect errors during read/write operation in file?
    (1) Using ferror()
    (2) Using error()
    (3) Using ferr()

43. By which function end-of-file is detected in text file?
    (1) feof()
    (2) end()
    (3) fend()

44.
```
void main()
{ FILE *fp;
  char ch;
  fp=fopen("newfile.txt","w");
  while((ch=getchar())!=EOF)
       putc(ch,fp);
  fclose(fp);
}
```
What does the above program segment do?
(1) Create a new file, "newfile.txt" by taking input from keyboards.

```
fp=fopen("newfile.txt","w");   /*creates newfile.txt*/
                               /*if same file already exists then deletes it */
while((ch=getchar())!=EOF)     /*this loop will run until a ^z is pressed */
    putc(ch,fp);               /*getchar will take input from keyboard to ch*/
                               /*putc() will write ch to the file*/
fclose(fp);                    /*closes the file*/
```

(2) Display the content of the file, "newfile.txt" to the VDU.
(3) Write a single character on the file, "newfile.txt".

45.
```
void main()
{ FILE *fptr1,*fptr2;
  char chr;
  fptr1=fopen("oldfile.txt","r");
  fptr2=fopen("newfile.txt","w");
  while((chr=getc(fptr1))!=EOF)
       putc(chr, fptr2);
  fclose(fptr1);
  fclose(fptr2);
}
```
What does the above program segment do?
(1) Copies the content of the file, "oldfile.txt" to the "newfile.txt".
(2) Display the content of the file, "newfile.txt" to the VDU.
(3) Moves the content of the file, "oldfile.txt" to the "newfile.txt".

46. Which of the following statement moves the file pointer fp by **m** bytes in backward direction from current position?
(1) fseek(fp,−m,1);
(2) fseek(fp,m,1);
(3) fseek(fp,−m,0);

47. Which of the following invocations of fseek() is equivalent to *rewind()*?
(1) fseek(fp,0,SEEK_SET);
(2) fseek(fp,0,SEEK_BEG);
(3) fseek(fp,0,1);

48. Which of the following function set will be appropriate for storing/retrieving a record consist of roll no, name and total marks in a file? Name may consist of any number of parts.
(1) fread()/fwrite()
(2) fscanf()/fprintf()
(3) fgets()/fputs()

49.
```
void main()
{ FILE *fptr;
  char s[80];
  fptr=fopen("sample.txt","r");
  while( fgets(s,79,fptr)!=NULL)
        puts(s);
  fclose(fptr);
}
```

What does the above program segment do?
(1) Reads strings from the file and displays them on screen.
(2) Reads strings from the keyboard and writes them on the file.
(3) Reads strings from the file and write them back on the file.

50.
```
struct emp
{ int empno;
   char ename[30];
   int basic;
};
void main()
{ FILE *fp;
  struct emp e;
  fp=fopen("employee.dat","rb");
  fseek(fp,0,2);
  n=ftell(fp);
  printf("%d",n/sizeof(e));
  fclose(fp);
}
```

What does the above program segment do?
(1) Display the total no. of records present in the file, "employee.dat".
(2) Display the size of the file, "employee.dat".
(3) Display the size of each record in the file, "employee.dat".

51. Assume "sample.txt" contains some lines where length of each line is less than 80 characters. Now consider the following code:
```
void main()
{ FILE *fp;
  char s[80]; int ln =0;
  fp=fopen("sample.txt","r");
  while( fgets(s,80,fp)!=NULL)
        ln++;
  printf("%d",ln);
  fclose(fp);
}
```

What does the above program segment do?
(1) Display the total number of lines in the file.
(2) Display the size of the file.
(3) Display the total number of character in the file.

52.
```
void filefn(FILE *fptr1, FILE *fptr2)
{ char ch;
  while((ch=fgetc(fptr1))!=EOF)
```

```
            fputc(ch,fptr2);
}
void main()
{ FILE *fileptr1,*fileptr2;
  fileptr1=fopen("oldfile.txt","r");
  fileptr2=fopen("newfile.txt","w");
  filefn(fileptr1,fileptr2);
  fclose(fileptr1);
  fclose(fileptr2);
}
```

What does the above program segment do?

(1) Copies the content of the file, "oldfile.txt" to the "newfile.txt".

(2) Display the content of the file, "newfile.txt" to the VDU.

(3) Moves the content of the file, "oldfile.txt" to the "newfile.txt".

53. The main() function can accept two parameters named argc and argv that can be used for retrieving command line arguments entered by the user. What is the data type of argc?

(1) int

(2) char*

(3) Bool

54. The main() function can accept two parameters named argc and argv that can be used for retrieving command line arguments entered by the user. What is the data type of argv?

(1) array of character pointer

(2) array of integer

(3) character pointer

55. The exe file name of a program is myprog.

The command entered at command prompt is as following:

myprog aa bb cc

What will be the value of argc?

(1) 4

(2) 3

(3) 0

56. The exe file name of a program is myprog.

The command entered at command prompt is as following:

myprog aa bb cc

What will be the value of argv[2]?

(1) bb

(2) aa

(3) cc

LEARN BY QUIZ – ANSWERS

Answer Explanations

1. **A file is a collection of bytes stored on a secondary storage device.** Depending on the interpretation of these bytes, several types of file may form. It may form textual document, a database file, an image file or file of any other form. The type of a particular file is decided entirely by the data structures and operations used by a program to process the file.

2. **File stores data permanently** – is the **correct statement**. Because files are stored on secondary memory, not in RAM. The type of data that we want to retain after the computer

is switched off, should be kept in file. Also unless we write the data in some file we cannot move it from one location to another computer in some different location using some media like disk or tape.

Array stores data permanently – is a **wrong statement**. Because arrays are stored in main memory and that is why it is volatile.

Structure stores data permanently – is a **wrong statement**. Because structures are stored in main memory and that is why it is volatile.

3. **In text file, data are stored as a character** – is the correct answer. So if we open an ASCII file using any word editor the data is readable.

4. In binary file data is stored as the binary equivalent of the data. e.g., if we save an integer 67 then its binary equivalent 0000000001000011 will be stored in file but if it is stored in a text file then ASCII value of 6 and that of 7, i.e., 54 and 55 will be stored in the file in binary, i.e., 0011011000110111 will be stored in the file.

5. In text file numbers are stored as strings of characters. As each character takes one byte and 24968 is a five digited number, **5 bytes is required to store the integer, 24968 in a text file.**

2 bytes is wrong answer because the number 24968 cannot be stored as integer in a text file.

6 bytes is wrong answer because like array here extra '\0' character will not be stored.

6. In text file, numbers are stored as strings of characters. As each character takes one byte, **6 bytes is required to store the floating point number, 24.968 in a text file.** This number consists of 5 digits and a decimal point.

4 bytes is wrong answer because the number 24.968 cannot be stored as floating point number in a text file.

5 bytes is wrong answer because for 5 digits 5 bytes are required and for decimal point(.) another 1 byte is required.

7. In binary file, numbers are stored in binary format. So, only 2 bytes is required to store any integer value. As 24968 is an integer number, **2 bytes is required to store it in a binary file.**

In binary file, the numbers are not stored as set of characters. So, 5 is wrong answer.

8. In binary file, the numbers are stored in binary format. So, 4 bytes is required to store any floating point number. As 24.968 is a floating point number, **4 bytes is required to store it in a binary file.**

In binary file, the numbers are not stored as set of characters. So, 6 is wrong answer.

9. **End-of-file is detected in text file by the character ^Z (whose ASCII value is 26).** In text mode, to mark the end of file a special character is inserted at the end of file, i.e., after the last character in the file. This character can be generated by holding down *Ctrl* and *Z* keys simultaneously (often represented by ^Z) or by pressing the key F6.

10. *fopen()* is used to open a file. It is a library function defined in **stdio.h** header file.

11. *fopen()* function is used to open a file. Before using a file in a program we have to open it.

The prototype of fopen() is:

FILE* fopen(const char*filename, const char *mode);

fopen() accept **filename** and **mode of opening the file** as arguments and returns a pointer, known as *file pointer*, to the **FILE** structure for the specified file.

12. To create a text file named myfile.txt, the file open statement will be:

FILE *fp;

fp=fopen("myfile.txt","w");

where fp is a pointer to a structure of type FILE. FILE is a structure defined in stdio.h.

fopen() function is used to open a file. Before using a file in a program we have to open it.

The prototype of fopen() is:

FILE* fopen(const char*filename, const char *mode);

fopen() accept **filename** and **mode of opening the file** as arguments and returns a pointer, known as *file pointer*, to the **FILE** structure for the specified file.

13. The correct statement to open a text file named myfile.txt for reading only will be

FILE *fp;

fp=fopen("myfile.txt","r");

fopen() function is used to open a file. Before using a file in a program we have to open it.

The prototype of fopen() is:

FILE* fopen(const char*filename, const char *mode);

fopen() accept **filename** and **mode of opening the file** as arguments and returns a pointer, known as *file pointer*, to the **FILE** structure for the specified file.

The statement

FILE *fp;

fp=fopen("myfile.txt","a");

is wrong because file open mode for read purpose is "r".

The statement

FILE *fp;

fp=fopen("myfile.txt");

is wrong because here file open mode is missing.

14. At most **only one file** can be opened with a single fopen().

For example, if we have to open two files for reading, the corresponding program segment will be:

            FILE *fp1, *fp2;

            Fp1 = fopen("file1.txt","r");

            fp2 = fopen("file2.txt","r");

So we can see and open multiple files in different modes in a single program using multiple fopen() function.

15. We can open and use any number of files at a time. However this number depends on the system we use.

16. *fclose()* function is used to close a file.

17. *fclose()* function is used to close a file.

To close the file a.txt and b.txt, the correct statement is:

fclose("a.txt");

fclose("b.txt");

18. To **read a character** from a file, the function **fgetc() is used**.

    The prototype is

    int fgetc(FILE *stream);

19. To **write a character** into the file, the function is **fputc()**.

    The prototype is

    int fputc(int c, FILE *stream);

    This function returns the character written. For **fputc** a return value of **EOF** indicates an error.

20. The correct statement to open a **binary file** named myfile.dat for **reading** only will be

    FILE *fp;

    fp=fopen("myfile.txt","rb");

    The statement

    FILE *fp;

    fp=fopen("myfile.txt","ab");

    is wrong because file open mode for read purpose is "rb".

    The statement

    FILE *fp;

    fp=fopen("myfile.txt");

    is wrong because the file open mode **"r"** is used for **reading in textfile**.

21. **If the file opening fails due to some reason** (like, incorrect filename, incorrect path, etc.), fopen() returns a value NULL (in stdio.h it is defined as #define NULL 0). So, **fp will contain NULL.**

22. **getc() reads a character from file**. Actually *getc* is a macro, defined in "stdio.h".

    Ex:

             FILE *fp;
             char ch;
             p=fopen("sample.c","r");
             ch=getc(fp);

    here, getc() will read the 1st character of the file, sample.c and this character will be stored within the variable ch.

    getch() and getchar() is used to read a character from console, i.e., keyboard, not from file.

23. **putc() writes a character into a file**. Actually *putc* is a macro, defined in "stdio.h".

    Ex:

             FILE *fp;
             char ch='A';
             fp=fopen("sample.c", "w");
             putc(ch,fp);

    here, **putc()** will write the character 'A' into the file, *sample.c*.

    Ultimately fputc() and putc() does same job but fputc() is a function where as putc() is a macro.

    getch() and getchar() is used to read a character from console, i.e., keyboard, not from file.

24. To modify the existing content of a file, the file opening mode for a text file is r+.

The file opening mode w is used to write new content on a file.

The file opening mode a+ is used to append new content at the end of a file.

25. The above program will **display the content of the file, "newfile.txt".**

Here, newfile.txt is opened in read mode. Next, each character is read by fgetc() and displayed into the VDU until the end-of-file is encountered. This end-of-file is detected by the macro EOF.

26. If we want to create a file containing only a series of integer numbers, **putw()** is appropriate for storing(writing) the number into the file.

The general form of **putw()** is:

> **putw(integer, filepointer);**

The integer value is written to the file pointed by the file pointer.

27. If we want to read numbers from a file containing only a series of integer numbers, **getw()** is appropriate for reading numbers from the file.

The general form of **getw()** is:

> **getw(file pointer);**

The getw() reads an integer from the file pointed by the file pointer and returns the integer.

28. The header file, **stdio.h**, contains the declaration of all the file handling functions and macros.

Any C program using a file handling function includes **stdio.h** in the following manner:

> **#include<stdio.h>**

29. **fgets** function is appropriate for reading a total line instead of a single character from a text file.

The syntax of the function is:

> **fgets(str,n,fp);**

where, **str** is an array of characters and specifies the address where the string is to be stored, **n** is the maximum length of the input string, and **fp** is a file pointer.

fgets( ) reads from the file pointed by **fp** and stores them in the array **str** until it reads n−1 characters or encountered a new line character or end of file marker, which one comes first.

30. **fputs** function is appropriate for storing(writing) a string instead of a single character into a text file.

The syntax of the function is:

> **fputs(str,fp);**

where, **str** is an array of characters or a string constant and **fp** is a file pointer.

fputs copies the null-terminated string **str** to the file pointed by the filepointer, **fp**. It does not append a new line character nor copy the terminating null character.

31. Instead of a single character or integer, if we want to write a group of mixed data into a text file, **fprintf** function is used.

The general format of **fprintf** is:

> **fprintf(fp, "control string", list);**

where **fp** is a file pointer which points a file. The **control string** contains conversion specifier for the items in the list. **List** is a list of variables whose content is to be written to the file.

printf() is used to display items in the VDU not to write in the file.

sprintf() is used to store formatted output into an array not to write in the file.

32. *fwrite()* is used to write a record(structure) into a binary file.

The general format of **fwrite** is:

> *fwrite(&var, sizeof(var),n,fp);*

where **var** is any variable (generally structure variable), **n** is the number of such variables to be written and **fp** is a file pointer which points a binary file that has been opened for writing. 1st argument indicates the address of the variable and 2nd argument indicates the size of the variable.

Generally, a record is a collection of heterogeneous data. As **fputs()** writes a string and **fputc()** writes a character into a file, these cannot be used for storing records.

33. *fread()* is used to read a record (structure) into a binary file.

The general format of **fread** is:

> *fread(&var, sizeof(var),n,fp);*

where **var** is any variable (generally structure variable), **n** is the number of such variables to be written and **fp** is a file pointer which points a binary file that has been opened for reading. 1st argument indicates the address of the variable and 2nd argument indicates the size of the variable.

34. *fseek()* is used to set the file pointer to the required location. The general form of this function is:

> *fseek(fp, offset, reference position);*

fp is the file pointer, **offset** specifies the number of bytes the file pointer is to be moved in terms of long integer from the **reference position**. The value of **reference position** will be one of the following values:

Meaning	Values	Corresponding Macros
Beginning of File	0	SEEK_SET
Current Position	1	SEEK_CUR
End of File	2	SEEK_END

35. The invocation, *fseek(fp,0,0);* sets the file pointer, fp at the beginning of file.

fseek() is used to set the file pointer to the required location. The general form of this function is:

> *fseek(fp, offset, reference position);*

fp is the file pointer, **offset** specifies the number of bytes the file pointer is to be moved in terms of long integer from the **reference position**. The value of **reference position** will be one of the following values:

Meaning	Values	Corresponding Macros
Beginning of File	0	SEEK_SET
Current Position	1	SEEK_CUR
End of File	2	SEEK_END

The invocation, *fseek(fp,0,1);* moves the file pointer, 0 byte from its current location, i.e., the filepointer remains at its position.

The invocation, *fseek(fp,1,1);* moves the file pointer, 1 byte from its current location.

36. The invocation, *fseek(fp,0,2);* sets the file pointer, fp at the end of the file.

    fseek() is used to set the file pointer to the required location. The general form of this function is:

    ### fseek(fp, offset, reference position);

    fp is the file pointer, *offset* specifies the number of bytes the file pointer is to be moved in terms of long integer from the *reference position*. The value of *reference position* will be one of the following values:

Meaning	Values	Corresponding Macros
Beginning of File	*0*	*SEEK_SET*
Current Position	*1*	*SEEK_CUR*
End of File	*2*	*SEEK_END*

37. The invocation, *fseek(fp,0,0);* is equivalent to *rewind()*.

    rewind() is used to set the file pointer at the beginning of the file, irrespective of its current position. The general form of this function is:

    ### rewind(fp);

    where, *fp* is the file pointer.

    fseek() is used to set the file pointer to the required location. The general form of this function is:

    ### fseek(fp, offset, reference position);

    fp is the file pointer, *offset* specifies the number of bytes the file pointer is to be moved in terms of long integer from the *reference position*. The value of *reference position* will be one of the following values:

Meaning	Values	Corresponding Macros
Beginning of File	*0*	*SEEK_SET*
Current Position	*1*	*SEEK_CUR*
End of File	*2*	*SEEK_END*

    The invocation, *fseek(fp,0,2);* sets the file pointer, fp at the end of the file.

    The invocation, *fseek(fp,0,1);* moves the file pointer, 0 byte from its current location i.e, the filepointer remains at its position.

38. Using *ftell()* we can know the current position of file pointer in a file. It is invoked as follows:

    ### n=ftell(fp);

    where *fp* is the file pointer. n would store number of bytes the file pointer is apart from beginning of a file.

    fseek() sets the file pointer at the desired position within the file.

    There is no library function called *fposition()*.

39. The above program segment will print the size of the file, *"newfile.txt"*.

    The *fseek(fp,0,2)* statement sets the file pointer at the end of the file. Then *ftell(fp)* statement returns the relative offset of the current position. As this is the last byte of the file, *n* will store actually the size of the file.

40. *remove()* is used to delete a file.

The syntax of this function is:

> *remove(filename);*

If the file is successfully deleted, then the *remove()* returns 0 but on failure returns −1. The reasons for its failure may be:
- File does not exist.
- File is open.
- File is read only.

41. *rename()* is used to rename a file.

The syntax of this function is:

> *rename(old filename, new filename);*

rename() changes the **old filename** to **new filename**.

If the file is renamed successfully, then the *rename()* returns 0 but on failure returns −1. The reasons for its failure may be:
- File does not exist.
- File is open.
- File is read only.

42. *Using ferror()* we can detect errors during read/write operation in file.

ferror() is a macro which is used to detect any error that might have occurred during a read or write operation on a file. It returns non zero value if any error is detected on read or write operation, otherwise returns 0 (zero).

43. *feof()* detects the end of file in any text file. When end of file is detected it returns true (1) otherwise returns false (0).

For example, to read a file we can write the following program segment :

```
void main()
{   FILE *fptr;
    char chr;
    fptr=fopen("newfile.txt","r");
    while(!feof(fptr))
    {   chr=fgetc(fptr);
        putchar(chr);
    }
    fclose(fptr);
}
```

44. The above program segment *will create a new file, "newfile.txt" by taking input from keyboards*.

It will accept character inputs from keyboard and write each character on to the file until it encounter the ^Z character.

EOF is a macro whose value is 26. When user press ^Z, it also returns 26. Then the loop will be terminated.

45. The above program segment *copies the content of the file, "oldfile.txt" to the "newfile.txt"*.

It will read each character from the file, "oldfile.txt" and write the character on to the file, "nexfile.txt" until it encounters the end-of-file.

46. *fseek(fp,−m,1);* moves the file pointer, fp m bytes in backward direction from current position.

   fseek() is used to set the file pointer to the required location. The general form of this function is:

   fseek(fp, offset, reference position);

   fp is the file pointer, *offset* specifies the number of bytes the file pointer is to be moved in terms of long integer from the *reference position*. The value of *reference position* will be one of the following values:

Meaning	Values	Corresponding Macros
Beginning of File	0	SEEK_SET
Current Position	1	SEEK_CUR
End of File	2	SEEK_END

47. The invocation, *fseek(fp,0,SEEK_SET);* is equivalent to *rewind().*

   rewind() is used to set the file pointer at the beginning of the file, irrespective of its current position. The general form of this function is:

   rewind(fp);

   where, *fp* is the file pointer.

   fseek() is used to set the file pointer to the required location. The general form of this function is:

   fseek(fp, offset, reference position);

   fp is the file pointer, *offset* specifies the number of bytes the file pointer is to be moved in terms of long integer from the *reference position*. The value of *reference position* will be one of the following values:

Meaning	Values	Corresponding Macros
Beginning of File	0	SEEK_SET
Current Position	1	SEEK_CUR
End of File	2	SEEK_END

48. *fread()/fwrite()* function set will be appropriate for storing/retrieving a record consist of roll no, name and total marks where name may consist of any number of parts.

49. The above program segment reads strings from the file, "sample.txt" and displays them on screen.

50. The above program segment will display the total no. of records present in the file, "employee. dat".

   The *fseek(fp,0,2)* statement sets the file pointer at the end of the file. Then *ftell(fp)* statement returns the relative offset of the current position. As this is the last byte of the file, *n* will store actually the size of the file. Again it is a binary file, so each record occupied same amount of memory. Dividing n by size of the record, we get the number of records in the file.

51. The above program segment will *display the total number of lines in the file.*

   fgets() will read a single line each time. So, to read n lines the loop will execute n times and the variable *ln* will also increment n times.

52. The above program segment **copies the content of the file, "oldfile.txt" to the "newfile. txt".**

    In the main() both files are opened. Then file pointers are passed as arguments to the **filefn()**. In the **filefn()**, each character will be read from the file, "oldfile.txt" and those character will be written on to the file, "nexfile.txt" until the end-of-file is encountered.

53. The argument argc is of int type. The declaration is

    int main(int argc, char *argv[])

    argc has the value of number of command line parameter passed. The argc parameter is always greater than or equal to 1.

54. The argument argv is an array of character pointers.

55. The value of argc will be 4.   The program name is considered an argument so aa, bb and cc are three arguments and myprog is the fourth. Since the program name is considered an argument, the value of argc is at least one and cannot be 0.

56. The value of argv[2] will be bb.

    The value of argv[1] will be aa

    The value of argv[3] will be cc

    Array index starts from 0. The program name is considered an argument and it is the first, i.e., 0th argument.

17

Bitwise Operators

Until now we have dealt with various operators. All these operators are operated on constants and variables of different data types, i.e., they are operated on byte level. But we are not able to get scope to see within these data types that how they are actually constructed with the individual bits. Also we are not able to set the individual bits within the bytes. If we write int x = 5; we know that the binary equivalent of 5, i.e., 101 will be stored in some memory location named x. As it is an integer variable it occupies 2 bytes of memory. So the total bit pattern of it will be 00000000 00000101. We know it but are never able to test that whether it is the actual bit pattern or not. This is an example but it was not possible for us to check or set the individual bit. But bit level operation is very important when a program interacts directly with the hardware. In this chapter, we will learn about bit by bit manipulation.

Another important feature of C language is it provides a set of operators that operate on individual bits of a variable. They are known as bitwise operators. Apart from hardware interaction these operators help us to save memory and make some computation faster. But these operators can only be applied to integral operands, i.e., integer and character operands, whether signed or unsigned. These operators are:

Table 17.1 Bitwise Operators

Operator	Meaning
&	Bitwise AND
|	Bitwise OR (Inclusive)
^	Bitwise Exclusive OR
~	One's Complement
<<	Left Shift
>>	Right Shift

All bitwise operators are binary except for one's complement, which is a unary operator. The bitwise AND operator and bitwise OR operator have higher precedence than the logical AND operator and logical OR operator. The shift operators have higher precedence than the relational operators. Associativity of all the bitwise operators is left to right except one's complement whose associativity is right to left.

17.1 BITWISE & OPERATOR

This operator is known as bitwise AND operator. It is a binary operator and both operands must be of same type (either char or int). This operator performs bitwise AND operation on their operand bit by bit starting from the least significant (i.e., rightmost) bit and sets each bit in the result. The bitwise AND operator returns 1 only when the corresponding bits in both operands are 1; if any one or both is 0, it returns 0. This rule is shown in the following table.

Table 17.2   Bitwise & operation on individual bits

bit1	bit2	bit1 & bit2
0	0	0
0	1	0
1	0	0
1	1	1

EXAMPLE 17.1

Let us consider three integer variable a, b and c where a = 21 and b = 25. The result of the operation, c = a & b; is shown in the following table.

Table 17.3   Illustration of bitwise & operation showing bit pattern

Variable	Bit pattern	Decimal equivalent
a	0000 0000 0001 0101	21
b	0000 0000 0001 1001	25
c = a & b	0000 0000 0001 0001	17

Following program shows the use of bitwise AND operator.

PROGRAM 17.1   Program to demonstrate the use of bitwise AND operator.

```
#include<stdio.h>
void main()
{
    int a,b,c;
    printf("Enter any two Integers: ");
    scanf("%d%d",&a,&b);
    c= a & b;
    printf("%d & %d = %d",a,b,c);
}
```

Sample output

    Enter any two integers: 21   25
    21 & 25 = 17

    Enter any two integers: 15   15
    15 & 15 = 15

The bitwise & operator is often used to test whether a particular bit is On or Off (i.e., 1 or 0). Suppose we want to check the *n*th bit. For this, we need to take a selected bit pattern whose all bits are set 0 except the *n*th bit. This pre-selected bit pattern is commonly known as **mask**. Now the bitwise AND operation between the original number (i.e., whose particular bit are going to check) and this mask produce zero or some non-zero value. As all other bits of the mask are set zero, the result depends on this *n*th bit. If the *n*th bit in the original number is 0, the corresponding bit in the resultant will be 0. So the result of the operation will be 0. On the other hand if the *n*th bit in the original number is 1, the corresponding bit in the resultant will be 1. So the result of the operation will be some non-zero value. Actually this resultant value will be same as the mask. This ANDing operation with a mask is known as **masking**. Following program illustrate this.

PROGRAM 17.2   Write a program to check whether the right most 3rd bit is set or not.

```
#include<stdio.h>
void main()
{
    int num,mask=4,result;
    printf("Enter any Number: ");
    scanf("%d",&num);
    result = num & mask;
    if(result == 0)
        printf("The right most 3rd bit is not set");
    else
        printf("The right most 3rd bit is set");
}
```

Sample output

    Enter any Number: 21
    The left most 3rd bit is set

    Enter any Number: 25
    The left most 3rd bit is not set

Using this concept, we can easily check whether an integer is odd or even. If a number is odd, its least significant bit (LSB) should be 1 but for even numbers the LSB would be 0. So, we need to test the LSB. Thus the mask value will be 1.

PROGRAM 17.3   Write a program to check whether an integer is odd or even.

```
#include<stdio.h>
void main()
{    int num,mask=1,result;
     printf("Enter any Number: ");
     scanf("%d",&num);
     result = num & mask;
     if(result == 0)
          printf("It is an Even Number.");
     else
          printf("It is an Odd Number.");
}
```

Sample output

Enter any Number: 15
It is an Odd Number.

Enter any Number: 20
It is an Even Number.

Another thing that can be done using bitwise AND operator is to set a particular bit off. If we want to set off the *n*th bit, the *n*th bit of the mask should be 0 and other bits need to be set as 1. When ANDing will be done with this mask, irrespective of whether the *n*th bit is 0 or 1 previously, the *n*th bit will be 0 and other bits remain same as previous. Following program shows this.

PROGRAM 17.4   Write a program to set off the right most 3rd bit.

```
#include<stdio.h>
void main()
{
     unsigned int num,mask=65531,result;
     printf("Enter any Number: ");
     scanf("%u",&num);
     result = num & mask;
     printf("After masking %d becomes %d",num,result);
}
```

Sample output

Enter any Number: 5
After masking 5 becomes 1

Enter any Number: 21
After masking 21 becomes 17

The binary equivalent of 5 is 0000 0000 0000 0101. As we want to set off right most 3rd bit, the all the bits of the mask should be 1 except the right most 3rd bit. So, the bit pattern of mask would be 1111 1111 1111 1011 whose decimal equivalent is 65531. After operation the 3rd bit from right is set off and the variable **result** contains 0000 0000 0000 0001 whose decimal equivalent is 1. Thus we get the output as 1. Similarly, 21 becomes 17 as its 3rd bit become 0.

17.2 BITWISE I OPERATOR

This operator is known as bitwise inclusive OR operator. It is also a binary operator and both operands must be of same type (either char or int). This operator performs bitwise OR operation on their operand bit by bit starting from the least significant (i.e., rightmost) bit and sets each bit in the result. The bitwise OR operator returns 0 only when the corresponding bits in both operands are 0; if any one or both is 1, it returns 1. The rules that decide the value of the resultant bit are shown in the following table:

Table 17.4   Bitwise | operation on individual bits

bit1	bit2	bit1 | bit2
0	0	0
0	1	1
1	0	1
1	1	1

EXAMPLE 17.2

Let us consider three integer variable a, b and c where a = 21 and b = 25. The result of the operation, c = a | b; is shown in the following table.

Table 17.5   Illustration of bitwise | operation showing bit pattern

Variable	Bit pattern	Decimal equivalent
a	0000 0000 0001 0101	21
b	0000 0000 0001 1001	25
c = a | b	0000 0000 0001 1101	29

Following program shows the use of bitwise OR operator.

PROGRAM 17.5   Program to demonstrate the use of bitwise OR operator.

```
#include<stdio.h>
void main()
{
    int a,b,c;
    printf("Enter any two Integers:  ");
    scanf("%d%d",&a,&b);
    c= a | b;
    printf("%d | %d = %d",a,b,c);
}
```

Sample output

Enter any two Integers: 21 25
21 | 25 = 29

Enter any two Integers: 5 6
5 | 6 = 7

The bitwise OR operator is usually used to set a particular bit ON which is just reverse of bitwise AND operator. Following program illustrate this.

PROGRAM 17.6   Write a program to set on the right most 3rd bit.

```c
#include<stdio.h>
void main()
{
    unsigned int num, mask=4, result;
    printf("Enter any Number: ");
    scanf("%u", &num);
    result = num | mask;
    printf("After masking %d becomes %d", num, result);
}
```

Sample output

Enter any Number: 1
After masking 1 becomes 5

Enter any Number: 17
After masking 17 becomes 21

17.3   BITWISE ^ OPERATOR

This operator is known as bitwise exclusive OR operator or commonly known as XOR. It is a binary operator and both operands must be of same type (either char or int). This operator performs bitwise Exclusive OR operation on their operand bit by bit starting from the least significant (i.e., rightmost) bit and sets each bit in the result. When both the operand bits are same, XOR operator returns 0; when operands are different, it returns 1. The rules that decide the value of the resultant bit are shown in the following table:

Table 17.6   Bitwise ^ operation on individual bits

bit1	bit2	bit1 ^ bit2
0	0	0
0	1	1
1	0	1
1	1	0

EXAMPLE 17.3

Let us consider three integer variable a, b and c where a = 21 and b = 25. The result of the operation, c = a ^ b; is shown in the following table.

Table 17.7   Illustration of bitwise ^ operation showing bit pattern

Variable	Bit pattern	Decimal equivalent
a	0000 0000 0001 0101	21
b	0000 0000 0001 1001	25
c = a ^ b	0000 0000 0000 1100	12

Following program shows the use of bitwise XOR operator.

PROGRAM 17.7   Program to demonstrate the use of bitwise XOR operator.

```
#include<stdio.h>
void main()
{
    int a,b,c;
    printf("Enter any two Integers: ");
    scanf("%d%d", &a, &b);
    c= a ^ b;
    printf("%d ^ %d = %d", a, b, c);
```

Sample output
```
Enter any two Integers: 21  25
21 ^ 25 = 12

Enter any two Integers: 5  6
5 ^ 6 = 3
```

The bitwise ^ operator is often used to toggle a particular bit is ON or OFF. Thus if a number is XORed twice with a particular mask, original number returns. Following example shows this.

PROGRAM 17.8   Program to demonstrate that XOR operator is used to toggle a particular bit ON or OFF.

```
#include<stdio.h>
void main()
{
    unsigned int num,mask=4,result;
    printf("Enter any Number: ");
    scanf("%u",&num);
    result = num ^ mask;
```

```
        printf("After 1st masking %d becomes %d", num, result);
        result = result ^ mask;
        printf("\nAfter 2nd masking it becomes %d", result);
}
```

Sample output

   Enter any Number: 21
   After 1st masking 21 becomes 17
   After 2nd masking it becomes 21

Using this concept, we can easily swap two integer variables without using third variable. We have to XORed thrice between those two variables. Suppose we have two integer variables, a = 5 whose binary equivalent in 4 bit machine is 0101 and b = 6 whose binary equivalent in 4 bit machine is 0110. Now XOR operation between these produces 0011. If we write a= a ^ b, a becomes 3 and b remains 6. Now XOR operation between these 3 (i.e., 0011) and 6 (i.e., 0110) again produce the first number, i.e., 5. For swapping this number needs to be stored within second variable, i.e., within b. So, our 2nd statement will be b= a ^ b. As a result **b** becomes 5 and **a** remains 3. Now XOR operation between these 3 (i.e., 0011) and 5 (i.e., 0101) will produce 6 and it needs to be stored within **a**. Thus the final statement would be a = a ^ b.

PROGRAM 17.9   Program to swap two integer variables using bitwise operator.

```
#include<stdio.h>
void main( )
{
    int var1,var2;
    printf("Enter any two Integers: ");
    scanf("%d%d",&var1,&var2);
    printf("Before swapping var1 = %d, var2= %d",var1,var2);
    var1= var1 ^ var2;
    var2= var1 ^ var2;
    var1= var1 ^ var2;
    printf("\nAfter swapping var1 = %d, var2= %d",var1,var2);
}
```

Sample output

   Enter any two Integers: 10   20
   Before swapping var1 = 10,   var2 = 20
   After swapping var1 = 20, var2 = 10

17.4   ~ OPERATOR

This operator is known as one's complement. It is a unary operator. It toggles the bit pattern, i.e., converts all 1s present in the number to 0s and all 0s to 1s. As 65 is represented as 0000 0000 0100 0001 in memory, One's complement of 65 therefore would be, 1111 1111 1011 1110. Following table defines the rule for bitwise one's complement operator.

Table 17.8   Bitwise ~ operation on individual bits

bit1	~bit1
0	1
1	0

Here is a program to show the use of one's complement operator (~).

PROGRAM 17.10   Program to demonstrate the use of one's complement operator.

```
#include<stdio.h>
void main()
{
    unsigned int n, comp;
    printf("Enter any Integer: ");
    scanf("%u",&n);
    comp= ~n;
    printf("n = %u, ~n = %u",n, comp);
}
```

Sample output

```
Enter any Integer: 0
n = 0, ~n = 65535
Enter any Integer: 65
n =65, ~n = 65470
```

In the first run of the above example, value of **a** is inputted as 0. So, its bit pattern is 0000 0000 0000 0000. Thus its one's complement will be 1111 1111 1111 1111 whose unsigned integer equivalent value is 65535. In the next run value of **a** is 65 whose bit pattern is 0000 0000 0100 0001. Therefore its one's complement would be, 1111 1111 1011 1110. Thus output is 65470.

17.5   LEFT SHIFT OPERATOR

The left shift operator is a bitwise operator in C. It is represented by <<. It is used to shift each bit of the first operand to the left. Second operand specifies the number of places the bits are shifted. On each shift the most significant bit (MSB) is lost and LSB is filled up with zero.

For example, the statement **var<<3** would shift all bits three places to the left. If the bit pattern of the variable, **var** is 0101011100101011, then **var<<3** gives 1011100101011000.

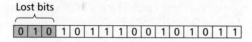

Lost bits

| 0 | 1 | 0 | 1 | 0 | 1 | 1 | 1 | 0 | 0 | 1 | 0 | 1 | 0 | 1 | 1 |

Before shifting bit pattern of the variable var.

Bits padded with Zeros

| 1 | 0 | 1 | 1 | 1 | 0 | 0 | 1 | 0 | 1 | 0 | 1 | 1 | 0 | 0 | 0 |

After execution of the statement, var ≪ 3.

Fig. 17.1 ≪ operation

It has to be remembered that shifting the operand **n** bit to the left is equivalent to multiplying it by 2^n. Consider the following table. In each row the operand is left shifted by one bit.

Table 17.9 Illustration of left shift operation showing bit pattern

Bit pattern	Decimal equivalent
0000 0000 0001 1001	25
0000 0000 0011 0010	50
0000 0000 0110 0100	100
0000 0000 1100 1000	200
0000 0001 1001 0000	400
....	...

Following program shows the effect of left shift operator.

PROGRAM 17.11 Program to demonstrate the use of left shift operator.

```c
#include<stdio.h>
void main()
{
    unsigned int n, i;
    printf("Enter any Integer: ");
    scanf("%u",&n);
    for(i=1;i<=5;i++)
    {
        printf("\n%u << %d = %u", n, i, n<<i);
    }
}
```

Sample output

```
Enter any Integer: 1
1 << 1 = 2
1 << 2 = 4
1 << 3 = 8
1 << 4 = 16
1 << 5 = 32
```

17.6 RIGHT SHIFT OPERATOR

The right shift operator is also a bitwise operator in C and its operation is similar to left shift operator except that the bits are shifted to right instead of left. It is represented by >>. It is used to shift each bit in the operand to right. On each shift the LSB is lost and MSB is filled up with zero. The number of places the bits are shifted depends on the number following the operator.

For example, var>>3 would shift all bits three places to the right. If the variable **var** contains the bit pattern 0101011100101011, then var >>3 gives 0000101011100101.

Before shifting bit pattern of the variable var.

After execution of the statement, var >> 3.

Fig. 17.2 >> operation

Note that shifting the operand **n** bit to the right is same as dividing (integer division) the number by 2^n. Consider the following table. In each row the operand is right shifted by one bit.

Table 17.10 Illustration of right shift operation showing bit pattern

Bit pattern	Decimal equivalent
0000 0000 0001 1001	25
0000 0000 0000 1100	12
0000 0000 0000 0110	6
0000 0000 0000 0011	3
0000 0000 0000 0001	1
....	...

Following program shows the effect of right shift operator.

PROGRAM 17.12   Program to demonstrate the use of right shift operator.

```
#include<stdio.h>
void main()
{
    unsigned int a,b,i;
    printf("Enter any Integers: ");
    scanf("%u",&a);
```

```
        for(i=1;i<=5;i++)
        {   printf("\n%u >> %d = %u", a, i, a>>i);
        }
    }
```

Sample output

```
Enter any Integer: 50
50 >> 1 = 25
50 >> 2 = 12
50 >> 3 = 6
50 >> 4 = 3
50 >> 5 = 1
```

17.7 PROGRAMMING EXAMPLES

Here are some programming examples to understand the various uses of bitwise operators.

PROGRAM 17.13   Write a program to check whether the *n*th bit is set or not.

```
#include<stdio.h>
void main()
{   unsigned int num,bitno,mask=1,result;
    printf("Enter any Number: ");
    scanf("%u",&num);
    printf("Enter The bit number: ");
    scanf("%d",&bitno);
    mask <<= bitno;               /* setting bitno th bit as 1 */
    result = num & mask;
    if(result == 0)
        printf("The %dth bit is not set", bitno);
    else
        printf("The %dth bit is set", bitno);
}
```

PROGRAM 17.14   Write a program to set off the right most *n*th bit.

```
#include<stdio.h>
void main()
{   unsigned int num,bitno,mask=1,result;
    printf("Enter any Number: ");
    scanf("%u",&num);
    printf("Enter The bit number: ");
    scanf("%d",&bitno);
    mask <<= bitno;          /* setting bitno th bit as 1 */
    mask = ~mask;    /* setting all the bits to 1 except bitno th bit */
    printf("%u",mask);
    result = num & mask;
```

```
    printf("After masking %d becomes %d", num, result);
}
```

PROGRAM 17.15   Write a program to set on the right most *n*th bit.

```
#include<stdio.h>
void main()
{    unsigned int num,bitno,mask=1,result;
     printf("Enter any Number: ");
     scanf("%u",&num);
     printf("Enter The bit number: ");
     scanf("%d",&bitno);
     mask <<= bitno;
     printf("%u",mask);
     result = num | mask;

     printf("After masking %d becomes %d", num, result);
}
```

PROGRAM 17.16   Write a program to display the bit pattern of an unsigned integer.

```
#include<stdio.h>
void main()
{    unsigned int num,bitno,mask=1,result,i;
     printf("Enter any Number: ");
     scanf("%u",&num);
     mask <<= 15;
     for(i=1;i<=16;i++)
     {    result = num & mask;
          if(result == 0)
               printf("0");
          else
               printf("1");
          mask >>= 1;
     }
}
```

PROGRAM 17.17   Write a function to change n number of bits starting from a particular bit position. Write a program to show this.

```
#include<stdio.h>
unsigned int change_bit(unsigned int ,int,int);
void showbit(unsigned int);
```

```c
void main ()
{
    unsigned number;
    int from, how;
    clrscr();
    printf ("\n Enter the positive integer number :");
    scanf ("%u", &number);
    printf("\n From starting position :");
    scanf("%d", &from);
    printf("\n How many number you want to change : ");
    scanf("%d", &how);

    clrscr();
    printf( "\n The original number is %u", number);
    printf( "\n Its bit pattern is ");
    showbit(number);
    number = change_bit(number, from, how);
    printf("\n After changing the number is %u", number);
    printf("\n After changing the bit pattern is ");
    showbit(number);
}

unsigned int change_bit(unsigned int n, int st, int no)
{
    unsigned mask=1;
    int i;
    mask=mask<<(st-1);
    for (i=1; i<=no; i++)
    {   n=n^mask;
        mask=mask<<1;
    }
    return(n);
}

void showbit(unsigned int no)
                /* Display the bit pattern of any unsigned integer */
{
    unsigned mask=1;
    mask=mask<<15;
    while (mask)
    {   if(no&mask)
            printf("1");
        else
            printf("0");
        mask>>=1;
    }
}
```

PROGRAM **17.18** Write a function to rotate left an unsigned integer n number of times. Write a program to show this.

```
#include<stdio.h>

unsigned int left_rotate(unsigned int, int);
void showbit(unsigned int);
void main ()
{
    unsigned number;
    int how;
    clrscr();
    printf ("\n Enter the positive integer number :");
    scanf ("%u", &number);
    printf("\n How many bits want to rotate : ");
    scanf("%d", &how);
    printf( "\n The original number is %u", number);
    printf( "\n its bit pattern is: ");
    showbit(number);
    number = left_rotate(number, how);
    printf("\n After rotation the number becomes %u", number);
    printf("\n Afetr rotation the bit pattern is ");
    showbit(number);
}

unsigned int left_rotate(unsigned int num, int no)          /* Rotate left n times */
{
    unsigned mask=1, chk;
    int i;
    mask = mask << 15;
    for (i=1; i<=no; i++)
    {   chk = num & mask;
        num <<=1;
        if(chk!=0)
        num = num | 1;
    }
    return(num);
}
void showbit(unsigned int no)    /* Display the bit pattern of any
                                              unsigned integer */
{   unsigned mask=1;
    mask=mask<<15;
    while (mask)
    {   if(no&mask)
            printf("1");
        else
            printf("0");
        mask>>=1;
    }
}
```

SUMMARY

➤ There are 6 bitwise operators are available in C.

➤ These are bitwise AND (&), bitwise OR (|), XOR (^), one's complement (~), left shift (<<) and right shift (>>) operator.

➤ Bitwise AND (&) operator is used to check a particular bit and to set a particular bit off.

➤ Bitwise OR (|) operator is used to set a particular bit.

➤ Bitwise XOR (^) operator may be used to toggle a particular bit is ON or OFF.

➤ One's complement (~) operator converts all 1s present in the bit pattern to 0s and all 0s to 1s.

➤ Left shift (<<) operator is used to shift each bit in the operand to left and right shift (>>) operator is used to shift each bit in the operand to right.

➤ Shifting the operand **n** bit to the left is same as multiplying it by 2^n and shifting the operand **n** bit to the right is same as dividing (integer division) the number by 2^n.

REVIEW EXERCISES

1. What do you mean by bitwise operation?

2. Explain the operations of bitwise operators &, | and ^.

3. What are the left shift and right shift operators? Give some examples which implement those operators.

4. What is one's complement operator?

5. What are the precedence and associativity of bitwise shift operators?

6. Using bitwise operator write a program in C to check whether an integer is odd or even.

7. Write a program to count number of 1s in the bit pattern of a given integer using bitwise operator.

8. Write a program to rotate right an unsigned integer n number of times. In each rotation each bit will be shifted one place and also recover the lost bit.

9. Write a program that sets one or more bits while other bits remain unchanged.

10. Write a program that inverts a set of bits while other bits remain unchanged.

LEARN BY QUIZ – QUESTIONS

1 Which of the following is not a bitwise operator?
  (1) !!
  (2) ^
  (3) &&

2 What will be value of c?

  int a=5, b=6;

  int c=a|b;

  (1) 0
  (2) 6
  (3) 7

3 What will be value of c?

int a=5, b=6;

int c=a&b;

(1) 4
(2) 7
(3) 1

4 What will be value of c?

int a=5, b=6;

int c=a^b;

(1) 3
(2) 6
(3) 0

5 What will be value of a and b after evaluating the expression?

int a=5, b=6;

a=a^b;

b=a^b;

a=a^b;

(1) a=6, b=5
(2) a=6, b=6
(3) a=5, b=5

6 What will be the value of b?

int a=4;

b=a<<2;

(1) 16
(2) 8
(3) 10

7. What will be the value of b?

int a=4,b;

b=a>>2;
(1) 1
(2) 0
(3) 2

8 What will be the value of b?

int a=0xfff0, b;

b=~a;

(1) 15
(2) 0
(3) 2

9. What will be the value of b?

int a=−3, b;

b=a>>2;

(1) −1

(2) 1

(3) 0

10. What will be the output?

int n = 15;

printf("%d", n << 3 >>5);

(1) Compilation error

(2) 3

(3) 5

LEARN BY QUIZ – ANSWERS

Answer Explanations

1. !! is not a bitwise operator.

   C supports a set of bitwise operators. The operators are as follows:

   1) &   (bitwise AND)

   2) | (bitwise OR)

   3) ^   (bitwise X-OR)

   4) ~   (One's complement)

   5) <<   (Left shift)

   6) >>   (right shift)

2. The value of **c** will be **7**.

   | is a bitwise (OR) operator in C

   Bitwise operators work on individual bits. To know the result of any expression using bitwise operators, the exact binary bit pattern of the operands should be considered. To find out the result we have to know the binary bit pattern of both the operands. Assuming int = 16 bits (2bytes), the binary bit pattern will be as follows:

a	0000000000000101
b	0000000000000110
a|b	0000000000000111

   Bitwise OR (|) generates result according to the following rule:

   0|0=0

   0|1=1

   1|0=1

   1|1=1

   So the above expression **a|b** has produced the binary 0000000000000111 which is 7 in decimal. Hence the correct answer is 7.

3. The value of c will be 4.

   & is a bitwise (AND) operators.

   Bitwise operators work on individual bits. To know the result of any expression using bitwise operators, the exact binary bit pattern of the operands should be considered.

To find out the result, we have to know the binary bit pattern of both the operands. Assuming int = 16 bits (2bytes), the binary bit pattern will be as follows:

a	0000000000000101
b	0000000000000110
a&b	0000000000000100

Bitwise AND (&) generates result according to the following rule:

    0&0=0
    0&1=0
    1&0=0
    1&1=1

So the above expression, a&b has produced the binary 0000000000000100 which is 6 in decimal. Hence the correct answer is 4.

4. The value of c will be 3.

    ^ is a bitwise (X-OR)operator.

Bitwise operators work on individual bits. To know the result of any expression using bitwise operators, the exact binary bit pattern of the operands should be considered.

To find out the result we have to know the binary bit pattern of both the operands. Assuming int = 16 bits (2bytes), the binary bit pattern will be as follows:

a	0000000000000101
b	0000000000000110
a^b	0000000000000011

Bitwise X-OR (^) generates result according to the following rule:

    0^0=0
    0^1=1
    1^0=1
    1^1=0

So the above expression a^b has produced the binary 0000000000000011, which is 3 in decimal. Hence the correct answer is 3.

5. The value of a and b will be a=6, b=5.

    ^ is bitwise operator (X-OR) in C.

Bitwise operators work on individual bits. To know the result of any expression using bitwise operators, the exact binary bit pattern of the operands should be considered.

To find out the result we have to know the binary bit pattern of both the operands. Assuming int = 16 bits (2bytes), the binary bit pattern will be as follows:

a	0000000000000101
b	0000000000000110
a^b	0000000000000011

Bitwise X-OR (^) generates result according to the following rule

    0^0=0
    0^1=0

$1 \wedge 0 = 0$

$1 \wedge 1 = 0$

Here bitwise X-OR operation has been done thrice. First a^b will produce the result 0000000000000011 which will be stored in a so a's value will be changed. Now this will be X-ORed with b and will be stored in b.

a	0000000000000011(modified)
b	0000000000000110
a^b	0000000000000101

After second X-OR operation, the result 0000000000000101 will be stored in b. So now b's content will be changed. Now after the third X-OR operation the result will become,

a	0000000000000011
b	0000000000000101 (modified)
a^b	0000000000000110

This result will finally be stored in a. So the final value of a will be 0000000000000110 (decimal 6) and value of b will be 0000000000000101 (decimal 5). We have observed that after three consecutive X-OR operation, the contents of a and b have been interchanged. So we conclude that interchanging the content of two variables is possible without using a third variable.

6. The value of b will be 16.

   Here the operator << has been used which is a bitwise left shift operator. To know the result of the expression we have to know the binary bit pattern of a. The binary equivalent of a is 0000000000000100.

   The expression a<<2 will shift the bits 2 positions left. As there are only 16 bits (int =2 bytes), the left most two bits will be dropped and the right most 2 bits will be vacant and will be filled up with 0.

   Drop off   <----- 0000000000000100<------insert 0.

   After the evaluation of the expression the a<<2 it will be 0000000000010000 and will be stored in b which is 16 in decimal.

7. The value of b will be is 1.

   Here the operator >> has been used which is a bitwise right shift operator. To know the result of the expression, we have to know the binary bit pattern of a. The binary equivalent of a is 0000000000000100.

   The expression a>>2 will shift the bits 2 positions right. As there are only 16 bits (int =2 bytes), the right most two bits will be dropped and the left most 2 bits will be vacant and will be filled up with 0.

   Insert 0   -----> 0000000000000100------> drop off.

   After the evaluation of the expression the a>>2, the result will be 0000000000000001 and it will be stored in b which is 1 in decimal.

8. The value of b will be 15.

   Here the operator ~ has been used which is a bitwise one's complement operator. To know the result of the expression, we have to know the binary bit pattern of a. The binary equivalent of a is 1111111111110000.

One's complement operator simply complements the binary bit pattern. As a result, all 1 will become 0 and all 0 will become 1. So the expression ~a will generate 0000000000001111 and will be stored in b.

So the content of b will be 15 in decimal.

9. The value of b will be −1.

Here the content of a is a negative number. In C, negative number is stored in 2's complement form. 2's complement of 3 is 1111111111111101. So a will have this value stored.

Now the expression a>>2 will shift all the bits 2 position right. As a result the left most two vacant positions will be filled up with 1.

Insert 1   ------->1111111111111101------->drop off

So the result will be 1111111111111111 and will be stored in b. The magnitude of b is −1. Actually negative numbers are stored in 2's complement form and 2's complement of 2's complement is the original number. 2's complement of 1111111111111111 is 0000000000000001 that is 1 (in decimal).

Note in case of left shift operation, right-most bits are always filed with 0s but in case of right operation for positive and unsigned number, the left-most bits are filled with 0s but in case of negative numbers they are filled with 1s.

10. The output will be 3

The binary equivalent of n is 0000000000001111.

After the operation n<<3 bit pattern will be 0000000001111000. This value will be right shifted by 5(>>5).

Thus the final bit pattern will be 0000000000000011 whose decimal value is 3.

18

Preprocessors

Another important feature of C language is that it may include instructions for the compiler. Though these instructions are not directly the part of C language, they expand the scope of programming environment. These are known as *preprocessor*. In this chapter, we will discuss about these preprocessors.

A unique feature of C language is the preprocessor. The C preprocessor, as its name implies, processes before the processing of C source program. It is a program that processes the source code before the compiler translates the source code into the object code. During processing, these preprocessors perform some modifications on the source code based on the instructions provided by the preprocessors. These instructions are known as *preprocessor commands* or *directives*. Each of the Preprocessor directives begin with a # symbol and do not require semicolon(;) at the end. The preprocessor is used to make the source code more readable, much easy to modify, portable and more efficient.

Some common Preprocessor directives are:
- #define directive – To define a symbolic constant or macro.
- #undef directive – To undefine a symbolic constant or macro.
- #include directive – To include another file in a source program.
- Conditional Compilation directive – To compile parts of source code conditionally.

We already discussed about #define and #include directive in brief. Here they would be discussed in details along with other directives.

18.1 #DEFINE DIRECTIVE

The processor directive #define is used to define symbolic constant. This statement is called 'macro definition' or simply '**macro**'. The macro substitution is a process where an identifier or symbolic constant is replaced by a predefined string each time it is encountered in a program. The syntax of declaring a macro is:

```
#define        identifier        string
```

EXAMPLE 18.1

```
#define PI          3.1415926
#define MAX            10
#define COUNTRY      "INDIA"
```

Note that all the identifiers are written in upper case. It is not mandatory. But the convention is to write the macros in upper case so that they can easily be separated from normal variables. Also note that the macro definition is not terminated by semicolon (;). The definition is terminated only by a new line. There may be one or more spaces before and after the identifier. Following example illustrates the use of macro.

PROGRAM 18.1   Program to show the use of macro.

```
#define SIZE 10

void main( )
{    int element[SIZE], i;
     for(i=0;i<SIZE;i++)
     {    printf("Enter Element %d: ",i+1);
          scanf("%d",&element[i]);
     }

     printf("\n\nThe Inputted Elements are : ");
     for(i=0;i<SIZE;i++)
     {
          printf("%d ", elements[i]);
     }
}
```

In the above program, all the occurrence of the symbolic constant SIZE will be replaced by 10 before the compilation. Thus the array will be declared of size 10 and the loops will be executed 10 times. One of the advantages of using macros is that if it is required to change the size of the array, we need not change every position which is related to the size of the array. We only have to change at the definition of the symbolic constant. This is very effective in the program where we use array.

Not only simple constant value but also macro definition can include any valid C expression. Following definition is a perfectly valid definition.

```
#define DISPLAY      printf("Hello!")
```

18.2 MACROS WITH ARGUMENTS

Macros can have arguments, just like functions. The preprocessor permits us to define more complex and more useful form of replacements. It takes the following form.

```
#define    identifier(a₁,a₂,…..aₙ)      string
```

Notice that there is no space between identifier and left parentheses and the identifier a_1, a2, ... a_n is analogous to formal arguments in a function definition.

A simple example of a macro with arguments is

```
#define SQUARE(x) x*x

void main( )
{
    printf("Square of 5 = %d", SQUARE(5));
}
```

When the program compiles, the printf( ) statement would look like,

```
printf("Square of 5 = %d", 5*5);
```

Macro replaces the predefined string in a stupid, unthinking, literal way. Thus use of macro is very risky if we do not use it very carefully. Consider the following example.

```
#define SQUARE(x) x*x

void main( )
{
    printf("Square of 5 = %d", SQUARE(2+3));
}
```

The output of the above program will be 11 instead of 25. Because the macro will be expanded as:

```
printf("Square of 5 = %d", 2+3 * 2+3);
```

And as the precedence of * operator is higher than that of + operator, 3*2 will be evaluated first. Next the statement 2+6+3 will execute which results 11.

This problem can be solved if we put the macro argument within parenthesis in the macro definition. Here is the corrected version of the above program.

```
#define SQUARE(x) (x)*(x)

void main( )
{
    printf("Square of 5 = %d", SQUARE(2+3));
}
```

Now the printf() statement will be expanded as,

```
printf("Square of 5 = %d", (2+3) * (2+3));
```

So, both the addition operation will execute before the multiplication and thus the output of the program will be 25 which is the expected result.

But the problem related to macro is not over. Consider the following example.

```
#define Increment(x) x++

void main( )
{    int a =5, b, c;
```

```
        b = Increment(a);
        c = Increment(5);
}
```

The statement, b = Increment(a); will execute fine. But what happens for the next statement? The statement will be expanded as, c = 5++; which is an error as a constant cannot be incremented. So, we need to be very careful in using the macros.

18.3 NESTING OF MACRO

Once an identifier has been defined it can be used to define another macro. Consider the following example.

```
        #define PI              3.1415926

        #define AREA(R)         PI*R*R
```

Not only for defining other macro, it can be a parameter of other macros. For example,

```
        #define MIN(A,B)       (A<B) ? A : B

        #define MIN3(A,B,C)    MIN(MIN(A,B),C)
```

Here is a complete program.

PROGRAM 18.2   Program to demonstrate nesting of macros.

```
#define MIN(A,B)        (A<B)? A : B
#define MIN3(A,B,C)     MIN(MIN(A,B),C)
void main( )
{
    int x, y, z, min_num;
    printf("Enter any three numbers:");
    scanf("%d%d%d", &x, &y, &z);
    min_num = MIN3(x,y,z);
    printf("Smallest Number is: %d",min_num);
}
```

18.4 MULTILINE MACRO

So far the macros are discussed their definitions are limited to single line only. We can spread macro definition in multiple line by adding backslash ('\') at the end of the line. This increases the readability.

```
#define SWAP(A,B) { A = A + B;   \
                    B = A - B;   \
                    A = A - B;   \
                  }
```

18.5   MACRO VS. FUNCTION

We have already noticed that macro calls are looked like function calls. But both are not actually the same. The differences between macro and function are:

- In macro substitution the preprocessor replaces an identifier or symbolic constant with predefined string in a thoughtless, stupid, literal way. Whereas when a function is called, the control is passed to the function with or without arguments. If any expression is passed as argument, instead of total expression is passed to the function, first the expression is evaluated and then the result is passed as function arguments. Within the function some operations are carried out and finally a useful value is returned or simply the control is returned from the function.
- Macros increase the program size, whereas functions make the program smaller and compact.
- Macros make the program run faster. But when a function is called, it takes a lot of extra time as there are some overheads associated with function calls such as jumping to the function call, saving registers, and pushing arguments into stack and therefore it slowdowns the program.
- Macro is very risky if we do not use it very carefully because it replaces the predefined string in a stupid, unthinking, literal way. For example,

```
#define SQR(A)    A*A
```

and in the main( ) if we write, x = SQR(2+3);
x will store 11 instead of 25. Because the macro will be expanded as:

```
x = 2 + 3 * 2 + 3;
```

But in case of function, this type of error will never occur.

18.6   #UNDEF DIRECTIVE

This directive is used to undefined, i.e., to remove a previously defined symbolic constant or macro. The general form of #undef directive is

```
#undef    identifier
```

For example, if a macro named MIN is already defined and if we want to remove it, the statement will be

```
#undef    MIN
```

This directive is basically useful when a macro definition is needed to restrict within a particular portion of the program.

18.7   #INCLUDE DIRECTIVE

The #include directive instructs the compiler to include another source file that may contain some functions and macros so that we need not rewrite them again. The general form is:

```
#include <filename>
```

As soon as the statement executes, the entire content of the file, mentioned as `filename`, is included at the point of the source code where the statement is written.

The nesting of file inclusion is also allowed. An included file can also include any other files which may include other files and so on. Suppose we have a source file named **sample.c** and it includes the file **test1.c**. This **test1.c** may include **test2.c** and so on.

sample.c

```
#include<test1.c>
    void main( )
    {
        printf("%d", SIZE);
    }
```

test1.c

```
#include<test2.c>
. . . . .
. . . . .
```

test2.c

```
#define SIZE 105
. . . . .
. . . . .
```

On execution of the program **sample.c**, the output will be: 105

In the above program the macro SIZE is not defined in the sample.c but it is available to the program due the #include directive. test2.c is first included to test1.c and then both these files will be included to sample.c.

The #include statement has two different forms. These are:

```
#include "filename"
```

```
#include <filename>
```

The difference between these forms is that the #include "filename" would look in the current directory first for the file mentioned in the double quotation. If the mentioned file is not found, the file will be searched in the specified list of directories as mentioned in the include search path. Whereas, the #include <filename> statement would search for the mentioned file in the angular bracket in the specified list of directories only.

18.8 CONDITIONAL COMPILATION DIRECTIVE

C provides a set of preprocessor directives which helps us in conditional compilation. Using these directives, we are able to compile or ignore selective portions of a program based on some conditions. These directives are: #if, #ifdef, #ifndef, #elif, #else, and #endif.

18.8.1   #if Directive

The #if directive is used to compile or skipped a certain portion of code. General form of #if directive is

```
#if constant_expression

        Statement(s)

#endif
```

If the constant_expression executed as true, the statement or statements between #if and #endif is compiled; but if it is false, the statement(s) will be ignored by the compiler. Consider the following example.

PROGRAM 19.3   Program to demonstrate #if directive.

```
#define   INDIA       1
#define   COUNTRY     INDIA
void main( )
{
      #if COUNTRY == INDIA
            char *currency = "Rupee";
      #endif
            puts(currency);
}
```

18.8.2   #else Directive

This directive cannot work independently. The #else directive works with #if directive in similar pattern as **else** statement works with **if** statement. The statement(s) between #else and #endif is compiled only when constant_expression with the #if directive executed as **false**. Previous example can be expanded with this directive.

PROGRAM 18.4   Program to demonstrate #if and #else directive.

```
#define INDIA      1
#define COUNTRY    INDIA
void main( )
{
      #if COUNTRY == INDIA
            char *currency = "Rupee";
      #else
            char *currency = "Dollar";
      #endif
            puts(currency);
}
```

18.8.3 #elif Directive

This directive also cannot work independently. Like #else directive, it works with #if directive. It indicates the form – else if. Its general form is

```
#if   constant_expression1
      Statement(s)
#elif   constant_expression2
      Statement(s)
#elif   constant_expression3
      Statement(s)
#elif   constant_expression4
      Statement(s)

      ..
      ..

#endif
```

Each #elif is followed by a constant_expression. If this constant_expression is true, the corresponding block of statement(s) is compiled and no other #elif expressions are tested. Following example illustrates the use of #elif statement.

PROGRAM 18.5 Program to demonstrate #elif directive.

```
#define  INDIA          1
#define  BANGLADESH     2
#define  JAPAN          3
#define  ENGLAND        4
#define  ITALY          5
#define  USA            6

#define  COUNTRY    INDIA
void main( )
{
    #if COUNTRY == INDIA
         char *currency = "Rupee";
    #elif COUNTRY == BANGLADESH
         char *currency = "Taka";
    #elif COUNTRY == JAPAN
         char *currency = "Yen";
    #elif COUNTRY == ENGLAND
         char *currency = "Pound";
    #elif COUNTRY == ITALY
         char *currency = "Lira";
    #elif COUNTRY == USA
         char *currency = "Dollar";
    #endif
    puts(currency);
}
```

#if directive can also be nested but matching #else and #endif directives must be in the same file as the #if.

18.8.4　#ifdef Directive

The #ifdef directive implies if defined. This directive checks whether a macro is already defined or not. The general form of #ifdef is

```
#ifdef  macro-name
        Statement(s)
#endif
```

If the macro-name is already defined with a #define directive the statement(s) between #ifdef and #endif is compiled. #else may also be used in conjunction with the #ifdef. Consider the following example.

```
#ifdef  SIZE
        #undef SIZE
#endif
```

Above directives ensures that if SIZE is already defined, its definition is removed.

18.8.5　#ifndef Directive

The #ifndef directive implies if not defined. It works just opposite to #ifdef. This directive returns true when a macro has not been defined. The general form of #ifndef is

```
#ifndef  macro-name
        Statement(s)
#endif
```

If the macro-name is not defined previously the statement(s) between #ifndef and #endif is compiled. #else may also be used in conjunction with the #ifndef. Consider the following example.

```
#ifndef  SIZE
        #define  SIZE  15
#endif
```

Here first it will be checked that the macro SIZE is already defined or not. If it is not defined it will be defined here.

18.9　ADDITIONAL DIRECTIVES

Apart from the above directives there are 3 other additional directives. These are #line, #error and #pragma.

18.9.1　#line Directive

The #line directive is used to change the contents of two predefined macros in turbo C named _LINE_ and _FILE_. The _LINE_ macro contains the line number of the line currently being compiled and _FILE_ contains the name of the source file being compiled. The general form of #line directive is

```
#line line_number [ input_file]
```

Where `line_number` is any positive integer which indicate the current line number and `input_file` is any valid filename which indicate the source filename. `input_file` is optional and if it is not specified, the current file name remains unchanged. For example,

```
#line 25 "sample.c"
```

changes the current line number to 25 and current source file name would be "sample.c".

18.9.2   #error Directive

The #error directive is used to produce an error message in turbo C. This directive also causes to stop the compilation procedure. The general form is

```
#error error-message
```

The `error-message` is the message that will be produced on execution of this statement and it need not be enclosed within double quotes. Consider the following example.

```
#ifndef STATUS
    #error   Status not Defined
#endif
```

18.9.3   #pragma Directive

The #pragma directive is an implement specific directive in ANSI C. The general form is

```
#pragma pragma_directive
```

With #pragma, turbo C can define whatever directives it desire without interfering with other compiler that supports #pragma. If the compiler is unable to understand the pragma_name, the pragma directive is ignored without generating any error message. Some pragma_directives are inline, warn, etc.

18.10   PREDEFINED MACROS

There are a set of predefined macros in ANSI C. these contains some useful information. Some of them are presented in the following table.

Table 18.1   Predefined macros

Macro name	Description
LINE	Current line number of the file being compiled.
FILE	Contains the name of the source file being compiled.
DATE	Date of the compilation.
TIME	Time of the compilation.
TURBOC	Version of TURBO C.

18.11 PROGRAMMING EXAMPLES

Here are some programming examples to understand the various uses of macro.

PROGRAM 18.6   Define a macro to find area of a rectangle. Write a program to find the area of a rectangle using the above macro.

```c
#include<stdio.h>
#define   AREA(L, B)  (L) * (B)
void main( )
{
    int len, breadth;
    printf(" Enter the Length of a rectangle :");
    scanf("%d", &len);
    printf(" Enter Breadth :");
    scanf("%d", &breadth);
    printf("Area = %d", AREA(len, breadth));
}
```

PROGRAM 18.7   Define a macro that will print an integer. Write a program to use the above macro.

```c
#define PRINTINT(A)    printf("%d", A)
void main( )
{
    int num;
    printf(" Enter any number :");
    scanf("%d", &num);
    printf("Inputted Number is :");
    PRINTINT(num);
}
```

PROGRAM 18.8   Define a macro that can swap two variables of any data type. Write a program that can swap variable of any data type.

```c
#include<stdio.h>
#define SWAP(TYPE,A,B) { TYPE t = A; A = B; B = t;}  /* Generic Macro */
void main()
{   int x=5, y=10;
    float a= 7.5, b= 3.2;
    printf("Before Swapping :-");
    printf("x=%d, y=%d",x,y);
    printf("a=%f, b= %f",a,b);
    SWAP(int,x,y);                /* 1st argument is data type, 2nd and
                                     3rd are the variables */
```

```
        SWAP(float,a,b);
        printf("After Swapping :-");
        printf("x=%d, y=%d",x,y);
        printf("a=%f, b= %f",a,b);
}
```

PROGRAM 18.9 Define a macro to print an array of integers. Write a program to use this macro.

```
#include<stdio.h>
/* Multi line Macro */
#define PRINTARRAY(ARR, SIZE)  { for(i=0;i<SIZE;i++) \
                                    printf("%d ",ARR[i]); }
void main()
{
    int my_array[10], i;
    for(i=0;i<10;i++)
    {   printf("Enter any Number: ");
        scanf("%d",&my_array[i]);
    }
    printf("\nElements of the array is : ");
    PRINTARRAY(my_array, 10);
}
```

PROGRAM 18.10 Define a macro that swap two integer variables. Define a macro to sort an array. Define a macro to print an array of integers. Write a program to sort an array using the above defined Macros.

```
#include<stdio.h>
/* Multi line and nested Macro */
#define SWAP(A,B) {int t = A; A = B; B = t;}
#define PRINTARRAY(ARR, SIZE)
{   for(i=0;i<SIZE;i++) \
    printf("%d ",ARR[i]);
}

#define SORT(ARR,SIZE)
{   for(k=0;k<SIZE-1;k++) \
    for(j=0;j<SIZE-1;j++) \
    if(ARR[j]>ARR[j+1])   \
    SWAP(ARR[j],ARR[j+1]) \
}

void main()
{   int my_array[10],i,k,j;
    for(i=0;i<10;i++)
```

```
    {    printf("Enter any Number: ");
         scanf("%d",&my_array[i]);
    }
    SORT(my_array,10);
    PRINTARRAY(my_array, 10);
         getch();
}
```

SUMMARY

➤ Preprocessors are processed before the processing of C source program.

➤ #define is used to define symbolic constant or macro.

➤ Macros can have arguments and it can be expanded in multiple lines.

➤ Though macro with argument(s) looks like a function, they are not same.

➤ #undef is used to undefine previously defined macro.

➤ #if directive is used to compile or skipped a certain portion of code.

➤ #ifdef directive checks whether a macro is already defined.

➤ #ifndef works just opposite to #ifdef. This directive returns true when a macro has not been defined.

REVIEW EXERCISES

1. What is C preprocessor? What is its use?

2. What is preprocessor directive?

3. What is macro? What is its use?

4. Differentiate between function and macro in C.

5. Differentiate between #if and #ifdef directive?

6. What is the utility of #include diective?

7. Differentiate between the following two declarations:
   (a) #include <filename > and
   (b) #include "filename"

8. Define a macro to find the radius of a circle.

9. Define a macro to find perimeter of a rectangle.

10. Define a macro to check whether an integer is odd or even?

11. Define a macro to find the largest number among three integer numbers.

12. Define a macro that will print all the elements of an array of integers.

LEARN BY QUIZ – QUESTIONS

1. What is Macro Substitution?
   (1) It is a process by which the value of a variable can be substituted by some other value.
   (2) It is a process by which an identifier is replaced by a predefined string.
   (3) It is a process by which a large program segment is substituted by small program segment.

2. What does the following program segment do?
```
#define PI   3.141

void main()
{    float r;
     printf("Enter the radius of a circle:");
     scanf("%f",&r);
     printf("%f",PI * r * r);
}
```
(1) It will calculate the area of a circle.
(2) It will calculate the circumference of a circle.
(3) It will show : PI * r * r

3. What will be the output of the following program segment:
```
#define SQR(A)   A * A
void main()
{ printf("%d",SQR(5));}
```
(1) 25
(2) SQR(5)
(3) 5

4. What will be the output of the following program segment:
```
#define SQR(A)    A * A
void main()
{printf("%d",SQR(2+3));}
```
(1) 11
(2) 25
(3) SQR(2+3)

5. What will be the output of the following program segment:
```
#define MAX(A,B)  (A>B)? A : B
void main()

{    int x=5,y=6,z;
     z= MAX(x,y);
     printf("%d",z);
}
```
(1) 6
(2) 5
(3) Garbage Value

6. What will be the output of the following program segment:
```
#define SQR(A)  (A) * (A)
void main()
{printf("%d",SQR(2+3));}
```
(1) 25
(2) 11
(3) SQR(2+3)

7. What will be the output of the following program segment:
```
#define MAX(A,B)   (A>B)? A : B
```

```
#define MAX3(A,B,C)   MAX(MAX(A,B),C)
void main()
{    int x=5,y=6,z=7,m;
     m= MAX3(x,y,z);
     printf("%d",m);
}
```

(1) 7
(2) 6
(3) 5

8. What does the following statement do?

```
#define PRINT_INT(A)   printf("%d",A)
```

   (1) It will print any integer without using control character.
   (2) It will print A.
   (3) It will print the content of a variable of any datatype.

9. Which of the following is a preprocessor directive (job of a preprocessor)?
   (1) Macro expansion
   (2) finding syntax error
   (3) Matching opening braces with closing ones.

10. Which of the following is a preprocessor directive (job of a preprocessor)?
    (1) conditional compilation
    (2) finding syntax error
    (3) Matching opening braces with closing ones.

11. Which of the following is a preprocessor directive (job of a preprocessor)?
    (1) File inclusion
    (2) finding syntax error
    (3) Making object file

12. Which of the following file inclusion statement is correct?
    (1) #include<a.h>
    (2) #INCLUDE<a.h>
    (3) #inlude{a.h}

13. Which of the following file inclusion statement is correct?
    (1) #include "a.h"
    (2) #INCLUDE<a.h>
    (3) #inlude{a.h}

14. To spread macro definition in multiple lines which character is used?
    (1) /
    (2) \
    (3) _

15. Which preprocessor is used to remove a previously defined symbolic constant or macro?
    (1) #remove macro_name
    (2) #undefine macro_name
    (3) #undef macro_name

16. Which of the following is used to compile or skipped a certain portion of code
    (1) #if
    (2) #ifdef
    (3) #skip

17. Which of the following statement is True?
    (1) #else is used only with #if directives
    (2) #else may be used with #if, #ifdef or # ifndef directives
    (3) #else can be used alone

18. Which of the following directive can work independently?
    (1) #elif
    (2) #else
    (3) #ifndef

19. Which directive is used to check whether a macro is already defined?
    (1) #ifdef
    (2) #isdef
    (3) #ifdefine

20. Which directive is used to check whether a macro is not defined?
    (1) #define
    (2) #ifndef
    (3) #ifdef

21. Which directive is used to change the line number of the line currently being compiled?
    (1) #line
    (2) #lineno
    (3) #file

22. Which directive is used to produce an error message in turbo C at the time of compilation?
    (1) #error
    (2) #errormsg
    (3) #errmessage

LEARN BY QUIZ – ANSWERS

Answer Explanations

1. **Macro Substitution is a process by which an identifier** or a symbolic constant **is replaced by a predefined string** each time it is encountered in a program. The **#define** directive is used to define a macro. The general form of *macro definitions*(or simply *macro*) are:
   (i) #define identifier string
   (ii) #define identifier(arg1,arg,...) string

   Before compilation the identifier will be replaced by the string.

2. It will calculate the area of a circle.

   Before compilation the identifier PI will be replaced by 3.141 and the printf() statement becomes printf("%f",3.141 * r * r);

3. Correct answer is 25.

   The printf statement will be expanded as: printf("%d", 5 * 5);

4. Correct answer is 11. As the argument of macro is 2+3,

   The printf statement will be expanded as: printf("%d", 2+3 * 2+3);

5. Correct answer is 6.

   Here MAX(x,y) statement will be substituted by the statement:(x>y)? x: y

   So, the maximum between x and y will be stored within z.

6. **Correct answer is 25.** Though the argument of macro is 2+3,

   The printf statement will be expanded as: printf("%d", (2+3) * (2+3));

7. Correct answer is 7.

   Here first MAX(x,y) will be find. Then that value will be compared with z.

   So, the maximum between x,y and z will be stored within m.

8. It will print any integer without using control character.

   For example,
   ```
   int x=5;
   PRINT_INT(x);
   ```
   Here, PRINT_INT(x); statement will be replaced by printf("%d",x);

   So, it will print the content of the variable x. Also note that, by this way we can print the content of any variable without using the control character '%d'.

9. Macro expansion is the role of the preprocessor. The preprocessor replaces macro templates by macro expansions. After preprocessor finishes its processing, the macro templates have no existence in the source code.

   Remaining two jobs are role of the compiler not the preprocessor.

10. Conditional compilation is the role of the preprocessor. We do it using the preprocessor commands #ifdef and #endif.

    Remaining two jobs are role of the compiler not the preprocessor.

11. File inclusion is the role of the preprocessor. We do it using the preprocessor commands #include. This statement causes the entire contents of a file to be inserted at that point in a program.

    Remaining two jobs are role of the compiler not the preprocessor.

12. #include<a.h> is correct. The preprocessor directive #include can be used in following two formats:
    1. #include<a.h>: the file a.h is searched only in the specified include directory of the compiler.
    2. #include"a.h": this directs the preprocessor to search the file a.h in the current directory as well as the specified list of directories mentioned in the search path of the operating system.

13. #include "a.h" is correct. The preprocessor directive #include can be used in following two formats:
    1. #include<a.h>: the file a.h is searched only in the specified include directory of the compiler.
    2. #include "a.h": this directs the preprocessor to search the file a.h in the current directory as well as the specified list of directories mentioned in the search path of the operating system.

14. To spread macro definition in multiple line backslash('\') is added at the end of the line.

15. #undef directive is used to undefined, i.e., to remove a previously defined symbolic constant or macro. The general form of is
    ```
    #undef    macro_name
    ```
    There is no such preprocessor named #undefine or #remove.

16. The #if directive is used to compile or skipped a certain portion of code.

    The #ifdef directive checks whether a macro is already defined or not.

    There is no such preprocessor named #skip.

17. #else may be used with #if, #ifdef or # ifndef directives.

    #else directive cannot work independently. The #else directive works with #if directive in similar pattern as else statement works with if statement. The statement(s) between #else and #endif is compiled only when contant_expression with the #if directive executed as false. #else may also be used in conjunction with the #ifdef and #ifndef.

18. #ifndef directive can work independently.

    #elif and #else cannot work independently. #elif is used in conjunction with #if and #else is used in conjunction with #if, #ifdef and #ifndef directives.

19. The #ifdef directive implies if defined. This directive checks whether a macro is already defined or not. The general form of #ifdef is

    ```
    #ifdef macro-name
            Statement(s)
    #endif
    ```

    If the macro-name is already defined with a #define directive the statement or statements between the #ifdef and #endif is compiled.

    There is no such preprocessor named #isdef or #ifdefine.

20. The #ifndef directive implies if not defined. It works just opposite to #ifdef. This directive returns true when a macro has not been defined. The general form of #ifndef is

    ```
    #ifndef macro-name
            Statement(s)
    #endif
    ```

    If the macro-name is not defined previously the statement(s) between #ifndef and #endif is compiled. #else may also be used in conjunction with the #ifndef.

21. The #line directive is used to change the contents of two predefined macros in turbo C named _LINE_ and _FILE_. The contents of _LINE_ and _FILE_ macro are the line number and file name which is currently being compiled.

22. The #error directive is used to produce an error message in turbo C at the time of compilation. This directive also causes to stop the compilation procedure. The general form is

    ```
            #error error-message
    ```

    The error-message is the message that will be produced on execution of this statement and it need not be enclosed within double quotes.

19

Linked List

We know that to store a set of elements we need to declare an array. But when we handle large set of elements there are some disadvantages of array. First of all the allocation of an array is static. Thus we need to mention the size of the array before compilation and this size cannot be changed throughout the program. We have to execute the program for fixed specified set of elements. But this is not possible in real life. Suppose, we want to write a program that will read student's name, roll number and marks of various subjects from user or from file and prepare a result sheet in descending order of total marks. If we write this program using an array, then it will be executed for fixed number of students. But generally in different classes or sections number of students varies. So, a single program is not sufficient. We need to write programs for each class/section; though the program logic is same for all cases. Different program is required only for different array size. One solution is to declare an array which is sufficiently large. But this may lead to the problem of wastage of memory. Again in certain situation, if more elements need to store than the defined one, then it also faces the lack of memory problems. Sometimes it may happen that requirement may changes with the time. In these cases, old programs are needed to modify. Solution of these problems is Dynamic Allocation. But only Dynamic Allocation is not the solution. Sometimes it is not always possible to predict the size of the array at the very beginning of the program. Again, if a very large array is required to define, then program may face the problem of allocation. As an array is a contiguous allocation, for very large size array, there may be some situations, where though total free space is much larger than requirement, an array cannot be defined only due to those free space, that are not contiguous. Another problem related to array is in insertion and deletion operation. If we want to insert an item at front or at any intermediate position, it cannot be done very easily as the existing elements need to be shifted to make room. Same problem is in case of deleting an item. Solution of all these problems is to create a Linked List.

In linked list we need not allocate memory for the entire list. Here only a single node is allocated at a time. This allocation takes place at runtime and as and when required. Thus unlike array, a large contiguous memory chunk is not allocated; instead very small memory pieces are allocated. When we need to store the first item, we have to allocate space for it only and will store the data at this place. Next when 2nd item need to store, we will again allocate space for the 2nd item and so on. As this memory spaces are not contiguous, to keep track this memory address along with the data part we have to store an extra information with each item and it is the address of next item. Thus to store an item we have to store two things. One is the data part of the item and the other is address part which store the address of next item. So, we need to declare a structure to implement it. In this chapter, we discuss about the representation of linked list and various operations on it.

19.1 LINKED LIST

A linked list is a linear collection of data items which is known as nodes. Each node is represented by a structure and each structure along with the data contains the address of next node. In this way, each node is linked with each other to form a list. Thus this type of list is popularly known as linked list.

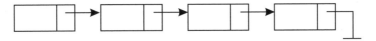

19.2 ADVANTAGES OF LINKED LIST

A linked list is a dynamic data structure. Hence the size of the linked list may increase or decrease at run time efficiently. We can create or delete node as and when required. As a result, there is no chance of wastage of memory due to prior allocation. Similarly there is no chance of lack of memory also. Unlike array, we need not allocate a large contiguous memory chunk. Every time when the allocation will be required, we will allocate a single node only. Thus instead of a large contiguous memory chunk, a large set of very small memory chunks will be required. So, how large may be our requirement if total free space in memory supports it, then there will be no problem in allocation. Moreover, it provides flexibility in rearranging the items efficiently. It is possible to insert and/or delete a node at any point in the linked list very efficiently with a very few and constant number of operations. Here we need not shift items. What we have to do is just updation of some pointers.

19.3 TYPES OF LINKED LIST

There are different kinds of linked lists. They are:
1. Linear singly linked list
2. Circular singly linked list
3. Two way or doubly linked list
4. Circular doubly linked list.

Linear singly linked list is simplest type of linked list. Here each node points to the next node in the list and the last node contains NULL to indicate the end of list. The problem of this type of list is once we move to next node, previous node cannot be traversed again.

Circular singly linked list is similar to linear singly linked list except a single difference. Here also each node points to the next node in the list but the last node instead of containing NULL it points to the first node of the list. The advantage of this list is that we can traverse circularly in this list. But the disadvantage is that to return the previous node we have to traverse the total list circularly which is time/effort consuming for large list.

Two way or doubly linked list solves this problem. Here each node has two address parts. One points to the previous node and the other points to the next node in the list. Both the ends of the list contain NULL. The advantage of this list is that we can traverse forward as well as backward according to our need. The disadvantage is that we cannot move circularly, i.e., to move from last node to first node we have to traverse the entire list.

Circular doubly linked list is the combination of doubly linked list and circular linked list. Here also each node has two address parts. One points to the previous node and the other points to the next node in the list. But instead of containing NULL the first node points to last node and the last node points to the first node of the list. The advantage of this list is that we can move in any direction, i.e., forward, backward as well as circular. Fig. 19.1 illustrates the different type of linked list.

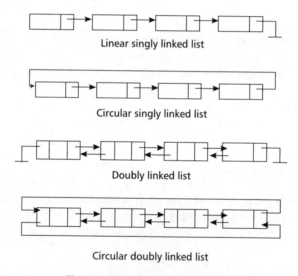

Linear singly linked list

Circular singly linked list

Doubly linked list

Circular doubly linked list

Fig. 19.1 Different type of linked list

In this chapter we discuss in details only the first one, i.e., linear singly linked list.

19.4 IMPLEMENTATION OF SINGLY LINKED LIST

A linked list is a chain of records or structures called **Nodes**. Each node has at least two members, one of which holds the data and the other points to the next node in the list. This is known as Single Linked Lists because the nodes of this type of list can only point to the next node in the list but not to the previous. Thus we can define the structure of the node as following:

```
struct   node
{       int data;
        struct node *next;
};
```

Here first member of the structure is an integer which represents the data part and next member is a pointer of this structure type which represents the address part. For simplicity the data part is taken as a single integer. But there may be more than one item with same or different data types. Thus the general form of a structure of a node is following:

```
struct node_name
{       data type      member1;
        data type      member2;
        data type      member3;
        . . . . . .
        . . . . . .
        struct node_name *pointer_name;
};
```

Here is some example of node structure of singly linked list.

EXAMPLE 19.1   Following structure can be used to create a list to maintain the student information.

```
struct node
{    int roll;
     char name[30];
     char address[60];
     int total;
     struct node * next;
};
```

EXAMPLE 19.2   Following structure can be used to create a list to maintain the list of books in a library.

```
struct node
{    int accession_no;
     char title[40];
     char author[40];
     float price;
     struct node * next;
};
```

As the structure refers the structure of same type, it is called **self-referential structure**. The self-referential structure is a structure which contains a member field that refers or points to the same structure type.

When a program will be written on linked list, we have to consider a variable (say, Head) which will be used to store the base address of the first node of the list. When there will be no node in the list, it will contain NULL. By this variable, we will access the list every time. Fig. 19.2 illustrates the representation of a singly linked list.

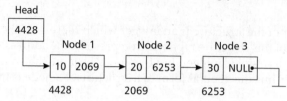

Fig. 19.2   Representation of a singly linked list in memory

In the Fig. 19.2, the linked list consists of 3 nodes. The data values of nodes are 10, 20 and 30, respectively. As the base address of Node1 is 4428, the Head variable contains 4428. Base address of Node2 is 2069 and that of Node3 is 6253. Thus address part of Node1 contains 2069 and address part of Node2 contains 6253 as Node1 points to Node2 and Node2 points to Node3. Node3 is the last node of this list. So, its address part contains NULL to indicate the end of list.

19.5   OPERATIONS ON SINGLY LINKED LIST

In this section, we will discuss various operations on singly linear linked list such as creating and traversing a list, inserting elements in a list, and deleting elements from a list. In all the following cases, we follow the following structure definition for the node.

```
typedef   struct node
{    int data;
     struct node *next;
}    Node;
```

19.5.1   Creating a Linked List

To create a list we may follow the following algorithm.
1. Create a node.
2. Assign the base address of the node to a pointer to make it current node.
3. Take input for the data part and store it.
4. Take input for the option whether another node will be created or not.
5. If option is 'yes', then
    (a) Create another new node.
    (b) Assign the base address of the new node to the address part of the current node.
    (c) Assign the base address of the new node to the pointer to make it current node.
    (d) Go to Step 3.
6. Else
    (a) Assign NULL to the address part of the current node.
    (b) Return to calling point.

Here is the C function of the above algorithm.

```
/* Function to create a linked list */
Node* create_list( )
{    Node * ptr,*cur;
     char ch;
     ptr = (Node*)malloc(sizeof(Node));
     cur = ptr;
     while(1)
     {    printf("Enter Data : ");
          scanf("%d",&cur->data);
          printf("Continue?(y/n): ");
          fflush(stdin);
          scanf("%c",&ch);
          if(toupper(ch)=='Y')
          {      /* New node is created and next part of current node
                                                      points it */
                 cur->next = (Node*)malloc(sizeof(Node));
                 cur = cur->next;  /* Current pointer points to next node
                                               to make it current */
          }
          else
          {    /* Null is assigned to next part of current node to make
                                                 it end node */
                 cur->next = NULL;
                 return(ptr);
          }
     }
}
```

In the above function no argument is sent but the base address of the first node is returned. Thus return type of the function is **Node***. Here first a node is created and inputted data is assigned to its data part. Next a choice has been taken to decide whether another node will be created or not. If we want to create another node, new node need to be created and next part of current node will point to it otherwise Null will be assigned to next part of current node to make it end node.

19.5.2 Displaying a Linked List

After creating a list we need to display it to see whether the values are stored properly. To display the list we have to traverse the list up to end. The algorithm may be described as:

1. Start from the first node.
2. Print the data part of the node.
3. Move to next node.
4. If the control not reached at end of the list go to Step 2.
5. Otherwise return to calling point.

The corresponding C function is as follows:

```
/* Function to display a linked list */
void display(Node * ptr)
{
     while(ptr!=NULL)
     {
          printf("%d->",ptr->data);
          ptr = ptr->next;
     }
     printf("Null");
}
```

In the above function the base address of the first node of the list, i.e., the content of Head will be received as an argument. Then it starts to print the data part of the current node and after printing each time, it moves to next node until the end of list is reached.

Here is a complete program that will create a linked list first and then display it.

PROGRAM 19.1   Write a program that will create a linked list and also display its content.

```
/*Program to Create a linked List */
# include<stdlib.h>
# include<conio.h>
# include<stdio.h>
# include<ctype.h>
typedef  struct node
      {    int data;
           struct node *next;
      }  Node;
Node * create_list( );
void display(Node *);
void main()
      {   Node *head;  /* head is the header node of linked list    */
          clrscr();
          head = create_list();
          printf("\nThe List is : ");
          display(head);
      }
Node * create_list( )            /* Function to Create a Linked List */
{
      Node * ptr,*cur;
      char ch;
      ptr = (Node*)malloc(sizeof(Node));
      cur = ptr;
      while(1)
      {
           printf("Enter Data : ");
           scanf("%d",&cur->data);
```

```
                printf("Continue?(y/n): ");
                fflush(stdin);
                scanf("%c",&ch);
                if(toupper(ch)=='Y')
                {                       /* Current node pointing to new node */
                    cur->next = (Node*)malloc(sizeof(Node));
                    cur = cur->next;
                }
            else
                {   cur->next = NULL;  /* Last node storing NULL at its address
                                                                    part */
                    return(ptr);
                }
            }
        }

    void display(Node * ptr)       /* Function to Display a Linked List */
    {
        while(ptr!=NULL)
        {
            printf("%d->",ptr->data);
            ptr = ptr->next;
        }
        printf("Null");
    }
```

Sample output
```
Enter Data: 10
Continue?(y/n): y
Enter Data: 20
Continue?(y/n): y
Enter Data:30
Continue?(y/n): n

The List is: 10->20->30->Null
```

19.6   INSERTING A NEW ELEMENT IN A LINKED LIST

To insert a node in a linked list, a new node has to be created first and assign the new value to its data part. Next we have to find the position in the list where this new node will be inserted. Then we have to update the address part of predecessor and/or successor nodes and also the new node. The insertion in the list can take place:

- At the beginning of the list
- At the end of the list
- At any intermediate position of the list. It may be
    - After specified node
    - Before specified node

19.6.1   Insert an Element at the Beginning of a List

As the element will be inserted at the beginning of the list, the content of head variable will be updated by the address of new node. So, the head variable, which is passed using call by value mechanism in the previous example, now needs to pass following call by reference mechanism. Thus instead of **Node*** the argument type will be **Node****. Do not confuse with Node* and Node**. When a pointer variable will be passed as function argument, a single '*' is required. Thus in the previous example, Node* is used to receive the head variable which is a pointer of type node. But now the address of the pointer variable needs to pass as call by reference mechanism needs to follow. So, here the argument type will be **Node****. Another argument of this function is the data part of new node. We can omit it by taking the input from the function. But sending it as argument is better as it is more generalized. Because inputs do not come always from keyboard, it may come from another list or from file, etc.

The general algorithm to insert an element at the beginning of the list may be defined as follows:
1.   Create a new node.
2.   Update its data part with the function argument.
3.   Update its address part with content of head variable whose address is also passed as argument.
4.   Update the content of head variable with the address of new node.

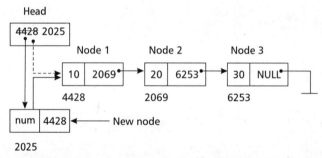

Fig. 19.3   Inserting a node at the beginning of a list

Fig. 19.3 shows the position of pointers after inserting a node at the beginning of a list. ⋯⋯⋯⋯▸ line shows old pointing path whereas ───▸ line shows the current pointing path.

Following is the function of above algorithm:

```
/* Function to insert a node at the beginning of the list   */
void insert_begin(Node **p, int num)
{    Node *new_node;
     new_node = (Node *)malloc(sizeof(Node));
     new_node->data = num;
     new_node->next = *p;    /* address part of new node storing the
                                address of next node or NULL if it is
                                                     a Null list. */
     *p = new_node;          /* Head pointing to new node. */
}
```

In the above function, if the list is empty, the address part of new node will store NULL as Head contains NULL for empty list. Otherwise it will store the address of next node. So, the new node becomes the first node and to point the first node of the list, Head will store the address of new node.

19.6.2 Insert an Element at the End of a List

When the node will be inserted at end, we have to face two situations. First, the list may be empty and secondly, there is an existing list. In first case we have to update the Head variable with the new node. But in 2nd case, we need not update the Head variable as the new node will be appended at end. For that we need to move at last node and then have to update the address part of last node. To find the last node, we can check the address part of the nodes. The node whose address part contains NULL, will be the last node.

The general algorithm to insert an element at the end of a list may be defined as follows:

1. Create a new node.
2. Update its data part with the function argument.
3. Update its address part with NULL as it will be the last node.
4. If the content of Head variable is NULL then
   (a) Update the content of head variable with the address of new node.
5. Else
   (a) Move to last node
   (b) Update the address part of last node with the address of new node.

Using the above algorithm we can write the following code.

```
/* Function to insert a node at the end of the list */

void insert_end(Node **p, int num)
{   Node *new_node,*cur;
    new_node = (Node *)malloc(sizeof(Node));
    new_node->data = num;
    new_node->next = NULL;

    if(*p == NULL)        /* For Null list it will be the 1st Node */
        *p = new_node;
    else
    {   cur = *p;
        while( cur->next != NULL)             /* Moving to last node */
        {
            cur = cur->next;
        }
        cur->next = new_node;
    }
}
```

Fig. 19.4 shows this insertion scheme.

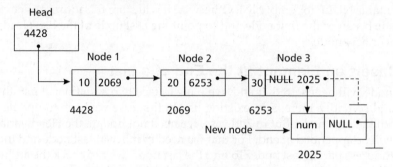

Fig. 19.4   Inserting a node at the end of a list

19.6.3   Insert a Node After a Specified Node

The specified node can be of two types. A node can be specified with the node number of the list, i.e., 1st node, 2nd node, … n-th node, etc. Another way is to mentioning the data part, i.e., we need to match the supplied data with the data of each node. Here we discuss the algorithm for the first case. Another thing we need to consider that what happens if the specified node is not in the list. At this situation, we can abort the insertion operation by specifying that 'the node does not exist' or we can insert the new node at end. Here we are considering the 2nd case. The following algorithm describes how a new node can be inserted after n-th node.

1. Create a new node.
2. Update its data part with the function argument.
3. If the content of Head variable is NULL then
   (a) Update the content of head variable with the address of new node.
4. Else
   (a) Move to n-th node
   (b) If the specified node not exists, stay at last node and update the address part of last node with the address of new node.
   (c) Update the address part of new node with the address part of n-th node.
   (d) Update the address part of n-th node with the address of new node.

Following function shows how a node can be inserted after n-th node.

```
/* Function to insert a node After Nth node */
void insert_after_nth(Node **p, int loc, int num)
{    Node *new_node ,*cur;
     int c;
     new_node = (Node *)malloc(sizeof(Node));
     new_node->data = num;
     new_node->next = NULL;
     if(*p == NULL)        /* For Null list it will be the 1st Node */
          *p = new_node;
     else
     {    cur = *p;
          for(c=1;c<=loc-1&&cur->next!=NULL;c++)/* to Move to Nth node */
```

```
{    cur = cur->next;
}
new_node->next = cur->next;
cur->next = new_node;
}
```

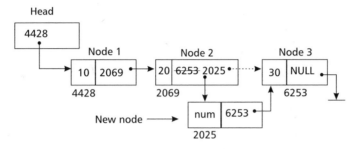

Fig. 19.5   Inserting a node after 2nd node

19.6.4   Insert a Node Before a Specified Node

Here also to mean a specified node we are considering n-th node. Thus our tusk is to insert a node before n-th node. In this case the new node may be inserted at the beginning of a list if is said to insert before first node, otherwise it will be inserted in some intermediate position. But if the value of n is larger than the node count, new node will be inserted at end.

The following algorithm describes how a new node can be inserted before n-th node.

1.   Create a new node.
2.   Update its data part with the function argument.
3.   If the content of Head variable is NULL or value of n is 1, then
     (a)   Update the address part of new node with content of head variable whose address is also passed as argument.
     (b)   Update the content of head variable with the address of new node.
4.   Else
     (a)   Move to previous node of nth node
     (b)   If the specified node not exists, stay at last node and update the address part of last node with the address of new node.
     (c)   Update the address part of new node with the address part of current node i.e. (n-1)th node.
     (d)   Update the address part of current node with the address of new node.

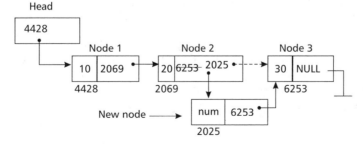

Fig. 19.6   Inserting a node before 3rd node

Following function shows how a node can be inserted before nth node.

```
/* Function to insert a node Before Nth node */

void insert_before_nth(Node **p, int loc, int num)
{    Node *new_node ,*cur;
     int c;
     new_node = (Node *)malloc(sizeof(Node));
     new_node->data = num;
     if(*p == NULL || loc==1)  /* If Null list or new node is inserted
                                         as 1st node */
     {    new_node->next = *p;
          *p = new_node;
     }
     else
     {    cur = *p;
          for(c=1;c<=loc-2&&cur->next!=NULL;c++)   /* to move to (n-1)
                                                          th node*/
          {
               cur = cur->next;
          }
          new_node->next = cur->next;
          cur->next = new_node;
     }
}
```

19.6.5 Deleting a Node from Linked List

To delete a node from a linked list, first we have to find the node which is to be deleted. Next we have to update the address part of predecessor and/or successor nodes and finally de-allocate the memory spaces that are occupied by the node. Like insertion there are several cases for deletion also. These may be:
- Deletion of first node
- Deletion of last node
- Deletion of any intermediate node. It may be:
  - Delete n-th node or
  - Delete the node whose data part matches with the given data, etc.

19.6.5.1 Deletion of First Node

In case of first node deletion we have to update the content of Head variable as now it points to 2nd node or NULL if the list becomes empty. So, like insertion here also the address of Head variable will be passed and the data type of the argument will be **Node****.

The general algorithm to delete the first node of the list may be defined as follows:
1. Update the content of head variable with the address part of first node, i.e., the address of 2nd node.
2. De-allocate the memory of first node.

Here is a function to delete the first node of a linked list.

```
/* Function to delete the first node of a linked list */
void delete_first( Node**p)
{    Node *cur = *p;
     if(*p == NULL)
     {    printf("\n\nEmpty List. Deletion not possible...");
          getch();
     }
     else
     {    cur = *p;
          *p = cur->next;
          free(cur);
          printf("\nNode Deleted Successfully. Press any key to
                                               Continue..");
          getch();
     }
}
```

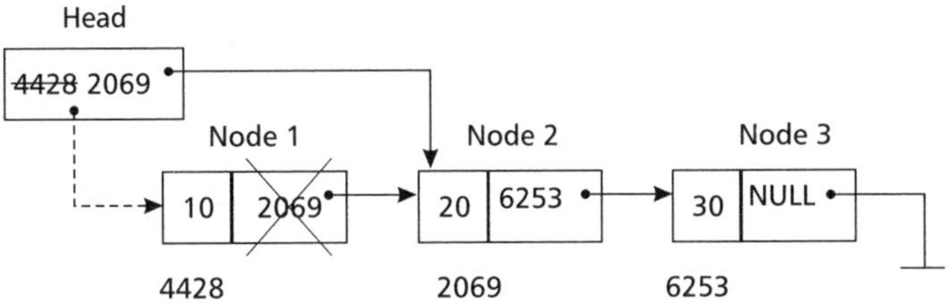

Fig. 19.7   Deletion of first node from a list

19.6.5.2 Deletion of Last Node

When we need to delete a node except the first node, first we have to move the predecessor node of the node which will be deleted. So, to delete the last node we have to move at previous node of last node. Though our task is to delete last node, the list may contain single node only. Then deletion of this node makes the list empty and thus the content of head variable will be updated with the NULL values.

The general algorithm to delete the last node of the list may be defined as follows:

1. Check whether one or more nodes in the list.
2. If the list contains a single node only, update the content of head variable with NULL and de-allocate the memory of the node.
3. Else
   (a) Move to previous node of last node.
   (b) De-allocate the memory of last node.
   (c) Update the address part of current node with NULL as it will be the last node now.

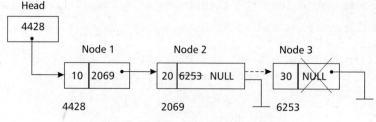

Fig. 19.8 Deletion of last node from a list

Following function shows how the last node can be deleted.

```
/* Function to delete the last node of a linked list */

void delete_last( Node**p)
{    Node *cur = *p;
     if(*p == NULL)
     {   printf("\n\nEmpty List. Deletion not possible...");
         getch();
     }
     else
     {   cur = *p;
         if(cur->next == NULL)   /* If the list contains single node only */
         {    *p = NULL;
              free(cur);
         }
         else
         {    while( cur->next->next != NULL)   /* to Move to previous
                                                    node of last node */
              {
                   cur = cur->next;
              }
              free(cur->next);
              cur->next = NULL;
         }
         printf("\nNode Deleted Successfully. Press any key to
                                                    Continue..");
         getch();
     }
}
```

19.6.5.3   *Deletion of Any Intermediate Node*

As we discussed that in case of deletion of node from any intermediate position, there may be several cases like n-th node deletion or deletion of the node whose data part matches with the given data. To delete the n-th node, we have to move the predecessor node of the n-th node. Next update the address part of $(n-1)$th node with the address part of deleted node and then de-allocate the memory of n-th node.

But in the 2nd case, we have to compare each node with the argument data. In this case, first node, last node or any intermediate node may be deleted. Again if the argument data does not match with any node, no node will be deleted.

The following algorithm describes how a node whose data part matches with the given data can be deleted.

1. Check the data of first node with the given data.
2. If it matches, then
    (a) Update the content of head variable with the address part of first node, i.e., the address of 2nd node.
    (b) De-allocate the memory of first node.
3. Else
    (a) Check the data of each node with the given data.
    (b) If searching fails, terminate operation mentioning appropriate message like 'Node not found.'.
    (c) If the match occurs, then
        (i) Move to previous node of the node whose data part matches with the given data.
        (ii) Update the address part of current node with the address part of next node (i.e., the node to be deleted).
        (iii) De-allocate the memory of next node (i.e., the node to be deleted).

Following function shows how the node whose data part matches with the given data can be deleted.

```
/* Functions to Delete a node whose Data matches with the given Data */
void delete_anynode (Node**p, int num)
{    Node *cur,*prev;
     int flag=0;
     if(*p == NULL)
     {    printf("\n\nEmpty List. Deletion not possible...");
          getch();
     }
     else
     {    cur = *p;
          if( cur->data == num)            /* For First Node   */
          {    *p = cur-> next;
               free(cur);
               printf("\nNode Deleted...Press any key to continue");
               getch();
          }
          else
          {    while( cur != NULL)          /* For Other Nodes  */
               {    if( cur->data == num)
                    {    flag = 1;
                         break;
                    }
               }
```

```
                prev = cur;  /* prev points to previous node of
                                current node */
                cur = cur-> next;   /* cur points to current node */
            }
            if(flag == 0)
            {   printf("\nData Not Found...");
                getch();
            }
            else
            {   prev->next = cur->next;
                free(cur);
                printf("\nNode Deleted...Press any key to continue");
                getch();
            }
        }
    }
}
```

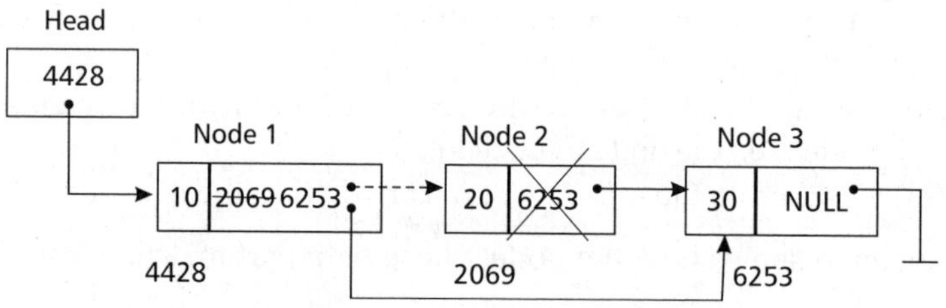

Head

Fig. 19.9   Deletion of an intermediate node from a list

Here is a complete program to show the various operations of Linked List.

PROGRAM 19.2   Write a program to demonstrate the various operations of Linked List.

```
/* Program to demonstrate Singly Linked List */
# include<stdlib.h>
# include<conio.h>
# include<stdio.h>
# include<ctype.h>

typedef  struct node
{    int data;
     struct node *next;
}    Node;
void insert_end(Node **,int);
void insert_begin(Node **,int);
void insert_before_nth(Node **,int,int);
void insert_after_nth(Node **,int,int);
void delete_first(Node **);
void delete_last(Node **);
void delete_anynode(Node **,int);
```

```
void display(Node *);
void main()
{   Node *head = NULL;
    int num, loc, choice;
    char opt;
    do
    {   clrscr();
        printf("PROGRAM TO IMPLEMENT SINGLE LINKED LIST");
        printf("\n=====================================");
        printf("\n\n1.Create/Appending The List");
        printf("\n2.Insert Node At Beginning");
        printf("\n3.Insert Node Before Nth node");
        printf("\n4.Insert Node After Nth node");
        printf("\n5.Delete First Node");
        printf("\n6.Delete Last Node");
        printf("\n7.Delete the Node whose Data matches with given Data");
        printf("\n8.Displaying the list");
        printf("\n9.Exit");
        printf("\n\nEnter your Choice : ");
        scanf("%d",&choice);

        switch(choice)
        {   case 1:
                do
                {   printf("Enter The Data : ");
                    scanf("%d", &num);
                    insert_end(&head, num);
                    printf("Enter more (y/n) :");
                    fflush(stdin);
                    opt=getchar();
                }   while(toupper(opt) !='N');
                    break;
            case 2:
                printf("Enter The Data : ");
                scanf("%d",&num);
                insert_begin(&head, num);
                break;
            case 3:
                printf("\nEnter The Node number Before which new
                                        node will be inserted :");
                scanf("%d",&loc);
                printf("\nEnter The Data : ");
                scanf("%d",&num);
                insert_before_nth(&head, loc, num);
                break;
            case 4:
                printf("\nEnter The Node number After which new
                                        node will be inserted :");
                scanf("%d",&loc);
                printf("\nEnter The Data : ");
```

```
            scanf("%d",&num);
            insert_after_nth(&head, loc, num);
            break;
        case 5:
            delete_first(&head);
            break;
        case 6:
            delete_last(&head);
            break;
        case 7:
            printf("\nEnter The Data You Want To Delete : ");
            scanf("%d", &num);
            delete_anynode(&head, num);
            break;
        case 8:
            display(head);
            getch();
            break;
        case 9:
            printf("\n\nQuiting.......");
            getch();
            exit(0);
        default:
            printf("Invalid choice. Please Enter Correct Choice");
            getch();
        }
    }   while(1);
}


/* Function to insert a node at the end of the list */
void insert_end(Node **p, int num)
{   Node *new_node,*cur;
    new_node = (Node *)malloc(sizeof(Node));
    new_node->data = num;
    new_node->next = NULL;
    if(*p == NULL)
    *p = new_node;
    else
    {   cur = *p;
        while( cur->next != NULL)  /* to Move to ast node  */
        {
            cur = cur->next;
        }
        cur->next = new_node ;
    }
}
```

```
void display(Node *p)        /* Function to display list */
{    if(p == NULL)
     {    printf("\n\nEmpty List.");
          getch();
     }
     else
     {    printf("\n\n");
          while(p!=NULL)
          {    printf("%d -> ", p->data);
               p = p->next;
          }
          printf("NULL");
     }
}


/* Function to insert a node at the beginning of the list */

void insert_begin(Node **p, int num)
{    Node *new_node;
     new_node = (Node *)malloc(sizeof(Node));
     new_node->data = num;
     new_node->next = *p;
     *p = new_node;
}


/* Function to insert a node Before Nth node */

void insert_before_nth(Node **p, int loc, int num)
{    Node *new_node ,*cur;
     int c;
     new_node = (Node *)malloc(sizeof(Node));
     new_node->data = num;
     if(*p == NULL || loc==1)
     {    new_node->next = *p;
          *p = new_node;
     }
     else
     {    cur = *p;
          for(c=1;c<=loc-2&&cur->next!=NULL;c++)
                                      /* to move to (n-1)th node*/
          {
               cur = cur->next;
          }
          new_node->next = cur->next;
          cur->next = new_node;
     }
}
```

```
/*    Function to insert a node After Nth node */
void insert_after_nth(Node **p, int loc, int num)
{    Node *new_node ,*cur;
     int c;
     new_node = (Node *)malloc(sizeof(Node));
     new_node->data = num;
     new_node->next = NULL;
     if(*p == NULL)
          *p = new_node;
     else
     {    cur = *p;
          for(c=1;c<=loc-1&&cur->next!=NULL;c++)
                                                  /* to Move to Nth node */
          {
               cur = cur->next;
          }
          new node->next = cur->next;
          cur->next = new_node;
     }
}


void delete_first( Node**p)    /* Functions to Delete First node */
{    Node *cur = *p;
     if(*p == NULL)
     {    printf("\n\nEmpty List. Deletion not possible...");
          getch();
     }
     else
     {    cur = *p;
          *p = cur->next;
          free(cur);
          printf("\nNode Deleted Successfully. Press any
                                        key to Continue..");
          getch();
     }
}


void delete_last( Node**p)      /* Functions to Delete Last node */
{  Node *cur = *p;
   if(*p == NULL)
   { printf("\n\nEmpty List. Deletion not possible...");
     getch();
   }
   else
      { cur = *p;
        if(cur->next == NULL)  /* If the list contains single node only */
        { *p = NULL;
          free(cur);
        }
```

```
      else
      { while( cur->next->next != NULL)
                        /* to Move to previous node of last node   */
          {
             cur = cur->next;
          }
          free(cur->next);
          cur->next = NULL;
      }
      printf("\nNodeDeletedSuccessfully. PressanykeytoContinue...");
      getch();
   }
}

/* Functions to Delete a node whose Data matches with given Data */
void delete_anynode ( Node**p, int num)
{  Node *cur,*prev;
   int flag=0;
   if(*p == NULL)
   { printf("\n\nEmpty List. Deletion not possible...");
     getch();
   }
   else
   { cur = *p;
     if( cur->data == num)        /* For First Node  */
     { *p = cur-> next ;
       free(cur);
       printf("\nNode Deleted...Press any key to continue");
       getch();
     }
     else
     {              /* For Other Nodes  */
       while( cur != NULL)
       {
          if( cur->data == num)
          { flag = 1;
            break;
          }
          prev = cur;  /* prev points to previous node of current node
                      */
          cur = cur-> next; /* cur  points  to  current  node  */
       }
       if(flag == 0)
       { printf("\nData Not Found...");
         getch();
       }
```

```
        else
        { prev->next = cur->next ;
          free(cur);
          printf("\nNode  Deleted...Press  any  key  to  continue");
          getch();
        }
      }
    }
  }
```

19.7 APPLICATIONS OF SINGLY LINKED LIST

Linked list is an important data structure in computer programming. It is used in a wide variety of programming application such as to implement various data structures such as stack, queue, and graph, to implement sparse matrix, and to perform arithmetic operation on large integers. Polynomials can also be represented using singly linked list.

The advantage of using linked list is that the size of a polynomial may grow or shrink as all the terms are not present always. Again if the size of the polynomial is very large, then also it can fit into the memory very easily as instead of total polynomial each term will be allocated at a time. The general form of a polynomial of degree n is:

$$f(x) = a_n x^n + a_{n-1} x^{n-1} + a_{n-2} x^{n-2} + \ldots\ldots\ldots + a_1 x + a_0$$

where $a_n, a_{n-1}, \ldots, a_1, a_0$ are coefficient and n, n–1, n–2,… are exponent or power of the each term of the polynomials. Thus we can easily implement it using a singly linked list whose each node will consist of three elements – coefficient, power and a link to the next term. So, the structure definition will be:

```
        struct polynomial
        {   int coff;
            int pwr;
            struct polynomial * next;
        };
```

Suppose a polynomial is, $f(x) = 3x^6 + 5x^3 + 9x + 2$. It will be represented as follows:

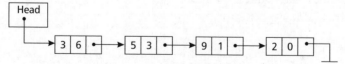

Fig. 19.10   Representation of a polynomial using linked list

To create the polynomial we can use a function similar to `insert_end` function which inserts node at the end of a list. But if we use this function we have to assume that the user should give the input in descending order of power of the terms. Alternatively we can write a function which will insert nodes in descending orders of power. But for simplicity we are following the `insert_end` function. Thus the functions to create a polynomial will be as follows:

```
/* Function to insert a node at end of a list to create a Polynomial */
typedef  struct polynomial Poly;  /*to make the structure name smaller
                                   typedef  statement is used  */
void insert_end(Poly **p, int c, int p)
{    Poly *new_node,*cur;
     new_node = (Poly *)malloc(sizeof(Poly));
     new_node->coff = c;
     new_node->pwr = p;
     new_node->next = NULL;

     if(*p == NULL)
         *p = new_node;
     else
     {   cur = *p;
         while( cur->next != NULL)
         {
             cur = cur->next;
         }
         cur->next = new_node ;
     }
}
```

By repetitively calling the above function we can create a polynomial.

```
/* Function to create a Polynomial */
void create_poly(Poly **p)
{    int cof, pr;
     char ch;
     while(1)
     {   printf("Enter Coefficient : ");
         scanf("%d",&cof);
         printf("Enter Power : ");
         scanf("%d",&pr);
         insert_end(p,cof,pr);
         printf("Continue?(y/n) : ");
         fflush(stdin);
         scanf("%c",&ch);
         if(toupper(ch)=='N')
             break;
     }
```

Now using the above structure we will write a complete program which will create two polynomials, display them, add these two polynomials and finally display the resultant polynomial.

PROGRAM 19.3   Write a program to add two polynomials.

```
/*Program to Add two Polynomials  */
# include<stdlib.h>
# include<conio.h>
# include<stdio.h>
# include<ctype.h>

typedef struct polynomial
{   int coff;
    int pwr;
    struct polynomial * next;
}   Poly;


/* Function to insert a node at the end of the list   */
void insert_end(Poly **ptr, int c, int p)
{   Poly *new_node,*cur;
    new_node = (Poly *)malloc(sizeof(Poly));
    new_node->coff = c;
    new_node->pwr = p;
    new_node->next = NULL;

    if(*ptr == NULL)
        *ptr = new_node;
    else
    {   cur = *ptr;
        while( cur->next != NULL)
        {
            cur = cur->next;
        }
        cur->next = new_node ;
    }
}


void create_poly(Poly **p)    /* Function to create a Polynomial */
{   int cof, pr;
    char ch;
    while(1)
    {   printf("Enter Coefficient : ");
        scanf("%d",&cof);
        printf("Enter Power : ");
        scanf("%d",&pr);
        insert_end(p,cof,pr);
        printf("Continue?(y/n) : ");
        fflush(stdin);
        scanf("%c",&ch);
        if(toupper(ch)=='N')
            break;
    }
}
```

```
void display(Poly * ptr)     /* Function to Display a Polynomial */
{    while(ptr!=NULL)
     {    printf("%dx^%d+",ptr->coff, ptr->pwr);
          ptr = ptr->next;
     }
     printf("\b ");
}

/* Function to Add two Polynomials */
void add_poly(Poly *h1, Poly *h2, Poly **h3)
{    while(h1 && h2)
     {    if(h1->pwr > h2->pwr)
          {    insert_end(h3,h1->coff,h1->pwr);
               h1 = h1->next;
          }
          else
          if(h1->pwr < h2->pwr)
          {    insert_end(h3,h2->coff,h2->pwr);
               h2 = h2->next;
          }
          else
          {    insert_end(h3,h1->coff+h2->coff,h1->pwr);
               h1 = h1->next;
               h2 = h2->next;
          }
     }
     while(h1)
     {    insert_end(h3,h1->coff,h1->pwr);
          h1 = h1->next;
     }
     while(h2)
     {    insert_end(h3,h2->coff,h2->pwr);
          h2 = h2->next;
     }
}

void main()
{
     Poly *head1=NULL, *head2=NULL, *head3=NULL;
     clrscr();
     printf("Enter values for 1st Polynomials:-\n");
     create_poly(&head1);
     printf("Enter values for 2nd Polynomials:-\n");
     create_poly(&head2);
     add_poly(head1,head2,&head3);
     clrscr();
     printf("\n1st Polynomial : ");
     display(head1);
     printf("\n2nd Polynomial : ");
```

```
            display(head2);
            printf("\nResultant Polynomial : ");
            display(head3);
      }
```

Sample output

    Enter values for 1st Polynomials:
        Enter Coefficient: 6
        Enter Power: 4
        Continue?(y/n): y
        Enter Coefficient: 2
        Enter Power: 3
        Continue?(y/n): n
        Enter values for 2nd Polynomials:
        Enter Coefficient: 5
        Enter Power: 3
        Continue?(y/n): y
        Enter Coefficient: 4
        Enter Power: 1
        Continue?(y/n): n

1st Polynomial: $6x^4+2x^3$
2nd Polynomial: $5x^3+4x^1$
Resultant Polynomial: $6x^4+7x^3+4x^1$

19.8 DISADVANTAGES OF LINKED LIST

Though there are several advantages of using linked list, some disadvantages are also there. The disadvantage of linked list is that it consumes extra space if compared to an array as each node in the list along with the data must contain the address of the next node. If the data part of the node is very small in size, this extra space is really a headache. For example if it contains a single integer, then to store a single item we need to allocate double space. To allocate 2 bytes, we have to allocate 4 bytes (2 bytes for integer data and 2 bytes for the address). But if the size of the data part is large, if it contains many items, then this wastage is negligible. For example, if we want to store data about student like roll no, name, father's name, local address, permanent address, and fees paid and suppose the size of this record structure is 300 bytes, then to store this 300 bytes we have to allocate 302 bytes which is negligible.

Another disadvantage is we can perform only sequential access on linked list. But array supports sequential access as well as random access.

19.9 PROGRAMMING EXAMPLES

Here are some programming examples to understand the various operations that can be performed using a Singly Linked List.

PROGRAM 19.4 **Write a function to count the number of nodes in a singly linked list.**

```
/* Function to count the node in a list */
int count(Node *p)
{
    int c=0;
    while(p!=NULL)
    {
        c++;
        p = p->next;
    }
    return(c);
}
```

PROGRAM 19.5 **Write a function to find the sum of data part in a singly linked list.**

```
/* Function to find the sum of data part in a list */
int calc_sum(Node *p)
{
    int sum=0;
    while(p!=NULL)
    {
        sum=sum+p->data;
        p = p->next;
    }
    return(sum);
}
```

PROGRAM 19.6 **Write a function to find a node with the given data in a singly linked list.**

```
/* Function to search a node in a list */
Node * search(Node *p, int num)
{
    while(p!=NULL)
    {
        if( p->data == num)
        return(p);
        p = p->next;
    }
    return(NULL);
}
```

PROGRAM 19.7 Write a function to find the largest node in a singly linked list.

```c
/* Function to find the largest node in a list */
Node * largest_node(Node *p)
{   int max = p->data;
    Node *max_node = p;
    while(p!=NULL)
    {   if( p->data > max)
        {   max = p->data;
            max_node = p;
        }
        p = p->next;
    }
    return(max_node);
}
```

PROGRAM 19.8 Write a function to display a singly linked list in reverse order.

```c
/* Function to display a list in reverse order */
void rev_display(Node *p)
{   int num;
    if(p!=NULL)
    {   num = p->data;
        rev_display(p->next);
        printf("%d ", num);
    }
}
```

PROGRAM 19.9 Write a function to physically reverse a singly linked list.

```c
/* Function to reverse a list physically */
void reverse_list(Node **p)
{   Node *prev, *cur, *nxt;
    cur = *p;
    nxt = cur->next;
    prev = NULL;
    cur->next = NULL;
    while( nxt != NULL)
    {   prev = cur;
        cur = nxt;
        nxt = cur->next;
        cur->next = prev;
    }
    *p = cur;
}
```

PROGRAM 19.10 **Write a function to insert a node at the proper position in a previously sorted linked list.**

```
/* Function to insert a node in a previously sorted list */
void insert_proper(Node **p, int num)
{    Node *new_node, *cur, *prev;
     new_node = (Node *)malloc(sizeof(Node));
     new_node->data = num;
     new_node->next = NULL;

     if(*p == NULL)
         *p = new_node;
     else
     {   cur = *p;
         if( cur->data > num)
         {   new_node->next = cur;
             *p = new_node;
         }
         else
         {
             while( cur != NULL)
             {   if( cur->data > num)
                 break;
                 prev = cur;
                 cur = cur->next;
             }
             new_node->next = cur;
             prev->next = new_node;
         }
     }
}
```

SUMMARY

➤ A linked list is a linear collection of data items which is known as nodes.

➤ Linked list is a dynamic data structure. Hence the size of the linked list may increase or decrease at run time, i.e., we can add or delete node as and when required.

➤ In contrast to array, it does not possess the problems of wastage of memory nor the lack of memory.

➤ Linked list provides flexibility in rearranging the items efficiently instead of allocating a large contiguous memory chunk.

➤ Insertion and deletion of nodes at any point in the list is very simple and require some pointer adjustment only.

➤ In Linear singly linked list each node points to the next node in the list and the last node contains NULL to indicate the end of list.

➤ In Circular singly linked list each node points to the next node in the list but the last node instead of containing NULL it points to the first node of the list.

➤ In Two way or doubly linked list each node has two address parts. One points to the previous node and the other points to the next node in the list. Both the ends of the list contain NULL.

➤ In Circular doubly linked list each node has two address parts. One points to the previous node and the other points to the next node in the list. But instead of containing NULL the first node points to last node and the last node points to the first node of the list.

➤ The self-referential structure is a structure which contains a member field that refers or points to the same structure type.

➤ Linked list is used to represent polynomials, to implement various data structures, sparse matrix, to perform arithmetic operation on large integers, etc.

➤ The disadvantage of linked list is that it consumes extra space since each node contains the address of the next item in the list and the nodes of the list can be accessed sequentially only.

REVIEW EXERCISES

1. What is linked list?
2. Why a linked list is called a dynamic data structure?
3. What is a self-referential structure?
4. What are the advantages of using linked list over arrays?
5. Is there any disadvantage of it?
6. What are the different types of linked list?
7. Write a C function to find the smallest element in a singly linked list.
8. Write a C function to find the average of data part in a singly linked list.
9. Write a C function to insert a node before a node whose data matches with given data in a singly linked list.
10. Write a C function to insert a node after a node whose data matches with given data in a singly linked list.
11. Write a C function to delete a node before a specified node.
12. Write a C function to delete a node after a specified node.
13. Write a C function to sort a singly linked list.
14. Write a C function to merge two sorted singly linked list.
15. Write a C function that will split a singly linked list into two different list one will contain Odd numbers and other will contain Even numbers.
16. Write a C function to multiply two polynomials.
17. Write a C function to remove alternate elements from a linked list.
18. Write a C function to delete entire list.

LEARN BY QUIZ – QUESTIONS

1. Which of the following statement is true?
   (1) Linked list is a static data structure.
   (2) Linked list is a dynamic data structure.
   (3) Linked list is a non linear data structure.

2. Which of the following statement is true?
   (1) Nodes of the Linked list are accessed sequentially only.
   (2) Nodes of the Linked list are accessed randomly only.
   (3) Nodes of the Linked list can be accessed sequentially as well as randomly.

3. What is the minimum number of fields in the node of a singly linear linked list?
   (1) 1
   (2) 2
   (3) 3

4. To insert a node at the beginning of a singly linear linked list how many pointers are needed to adjust?
   (1) 1
   (2) 2
   (3) 3

5. To insert a node at the end of a singly linear linked list, the next part of new node always contains NULL. Apart from this how many pointers are needed to adjust?
   (1) 1
   (2) 2
   (3) 3

6. To insert a node at any intermediate position of a singly linear linked list how many pointers are needed to adjust?
   (1) 1
   (2) 2
   (3) 3

7. To delete the first node of a singly linear linked list how many pointers are needed to adjust?
   (1) 1
   (2) 2
   (3) 3

8. To delete the last node of a singly linear linked list how many pointers are needed to adjust?
   (1) 1
   (2) 2
   (3) 3

9. To delete any intermediate node of a singly linear linked list how many pointers are needed to adjust?
   (1) 1
   (2) 2
   (3) 3

10. Which of the following statement is not true?
    (1) Linked list is a linear data structure.
    (2) Linked list is a dynamic data structure.
    (3) Linked list is a non linear data structure.

11. Which of the following statement is not true?
    (1) Allocation of array in memory is contiguous.
    (2) Allocation of structure in memory is contiguous.
    (3) Allocation of linked list in memory is contiguous.

12. Which of the following statement is true?
    (1) In a linked list, new nodes are added only at end of the list.
    (2) Linked list are represented in computer memory using self referential structure.
    (3) In singly linked list, pointer field of a node contains the address of the predecessor node.

13. How many pointer fields are required in a node in case of doubly linked list?
    (1) 1
    (2) 2
    (3) 4

14. Suppose we have to create a linked list to store some data (Roll no, Name and Fees Paid) of students. Which of the following is not a valid node structure for this purpose?
    ```
    (1) struct student
        {  int roll;
           char name[30];
           int fees_paid;
        };
    (2) struct student
        {  int roll;
           char name[30];
           int fees_paid;
           struct student *next_node;
        };
    (3) struct student
        {  int roll;
           char name[30];
           int fees_paid;
        };
        struct node
        {  struct student stud;
           struct node *next_node;
        };
    ```

15. To represent a Polynomial how many member fields are required in node structure?
    (1) 2
    (2) 3
    (3) 4

16. Suppose to maintain an inventory we have to create a linked list to store data (Product Code, Description, and Quantity) of products. Which of the following is not a valid node structure for this purpose?
    ```
    (1) struct product
        {  char pcode[10];
           char description[30];
           int qty;
        };
        struct node
        {  struct product prod;
           struct product *next_node;
        };
    ```

```
(2) struct product
    {   char pcode[10];
        char description[30];
        int qty;
    };
    struct node
    {   struct product prod;
        struct node *next_node;
    };
(3) struct node
    {   struct
        {   char pcode[10];
            char description[30];
            int qty;
        }
        product;
        struct node *next_node;
    };
```

17. Is it possible to represent very large integers, which cannot be stored in variables of long int data type, using linked list?

   If possible, specify the members of the node structure.

   (1) Not possible. It is not related to linked list.
   (2) Possible. Each node will consist of three member fields – coefficient, power and a link to the next node.
   (3) Possible. Each node will consist of two member fields – a string containing the integer as a string and a link to the next node.

LEARN BY QUIZ – ANSWERS

Answer Explanations

1. Linked list is a dynamic data structure.

2. Nodes of the linked list are accessed sequentially only.

3. 2.

   One is for data part and other is to store the address of successor node.

4. 2.

   Only 2 pointers are needed to adjust to insert a node at the beginning of a singly linear linked.

   Next pointer of new node will point to first node of the list (or Null if it is an empty list) and Head pointer will point to new node.

5. 1.

   Only single pointer is needed to adjust. If the list is empty, Head pointer will point to new node. Otherwise next pointer of last node will point to new node.

6. 2.

   Predecessor node will point to new node and new node will point to successor node.

7. 1.

Only single pointer is needed to adjust. Head pointer will point to 2nd node. If the list contain single node only, Head pointer will contain NULL.

8. 1.

Only single pointer is needed to adjust. Predecessor node of last node will point to NULL. If the list contain single node only, Head pointer will contain NULL.

9. 1.

Only single pointer is needed to adjust. Predecessor node of deleted node will point to the successor node of deleted node.

10. Option 3, i.e., linked list is a non linear data structure – is not true.

Linked list is a linear and dynamic data structure.

11. Option 3, i.e., allocation of linked list in memory is contiguous – is not true.

Allocation of array and structure in memory is contiguous but not in case of linked list. Each node in the list is created separately as and when required. Thus allocations take place in different memory locations.

12. Linked lists are represented in computer memory using self referential structure.

In a linked list, new nodes can be added anywhere in the list. It may be at beginning or at end or any intermediate position of the list.

In singly linked list, pointer field of a node contains the address of the successor node, not the predecessor node or NULL if it is the last node.

13. 2.

There are 2 pointer fields are required in a node in case of doubly linked list. One to store the address of predecessor and one to store the address of successor.

14. Option 1 is not a valid node structure for this purpose.

Options 2 and 3 both are correct. In case of option 3 nested structure is used.

15. 3.

Each node will consist of three member fields – coefficient, power and a link to the next node.

16. Option 1 is not a valid node structure for this purpose as in struct node, the next_node pointer is of type struct product. It should be of type struct node. It is shown in option 2.

In option 3 unnamed nested structure is defined within struct node which is a valid definition.

17. Possible. It can be represented as a polynomial. For example, the number 5000000000000000000000006 can be represented as $5 \times 10^{25} + 6 \times 10^{0}$. So, each node will consist of three member fields – coefficient, power and a link to the next node.

Large integer can be stored as string but to operate it as integer is very difficult. Again if it is stored as string, then linked list data structure is not required.

PART C

Technical Questions for Interview

Model Question Set–I

What will be the output for following code segments? If there is any compilation error or runtime error, mention it.

```
(1)  main()
     {   int num;
         printf("%d", scanf("%d", &num));      /* Suppose, 15 is given as input here */
     }
```

```
(2)  main()
     {
         float Hi = 1.3;
         double Fi = 1.3;
         if(Hi==Fi)
                 printf("Both are Equal");
         else
                 printf("Not Equals");
     }
```

```
(3)  main()
     {   extern int num;
         num = 15;
         printf("%d", num);
     }
```

```
(4)  main()
     {   int choice = 3;
         switch(choice)
         {   default:  printf("zero");
             case 1:   printf("one");
                       break;
             case 2:   printf("two");
                       break;
             case 3:   printf("three");
                       break;

         }
     }
```

(5) #define int char
     main()
     {   int var = 97;
         printf("Size of (var) = %d", sizeof(var));
     }

(6) main()
     {   int num = 12;
         num = !num>15;
         printf ("num = %d", num);
     }

(7) main()
     {   int p=7;
         printf("%d %d %d %d %d %d", p++, p--, ++p,--p, p);
     }

(8) main()
     {
         int *ptr;
         {
             int num1 = 10, num2 = 20;
             ptr = &num1;
         }
         printf("%d",*ptr);
     }

(9) #define fn(a1,a2) a1##a2
     main()
     {   int num1= 50;
         printf("%d", fn(num,1));
     }

(10) main()
      {
          char arr[]="abc\0def\0";
          int ln=strlen(arr);
          printf("Length of the string is: %d", ln);
      }

(11) main()
      {   int const * ptr = 1;
          printf("%d", ++(*ptr));
      }

(12) main()
      {   int arr[ ]={2.7,3.3,4,6.6,5};
          int j,*pptr=arr,*qptr=arr;
          for(j=0;j<5;j++)
          {   printf(" %d ",*arr);
              ++qptr;
          }

```
        for(j=0;j<5;j++)
        {   printf(" %d ",*pptr);
            ++pptr;
        }
    }
(13)    main()
    {   unsigned int num = 65000;
        while(num++!=0);
        printf("%d", num);
    }
(14)    main()
    {   static char lanuages[5][20]={"Basic", "C", "Python", "Java", "Ada"};
        int i; char *temp;
        temp=languages[3];
        languages[3]=languages[4];
        languages[4]=temp;
        for (i=0;i<5;i++)
            printf("%s", languages[i]);
    }
(15)    main ( )
    {   static char *sptr[ ] = {"white", "black", "green", "blue"};
        char **dptr[ ] = {sptr+3, sptr+2, sptr+1, sptr}, ***tptr;
        tptr = dptr;
        **++tptr;
        printf("%s", *--*++tptr + 3);
    }

(16)    main()
    {   float x=3, y=5;
        enum{a=50, b=60,c};
        printf("\n%f",x%y);
        printf("\n%f",fmod(x, y));
        printf("\n%f",x<<2);
        printf("\n%d",++c);
    }
(17)    int one_dim[]={15,25,35};
    main()
    {   int *iptr;
        iptr=one_dim;
        iptr+=3;
        printf("%d", *iptr);
    }
(18)    main()
    {   char *ptr;
        ptr="%d\n";
        ptr++;
```

```
        ptr++;
        printf(ptr-2,2);
    }
(19) main()
    {   int arr[5];
        printf("%d",*arr+2-*arr+4);
    }
(20) main()
    {   struct sample
        {   int num = 5;
            char strn[]="hello";
        };
        struct sample *sptr;
        printf("%d",sptr->num);
        printf("%s",sptr->strn);
    }
```

Answer of Model Question Set – I

(1) 1

Explanation: Scanf returns number of items successfully read

(2) Not Equals

(3) Linker Error: Undefined symbol '_num'.

(4) three

(5) Size of (var) = 1

Explanation: Since the #define replaces the string **int** by the macro **char**

(6) num = 0

Explanation: Priority of '!' operator is higher than '>' operator. So, !num executes first which returns 0. Next 0>15 – this expression is executed. This is also false and returns 0.

(7) 6 7 7 6 7

(8) 10

Explanation: The variable num1 and num2 is block level variables. Their visibility is within the block only. But lifetime is upto the exit of the function. Hence num1 is still allocated on that memory location and *ptr prints the value from that location.

(9) 50

(10) 3

Explanation: As soon as a '\0' character is found the string operations will be terminated. Thus strlen() terminates 3.

(11) Compiler error: Cannot modify a constant value.

Explanation: ptr is a pointer to a "constant integer". Here it is tried to modify the value of a "constant integer".

(12) 2 2 2 2 2 2 3 4 6 5

Explanation: Both **pptr** and **qptr** are initialized with the base address of the array arr. In first loop, **qptr** is incremented but printing is done through arr which is not modified. Thus 5 times the value 2 is printed. In second loop, **pptr** is incremented and printing is also done through **pptr**. So the values 2 3 4 6 5 is printed.

(13) 1

Explanation: As there is a semicolon after the while statement, the loop will be terminated when the value of num becomes 0. Due to post-increment, after checking the condition num will be incremented by 1.

(14) Compiler error: Lvalue required in function main

Explanation: Array names are pointer constants; it cannot be modified.

(15) te

Explanation: Here tptr holds the initial value of dptr, i.e. tptr becomes sptr+3. In next statement tptr is incremented by 1. So, tptr now becomes sptr+2. In the printf statement, first tptr incremented and *++tptr gets the value sptr+1. Next the pre-decrement operator is executed and results sptr+1 – 1 = sptr. Now the indirection operator gets the value from the array of sptr and adds 3 to the base address. The printing is starteded from this position. Hence, output is 'te'.

(16) Line no 5: Cannot apply mod to float
Line no 7: Cannot apply leftshift to float
Line no 8: Error: Lvalue required

Explanation: % operator and bitwise operators cannot be operated on float values.   fmod() is used to find the modulus values i.e. remainder value of some division for float variables. Enumeration constants cannot be modified, so ++ operator cannot be applied on it.

(17) Garbage value

Explanation: iptr pointer is pointing to a memory location which is out of the range of the array, one_dim.

(18) 2

Explanation: Since the pointer is incremented twice and again decremented by 2, it points to same memory location. Thus the format string is used as '%d\n' and 2 is printed.

(19) 6

Explanation: Though the array contains garbage value, we need not to concentrate on it. *arr and -*arr simply cancels out and the result is 2 + 4 = 6 .

(20) Compiler Error

Explanation: We can not initialize variables at the time of defining a structure.

Model Question Set–II

What will be the output for following code segments? If there is any compilation error or runtime error, mention it.

(1)
```
main()
{   int num=0;
    for(;num++;printf("%d",num)) ;
            printf("%d",num);
}
```

(2)
```
main()
{   static int num = 4;
    printf("%d ", num--);
    if(num)
        main();
}
```

(3)
```
main()
{   int p=-1, q=-1, r=0, s=2, t;
    m=p++&&q++&&r++||s++;
    printf("%d %d %d %d %d", p, q, r, s, t);
}
```

(4)
```
main()
{   int num = - -5;
    printf("Num = %d", num);
}
```

(5)
```
#define int char
main()
{   int num = 130;
    printf("Num = %d", num);
}
```

(6)
```
main()
{   printf("\not");
    printf("\bst");
    printf("\rra");
}
```

(7)   #define sqre(num) num*num
```
main()
{   int var;
    var = 64/sqre(4);
    printf("%d", var);
}
```

(8)   #define clrscr() 5000
```
main()
{   clrscr();
    printf("%d", clrscr());
}
```

(9)
```
main()
{   printf("%p",main);
}
```

(10)
```
main()
{   int n1=10, n2=20, n3, n4=40, n5=50;
    printf("%d %d");
    printf("%d %d %d %d %d");
}
```

(11)
```
main()
{   char arr[ ]="cat";
    int j;
    for(j=0;arr[ j ];j++)
    printf("%c%c%c%c\n", arr[ j ], *(arr+j), *(j+arr), j[arr]);
}
```

(12)
```
main()
{   char *ptr;
    printf("%d \t %d ",sizeof(*ptr),sizeof(ptr));
}
```

(13)
```
cat()  {
            printf("cat");
        }
mat() {
            printf("mat");
        }
rat()  {
            printf("rat");
        }
main()
{
    int (*fptr[3])();
    fptr[0]=cat;
    fptr[1]=mat;
    fptr[2]=rat;
    fptr[2]();
}
```

```
(14)   main()
       {   char my_arr[100];
           my_arr[0]='1'; my_arr[1]]='2'; my_arr[2]='3'; my_arr[4]='4';
           func(my_arr);
       }
       func(char ptr[])
       {
           ptrr++;
           printf("%c",*ptr);
           ptr++;
           printf("%c",*ptr);
       }
(15)   void main()
       {
           void *vptr;
           int integr=2;
           int *iptr=&integr;
           vptr=iptr;
           printf("%d",(int*)*vptr);
       }
(16)   Is the following code legal?
       typedef struct sample
       {
           int num;
           sampleType *ptr;
       }   sampleType;
(17)   struct points
       {
           int x_co;
           int y_co;
       };
       struct points origin,*ptr;
       void main()
       {
           ptr=&origin;
           printf("\norigin is (%d, %d)", (*ptr).x_co,(*ptr).y_co);
           printf("\norigin is (%d, %d)", ptr->x_co, ptr->y_co);
       }
(18)   sum(var1, var2)
       int var1, var2;
       {
           return var1+var2;
       }
       main(int x, char **y)
       {
           int s;
           s = sum(y[1], y[2]);
       }
```

(19) void main()
```
{
    FILE *fptr1,*fptr2;
    fptr1=fopen("file1","w");
    fptr2=fopen("file1","w");
    fputc('X',fptr1)
    fputc('Y',fptr2)
    fclose(fptr1)
    fclose(fptr2)
}
```
Is there any error in the above code?

(20) void main()
```
{
    static int num = 5;
    if(--num)
    {
        main();
        printf("%d ", num);
    }
}
```

Answer of Model Question Set – II

1. 1
    Explanation: As the value of num is 0, the condition of for loop will be false at very first time. But due to post-increment operator, num will be incremented to 1.

(2) 4 3 2 1

(3) 0 0 1 3 1

(4) Num = 5

(5) –126

(6)

 rat

(7) 64

(8) 5000

(9) Some address will be printed.

(10) 50 40
     50 40 20 10 0

(11) cccc
     aaaa
     tttt
     Explanation: arr[j], *(j+arr), *(arr+j), j[arr] all are equivalent statement.

(12) 1   2

(13) rat
     Explanation: fptr is an array of pointers to functions of return type int. fptr[0] will store the address of the function cat, fptr[1] and fptr[2] will strore the address of mat and rat respectively. As fptr[2] points to rat, fptr[2]() is in effect of writing rat().

(14)   23

      Explanation: In the function ptr is basically a pointer. So, it does not have any problem to increment. On first increment it points to 2nd element i.e. '2' then on next increment it points to '3'. So 23 will be printed.

(15)   Compiler Error. We cannot apply indirection on type void*.

(16)   No.

      Explanation: The type name sampleType is not known at the point of declaring the structure. To solve the problem forward declaration are required.

(17)   origin is(0,0)

      origin is(0,0)

      Explanation: Since the structure variable origin is declared globally, x_co & y_co are initialized as zeroes.

(18)   Compiler error: can not convert char* to int

      Explanation: y[1] & y[2] are strings. They are passed to the function sum without converting it to integer values.

(19)   No error. But it will overwrite on the same file.

(20)   0 0 0 0

Model Question Set–III

What will be the output for following code segments? If there is any compilation error or runtime error, mention it.

(1)
```c
void main()
{   int num=15;
    printf("%d",num++ + ++num);
}
```

(2)
```c
void main()
{   int index=1;
    while (index<=5)
    {   printf("%d",index);
        if (index>=3)
            goto out;
        index++;
    }
}
func()
{
    out:
    printf("welcome");
}
```

(3)
```c
void main()
{
    extern out_var;
    printf("%d", out_var);
}
int out_var=20;
```

(4)
```c
main()
{
    main();
}
```

```
(5)   main()
      {   char ch;
          ch=!5;
          printf("%d", ch);
      }
(6)   #define NULL  -1
      #define TRUE   1
      #define FALSE  0
      main()
      {   if(FALSE)
              puts("FALSE");
          else if(NULL)
              puts("TRUE");
          else
              puts("NULL");
      }
(7)   main()
      {   char *ptr = "C programming",*ptr1;
          ptr1=ptr;
          while(*ptr!='\0') ++*ptr++;
          printf("%s   %s",ptr,ptr1);
      }
(8)   main()
      {    char *ptr;
          ptr = "Welcome";
          printf("%c\t",*&*p);
      }
(9)   #include<stdio.h>
      main()
      {
          char arr[]={'1','2','3','\n','4','\0'};
          char *ptr,*strn,*strn1;
          ptr=&arr[3];
          strn=ptr;
          strn1=arr;
          printf("%d",++*ptr + ++*strn1);
      }
(10)  main()
      {
          int  i, ln;
          char *ptr = "abcd";
          ln = strlen(ptr);
          *ptr = ptr[ln];
          for(i=0; i<ln; ++i)
          {
              printf("%s\n",ptr);
```

```
            ptr++;
          }
     }
(11)  main()
      {   char *cp, ch;
          void *vp, vd;
          ch=10; vd=0;
          cp = &ch; vp = &vd;
          printf("%c %v", ch, vd);
      }
(12)  function1(m, n)
      int m, n;
      {
          return( m= (m==n) );
      }
      main()
      {
          int function2(),function1();
          printf("The value of function 2 is %d\n", function2 (function1, 4, 5));
      }
      function2(func_ptr,num1, num2)
      int (*func_ptr) ();
      int num1,num2;
      {
          return((*func_ptr) (num1, num2));
      }
```

(13) Is the following code legal?
```
      typedef struct sample  sampleType;
      struct sample
      {
          int num;
          sampleType *ptr;
      };
```

(14)
```
      main()
      {   int num = 5,*int_ptr;
          void *vptr;
          int_ptr=vptr=&num;
          int_ptr++;
          vptr++;
          printf("%u  %u ",int_ptr, vptr);
      }
```

(15) What will be the position of the file marker in the following cases?
      (i) fseek(fp,0,SEEK_SET);
      (ii) fseek(fp,0,SEEK_CUR);

(16)
```
      void main()
      {
          int val = retn(sizeof(float));
```

```
            printf("It is %d",++val);
        }
        int retn(int retn)
        {
            retn += 2.6;
            return(retn);
        }
(17)   int add( int x, int y)
        {
            int z = x + y;
        }
        void main( )
        {
            int x= '5', y = '6';
            printf("%d %d %d", x, y, add(x, y));
        }
(18)   void main( )
        {
            int n = 15;
            printf("%d", n << 3 >>5);
        }
(19)   void main( )
        {
            int x = y = z = 5;
            printf("%d %d %d", x, y, z);
        }
(20)   void  main()
        {
            printf("%x",-1<<4);
        }
```

Answer of Model Question Set – III

(1)   32

(2)   Compiler error: Undefined label 'out' in function main.

     Explanation: The label 'out' is available only within function func(). Thus in the function main it will not be visible.

(3)   20

(4)   Runtime error: Stack overflow.

     Explanation: Here main function recursively calls ownself again and again. So, function calls will be stored with in the stack. As there is no terminating condition, after sometimes the stack will be overflowed at runtime.

(5)   0

(6)   TRUE

(7)   D!qsphsbnnjoh

     Explanation: In the expression ++*ptr++, first *ptr i.e. the value of the location currently pointed by ptr will be incremented due to the pre-increment operator and then the pointer ptr will be incremented i.e. ptr++ will be executed

So, in each iteration, each character is converted to its next character. Thus 'C' is converted to 'D', blank space is converted to '!', 'p' is converted to 'q' and so on. Thus, the string converted to "D!qsphsbnnjoh". But ptr reaches to '\0', hence it prints nothing. As ptr1 stores the base address of the string, it prints the converted string.

(8)   W

(9)   61

Explanation: ptr is pointing to '\n' and strn1 is pointing to the character '1'. ++*ptr indicates that the content of the pointer ptr will be incremented by one. As the ASCII value of '\n' is 10, it will be incremented to 11. Similarly ++*strn1 returns '2'. ASCII value of '2' is 50. now 11 and 50 will be added and will print 61.

(10)   (blank space)

bcd

cd

d

Explanation: Here strlen function returns 4. Now the value of ptr[4] i.e. '\0' will be stored at ptr[0]. So, the string becomes "\0bcd". In first iteration, the printf statement will ptr[0] = '\0' and hence it prints nothing and pointer value is incremented. In 2nd iteration it prints from ptr[1]. So, "bcd" will be printed. Similarly in next irerations "cd" and "d" will be printed.

(11)   Compiler error : size of vd is Unknown.

Explanation: Since void is an empty type we can not create a variable of void type. But a pointer of type void (i.e. void* vp;) can be created.

(12)   The value of function2 is 0 !

Explanation: The function 'function2' has 3 parameters - a pointer to another function and two integers. function2 returns the result of the operation of function1. function1 returns 0, as m==n returns 0. So, function2 also return 0.

(13)   Yes

Explanation: As sampleType is already typedefined, the type name sampleType is known to the compiler.

(14)   Compiler error: Cannot increment a void pointer

Explanation: No pointer arithmetic can be done on void pointers and indirection operator (*) also cannot be applied on void pointers.

(15)   (i) Sets the file pointer at the beginning of file.

(ii) Sets the file pointer at the current position.

(16)   It is 7

Explanation: Function name and the argument name can be the same. So, the declaration int retn(int retn) is valid. In the function retn, 4 is added with 2.6 and thus return 6 as the function returns an int. So, val becomes 6 and next it incremented to 7 and be printed.

(17)   53 54 107

(18)   3

(19)   Compiler error: Undefined symbol 'y', 'z'.

(20)   fff0

Explanation: Internally-1 is represented as all 1's. This values will be left shifted four times. So, the least significant 4 bits are filled with 0's.

What will be the output for following code segments? If there is any compilation error or runtime error, mention it.

(1)
```c
#include <stdio.h>
#define number 20
void main( )
{
    #define number 30
    printf("%d", number);
}
```

(2)
```c
void main( )
{
    char *ptr;
    ptr="Hello";
    printf("%c\n",*&*ptr);
}
```

(3)
```c
void main()
{   int p=7;
    printf("%d", p+++++p);
}
```

(4)
```c
void main()
{   int opt =1, val= 2;
    switch(opt)
    {   case 1:  printf("This is Case 1");
                break;
        case val:  printf("This is Case 2");
                break;
    }
}
```

(5)
```c
void main()
{
    struct sample1
```

```
        {
            char ch;
            struct sample2
            {
                int num;
                struct sample *p;
            };
            struct sample2 *q;
        };
    }
```

(6) void main()
```
    {
        extern int x;
        x = 50;
        printf("%d", sizeof(x));
    }
```

(7) void main( )
```
    {
        int arr[2][3][2] = {{{1,2},{3,4},{5,6}},{{4,5},{6,7},{8,9}}};
        printf("%p %p %p %d \n", arr, *arr, **arr, ***arr);
        printf("%p %p %p %d \n", arr+1, *arr+1, **arr+1, ***arr+1);
    }
```
Consider the base address of the array is 2000.

(8) void main( )
```
    {   int arr[ ] = {5,15,25,35,45,55},i,*ptr;
        for(i=0; i<=5 i++)
        {   printf("%d" ,*arr);
            arr++;
        }
        ptr = arr;
        for(i=0; i<=5; i++)
        {   printf("%d " ,*ptr);
            ptr++;
        }
    }
```

(9) void main( )
```
    {
        char *ptr;
        int  x;
        for (x=0; x<3; x++) scanf("%s" ,(ptr+x));
        for (x=0; x<3; x++) printf("%c " ,*(ptr+x));
        for (x=0; x<3; x++) printf("\n%s " ,(ptr+x));
    }
```
Suppose the inputs are: ANIL, BIKASH and CHOWDHURY.

(10) void main( )
```
    {
        printf("%d", var);
```

```
        }
        int var=50;
(11)    void main()
        {
            int num=-1;
                +num;
            printf("num = %d, +num = %d \n",num,+num);
        }
(12)    void main()
        {
            char *strn1="Hello!";
            char strn2[]="Hello!";
            printf("%d %d %d",sizeof(strn1),sizeof(strn2),sizeof("Hello!"));
        }
(13)    void main()
        {
            int num=2,*ptr1,*ptr2;
            ptr1=ptr2=&num;
            *ptr1+=*ptr2+=num+=2.5;
            printf("\n%d %d %d",num,*ptr1,*ptr2);
        }
(14)    char *Function1()
        {
            char arr[ ] = "String";
            return arr;
        }
        char *Function2()
        {
            char arr[ ] = {'S', 't', 'r', 'i', 'n', 'g'};
            return arr;
        }
        void main()
        {
            puts(Function1());
            puts(Function2());
        }
(15)    void main()
        {
            char *ptr1="Technology";
            char *ptr2;
            ptr2=(char *)malloc(15);
            while(*ptr2++ = *ptr1++);
            printf("%s ",ptr2);
        }
(16)    void main()
        {
            char *ptr = "C Programming";
```

```
        (*ptr)++;
        printf("%s\n",ptr);
        ptr++;
        printf("%s\n",ptr);
    }
(17)  void main()
    {
        int m =0, n =0;
        if(m && n++)
            printf("%d, %d", m++, n);
        printf("%d, %d", m, n);
    }
(18)  int num;
    main()
    {
        int i;
        for ( i=4; scanf("%d",&num) - i; printf("%d\n",num))
            printf("%d--", i--);
    }
                    /* If the inputs are 0,1,2,3 find the Output. */
(19)  void main()
    {
        int x= 0, y = 1;
        char ch1 = 49, ch2 =65;
        if(x,y,ch1,ch2)
        printf("Welcome");
    }
(20)  void main()
    {
        unsigned int loop;
        for(loop=1;loop>-2;loop--)
        printf("%u", loop);
        printf("%u", loop);
    }
```

Answer of Model Question Set – IV

(1) 30

Explanation: We can redefine the preprocessor directives anywhere and any number of times. But the latest declaration will be considered.

(2) H

Explanation: Here ptr points to the first character of the string "Hello". Thus *ptr returns H. Next & references its address and * dereferences again to the value H.

(3) Compiler Error

Explanation: The expression p+++++p will be parsed as p ++ ++ + p which is an illegal combination of operators.

(4) Compiler Error: Constant expression required in function main.

Explanation: Within the switch-case statement variables cannot be used directly; only constant expressions can be used.

(5) Compiler Error

Explanation: As the structure sample2 is declared within the structure sample1, it is necessary to declare variable at the end of declaration of sample2.

(6) Linker error: undefined symbol '_x'.

Explanation: extern declaration state that the variable is defined elsewhere in the program. Thus compiler passes external variables to be resolved by the linker. So there is no compilation error. At the time of linking, linker searches for the variable, x. Since it is not declared at all, linker error occurs.

(7) 2000, 2000, 2000, 1
2012, 2004, 2002, 2

Explanation: It is a 3-D array. But in memory allocation are linear and contiguous. Thus it will be treated as the following single dimensional array.

1	2	3	4	5	6	4	5	6	7	8	9
2000	2002	2004	2006	2008	2010	2012	2014	2016	2018	2020	2022

First printf statement arr, *arr, **arr provide the address of first element and ***arr specifies the value of this location. In second printf arr+1 increments in the 3rd dimension. So, it points to the address 2012. *arr+1 increments in 2nd dimension. So, it points to the address 2004 and **arr +1 increments in 1st dimension. So,it points 2002 and ***arr+1 adds 1 to the value of first location.

(8) Compiler error: lvalue required.

Explanation: Error is in the statement arr++. Array name is a constant pointer and thus cannot be modified.

(9) A B C
ABCHOWDHURY
BCHOWDHURY
CHOWDHURY

Explanation: Here only one pointer is used to take input of 3strings. Thus inputs are taken in the almost same memory location. Just each time shifted by 1. As the inputs are: ANIL, BIKASH and CHOWDHURY , then the first input will be stored as:

A	N	I	L	\0

At the time of second input the pointer is incremented by 1, so the input will be stored from next memory location.

A	B	I	K	A	S	H	\0

Similarly, third input will be stored from arr[2].

A	B	C	H	O	W	D	H	U	R	Y	\0

Thus first printf prints the content of the address pointed by ptr, ptr+1 and ptr+2. Second printf prints three strings starting from locations ptr, ptr+1and ptr+2.

(10) Compiler error: undefined symbol var in function main.

(11) num = –1, +num = –1

(12)   2 7 7

(13)   16 16 16

Explanation: ptr1 and ptr2 both points to the same memory location i.e. the address of num. Thus changes through ptr1 and ptr2 ultimately affects only the value of num.

(14)   Garbage values.

Explanation: Both strings are allocated locally to their functions. Thus when control returns back to the main, the strings will be de-allocated.

(15)   An empty string

Explanation: Within the while loop, the entire string pointed by ptr1 will be copied to ptr2. But after copying, ptr2 will point to the '\0' character of the copied string. Thus an empty string i.e. nothing will be printed.

(16)   D Programming

Programming

(17)   0, 0

Explanation: The value of i is 0. Since this information is enough to determine the truth value of the Boolean expression. So the statement following the if statement is not executed. The values of i and j remain unchanged and get printed.

(18)   4--0

3--1

2--2

Explanation: The values of the variables during execution will be,

i	num	scanf("%d",&num)–i
4	0	–4
3	1	–2
2	2	0

(19)   Welcome

Explanation: The associativity of comma operator is from left to right. Thus only rightmost value will be returned. As it is a non zero value the if statement becomes true.

(20)   1

Explanation: When the variable loop (an unsigned integer) is compared with -2 (i.e, a signed value), signed is promoted to unsigned value. So, -2 is converted to its unsigned equivalent i.e, 65534. Thus condition becomes false and control comes out from the loop.

Model Question Set–V

What will be the output for following code segments? If there is any compilation error or runtime error, mention it.

(1)
```c
void main()
{
    int num=-1;
    -num;
    printf("num = %d, -num = %d \n",num,-num);
}
```

(2)
```c
#include<stdio.h>
void main()
{
    const int i=5;
    float j;
    j = ++i;
    printf(„%d  %f", i,++j);
}
```

(3)
```c
void main()
{
    int x=5,y=6,z;
    printf("%d",x+++y);
}
```

(4)
```c
void main()
{
    int i=_1_func(10);
    printf("%d\n",--i);
}
int _1_func(int i)
{
    return(i++);
}
```

(5)
```c
char *Function1()
{
    static char arr[ ] = "String";
```

```
            return arr;
        }
        char *Function2()
        {    char arr[ ] = {'S', 't', 'r', 'i', 'n', 'g'};
            return arr;
        }
        void main()
        {    puts(Function1());
            puts(Function2());
        }
(6)    void main()
        {
            display();
        }
        void display()
        {
            printf("How fun it is!");
        }
(7)    void main()
        {
            char arr[]="\0";
            if(printf("%s\n",arr))
                printf("Good \n");
            else
                printf("Nice \n");
        }
(8)    void main()
        {
            static int x=x++, y=y++, z=z++;
            printf("x = %d y = %d z = %d", x, y, z);
        }
(9)    void main()
        {
            while(1)
            {
                if(printf("%d", printf("%c")))
                        break;
                else
                        continue;
            }
        }
(10)   void main()
        {
            unsigned int num=5;
            while(num-->=0)
                printf("%u ",num);
        }
(11)   #define product(m,n) m*n
        void main( )
        {
            int a=5,b=6;
```

```
            printf("%d",product(a+2,b-1));
    }
(12)    void main()
        {
            int a=0;
            while(+(+a--)!=0)
                    a-=a++;
            printf("%d",a);
        }
(13)    void main()
        {
            int num=5;
            printf("%d", ++num++);
        }
(14)    void main()
        {
            char *ptr = "India";
            char ch;
            ch = ++*ptr++;
            printf("%c", ch);
        }
(15)    void main()
        {
            char ptr[ ]="%d\n";
            ptr[1] = 'c';
            printf(ptr,65);
        }
(16)    void main()
        {
            int x=5;
            printf("%d",x=++x ==6);
        }
(17)    void main()
        {
            while (strcmp("Hello","Hello\0"))
                printf("Strings are Identical\n");
        }
(18)    void main()
        {
            static int num;
            while(num<=0)
            (num>2)?num++:num--;
            printf("%d", num);
        }
(19)    void main()
        {
            int x= 5, y= 6;
            y = (x, y) ? (x, y) ? x : y : y;
            printf("x=%d, y=%d", x, y);
        }
```

(20) void main()
      {
          int a=5, b=6, c=6;
          a = a & = b&&c;
          printf("%d %d", a, b);
      }

Answer of Model Question Set – V

(1) num = –1, -num = 1
     Explanation: -num is executed and this execution doesn't affect the value of num. In printf first the value of num is printed. After that the value of the expression -num = -(-1) i.e. 1 is printed.

(2) Compiler error
     Explanation: i is a constant. the value of constant cannot be changed.

(3) 11
     Explanation: The expression x+++y is treated as (x++ + y)

(4) 9
     Explanation: return(i++) it will first return i and then increments. i.e. 10 will be returned.

(5) String
     Garbage value
     Explanation: In the Function1 the arr array is declared as static. Thus its lifetime is through out the program and it will be printed from main. But in Function2 the arr array is declared as auto. Thus when control returns to the main function, the string will be de-allocated and produce some garbage value.

(6) Compiler error: Type mismatch in re-declaration of display.
     Explanation: When the compiler sees the function display it doesn't know anything about it. So the default return type (ie, int) is assumed. But when compiler sees the actual definition of display mismatch occurs since it is declared as void. Hence the error.
     The solutions are as follows:
     (1) declare void display() in main().
     (2) define display() before main().
     (3) declare extern void display() before the use of display().

(7) Good
     Explanation: printf( ) returns number of characters it prints. As it prints only a null character, it returns 1 which makes the if statement true, thus "Good" is printed.

(8) x = 1 y = 1 z = 1
     Explanation: An identifier is available to use in program from the point where it is declared. Thus expressions such as x = x++ are valid statements. As x, y and z are static variables, by default they are initialized to zero.

(9) Garbage values(single character) and 1
     Explanation: The inner printf( ) executes first and print a character which is basically garbage value. But as it will prints a character, the inner printf( ) returns 1. So, the outer printf prints 1 and also return 1. Thus the if statement becomes true and the break statement encountered and comes out from the infinite loop.

(10)   5 4 3 2 1 0 65535 65534.....
       Explanation: Since num is an unsigned integer it can never become negative. So the expression num-- >=0 will always be true, leading to an infinite loop.

(11)   10
       Explanation: The macro will be expanded and evaluated as:
          a+2*b-1 => a+(2*b)-1 => 5+(2*6)-1 => 16

(12)   -1
       Explanation: Unary + operator is a dummy operator; it does not have any affect on code. Thus the while loop becomes, while(a--!=0) which is false and the loop terminated. –1 is printed due to post-decrement operator.

(13)   Compiler error: Lvalue required in function main
       Explanation: ++num yields a constant. Thus postfix ++ cannot operate on it.

(14)   J
       Explanation: ++*ptr++ will be executed as ++*(ptr++).

(15)   A
       Explanation: After executing the statement ptr[1] = 'c' the string becomes, "%c\n". Now this string becomes the format string for printf and ASCII character of 65 is 'A', So, the output is: A.

(16)   1
       Explanation: The == poperator has the higher precedence than = operator. So, the expression will be considered as x = (++x==6). Now, ++x is equal to 6 and returns 1(true).

(17)   No output
       Explanation: Adding an extra '\0' at end with a string constant does not make any difference when they are compared with strcmp(). So, strcmp returns 0; hence breaking out of the while loop.

(18)   32767
       Explanation: num is initialized to 0 as it is declared as static. Within the loop the conditional operator evaluates to false and num-- will execute. It will be continued until the integer value rotates to positive value (32767). Then the loop condition becomes false and control comes out from it. Finally prints the value of num.

(19)   x=5, y=5;
       Explanation: The statement which is consist of nested ?: operator can be considered as following if-else statement.
       if(x, y)
       {   if(x ,y)
               y = x;
           else
               y = y;
       }
       else
           y = y;

(20)   1 6
       Explanation: The expression will be executed as a=(a&=(b&&c)); The expression (b&&c) evaluates to 1 because both the value of b and c are 6. So, the expression becomes a = 5&1. Hence the result.

Common Questions and Answers

1. What is the difference between Compiler and Interpreter?

Ans:

Compiler	Interpreter
1. A compiler scans the entire program first and then translates it into machine code.	1. An interpreter translates the program line by line.
2. A compiler creates a list of errors after compilation.	2. An interpreter stops after the first error.
3. A compiler produces an independent executable file.	3. An interpreted program needs the interpreter each time it is run.
4. A compiler is faster than an interpreter.	4. An interpreter is much slower than as compared to compiler.
5. A compiler requires larger memory space.	5. An interpreter occupies less memory space.
6. Compiler is slow for debugging.	6. Interpreter is good for fast debugging.

2. What is ternary operator?

Ans: Ternary operator is an operator which has three operands. In C, there is a ternary operator named conditional operator or ' ? : ' operator. The general form of conditional operator is:

Expression 1 ? Expression 2 : Expression 3

First expression1 is evaluated. If the expression1 is true, then expression2 is evaluated otherwise expression3 is evaluated.

EXAMPLE

```
void main( )
{    int a, b, max;
     printf("Enter any two number :");
     scanf("%d%d",&a, &b);
     max = (a>b) ? a: b;
     printf("Max = %d",max);
}
```

The above program prints the maximum between two inputted numbers.

Ternary operator can also be nested.

For example,

```
max = (a>b)? ((a>c)? a: c) : ((b>c) ? b: c);
```

The above statement finds the maximum between three inputted numbers. Here, after evaluation of expression1, it faces another conditional operator at the position of expression2 or expression3.

3. What are the functions of the typecast operator and size of operator?

Ans: Typecast operator: The typecast operator is used to convert the value of any data type to the specified data type explicitly. The typecast operator is written as

```
(data type) expression
```

For Example,   int a = 5, b=2;

   float c;

   c = a/b;

In the above example, though c is a float variable, it will contain 2 as **a** and **b** both are integer variable and operation on both integers produce integer. So, to get the exact result, typecast operator is required. And we have to write,

   c = (float) a / b;

Now, the value of **a** will be first converted to **float**. Then division will be performed. So, we get the exact result, i.e., 2.5.

Size of operator: The sizeof operator is used to find the number of bytes occupied in memory by a variable, a constant or a data type qualifier. For example,

   sizeof(int) will return 2.

   sizeof('a') will return 1.

   float f;

   sizeof(f) will return 4.

This operator is effectively used to find the size of array and structure, if their sizes are not known to the programmer or there is a chance to change their size. It is also used at the time of dynamically memory allocation.

4. What do you mean by operator precedence and associativity? Explain with an example.

Ans: If number of operators used in an expression is more than one, the order of execution depends on *precedence* and *associativity*. Precedence determines the priority or order in which the operations are performed. In C language, some specific levels of precedence have been defined. All the operators belong to any one of that level. Expressions with higher-precedence operators are evaluated first. The highest precedence is given to the function expression operator, '( )' whereas the lowest precedence is given to the comma operator, ','. The grouping of operands can be forced by using parentheses.

For example, consider the expression,

$$X - y / z$$

Here the / operation is performed before - as the precedence of / is higher than that of -.

On the other hand, associativity is the right-to-left or left-to-right order of execution for a group of operands to operators that have the same precedence. The precedence of an operator is important only when the other operators in the expression are of higher or lower precedence but within same precedence associativity determines the order in which direction it will be executed.

Consider the following example:

$$x - y * z + p$$

Here as * operator has higher precedence than - and +, * is executed before + and -. But between + and -, which is executed first will be determined by their associativity as both have the same precedence. The associativity of + and - operators is left to right, hence in the above example the result of y * z is subtracted from x first, and then this result will be added with p.

[The precedence of all operators and their associativity are shown in Table 7.7]

5. Distinguish between i++ and ++i statements.

Ans: i++ denotes post increment whereas ++i denotes pre-increment. Both statements increment the value of i by 1. Both have same effect when they are used in an isolated statement.

For example,

> i++;

> and ++i; have same effect.

But they are different when used in association with some other operator in a C statement. ++i first increments the value of i and then that incremented value is used in the statement to execute the other operator. But i++ uses the old value in the statement to execute the other operator and at the end it increments the value of i.

For example,

> i = 5;

> j = ++i;

Here, first i will be incremented to 6 and this incremented value (i.e., 6) will be stored to j.

> i = 5;

> j = i++;

Here, first i will be assigned to j. So, 5 will be store within j. And after assignment i will be incremented to 6.

6. Why & is used in case of scanf() statement in C, though it is not used in printf() statement?

Ans: The scanf ( ) requires the address of variable(s) as arguments. That is why '&' is used in case of scanf ( ) statement in C. But printf( ) requires the value of variable(s) as arguments. So, '&' is not used in case of printf ( ) statement.

7. What is automatic type conversion?

Ans: When the conversion of one data type to another take place automatically, it is known as automatic type conversion or implicit type conversion. It is also known as **coercion**.

In a mixed-type expression, data of one or more lower types is automatically converted to higher type during execution. Following are the example of automatic type conversion.

```
float   num1;
long    num2;
int     num3;

num2 = num3;
num3 = num1 / num2;
```

Though num1, num2 and num3 are of different data types, the variables of lower data type will be automatically converted to corresponding higher data types each time an operation take place. Programmer should be cautious about automatic type conversion as there is a chance of losing fractional part.

8. Compare the use of the *switch* statement with the use of the nested *if-else* statement. Which is more convenient and why?

Ans: The switch statement allows the user to make a decision from the number of choice. The syntax of switch statement:

```
switch(expression)
{    case   value-1:
            statement(s);
            [break;]
     case   value-2:
            statement(s);
            [break;]
     case value-3:
            statement(s);
            [break;]
     . . . .
     . . . .
     default:
            statement(s);
}
```

Here, the expression is first evaluated. Value of the expression is tested with the different case values sequentially. Then this value compared with the constant values that follow the case statement. If this matches any of the constant values in a case, the statements following that case are executed. If the value does not match any of the case value, the **default** is chosen.

The nested if-else statement also allows the user to make a decision from the number of choice. If we write an if or if-else statement within an if/if-else statement, it is called nested if-else statement. There is no limitation on level of nesting, we can write as many if statement within if statement as we required.

EXAMPLE

```
if(cond.)
  {  if(cond.)
     {  if(cond.)
        . . . .
        else
        . . . .
     }
     else
     {  if(cond.)
        . . . .
        else
        . . . .
     }
  }
```

The difference between switch and nested if-else statement is that the switch statement is only checks the equality, whereas nested if-else statement check all type of relations, i.e., >,<,>=,<=,= = and !=. So, if we have to check all possibilities with in a range, different types of conditions (not only equality), *nested if-else is more convenient*. But if our option is to choose one among a set of alternative integral values, *switch is more convenient*.

9. Write down the differences between entry-controlled and exit-controlled loop statements.

Ans:

Entry-controlled loop statements	Exit-controlled loop statements
1. Here condition is checked before the execution of the body of the loop.	1. Here condition is checked after the execution of the body of the loop.
2. In C, while and for are of entry controlled type loop statement.	2. In C, do-while is of exit-controlled type loop statement.
3. As the condition is tested first, body of the loop may not execute at all.	3. As the body of the loop is executed first before the condition checked, the body of the loop is always executed at least once.

10. Differentiate between do-while and while statements with suitable example.

Ans: while statement: In 'C', while statement is a pre-test iteration or entry controlled loop statement. Here condition is tested first. If the condition is true, then body of the loop is executed. This continues until the condition become false. *As the condition is tested first, body of the loop may not execute at all.* The general form of while loop:

```
while (condition)
```

```
{
    ... // body of the loop
    ...
}
```

EXAMPLE

```
int i = 5;
while(i<= 10)
{   printf("%d ", i);
    i++;
}
```

The above example, will print: 5 6 7 8 9 10 . . . .

But, `int i = 5;`

```
while(i>= 10)
{ printf("%d ", i);
    i++;
}
```

The above example will print nothing as the condition is false at very beginning.

do-while statement: In 'C', do-while statement is a post-test iteration or exit controlled loop statement. Here, body of the loop is executed first. Then the condition is tested whether the loop will execute next time or not. If the condition is true, the control continues to evaluate the body of the loop once again. When the condition becomes false, the loop will be terminated. *As the body of the loop is executed first before the condition checked, the body of the loop is always executed at least once.* The general form of do-while loop:

```
do
{
    ... // body of the loop
    ...
}   while (condition);
```

EXAMPLE

```
int i = 5;
do
{ printf("%d ", i);
    i++;
} while(i<= 10);
```

The above example, will print: 5 6 7 8 9 10

But, `int i = 5;`

```
do
{  printf("%d ", i);
   i++;
}  while(i>= 10);
```

The above example, will print: 5. Because before condition checking, body of the loop will execute and will print 5.

11. What is the difference between break and continue statement.

Ans: Break statement forces to jump out from a loop instantly. When *break* is encountered inside any loop, control automatically passes to the first statement after the loop. Break statement is also used to come out from the switch-case statement.

EXAMPLE

```
int i = 5;
while(i<= 10)
{    printf("%d ", i);
     if( i == 7)
          break;
     i++;
}
printf("%d ", i);
```
The above example will print: 5 6 7 7

Whereas the continue statement is used to transfer the control to the beginning of the loop, bypassing the statements between the continue statement and end of loop.

EXAMPLE

```
int i = 5;
while(i<= 10)
{    printf("%d ", i);
     if( i == 7)
          continue;
     i++;
}
printf("%d ", i);
```
The above example will print: 5 6 7 7 7 7

In the above example, same code (which is used as example of break statement) is used. Only difference is instead of break statement here we use continue statement. As a result, when the value of **i** becomes 7, control looped back to the beginning of the loop. so, i does not get chance to increment and the loop becomes an infinite loop.

12. Compare the purpose of break statement with that of exit().

Ans: Break statement forces to jump out from a loop instantly. When *break* is encountered inside any loop, control automatically passes to the first statement after the loop. Break statement is also used to come out from the switch-case statement.

On the other hand, exit( ) is used to terminate the program. When some abnormal situation arise in the program such as file not opened or required memory is not allocated, we can use exit( ) to terminate the execution of the program.

EXAMPLE

```
int i = 5;
while(i<= 10)
{ printf("%d ", i);
   if( i == 7)
         break;
   i++;
}
printf("%d ", i);
```

Here, in the above program when the value of **i** becomes 7, the control will come out from the loop because then break statement will be executed. And the printf statement will print the value of **i**, i.e., 5. So, the output will be: 5 6 7 7

But instead of break statement if we use exit( ), the moment the condition will be satisfied, the execution of the program will terminate without executing the printf statement. So, the output will be: 5 6 7.

13. What is a null statement? What is a null string?

Ans: null statement: The statement which contains nothing is known as null statement. It is denoted only by a single ';'. Generally this null statement is used with loop statement.

EXAMPLE

```
for(i=0;i<10000;i++);
```

Here, this actually treated as:

```
for(i=0;i<10000;i++)
{   ;
}
```

The body of the for loop contains only a semicolon, known as null statement. The above for statement is used to delay some time.

null string: The string which contain only '\0' value at its first position is known as null string. Its length is zero.

EXAMPLE

```
char arr[30];
    arr[0] = '\0';
```

Here, arr is a null string.

14. What is the difference between x, 'x' and "x"?

Ans: x represents a variable named **x** but **'x'** is a character constant which represents a character value x whose ASCII value is 120. Whereas **"x"** represents a string constant, i.e., a character array whose size is 2 and consist of two character 'x' and '\0'.

15. What are the disadvantages of an array?

Ans: The disadvantages of an array are:

- **Staic allocation:** The allocation of an array is static and done at compile time. So, we have to declare an array which is sufficiently large. For this reason there is *wastage of memory*. Again in certain situation, if more memory is required than the defined one, then it also faces the *lack of memory* problems. [Solution of this problem is Dynamic Allocation.]
- **Contiguous allocation:** If a very large array is required to define, then program may face the problem of allocation. As an array is a contiguous allocation, for very large size array, there may be some situations, where though total free space is much larger than requirement, an array cannot be defined only due to those free space, that are not contiguous. [Solution of this problem is Linked List.]

16. What is meant by the scope of a variable within a program?

Ans: A scope specifies the part of the program where a variable name is visible, that is the accessibility of the variable by its name. In other word, scope of a variable means in which portion that variable is accessible. Scopes are of two types – local and global.

The scope of a variable depends on the type of storage class. Scope of auto, register and static variable is local to the block in which the variable is declared. Means the variable is accessible only from the block in which it is declared but the variable is not accessible from outside this block. The scope of external variables is global which means these variables are accessible from not only within the block it is declared, but also from outside this block and from all other functions in a program file.

17. Distinguish between automatic and static variables.

Automatic variables	Static variables
1. Default value is garbage value.	1. Default value is zero.
2. Life of automatic variable persists till the control remains within the block in which it is defined.	2. Life of static variable persists till the program ends and value of the variable persists between different function calls.
3. By default variable is declared as automatic. The keyword auto can also be used to declare automatic variable.	3. The keyword 'static' is used to declare static variable.

18. What is the difference between global & local variable.

Local variable: The variables whose scope is limited within the block (or function) are known as local variable. A local variable is only visible to the block or function in which it is declared. For example, formal arguments and variables declared within a function are local variable.

Global variable: The variables which are declared outside of all functions are called global variables. A global variable is visible to all the functions in a program. A global variable may be accessed from more than one file with the help of extern keyword.

EXAMPLE

```
#include <stdio.h>
int m;              // global variable declaration
void main( )
{   int x,y;        // local variable declaration
    .......
    .......
}
```

In the above example, global variable is m and local variables are x and y.

19. Write down the difference between global variable and static variable

Ans: A global variable is accessible from any portion of the program but the scope of static variable is limited to the block in which it is declared.

A global variable may be accessed from more than one file. But it is not possible for static variable.

If it be required to pass the same value in different functions or programs, global variable is required. But, if it be required that the value of a variable persists between different function calls, the solution is static variable.

20. What are the advantages of using functions in 'C' programming? What is the difference between users defined functions & library functions?

Ans: The advantages of using functions are:

- Increases readability.
- Decreases LOC.
- Minimize the effort in testing, debugging and maintenance.
- Increases reusability.
- Helps in top down modular programming.

The difference between user defined functions and library functions is library functions are already defined in library and that are ready to use whereas user defined functions are those functions that have to be defined by the programmer and then only that can be used.

21. Briefly describe actual & formal arguments.

Ans: We can classify the arguments into two types – actual argument and formal argument. The arguments we send at the time of function call is known as actual arguments. They are called actual arguments because these arguments hold the actual value; whereas the arguments defined at the argument list in a function definition is known as formal arguments. They are called formal arguments because they are formal place holder. With the following example these can be explained clearly.

```
int factorial(int n)        // formal argument
{  int i, f=1;
   for(i=1;i<=n;i++)
         f=f*i;
   return(f);
}
void main( )
{  int x,fact;
   printf("Enter any Number : ");
   scanf("%d",&x);
   fact = factorial(x);        // Actual argument
   printf("Factorial of %d is %d", x,fact);
}
```

In the above example, x is actual argument in the statement

```
fact = factorial(x);
```

and n is formal argument in the definition of the function, factorial( ).

22. When is it necessary to declare prototype of a function?

Ans: We can define a function any where in the program, i.e., before or after any function including main( ). But the function should be defined before its calling. If a function is not defined before its calling, it is necessary to declare the prototype of the function.

Again in turbo C, the default return type of any user defined function is int. If the return type of any function is not integer, it is necessary to declare the prototype of the function.

23. What is function overhead? Explain with an example.

Ans: When a function is called, it takes a lot of extra time in executing a series of instructions for tasks such as jumping to the function, saving registers, pushing arguments into the stack and on returning to the calling function and retrieving the values from stack. When a function is very small, a substantial percentage of execution time is spent in such operations. This is called function overhead.

For example, consider the code segment:

```
int square(int x)
{
      return (x*x);
}
```

```
void main( )
{    int a,b;
     printf("Enter any number : ");
     scanf("%d",&a);
     b = square(a);
     printf("Square of %d is %d", a, b);
}
```

In the above example, when the function will be called, the variables of main( ) along with value of the program counter will be saved in a stack first. Then the control will jump to the function. And after executing the statements in the function, control will again jump back to the calling point and will retrieve the saved values from stack. So, to execute a single line function a set of extra statements are required to execute. This is function overhead.

24. What do you mean by recursion? What advantages are there in its use?

Ans: Every function in 'C' may be called from any other function or itself. When a function is called by itself, the function is called recursive function. And the process is called recursion. So, we can define, **Recursion** is the process where a function is called by itself. Though it is more memory consuming process, but it is very effective in implementation where algorithm demands same repetitive process.

Advantage of Recursion:

1. Reduce the code.
2. Helps in implementation of divide and conquer algorithm.
3. Helps in implementation where algorithms use STACK.
4. Helps to reverse the order of some sequence.

25. Write down the differences between recursion and iteration.

Ans: Both iteration and recursion involve in repetition. But the way of implementation is different. Iteration explicitly uses a repetition structure, i.e., loop; recursion achieves repetition through repeated function calls. In comparison to iteration, there is usually significant time and space cost associated with recursion, due to the overhead required to manage the stack and the relative slowness of function calls. But in some situation, recursion is very effective in implementation where algorithm demands same repetitive processes such as implementation of tree, sorting methods that follow divide and conquer method.

26. What are the major drawbacks of using recursion?

Ans: The major drawbacks of using recursion are it is not as good as iteration regarding time and space complexity. Recursion achieves repetition through repeated function calls.

In iteration same set of variables is used. But in recursion, every time the function is called, the complete set of variables is allocated again and again. So, a significant space cost is associated with recursion.

Again there is also a significant time cost associated with recursion, due to the overhead required to manage the stack and the relative slowness of function calls.

27. What is a pointer? What are the different characteristics of a pointer?

Ans: Pointer is a very important feature in C language. It is a very powerful tool. The variable which holds the address of another variable is called pointer variable. A pointer variable is used to access variable by its address.

There are several advantages of using pointers. Some of them are:

- Able to return more than one value from a function using call by reference method.
- Pass arrays and strings more efficiently as arguments to a function.
- Dynamic memory allocation.
- Implements complex data structures such as linked list, trees, and graph.
- Increase execution speed.
- Better memory utilization.

Some characteristics of a pointer:

- Every pointer variable can hold the address of only corresponding data type.
- Only void pointer can store the address of any data type.
- To get the content of the memory location pointed by the pointer variable '*'(dereferencing) operator is required.
- Only 3 arithmetic operations are permitted on pointer. These are:
  ◆ Addition of a number to a pointer.
  ◆ Subtraction of a number from a pointer.
  ◆ Subtraction of a pointer from another.

28. What do you understand by pointer to pointer?

Ans: When a pointer variable contains the address of another pointer variable, it is called pointer to pointer. Consider the following code snippet:

```
int a = 5;

int *ptr = &a;

int **pptr = &ptr;
```

here, ptr is a pointer variable which holds the address of the variable, a and pptr is a pointer to pointer which holds the address of pointer variable, ptr.

29. What are call by value and call by reference? Explain with examples.

Ans: The arguments passed to any function can be of two types – call by value and call by reference.

Call by value: When we pass the arguments as a call by value, we pass the value of variables to the function. For example consider the following code snippet.

```
int sum(int a, int b)
{
    int c;
    c=a+b;
    return(c);
}
```

```
void main( )
{
     int x, y, z;
     printf("Enter any two Numbers:");
     scanf("%d%d",&x,&y);
     z = sum(x,y);
     printf("Sum =%d ",z);
}
```

Here, value of x and y will be passed to sum( ) and those value will be accepted by the formal arguments of sum( ), a and b.

Call by reference: When we pass the address of variables to the function as arguments, it is called call by reference. The main advantage of call by reference is that we can change/modify the content of more than one variable through some function. This is not possible if we invoke a function using call by value mechanism as any function can return at most one value. For example, consider the following code snippet.

```
void swap(int *p, int *q)
{
     int temp;
     temp = *p;
     *p = *q;
     *q = temp;
}
void main( )
{
     int x, y;
     printf("Enter any two Numbers:");
     scanf("%d%d",&x,&y);
     printf("Before Swaping, X = %d, Y = %d ",x, y);
     swap(&x, &y);
     printf("After Swaping, X = %d, Y = %d ",x, y);
}
```

Here, instead of value of x and y, address of x and y is sent to swap( ). So, from swap() function, we can directly access the address of x and y variable and can change the content of those location.

30. What is the relationship between an array name and pointer?

Ans: An array name is a constant pointer. A pointer holds the address of some variable and an array name represents the base address of an array variable. Whatever operations are done on pointer are also applicable to array name. But the only difference is that the content of array name can not be changed.

For example,   int a[10],*p;

                      p=a;

           now,   p++ is a valid statement.

           But, we can not write a++ .

31. What is the difference between array of pointers and pointer to an array?

Ans: Array of pointers means an array whose each element is a pointer. As pointer variable contains an address, an array of pointer is basically a collection of addresses. The addresses stored in the array of pointers can be addresses of isolated variables or addresses of some array or any other addresses. All rules that is applicable to an array, is also applicable for array of pointers.

EXAMPLE

```
int *arr[3];
int x, y[5],z[10];
arr[0]= &x;
arr[1]= y;
arr[2]= z;
```

Here, arr is an array of pointers which contains the address of variable x and the base address of two array y and z.

On the other hand, pointer to an array means a pointer which holds the address of an array. For example,

int *p, arr[10];

p = arr ;

Here, p is a pointer to an array.

32. Are the expressions *ptr++ and ++*ptr same? Explain.

Ans: No. *ptr++ and ++*ptr are not same. *ptr++ first returns the content of the location pointed by ptr and after that increase the address by one. So, it is equivalent to *ptr , then ptr++. But ++*ptr increment the content of the address pointed by ptr by one. So, it is equivalent to ++(*ptr).

For example, consider the following code snippet.

```
int a[4]={5,10,15,20},*ptr;
ptr=a;
clrscr();
printf("\n%d ",*ptr++);
printf("%d ",*ptr);
printf("%d ",++*ptr);
printf("%d ",*ptr);
output: 5   10   11   11
```

Explanation: here ptr first return 5 as it is pointing to the element in the array and then increment to next element in the array. So, second printf prints 10. Now, ++*ptr increment the content of this location. So, it prints 11.

33. What is the difference between two declarations?

```
int  *a[20];
int  (*a)[21];
```

Ans: The first declaration, i.e., int *a[20] describes that a is an array of pointer to int of size 20; whereas, the second declaration states that a is pointer to array of int of size 21.

34. Is it possible to pass a portion of an array to a function? Illustrate with an example.

Ans: Yes. It is possible to pass a portion of an array to a function. For this, we need to pass the index of staring position and end position of the portion of the array as well as base address of the array. The following example shows it clearly.

EXAMPLE

```
void display(int *p, int start, int end)
{    int i=0;
     for(i=start; i<=end; i++)
         printf("%d   ", *(p+i));
}
```

The above function can display any portion of any integer array.

If it is called as: display(arr,0,5);

Then it will display the first 6 elements of arr array.

If it is called as: display(arr,2,4);

Then it will display the 3rd, 4th and 5th elements of arr array.

35. (a) Give example of each of the following:

    (i)   Function returning a pointer to an array of float.

    (ii) Function returning a pointer to a function returning float.

    (iii) Pointer to pointer to integer.

    (iv) Pointer to an array of integers.

    (v)   Pointer to an array of pointers to a function returning character.

Ans:

    (i)

```
float * f1()
{ static float arr[10], *p;
  p = arr;
  return(p);
}
```

Here, f1() is a function which returns a pointer to an array of float.

    (ii)

```
(float ( *func_ptr)( ))  f2( )
{ static float avg();
  float( *func_ptr)( );
  func_ptr = avg( );
  ...
  ...
  return(func_ptr);
}
```

Here, f2( ) is a function which returns a pointer to a function returning float. func_ptr is a pointer to a function which returns a float.

(iii)   `int x, *p, **ptr;`

   `p = &x;`   `/* p is a pointer to integer */`

   `ptr = & p;`

   Here, ptr is a pointer to pointer to integer.

(iv)   `int arr[10], *p;`

   `p = arr;`

   Here, p is a pointer to an array of integers.

(v)   `char f3( );`

   `char( *func_ptr)( );`

   `func_ptr = f3( );`

   `char( *func_ptr)( ) arr[10], *ptr;`

   `ptr = arr;`

   Here, ptr is a pointer to an array of pointers to a function returning character.

36. (a) Explain the meaning of the following declarations:

   (i)   **float (*p) [25];**

   (ii)   **int (*p) (char *a);**

Ans: In the declaration, **float (*p) [25];**

   p is pointer to array[25] of float.

In the declaration, **int (*p) (char *a);**

   p is pointer to function expecting (char *) and returning integer.

37. What do you mean by dynamic memory allocation?

Ans: The process of allocating memory at the time of program execution, i.e., at run time is known as dynamic memory allocation. The advantage of dynamic memory allocation is that we can allocate memory according to our requirement. So, like static allocation we do not have any wastage of memory neither we face lack of memory. malloc(), calloc(), and realloc() are used in 'C' to allocate memory and free() is used to de-allocate memory during the program execution.

38. Compare between static memory allocation and dynamic memory allocation.

Ans: The process of allocating memory at compile time is known as static memory allocation. When we declare a variable or an array or structure, actually we declare them as statically. This type of allocation is known as static memory allocation. In case of static allocation, there is a disadvantage when we declare an array. We have to mention the size of the array at the time of coding, i.e., much earlier of program execution. As a result we may have to face the problem of wastage of memory or lack of memory.

On the other hand, the process of allocating memory at the time of program execution, i.e., at run time is known as dynamic memory allocation. The advantage of dynamic memory allocation is that we can allocate memory according to our requirement. So, like static allocation we do not have any wastage of memory neither we face lack of memory. We can allocate memory dynamically using malloc( ) or calloc( ).

39. What are the differences between malloc( ) and calloc( ) functions.

Ans:

malloc( )	calloc( )
• The memory allocated by malloc( ) contains garbage values.	• The memory allocated by calloc( ) contains all zeros.
• It is a single argument function and accept the total number of bytes to allocate.	• It is a two argument function and the arguments are number of blocks and size of each block.
• General form: pntr=(type-to-cast*)malloc(block_size);	• General form: pntr=(type-to-cast*)calloc(number of block, size of each block in byte);

40. What is memory leakage?

Ans: A memory leakage is a kind of unintentional memory consumption by computer program where the program allocates some memory but does not release that allocated memory when it is no longer needed. Memory leakage may occur due to various reasons. One common reason is that memory is allocated to a pointer and before de-allocation the pointer goes out of scope. This allocated memory never gets de-allocated and remains in the heap until the system is restarted.

For example,

```
void func1()
{
    int* pntr = (int*)malloc(20);
    ....
    *pntr = (int*)malloc(30);
    ....
    ...
}
```

In the above example, pntr is allocated memory using 'malloc', but without de-allocating that memory second time another block of memory is allocated and assigned to pntr. Thus previous allocation will never get scope to de-allocate and will leak.

41. Compare and contrast between structure and union in C.

Ans: Both structures and unions are user-defined data types and are used to group a number of variables of different type in single unit. But, while all the members of a structure have their own separate memory, the members of a union share the common space in memory. Thus, in case of union same memory location sometimes may be treated as a variable of one type, and sometimes may be considered as different type. So, in the group of elements if all elements may require at a time, the choice is structure. But every time if any one among different data type is required, not all elements at a time, the choice is union.

For example, consider the following structure and union.

```
struct sample_struct  { char var1;
                        int var2;
                        float var3;
                        } s1;
```

```
union sample_union  {  char v1;
                        int v2;
                        float v3;
                     } u1;
```

As in structure, all member elements are allocated at different but contiguous memory location, total size of the structure variable, s1 is 7(1+2+4). But the size of the union variable, u1 is 4 because each member element in union shares the common memory space. The compiler allocates a piece of storage which is large enough to hold the largest variable type in the union. Here, v3 requires 4 bytes which is the largest among members.

42. What is a self-referential structure?

Ans: When a structure refers the structure of same type, it is called self-referential structure. The self-referential structure is a structure which contains a member field that refers or points to the same structure type. For example, the structure we use to implement linked list is a self referential structure.

```
struct   node
{    int data;
     struct node *p;
};
```

The above structure is a self referential structure.

43. What is the difference between arrays within a structure and the array of structure?

Ans: Arrays within a structure indicate that a structure contains arrays as member.

For example,

```
struct student
{  int roll;
   char name[30];
   int marks_theory[5];
   int marks_lab[3];
};
```

Here name, marks_theory and marks_lab are the three arrays within the structure student.

The array of structure is an array whose each element represents a structure variable.

For example,

```
struct student stud[10];
```

defines an array called stud, that consists of 10 elements. Each element is of the type **struct student.**

44. What is the difference between array and structure?

Ans:

Array	Structure
• Array is a collection of homogeneous elements.	• Structure is a collection of heterogeneous elements.
• An array may consist of structure.	• Structure may contain array as member element.
• No keyword is required to declare an array.	• The keyword struct is used to declare a structure.
• An array cannot have bit fields.	• A structure may contain bit fields.

• The general form to declare an array:
 	
 data type array-name[size];
	• The general form to declare an array:
	
	```struct [structure name] {```
	
	```structure members;```
	
	```};```

45. What is special about void pointer and what are the advantage and disadvantage of using void pointer?

Ans: Pointer to void, or a void pointer, is a special type of pointer that has a great facility of pointing to any data type. Except void pointer, all pointer variables can store the address of only corresponding data type. The address placed in a pointer must have the same type as the pointer. But the Void Pointer is a special type of pointer that the programmer can use to point to any data type. We can declare void pointer in this manner:

```
void* sample;
```

Now assigning the void pointer to the address of any integer, float or variable of any other data type is perfectly correct. For example,

```
int i; float f;
sample=&i;
sample=&f;
```

So, the **advantage** of void pointer is that it can be used to store address of any data type.

Disadvantage: The disadvantage of void pointer is that as the void pointer does not know what type of variable it is pointing to, it cannot be dereferenced. Rather, the void pointer must first be explicitly cast to another pointer type before it is dereferenced. Similarly, it is not possible to do pointer arithmetic on a void pointer.

46. Distinguish between printf ( ) and fprintf ( ) functions.

Ans: printf( ) is a formatted output function. It is used to print captions and content of variables to the VDU. The general form of printf( ) is:

```
printf("control string", var1, var2,...,var n);
```

On the other hand, the fprintf( ) is used to write group of heterogeneous data in file in a formatted way. The general form of fprintf( ) is:

```
fprintf(file-pointer, "control string", var1, var2,...,var n);
```

47. Distinguish between rewind( ) and fseek( ) functions.

Ans: The rewind( ) function places the file pointer to the beginning of the file, irrespective of where it is present now. The general form of rewind( ) is:

```
rewind(file-pointer);
```

But fseek( ) is used to move the file pointer to a desired location within a file. The general form of rewind( ) is:

```
fseek(file-pointer, offset, ref-position);
```

where offset specifies the number of bytes to move from the location specified by ref-position and data type of offset is long integer. −ve value of offset indicates that the file pointer will move in backward direction. There are 3 reference positions. These are:

Ref-position	Value	Macro
Beginning of the file	0	SEEK_SET
Current position	1	SEEK_CUR
End of the file	2	SEEK_END

So, we can say, fseek(fp,0,0) is same as rewind(fp); where fp is a file pointer.

48. What is the significance of EOF?

Ans: EOF is a macro defined in the 'stdio.h' header file. It is a constant indicating that end-of-file has been reached on a file.

49. What is the difference between fscanf( ) and fread( )?

Ans: Both fscanf( ) and fread( ) are used to read group of mixed data from a file. But there are some differences also.

fscanf( )	fread( )
1. fscanf( ) reads formatted data from a file.	1. fread( ) reads data bytewise.
2. Used on text file only.	2. Used on both binary and text file.
3. If any field consists of variable number of words (like name), it is not very useful.	3. If any field consists of variable number of words, it is very much useful.
4. If end-of-file is encountered, it returns EOF.	4. If end-of-file is encountered, it returns 0.
5. General form: fscanf(filepointer, "format string",&vars..);	5. General form: fread(&var, sizeof(var), n, file pointer);

50. What are the command line arguments?

Ans: Command line arguments are the parameters supplied to a 'C' program when the program will execute. Using command line argument we can supply inputs to a program. This input may contain filename as well as any other value. In any 'C' function number of argument is fixed. But the advantage of command line argument is that we can supply variable number of arguments to a program. To accept command line argument in a 'C' program, we have to define the main function as:

```
main( int argc, char*argv[])
{
    . . . .
}
```

The argument **argc** tells the number of arguments (i.e., argument count) on the command line and **argv** represents argument value, i.e., arguments.

For example, if we want to execute a 'C' program (named mycopy) that copies the content of one file to another, we may write the command line as:

```
C:\TC> mycopy    A.TXT    B.TXT
```

Then, argc will contain 3 and argv[0], argv[1] and argv[2] will store the address of three string "mycopy", "A.TXT", "B.TXT", respectively.

51. Write down the difference between macro and function.

Ans: The differences between macro and function are:
- In macro substitution the preprocessor replaces an identifier or symbolic constant with predefined string in a thoughtless, stupid, literal way. Whereas when a function is called with some argument and if any expression is passed as argument, instead of total expression is passed to the function, first the expression is evaluated and then the result is passed as function arguments.
- Macros increase the program size, whereas functions make the program smaller and compact.
- Macros make the program run faster. But when a function is called, it takes a lot of extra time as there are some overheads associated with function calls such as jumping to the function call, saving registers, and pushing arguments into stack and therefore it slows down the program.
- Macro is very risky if we do not use it very carefully because it replaces the predefined string in a stupid, unthinking, literal way. For example,

```
#define SQR(A)    A*A
```

and in the main( ) if we write, x = SQR(2+3);

x will store 11 instead of 25. Because the macro will be expanded as:

$$x = 2+3 * 2+3;$$

But in case of function this type of error will never occur.

52. Why a linked list is called a dynamic data structure?

Ans: Linked list is consisting of nodes. Each node is created dynamically as and when it is required. Like array declaration which is static allocation, we need not mention the node number of the list. According to our requirement we can add or remove node from the linked list very efficiently with a very few and constant number of operations. That is why linked list is called dynamic data structure.

53. Compare array and linked list.

Ans:

Array	Linked list
1. Allocation of array is contiguous.	1. There is no such restriction in case of allocation of nodes of linked list.
2. Allocation of array is static. So, size of an array is fixed.	2. Allocation of nodes of linked list is dynamic. So, it can grow or shrink in size at runtime.
3. Insertion and deletion of elements is much time-consuming than linked list.	3. Insertion and deletion of elements is less time-consuming than array.
4. It supports sequential access as well as direct access.	4. Only sequential access can be performed on linked list.

54. What are the advantages of using linked list over arrays?

Ans: The advantages of using linked list over arrays are:

1. A linked list is a dynamic data structure. Hence the size of the linked list can grow or shrink in size at run time. But array is static allocation. So, its size is fixed during the program.

2. We can create or delete node as and when required. As a result, there is no chance of wastage of memory due to prior allocation. But in case of array, there is a possibility of wastage of memory or lack of memory as we have to declare the array size much earlier.

3. As allocation of array is contiguous, some times it may happen to allocate a very large array that though total free space is much larger than the requirement, an array cannot be allocated as there is not enough contiguous free space. But in case of linked list this type of problem can not be arise.

4. Linked lists provide flexibility in rearranging the items efficiently. It is possible to insert and/or delete a node at any point in the linked list very efficiently with a very few and constant number of operations. But in case of array, to insert or to remove an item we have to shift a large number of elements which is very much time consuming.

ASCII Characters

ASCII Control Characters

Decimal	Character	Description	Control Character
0	NUL	Null character	CTRL+@
1	SOH	Start of Heading	CTRL+A
2	STX	Start of Text	CTRL+B
3	ETX	End of Text	CTRL+C
4	EOT	End of Transmission	CTRL+D
5	ENQ	Enquiry	CTRL+E
6	ACK	Acknowledgment	CTRL+F
7	BEL	Bell	CTRL+G
8	BS	Back Space	CTRL+H
9	HT	Horizontal Tab	CTRL+I
10	LF	Line Feed	CTRL+J
11	VT	Vertical Tab	CTRL+K
12	FF	Form Feed	CTRL+L
13	CR	Carriage Return	CTRL+M
14	SO	Shift Out / X-On	CTRL+N
15	SI	Shift In / X-Off	CTRL+O
16	DLE	Data Line Escape	CTRL+P
17	DC1	Device Control 1 (XON)	CTRL+Q
18	DC2	Device Control 2	CTRL+R
19	DC3	Device Control 3 (XOFF)	CTRL+S
20	DC4	Device Control 4	CTRL+T

Decimal	Character	Description	Control Character
21	NAK	Negative Acknowledgement	CTRL+U
22	SYN	Synchronous Idle	CTRL+V
23	ETB	End of Transmit Block	CTRL+W
24	CAN	Cancel	CTRL+X
25	EM	End of Medium	CTRL+Y
26	SUB	Substitute	CTRL+Z
27	ESC	Escape	CTRL+[
28	FS	File Separator	CTRL+\
29	GS	Group Separator	CTRL+]
30	RS	Record Separator	CTRL+ ^
31	US	Unit Separator	CTRL+_
127	DEL	Delete	CTRL+?

ASCII Printable Characters

Decimal	Character	Decimal	Character	Decimal	Character
32	(Space)	65	A	98	B
33	!	66	B	99	C
34	"	67	C	100	D
35	#	68	D	101	E
36	$	69	E	102	F
37	%	70	F	103	G
38	&	71	G	104	H
39	'	72	H	105	I
40	(	73	I	106	J
41	)	74	J	107	K
42	*	75	K	108	L
43	+	76	L	109	M
44	,	77	M	110	N
45	–	78	N	111	O
46	.	79	O	112	P
47	/	80	P	113	Q
48	0	81	Q	114	R
49	1	82	R	115	S
50	2	83	S	116	T
51	3	84	T	117	U
52	4	85	U	118	V
53	5	86	V	119	W
54	6	87	W	120	X
55	7	88	X	121	Y
56	8	89	Y	122	Z
57	9	90	Z	123	{
58	:	91	[	124		
59	;	92	\	125	}
60	<	93	]	126	~
61	=	94	^		
62	>	95	_		
63	?	96	`		
64	@	97	a		

Extended ASCII Characters

Decimal	Character	Decimal	Character	Decimal	Character
128	Ç	161	í	194	┬
129	ü	162	ó	195	├
130	é	163	ú	196	─
131	â	164	ñ	197	┼
132	ä	165	Ñ	198	╞
133	à	166	ª	199	╟
134	å	167	º	200	╚
135	ç	168	¿	201	╔
136	ê	169	®	202	╩
137	ë	170	¬	203	╦
138	è	171	½	204	╠
139	ï	172	¼	205	═
140	î	173	¡	206	╬
141	ì	174	«	207	╧
142	Ä	175	»	208	╨
143	Å	176	░	209	╤
144	É	177	▒	210	╥
145	Æ	178	▓	211	╙
146	Æ	179	│	212	╘
147	ô	180	┤	213	╒
148	ö	181	╡	214	╓
149	ò	182	╢	215	╫
150	û	183	╖	216	╪
151	ù	184	╕	217	┘
152	ÿ	185	╣	218	┌
153	Ö	186	║	219	█
154	Ü	187	╗	220	▄
155	ø	188	╝	221	▌
156	£	189	╜	222	▐
157	Ø	190	╛	223	▀
158	Pts	191	┐	224	α
159	ƒ	192	└	225	β
160	á	193	┴	226	Γ

Decimal	Character	Decimal	Character	Decimal	Character
227	π	237	φ	247	≈
228	Σ	238	ε	248	°
229	σ	239	∩	249	··
230	μ	240	≡	250	·
231	τ	241	±	251	√
232	Φ	242	≥	252	ⁿ
233	Θ	243	≤	253	²
234	Ω	244	⌠	254	■
235	δ	245	⌡	255	nbsp
236	∞	246	÷		

Some Useful Library Functions

Every C compiler has a large number of library functions. Some of the library functions are discussed in the relevant chapters. Most of the library functions and macros that are frequently used are tabulated in this appendix under their header files.

conio.h

Function	Prototype	Description
clrscr()	void clrscr(void)	Clears the output screen.
getch()	int getch(void)	Reads a character from console(keyboard) but does not echo to the screen.
getche()	int getche(void)	Reads a character from console(keyboard) and echoes to the screen.
gotoxy()	void gotoxy(int x, int y)	Moves the cursor to the given position in the current text window.
kbhit()	int kbhit(void)	Checks for currently available keystrokes.
putch()	int putch(int)	Prints a character to the text window on the screen.
textbackground()	void textbackground(int newcolor)	Selects a new back ground color.
textcolor()	void textcolor(int newcolor)	Selects a new color in text mode.

ctype.h

Function	Prototype	Description
isalnum()	int isalnum(int)	checks whether character is alphanumeric
isalpha()	int isalpha(int)	checks whether character is an alphabet
isascii()	int isascii(int)	checks whether character is a 7 bit ASCII character
iscntrl()	int iscntrl(int)	checks whether character is a control character
isdigit()	int isdigit(int)	checks whether character is a digit

Function	Prototype	Description
isgraph()	`int isgraph(int)`	checks whether character is a graphical character
islower()	`int islower(int)`	checks whether character is in lower case
isprint()	`int isprint(int)`	checks whether character is a printable character
ispunct()	`int ispunct(int)`	checks whether character is a punctuation
isspace()	`int isspace(int)`	checks whether character is a space
isupper()	`int isupper(int)`	checks whether character is in upper case
isxdigit()	`int isxdigit(int)`	checks whether character is a hexadecimal digit
tolower()	`int tolower(int)`	converts a upper case character to lower case
toupper()	`int toupper(int)`	converts a lower case character to upper case

math.h

Function	Prototype	Description
abs()	`int abs(int)`	Returns absolute value of an integer
acos()	`double acos(double)`	Computes arc cosine of the argument
asin()	`double asin(double)`	Computes arc sine of the argument
atan()	`double atan(double)`	Computes arc tangent of the argument
atan2()	`double atan2(double, double)`	Computes arc tangent and determine the quadrant using sign
ceil()	`double ceil(double)`	Returns nearest integer greater than argument passed
cos()	`double cos(double)`	Computes the cosine of the argument
cosh()	`double cosh(double)`	Computes the hyperbolic cosine of the argument
exp()	`double exp(double)`	Computes the e raised to given power
fabs()	`double fabs (double)`	Computes absolute argument of floating point argument
floor()	`double floor(double)`	Returns nearest integer lower than the argument passed.
fmod()	`double fmod(double x, double y)`	Divide x by y with integral quotient and return remainder.
hypot()	`double hypot(double, double)`	Computes hypotenuse of right triangle (i.e., computes square root of sum of two arguments)
labs()	`labs(long)`	Find absolute value of long integer.
log()	`double log(double)`	Computes natural logarithm
log10( )	`double log10(double)`	Computes logarithm of base argument 10
pow()	`double pow(double number, double power)`	Computes the number raised to given power
sin()	`double sin(double)`	Computes sine of the argument
sinh()	`double sinh(double)`	Computes hyperbolic sine of the argument
sqrt()	`double sqrt(double)`	Computes square root of the argument
tan()	`double tan(double)`	Computes tangent of the argument
tanh()	`double tanh(double)`	Computes hyperbolic tangent of the argument

stdio.h

Function	Prototype	Description
clearerr()	`void clearerr(FILE *stream)`	Resets the error indication for a given stream.
fclose()	`fclose(FILE *stream)`	Closes an opened file
feof()	`int feof(FILE *stream)`	Finds end of file
ferror()	`int ferror(FILE *stream)`	Tests if an error has occurred on a stream.
fflush()	`int fflush(FILE *stream)`	Flushes a stream
fgetc()	`int fgetc(FILE *stream)`	Reads a character from file
fgets()	`char *fgets(char *str, int n, FILE *stream)`	Reads string from a file, one line at a time
fopen()	`FILE *fopen(char *name, char *mode)`	Opens the filename pointed to by filename using the given mode.
fprintf()	`int fprintf(FILE *stream, char *format, args..)`	Writes formatted data to a file
fputc()	`int fputc(int char, FILE *stream)`	writes a character to file
fputs()	`int fputs(const char *str, FILE *stream)`	Writes string to a file
fread()	`size_t fread(void *ptr, size_t size, size_t nmemb, FILE *stream)`	Reads data from the given stream into the array pointed to by ptr.
fscanf()	`int fscanf(FILE *stream, char *format, args..)`	Reads formatted data from a file
fseek()	`int fseek(FILE *stream, long int offset, int ref_position)`	Moves the file pointer offset byte position from ref_position.
ftell()	`long int ftell(FILE *stream)`	Gives current position of file pointer
fwrite()	`size_t fwrite(const void *ptr, size_t size, size_t nmemb, FILE *stream)`	Writes data from the array pointed to by ptr to the given stream.
getc()	`int getc(FILE *stream)`	Reads character from file
getchar()	`int getchar(void)`	Reads character from stdin(keyboard).
gets()	`char *gets(char *str)`	Reads a string of characters terminated by a new line from stdin and stores it into str.
getw()	`int getw(FILE *stream)`	Reads an integer from file
printf()	`int printf(const char *format, ...)`	print the arguments onto the output screen using format string
putc()	`int putc(int char, FILE *stream)`	Writes a character to file
putchar()	`int putchar(int char)`	Writes a character to stdout
puts()	`int puts(const char *str)`	Writes a string to stdout excluding the null character and appends a newline character.
putw()	`int putw(int, FILE *stream)`	Writes an integer to file

Function	Prototype	Description
remove()	`int remove(const char *file-name)`	Deletes a file
rename()	`int rename(const char *old_filename, const char *new_filename)`	Causes the filename referred to, by old_file-name to be changed to new_filename.
rewind()	`void rewind(FILE *stream)`	Moves file pointer position to the beginning of the file
scanf()	`int scanf(const char *for-mat, ...)`	Reads a series of input fields from stdin(keyboard) and stores at addresses passed as arguments.
sprint()	`int sprintf(char *string, char *format, args..)`	Writes formatted output to string
sscanf()	`int sscanf(char *string, char *format, args..)`	Reads formatted input from a string

string.h

Functions	Prototype	Description
memchr()	`void *memchr(const void *, int, size_t)`	It is used to locate the first occurrence of the character in the specified string
memcmp()	`int memcmp(const void *, const void *, size_t)`	It is used to compare specified number of characters from two buffers
memcpy()	`void *memcpy(void *, const void *, size_t)`	It is used to copy a specified number of bytes from one memory to another
memicmp()	`int memicmp(const void *, const void *, size_t)`	It is used to compare specified number of characters from two buffers regardless of the case of the characters
memmove()	`void *memmove(void *, const void *, size_t)`	It is used to copy a specified number of bytes from one memory to another or to overlap on same memory.
memset()	`void *memset(void *, int, size_t)`	It is used to initialize a specified number of bytes to null or any other value in the buffer
strcat()	`char *strcat(char *, const char *)`	Concatenates 2nd string at the end of 1st string.
strchr(str1,char)	`char *strchr(const char *, int)`	Returns pointer to first occurrence of char in the string.
strcmp()	`int strcmp(const char *, const char *)`	Returns 0 if 1st string is same as 2nd string. Returns <0 if 1st string < 2nd string. Returns >0 if 1st string > 2nd string.
strcmpi(str1,str2)	`int strcmpi(const char *, const char *)`	Same as strcmp() function. But, this function ignores case.
strcpy()	`char *strcpy(char *, const char *)`	Copies 2nd string into 1st string
strdup()	`char *strdup(const char *)`	duplicates the string

Functions	Prototype	Description
strlen()	`size_t strlen(const char *)`	Gives the length of the string excluding '\0'
strlwr()	`char *strlwr( char *)`	converts string to lowercase
strncat()	`char *strncat(char *, const char *, size_t)`	appends a portion of string to another
strncmp()	`int strncmp(const char *, const char *, size_t)`	Same as strcmp() but compares up to n characters
strncpy()	`Char *strncpy(char *, const char *, size_t)`	copies given number of characters of one string to another
strnicmp()	`int strnicmp(const char *, const char *, size_t)`	Same as strcmpi() but compares up to n characters
strnset()	`char *strnset(char *, int)`	sets first n character in a string to given character
strrchr()	`char *strrchr(const char *, int)`	Returns pointer to last occurrence of char in the string.
strrev()	`char *strrev(char *)`	reverses the given string
strset()	`char *strset(char *, int)`	sets all character in a string to given character
strstr()	`Char *strstr(const char *, const char *)`	Returns pointer to first occurrence of 2nd string in 1st string.
strtok()	`char *strtok(char *, const char *)`	tokenizing given string using delimiter
strupr()	`char *strlwr( char *)`	converts string to uppercase

stdlib.h

Function	Prototype	Description
abort()	`Void abort(void)`	It terminates the C program
abs()	`int abs(int)`	Returns absolute value of an integer
atof()	`double atof(const char *)`	Converts string to float
atoi()	`int atoi(const char *)`	Converts string to int
atol()	`long atol(const char *)`	Converts string to long
calloc()	`void *calloc(size_t, size_t)`	Allocate space in memory at runtime and initializes the allocated memory to zero.
delay()	`void delay(unsigned)`	Suspends the execution of the program for specified milliseconds
div()	`div_t div(int, int)`	Performs division operation
exit()	`void exit(int)`	Terminates the program.
free()	`void free(void *)`	Frees the allocated memory by malloc (), calloc (), realloc () functions and returns the memory to the system.
getenv()	`char* getenv(const char *)`	Gets the current value of the environment variable

Function	Prototype	Description
malloc()	`void* malloc(size_t)`	Allocate space in memory during the execution of the program.
putenv()	`int putenv(char *)`	Modifies the value for environment variable
rand()	`int rand(void)`	Returns the random integer numbers
random()	`long random(void)`	Returns a random number between 0 and specified number 1.
random-ize()	`void randomize(void)`	Initializes the random number generator with a random value.
realloc()	`void* realloc(void *, size_t)`	Modifies the allocated memory size by malloc () and calloc () functions to new size
srand()	`void srand(unsigned)`	The random number generator is reinitialized by calling srand with an argument value of 1. It can be set to a new starting point by calling srand with a given number.
strtod()	`double strtod(const char *, char **);`	Converts string to double
strtol()	`long strtol(const char *, char **, int);`	Converts string to long
system()	`int system(const char *)`	Execute commands outside the C program.

time.h

Function	Prototype	Description
asctime()	`char *asctime(const struct tm *)`	Tm structure contents are interpreted by this function as calendar time. This time is converted into string.
clock()	`clock_t clock(void)`	Get current system time
ctime()	`char *ctime(const time_t *)`	Returns string that contains date and time information
difftime()	`double difftime(time_t, time_t)`	Returns the difference between two given times
getdate()	`struct tm *getdate(const char *)`	Get the system date
gmtime()	`struct tm *gmtime(const time_t *)`	Converts date and time to Greenwich Mean Time (GMT)
localtime()	`struct tm localtime(const time_t *)`	Shares the tm structure that contains date and time information
mktime()	`time_t mktime(struct tm *)`	Interprets tm structure as calendar time
setdate()	`struct tm *setdate(const char *)`	Modify the system date
strftime()	`size_t strftime(char *,size_t, const char *,const struct tm *)`	Modify the actual time format
time()	`time_t time(time_t *)`	Get current system time as structure

Graphics.h

Function	Prototype	Description
arc()	`void far arc(int x, int y, int stangle, int endangle, int radius)`	Draws a circular arc
bar()	`void far bar(int left, int top, int right, int bottom)`	Draws a bar
circle()	`void far circle(int x, int y, int radius)`	Draws a circle
closegraph()	`void far closegraph( void )`	Shuts down the graphics screen
drawpoly()	`void far drawpoly(int numpoints, int far *polypoints)`	Draws the outline of a polygon
ellipse()	`void far ellipse(int x, int y, int stangle, int endangle, int xradius, int yradius)`	Draws an elliptical arc
fillellipse()	`void far fillellipse(int x, int y, int xradius, int yradius)`	Draws and fills an ellipse
fillpoly()	`void far fillpoly(int numpoints, int far *polypoints)`	Draws and fills a polygon
floodfill()	`void far floodfill(int x, int y, int border)`	Flood fills a bounded region
getbkcolor()	`int far getbkcolor( void )`	Returns current back ground color
getcolor()	`int far getcolor( void )`	Returns current drawing color
getmaxx()	`int far getmaxx( void )`	Returns maximum x screen coordinate
getmaxy()	`int far getmaxy( void )`	Returns maximum y screen coordinate
getpixel()	`unsigned far getpixel(int x, int y)`	Gets the color of a specified pixel
getx()	`int far getx( void )`	Returns the current position's x coordinate
gety()	`int far gety( void )`	Returns the current position's y coordinate
graphresult()	`int far grapfresult( void )`	Returns an error code for the last unsuccessful graphics operation
initgraph()	`void far initgraph(int far *graphdriver, int far *graphmode, char far *pathtodriver)`	Initializes the graphics screen
line()	`void far line(int x1, int y1, int x2, int y2)`	Draws a line between two specified points
outtextxy()	`void far outtextxy(int x, int y, char far *textstring)`	Displays a string at the specified location(graphics mode)
putpixel()	`void far getpixel(int x, int y, int color)`	Plots a pixel at a specified color
rectangle()	`void far rectangle(int left, int top, int right, int bottom)`	Draws a rectangle(graphics mode)

Function	Prototype	Description
restorecrt-mode	`void far restorecrtmode( void )`	Restores screen mode to pre-initgraph setting
sector()	`void far sector(int x, int y, int stangle, int endangle, int xradius, int yradius)`	Draws and fills an elliptical pie slice
setbkcolor()	`void far setbkcolor( int color )`	Sets back ground color using the palette
setcolor()	`int far setcolor(int color )`	Sets current drawing color
settextjustify()	`void far settextjustify(int horiz, int vert)`	Sets text justification for graphics mode
settextstyle()	`void far settextstyle(int font, int direction, int charsize)`	Sets the current text characteristics

size_t   Unsigned integer type of the result of the *sizeof* operator.

div_t   is a structure of integers defined (with **typedef**) in stdlib.h as follows:

```
typedef struct
    {
        int quot; /* quotient */
        int rem; /* remainder */
    } div_t;
```

In **time.h** header file the structure **tm** is declared which includes the following members:

```
int    tm_sec      seconds [0,61]
int    tm_min      minutes [0,59]
int    tm_hour     hour [0,23]
int    tm_mday     day of month [1,31]
int    tm_mon      month of year [0,11]
int    tm_year     years since 1900
int    tm_wday     day of week [0,6] (Sunday = 0)
int    tm_yday     day of year [0,365]
int    tm_isdst    daylight savings flag
```

File control structure for streams defined in stdio.h header file is:

```
typedef struct {
                short level;
                unsigned flags;
                char fd;
                unsigned char hold;
                short bsize;
                unsigned char *buffer, *curp;
                unsigned istemp;
                short token;

            } FILE;
```